WORLD TRADE ORGANIZATION

Dispute Settlement Reports

2014
Volume V

Pages 1725-2186

CAMBRIDGE
UNIVERSITY PRESS

University Printing House, Cambridge CB2 8BS, United Kingdom

Cambridge University Press is part of the University of Cambridge.

It furthers the University's mission by disseminating knowledge in the pursuit of education, learning and research at the highest international levels of excellence.

www.cambridge.org
Information on this title: www.cambridge.org/9781107139190

First published 2016

Printed in the United Kingdom by Clays, St Ives plc

A catalogue record for this publication is available from the British Library

ISBN 978-1-107-13919-0 Hardback

THE WTO DISPUTE SETTLEMENT REPORTS

The *Dispute Settlement Reports* of the World Trade Organization (the "WTO") include panel and Appellate Body reports, as well as arbitration awards, in disputes concerning the rights and obligations of WTO Members under the provisions of the *Marrakesh Agreement Establishing the World Trade Organization*. The *Dispute Settlement Reports* are available in English. Volumes comprising one or more complete cases contain a cumulative list of published disputes. The cumulative list for cases that cover more than one volume is to be found in the first volume for that case.

This volume may be cited as DSR 2014:V

TABLE OF CONTENTS

UNITED STATES - COUNTERVAILING MEASURES ON CERTAIN HOT-ROLLED CARBON STEEL FLAT PRODUCTS FROM INDIA

Report of the Appellate Body
WT/DS436/AB/R

Adopted by the Dispute Settlement Body
on 19 December 2014

India, *Appellant/Appellee*	Appellate Body Division:
United States, *Other Appellant/Appellee*	Ramírez-Hernández, Presiding Member
Australia, *Third Participant*	Bhatia, Member
Canada, *Third Participant*	Graham, Member
China, *Third Participant*	
European Union, *Third Participant*	
Saudi Arabia, *Third Participant*	
Turkey, *Third Participant*	

TABLE OF CONTENTS

ABBREVIATIONS USED IN THIS REPORT

Abbreviation	Description
Anti-Dumping Agreement	Agreement on Implementation of Article VI of the General Agreement on Tariffs and Trade 1994
DSB	Dispute Settlement Body
DSU	Understanding on Rules and Procedures Governing the Settlement of Disputes
f.o.b	free on board
GATT 1994	General Agreement on Tariffs and Trade 1994
GOI	Government of India
Hoda Report	National Mineral Policy, Report of the High Level Committee (December 2006), attached to 2006 New Subsidy Allegations (Tata) (Panel Exhibit USA-71)
JPC	Joint Plant Committee
JSW	Jindal Steel Works
NMDC	National Mineral Development Corporation
OTR	Off-the-road
Panel Report	Panel Report, *United States – Countervailing Measures on Certain Hot-Rolled Carbon Steel Flat Products from India* (WT/DS436/R)
PSNR	Permanent sovereignty over one's natural resources
SCM Agreement	Agreement on Subsidies and Countervailing Measures
SDF	Steel Development Fund
SOCB	State-owned commercial bank
Tata	Tata Steel Limited
TPS	Target Plus Scheme
US Tariff Act	United States Tariff Act of 1930, Public Law No. 1202-1527, 46 Stat. 741
US Regulations	*United States Code of Federal Regulations*, Title 19, Volume 3, Chapter III, Part 351
US Statute	*United States Code*, Title 19, Chapter 4, Subtitle IV
USDOC	US Department of Commerce
USITC	US International Trade Commission
VMPL	Vijayanagar Minerals Pvt. Ltd.
Working Procedures	Working Procedures for Appellate Review, WT/AB/WP/6, 16 August 2010
WTO	World Trade Organization
WTO Agreement	Marrakesh Agreement Establishing the World Trade Organization

CASES CITED IN THIS REPORT

Short title	Full case title and citation
Australia – Apples	Appellate Body Report, *Australia – Measures Affecting the Importation of Apples from New Zealand*, WT/DS367/AB/R, adopted 17 December 2010, DSR 2010:V, p. 2175
Australia – Salmon	Appellate Body Report, *Australia – Measures Affecting Importation of Salmon*, WT/DS18/AB/R, adopted 6 November 1998, DSR 1998:VIII, p. 3327
Brazil – Desiccated Coconut	Appellate Body Report, *Brazil – Measures Affecting Desiccated Coconut*, WT/DS22/AB/R, adopted 20 March 1997, DSR 1997:I, p. 167
Brazil – Retreaded Tyres	Appellate Body Report, *Brazil – Measures Affecting Imports of Retreaded Tyres*, WT/DS332/AB/R, adopted 17 December 2007, DSR 2007:IV, p. 1527
Canada – Aircraft	Appellate Body Report, *Canada – Measures Affecting the Export of Civilian Aircraft*, WT/DS70/AB/R, adopted 20 August 1999, DSR 1999:III, p. 1377
Canada – Aircraft	Panel Report, *Canada – Measures Affecting the Export of Civilian Aircraft*, WT/DS70/R, adopted 20 August 1999, upheld by Appellate Body Report WT/DS70/AB/R, DSR 1999:IV, p. 1443
Canada – Aircraft (Article 21.5 – Brazil)	Appellate Body Report, *Canada – Measures Affecting the Export of Civilian Aircraft – Recourse by Brazil to Article 21.5 of the DSU*, WT/DS70/AB/RW, adopted 4 August 2000, DSR 2000:IX, p. 4299
Canada – Autos	Appellate Body Report, *Canada – Certain Measures Affecting the Automotive Industry*, WT/DS139/AB/R, WT/DS142/AB/R, adopted 19 June 2000, DSR 2000:VI, p. 2985
Canada – Continued Suspension	Appellate Body Report, *Canada – Continued Suspension of Obligations in the EC – Hormones Dispute*, WT/DS321/AB/R, adopted 14 November 2008, DSR 2008:XIV, p. 5373
Canada – Dairy	Appellate Body Report, *Canada – Measures Affecting the Importation of Milk and the Exportation of Dairy Products*, WT/DS103/AB/R, WT/DS113/AB/R and Corr.1, adopted 27 October 1999, DSR 1999:V, p. 2057
Canada – Dairy (Article 21.5 – New Zealand and US)	Appellate Body Report, *Canada – Measures Affecting the Importation of Milk and the Exportation of Dairy Products – Recourse to Article 21.5 of the DSU by New Zealand and the United States*, WT/DS103/AB/RW, WT/DS113/AB/RW, adopted 18 December 2001, DSR 2001:XIII, p. 6829
Canada – Dairy (Article 21.5 – New Zealand and US II)	Appellate Body Report, *Canada – Measures Affecting the Importation of Milk and the Exportation of Dairy Products – Second Recourse to Article 21.5 of the DSU by New Zealand and the United States*, WT/DS103/AB/RW2, WT/DS113/AB/RW2, adopted 17 January 2003, DSR 2003:I, p. 213
Canada – Periodicals	Appellate Body Report, *Canada – Certain Measures Concerning Periodicals*, WT/DS31/AB/R, adopted 30 July 1997, DSR 1997:I, p. 449

Short title	Full case title and citation
Canada – Renewable Energy /Canada – Feed-in Tariff Program	Appellate Body Reports, *Canada – Certain Measures Affecting the Renewable Energy Generation Sector / Canada – Measures Relating to the Feed-in Tariff Program*, WT/DS412/AB/R / WT/DS426/AB/R, adopted 24 May 2013
Chile – Price Band System (Article 21.5 – Argentina)	Appellate Body Report, *Chile – Price Band System and Safeguard Measures Relating to Certain Agricultural Products – Recourse to Article 21.5 of the DSU by Argentina*, WT/DS207/AB/RW, adopted 22 May 2007, DSR 2007:II, p. 513
China – Auto Parts	Appellate Body Reports, *China – Measures Affecting Imports of Automobile Parts*, WT/DS339/AB/R / WT/DS340/AB/R / WT/DS342/AB/R, adopted 12 January 2009, DSR 2009:I, p. 3
China – Autos (US)	Panel Report, *China – Anti-Dumping and Countervailing Duties on Certain Automobiles from the United States*, WT/DS440/R and Add.1, adopted 18 June 2014
China – Broiler Products	Panel Report, *China – Anti-Dumping and Countervailing Duty Measures on Broiler Products from the United States*, WT/DS427/R and Add.1, adopted 25 September 2013
China – GOES	Appellate Body Report, *China – Countervailing and Anti-Dumping Duties on Grain Oriented Flat-Rolled Electrical Steel from the United States*, WT/DS414/AB/R, adopted 16 November 2012, DSR 2012:XII, p. 6251
China – GOES	Panel Report, *China – Countervailing and Anti-Dumping Duties on Grain Oriented Flat-Rolled Electrical Steel from the United States*, WT/DS414/R and Add.1, adopted 16 November 2012, upheld by Appellate Body Report WT/DS414/AB/R, DSR 2012:XII, p. 6369
China – Rare Earths	Appellate Body Reports, *China – Measures Related to the Exportation of Rare Earths, Tungsten, and Molybdenum*, WT/DS431/AB/R / WT/DS432/AB/R / WT/DS433/AB/R, adopted 29 August 2014
China – Raw Materials	Appellate Body Reports, *China – Measures Related to the Exportation of Various Raw Materials*, WT/DS394/AB/R / WT/DS395/AB/R / WT/DS398/AB/R, adopted 22 February 2012, DSR 2012:VII, p. 3295
Dominican Republic – Import and Sale of Cigarettes	Appellate Body Report, *Dominican Republic – Measures Affecting the Importation and Internal Sale of Cigarettes*, WT/DS302/AB/R, adopted 19 May 2005, DSR 2005:XV, p. 7367
EC – Asbestos	Appellate Body Report, *European Communities – Measures Affecting Asbestos and Asbestos-Containing Products*, WT/DS135/AB/R, adopted 5 April 2001, DSR 2001:VII, p. 3243
EC – Bed Linen	Appellate Body Report, *European Communities – Anti-Dumping Duties on Imports of Cotton-Type Bed Linen from India*, WT/DS141/AB/R, adopted 12 March 2001, DSR 2001:V, p. 2049
EC – Bed Linen (Article 21.5 – India)	Appellate Body Report, *European Communities – Anti-Dumping Duties on Imports of Cotton-Type Bed Linen from India – Recourse to Article 21.5 of the DSU by India*, WT/DS141/AB/RW, adopted 24 April 2003, DSR 2003:III, p. 965
EC – Chicken Cuts	Appellate Body Report, *European Communities – Customs Classification of Frozen Boneless Chicken Cuts*, WT/DS269/AB/R, WT/DS286/AB/R, adopted 27 September 2005, and Corr.1, DSR 2005:XIX, p. 9157

Short title	Full case title and citation
EC – Countervailing Measures on DRAM Chips	Panel Report, *European Communities – Countervailing Measures on Dynamic Random Access Memory Chips from Korea*, WT/DS299/R, adopted 3 August 2005, DSR 2005:XVIII, p. 8671
EC – Export Subsidies on Sugar	Appellate Body Report, *European Communities – Export Subsidies on Sugar*, WT/DS265/AB/R, WT/DS266/AB/R, WT/DS283/AB/R, adopted 19 May 2005, DSR 2005:XIII, p. 6365
EC – Fasteners (China)	Appellate Body Report, *European Communities – Definitive Anti-Dumping Measures on Certain Iron or Steel Fasteners from China*, WT/DS397/AB/R, adopted 28 July 2011, DSR 2011:VII, p. 3995
EC – Hormones	Appellate Body Report, *EC Measures Concerning Meat and Meat Products (Hormones)*, WT/DS26/AB/R, WT/DS48/AB/R, adopted 13 February 1998, DSR 1998:I, p. 135
EC – Poultry	Appellate Body Report, *European Communities – Measures Affecting the Importation of Certain Poultry Products*, WT/DS69/AB/R, adopted 23 July 1998, DSR 1998:V, p. 2031
EC – Sardines	Appellate Body Report, *European Communities – Trade Description of Sardines*, WT/DS231/AB/R, adopted 23 October 2002, DSR 2002:VIII, p. 3359
EC – Seal Products	Appellate Body Reports, *European Communities – Measures Prohibiting the Importation and Marketing of Seal Products*, WT/DS400/AB/R / WT/DS401/AB/R, adopted 18 June 2014
EC – Selected Customs Matters	Appellate Body Report, *European Communities – Selected Customs Matters*, WT/DS315/AB/R, adopted 11 December 2006, DSR 2006:IX, p. 3791
EC – Tube or Pipe Fittings	Appellate Body Report, *European Communities – Anti-Dumping Duties on Malleable Cast Iron Tube or Pipe Fittings from Brazil*, WT/DS219/AB/R, adopted 18 August 2003, DSR 2003:VI, p. 2613
EC and certain member States – Large Civil Aircraft	Appellate Body Report, *European Communities and Certain Member States – Measures Affecting Trade in Large Civil Aircraft*, WT/DS316/AB/R, adopted 1 June 2011, DSR 2011:I, p. 7
India – Patents (US)	Appellate Body Report, *India – Patent Protection for Pharmaceutical and Agricultural Chemical Products*, WT/DS50/AB/R, adopted 16 January 1998, DSR 1998:I, p. 9
Japan – Agricultural Products II	Appellate Body Report, *Japan – Measures Affecting Agricultural Products*, WT/DS76/AB/R, adopted 19 March 1999, DSR 1999:I, p. 277
Japan – Apples	Appellate Body Report, *Japan – Measures Affecting the Importation of Apples*, WT/DS245/AB/R, adopted 10 December 2003, DSR 2003:IX, p. 4391
Japan – DRAMs (Korea)	Appellate Body Report, *Japan – Countervailing Duties on Dynamic Random Access Memories from Korea*, WT/DS336/AB/R and Corr.1, adopted 17 December 2007, DSR 2007:VII, p. 2703
Japan – DRAMs (Korea)	Panel Report, *Japan – Countervailing Duties on Dynamic Random Access Memories from Korea*, WT/DS336/R, adopted 17 December 2007, as modified by Appellate Body Report WT/DS336/AB/R, DSR 2007:VII, p. 2805

Short title	Full case title and citation
Korea – Alcoholic Beverages	Appellate Body Report, *Korea – Taxes on Alcoholic Beverages*, WT/DS75/AB/R, WT/DS84/AB/R, adopted 17 February 1999, DSR 1999:I, p. 3
Korea – Commercial Vessels	Panel Report, *Korea – Measures Affecting Trade in Commercial Vessels*, WT/DS273/R, adopted 11 April 2005, DSR 2005:VII, p. 2749
Korea – Dairy	Appellate Body Report, *Korea – Definitive Safeguard Measure on Imports of Certain Dairy Products*, WT/DS98/AB/R, adopted 12 January 2000, DSR 2000:I, p. 3
Korea – Procurement	Panel Report, *Korea – Measures Affecting Government Procurement*, WT/DS163/R, adopted 19 June 2000, DSR 2000:VIII, p. 3541
Mexico – Anti-Dumping Measures on Rice	Appellate Body Report, *Mexico – Definitive Anti-Dumping Measures on Beef and Rice, Complaint with Respect to Rice*, WT/DS295/AB/R, adopted 20 December 2005, DSR 2005:XXII, p. 10853
Mexico – Anti-Dumping Measures on Rice	Panel Report, *Mexico – Definitive Anti-Dumping Measures on Beef and Rice, Complaint with Respect to Rice*, WT/DS295/R, adopted 20 December 2005, as modified by Appellate Body Report WT/DS295/AB/R, DSR 2005:XXIII, p. 11007
Mexico – Corn Syrup (Article 21.5 – US)	Appellate Body Report, *Mexico – Anti-Dumping Investigation of High Fructose Corn Syrup (HFCS) from the United States – Recourse to Article 21.5 of the DSU by the United States*, WT/DS132/AB/RW, adopted 21 November 2001, DSR 2001:XIII, p. 6675
Philippines – Distilled Spirits	Appellate Body Reports, *Philippines – Taxes on Distilled Spirits*, WT/DS396/AB/R / WT/DS403/AB/R, adopted 20 January 2012, DSR 2012:VIII, p. 4163
Thailand – H-Beams	Appellate Body Report, *Thailand – Anti-Dumping Duties on Angles, Shapes and Sections of Iron or Non-Alloy Steel and H-Beams from Poland*, WT/DS122/AB/R, adopted 5 April 2001, DSR 2001:VII, p. 2701
US – Anti-Dumping and Countervailing Duties (China)	Appellate Body Report, *United States – Definitive Anti-Dumping and Countervailing Duties on Certain Products from China*, WT/DS379/AB/R, adopted 25 March 2011, DSR 2011:V, p. 2869
US – Anti-Dumping and Countervailing Duties (China)	Panel Report, *United States – Definitive Anti-Dumping and Countervailing Duties on Certain Products from China*, WT/DS379/R, adopted 25 March 2011, as modified by Appellate Body Report WT/DS379/AB/R, DSR 2011:VI, p. 3143
US – Carbon Steel	Appellate Body Report, *United States – Countervailing Duties on Certain Corrosion-Resistant Carbon Steel Flat Products from Germany*, WT/DS213/AB/R and Corr.1, adopted 19 December 2002, DSR 2002:IX, p. 3779
US – Carbon Steel	Panel Report, *United States – Countervailing Duties on Certain Corrosion-Resistant Carbon Steel Flat Products from Germany*, WT/DS213/R and Corr.1, adopted 19 December 2002, as modified by Appellate Body Report WT/DS213/AB/R, DSR 2002:IX, p. 3833
US – Carbon Steel (India)	Panel Report, *United States – Countervailing Measures on Certain Hot-Rolled Carbon Steel Flat Products from India*, WT/DS436/R and Add.1, circulated to WTO Members 14 July 2014

Short title	Full case title and citation
US – Clove Cigarettes	Appellate Body Report, *United States – Measures Affecting the Production and Sale of Clove Cigarettes*, WT/DS406/AB/R, adopted 24 April 2012, DSR 2012: XI, p. 5751
US – Continued Suspension	Appellate Body Report, *United States – Continued Suspension of Obligations in the EC – Hormones Dispute*, WT/DS320/AB/R, adopted 14 November 2008, DSR 2008:X, p. 3507
US – Continued Zeroing	Appellate Body Report, *United States – Continued Existence and Application of Zeroing Methodology*, WT/DS350/AB/R, adopted 19 February 2009, DSR 2009:III, p. 1291
US – Corrosion-Resistant Steel Sunset Review	Appellate Body Report, *United States – Sunset Review of Anti-Dumping Duties on Corrosion-Resistant Carbon Steel Flat Products from Japan*, WT/DS244/AB/R, adopted 9 January 2004, DSR 2004:I, p. 3
US – Corrosion-Resistant Steel Sunset Review	Panel Report, *United States – Sunset Review of Anti-Dumping Duties on Corrosion-Resistant Carbon Steel Flat Products from Japan*, WT/DS244/R, adopted 9 January 2004, as modified by Appellate Body Report WT/DS244/AB/R, DSR 2004:I, p. 85
US – Countervailing and Anti-Dumping Measures (China)	Appellate Body Report, *United States – Countervailing and Anti-Dumping Measures on Certain Products from China*, WT/DS449/AB/R and Corr.1, adopted 22 July 2014
US – Countervailing Duty Investigation on DRAMS	Appellate Body Report, *United States – Countervailing Duty Investigation on Dynamic Random Access Memory Semiconductors (DRAMS) from Korea*, WT/DS296/AB/R, adopted 20 July 2005, DSR 2005:XVI, p. 8131
US – Countervailing Duty Investigation on DRAMS	Panel Report, *United States – Countervailing Duty Investigation on Dynamic Random Access Memory Semiconductors (DRAMS) from Korea*, WT/DS296/R, adopted 20 July 2005, as modified by Appellate Body Report WT/DS296/AB/R, DSR 2005:XVII, p. 8243
US – Countervailing Measures on Certain EC Products	Appellate Body Report, *United States – Countervailing Measures Concerning Certain Products from the European Communities*, WT/DS212/AB/R, adopted 8 January 2003, DSR 2003:I, p. 5
US – FSC	Appellate Body Report, *United States – Tax Treatment for "Foreign Sales Corporations"*, WT/DS108/AB/R, adopted 20 March 2000, DSR 2000:III, p. 1619
US – Gambling	Appellate Body Report, *United States – Measures Affecting the Cross-Border Supply of Gambling and Betting Services*, WT/DS285/AB/R, adopted 20 April 2005, DSR 2005:XII, p. 5663 (Corr.1, DSR 2006:XII, p. 5475)
US – Gasoline	Appellate Body Report, *United States – Standards for Reformulated and Conventional Gasoline*, WT/DS2/AB/R, adopted 20 May 1996, DSR 1996:I, p. 3
US – Hot-Rolled Steel	Appellate Body Report, *United States – Anti-Dumping Measures on Certain Hot-Rolled Steel Products from Japan*, WT/DS184/AB/R, adopted 23 August 2001, DSR 2001:X, p. 4697
US – Lamb	Appellate Body Report, *United States – Safeguard Measures on Imports of Fresh, Chilled or Frozen Lamb Meat from New Zealand and Australia*, WT/DS177/AB/R, WT/DS178/AB/R, adopted 16 May 2001, DSR 2001:IX, p. 4051

Short title	Full case title and citation
US – Lamb	Panel Report, *United States – Safeguard Measures on Imports of Fresh, Chilled or Frozen Lamb Meat from New Zealand and Australia*, WT/DS177/R, WT/DS178/R, adopted 16 May 2001, as modified by Appellate Body Report WT/DS177/AB/R, WT/DS178/AB/R, DSR 2001:IX, p. 4107
US – Large Civil Aircraft (2nd complaint)	Appellate Body Report, *United States – Measures Affecting Trade in Large Civil Aircraft (Second Complaint)*, WT/DS353/AB/R, adopted 23 March 2012, DSR 2012:I, p. 7
US – Lead and Bismuth II	Appellate Body Report, *United States – Imposition of Countervailing Duties on Certain Hot-Rolled Lead and Bismuth Carbon Steel Products Originating in the United Kingdom*, WT/DS138/AB/R, adopted 7 June 2000, DSR 2000:V, p. 2595
US – Line Pipe	Appellate Body Report, *United States – Definitive Safeguard Measures on Imports of Circular Welded Carbon Quality Line Pipe from Korea*, WT/DS202/AB/R, adopted 8 March 2002, DSR 2002:IV, p. 1403
US – Oil Country Tubular Goods Sunset Reviews	Appellate Body Report, *United States – Sunset Reviews of Anti-Dumping Measures on Oil Country Tubular Goods from Argentina*, WT/DS268/AB/R, adopted 17 December 2004, DSR 2004:VII, p. 3257
US – Section 211 Appropriations Act	Appellate Body Report, *United States – Section 211 Omnibus Appropriations Act of 1998*, WT/DS176/AB/R, adopted 1 February 2002, DSR 2002:II, p. 589
US – Section 301 Trade Act	Panel Report, *United States – Sections 301-310 of the Trade Act of 1974*, WT/DS152/R, adopted 27 January 2000, DSR 2000:II, p. 815
US – Shrimp	Appellate Body Report, *United States – Import Prohibition of Certain Shrimp and Shrimp Products*, WT/DS58/AB/R, adopted 6 November 1998, DSR 1998:VII, p. 2755
US – Softwood Lumber IV	Appellate Body Report, *United States – Final Countervailing Duty Determination with Respect to Certain Softwood Lumber from Canada*, WT/DS257/AB/R, adopted 17 February 2004, DSR 2004:II, p. 571
US – Softwood Lumber IV	Panel Report, *United States – Final Countervailing Duty Determination with Respect to Certain Softwood Lumber from Canada*, WT/DS257/R and Corr.1, adopted 17 February 2004, as modified by Appellate Body Report WT/DS257/AB/R, DSR 2004:II, p. 641
US – Softwood Lumber VI (Article 21.5 – Canada)	Appellate Body Report, *United States – Investigation of the International Trade Commission in Softwood Lumber from Canada – Recourse to Article 21.5 of the DSU by Canada*, WT/DS277/AB/RW, adopted 9 May 2006, and Corr.1, DSR 2006:XI, p. 4865
US – Stainless Steel (Mexico)	Appellate Body Report, *United States – Final Anti-Dumping Measures on Stainless Steel from Mexico*, WT/DS344/AB/R, adopted 20 May 2008, DSR 2008:II, p. 513

Short title	Full case title and citation
US – Steel Safeguards	Appellate Body Report, *United States – Definitive Safeguard Measures on Imports of Certain Steel Products*, WT/DS248/AB/R, WT/DS249/AB/R, WT/DS251/AB/R, WT/DS252/AB/R, WT/DS253/AB/R, WT/DS254/AB/R, WT/DS258/AB/R, WT/DS259/AB/R, adopted 10 December 2003, DSR 2003:VII, p. 3117
US – Tyres (China)	Appellate Body Report, *United States – Measures Affecting Imports of Certain Passenger Vehicle and Light Truck Tyres from China*, WT/DS399/AB/R, adopted 5 October 2011, DSR 2011:IX, p. 4811
US – Upland Cotton	Appellate Body Report, *United States – Subsidies on Upland Cotton*, WT/DS267/AB/R, adopted 21 March 2005, DSR 2005:I, p. 3
US – Upland Cotton	Panel Report, *United States – Subsidies on Upland Cotton*, WT/DS267/R, Add.1 to Add.3 and Corr.1, adopted 21 March 2005, as modified by Appellate Body Report WT/DS267/AB/R, DSR 2005:II, p. 299
US – Upland Cotton (Article 21.5 – Brazil)	Appellate Body Report, *United States – Subsidies on Upland Cotton – Recourse to Article 21.5 of the DSU by Brazil*, WT/DS267/AB/RW, adopted 20 June 2008, DSR 2008:III, p. 809
US – Wheat Gluten	Appellate Body Report, *United States – Definitive Safeguard Measures on Imports of Wheat Gluten from the European Communities*, WT/DS166/AB/R, adopted 19 January 2001, DSR 2001:II, p. 717
US – Wool Shirts and Blouses	Appellate Body Report, *United States – Measure Affecting Imports of Woven Wool Shirts and Blouses from India*, WT/DS33/AB/R, adopted 23 May 1997, and Corr.1, DSR 1997:I, p. 323
US – Zeroing (EC)	Panel Report, *United States – Laws, Regulations and Methodology for Calculating Dumping Margins ("Zeroing")*, WT/DS294/R, adopted 9 May 2006, as modified by Appellate Body Report WT/DS294/AB/R, DSR 2006:II, p. 521

PANEL EXHIBITS CITED IN THIS REPORT

Exhibit No.	Short title (if any)	Description
IND-4	Statement of Administrative Action	Uruguay Round Agreements Act, Statement of Administrative Action, H.R. Doc. No. 103-316 (1994)
IND-7	2001 AR Issues and Decision Memorandum	USDOC, Issues and Decision Memorandum: Final Results of the Countervailing Duty Investigation, Certain Hot-Rolled Carbon Steel Flat Products from India (C-533-821) for the period 01/04/1999-31/03/2000 (21 September 2001)
IND-9	USITC Final Determinations	USITC, Hot Rolled Steel Products from Argentina and South Africa, Investigations Nos. 701-TA-404 (Final) and 731-TA-898 and 905 (Final), Publication 3446 (August 2001)
IND-15A		United States Steel Corporation, Letter dated 2 May 2005 to USDOC alleging additional government subsidies (Essar) in Certain Hot-Rolled Carbon Steel Flat Products from India (C-533-821)
IND-15B		United States Steel Corporation, Letter dated 29 June 2005 in response to USDOC request for clarification regarding new subsidy allegations (Essar) of 2 May 2005 in Certain Hot-Rolled Carbon Steel Flat Products from India (C-533-821)
IND-17	2004 AR Preliminary Results	USDOC, Notice of Preliminary Results of Countervailing Duty Administrative Review: Certain Hot-Rolled Carbon Steel Flat Products from India (C-533-821) for the period 01/01-31/12/2004, *United States Federal Register*, Vol. 71, No. 6 (10 January 2006), pp. 1512-1519
IND-24		United States Steel Corporation, Letter dated 23 May 2007 alleging additional government subsidies (Ispat) in Certain Hot-Rolled Carbon Steel Flat Products from India (C-533-821)
IND-25		United States Steel Corporation, Letter dated 23 May 2007 alleging additional government subsidies (JSW) in Certain Hot-Rolled Carbon Steel Flat Products from India (C-533-821)
IND-26		United States Steel Corporation, Letter dated 23 May 2007 alleging additional government subsidies (Tata) in Certain Hot-Rolled Carbon Steel Flat Products from India (C-533-821)
IND-27		United States Steel Corporation, Letter dated 23 May 2007 alleging additional government subsidies (Essar) in Certain Hot-Rolled Carbon Steel Flat Products from India (C-533-821)

Exhibit No.	Short title (if any)	Description
IND-32	2006 AR Preliminary Results	USDOC, Certain Hot-Rolled Carbon Steel Flat Products from India: Notice of Preliminary Results of Countervailing Duty Administrative Review (C-533-821) for the period 01/01-31/12/2006, *United States Federal Register*, Vol. 73, No. 6 (9 January 2008), pp. 1578-1599
IND-33	2006 AR Issues and Decision Memorandum	USDOC, Issues and Decision Memorandum: Final Results of Administrative Review, Certain Hot-Rolled Carbon Steel Flat Products From India (C-533-821) for the period 01/01-31/12/2006, 7 July 2008
IND-37		USDOC, Certain Hot-Rolled Carbon Steel Flat Products from India: Notice of Preliminary Results and Partial Rescission of Countervailing Duty Administrative Review (C-533-821) for the period 01/01-31/12/2007, *United States Federal Register*, Vol. 73, No. 250 (30 December 2008), pp. 79791-79802
IND-38	2007 AR Issues and Decision Memorandum	USDOC, Issues and Decision Memorandum: Final Results and Partial Rescission of Countervailing Duty Administrative Review, Certain Hot-Rolled Carbon Steel Flat Products from India (C-533-821) for the period 01/01-31/12/2007, 29 April 2009
IND-47	Hyosung Corporation v. United States	United States Court of International Trade, Hyosung Corporation v. United States, 2011 WL 1882519 (CIT) (31 March 2011)
IND-48	Rhone Poulenc, Inc. v. United States	United States Court of Appeals for the Federal Circuit, Rhone Poulenc, Inc. v. The United States, 899 F.2d 1185 (Fed. Cir. 1990) (27 March 1990)
IND-49A	Mueller Comercial de Mexico v. United States	United States Court of International Trade, Mueller Comercial de Mexico v. United States, 807 F.Supp.2d 1361 (CIT 2011) (16 December 2011)
IND-49B	Essar Steel Ltd v. United States	United States Court of Appeals for the Federal Circuit, Essar Steel Limited v. United States, 678 F.3d 1268 (Fed. Cir. 2012) (27 April 2012)
IND-54B		Supreme Court of India, Tata Iron and Steel Co. Ltd. v. Collector of Central Excise, Jamshedpur (2002) 8 SCC, pp. 338-351
IND-57		Essar Steel Limited, Response dated 12 April 2005 to USDOC questionnaire of 3 February 2005 in administrative review of Certain Hot-Rolled Carbon Steel Flat Products from India (C-533-821) for the period 01/01-31/12/2004

Exhibit No.	Short title (if any)	Description
IND-58	2005 GOI Supplemental Questionnaire Response for 2004 AR	Government of India, Response dated 2 September 2005 to USDOC supplemental questionnaire of 3 August 2005 in administrative review of Certain Hot-Rolled Carbon Steel Flat Products from India (C-533-821) for the period 01/01-31/12/2004
IND-59	2007 GOI Questionnaire Response for 2006 AR	Government of India, Response dated 23 April 2007 to USDOC questionnaire in administrative review of Certain Hot-Rolled Carbon Steel Flat Products from India (C-533-821) for the period 01/01-31/12/2006
IND-61		Government of India, Response dated 8 February 2008 to USDOC supplemental questionnaire of 11 January 2008 in administrative review of Certain Hot-Rolled Carbon Steel Flat Products from India (C-533-821) for the period 01/01-31/12/2006
IND-65	2007 Tata Questionnaire Response for 2006 AR	Tata Steel Limited, Response dated 1 November 2007 to USDOC Countervailing Duty New Subsidies Allegations Questionnaire 27 September 2007 in administrative review of Certain Hot-Rolled Carbon Steel Flat Products from India (C-533-821) for the period 01/01-31/12/2006
IND-67		Tata Steel Limited, Response dated 8 February 2008 to USDOC supplemental questionnaire of 11 January 2008 in administrative review of Certain Hot-Rolled Carbon Steel Flat Products from India (C-533-821) for the period 01/01-31/12/2006
IND-68A		Tata Steel Limited, Expert Statement of Professor James Otto on behalf of Tata Steel Limited in administrative review of Certain Hot-Rolled Carbon Steel Flat Products from India (C-533-821) for the period 01/01-31/12/2006 (6 November 2007)
IND-68B		Tata Steel Limited, Additional Statement of James Otto on Ore Royalties on behalf of Tata Steel Limited in administrative review of Certain Hot-Rolled Carbon Steel Flat Products from India (C-533-821) for the period 01/01-31/12/2006 (28 November 2007)
IND-70	Tata Verification Report	Tata Steel Limited, Certification of Service of Verification Exhibits and Minor Corrections identified by the USDOC in Countervailing Duty Investigation of Certain Hot-Rolled Carbon Steel Flat Products from India (C-533-831) for the period 01/01-31/12/2006 (17 March 2008)

Exhibit No.	Short title (if any)	Description
IND-71		Table of relevant USDOC determinations regarding the application of "adverse facts available" provisions in administrative reviews
IND-72-1(2)		DPE Guidelines, Chapter IX: Navratna/Miniratna Status of PSUs, section 1, "Turning selected public sector enterprises into global giants – grant of autonomy"
IND-72-2(1)		DPE Guidelines, Chapter IX: Navratna/Miniratna Status of PSUs, section 5, "Financial and operational autonomy for profit making public sector enterprises – Mini-Ratnas"
USA-4		Countervailable subsidy – Benefit conferred, *United States Code*, Title 19, Chapter 4, Subtitle IV, Section 1677(5)(E)
USA-12		Determinations on basis of facts available, *United States Code*, Title 19, Chapter 4, Subtitle IV, Section 1677e
USA-13		Determinations on the basis of the facts available, *United States Code of Federal Regulations*, Title 19, Vol. 3, Chapter III, Part 351, Section 351.308
USA-14	Final Rule on Antidumping and Countervailing Duties	USDOC, Antidumping Duties; Countervailing Duties: Final Rule, *United States Federal Register*, Vol. 62, No. 96 (19 May 1997), pp. 27296 and 27339-27341
USA-15		USDOC, Final Affirmative Countervailing Duty Determination: Certain Cut-to-Length Carbon-Quality Steel Plate from Indonesia, *United States Federal Register*, Vol. 64, No. 249 (29 December 1999), pp. 73155-73164
USA-17		USDOC, Issues and Decision Memorandum: Final Determination in the Countervailing Duty Investigation of Stainless Steel Bar From Italy (C-475-830) (15 January 2002), pp. 1 and 15-19
USA-19		USDOC, Issues and Decision Memorandum: Final Results of Countervailing Duty Administrative Review: Certain In-shell Pistachios from the Islamic Republic of Iran (C-507-501) (6 September 2005)
USA-47		USDOC, Initiation of Antidumping and Countervailing Duty Administrative Reviews and Request for Revocation in Part, *United States Federal Register*, Vol. 72, No. 22 (2 February 2007), pp. 5005-5007

Exhibit No.	Short title (if any)	Description
USA-66	2004 GOI Verification Report	USDOC, Verification of Questionnaire Responses Submitted by the Government of India in Countervailing Duty Administrative Review of Certain Hot-Rolled Carbon ("HRC") Steel Flat Products from India (C-533-821), for the period 01/01-31/12/2004 (3 January 2006), pp. 1-9
USA-69	2004 New Subsidy Allegations (Essar)	United States Steel Corporation, Letter dated 2 May 2005 alleging additional government subsidies (Essar) in Certain Hot-Rolled Carbon Steel Flat Products from India (C-533-821)
USA-71	2006 New Subsidy Allegations (Tata)	United States Steel Corporation, Letter dated 23 May 2007 alleging additional government subsidies (Tata) in Certain Hot-Rolled Carbon Steel Flat Products From India (C-533-821)
USA-74	2001 Investigation Verification Report of GOI Responses	USDOC, Verification of the Questionnaire Responses Submitted by the Government of India (GOI) in Countervailing Duty Investigation of Certain Hot-Rolled Carbon Steel Flat Products from India (C-533-821), for the period 01/01-31/12/2001 (17 July 2001)
USA-75	2001 GOI Supplemental Questionnaire Response	Government of India, Response dated 20 March 2001 to USDOC supplemental questionnaire in Countervailing Duty Investigation of Certain Hot-Rolled Carbon Steel Flat Products from India (Section 701 Investigation) (C-533-821)
USA-78		National Steel Corporation and United States Steel Corporation, Letter dated 19 May 2003 alleging additional government subsidies (Essar) in Certain Hot-Rolled Carbon Steel Flat Products from India (C-533-821)
USA-80		USDOC, Initiation of Antidumping and Countervailing Duty Administrative Reviews and Request for Revocation in Part, *United States Federal Register*, Vol. 68, No. 14 (22 January 2003), pp. 3009-3011
USA-81		USDOC, Initiation of Antidumping and Countervailing Duty Administrative Reviews and Request for Revocation in Part, *United States Federal Register*, Vol. 70, No. 19 (31 January 2005), pp. 4818-4820
USA-82		USDOC, Initiation of Antidumping and Countervailing Duty Administrative Reviews and Request for Revocation in Part, *United States Federal Register*, Vol. 73, No. 18 (28 January 2008), pp. 4829-4831

Exhibit No.	Short title (if any)	Description
USA-114	2004 GOI Verification Report	USDOC, Verification of the Questionnaire Responses Submitted by the Government of India in Countervailing Duty Administrative Review of Certain Hot-Rolled Carbon ("HRC") Steel Flat Products from India (C-533-821) for the period 01/01-31/12/2004 (3 January 2006)
USA-118		Essar Steel Ltd., Response dated 14 November 2007 to USDOC supplemental questionnaire of 6 November 2007 in Certain Hot-Rolled Carbon Steel Flat Products from India (C-533-821), including attachments and internal Exhibit 1, table of "2006 iron ore prices in the Japanese market", sourced from Tex Report
USA-119		Essar Steel Ltd., Response dated 21 November 2008 to USDOC fourth supplemental questionnaire in Certain Hot-Rolled Carbon Steel Flat Products from India (C-533-821), including attachments and internal Exhibit 4, table of "2007 iron ore prices in the Japanese market", sourced from Tex Report

1. INTRODUCTION

1.1 India and the United States each appeals certain issues of law and legal interpretations developed in the Panel Report, *United States – Countervailing Measures on Certain Hot-Rolled Carbon Steel Flat Products from India*[1] (Panel Report). The Panel was established[2] to consider a complaint by India[3] with respect to the imposition, by the United States, of countervailing duties on certain hot-rolled carbon steel flat products from India.

1.1 Panel Proceedings

1.2 India challenged two types of measures related to the imposition by the United States of countervailing duties on imports of certain hot-rolled carbon steel flat products from India, namely: (i) the relevant legislation; and (ii) the specific determinations leading to the imposition of countervailing duties. First, India brought claims against certain provisions of the United States Tariff Act of 1930[4] (US Tariff Act) as codified in the *United States Code*, Title 19, Chapter 4, Subtitle IV (US Statute)[5], and of the *United States Code of Federal Regulations*, Title 19, Volume 3, Chapter III, Part 351 (US Regulations).[6] Second, India challenged several measures related to the United States' original investigation initiated in December 2000, the 2002, 2004, 2006, 2007, and 2008 administrative reviews, and the 2006 sunset review. For both these types of measures, India also challenged their amendments, replacements, implementing acts, or any other related measure in connection with them.[7] The measures at issue in this dispute are set forth in greater detail at paragraphs 2.1 and 2.2 of the Panel Report.

1.3 India claimed that the US measures were inconsistent with several of the obligations under the Agreement on Subsidies and Countervailing Measures (SCM Agreement), the General Agreement on Tariffs and Trade 1994 (GATT 1994), and the Marrakesh Agreement Establishing the World Trade Organization (WTO Agreement). These obligations pertain to the determination of the existence of a subsidy, specificity, initiation of investigations, evidence, requirements for consultations, calculation of benefit, determination of injury, imposition and collection of anti-dumping duties, review of countervailing

---

1 WT/DS436/R, 14 July 2014.

2 At its meeting on 31 August 2012, the Dispute Settlement Body (DSB) established a panel pursuant to the request of India in document WT/DS436/3, in accordance with Article 6 of the Understanding on Rules and Procedures Governing the Settlement of Disputes (DSU). (Panel Report, para. 1.3)

3 Request for the Establishment of a Panel by India, WT/DS436/3.

4 United States Tariff Act of 1930, Public Law No. 1202-1527, 46 Stat. 741.

5 Specifically, Sections 1677(7)(G); 1675a(a)(7); 1675b(e)(2); and 1677e(b).

6 Specifically, Sections 351.511(a)(2)(i)-(iv); and 351.308.

7 Panel Report, paras. 2.1 and 2.2.

duties, and public notice requirements.[8] In addition, pursuant to Article 19 of the Understanding on Rules and Procedures Governing the Settlement of Disputes (DSU), India requested the Panel to suggest two specific ways for the United States to bring its measures into conformity with the three Agreements: (i) that the United States repeal or amend the impugned provisions of the law; and (ii) that the United States withdraw the countervailing duty on hot-rolled carbon steel flat products from India.[9] India's claims and requests for findings and recommendations are set forth in greater detail at paragraphs 3.1 and 3.2 of the Panel Report.

1.4 On 3 May 2013, the United States submitted to the Panel two requests for preliminary rulings concerning the consistency of India's panel request with Article 6.2 of the DSU. The United States' first request concerned India's claim under Article 11 of the SCM Agreement, which was set out in India's panel request as follows: "[T]he determinations made, and the countervailing measures imposed, by the United States are inconsistent with ... Article 11 of the [SCM Agreement] because no investigation was initiated or conducted to determine the effects of new subsidies included in the administrative reviews".[10] The United States argued that India's claims relating to the alleged initiation of an investigation despite the insufficiency of evidence in the domestic industry's written application, as contained in India's first written submission, fell outside the Panel's terms of reference. The United States' second request concerned India's claim that the United States' 2013 sunset review was inconsistent with Article 12.7 of the SCM Agreement. The United States argued that, because India had not explicitly referred to the 2013 sunset review in its panel request, India's claim in this respect fell outside the Panel's terms of reference. On 21 May 2013, in advance of the first substantive meeting of the Panel with the parties, India provided a written response to the United States' requests for preliminary rulings. On 16 August 2013, the Panel issued preliminary rulings to the parties to the dispute. The contents of the Panel's preliminary rulings are reproduced in Section 1.3.3 of the Panel Report.

1.5 The Panel Report was circulated to Members of the World Trade Organization (WTO) on 14 July 2014. With respect to the United States' requests for preliminary rulings, the Panel found that:

a. the 2013 sunset review was within the Panel's terms of reference;

b. India's claim that the United States acted inconsistently with Article 11.1 of the SCM Agreement by failing to "initiate" an investigation into new subsidies was within the Panel's terms of reference; and

8 Panel Report, para. 3.1.

9 Panel Report, para. 3.2.

10 WT/DS436/3.

c. India's claims that the United States acted inconsistently with Articles 11.1, 11.2, and 11.9 of the SCM Agreement in connection with the alleged initiation of an investigation, despite the insufficiency of evidence in the domestic industry's written application, fell outside the Panel's terms of reference.[11]

1.6 In connection with the provision of high-grade iron ore by the National Mineral Development Corporation (NMDC), the Panel upheld two of India's claims. These claims related to the determination of specificity by the US Department of Commerce (USDOC), and its methodology in the calculation of benefit to the recipients. Specifically, the Panel found that the United States acted inconsistently with:

a. Article 2.1(c) of the SCM Agreement by failing to take account of all the mandatory factors in its determination of *de facto* specificity regarding the NMDC[12]; and

b. Article 14(d) of the SCM Agreement by failing to consider the relevant domestic pricing information for use as Tier I benchmarks[13], in respect of which the United States sought to rely on *ex post* rationalization.[14]

1.7 In connection with the Captive Mining of Iron Ore Programme and the Captive Mining of Coal Programme[15], the Panel upheld three claims by India. These claims related to, *inter alia*, the USDOC's appreciation of the evidence, its determination that the Government of India (GOI) provided a financial contribution by providing iron and coal for less than adequate remuneration, and its methodology in the calculation of benefit to the recipients. In particular, the Panel found that the United States acted inconsistently with:

---

[11] Panel Report, para. 8.1. See also paras. 1.42 and 1.43.

[12] Panel Report, para. 8.2.a.i. See also para. 7.193.

[13] Section 351.511(a)(2)(i)-(iii) of the US Regulations contains the price benchmarking mechanism to be applied by the USDOC when determining whether or not the provision of goods by a government or public body confers a benefit on the recipient. The mechanism provides for three tiers against which the government price is to be compared: Tier I – actual market-determined price; Tier II – world market price; and Tier III – consistency with market principles. (See Panel Report, para. 7.15)

[14] Panel Report, para. 8.2.a.ii. See also para. 7.194.

[15] These "captive mining" programmes refer to those in respect of which the Government of India (GOI) provided iron ore and coal through the grant of the right to mine those minerals. The mining rights at issue were known as "captive mining rights" in that they allowed the beneficiary an exclusive right to mine iron ore or coal for their own use in the production of steel. With particular respect to the coal mining rights, these were granted under the Coal Mining Nationalization Act. The Panel addressed India's challenge of the USDOC's determination that Tata Iron and Steel Company Limited, which later became known as Tata Steel Limited (Tata), was a beneficiary of the Captive Mining of Coal Programme. (See Panel Report, paras. 7.220, 7.233, 7.240, 7.242 (and fn 435 thereto), and 7.245-7.252)

a. Article 12.5 of the SCM Agreement, by failing to determine the existence of the Captive Mining of Iron Ore Programme on the basis of accurate information[16];

b. Article 1.1(a)(1)(iii) of the SCM Agreement, by determining without sufficient evidentiary basis that the GOI granted Tata Steel Limited (Tata) a financial contribution in the form of a captive coal mining lease under the Captive Mining of Coal Programme/Coal Mining Nationalization Act[17]; and

c. Article 14(d) of the SCM Agreement, in connection with the USDOC's rejection of certain domestic pricing information when assessing benefit in respect of mining rights for iron ore.[18]

1.8 Additionally, the Panel upheld several more of India's claims. These claims related to, *inter alia*, the US International Trade Commission's (USITC) assessment of injury including its use of cross-cumulation[19], its application of "facts available", and its failure to observe its public notice obligations. In particular, the Panel found that the United States acted inconsistently with:

a. Article 15.3 of the SCM Agreement, with respect to Section 1677(7)(G) of the US Statute "as such" and "as applied" in the original investigation at issue, in connection with the "cross-cumulation" of the effects of imports that are subject to a countervailing duty investigation with the effects of imports that are not subject to simultaneous countervailing duty investigations[20];

b. Articles 15.1, 15.2, 15.4, and 15.5 of the SCM Agreement, with respect to Section 1677(7)(G) of the US Statute "as such" and "as applied" in the original investigation at issue, in connection with injury assessments based on, *inter alia*, the volume, effects, and impact of non-subsidized, dumped imports[21];

c. Article 12.7 of the SCM Agreement, by applying "facts available" devoid of any factual foundation in connection with several determinations concerning Jindal Steel Works (JSW), Vijayanagar Minerals Pvt. Ltd. (VMPL), and Tata[22]; and

d. Article 22.5 of the SCM Agreement, by failing to provide adequate notice of the USDOC's consideration of certain in-

16 Panel Report, para. 8.2.b.i. See also paras. 7.217 and 7.265.

17 Panel Report, para. 8.2.b.ii. See also paras. 7.252 and 7.265.

18 Panel Report, para. 8.2.b.iii. See also paras. 7.263 and 7.265.

19 The Panel defined "cross-cumulation" as the cumulative assessment of the effects of imports that are subject to a countervailing duty investigation with the effects of imports that are subject to only a parallel anti-dumping investigation. (See Panel Report, para. 7.339)

20 Panel Report, para. 8.2.c. See also para. 7.356.

21 Panel Report, para. 8.2.d. See also para. 7.369.

22 Panel Report, para. 8.2.e. See also paras. 7.452, 7.456, 7.465, 7.468, 7.471, 7.473, and 7.475.

country benchmarks when assessing benefit conferred by the NMDC's sales of iron ore.[23]

1.9 However, the Panel rejected several of India's claims. These claims related to, *inter alia*, the USDOC's appreciation of the evidence, its assessment of adequacy of remuneration and its determination of benefit, its assessment of "prevailing market conditions" within the meaning of Article 14(d) of the SCM Agreement, its determination of whether the Steel Development Fund (SDF) constituted a public body, its examination of new subsidy allegations in the conduct of administrative reviews, and the USITC's assessment of injury. Specifically, the Panel rejected India's claims that the United States acted inconsistently with:

a. Article 14(d) of the SCM Agreement, with respect to Section 351.511(a)(2)(i)-(iii) of the US Regulations "as such"[24];

b. Articles 14(d), 19.3, and 19.4 of the SCM Agreement, with respect to Section 351.511(a)(2)(iv) of the US Regulations "as such"[25];

c. Articles 1.1(a)(1), 1.1(b), 2.4, 14(d), and the chapeau of Article 14 of the SCM Agreement, in connection with the provision of high-grade iron ore by the NMDC[26];

d. Articles 1.1(a)(1)(iii), 1.1(b), and 14(d) of the SCM Agreement, in connection with the Captive Mining of Iron Ore Programme and the Captive Mining of Coal Programme[27];

e. Articles 1.1(a)(1), 1.1(a)(1)(i), 1.1(b), 14(b), and the chapeau of Article 14 of the SCM Agreement in connection with the SDF[28];

f. Articles 15.1, 15.2, 15.3, 15.4, and 15.5 of the SCM Agreement, in connection with Sections 1675a(a)(7) and 1675b(e)(2) of the US Statute "as such", and in connection with Section 1675a(a)(7) of the US Statute "as applied" in the sunset review at issue[29];

g. Articles 15.1 and 15.4 of the SCM Agreement in connection with the USITC's evaluation of certain economic factors in its injury determination[30];

h. Article 12.7 of the SCM Agreement, in connection with Section 1677e(b) of the US Statute and Section 351.308(a), (b), and (c) of the US Regulations "as such"[31];

---

23 Panel Report, para. 8.2.f. See also para. 7.352.

24 Panel Report, para. 8.3.a. See also paras. 7.35, 7.52, and 7.64.

25 Panel Report, para. 8.3.b. See also paras. 7.63 and 7.64.

26 Panel Report, para. 8.3.c. See also paras. 7.89, 7.140, 7.171, 7.193, and 7.194.

27 Panel Report, para. 8.3.d. See also paras. 7.241, 7.260, and 7.264.

28 Panel Report, para. 8.3.e. See also paras. 7.279, 7.297, 7.301, and 7.311-7.313.

29 Panel Report, para. 8.3.f. See also para. 7.392.

30 Panel Report, para. 8.3.g. See also para. 7.408.

31 Panel Report, para. 8.3.h. See also para. 7.445.

i. Article 12.7 of the SCM Agreement, in connection with the application of "facts available" concerning: (i) the USDOC's "rule" to use the highest non-*de minimis* subsidy rate; and (ii) several of the USDOC's determinations[32];

j. Articles 11.1, 13.1, 21.1, 21.2, 22.1, and 22.2 of the SCM Agreement, in connection with the examination of new subsidy allegations in the administrative reviews at issue[33]; and

k. Article 22.5 of the SCM Agreement, by failing properly to explain in the public notices the reasons for rejecting: (i) the interested parties' argument relating to the treatment of SDF levies; and (ii) the use of NMDC export prices as a price benchmark.[34]

1.10 Finally, the Panel exercised judicial economy in respect of India's claims under:

a. Articles 2.1(c) and 2.4 of the SCM Agreement, in connection with the USDOC's determination that the Captive Mining of Iron Ore Programme is *de facto* specific[35];

b. Article 2.1(a) and (b) of the SCM Agreement, in connection with the USDOC's determination that the Captive Mining of Coal Programme/Coal Mining Nationalization Act is *de jure* specific[36];

c. Article 22.5 of the SCM Agreement, in connection with the USDOC's public notice concerning: (i) the GOI's grant of captive coal mining rights to Tata; and (ii) the *de facto* specificity of the Captive Mining of Iron Ore Programme[37]; and

d. Articles 10, 19.3, 19.4, 32.1, and 32.5 of the SCM Agreement, Article VI of the GATT 1994, and Article XVI:4 of the WTO Agreement, in connection with India's consequential claims.[38]

1.11 Pursuant to Article 19.1 of the DSU, having found that the United States acted inconsistently with certain provisions of the SCM Agreement, the Panel recommended that the United States bring its measures into conformity with its obligations under that Agreement. Given the complexities to which implementation may give rise, the Panel declined India's request to exercise its discretion under the second sentence of Article 19.1 to suggest ways in which the United States might implement the recommendation.[39]

---

32 Panel Report, para. 8.3.i. See also paras. 7.450, 7.458, 7.459, and 7.480.

33 Panel Report, para. 8.3.j. See also para. 7.508.

34 Panel Report, para. 8.3.k. See also paras. 7.531 and 7.535.

35 Panel Report, para. 8.4.a. See also paras. 7.218 and 7.219.

36 Panel Report, para. 8.4.b. See also para. 7.253.

37 Panel Report, para. 8.4.c. See also paras. 7.533 and 7.534.

38 Panel Report, para. 8.4.d. See also para. 7.537.

39 Panel Report, para. 8.6.

1.2 Appellate Proceedings

1.12 On 8 August 2014, India notified the Dispute Settlement Body (DSB), pursuant to Articles 16.4 and 17 of the DSU, of its intention to appeal certain issues of law covered in the Panel Report and certain legal interpretations developed by the Panel, and filed a Notice of Appeal[40] and an appellant's submission pursuant to Rule 20 and Rule 21, respectively, of the Working Procedures for Appellate Review[41] (Working Procedures). On 13 August 2014, the United States notified the DSB, pursuant to Articles 16.4 and 17 of the DSU, of its intention to appeal certain issues of law covered in the Panel Report and certain legal interpretations developed by the Panel, and filed a Notice of Other Appeal[42] and an other appellant's submission pursuant to Rule 23 of the Working Procedures.

1.13 On 11 August 2014, the United States requested the Appellate Body Division hearing the appeal to extend the deadline for filing the United States' appellee's submission in this appeal by seven calendar days, to 2 September 2014, due to the size and complexity of India's appeal. On 12 August 2014, the Division invited India and the third parties to comment in writing, no later than 15 August 2014, on the United States' request. India and the European Union provided comments. India requested that any extension of the deadline for the United States to file its appellee's submission be equally granted to India. The European Union requested the Division, if it accepted the United States' request, to consequently extend the deadline for third participants to file their notifications and written submissions. On 19 August 2014, the Division issued a Procedural Ruling to the participants and third parties in respect of the United States' request. The Division decided, pursuant to Rule 16 of the Working Procedures, to extend the date for filing the appellees' submissions to 1 September 2014. Consequently, the Division also decided to extend the date for filing the third participants' written submissions and notifications to 3 September 2014. This Procedural Ruling is attached to this Report as Annex 3.

1.14 On 1 September 2014, India and the United States each filed an appellee's submission.[43] On 3 September 2014, five third participants (Australia, Canada, China, the European Union, and Saudi Arabia) each filed a third participant's submission.[44] On the same day, Turkey notified its intention to appear at the oral hearing as a third participant.[45]

1.15 The oral hearing in this appeal was held on 24-26 September 2014. The participants each made an opening oral statement. Four third participants

[40] WT/DS436/6 (attached as Annex 1 to this Report).
[41] WT/AB/WP/6, 16 August 2010.
[42] WT/DS436/7 (attached as Annex 2 to this Report).
[43] Pursuant to Rules 22 and 23(4) of the Working Procedures.
[44] Pursuant to Rule 24(1) of the Working Procedures.
[45] Pursuant to Rule 24(4) of the Working Procedures.

(Australia, Canada, China, and Saudi Arabia) made oral statements. The participants and third participants responded to questions posed by the Members of the Appellate Body Division hearing the appeal.

1.16 By letter dated 6 October 2014, the Chair of the Appellate Body notified the Chair of the DSB that the Appellate Body would not be able to circulate its report within the 60-day period stipulated in Article 17.5 of the DSU, or within the 90-day period pursuant to the same provision. The Chair of the Appellate Body explained that this was due to scheduling issues arising from the substantial workload in the Appellate Body in the second half of 2014 including: (i) the request for the extension of the deadlines for filing the appellees' and third participants' submissions in this appeal; (ii) the fact that the Appellate Body comprised only six Members when the appeal was filed; (iii) the overlap in the composition of the Divisions hearing the different appeals during this period; (iv) the number and complexity of the issues raised in these and concurrent appeal proceedings; and (v) the additional time required for translation of the report for circulation in all three official languages. Consequently, the Chair of the Appellate Body informed the Chair of the DSB that the report in this appeal would be circulated no later than 8 December 2014.

2. ARGUMENTS OF THE PARTICIPANTS AND THIRD PARTICIPANTS

2.1 Claims of Error by India – Appellant

2.1.1 The Panel's terms of reference

2.1 India requests the Appellate Body to reverse the Panel's preliminary ruling that the claims in Sections XII.C.1 and XII.C.2 of India's first written submission to the Panel were outside the Panel's terms of reference. India further requests the Appellate Body to complete the analysis in respect of these claims on appeal. India's appeal in this regard is contingent on the Appellate Body rejecting its appeal that the sale of high-grade iron ore by the NMDC does not constitute an actionable subsidy under the SCM Agreement.

2.2 In its appellant's submission, India claims that the Panel acted inconsistently with Article 11 of the DSU, and erred in its application of Article 6.2 of the DSU, by failing to address the meaning of the term "initiated" in India's panel request. India also claims that the Panel acted inconsistently with Article 11 of the DSU by failing to take into account: (i) the fact that the United States did not suffer prejudice by the alleged lack of clarity of the panel request; and (ii) certain questions circulated during consultations.

2.1.1.1 The meaning of the word "initiated" in India's panel request

2.3 India argues that the Panel erred in its construction of the term "initiated", as used in India's panel request. India recalls that paragraph 12(f)(i) of its panel request stated that "no investigation was initiated or conducted", in violation of Article 11 of the SCM Agreement[46], and Sections XII.C.1 and XII.C.2 of its first written submission referred to "initiating investigation[s] ... [without] sufficient evidence", in violation of Articles 11.1, 11.2, and 11.9 of the SCM Agreement.[47] In India's view, the term "initiated" is defined as a term of art in footnote 37 of the SCM Agreement to mean a "procedural action by which a Member formally commences an investigation as provided in Article 11". Thus, the term "initiated" in India's panel request should be construed in the light of that definition, such that the phrase "no investigation was initiated or conducted" should be understood to mean "such investigations not being commenced and performed in a manner '*provided in Article 11*' of the SCM agreement".[48] According to India, such reading of its panel request would automatically cover violations of Articles 11.1, 11.2, and 11.9 of the SCM Agreement, including the commencement of investigations without sufficient evidence.

2.4 India submits that, although its panel request referred to Article 11 of the SCM Agreement only generally, the interlinked nature of its provisions and their common relationship to the initiation and conduct of investigations means that its panel request was sufficient to present the problem clearly in relation to all of the provisions of Article 11, except Articles 11.6, 11.8, 11.10, and 11.11. India's decision to limit its claims in its first written submission to Articles 11.1, 11.2, and 11.9 of the SCM Agreement should not influence the construction of its panel request. In India's view, by failing to examine the meaning of the term "initiated" as set out in India's panel request, the Panel failed to apply correctly the legal standard under Article 6.2 of the DSU to the facts of this case.

2.5 Furthermore, India argues that the Panel failed to conduct an objective assessment because the Panel, "[i]n a mere footnote", dismissed India's claim in relation to the meaning of the term "initiated".[49] In India's view, in order to discharge its duties under Article 11 of the DSU, the Panel should have, first, examined whether the term "initiated" should be construed in the light of the definition provided in footnote 37 of the SCM Agreement, and, second, should have examined whether the claims in Sections XII.C.1 and XII.C.2 of India's first written submission were captured by that definition.

2.1.1.2 Relevance of prejudice and questions during consultations

2.6 India argues that the Panel erred by failing to apply the findings of the Appellate Body in *Korea – Dairy* and of the panel in *US – Lamb*. India recalls its

---

46 India's appellant's submission, para. 663 (quoting India's panel request, para. 12).

47 India's appellant's submission, para. 664 (quoting India's first written submission to the Panel, section XII.C.1).

48 India's appellant's submission, para. 674 (quoting India's response to United States' requests for preliminary rulings, para. 10 (emphasis original)).

49 India's appellant's submission, para. 675.

argument before the Panel that, pursuant to the Appellate Body's finding in *Korea – Dairy*, an assessment of compliance with Article 6.2 of the DSU must take into account whether the ability of the respondent to defend itself was actually prejudiced by an alleged defect in the panel request. In India's view, the United States "merely asserted" that it sustained prejudice, but offered no supporting particulars.[50] According to India, in rejecting India's argument, the Panel failed to assess the relevance and implications of the Appellate Body's finding in *Korea – Dairy* in relation to its argument.

2.7 India further recalls its argument before the Panel that, based on the panel's finding in *US – Lamb*, one of the "attendant circumstances" to consider in assessing whether a panel request complies with Article 6.2 is the consultations held between the parties, including the written questions circulated for that purpose.[51] In India's view, therefore, the Panel should have taken into account the questions circulated by India during the consultations stage in construing its panel request. India contends that the Panel mistakenly relied on the Appellate Body report in *US – Upland Cotton* in finding that it could not refer to events that had occurred at the consultations stage of the dispute.[52] According to India, unlike the panel in *US – Lamb*, the Appellate Body in *US – Upland Cotton* was not dealing with the relevance of what took place during consultations in the context of Article 6.2 of the DSU, and the Appellate Body in that case was not seized with the question of harmoniously applying Article 6.2 of the DSU with Article 4.6 of the DSU.[53]

2.8 India submits that prior adopted findings of the Appellate Body and panels form part of the *acquis* of the WTO system and, unless cogent reasons permit, a subsequent panel cannot disregard such earlier findings.[54] Thus, in order to discharge its duties under Article 11 of the DSU, the Panel should have considered and assessed the relevance and implications of such findings, and should have justified its failure to apply those findings with cogent reasons.[55]

2.1.1.3 Completion of the analysis

2.9 India requests the Appellate Body to complete the analysis of the claims in Sections XII.C.1 and XII.C.2 of its first written submission to the Panel in the event that it reverses the Panel's preliminary ruling under appeal.

2.10 In India's view, there are sufficient undisputed facts on the record and factual findings by the Panel to facilitate completion of the analysis. In

---

[50] India's appellant's submission, para. 668.

[51] India's appellant's submission, para. 669 (referring to India's response to United States' requests for preliminary rulings, para. 25; and Panel Report, *US – Lamb*, para. 5.40).

[52] India's appellant's submission, para. 671 (referring to Panel Report, para. 1.37).

[53] India's appellant's submission, para. 672 (referring to Appellate Body Report, *US – Upland Cotton*, para. 286).

[54] India's appellant's submission, para. 670, (fn omitted)

[55] India's appellant's submission, para. 670.

particular, India's claims relate to the sufficiency of evidence contained in the application of the domestic industry for the initiation of investigations into two specific subsidy programmes. The presence of that application on the panel record provides a sufficient basis on which to assess compliance with Articles 11.1, 11.2, and 11.9 of the DSU.

2.11 According to India, during the 2004 administrative review, the USDOC initiated an investigation into the alleged sale of high-grade iron ore by the NMDC for less than adequate remuneration. However, an examination of the relevant documents and evidence provided by the domestic industry reveal that the domestic industry did not allege that the NMDC is a "public body" selling high-grade iron ore for less than adequate remuneration, but, rather, alleged that the imposition of an export restraint on iron ore resulted in low-priced inputs to steel producers.[56] According to India, this means that the application contained no evidence in respect of sales by the NMDC for less than adequate remuneration. In respect of the Target Plus Scheme (TPS), India asserts that the documents and evidence submitted by the domestic industry made no allegations in respect of that alleged programme.[57]

2.12 Thus, according to India, the omission by the domestic industry to provide any evidence on these two alleged subsidy programmes means that the United States violated Articles 11.1 and 11.2 of the SCM Agreement by initiating investigations without sufficient evidence, and violated Article 11.9 of the SCM Agreement by failing to terminate the investigations promptly in the absence of sufficient evidence.

2.13 On that basis, the Appellate Body should complete the analysis and find that the United States acted inconsistently with Article 11.1, 11.2, and 11.9 of the SCM Agreement.

2.1.2 Public Body

2.14 India alleges that the Panel erred when it rejected India's claims that the USDOC acted inconsistently with Article 1.1(a)(1) of the SCM Agreement in determining that the NMDC constitutes a "public body". India contends that the Panel's findings were based on a flawed legal interpretation of Article 1.1(a)(1) of the SCM Agreement and that the Panel failed to make an objective assessment of the matter before it, as required under Article 11 of the DSU. India requests

---

56 India's appellant's submission, para. 686 (referring to United States Steel Corporation, Letter dated 2 May 2005 to USDOC alleging additional government subsidies (Essar) in Certain Hot-Rolled Carbon Steel Flat Products from India (C-533-821) (Panel Exhibit IND-15A); and United States Steel Corporation, Letter dated 29 June 2005 in response to USDOC request for clarification regarding new subsidy allegations (Essar) of 2 May 2005 in Certain Hot-Rolled Carbon Steel Flat Products from India (C-533-821) (Panel Exhibit IND-15B)).

57 India's appellant's submission, para. 688 (referring to Essar Steel Limited, Response dated 12 April 2005 to USDOC questionnaire in administrative review of Certain Hot-Rolled Carbon Steel Flat Products from India (C-533-821) for the period 01/01-31/12/2004 (Panel Exhibit IND-57)).

the Appellate Body to reverse the Panel's findings upholding the USDOC's determination that the NMDC is a "public body". India also requests the Appellate Body to complete the legal analysis and to find that the USDOC acted inconsistently with Article 1.1(a)(1) of the SCM Agreement in determining that the NMDC is a "public body".

2.1.2.1 Interpretation and application of Article 1.1(a)(1) of the SCM Agreement: Public Bodies

2.15 Referring to the meaning of the term "public body" as clarified by the Appellate Body in *US – Anti-Dumping and Countervailing Duties (China)*, India submits that the Panel misunderstood the findings of the Appellate Body in that dispute and thus erred when it construed the term "public body" to mean any entity that is "meaningfully controlled" by a government.

2.16 India refers to the Appellate Body report in *US – Anti-Dumping and Countervailing Duties (China)* to argue that, for an entity to be a "public body" within the meaning of Article 1.1(a)(1), it must have the power to regulate, control, or supervise individuals or otherwise restrain the conduct of "private bodies".[58] In addition, India claims that a "public body" must also be able to entrust or direct a "private body" – i.e. give responsibility to, or exercise authority over a "private body". India further alleges that the Panel erroneously considered proof of "meaningful control" to be a "necessary and sufficient" condition in order to establish that an entity is a public body, and points out that the Panel's entire evaluation "revolves around whether GOI had 'meaningful control' over NMDC".[59] India observes, however, that the Appellate Body did not refer to the exercise of "meaningful control" as a substitute to the test of "governmental authority to perform [a] governmental function".[60] Rather, the Appellate Body found that evidence that the government is exercising "meaningful control" over an entity and its conduct may, in certain circumstances, be considered relevant in inferring that the entity is exercising governmental authority.[61]

2.17 India submits that the Panel erred in its application of Article 1.1(a)(1) of the SCM Agreement to the determinations made by the USDOC in the underlying investigation, by failing to examine if the USDOC had considered whether the NMDC performed governmental functions. Specifically, the Panel should have examined if the USDOC considered whether the NMDC: (i) was vested with the power and authority to perform governmental functions; (ii) had

58 See India's appellant's submission, para. 307 (referring to Appellate Body Report, *US – Anti-Dumping and Countervailing Duties (China)*, para. 290).

59 India's appellant's submission, para. 321.

60 India's appellant's submission, para. 336.

61 India's appellant's submission, para. 322 (referring to Appellate Body Report, *US – Anti-Dumping and Countervailing Duties (China)*, para. 318).

the power and authority to direct or entrust a private body; and (iii) was in fact exercising governmental functions. Furthermore, India contends that the Panel erred in its application of Article 1.1(a)(1) by giving a dispositive role to the existence of "meaningful control". India adds that the Panel wrongly relied on the United States' assertion that the NMDC was "governed by the Ministry of Steel"[62], without providing an adequate explanation as to how such "governance" demonstrates that the government exercised meaningful control. India argues, in the alternative, that the Panel erred in finding that the GOI's alleged involvement in the NMDC's board of directors together with the government ownership of the NMDC was sufficient to fulfil the requirements of "meaningful control", as was referred to by the Appellate Body in *US – Anti-Dumping and Countervailing Duties (China)*.[63]

2.18 Furthermore, India submits that the Panel erred in finding that the involvement of the GOI in the appointment of the NMDC's directors was "more 'substantive' or 'meaningful' than mere shareholding".[64] According to India, shareholding and appointment of directors are "necessarily indistinguishable from each other"[65] as they are "merely two sides of the same coin".[66] That being the case, a finding of government shareholding and the government's concomitant right to appoint directors cannot be sufficient, taken alone, to support a finding that an entity is a public body. Thus, according to India, the USDOC's determination that the NMDC is a public body was based solely on the GOI's shareholding, given that the appointment of directors could not be considered separate and additional to shareholding. India maintains that, in reaching its finding, the Panel's reliance on the Appellate Body's finding in *US – Anti-Dumping and Countervailing Duties (China)* was misplaced. This is because the Appellate Body's findings concerned the appointment of chief executives rather than of a board of directors, and, in any event, the Appellate Body relied on other factors in support of its findings.[67]

2.1.2.2 Article 11 of the DSU

2.19 India also claims that the Panel failed to comply with its obligation to make an objective assessment of the matter before it, as required under Article 11 of the DSU. In this respect, India identifies four discrete errors in the Panel's review of the evidence underlying the USDOC's finding that the NMDC is a "public body". Specifically, India contends that the Panel: (i) disregarded an admission made by the United States in the context of the panel proceedings in *US – Anti-Dumping and Countervailing Duties (China)*; (ii) relied on an *ex post*

62 India's appellant's submission, para. 323 (quoting Panel Report, para. 7.82).
63 India's appellant's submission, para. 301.
64 India's appellant's submission, para. 291 (referring to Panel Report, para. 7.85).
65 India's appellant's submission, para. 290.
66 India's appellant's submission, para. 291.
67 India's appellant's submission, paras. 293-296.

rationalization of the USDOC's "public body" determination; (iii) ignored certain evidence regarding the GOI's involvement in the appointment of directors of the NMDC; and (iv) failed to assess properly evidence regarding the NMDC's status as a *Miniratna* or *Navratna* company.

2.20 First, India challenges the Panel's acceptance of the United States' assertion that, in finding the NMDC to be a "public body", the USDOC considered factors other than the GOI's shareholding in the NMDC. India contends that, by accepting the United States' assertion on this point, the Panel improperly disregarded an admission allegedly made by the United States in the panel proceedings in *US – Anti-Dumping and Countervailing Duties (China)*. According to India, the United States admitted that, in the investigation under challenge in that dispute, the USDOC considered the shareholding of the GOI "as the sole factor" relevant for its "public body" determinations, "without reference to any more factors".[68] India submits that admissions made by a party on a specific fact in prior WTO dispute settlement proceedings are relevant in subsequent disputes[69], and argues, therefore, that the Panel ought to have considered the alleged admission of the United States rather than "disregarding it outright".

2.21 Second, India argues that the Panel improperly upheld the USDOC's determination on the basis of *ex post facto* explanations provided by the United States in the panel proceedings. India posits that the USDOC's reference to the NMDC being "governed by" the GOI was at the root of the Panel's rejection of India's claim. Yet, India argues, the term "governed by" is not defined in any of the determinations under challenge. Rather, the United States explained what the term actually meant for the first time during the panel proceedings. India argues that reliance by a panel on supplementary information in this way results in a standard of review falling short of what is required by Article 11 of the DSU. Further, India contends that evidence on the record before the USDOC was irrelevant to the Panel's consideration, unless it formed part of the evaluation or determination of the USDOC itself. According to India, in order to rely on such evidence, the United States would have had to demonstrate that the USDOC had actually considered and evaluated that evidence, and that such evaluation was reflected in the USDOC's determination at issue.

2.22 Third, assuming that the United States' explanations of the meaning of the term "governed by" are not deemed to constitute *ex post facto* rationalizations, India submits that the Panel disregarded material evidence in finding that the United States actually relied on something other than government shareholding. In support of its contention, India recalls that the term "governed by" was defined by the United States by reference to three factors: (i) evidence of GOI involvement in the board of directors of the NMDC; (ii) the "administrative control" of the NMDC by the GOI; and (iii) evidence in the 2007 administrative

---

68 India's appellant's submission, para. 252. (emphasis omitted)

69 India's appellant's submission, para. 254.

review that the GOI appointed seven of the 13 directors of the NMDC. India then points to the following evidence that it sees as contradicting this proposition and which the Panel allegedly failed to consider.

2.23 India argues that, as the interested parties pointed out during the investigation, the majority of the directors whose appointment the GOI was allegedly involved in were all independent. However, the USDOC never considered this to be a relevant factor in the analysis. Furthermore, although the USDOC itself distinguished between the GOI "appointing" two directors and having mere "approval power" over the appointment of seven other directors, it never sought further information or examined the difference between the two. In India's view, the USDOC's "disregard and disinterest" in further examining such information can be explained by its statements of law that "majority ownership of an input supplier qualifies it as a government authority within the meaning of [19 USC § 1677(5)(D)(i))]" and that "[a]nalyzing additional factors is not necessary absent information that calls into question whether government ownership does not mean government control".[70] India claims that the Panel relied on isolated statements from the Issues and Decision Memorandum for the 2007 administrative review[71] (2007 AR Issues and Decision Memorandum), giving the appearance that the USDOC actually fully considered the GOI's involvement in the selection of the board of directors of the NMDC.

2.24 Second, India refers to an alleged admission by the United States before the Panel that "administrative control" was not used in its determinations. According to India, administrative control is not an independent factor because the United States equates the notion of "administrative control" with "governed by", which in turn is equated with ownership and appointment of board of directors. India posits, however, that the Panel referred to the notion of "administrative control" as if it were "something unique and additional".[72] India submits that an objective assessment of the facts in the underlying investigation should have led the Panel to discard administrative control as a relevant factor in reaching its determination.

2.25 Third, according to India, the USDOC's reference to the appointment of board directors was only to reject arguments raised by interested parties that the GOI did not control the board of directors, and was not an independent factor supporting the USDOC's finding. India submits that the Panel erred, therefore, by concluding that the USDOC considered something more than government shareholding in the 2004 and 2006 administrative reviews in the underlying investigation.

2.26 Finally, India argues that the Panel erred by ruling on whether the NMDC's status as a *Miniratna* or *Navratna* company during certain periods

---

[70] India's appellant's submission, para. 273 (quoting 2007 AR Issues and Decision Memorandum (Panel Exhibit IND-38), Analysis of Comment 10, p. 45).

[71] See *supra*, fn 70.

[72] India's appellant's submission, para. 269.

meant that it could not be a "public body". Instead of making "a finding on the implication of 'Miniratna' or 'Navaratna' status of NMDC", the Panel should have considered only the USDOC's "failure" to evaluate the evidence before it.[73] Therefore, India claims, the Panel made a finding on a matter not before it, "in direct breach of its function under Article 11 of the DSU".[74]

2.1.2.3 Completion of the analysis

2.27 In the event that the Appellate Body reverses the Panel's finding upholding the USDOC's determination that the NMDC is a "public body", India requests the Appellate Body to complete the analysis and find that the USDOC acted inconsistently with Article 1.1(a)(1) of the SCM Agreement in determining that the NMDC is a "public body". India notes that the factual findings of the Panel and the undisputed facts on record constitute a sufficient basis for the Appellate Body to complete the analysis.

2.28 India maintains that the USDOC's determination that the NMDC is a public body is inconsistent with Article 1.1(a)(1) because the USDOC relied solely on the GOI's shareholding in the NMDC to support its finding. India recalls the argument of the United States before the Panel that the USDOC considered something beyond just the GOI's shareholding because the determination also refers to the NMDC as being "governed by" the GOI. India contends that the explanations provided by the United States on the term "governed by" are, at best, *ex post facto* clarifications that cannot be considered at this stage of the proceedings, and that even those *ex post facto* explanations are contrary to the evidence on record. India points out that the USDOC foreclosed any arguments regarding the composition of the board of directors and the fact that they were "independent directors". India further notes that it is undisputed on the record that the GOI pointed to the *Miniratna* status of the NMDC, which grants the latter significant autonomy in conducting its affairs.

2.29 India further argues that the determination reveals that the USDOC failed to determine if the NMDC was vested with the power and authority to perform governmental functions, or to direct or control a private body, or was in fact performing governmental functions. Specifically, even assuming that the GOI had a significant role to play in the appointment of the NMDC's board of directors, there was nothing in the USDOC's determination to support a finding that this would amount to the GOI exercising meaningful control over the NMDC. India recalls that, in *US – Anti-Dumping and Countervailing Duties (China)*, the Appellate Body suggested "the possibility of a government's exercise of meaningful control as a proxy ... may indicate, on a case-to-case basis, the existence of 'governmental authority to perform governmental function'".[75] According to India, the USDOC ought to have examined whether

[73] India's appellant's submission, para. 282. (emphasis omitted)
[74] India's appellant's submission, para. 282.
[75] India's appellant's submission, para. 336.

any alleged control meant that the NMDC performed governmental functions on behalf of the GOI. India submits that the USDOC performed no such examination and, instead, applied a straightforward presumption that the alleged existence of potential control of the NMDC by the GOI was sufficient for a "public body" determination.

2.1.3 Financial contribution

2.1.3.1 Captive mining rights

2.30 India claims that the Panel erred in finding that the USDOC's determination that India provided goods through the grant of mining rights for iron ore and coal is not inconsistent with Article 1.1(a)(1)(iii) of the SCM Agreement. India principally contends that Article 1.1(a)(1)(iii) does not cover grants for which the beneficiaries have to engage in significant intervening acts to make a good available for use or enjoyment. India requests the Appellate Body to find that the Panel erred in the interpretation and application of Article 1.1(a)(1)(iii), and that the Panel failed to discharge its duty under Article 11 of the DSU. India further requests the Appellate Body to reverse the Panel's finding and to complete the legal analysis and find that the United States acted inconsistently with Article 1.1(a)(1)(iii) of the SCM Agreement in determining that the grant of mining rights for iron ore and coal is a financial contribution.

2.31 India recalls that, in *US – Softwood Lumber IV*, the Appellate Body rejected Canada's contention that the meaning of the term "provides" in Article 1.1(a)(1)(iii) should be limited to the "supplying" or "giving" of goods or services, and cannot be broadly interpreted to mean "making available".[76] India also notes, however, that the Appellate Body warned that the meaning of the term "provides" cannot be stretched to its extreme. India adds that the Appellate Body emphasized the need to ensure that only governmental actions that bear a "reasonable proximate connection" to the use or enjoyment of the goods in question could be covered under Article 1.1(a)(1)(iii).[77]

2.32 India considers that the relevant context also supports this conclusion. India argues that the term "contribution" in the chapeau of Article 1.1(a)(1) normally refers to a "gift or payment to a common fund or collection" or "the part played by a person or thing in bringing about a result or helping something to advance", and that the use of the term "financial" makes it clear that the contribution in question must be related to monetary resources or providing funding.[78] Furthermore, the word "by" means that there is a specific action that is to be undertaken by the government or any public body and that this specific

---

[76] India's appellant's submission, para. 491 (referring to Appellate Body Report, *US – Softwood Lumber IV*, paras. 70 and 71).
[77] *Ibid.*
[78] India's appellant's submission, para. 492 (referring to *Oxford Dictionary of English*, 3rd edn, A. Stevenson (ed.) (Oxford University Press, 2010), pp. 379 and 653).

action involves "contributing" something of economic value.[79] India adds that the presence of the phrase "i.e. where" clarifies that the four subparagraphs under Article 1.1(a)(1) are all meant to explain the situations or conditions as to when a financial contribution by a government or a public body is deemed to exist under the SCM Agreement. In India's view, it is therefore clear from this context that the "goods or services" referred to in Article 1.1(a)(1)(iii) correspond to the "financial contribution" referred to in the chapeau, and that the specific action undertaken by the government or public body must be "providing" the "goods" such that the governmental action itself, rather than the intervening acts of non-governmental bodies, directly results in the provision of the goods.

2.33 India contends that the grant of mining rights is a situation where the government does not really "provide" the mineral in question, because "significant efforts, risks and investment have to be undertaken by the miner to actually make the mineral available for use or enjoyment".[80] In India's view, the Panel applied a "but for" test instead of a reasonably proximate connection test, whereby the Panel considered that, "but for" the government's granting of the rights, mining companies could not have used or enjoyed the mineral in the first place. However, this logic would apply equally to other governmental acts, such as allowing the mining company to be registered as a legal person within domestic law, or to be able to transact in the domestic legal framework through registration procedures in the domestic tax system, or to own or lease equipment or vehicles for mining or transportation. India maintains that this results in the very "slippery slope" that the Appellate Body sought to avoid in *US – Softwood Lumber IV* when it clarified the need to show a reasonable proximate connection under Article 1.1(a)(1)(iii).[81]

2.34 India submits that there is no reasonably proximate relationship between the grant of mining rights, on the one hand, and the availability of the mined iron ore or coal, on the other hand. India recalls the panel's finding, in *US – Softwood Lumber IV*, that the "right to harvest standing timber" is not severable from "standing timber".[82] There was therefore no intervening act in *US – Softwood Lumber IV* between granting the "right to harvest standing timber" and "standing timber". This is not the case with mining, India argues, because the connection between the grant of mining rights and the provision of the mineral itself is severed by a series of significant actions performed by the beneficiary at its own risk and cost. India further contends that, unlike the harvesting rights for timber, the exploitation of a mining right, apart from involving considerable expenses incurred in procurement of the right itself, also involves costs of labour,

---

[79] India's appellant's submission, para. 492 (referring to *Oxford Dictionary of English*, 3rd edn, A. Stevenson (ed.) (Oxford University Press, 2010), p. 240).

[80] India's appellant's submission, para. 495.

[81] India's appellant's submission, para. 496.

[82] India's appellant's submission, para. 499 (referring to Panel Report, *US – Softwood Lumber IV*, para. 7.17).

exploration, extraction, and a number of industrial processes that make the minerals marketable and usable.

2.35 India notes the Panel's consideration that India's argument – regarding the remoteness of the mining lease and the extraction of mined material – would create legal uncertainty. India argues that the Panel's concern was "entirely exaggerated"[83] since the SCM Agreement is filled with provisions that reflect a certain amount of subjectivity in application. In addition, both the panel and the Appellate Body are required to interpret and apply the covered agreements in accordance with customary rules of international law, and where such interpretation imposes the need for a case-by-case analysis, the panel and Appellate Body "must not cower away from such requirements citing alleged legal uncertainty".[84] India argues, therefore, that a panel "cannot cite difficulties in application to simply dilute this very requirement into redundancy".[85]

2.36 India also claims that the Panel erred under Article 11 of the DSU in not giving appropriate consideration to India's evidence relating to the amount of royalty paid to the GOI and the GOI's lack of control over the extraction process. India maintains that, despite the Panel's statements to the contrary, India had explained the significance of mining rights constituting only about 9% of the total price of the mined ore. Recalling its view that there is no proximate linkage in this case between the grant of mining rights and the use or enjoyment of the mined mineral, India points to the significance of the intervention of other acts of extraction, crushing, grinding, separation, and classification that are undertaken by the beneficiary. In that respect, the "most credible proof of existence and importance of such intervening processes is the fact that the royalties paid for the mining rights only account for 9.03% and it is the remaining 90.97% cost incurred by the miner, which makes the ore usable or marketable".[86] India recalls the evidence of cost allocation submitted before the Panel, which, in its view, presents an accurate image of how insufficient the government grant of mining rights is. This is highly relevant in assessing whether there is a "reasonable proximate connection" between the grant of mining rights and the use or enjoyment of the mined mineral. India therefore concludes that the Panel failed in its duty under Article 11 of the DSU by refusing to evaluate India's explanation and ultimately rejecting it as irrelevant.

2.1.3.2 SDF loans

2.37 India claims that the Panel erred in finding that the USDOC's determination that the SDF Managing Committee provided direct transfers of funds is not inconsistent with Article 1.1(a)(1)(i) of the SCM Agreement. India contends that the SDF loans do not constitute a "direct transfer" of funds because

83 India's appellant's submission, para. 502.
84 India's appellant's submission, para. 503.
85 *Ibid.*
86 India's appellant's submission, para. 488.

the loan proceeds were transferred by an intermediary entity that is not the government or a public body. India requests the Appellate Body to find that the Panel erred in the interpretation and application of Article 1.1(a)(1)(i). India further requests the Appellate Body to reverse the Panel's findings and to complete the legal analysis and find that the United States acted inconsistently with Article 1.1(a)(1)(i) of the SCM Agreement in determining that the SDF loans are a "financial contribution".

2.38 India argues that, despite the fact that its claim was based on the interpretation of the terms "direct" and "transfer" in Article 1.1(a)(1)(i), the Panel never provided an interpretation in accordance with customary rules of international law. India maintains that, if an action is "direct", the action and its consequence should be immediately connected or linked, without involving any intermediary or intervening agency. India argues that this is supported by the context of the provision and the preamble to Article 1.1(a)(1), which, India argues, indicate that a financial contribution consists of a specific action that is to be undertaken by the government or any public body. India further contends that the use of the phrase "i.e. where" highlights that what is covered is the action undertaken by the government, and that it is this action that should actually include or contain the fund transfer. India maintains that, where the action undertaken by the government is only decision-making on the issuance or terms of the transfer, it precedes the actual transfer of the funds by an intermediary or intervening agency and therefore is not a government practice that involves the direct transfer of funds.

2.39 India also finds contextually significant the absence of the word "direct" in other subparagraphs of Article 1.1(a)(1), which suggests, in its view, that Article 1.1(a)(1)(i) is not intended to cover indirect transfers of funds. This implication becomes crucial when read in the light of the language in Article 1.1(a)(1)(iv) relating to situations where a government "entrusts or directs a private body to carry out … the type of functions illustrated in (i)". India notes that the Appellate Body has interpreted "direction" as referring to situations where a government exercises its authority, including some degree of compulsion, over a private body, and "entrustment" as referring to situations in which a government gives responsibility to a private body. Thus, whereas subparagraph (i) deals with governmental actions directly providing a financial contribution, subparagraph (iv) deals with governmental actions indirectly providing a financial contribution through the direct action of a private body. Consequently, where a government takes the decision that it is an intermediate private body or agency who issues a loan on certain terms or waives a loan already issued, the scenario is addressed under Article 1.1(a)(1)(iv). India argues that the Panel's interpretation, however, renders Article 1.1(a)(1)(iv) of the SCM Agreement inutile, because the Panel considered that, where a government takes the decision to issue a loan, this would be a direct transfer of funds even if the actual funds are transferred by a private entity such as the Joint Plant Committee (JPC). In India's view, if this understanding were correct, subparagraph (iv) would not need to exist.

2.40 India further argues that the SCM Agreement reflects a delicate balance between those Members that seek to impose more disciplines on the use of subsidies and those that seek to impose more disciplines on the application of countervailing measures. In addition, the negotiating history of the SCM Agreement indicates that the words used to create the definition of a subsidy were carefully chosen. According to India, the list contained in Article 1.1(a)(1) is exhaustive and the conditions prescribed therein reflect the delicate balance the drafters intended to achieve. Any attempt "to circumvent the conditions in Article 1.1(a)(1)(iv) by subsuming the concept within Article 1.1(a)(1)(i) cannot be permitted".[87] Therefore, India contends, the Panel's interpretation is contrary to the object and purpose of the SCM Agreement.

2.41 India recalls the Panel's finding that the JPC formally administered the disbursement and collection of funds, and the day-to-day operations of the SDF. According to India, evidence that was before the USDOC shows that the issuance and administration of loans provided under the SDF was supervised by the JPC and, therefore, that it was the JPC that transferred the funds. Thus, there is no direct link between the "governmental practice" of the SDF Managing Committee and the transfer of funds to the participating members because there was an intervening agency between the actions of the SDF Managing Committee and the recipients. Accordingly, India contends, the issuance of SDF loans is not a governmental practice that involves a "direct" transfer of funds for the purposes of Article 1.1(a)(1)(i).

2.42 In addition, India argues that the issuance of SDF loans cannot amount to a "transfer of funds" within the meaning of Article 1.1(a)(1)(i). India considers that the ordinary meaning of the phrase "transfer of funds" would require a person to convey the title over money or financial resources to another person. Therefore, the "transfer of funds" only refers to situations where the government gives up the rights and interests it has over the funds in question, while simultaneously creating the rights and interests over the funds in favour of the beneficiaries. According to India, "[u]nless the 'government' incurs a financial charge on its own account, such that the funds being transferred would have otherwise been at the disposal of the government but for the alleged 'transfer' in question, there cannot be a financial contribution under Article 1.1(a)(1)(i) of the SCM Agreement."[88]

2.43 India contrasts the use of the term "transfer" in Article 1.1(a)(1)(i) with the use of the term "provides" in Article 1.1(a)(1)(iii). In India's view, the term "provides" is much wider in that it means to "make available" or "put at the disposal of".[89] Thus, "[h]ad the drafters intended sub-paragraph (i) to cover any governmental action that may ultimately lead to funds being made available or

---

87 India's appellant's submission, para. 557.

88 India's appellant's submission, para. 564.

89 India's appellant's submission, para. 565 (quoting Appellate Body Report, *US – Softwood Lumber IV*, para. 69).

accessible to beneficiaries, a broader term such as 'provides' would have been used."[90] India also refers to the preambular language in Article 1.1(a)(1), and in particular to the indication that each of the subparagraphs relate to a "financial contribution by a government or any public body". India argues that the use of the term "financial" makes it clear that the contribution in question must relate to resources capable of being valued monetarily, and that such a financial contribution has to be "by" a government or public body. India thus considers that subsidies intended to be covered in Article 1.1(a)(1)(i) are to be drawn from government sources of revenue and result in a charge on the public account.

2.44 India considers that its understanding of Article 1.1(a)(1)(i) is confirmed by the negotiating history of the SCM Agreement. India points to various statements, including those by the Group of Experts on the Calculation of the Amount of a Subsidy, which considered that "subsidies exist where the government exercises its authority to impose tax and to expend revenue, whether directly or through delegation of its taxing and authority."[91] In India's view, subsidies have generally been linked directly to the taxation function of the government and monetary resources or contributions derived from this taxation function must be owned and under the complete control of the government. India submits that "it is this understanding that is reflected in Article 1.1(a)(1)(i) ... and hence, a direct transfer of funds by a government must involve financial contributions from out of public funds or involve a charge on the public account."[92]

2.45 India contends that the Panel's only basis for rejecting India's claim is the fact that the SDF Managing Committee was instrumental, because of its role as decision-maker regarding the issuance, terms, and waivers of SDF loans, in transferring those funds from the SDF to the loan beneficiaries. India maintains, however, that it is an admitted fact that the funds were garnered for the SDF only through the JPC, which is a private body. India asserts that there was no finding by the USDOC or the Panel that the SDF funds were actually owned by the government or that the release of these funds resulted in a charge on the public account. Furthermore, the decision to add an extra element to the price of steel products towards the SDF was made by the JPC, which is majority controlled by participating steel plants. In India's view, all of these indicators point to the conclusion that the SDF funds were not government funds and that the SDF was financed solely by producer levies and other non-governmental sources. India also points to the holding by the Supreme Court of India that the JPC did not have the power to tax; the SDF levy was not a tax; but rather consisted of producer funds; the SDF levy was only an element of price added to

---

90 India's appellant's submission, para. 565.

91 India's appellant's submission, para. 569 (quoting Group of Experts on the Calculation of the Amount of a Subsidy, contained in Negotiating Group on Subsidies and Countervailing Measures, *Note by the Secretariat*, MTN.GNG/NG10/W/4, p. 9).

92 India's appellant's submission, para. 571.

the *ex works* price; and the ultimate beneficiaries of this added element were the steel plants themselves. Both the Panel and the United States disregarded these features of the SDF programme. India concludes that the mere instrumental role played by the SDF Managing Committee in issuing the SDF loans do not *ipso facto* make the SDF loans a direct 'transfer' of funds under Article 1.1(a)(1)(i) of the SCM Agreement.

2.1.4 Benefit – "As such" claims

2.46 India appeals the Panel's conclusion that the US benchmarking mechanism for assessing the adequacy of remuneration for government-provided goods, as reflected in Section 351.511(a)(2)(i)-(iv) of the US Regulations, is not inconsistent with Article 14(d) of the SCM Agreement.[93] India claims that, in making its findings, the Panel incorrectly interpreted and applied Article 14(d), and acted inconsistently with its mandate under Article 11 of the DSU. India requests the Appellate Body to reverse the Panel's conclusion and find that the US benchmarking mechanism, as reflected in Section 351.511(a)(2)(i)-(iv), is inconsistent with Article 14(d) of the SCM Agreement. India also requests the Appellate Body to find, as a necessary consequence, that the United States acted inconsistently with Article 14(d) in the underlying countervailing duty investigation at issue.[94]

2.1.4.1 Assessment of the adequacy of remuneration for government-provided goods required under Article 14(d) of the SCM Agreement

2.47 India appeals the Panel's dismissal of its claim that the US benchmarking mechanism, reflected in Section 351.511(a)(2)(i)-(iii) of the US Regulations, is inconsistent with Article 14(d) of the SCM Agreement because it fails to require, in every case, that the adequacy of remuneration for government-provided goods be assessed from the perspective of the government provider, prior to assessing

[93] Section 351.511 of the US Regulations implements Section 1677(5)(E) of the US Statute, which concerns the determination of "benefit" conferred by the provision of goods or services. For this purpose, Section 351.511(a)(2) defines "adequate remuneration". Subparagraphs (i)-(iii) of that provision establish a three-tier hierarchy for determining whether remuneration for the provision of goods by the government is adequate. Under subparagraph (i), the USDOC will normally seek to measure the adequacy of remuneration by comparing the government price to a market-determined price for the good or service resulting from actual transactions in the country in question. Subparagraph (ii) provides that, where an actual market-determined price is "unavailable", adequacy of remuneration may be measured by comparison to a world market price. If world market prices are "unavailable" to purchasers in the country in question, subparagraph (iii) provides that adequacy of remuneration will "normally" be measured by "assessing whether the government price is consistent with market principles". Subparagraph (iv) provides that, where adequacy of remuneration is assessed under either subparagraph (i) or subparagraph (ii), the comparison price must be adjusted to reflect the price that a firm actually paid or would pay if it imported the product (including delivery charges and import duties).

[94] India's appellant's submission, paras. 18 and 162.

whether a benefit has been conferred on a recipient. In rejecting India's claim, the Panel erred in its interpretation of Article 14(d), and acted inconsistently with its duty under Article 11 of the DSU.

2.48 India asserts that, in finding that a determination of inadequate remuneration from the perspective of the recipient necessarily results in a finding of benefit within the meaning of Article 14(d), the Panel incorrectly interpreted the first sentence of Article 14(d). Noting that the first sentence of Article 14(d) refers to the terms "benefit" and "remuneration", India submits that the fact that separate terms are used implies that, conceptually, "benefit" and "remuneration" are not the same. Moreover, the text of Article 14(d) does not state that a benefit is conferred on a recipient "each and every time" that remuneration is found to be inadequate. The presence of the term "unless" in the first sentence of Article 14(d), as well as the phrase "shall not be considered as conferring a benefit unless", implies that, without establishing that the government provided the good in question for less than adequate remuneration, there can be no benefit conferred on a recipient of that good. This does not suggest, however, that inadequacy of remuneration must always result in a determination of benefit. In other words, inadequacy of remuneration under Article 14(d) is necessary, but not always sufficient, to establish that a benefit, within the meaning of that provision, has been conferred on a recipient of government-provided goods.[95]

2.49 India submits that the Panel erred in its interpretation of Article 14(d) of the SCM Agreement in finding that the adequacy of remuneration for government provided-goods is to be assessed from the perspective of the recipient, rather than the government provider. Noting that the first sentence of Article 14(d) refers to "the provision of goods or services ... by a government", India considers that the text and context of Article 14(d) support its contention that the adequacy of remuneration must be assessed from the perspective of the government provider. Moreover, because "benefit", under Article 14(d), is determined from the perspective of the recipient, it is "logical" that the adequacy of remuneration for government-provided goods be assessed from the perspective of the government provider. If the remuneration is found to be inadequate, the investigating authority would then have to assess whether a benefit has been conferred on the recipient. India considers that the Panel's conclusion that adequacy of remuneration need not be assessed separately from, and prior to, assessing whether a benefit has been conferred on the recipient is contrary to "the ordinary and contextual understanding" of the first sentence of Article 14(d).[96]

2.50 India considers further that the Panel's interpretation of Article 14(d) suffers from inherent contradictions. First, India sees a contradiction between, on the one hand, the Panel's statement that "remuneration" and "benefit" relate to

95 India's appellant's submission, paras. 22-27

96 India's appellant's submission, paras. 28-32.

"different notions" and, on the other hand, the Panel's conclusion that a finding of inadequate remuneration necessarily results in a finding of benefit. Second, India considers that the Panel's interpretation of the term "remuneration" to mean "the sum that is paid for the good provided by the government"[97] does not reconcile with its finding that Article 14(d) does not require separate analyses of "adequacy of remuneration" and of "benefit". India questions how one can logically assess the adequacy of remuneration paid to the government from the perspective of any entity other than the government. Third, India considers that, if a competitor's price is adopted to determine simultaneously both the adequacy of remuneration and the amount of benefit conferred (by assessing whether if the government price is less than the benchmark), there would be no difference between the "standards" applicable to each concept. This, argues India, would result in "circularity" in the first sentence of Article 14(d).[98]

2.51 For these reasons, India requests the Appellate Body to reverse the Panel's finding that, under Article 14(d) of the SCM Agreement, Members are not required to assess the adequacy of remuneration for government-provided goods from the perspective of the government provider, prior to assessing the quantum of benefit conferred on a recipient. Instead, the Appellate Body should find that Article 14(d) requires an assessment of the adequacy of remuneration actually received by the government provider of goods prior to determining the quantum of benefit received by the recipient. India further requests the Appellate Body to find that the US benchmarking mechanism, as reflected in Section 351.511(a)(2)(i)-(iii) of the US Regulations, is inconsistent with Article 14(d) of the SCM Agreement because it does not require, in every case, that the adequacy of remuneration for government-provided goods be assessed from the perspective of the government provider, prior to assessing the amount of benefit conferred on a recipient. It follows, submits India, that the Appellate Body must also find that the United States acted inconsistently with Article 14(d) of the SCM Agreement by applying its benchmarking mechanism in the underlying investigations concerning the sale of iron ore by the NMDC and the GOI's grant of captive mining rights for iron ore and coal.

2.1.4.2 Exclusion of government prices as benchmarks under the US benchmarking mechanism

2.52 India notes that it had argued before the Panel that the US benchmarking mechanism is inconsistent with Article 14(d) of the SCM Agreement because, under Tier I of that mechanism, the United States simply rejects government prices that do not emanate from competitive government auctions. India submits that the Panel found that "government transactions and prices can be presumptively and conclusively ignored" in the assessment of "prevailing market

[97] India's appellant's submission, para. 34 (quoting Panel Report, para. 7.28). (emphasis omitted)

[98] India's appellant's submission, paras. 32-37.

conditions" under Article 14(d).[99] In making this finding, the Panel erred in its interpretation of Article 14(d).

2.53 Noting that the first sentence of Article 14(d) states that the provision of goods by a government is not to be considered as conferring a benefit unless proved otherwise, India contends that the direct implication of this is that Article 14(d) does not permit investigating authorities to reject presumptively the government price under challenge as not being market driven. Yet the Panel, contrary to Article 14(d), simply assumed that all government prices are *ipso facto* presumed to cater to public policy objectives and, hence, can be disregarded for the purposes of Article 14(d). India considers that the Panel's interpretation renders the first sentence of Article 14(d) otiose. Moreover, Article 14(d) is concerned with the market on an "as is" basis, and therefore does not permit government prices to be disregarded in the analysis of benefit. In this regard, the Appellate Body found, in *US – Softwood Lumber IV*, that the term "market conditions" in Article 14(d) does not refer to a market undistorted by the government's financial contribution.[100] In addition, the Panel's interpretation of Article 14(d) fails to account for the implications of the Appellate Body's findings, in *US – Anti-Dumping and Countervailing Duties (China)*, that governmental loans cannot *ipso facto* be rejected as "non-commercial".[101] This means that there is no presumption that government prices are *ipso facto* unusable as benchmarks for assessing benefit under Article 14(d). Instead, investigating authorities are required to establish whether government presence or influence in the relevant market causes distortions that render the relevant government prices unusable.

2.54 For the above reasons, India requests the Appellate Body to reverse the Panel's finding that government prices can be presumptively rejected by investigating authorities as potential benchmarks under Article 14(d) of the SCM Agreement. Because this finding led the Panel to reject India's claim that Section 351.511(a)(2)(i)-(ii) of the US Regulations is inconsistent with Article 14(d), India further requests the Appellate Body to find that Section 351.511(a)(2)(i)-(ii) is inconsistent with Article 14(d) because it presumptively excludes government prices that do not emanate from competitive government auctions as benchmarks under Tiers I and II of the US benchmarking mechanism. In addition, India requests the Appellate Body to find that the USDOC's "presumptive and conclusive" rejection of NMDC export prices as a relevant benchmark for assessing the adequacy of remuneration in respect of

[99] India's appellant's submission, para. 42.

[100] India's appellant's submission, para. 47 (referring to Appellate Body Report, *US – Softwood Lumber IV*, para. 87).

[101] India's appellant's submission, para. 48 (referring to Appellate Body Report, *US – Anti-Dumping and Countervailing Duties (China)*, para. 479).

iron ore provided by the NMDC is inconsistent with Article 14(d) of the SCM Agreement.[102]

2.1.4.3 Use of world market prices under Tier II of the US benchmarking mechanism

2.55 India claims that the Panel erred in rejecting its claim that the US benchmarking mechanism is inconsistent with Article 14(d) of the SCM Agreement because it permits the use of world market prices as benchmarks under Tier II of the US benchmarking mechanism without requiring the USDOC to first exhaust fully all sources of in-country benchmarks. India argues that, in rejecting its claim, the Panel acted inconsistently with its duties under Articles 11 and 12.7 of the DSU, and erred in its interpretation and application of Article 14(d) of the SCM Agreement.

2.56 India notes that the Panel understood India's argument to be that out-of-country benchmarks may only be used in situations where the market in the country of provision is distorted due to the predominant role of the government provider in that market. India claims that the Panel understood its argument in a very narrow manner, and ignored India's argument that the measure at issue effectively permits the USDOC to use out-of-country benchmarks without exhausting all possible sources of in-country benchmarks. Thus, India contends that it had effectively challenged the use of world market prices as benchmarks under Tier II of the US benchmarking on two different grounds. First, the US benchmarking mechanism is inconsistent with Article 14(d) because it permits recourse to out-of-country benchmarks in situations other than where the market in the country of provision is distorted due to the predominant role played by government in the market. Second, the US benchmarking mechanism is inconsistent with Article 14(d) because it permits recourse to out-of-country benchmarks without requiring the USDOC to first exhaust all possible sources of in-country benchmarks. India claims that the Panel ignored the latter ground of its claim. In India's view, the Panel's assessment falls short of the standard imposed on panels under Article 11 of the DSU.

2.57 India also challenges, under Articles 11 and 12.7 of the DSU, the Panel's finding that Article 14(d) of the SCM Agreement permits recourse to an out-of-country benchmark in "other situations" besides where the market in the country of provision is distorted as a result of governmental interference in that market. The Panel failed to provide basic guidelines to determine what these "other situations" are, and therefore failed to provide a basic rationale for its findings as required by Article 12.7 of the DSU, "read with" Article 11 of the DSU.[103]

2.58 Furthermore, India challenges the Panel's interpretation of Article 14(d) of the SCM Agreement as permitting recourse to an out-of-country benchmark

[102] India's appellant's submission, para. 56.
[103] India's appellant's submission, para. 64.

in "other situations" besides where the market in the country of provision is distorted by governmental interference in that market. According to India, the Panel failed to appreciate the implications of previous panel and Appellate Body reports in interpreting Article 14(d). These previous reports highlight the exceptional nature of the circumstances in which out-of-country benchmarks may be used under Article 14(d). In *US – Softwood Lumber IV* and *US – Anti-Dumping and Countervailing Duties (China)*, the Appellate Body did not endorse the use of out-of-country benchmarks in circumstances unrelated to governmental interference in the relevant market. India emphasizes that all these cases involved situations of governmental interference in the market to varying degrees, including where the government (i) is the predominant supplier of the goods in question in the market, (ii) is the only suppliers of the particular goods in the country, or (iii) administratively controls all of the prices for the goods in the country. In *US – Anti-Dumping and Countervailing Duties (China)*, the Appellate Body considered the predominant role of the government in the market as the "very limited" circumstance in which the investigating authorities may use a benchmark other than private prices in the country of provision.[104] For India, this does not permit authorities to use out-of-country benchmarks simply because a limited set of in-country benchmarks are unavailable.[105]

2.59 India also challenges the Panel's rejection of its claim that the US benchmarking mechanism is inconsistent with Article 14(d) of the SCM Agreement because it does not require, in every case, that Tier II benchmarks be adjusted to reflect prevailing market conditions in the country of provision. India submits that, in rejecting its claim, the Panel acted inconsistently with Article 11 of the DSU, and erred in its application of Article 14(d) of the SCM Agreement.

2.60 India notes that the Panel rejected its claim on the basis that, because the US statutory provision, implemented by the US Regulations setting forth the US benchmarking mechanism, requires that the adequacy of remuneration for government-provided goods be assessed in relation to the prevailing market conditions in the country of provision, Tier II benchmarks applied pursuant to the implementing Regulation must, in law, also relate to the prevailing market conditions in the country of provision. Noting that the specific measure challenged by India is the US Regulations setting forth the US benchmarking mechanism, rather than the overarching statutory provision that they implement, India argues that the Panel acted inconsistently with Article 11 by ignoring the plain text and meaning of the specific measure at issue. In addition, the Panel violated Article 11 of the DSU by simply accepting the United States' assertions about the meaning and implications of the overarching statutory provision implemented by the US Regulations setting forth the US benchmarking mechanism.[106]

[104] India's appellant's submission, para. 70.
[105] India's appellant's submission, paras. 65-70.
[106] India's appellant's submission, paras. 79-84.

2.61 Furthermore, India recalls the Appellate Body's finding that, where proxies such as prices for similar goods quoted on world markets are used as benchmarks under Article 14(d), investigating authorities are under an obligation to ensure that the resulting benchmark relates or refers to, or is connected with, prevailing market conditions in the country of provision.[107] India emphasizes that, because market conditions are not presumed to be the same inside and outside the country of provision, Members are mandated to make necessary adjustments to ensure that out-of-country benchmarks selected for the purpose of assessing benefit under Article 14(d) reflect prevailing market conditions in the country of provision. India argues that there is no presumption that market conditions prevailing outside a Member can relate to, refer to, or be connected with, prevailing market conditions in the country of provision. According to India, the Appellate Body, in *US – Softwood Lumber IV*, acknowledged that it may be close to impossible to adjust out-of-country benchmarks to reflect prevailing market conditions in the country of provision.[108] India highlights, in addition, that countervailing duties are not intended to countervail differences in comparative advantages between countries. By not requiring adjustments to ensure that out-of-country benchmarks reflect prevailing market conditions in the country of provision, the challenged measure does not account for comparative advantages that a Member may have. India therefore contends that, in rejecting its above claim, the Panel erred in its application of Article 14(d) of the SCM Agreement, because neither the US Regulations, nor the overarching statutory provision that they implement, mandate the need to make adjustments in the case of Tier II benchmarks.

2.62 For these reasons, India requests the Appellate Body to reverse the Panel's finding that the use of world market prices as Tier II benchmarks under the US benchmarking mechanism is consistent with Article 14(d) of the SCM Agreement, and to find, instead, that the US benchmarking mechanism is inconsistent with Article 14(d) because: (i) it requires the use of out-of-country benchmarks without first establishing that the market in question is distorted by governmental interference in that market; (ii) it requires the use of out-of-country benchmarks without first exhausting all possible sources of in-country benchmarks; and (iii) it does not require that Tier II benchmarks be adjusted to reflect prevailing market conditions in the country of provision. In India's view, it follows that the Appellate Body must also find that the USDOC's determinations of benefit in the underlying countervailing duty investigation concerning the provision of iron ore by the NMDC and the GOI's grant of captive mining rights for iron ore and coal are inconsistent with Article 14(d) of the SCM Agreement.

---

[107] India's appellant's submission, para. 87 (referring to Appellate Body Report, *US – Softwood Lumber IV*, paras. 106 and 120).

[108] India's appellant's submission, paras. 71 and 73 (referring to Appellate Body Report, *US – Softwood Lumber IV*, para. 108).

2.1.4.4 The Panel's failure to assess two grounds of India's "as such" claim against the US benchmarking mechanism

2.63 India appeals the Panel's assessment of India's claim that the US benchmarking mechanism, as reflected in Section 351.511(a)(2)(i)-(iii) of the US Regulations, is inconsistent with Article 14(d) of the SCM Agreement. India recalls that it submitted six "different grounds" before the Panel in support of its claim that the US benchmarking mechanism is inconsistent with Article 14(d).[109] These grounds focused on different aspects of Article 14(d) and are "akin to six different sub-claims" that the Panel was required to assess independently. However, India submits, the Panel failed to assess two of the six grounds submitted by India and thereby acted inconsistently with its duty under Article 11 of the DSU.[110]

2.64 First, India notes that, on the basis of the text of the second sentence of Article 14(d), and a comparison with Articles 14(b) and 14(c) of the SCM Agreement, India had argued before the Panel that a government price in accordance with "commercial considerations" cannot constitute remuneration that is "less than adequate" within the meaning of Article 14(d). Second, India notes that it had argued before the Panel that the US benchmarking mechanism is inconsistent with Article 14(d) because it permits a government price that is "adequate" under Tier III of the US benchmarking mechanism to be rejected on the basis of the application of benchmarks under Tiers I and II of that mechanism. According to India, the Panel failed to evaluate either of these arguments independently and, instead, dismissed them on the basis of its rejection of India's argument that, under Article 14(d), the adequacy of remuneration must be assessed from the perspective of the government provider before assessing whether a benefit has been conferred on the recipient.[111]

2.65 India requests the Appellate Body to examine the above two grounds for its claim and to find that the US benchmarking mechanism is inconsistent with Article 14(d) of the SCM Agreement. With respect to the first of these grounds, India requests the Appellate Body to find that Article 14(d) does not permit

---

[109] India alleges that these six grounds were as follows: (i) the US benchmarking mechanism is inconsistent with the first sentence of Article 14(d) because it fails to assess the adequacy of remuneration from the perspective of the government provider, before assessing whether there is a benefit to the recipient; (ii) the US benchmarking mechanism is inconsistent with the second sentence of Article 14(d) because it does not require a consideration of whether the difference between a government and a competitor's price is justified by "commercial considerations"; (iii) a government price that is "adequate" under Tier III will be deemed "less than adequate" merely based on the benchmark method under Tiers I or II; (iv) under Tiers I and II, all government prices are not considered as a "price" in relation to the prevailing market conditions; (v) world market prices prescribed under Tier II are not in relation to prevailing market conditions in the country of provision of goods; and (vi) Tiers II and III are inconsistent with Article 14(d) of the SCM Agreement since it prioritizes the Tier-II methodology above Tier-III. (India's appellant's submission, para. 19)

[110] India's appellant's submission, paras. 103-122.

[111] India's appellant's submission, paras. 99, 100, 104, 105, and 111-115.

investigating authorities to determine the existence of "benefit" merely because a government price is less than a certain benchmark price. India requests the Appellate Body to further find that, where an investigating authority finds a difference between the government price and a certain benchmark price, the investigating authority is under an obligation to assess whether the difference in price is justified by "commercial considerations". In support of this argument, India relies on the text of the second sentence of Article 14(d), as well as the context provided by the other subparagraphs of Article 14, and Article XVII:1(b) of the GATT 1994. The second sentence of Article 14(d) states that the adequacy of remuneration shall be determined "in relation to prevailing market conditions" for the good or service in question in the country of provision. In India's view, the text of Article 14(d) thus necessarily limits the relevant market to only the "goods in question" and the "country of provision".[112]

2.66 Turning to the context provided by other subparagraphs of Article 14, India submits that it is clear that determinations under Article 14(b) or (c) have to be made using a rigid comparison, and the existence of a benefit is established once there is a difference in the amounts being compared. By contrast, Article 14(d) does not state that the provision of goods confers a benefit if there is a difference between, on the one hand, the amount paid by the recipient for the goods provided by the government and, on the other hand, the amount the recipient would have to pay to obtain the same goods on the market. Instead, by using the phrases "in relation to" and "prevailing market conditions", Article 14(d) implies a much broader and more comprehensive analysis using the "prevailing market conditions" as the framework, rather than as a "rigid" comparison. The substantial differences in the structure, language, and approaches of Articles 14(b) and 14(c), on the one hand, and Article 14(d), on the other hand, suggest that, under the latter provision, a given amount of "remuneration" for government-provided goods may be "adequate", even if there is a difference between the government price and the price for similar goods transacted between private parties in the relevant market.[113]

2.67 India points to further context found in Article XVII:1(b) of the GATT 1994. Noting that price, quality, availability, marketability, transportation, and other conditions of purchase or sale are all factors to be taken into account in determining whether the purchases or sales of a state trading enterprise are in accordance with "commercial considerations" under Article XVII:1(b), India submits that "the duplication of the very same factors"[114] in Article 14(d) shows equivalence in the concepts underlying Article XVII:1(b) of the GATT 1994 and Article 14(d) of the SCM Agreement. Thus, prices set in accordance with "commercial considerations" would be prices reflective of the supply and demand of both sellers and buyers in the market. Moreover, the "prevailing

[112] India's appellant's submission, paras. 127-129.

[113] India's appellant's submission, paras. 130-132.

[114] India's appellant's submission, para. 133.

market conditions" cannot be anything other than those arising from enterprises engaged in the purchase and sale of goods based on considerations and factors that are characteristic of commerce and trade. Thus, in India's view, an assessment of whether prices are set in "accordance with commercial considerations" cannot be any different from an assessment of whether a given price is "less than adequate" with respect to "prevailing market conditions".[115]

2.68 Accordingly, India argues that, when properly interpreted, the second sentence of Article 14(d) has a "far wider import than a mere minimalist price-benchmark" comparison. While it may not be incorrect for an investigating authority to start its examination by using a private price as a benchmark, it is certainly incorrect for the investigating authority to stop its analysis with such comparison. Instead, if this comparison shows a difference between prices, the investigating authority is bound to examine further whether "commercial considerations" explain this difference. India maintains, therefore, that the US benchmarking mechanism is inconsistent with Article 14(d) because it does not require, in every case, a determination of whether the government acts in accordance with commercial considerations and has provided goods for adequate remuneration when assessed in relation to prevailing market conditions in the country of provision.[116]

2.69 Turning to the second ground that the Panel failed to evaluate, India submits that the use of the phrase "shall not be considered as conferring a benefit unless" in Article 14(d) means that, unless proven otherwise, the provision of goods by a government is not considered to confer a benefit. Thus, the "logical corollary" to the first sentence of Article 14(d) is that, where the "remuneration" for government-provided goods is "adequate" under a method consistent with Article 14(d), such remuneration cannot be considered as conferring a benefit. Noting that, under Tier III of the US benchmarking mechanism, the USDOC examines whether the government price for the relevant good is consistent with "market principles", India contends that, because the Tier III methodology is itself consistent with Article 14(d) of the SCM Agreement, a price that is "adequate" under that methodology cannot become inadequate as a result of the application of benchmarks under Tiers I and II of the US benchmarking mechanism. India submits that, for this reason, the "hierarchical approach" that characterizes the US benchmarking mechanism is inconsistent with Article 14(d).[117]

2.70 For these reasons, India requests the Appellate Body to find that the Panel acted inconsistently with Article 11 of the DSU by failing to evaluate separately two of the grounds on which it rested its claim that the US benchmarking mechanism, as reflected in Section 351.511(a)(2)(i)-(iii) of the US Regulations, is inconsistent with Article 14(d) of the SCM Agreement. India further requests

[115] India's appellant's submission, paras. 134 and 135.

[116] India's appellant's submission, paras. 146-151.

[117] India's appellant's submission, paras. 156-159.

the Appellate Body to examine these grounds, complete the analysis, and find that the US benchmarking mechanism is inconsistent with Article 14(d). In India's view, it follows as a "necessary consequence" that the Appellate Body must find that the United States acted inconsistently with Article 14(d) of the SCM Agreement in the underlying countervailing duty investigation concerning the provision of iron ore by the NMDC and the GOI's grant of captive mining rights for iron ore and coal.

2.1.4.5 Mandatory use of "as delivered" prices as benchmarks under the US benchmarking mechanism

2.71 India appeals the Panel's finding that the mandatory use of "as delivered" prices as benchmarks under Section 351.511(a)(2)(iv) of the US Regulations is not inconsistent with Article 14(d) of the SCM Agreement. India submits that, in reaching this finding, the Panel acted inconsistently with its duty under Article 11 of the DSU, and erred in its interpretation and application of Article 14(d).

2.72 India advances two claims under Article 11 of the DSU in relation to the Panel's above finding. First, India takes issue with the Panel's statement that India had conflated the term "prevailing market conditions", in Article 14(d), with the contractual terms and conditions of the government provision under investigation. Contrary to the Panel's statement, India's case before the Panel was that the term "conditions of sale", within the meaning of Article 14(d), refers to the "general or common stipulation"[118] present in contracts for the provision of the relevant goods in the country of provision. The Panel read India's submissions out of context, and construed India's claim "so narrowly" that the "very claim" made by India was altered. In so doing, India asserts, the Panel effectively engaged in an assessment of a matter that was not before it, and thereby acted inconsistently with Article 11 of the DSU.[119]

2.73 Second, India claims that the Panel acted inconsistently with Article 11 of the DSU by failing to apply its own interpretation of Article 14(d) to its assessment of India's claim. India recalls that, in the course of rejecting India's claim, the Panel interpreted Article 14(d) and found that the terms "prevailing market conditions" and "conditions of sale" relate to "the general conditions of the relevant market, in the context of which market operators engage in sales transactions".[120] The Panel did not, however, make a finding on whether the sale of a good in the market generally on an *ex works* basis constitutes one of such "general conditions". India argues that a finding on this specific issue would have "materially affected"[121] the Panel's decision to reject India's claim. This is

---

[118] India's appellant's submission, para. 168 (quoting India's first written submission to the Panel, para. 88).
[119] India's appellant's submission, paras. 168-174.
[120] India's appellant's submission, para. 176 (quoting Panel Report, para. 7.60).
[121] India's appellant's submission, para. 176.

because, if the fact that a given good in the market is being sold generally on an *ex works* basis constitutes one of the "general conditions" referred to by the Panel, then, determining the adequacy of remuneration on an "as delivered" basis, in every case, would result in disregarding "prevailing market conditions" where the good in question is generally sold on an *ex works* basis in the country of provision. Thus, in its assessment of India's claim against the mandatory use of "as delivered" prices under the US benchmarking mechanism, the Panel was required to apply its interpretation of Article 14(d) to that measure. India alleges that, by not doing so, the Panel failed to assess the claim that was before it and, therefore, acted inconsistently with Article 11 of the DSU.

2.74 For India, the Panel's rejection of its claim against the mandatory use of "as delivered" prices under the US benchmarking mechanism was partly based on the Panel's erroneous interpretation that government prices can *ipso facto* be rejected under Article 14(d) of the SCM Agreement. India notes that it has challenged this interpretation of the Panel in the context of its claim regarding the exclusion of government prices as benchmarks under the US benchmarking mechanism. For the same reasons advanced in relation to that claim, India submits that the Panel erred in rejecting its claim on the basis that government prices can *ipso facto* be rejected under Article 14(d).[122]

2.75 India further notes that it had argued before the Panel that the use of "as delivered" out-of-country prices as benchmarks under the US benchmarking mechanism nullifies the comparative advantage of the country of provision in terms of being able to provide the goods in question locally. India notes that the Panel rejected this argument based on the alleged existence of an import transaction in the underlying investigation, which, in the Panel's view, meant that import transactions necessarily relate to prevailing market conditions in India. However, India argues that the alleged existence of one import transaction in the underlying investigation only justifies the use of "as delivered" prices in one isolated circumstance, whereas India's claim relates to the adjustment of out-of-country benchmarks to reflect delivery charges in *all* circumstances. Thus, India maintains that the Panel failed to provide a "basic rationale" to justify its rejection of India's claim concerning the countervailing of "comparative advantages" and, therefore, acted inconsistently with its mandate under Article 11 of the DSU, "read with" Article 12.7 of the DSU.

2.76 According to India, in rejecting its above argument, the Panel also erred in its interpretation and application of Article 14(d). The "underlying premise" on which the Panel rejected its argument is that import transactions reflect prevailing market conditions in the country of provision. Based on that premise, the Panel concluded that the existence of even a single import transaction, inclusive of all delivery and import charges, "necessarily" relates to prevailing market conditions in India. The Panel thus conflated the term "prevailing market

---

[122] India's appellant's submission, para. 180.

conditions" with the existence of import transactions. Yet, as the Panel itself recognized, "prevailing market conditions" relate to the general conditions of the relevant market, in the context of which market operators engage in sales transactions. Noting that the Appellate Body has considered that Article 14(d) demands an examination of the entire market, accounting for both sides of the transaction (i.e. demand and supply), India submits that the Panel's premise places a disproportionate emphasis on import transactions. However, where there is domestic supply for the good in question, as well as one or more import transactions for that good, the "prevailing market conditions" in the country of provision can only be determined by comprehensively accounting for both types of transactions. The measure under challenge forecloses any such examination. India therefore submits that the premise on which the Panel rejected its claim is "fundamentally flawed" and "ignores the ordinary understanding" of Article 14(d).[123]

2.77 For the above reasons, India requests the Appellate Body to reverse the Panel's finding that the mandatory use of "as delivered" prices under the US benchmarking mechanism is not inconsistent with Article 14(d) of the SCM Agreement. Further, India requests the Appellate Body to complete the legal analysis and find that the mandatory use of "as delivered" benchmarks, provided for under Section 351.511(a)(2)(iv) of the US Regulations, is inconsistent with Article 14(d). In India's view, it follows as a "necessary consequence" that the Appellate Body must also find that the United States acted inconsistently with Article 14(d) of the SCM Agreement in the underlying countervailing duty investigation concerning the provision of iron ore by the NMDC and the GOI's grant of captive mining rights for iron ore and coal. India advances the following arguments in support of its request for completion of the analysis.

2.78 India submits that the fact that goods are sold generally in the market in question on an *ex works* or "as delivered" basis is a "condition of sale" and hence one of the "prevailing market conditions" referred to in Article 14(d). In support of this interpretation of Article 14(d), India first notes that, in its ordinary sense, the term "condition" refers to a rule or a decision that one must agree to, sometimes forming part of a contract or a formal agreement[124]; it also refers to a stipulation or a prerequisite in a contract, or a will or any legal instrument, constituting the essence of the instrument.[125] Therefore, India submits that the term "conditions of sale", as it appears in Article 14(d), refers to the general or common stipulation present in contracts for the provision of the goods in question in the country of provision.

---

[123] India's appellant's submission, para. 189.

[124] India's appellant's submission, para. 193 (referring to *Oxford Dictionary of English*, 3rd edn, A. Stevenson (ed.) (Oxford University Press, 2010), p. 363).

[125] India's appellant's submission, para. 193 (referring to *Black's Law Dictionary*, 9th edn, B.A. Garner (ed.) (West Group, 2009), p. 333).

2.79 In addition, India notes that these conditions in commercial contracts materially alter the rights and liabilities of the parties to the transaction. This implies that the United States cannot assess the adequacy of remuneration for government-provided goods using "as delivered" benchmarks in all cases. Instead, there must be an evaluation of whether the sale of a good on an "as delivered" basis is actually one of the "conditions of sale" prevailing in the relevant market. Under the US benchmarking mechanism, the adequacy of remuneration for government-provided goods is assessed using "as delivered" prices as benchmarks, irrespective of the "conditions of sale" prevailing in the country of provision. In India's view, this is inconsistent with the ordinary meaning of the second sentence of Article 14(d).

2.80 India submits that "the sole objective" of requiring comparisons to be made at an "as delivered" level is to "arbitrarily increase" the benchmark price to a higher level so that benefit is established even in situations where no benefit has actually been conferred. Where the USDOC adopts out-of-country benchmarks (import prices under Tier I or world market prices under Tier II) to assess the adequacy of remuneration for government-provided goods, an affirmative determination of "benefit" is a foregone conclusion, because international freight and import duties are almost always higher than domestic freight and local taxes. India maintains that this cannot be a reasonable and good faith understanding of Article 14(d) of the SCM Agreement.[126]

2.81 India further submits that the use of "as delivered" prices as benchmarks is inconsistent with the Appellate Body's finding, in *US – Softwood Lumber IV*, that Article 14(d) cannot be used to countervail "comparative advantages" of Members.[127] Specifically, the use of "as delivered" out-of-country price benchmarks provided for under the US benchmarking mechanism effectively countervails comparative advantages of the country of provision. The use of "as delivered" import prices under Tier I, or "as delivered" world market prices under Tier II, of the US benchmarking mechanism creates the "hypothetical situation"[128] that the good in question is not available in the country of provision. Thus, the measure at issue presumes that, under the "prevailing market conditions" in the country of provision, users of the relevant good would necessarily import the good at a price inclusive of international freight, import duties, and all other delivery charges. However, India contends, in a given set of facts, there may actually be no import transactions of this nature in the country of provision, and, even if such transactions exist, they could occupy a significantly small percentage of the entire supply-demand matrix in the country of provision. Therefore, India reiterates that, where out-of-country benchmarks are used under the US benchmarking mechanism, the adjustment of these benchmarks to include all delivery charges, as if the good were generally

126 India's appellant's submission, para. 201.
127 India's appellant's submission, para. 202.
128 India's appellant's submission, para. 203.

imported, nullifies the comparative advantage of the country of provision in terms of being able to provide the goods in question locally.[129]

2.1.5 Benefit – "As applied" claims

2.1.5.1 The USDOC's determination that the NMDC provided iron ore for less than adequate remuneration

2.82 In relation to the USDOC's determination that the NMDC provided iron ore for less than adequate remuneration, India appeals the Panel's findings concerning: (i) the *ex post* rationale put forward by the United States to justify the USDOC's rejection of certain domestic pricing information as Tier I benchmarks for assessing the adequacy of remuneration for iron ore provided by the NMDC; (ii) the USDOC's use of "as delivered" prices from Australia and Brazil as benchmarks for assessing the adequacy of remuneration for iron ore provided by the NMDC; and (iii) the USDOC's rejection of certain NMDC export prices as Tier II benchmarks in the 2006, 2007, and 2008 administrative reviews. India claims that, in making its findings, the Panel erred in its interpretation and application of Article 14(d), the chapeau of Article 14, and Articles 12.1, 12.4, and 12.7 of the SCM Agreement. Moreover, the Panel acted inconsistently with its duty under Article 11 of the DSU. India requests the Appellate Body to reverse the challenged Panel findings and find instead that, in determining that the NMDC provided iron ore for less than adequate remuneration, the United States acted inconsistently with Article 14(d) and the chapeau of Article 14 of the SCM Agreement. Moreover, because the USDOC used the benchmarks that it had selected for the NMDC investigation in the investigation concerning the GOI's grant of captive mining rights for iron ore and coal, India requests the Appellate Body to find that the USDOC's determinations that the GOI provided iron ore and coal for less than adequate remuneration are also inconsistent with Article 14(d) of the SCM Agreement.[130]

2.1.5.1.1 The Panel's findings concerning the USDOC's rejection of certain domestic pricing information

2.83 India notes that the Panel found that the explanation put forward by the United States for the USDOC's rejection of the domestic pricing information as Tier I benchmarks constitutes *ex post* rationalization and, on that basis, the Panel found that the USDOC's failure to consider the domestic pricing information at issue was inconsistent with Article 14(d), and therefore Article 1.1(b), of the SCM Agreement. Noting that the Panel proceeded to consider, and make findings on, the *ex post* rationalizations that the United States had put forward,

[129] India's appellant's submission, paras. 203 and 204.
[130] India's appellant's submission, paras. 422, 435, 458-460, 468, and 478.

India argues that the Panel assessed a matter that was not before it, and thereby acted inconsistently with its mandate under Article 11 of the DSU. In this regard, the Appellate Body has established that a panel can examine only information contained in the record and the explanations given by the investigating authority in its published report.[131] Thus, India submits that any *ex post* rationalization offered in these Panel proceedings was information that fell outside the Panel's jurisdiction.

2.84 India therefore requests the Appellate Body to declare moot the Panel's findings and observations in respect of the *ex post* rationalization put forward by the United States. In the event that the Appellate Body declines this request, India requests the Appellate Body to examine the findings made by the Panel on the merits of the *ex post* rationalization advanced by the United States, and find that, in making these findings, the Panel erred in its interpretation and application of Articles 12.1, 12.4, 12.7, and 14 of the SCM Agreement.[132] India advances the following four arguments in support of its requests.

2.85 First, India asserts that the Panel erred in its interpretation of Article 14(d) in finding that the United States can *ipso facto* reject information concerning sales identified as having been made by government-owned entities as relevant benchmarks. According to India, this Panel finding clearly relates to the Panel's earlier finding that prices of government-owned enterprises can be rejected as benchmarks for assessing the adequacy of remuneration in respect of government-provided goods. However, India contends, the prices of the alleged government providers covered in the price charts submitted by the GOI and Tata[133] were not under challenge and, therefore, ought not to have been rejected by the USDOC in determining Tier I benchmarks for assessing the adequacy of remuneration for iron ore provided by the NMDC.

2.86 India further asserts that, in finding that the USDOC would have been entitled to reject the price quote submitted by Tata[134] as a Tier I benchmark on the basis that it did not specify the exact percentage of iron ore content, the Panel erred in applying Articles 12.1, 12.7, and 14 of the SCM Agreement. India submits that, by harmoniously construing Article 14(d) with Articles 12.1 and 12.7 of the SCM Agreement, the USDOC could have used the price quote in determining a benchmark by determining the iron ore content on the basis of "facts available". Moreover, insofar as Article 12 of the SCM Agreement as a whole embodies due process rights of the interested parties, at a minimum, the United States had an obligation to identify the alleged defects in the information submitted on record such that the interested parties could have provided

---

[131] India's appellant's submission, paras. 416 and 417 (referring to Appellate Body Reports, *US – Tyres (China)*, para. 329; and *US – Wheat Gluten*, para. 162).

[132] India's appellant's submission, paras. 423-435.

[133] India's appellant's submission, paras. 424 and 425 (referring to price charts submitted by the GOI and by Tata in Panel Exhibits IND-61, IND-67, and IND-70 (see table of Panel Exhibits at pp. 13-16 of this Report)).

[134] This price quote was submitted in Tata Verification Report (Panel Exhibit IND-70), p. 23.

clarifications or sought to correct any alleged defects. In fact, the price quote in question formed part of the Tata Verification Report[135], and the United States therefore had every conceivable opportunity to verify this data and seek all possible clarifications. In failing to do so, India submits that the United States violated the due process obligations under Article 12.

2.87 India additionally submits that, in finding that an investigating authority is not required to determine price benchmarks on the basis of information that is not shown to pertain to actual transactions, the Panel erred in interpreting Articles 12.1 and 14 of the SCM Agreement. The Panel's finding that Article 14 provides investigating authorities with sufficient discretion to disregard pricing information that does not pertain to actual transactions creates an unreasonable burden by requiring interested parties to file prices of actual transactions. India submits that pricing information from actual transactions is confidential, as recognized by Article 12.4 of the SCM Agreement. Thus, a given exporter would not have access to information pertaining to sales transactions of other parties where this exporter has purchased its entire supply through the alleged subsidy. In India's view, this leaves the exporter "at the mercy of" the investigating authority.[136]

2.88 Finally, India submits that, in finding that the USDOC was not required to use the price quote submitted by Tata for the purpose of determining a Tier I benchmark because Tata had claimed confidentiality with respect to this price quote, the Panel erred in applying Articles 12.4, 12.1, and 14 of the SCM Agreement. India argues that Article 12.1, "read with" Article 14, requires investigating authorities to use confidential information at least in favour of the party providing such information. Thus, even assuming that the price quote in question was confidential information of Tata, Article 12.4 of the SCM Agreement does not preclude the use of such confidential information for Tata itself. Furthermore, it is not disputed that the benchmarks that were used to assess the adequacy of remuneration in respect of iron ore provided by the NMDC were also applied by the USDOC in determining the adequacy of remuneration in respect of the GOI's grant of captive mining rights for iron ore to Tata. In addition, in the 2008 administrative review and the 2013 sunset review, the provision of iron ore by the NMDC to Tata was also countervailed on the basis of adverse facts available. Thus, the price quote submitted by Tata ought to have been used throughout the investigation to calculate the existence and amount of benefit allegedly obtained by Tata through the GOI's grand of captive mining right for iron ore. This price quote should also have been used in the 2008 administrative review and the 2013 sunset review to calculate the benefit allegedly obtained by Tata through the provision of iron ore by the

[135] India's appellant's submission, para. 429 (referring to Tata Verification Report).
[136] India's appellant's submission, para. 430.

NMDC. Accordingly, the Panel's finding is "an erroneous application" of Articles 12.4, 12.1, and 14 of the SCM Agreement.[137]

2.1.5.1.2 The USDOC's use of "as delivered" prices from Australia and Brazil as benchmarks

2.89 India appeals the Panel's finding that the use of "as delivered" prices from Australia and Brazil as benchmarks for assessing the adequacy of remuneration in respect of iron ore provided by the NMDC is consistent with Article 14(d) of the SCM Agreement. According to India, in making this finding, the Panel acted inconsistently with its duty under Article 11 of the DSU, and erred in its interpretation and application of Article 14(d).

2.90 India challenges, under Article 11 of the DSU, the Panel's reliance on a statement made by NMDC officials to support its finding that Australian and Brazilian prices for iron ore, adjusted for delivery to steel producers in India, indicate what a steel producer in India would be "willing to pay", and thus necessarily relate to the prevailing market conditions in India. India claims that "the Panel assumed that the reference to 'willing to pay to import' necessarily implies a reference to the final payment for the import inclusive of ocean freight, import duties and other delivery charges."[138] The Panel's reference to an isolated statement on the record to infer that the use of delivered prices of imported iron ore was appropriate disregards and contradicts actual evidence on the record. India highlights that the statements referred to by the Panel were never referred to by the USDOC in its findings in the underlying investigation. Thus, the Panel re-evaluated the record of the investigation, and justified the USDOC's determination on a basis that the USDOC itself had not referred to in its determination. According to India, this in itself suffices to establish that the Panel acted inconsistently with Article 11 of the DSU.

2.91 In any event, India points to evidence on the record that, in its view, contradicts the Panel's assessment. According to India, a questionnaire response from the GOI, in the context of the 2006 administrative review, establishes that "the domestic prices for iron ore were determined by NMDC based on its export price for iron ore (F.O.B.) to Japan as published in the Tex Report, after accounting for currency conversion and rail freight, port charges etc."[139] Thus, the NMDC's sales of iron ore to Japan competed with sales of iron ore from Australia and, therefore, the NMDC's f.o.b. export prices were comparable to

[137] India's appellant's submission, para. 434.

[138] India's appellant's submission, para. 442.

[139] India's appellant's submission, para. 444 (referring to 2007 GOI Questionnaire Response for 2006 AR (Panel Exhibit IND-59), p. 6; and Tex Reports of 2006 and 2007 iron ore prices from foreign suppliers paid by purchasers in Japan, Supplemental questionnaire responses of Essar Steel Ltd., dated 14 November 2007 (Panel Exhibit USA-118) and dated 21 November 2008 (Panel Exhibit USA-119) (referred herein jointly as "Tex Report").

Australian f.o.b. prices. Because the NMDC's export prices were used to determine the NMDC's domestic prices, these domestic prices are "indirectly comparable to Australian prices as well".[140] Thus, the statement by NMDC officials that the NMDC took into account what steel producers were willing to pay to import, could have been a reference not to delivered import prices, but rather to the *ex mine* or the f.o.b. prices of imported iron ore.[141]

2.92 Moreover, India submits that the Panel's "assumption" that NMDC officials were referring to the delivered prices of imported iron ore is "illogical".[142] In this regard, India contends that "every single market participant, including NMDC and purchasers of iron ore", would be aware that the costs of procuring iron ore from Australia or Brazil would be significantly higher than procuring it locally, as a result of the costs of ocean freight, international insurance, and applicable import duties. In addition, evidence on the record establishes that import transactions were minimal, and that the NMDC itself was not catering to the entire market for iron ore in India. This evidence highlights that the NMDC also competes with local players and, therefore, in its pricing policy, had to account for the prices charged by other domestic suppliers. In India's view, therefore, the Panel erroneously assumed that the NMDC's pricing policy was only dictated by the "delivered prices" of imported iron ore.

2.93 In the light of the above, India asserts that the Panel's reference to an isolated statement by NMDC officials to infer that the use of "as delivered" prices from Australia and Brazil as benchmarks was appropriate under Article 14(d) disregards material evidence on the record. Thus, India submits that the Panel acted inconsistently with its duty under Article 11 of the DSU.[143]

2.94 India further contends that the Panel erred in its interpretation and application of Article 14(d) in finding that the "as delivered" prices from Australia and Brazil reflect "prevailing market conditions" in India. In India's view, the term "prevailing market conditions" refers to the conditions prevailing in the market in general, as opposed to isolated acts of individual players in the market in question. Thus, the assessment of "prevailing market conditions" for countries having both import and domestic transactions for a particular good will depend on a qualitative and quantitative analysis of both types of transactions. The mere fact that one steel producer procured iron ore from Brazil in one isolated transaction in which it paid an "as delivered" price for the iron ore cannot be expanded into the generic conditions applicable to the market in India. Similarly, the Panel's reliance on a statement by NMDC officials that the NMDC allegedly prices iron ore based on what steel producers are willing to pay to import iron ore does not mean that all suppliers of iron ore in the market behaved in such a manner. In addition, India reiterates that evidence on the

140 India's appellant's submission, para. 444.
141 *Ibid.*
142 India's appellant's submission, para. 445.
143 India's appellant's submission, para. 448.

record shows that there were other domestic suppliers of iron ore in India, and that iron ore was not being supplied on an "as delivered" basis. Moreover, evidence on the record demonstrates that imports of iron ore are not physically able to enter the domestic market because foreign ships are too large for India's ports. This implies that there were a large number of transactions in India where the price for iron ore was not an "as delivered" price, and that the "as delivered" prices for iron ore did not constitute a "prevailing market condition" in India, within the meaning of Article 14(d). Thus, India argues that the Panel's reliance on "isolated import transactions" involving payment for iron ore on an "as delivered" basis to establish that these transactions reflected "prevailing market conditions" in India was based on an incorrect understanding of the term "prevailing market conditions" in Article 14(d).[144]

2.95 Finally, India contends that the Panel erred in its interpretation of Article 14(d) in finding that the use of "as delivered" prices of iron ore from Australia and Brazil did not countervail India's comparative advantage in terms of its ability to supply the domestic demand for iron ore. India notes that its case before the Panel was that India had a comparative advantage whereby users of iron ore could procure iron ore locally without "having to suffer the costs and risks associated with" importing the good from a different country, and that the use of "as delivered" benchmarks countervailed this comparative advantage since it created the hypothetical scenario that iron ore does not exist in India, forcing Indian steel producers to import it.[145] India submits that the Panel dismissed its claim concerning the countervailing of India's comparative advantage through the use of "as delivered" benchmarks also on the basis of an isolated import transaction from Brazil by one steel producer, and an isolated statement by NMDC officials that the NMDC prices its iron ore based on what steel producers are willing to pay to import iron ore. India asserts that the Panel's dismissal of its claim concerning the countervailing of India's comparative advantage was thus also based on an erroneous interpretation of Article 14(d) of the SCM Agreement.[146]

2.1.5.1.3 The USDOC's rejection of NMDC export prices as Tier II benchmarks

2.96 India appeals the Panel's dismissal of India's claim that the USDOC's exclusion of NMDC export prices from India to Japan as Tier II benchmarks, in the 2006, 2007, and 2008 administrative reviews, for assessing the adequacy of remuneration for iron ore provided by the NMDC is inconsistent with Article 14(d) and the chapeau of Article 14 of the SCM Agreement. In dismissing this

144 India's appellant's submission, paras. 452-454.

145 India's appellant's submission, para. 455 (referring to India's first written submission to the Panel, paras. 305-309).

146 India's appellant's submission, para. 457.

claim, the Panel erred in its interpretation and application of Article 14(d), and failed to assess objectively India's claim under the chapeau of Article 14.

2.97 India submits that the Panel's finding – made in the context of India's "as such" challenge against the US benchmarking mechanism – that government prices can be presumptively rejected as benchmarks under Article 14(d) led the Panel to reject India's claim concerning the USDOC's rejection of the NMDC's export prices as Tier II benchmarks. Because the Panel erred in finding that government prices can be presumptively rejected as benchmarks under Article 14(d), India requests the Appellate Body to find that the Panel erred in its interpretation and application of Article 14(d) in finding that the rejection of the NMDC's export prices as Tier II benchmarks is consistent with that provision.

2.98 Finally, India submits that the Panel failed to assess objectively India's claim against the requirements of the chapeau of Article 14, and therefore did not assess whether the USDOC "adequately explained" its inconsistent treatment of the NMDC's export prices in the 2004 administrative review, on the one hand, and in the 2006, 2007, and 2008 administrative reviews, on the other hand.[147] Specifically, the Panel was required to evaluate whether the USDOC, clearly and intelligibly, and in a manner that could be easily understood and discerned, explained adequately why the NMDC export prices at issue did not constitute Tier II (world market price) benchmarks under Section 351.511(a)(2)(ii) of the US Regulations.[148] India therefore requests the Appellate Body to find that the Panel erred in "understanding and applying" the requirements of the chapeau of Article 14. Moreover, India further requests the Appellate Body to complete the legal analysis and find that the United States acted inconsistently with the chapeau of Article 14 because of the USDOC's rejection of the NMDC's export prices as a relevant benchmark.[149]

2.1.5.2 The USDOC's determination that the GOI provided iron ore for less than adequate remuneration through its grant of captive mining rights

2.99 India appeals the Panel's finding that the USDOC's determination that the grant of mining rights for iron ore and coal by India conferred a benefit is not inconsistent with Article 14(d) of the SCM Agreement. According to India, the USDOC relied on a notional pricing methodology that was inconsistent with the requirement to assess whether there was "adequate remuneration" within the meaning of Article 14(d). India also contends that the Panel acted inconsistently with Article 11 of the DSU by failing to assess India's claim that the USDOC's benefit assessment was not in accordance with a good faith interpretation of

[147] India's appellant's submission, para. 463.
[148] India's appellant's submission, para. 466.
[149] India's appellant's submission, para. 478.

Article 14(d). India requests the Appellate Body to reverse the Panel's findings, and to complete the legal analysis and find that the United States acted inconsistently with Article 14(d) in determining benefit for the GOI's grant of captive mining rights by comparing iron ore and coal prices with a "notional price" for extracted iron ore and coal.[150]

2.100 India submits that the USDOC established that the remuneration received by the GOI was based on a price for the extracted mineral that included the cost of extraction, the royalty rate, and a notional reasonable profit. This "notional" price was then compared to a Tier II, out-of-country benchmark that was adjusted for freight and delivery charges. India maintains that the USDOC determined the benefit for an upstream product by comparing the extraction cost with an out-of-country benchmark, both of which pertained to a downstream product.

2.101 India argues that, since Article 14(d) requires an assessment as to the adequacy of remuneration, such remuneration cannot be anything other than the actual amount received by the GOI. India considered several definitions of the word "remuneration", and found that they closely resemble the definitions provided by the Appellate Body in *US – Softwood Lumber IV*, consisting of "reward, recompense; payment, pay".[151] According to the Appellate Body, "a benefit is conferred when a government provides goods to a recipient and, in return, receives insufficient payment or compensation for those goods."[152] India contends that, in the case of mining rights, the only amount paid by the miner to the GOI is the royalty, and it is therefore the adequacy of these mining rights that is to be examined under Article 14(d) of the SCM Agreement.

2.102 India argues that extracted iron ore and coal are the results of the activities of Indian miners, and that any such expenditure cannot be attributed to the GOI as the latter's remuneration. To do otherwise would result in an affirmative finding of benefit in every case of a grant of extraction rights because the compensation to the government for taking the risk associated with extraction is not factored into the equation employed by the USDOC. India further maintains that the USDOC could have, instead, used an alternative methodology that it employs for benefit determinations in the context of providing electricity, land leases, or water, where it determines whether the government price is set in accordance with market principles. Such a methodology is consistent with Article 14(d) of the SCM Agreement. India suggests that the reason such a methodology was not applied by the USDOC was that uncontested evidence on the Panel record showed the royalty rates charged

[150] India's appellant's submission, para. 520.

[151] India's appellant's submission, para. 514 (quoting Appellate Body Report, *US – Softwood Lumber IV*, para. 84, in turn quoting *Shorter Oxford English Dictionary*, 5th edn, W.R. Trumble, A. Stevenson (eds.) (Oxford University Press, 2002), Vol. II, p. 2529).

[152] India's appellant's submission, para. 514 (quoting Appellate Body Report, *US – Softwood Lumber IV*, para. 84).

by the GOI to be at similar levels as those charged by other WTO Members. India referred to an expert statement it had introduced before the Panel showing that India's pricing policies in respect of iron ore and coal were "consistent with market principles", and "not significantly lower than other ore producing nations".[153]

2.103 In addition, India contends that the Panel erred in rejecting India's claim that the USDOC's methodology for determining benefit is inconsistent with a good faith interpretation of Article 14(d) of the SCM Agreement. According to India, "a good faith obligation flows through the text of [an] entire treaty including each and every article of a treaty, which is the subject matter of interpretation before a Panel".[154] By rejecting its claim as being outside the Panel's terms of reference, the Panel erred in refusing to assess India's claim that the USDOC's methodology is not in accordance with a good faith interpretation of Article 14(d). India therefore maintains that the Panel failed to assess the matter before it, as required by Article 11 of the DSU.

2.1.5.3 The USDOC's determination that SDF loans conferred a benefit within the meaning of Article 14(b) of the SCM Agreement

2.104 India appeals the Panel's finding that the USDOC's determination that the issuance of SDF loans conferred a benefit is not inconsistent with Articles 1.1(b) and 14(b) of the SCM Agreement. India principally contends that the Panel failed to appreciate that the benchmark used under Article 14(b) must be comparable to the terms of loans provided under the SDF. India further contends that the Panel acted inconsistently with Article 11 of the DSU in disregarding material evidence on the Panel record relating to the manner in which consumers paid for increased levies on steel products. India requests the Appellate Body to reverse the Panel's findings in this regard and to complete the legal analysis and find that the United States acted inconsistently with Articles 1.1(b) and 14(b) of the SCM Agreement by determining that a benefit was conferred in respect of SDF loans.

2.105 India notes that Article 14(b) requires a comparison of the amounts paid on a loan with those paid on a "comparable commercial loan". India submits that a proper understanding of the term "comparable commercial loan" would have led the Panel to agree with India that the deposits made by the participating steel

---

[153] India's appellant's submission, para. 518 (referring to Tata Steel Limited, Expert Statement of Professor James Otto on behalf of Tata Steel Limited in administrative review of Certain Hot-Rolled Carbon Steel Flat Products from India (C-533-821) for the period 01/01-31/12/2006 (6 November 2007) (Panel Exhibit IND-68A); and Tata Steel Limited, Additional Statement of James Otto on Ore Royalties on behalf of Tata Steel Limited in administrative review of Certain Hot-Rolled Carbon Steel Flat Products from India (C-533-821) for the period 01/01-31/12/2006 (28 November 2007) (Panel Exhibit IND-68B)).

[154] India's appellant's submission, para. 522.

producers to become eligible for SDF loans had to be accounted for in the benefit analysis. In accordance with the guidance from the Appellate Body in *US – Anti-Dumping and Countervailing Duties (China)*, the benchmark to be chosen must have a similar structure as the loan under challenge. India observes that the decision of the Supreme Court of India that it had introduced before the Panel categorically states that "steel producers who did not contribute to the SDF program in the first place cannot obtain the SDF loans".[155] Thus, in order to ensure that the comparable commercial loan incorporates a similar structure as well, the United States should first have considered using loans that have a similar entry fee. According to India, the United States is not permitted to use a benchmark loan that is so markedly different from the government loan in question that it renders redundant the term "comparable" in Article 14(b).

2.106 India adds that the existence of an entry deposit into a loan programme significantly affects the rate at which loans would later be disbursed using the same funds. Under normal market and commercial conditions in this scenario, commercial players would expect a lower rate of interest. India further contends that, although the USDOC could have made relevant adjustments to the benchmark, it is undisputed that it did not make any such adjustments to the benchmark in the underlying investigation at issue.

2.107 India also maintains that the Panel disregarded material evidence on the Panel record relating to the manner in which consumers paid for increased levies on steel products. In particular, the Panel's assessment fails to consider the Supreme Court of India's decision that "the SDF program was not open to those who did not make investments into the fund in the first place".[156] This decision, India argues, is a relevant domestic interpretative tool in determining the features of the SDF loans. The decision of the Supreme Court shows that "the SDF levy was on the producers; and the ultimate beneficiaries of this added element were the steel plants themselves, i.e. the fund was not open to other steel producers."[157] Had the Panel been correct in that the SDF funds were consumer levies managed by the government, the SDF loans would have been open to all steel producers. India considers, however, that participating steel members had a right over the SDF funds, where others did not. Specifically, it is only the participating steel producers who had any title or interest to the SDF funds because it was their decision to create and contribute to the fund. Moreover, "it was the private entities who decided to increase prices of their products so as to direct this additional element of price to create the SDF fund".[158] In India's view, therefore, the SDF funds were akin to collective "profits" of the participating steel enterprises. India argues that the Panel did not refer to this evidence in its

[155] India's appellant's submission, para. 589 (referring to Supreme Court of India, Tata Iron and Steel Co. Ltd. v. Collector of Central Excise, Jamshedpur (2002) 8 SCC, pp. 338-351 (Panel Exhibit IND-54B)).

[156] India's appellant's submission, para. 583.

[157] *Ibid.*

[158] India's appellant's submission, para. 584.

Report, and therefore did not objectively assess the facts and evidence before it, as required under Article 11 of the DSU.

2.1.6 Specificity

2.108 India claims that the Panel erred in finding that the USDOC's determination that the sale of iron ore by the NMDC is specific is not inconsistent with Articles 1.2 and 2.1(c) of the SCM Agreement. India requests the Appellate Body to reverse the Panel's findings in this regard and to complete the legal analysis and find that the United States acted inconsistently with Article 2.1(c) of the SCM Agreement in determining that the sale of iron ore by the NMDC is *de facto* specific. India further requests that, in the event that the Appellate Body finds that the United States acted inconsistently with Article 2.1(c), the Appellate Body must also find that the United States acted inconsistently with Article 2.4 of the SCM Agreement. India adds that the violation of Article 2.4 follows from the United States' failure to substantiate with positive evidence that the NMDC sold iron ore to a limited number of certain enterprises.

2.1.6.1 Discrimination in favour of "certain enterprises"

2.109 India considers that the Panel's finding, that Article 2.1(c) did not require an examination of whether the programme *de facto* discriminates between "certain enterprises" and other similarly situated enterprises, is self-contradictory. On the one hand, the Panel recognized that "the specificity determination under both Articles 2.1(a) and 2.1(c) is about '... existence of a restriction on access to the subsidy, in the sense that the subsidy is available to [certain enterprises], but not to others'."[159] Yet, on the other hand, "the Panel [held] that the test of 'specificity' is not about 'discrimination'."[160] In this regard, India considers that the fact that a subsidy is being given to some but not to other entities is exactly how one would normally define discrimination. India further submits that these "other" entities that are denied the subsidy would have to be "like" the "certain enterprises" that are granted the subsidy.

2.110 India argues that its position is supported by the text and context of Article 2.1 of the SCM Agreement. Article 2.1(a) "impliedly suggests that the 'other' entities which are denied access to the subsidy are otherwise 'like' enough for them to have got that subsidy as well".[161] Similarly, under Article 2.1(b), if the objective criteria or conditions of a subsidy privilege "certain enterprises" over "others", a determination of non-specificity cannot be reached. India

159 India's appellant's submission, para. 351.
160 India's appellant's submission, para. 353.
161 India's appellant's submission, para. 355.

submits that, since Article 2.1(c) applies in the same context and within the same analytical framework, this logic would extend to this provision as well.

2.111 India finds support for its position in the Appellate Body report in *US – Large Civil Aircraft (2nd complaint)*, where the Appellate Body concluded that the inquiry under Article 2.1(c) "requires a panel to examine the reasons as to why the actual allocation of 'amounts of subsidy' differs from an allocation that would be expected to result if the subsidy were administered in accordance with the conditions for eligibility for that subsidy".[162] India emphasizes that the Appellate Body's analysis involved a comparative approach between the expected allocation of the subsidy in the ordinary course and the actual allocation of the subsidy in practice. Even when there was a *de facto* disparity in the way in which the subsidy was allocated, the Appellate Body explored whether this position could have been justified nonetheless on a logical basis. In India's view, had evidence in this regard been presented, the United States in that dispute could have demonstrated that the programme was in fact, not specific. India submits that the Appellate Body's reasoning highlights a comparative approach underlying the *de facto* specificity analysis, requiring an examination of factors that would explain or justify why only a few entities *de facto* benefited from the subsidy. This examination, according to India, is an analysis of whether or not there is *de facto* discrimination.

2.112 With respect to the underlying investigation at issue in this dispute, India argues that the sale of iron ore by the NMDC is neutral from the perspective of governmental instruments and actions. Moreover, the sale of iron ore by the NMDC is potentially available only to users of iron ore. Thus, India contends that "there is no recorded disparity between the expected allocation and the actual allocation of the subsidy – the USDOC does not record that among the various users of iron ore, iron ore was sold by NMDC only to a limited number of them."[163] India highlights that those who were allegedly denied this iron ore, i.e. non-users of iron ore, are clearly not "like" users of iron ore. Thus, the non-existence of iron ore sales to non-users of iron ore does not justify a finding of *de facto* specificity under Article 2.1(c). Accordingly, India considers that the United States did not demonstrate that the sale of iron ore was limited to only a few entities but not to others who were similarly situated from an eligibility perspective but were not provided iron ore, as required by Article 2.1(c). India further claims that this requirement relates to the overall object and purpose of disciplining trade-distorting subsidies. As India argues, "[t]he sale of iron ore to persons who would in the ordinary course of business purchase iron ore, cannot be trade distortive in nature".[164]

---

[162] India's appellant's submission, para. 358 (quoting Appellate Body Report, *US – Large Civil Aircraft (2nd complaint)*, para. 877).

[163] India's appellant's submission, para. 362.

[164] India's appellant's submission, para. 364.

2.1.6.2 The meaning of the phrase "limited number of certain enterprises"

2.113 Under its second line of argumentation, India submits that the Panel erred in interpreting the phrase "limited number of certain enterprises" in Article 2.1(c) of the SCM Agreement. India observes that the term "limited number" is preceded by "use ... by" and, therefore, Article 2.1(c) clearly focuses on the users of the subsidy programme being limited in number. Moreover, the term "limited number" is followed by the term "of certain enterprises". The word "of", in its ordinary sense, is used to denote a "sub-set – super-set" relationship between "limited number" and "certain enterprises". Thus, in India's view, when understood in the light of the earlier inference that the provision deals with a "limited number" of "users", it is evident that these "limited number" of users form a sub-set of "certain enterprises". Additionally, India considers that the term "certain enterprises" in Article 2.1(c) refers to the person or persons or group of persons that benefit from the subsidy programme.

2.114 India submits that, in rejecting its claim, the Panel ignored these significant inferences from the text of Article 2.1(c) because it concluded that the relevant category for the required numerical exercise is the category of "certain enterprises". India emphasizes that, on the contrary, the relevant category for the numerical exercise is the users of the programme within the category of "certain enterprises". In particular, according to the United States' own determination, the "certain enterprises" in this case are the "users of iron ore".[165] As a result, Article 2.1(c) requires the United States to have demonstrated that the alleged NMDC programme was being used by a limited number of entities within the set of "users of iron ore". In India's view, the United States, however, did not conduct any such analysis and thus, its specificity determination is not justified under Article 2.1(c).

2.1.6.3 Provision of goods and specificity

2.115 Under its third line of argumentation, India contends that the Panel erred in finding that a government provision of goods can be *de facto* specific merely based on the "inherent limitations" on use of the goods provided. India contends that, under the Panel's interpretation, investigating authorities can determine the provision of goods to be *de facto* specific to certain enterprises even if this arises only based on the inherent limitations of the goods. In India's view, the Panel's interpretation creates redundancy in the SCM Agreement, given that it permits the investigating authority to find specificity as a matter of course, diluting the requirements enshrined in Articles 1.2 and 2.1. In particular, under the Panel's interpretation, "[i]f an authority is permitted to determine *de facto* specificity based on the inherent characteristics of the goods provided by a government, all government provisions of goods that amount to a subsidy under

[165] India's appellant's submission, para. 376.

Article 1.1(a)(1)(iii) would *ipso facto* be *de facto* specific in every case."[166] Thus, according to India, the Panel's interpretation renders Article 2.1(c) inutile in the context of the subsidy programmes covered by Article 1.1(a)(1)(iii).

2.116 Next, India addresses the Panel's statement that there are goods that can be provided to an "indefinite number" of certain enterprises, and are thus not specific, such as oil, gas, and water. India contends that the Panel's examples are not correct. Oil and gas need not be required in all industries in the economy, where the energy required is obtained through electricity. Water also is not a raw material required to manufacture all products in the economy. In any event, India considers that these are examples of goods that constitute "general infrastructure" within the meaning of Article 1.1(a)(1)(iii), and thus do not amount to a financial contribution.

2.117 India further submits that the "absurdity"[167] of the Panel's interpretation is clear from the application of the specificity requirement by the United States in the underlying investigation. In particular, India points out that the purchase of iron ore from the NMDC is open to any person willing to pay the market consideration sought by the NMDC. However, the good in question in this case is iron ore, which by its inherent nature cannot be used by all industries. According to the Panel's interpretation, the only circumstance in which the provision of iron ore will not be specific under Article 2.1 is when the NMDC forcibly provides iron ore even to those industries that do not have the capability to consume or otherwise make use of iron ore. Consequently, India argues that the United States' understanding, upheld by the Panel, results in the automatic and mechanistic application of the specificity requirement, thereby robbing it of its value and purpose.

2.118 In addition, India argues that the Panel erred in dismissing its argument that the negotiating history supports the position that an affirmative finding of *de facto* specificity will not be reached merely based on the inherent characteristics of the goods in question. According to India, the negotiating history of Article 2 of the SCM Agreement indicates that there was no consensus among the negotiators on the issue of determining specificity based solely on the inherent characteristics of the goods. Consequently, India emphasizes that "Article 2.1(c) of the SCM Agreement cannot be interpreted in a manner that would indirectly incorporate into the treaty what the negotiators could not originally agree on."[168] India therefore submits that the Panel erred by failing to accept this inference from the negotiating history.

2.119 Finally, India claims that the Panel acted inconsistently with its obligation under Article 11 of the DSU because it failed to record and evaluate the "cogent reasons" offered by India for not following certain findings set out in the panel

---

[166] India's appellant's submission, para. 388. (emphasis omitted)

[167] India's appellant's submission, para. 389.

[168] India's appellant's submission, para. 397.

report in *US – Softwood Lumber IV*. According to India, the Panel based its conclusion regarding *de facto* specificity under Article 2.1(c) of the SCM Agreement solely on the findings in *US – Softwood Lumber IV*, despite the fact that India had submitted that such findings could not be relied upon in this case for various reasons. India argues that, although the Panel had every discretion to disagree with India and issue a finding that the "cogent reasons" offered by India were not sufficient to depart from an earlier view, the Panel could not ignore material submissions placed on the record by India. On this basis, India contends that the Panel's failure to record and evaluate the "cogent reasons" offered by India violates the due process rights of India in a manner inconsistent with Article 11 of the DSU.

2.1.7 Facts available

2.120 India requests the Appellate Body to reverse the Panel's finding that the measure at issue, Section 1677e(b) of the US Statute and Section 351.308(a)-(c) of the US Regulations, is not inconsistent, "as such" and "as applied", with Article 12.7 of the SCM Agreement. India submits that the Panel erred in its interpretation of Article 12.7 of the SCM Agreement and, even if the Panel's interpretation is upheld, the Panel nonetheless failed to apply the correct legal standard for construing municipal law, and consequently failed to take into account material evidence in reaching its "as such" finding, contrary to Article 11 of the DSU. Furthermore, India claims that the Panel erred in finding that the application of a "rule" on highest non-*de minimis* subsidy rates in numerous instances does not give rise to "as applied" inconsistencies with Article 12.7. India also asserts that the Panel acted inconsistently with Article 11 of the DSU in finding that India failed to make a *prima facie* case in respect of its claim that the 2013 sunset review is inconsistent with Article 12.7 of the SCM Agreement. India requests the Appellate Body to complete the legal analysis in respect of both its "as such" and "as applied" claims under Article 12.7 and find that the measure at issue is inconsistent "as such" and "as applied" with Article 12.7 of the SCM Agreement.

2.1.7.1 Interpretation of Article 12.7 of the SCM Agreement

2.121 India claims that the Panel erred in rejecting its interpretation of Article 12.7 of the SCM Agreement. India asserts that, based on a correct interpretation of Article 12.7, only the most fitting or appropriate facts determined by way of an "evaluative, comparative assessment" of all available evidence can be used, and that Article 12.7 cannot be used to punish or penalize non-cooperation.[169] India argues that, although both its and the Panel's views on the interpretation of Article 12.7 stem from the findings of the panel and the Appellate Body in

[169] India's appellant's submission, paras. 210 and 237.

Mexico – Anti-Dumping Measures on Rice, the Panel's view represents an incomplete and inaccurate understanding of those findings.

2.122 In India's view, the Appellate Body's findings in *Mexico – Anti-Dumping Measures on Rice* indicate that both Article 12.7 of the SCM Agreement and Article 6.8 of the Agreement on Implementation of Article VI of the General Agreement on Tariffs and Trade 1994 (Anti-Dumping Agreement) are part of the due process requirements embodied in each agreement, and are intended to fulfil the very same objective and cannot be interpreted in a "markedly different" manner.[170] In particular, India argues that the Appellate Body actually applied the very same standard for both Article 6.8 of the Anti-Dumping Agreement and Article 12.7 of the SCM Agreement in that case, and further, that the Appellate Body upheld the panel's approach in that case that both provisions were contravened for the very same reasons.[171] In India's view, the Panel failed to account for these aspects of the *Mexico – Anti-Dumping Measures on Rice* rulings when finding that the interpretation of Article 12.7 advanced by India, which was based on the panel's finding in *Mexico – Anti-Dumping Measures on Rice*, is applicable only to Article 6.8 of the Anti-Dumping Agreement and not to Article 12.7 of the SCM Agreement.

2.123 India argues that, contrary to the Panel's finding, the absence in the SCM Agreement of an equivalent to Annex II to the Anti-Dumping Agreement does not result in the general standards applicable under Article 12.7 of the SCM Agreement to be different to those under Article 6.8 of the Anti-Dumping Agreement.[172] India points out that the first sentence of Article 6.8 of the Anti-Dumping Agreement and of Article 12.7 of the SCM Agreement are identical, and argues that, based on a detailed review of Annex II to the Anti-Dumping Agreement, nothing in Annex II prescribes any standard by which an investigating authority is required to select from among the many alternatives that may exist to fill a gap. Therefore, the Panel's reliance on the absence in the SCM Agreement of an equivalent to Annex II to the Anti-Dumping Agreement as a basis for prescribing a "markedly different" standard for Article 12.7 of the SCM Agreement from that in Article 6.8 of the Anti-Dumping Agreement was "erroneous and misplaced".[173]

2.124 India argues that the understanding that Article 12.7 of the SCM Agreement and Article 6.8 of the Anti-Dumping Agreement refer to the very "same general requirements" has been consistently applied by panels in *China –*

[170] India's appellant's submission, para. 216 (referring to Appellate Body Report, *Mexico – Anti-Dumping Measures on Rice*, para. 295).

[171] India's appellant's submission, para. 218 (referring to Appellate Body Report, *Mexico – Anti-Dumping Measures on Rice*, para. 298; and Panel Report, *Mexico – Anti-Dumping Measures on Rice*, para. 7.242).

[172] India's appellant's submission, para. 220.

[173] India's appellant's submission, para. 223.

GOES, *China – Broiler Products*, and *China – Autos (US)*.[174] India further argues that the Ministerial Declaration on Dispute Settlement Pursuant to the Agreement on Implementation of Article VI of the General Agreement on Tariffs and Trade 1994 or Part V of the Agreement on Subsidies and Countervailing Measures supports the view that similar standards are to be applied across similar provisions in the Anti-Dumping Agreement and in the SCM Agreement.

2.125 Finally, India submits that comparatively evaluating all the available facts should logically be part of the standard articulated by the Panel, which refers to the need to account for all substantiated facts on the record and ensure that only information that can "reasonably" replace the missing information is used. India argues that, as part of that standard, a panel would need to determine what a "reasonable" replacement for the missing information would be, taking account of all substantiated facts on the record. In India's view, it is unclear how an assessment of what is "reasonable", after having taken into account all substantiated facts on the record, is different than comparatively evaluating all the available facts with a view to selecting the best information.

2.1.7.2 The Panel's "as such" finding

2.126 India appeals the Panel's rejection of India's "as such" claim under Article 12.7 of the SCM Agreement on the ground that the Panel failed to meet the requirements of Article 11 of the DSU by applying an incorrect standard for construing municipal law, and by consequently disregarding material evidence on its operation in reaching its finding. This claim is conditional upon the Appellate Body rejecting India's claim that the Panel erred in interpreting Article 12.7 of the SCM Agreement.

2.127 India argues that the legal standard by which a Member's municipal law is to be construed involves, in addition to the text of the measure itself, a consideration of "other domestic interpretive tools", such as judicial interpretations and the legislative history. Thus, the Panel was correct in starting its analysis with the text of the law in question, namely, Section 1677e(b) of the US Statute and Section 351.308(a)-(c) of the US Regulations, but should have proceeded further to examine other evidence submitted relating to the construction of the measure. India therefore argues that the Panel erred in failing to consider the evidence placed on the record by India, namely, an excerpt of the Statement of Administrative Action, decisions issued by the Federal Circuit and the Court of International Trade (as well as the United States' failure to contest India's reliance on these), determinations of the USDOC, and a data sheet covering 245 USDOC determinations under the measure at issue.

[174] India's appellant's submission, paras. 224 and 225 (referring to Panel Report, *China – Autos (US)*, para. 7.172).

2.128 In India's view, these domestic interpretative tools demonstrate that Section 1677e(b) of the US Statute and Section 351.308(a)-(c) of the US Regulations do not require the USDOC to take into account all substantiated facts and are not intended to provide a reasonable replacement for the missing information. Rather, India submits that the evidence it submitted demonstrates that Section 1677e(b) of the US Statute and Section 351.308(a)-(c) of the US Regulations actually require adverse inferences to be drawn in each and every case of non-cooperation, so as to "penalize" the non-cooperating party.[175] India asserts that this evidence is very clearly material, and that the Panel's disregard of this evidence violates Article 11 of the DSU.[176]

2.129 India requests the Appellate Body to complete the legal analysis and find that the measure at issue is inconsistent, "as such", with Article 12.7 of the SCM Agreement.[177] India argues that, on the basis of a correct interpretation of Article 12.7, there are three separate and independent grounds for demonstrating an inconsistency with Article 12.7, namely, that the measure at issue: (i) does not require the use of facts that are most fitting or most appropriate, but instead requires the use of information that is adverse to the non-cooperating party so as to penalize that party; (ii) enables the use of adverse facts without engaging in an evaluative, comparative assessment of all the available evidence; and (iii) enables a punitive application of the facts available standard whereby, as a matter of rule in this case, the USDOC is required to draw the worst possible inference as well as choose the highest prior margin to ensure that the party concerned is penalized for non-cooperation. India argues that, although the text of the measure at issue is "innocuous" and appears to provide discretion, the evidence submitted by India on its meaning and scope, as actually understood and applied by the USDOC, suggests that the USDOC "routinely and mechanically determines to draw the worst possible inference" in every case of non-cooperation by an interested party.[178] India argues that the evidence suggests that, in drawing adverse inferences, the USDOC does not engage in a comparative evaluation of the possible facts, evidence, or inferences, nor does it assess which facts or evidence may best fit and replace the missing information.[179]

2.130 India further submits that, even under the interpretation articulated by the Panel, the same evidence demonstrates a violation of Article 12.7 of the SCM Agreement. The standard articulated by the Panel would require the USDOC to account for all facts available on record, and to ensure that only what can reasonably replace the missing information is used. India asserts that, since the USDOC makes a conclusive assumption that the highest prior margin must

[175] India's appellant's submission, para. 232.
[176] India's appellant's submission, para. 233.
[177] India's appellant's submission, paras. 234-236.
[178] India's appellant's submission, para. 239.
[179] *Ibid.*

necessarily be a reasonable substitute for the missing information, there is no meaningful assessment as to whether the adverse inference drawn is actually a "reasonable" substitute for the missing information. Thus, irrespective of whether the Appellate Body agrees with the Panel's interpretation of Article 12.7, India argues that the measure at issue is inconsistent with Article 12.7 of the SCM Agreement.

2.1.7.3 The Panel's "as applied" finding

2.131 India appeals the Panel's rejection of its claim that the USDOC applied a "rule" in "about 230 instances" that is inconsistent with Article 12.7 of the SCM Agreement.[180] India raises this appeal firstly on the ground that the Panel applied an incorrect interpretation of Article 12.7 of the SCM Agreement to the claim, and secondly that, even if the Appellate Body upholds the Panel's interpretation of Article 12.7, the Panel nonetheless erred by imposing an unnecessary burden of proof on India. On either ground, India requests the Appellate Body to reverse the Panel's finding, complete the legal analysis, and find that the United States has acted inconsistently with Article 12.7 in these instances.

2.132 As to the first ground, assuming that Article 12.7 of the SCM Agreement requires an investigating authority to engage in an evaluative, comparative exercise and choose among those facts available which best fit the missing information, according to India, the mere fact that the USDOC applies the highest non-*de minimis* rate itself shows that this requirement is not fulfilled. In India's view, the USDOC consistently applies a "rule" pursuant to which it would firstly opt for data on the highest non-*de minimis* subsidy rate for an identical programme, and absent such data, would then opt for the highest non-*de minimis* subsidy rate for a similar programme, and, as a last preference, would opt for data on the highest non-*de minimis* subsidy rate for any programme in any countervailing duty investigation involving the same country, so long as the industry in question could have accessed that programme. Based on this "rule", India argues that the USDOC starts with the conclusive non-rebuttable presumption that the highest non-*de minimis* rate is the best substitute for the missing information, which, in India's view, demonstrates a violation of Article 12.7 of the SCM Agreement.

2.133 As to the second ground, India asserts that the Panel's standard of proof, under which India was required to show how the highest non-*de minimis* subsidy rate was not a reasonable substitute for the missing information in each claimed instance, represents an "illogical and self-contradictory" application of the Panel's interpretation of Article 12.7.[181] Rather, India argues that, even based on the Panel's approach to interpreting Article 12.7, the purpose of Article 12.7 is to ensure non-cooperation does not "impede the investigation", rather than "to

[180] India's appellant's submission, paras. 592 and 593.

[181] India's appellant's submission, para. 602.

punish" non-cooperation.[182] On this basis, the fact that the USDOC necessarily applies the highest non-*de minimis* subsidy rate pursuant to the "rule" is "*ipso facto* a violation" of Article 12.7.[183] Thus, according to India, any application of the "rule" necessarily establishes an "as applied" violation, and therefore India need not show further why in each instance the application of the "rule" is inconsistent with Article 12.7.

2.134 India further requests the Appellate Body to find that the Panel did not reasonably consider the evidence and legal arguments raised by India in support of its claim regarding the 2013 sunset review, in contravention of Article 11 of the DSU. India thus requests the Appellate Body to reverse the Panel's finding that India failed to make a *prima facie* case, and to complete the legal analysis of its claim.

2.135 In respect of the 2013 sunset review, India first notes that the review is a published and publicly available document, the contents of which "cannot be disputed", and that India challenged "every single finding" in the 2013 sunset review before the Panel.[184] On this basis, the fact that India did not identify specific instances of breach is not a material defect in India's submission.

2.136 Second, India contends that, since its first written submission to the Panel stated that, "for substantially the same reasons as enunciated above", and since the 2013 sunset review did not make any new determinations but, rather, cited prior determinations in the same investigation, India was merely avoiding repeating the same arguments to avoid duplication by expressing its claim in one paragraph only.[185] In India's view, it was anomalous for the Panel to find, on the one hand, breaches of Article 12.7 of the SCM Agreement in a number of instances in the context of administrative reviews and, on the other hand, reject India's claim regarding the same breaches repeated in the context of the 2013 sunset review.

2.1.8 New subsidy allegations

2.137 India appeals the Panel's findings rejecting India's claims that the examination by the USDOC of new subsidy allegations in administrative reviews related to the imports at issue was inconsistent with Articles 11.1, 13.1, 21.1, 21.2, 22.1, and 22.2 of the SCM Agreement. India presents two main arguments in support of its contention. First, India argues that the Panel erred in interpreting the relationship between Articles 11 and 21 of the SCM Agreement. Second, India alleges that the Panel breached its duties under Articles 11 and 12.7 of the DSU to conduct an objective assessment of the matter before it and

[182] India's appellant's submission, para. 604.
[183] India's appellant's submission, para. 605.
[184] India's appellant's submission, para. 610.
[185] India's appellant's submission, para. 611 (quoting India's first written submission to the Panel, para. 576). (emphasis omitted)

to provide a basic rationale for its findings. Consequently, India requests the Appellate Body to reverse the Panel's rejection of India's claims under Articles 11.1, 13.1, 22.1, and 22.2 of the SCM Agreement, and further requests the Appellate Body to complete the legal analysis in respect of these claims.[186]

2.138 As regards the relationship between Articles 11 and 21 of the SCM Agreement, India argues that the Panel "simply failed to evaluate Article 11".[187] According to India, Article 11 is the sole provision in the SCM Agreement that deals with the initiation of an investigation into the existence, degree, and effect of any alleged subsidy. Thus, Article 11 applies so long as the purpose of an investigation is to determine the existence, degree, and effect of a subsidy, regardless of whether it is an original investigation. India submits that such an interpretation does not result in unnecessary overlap between Articles 11 and 21, because reviews under Article 21 concern the continuation or recurrence of subsidization in relation to a subsidy that has already been found to exist pursuant to investigations conducted under Article 11.

2.139 India further argues that the Panel's assumption that the applicability of Article 21 *ipso facto* excludes the applicability of Articles 11, 13.1, 22.1, and 22.2 does not correspond to a good faith interpretation of Articles 21 and 11. In India's view, Articles 11, 13, and 22 of the SCM Agreement contain the due process requirements set forth in the SCM Agreement when a subsidy is investigated for the first time. Where a review under Article 21 deals, for the first time, with the existence of new subsidies, an investigating authority must comply with the requirements of Articles 11, 13, and 22. The Panel's "assumption" that Article 11 is inapplicable to investigations into new subsidies in the context of reviews under Article 21 allows for the circumvention, by investigating authorities, of the due process protections contained in Articles 11, 13, and 22 in respect of new subsidies.[188] Such an interpretation would disturb the delicate balance in the SCM Agreement between disciplining the use of subsidies, on the one hand, and disciplining the use of countervailing measures, on the other hand. Accordingly, India requests the Appellate Body to reverse the Panel's finding that Articles 11.1, 13.1, 22.1, and 22.2 are not applicable to administrative reviews conducted pursuant to Articles 21.1 and 21.2 of the SCM Agreement, as well as the Panel's rejection of India's claims under these provisions.

2.140 India argues that the Panel breached its duties under Articles 11 and 12.7 of the DSU to conduct an objective assessment of the matter before it and to provide a basic rationale for its findings. India states that the Panel erroneously narrowed the scope of India's claim to focus on whether Articles 21.1 and 21.2 of the SCM Agreement permit the examination of new subsidy allegations in

[186] India's appellant's submission, paras. 628 and 645.
[187] India's appellant's submission, para. 633.
[188] India's appellant's submission, paras. 637 and 642.

administrative reviews. In doing so, the Panel failed separately to address the "independent claims"[189] of India that the USDOC acted inconsistently with Articles 11.1, 13.1, 22.1, and 22.2 of the SCM Agreement by not initiating investigations into the new subsidies pursuant to these provisions. Thus, the Panel acted inconsistently with Article 11 of the DSU by exercising false judicial economy. In addition, the Panel simply assumed that Articles 11 and 21 are mutually exclusive without explaining why such an interpretation is appropriate in the light of the customary rules of treaty interpretation. Therefore, the Panel also acted inconsistently with Article 12.7 of the DSU by failing to provide a basic rationale for its findings. Consequently, India requests the Appellate Body to reverse the Panel's rejection of India's claims under Articles 11.1, 13.1, 22.1, and 22.2 of the SCM Agreement, and to complete the legal analysis of these claims on the basis of the following considerations.

2.141 With respect to its claim under Article 11.1 of the SCM Agreement, India refers to the US Regulations governing original investigations, highlighting that one of the requirements is for the USDOC to issue a "New Subsidies Allegation Memorandum" each time it initiated an original investigation. India argues that, during the 2004, 2006, and 2007 administrative reviews, the USDOC took no procedural action to formally commence investigations in administrative reviews, and in particular did not issue new subsidy allegations memoranda. Instead, the USDOC directly proceeded to issue questionnaires regarding the alleged new subsidies, in the conduct of the administrative reviews. Thus, India claims that the United States acted contrary to Article 11.1 of the SCM Agreement.

2.142 Concerning its claim under Article 13.1 of the SCM Agreement, India asserts that "[a] combined reading of Article 13.1 and Article 11.2(iii) of the SCM Agreement requires the United States to invite India for consultations to clarify the *existence, amount and nature of* each and every subsidy alleged to have been granted by India."[190] The United States did not invite India for consultations "prior to initiation of the investigation" regarding the new subsidies, thereby failing to provide India any opportunity to clarify the situation in relation all the new subsidies.[191] India contends that this "initiation of investigations by the United States into the New Subsidies, without providing an opportunity to India for consultations", is inconsistent with Article 13.1 of SCM Agreement.[192]

2.143 In respect of its claims under Articles 22.1 and 22.2 of the SCM Agreement, India asserts that, during the 2004, 2006, and 2007 administrative reviews, the USDOC conducted investigations into several new

189 India's appellant's submission, para. 623.
190 India's appellant's submission, para. 657. (emphasis original)
191 India's appellant's submission, para. 657.
192 India's appellant's submission, para. 659.

subsidy programmes[193], without issuing a public notice through a New Subsidies Allegation Memorandum. According to India, the United States did not issue any public notice containing the "description of the subsidy practice or practices to be investigated".[194] Instead, the USDOC directly investigated the same by issuing questionnaires to the GOI and the interested parties under Article 12 of the SCM Agreement. Thus, India maintains that the United States failed to comply with its obligation under Articles 22.1 and 22.2 of the SCM Agreement.

2.2 Arguments of the United States – Appellee

2.2.1 The Panel's terms of reference

2.144 The United States requests that the Appellate Body uphold the Panel's preliminary ruling regarding the compliance of India's panel request with Article 6.2 of the DSU on the grounds that the Panel applied the correct legal standard for Article 6.2 and that India's reliance on the definition of "initiation" under the SCM Agreement does not cure its defective panel request.

2.145 In the United States' view, India's appeal on the Panel's preliminary ruling was not properly raised, because India raises a claim under Article 11 of the DSU as its primary claim, and raises a subsidiary claim based on the same reasoning of its Article 11 claim regarding the Panel's application of the law in Article 6.2 of the DSU to the facts of this case. According to the United States, this approach to a claim under Article 11 of the DSU has been held to be "unacceptable" in WTO jurisprudence, since such a claim must rest on independent grounds going to specific errors regarding the objectivity of a panel's assessment, and may not simply recast arguments made before a panel.[195] In any event, the United States argues that the substance of India's claims fails under either Article 6.2 or Article 11 of the DSU.

2.2.1.1 The meaning of the word "initiated" in India's panel request

2.146 The United States argues that, according to WTO jurisprudence, Article 6.2 of the DSU contains two distinct requirements in respect of panel requests, namely, that they identify the specific measures at issue, and that they provide a brief summary of the legal basis of the complaint. Under the second requirement, the United States points to WTO jurisprudence suggesting that the brief summary of the legal basis must be sufficient to present the problem clearly, and

---

[193] India's appellant's submission, para. 655 (referring to the following subsidy programmes: Target Plus Scheme; Status Certificate programme; EPZ & EOU, EPZ; Income Tax under 10A & 10B; Market Development Assistance; Market Access Initiative; and Long term loan from GOI).

[194] India's appellant's submission, para. 656. (emphasis omitted)

[195] United States' appellee's submission, paras. 617 and 618 (referring to Appellate Body Reports, *EC – Fasteners (China)*, para. 442; *China – Rare Earths*, paras. 5.173 and 5.178; *US – Steel Safeguards*, para. 498; and *Chile – Price Band System (Article 21.5 – Argentina)*, para. 238).

must plainly connect the challenged measure with the provisions of the covered agreements claimed to have been infringed.[196] A panel request must be assessed as a whole, in the light of attendant circumstances, and on its face at the time of filing.[197] Later submissions made during the panel proceedings cannot cure defects in a panel request.

2.147 The United States recalls the Panel's finding that, "by clearly and only stating that an investigation was *not* initiated or conducted, India's panel request precludes claims relating to the alleged initiation of an investigation, or the manner in which an investigation was conducted, being included in the scope of the dispute."[198] According to the United States, India's arguments regarding the definition of the word "initiation" do not explain how India's panel request can be read as encompassing, on its face, issues concerning whether sufficient evidence existed to initiate investigations.[199] In particular, the definition of "initiation" in footnote 37 of the SCM Agreement does not serve to provide a sufficiently clear identification of which particular obligations in Article 11 of the SCM Agreement form the legal basis of India's complaints.

2.148 Contrary to India's argument that the provisions of Article 11 of the SCM Agreement are "interlinked", the United States notes that Article 11 contains 11 subparagraphs, and numerous disparate obligations. According to the United States, WTO jurisprudence suggests that, where a provision contains several distinct obligations that are capable of being separately breached, a cursory reference to that provision in a panel request may not reveal which of those obligations is at issue.[200] Thus, the Panel correctly found that India's panel request is not reasonably open to the reading advanced by India that the phrase "no investigation was initiated or conducted" covers "initiating investigation[s] ... [without] sufficient evidence".[201]

2.149 Finally, with regard to India's claim under Article 11 of the DSU, the United States asserts that India identifies nothing in the Panel Report to suggest that the Panel's assessment and rejection of India's argument lacked objectivity.[202]

[196] United States' appellee's submission, para. 623 (referring to Appellate Body Reports, *US – Oil Country Tubular Goods Sunset Reviews*, para. 162; and *China – Raw Materials*, para. 220).

[197] United States' appellee's submission, para. 623 (referring to Appellate Body Report, *US – Carbon Steel*, para. 127).

[198] United States' appellee's submission, para. 634 (quoting Panel Report, para. 1.34). (emphasis original)

[199] United States' appellee's submission, para. 635.

[200] United States' appellee's submission, para. 636 (referring to Appellate Body Report, *Korea – Dairy*, para. 128).

[201] United States' appellee's submission, paras. 632-634 (referring to Panel Report, para. 1.34)

[202] United States' appellee's submission, para. 637.

2.2.1.2 Relevance of prejudice and questions during consultations

2.150 The United States submits that the Panel was correct in not applying the findings of the Appellate Body in *Korea Dairy* and the panel in *US – Lamb*, relied upon by India. In particular, India's assertion based on the Appellate Body's finding in *Korea – Dairy* that Article 6.2 of the DSU requires a showing of actual prejudice by the respondent is "simply wrong".[203] Nothing in the text of Article 6.2 supports this assertion, and it has been rejected in recent Appellate Body reports.[204]

2.151 In respect of India's reliance on the panel's finding in *US – Lamb*, the United States argues that past panel reports are not binding on a panel in a dispute, and there was thus no obligation for a separate consideration of that case by the Panel. In any event, the consultations questions that India argues should have been taken into account, based on the panel's finding in *US – Lamb*, were not furnished to the panel record, and therefore could not have been taken into account. Even if they had been taken into account, the United States contends that they would not have assisted India's case, and, in any event, the universe of claims from which India might have selected in formulating its panel request is not relevant to determining what was actually contained in the panel request.

2.152 The United States further argues that the fact that a panel does not address an argument presented by a party does not rise to the level of a violation of Article 11 of the DSU. In order for India's claim under Article 11 of the DSU to succeed, India would have had to identify specific errors regarding the objectivity of the Panel's assessment, including an explanation of why the alleged error meets the threshold for a breach of Article 11. In the United States' view, India "simply re-aired the same arguments made before the Panel", without impugning the Panel's objectivity or findings.[205]

2.2.1.3 Completion of the legal analysis

2.153 The United States requests the Appellate Body to decline India's request for completion of the legal analysis of the claims in Sections XII.C.1 and XII.C.2 of its first written submission to the Panel.

2.154 The United States argues, first, that India's claims under Articles 11.1, 11.2, and 11.9 of the SCM Agreement fail because, as the Panel found in respect of Article 11.1, those provisions apply only in the context of original investigations, and not in the context of administrative review proceedings, which are the subject of India's claims.

---

[203] United States' appellee's submission, para. 626.

[204] United States' appellee's submission, para. 626 (referring to Appellate Body Reports, *China – Raw Materials*, para. 233; and *EC – Fasteners (China)*, paras. 132, 139, 562-564, and 595-598).

[205] United States' appellee's submission, para. 630.

2.155 Second, the United States argues that the Panel made no factual findings in relation to India's claims, and the facts on the panel record on which a completion of the analysis would be grounded are not undisputed. As an example, the United States points to the preliminary determination in the USDOC's 2004 administrative review, which it considers "directly contradicts" India's assertion that no allegation was made regarding the sale of high-grade iron ore by the NMDC.[206]

2.156 In respect of the TPS, the United States argues that its examination was not initiated based on a written request, and thus Article 11.6 of the SCM Agreement would apply; however, India has raised no claim under that provision.

2.157 Thus, the United States considers that there is no legal or factual basis on which to complete the analysis of India's claims under Articles 11.1, 11.2, and 11.9 of the SCM Agreement.

2.2.2 Public Body

2.158 The United States requests the Appellate Body to uphold the Panel's finding that the USDOC did not act inconsistently with Article 1.1(a)(1) of the SCM Agreement when it determined that the NMDC is a "public body". The United States contends that the Panel interpreted and applied Article 1.1(a)(1) of the SCM Agreement in a manner consistent with the interpretation given by the Appellate Body in *US – Anti-Dumping and Countervailing Duties (China)*. The United States further submits that India has not established that the Panel failed to make an objective assessment of the matter before it, as required by Article 11 of the DSU. Finally, should the Appellate Body decide to complete the legal analysis, the United States maintains that the evidence on the USDOC's administrative record supports the USDOC's determination that the NMDC is a 'public body', even under an interpretation of that term that requires evidence beyond 'meaningful control'".[207]

2.2.2.1 Interpretation and application of Article 1.1(a)(1) of the SCM Agreement: Public Bodies

2.159 The United States contends that India's understanding of the term "public body" is incorrect and inconsistent with the Appellate Body's interpretation and application of Article 1.1(a)(1) of the SCM Agreement in *US – Anti-Dumping and Countervailing Duties (China)*. The United States acknowledges that the Appellate Body found, in that dispute, that the "defining elements of the word

---

[206] United States' appellee's submission, para. 641 (referring to 2004 AR Preliminary Results (Panel Exhibit IND-17), internal p. 5).
[207] United States' appellee's submission, para. 504.

'government' inform the meaning of the term 'public body'".[208] The United States further notes that, in making this finding, the Appellate Body referred to its earlier finding, in *Canada – Dairy*, that the "essence of government is that it enjoys the effective power to regulate, control, or supervise individuals, or otherwise restrain their conduct".[209] However, the United States submits that the Appellate Body did not find that every public body must, like the government, have the power to regulate, control, supervise or restrain the conduct of individuals. The Appellate Body also did not find that every public body must have the power to entrust or direct private bodies. Rather, according to the United States, the Appellate Body found in that dispute, that an entity "meaningfully controlled" by the government can be a public body.[210]

2.160 The United States recalls that, in *US – Anti-Dumping and Countervailing Duties (China)*, the Appellate Body upheld the USDOC's determination that state-owned commercial banks (SOCBs) were public bodies. Moreover, the United States submits that the Appellate Body did not examine or discuss any evidence as to whether SOCBs had the power to regulate, control, supervise, or restrain the conduct of others, or whether they could entrust or direct private bodies. For the United States, this is hardly surprising given that banks typically do not possess such authority. The United States further submits that, in spite of SOCBs not possessing such powers, the Appellate Body nevertheless found them to be public bodies. For these reasons, the United States argues, India's interpretation of the term "public body" is, in reality, a deviation from the interpretation articulated by the Appellate Body in *US – Anti-Dumping and Countervailing Duties (China)*.

2.161 Furthermore, the United States points out that, in *US – Anti-Dumping and Countervailing Duties (China)*, the Appellate Body "repeatedly referred" to the government's "meaningful control" over an entity in its analysis of whether SOCBs were "public bodies"[211] and focused its analysis on evidence that demonstrated that the SOCBs were "meaningfully controlled" by the government. Hence, the United States contends that the implication of the Appellate Body's reasoning is that evidence of government ownership plus additional evidence of government control could be sufficient to establish "meaningful control", which in turn is sufficient to establish that the entity is a public body.

2.162 Turning to the Panel's interpretation of the term "public body", the United States observes that the Panel understood the Appellate Body to have found that "the critical consideration in identifying a public body is the question of

---

[208] United States' appellee's submission, para. 510 (quoting Appellate Body Report, *US – Anti-Dumping and Countervailing Duties (China)*, para. 290).

[209] *Ibid.*

[210] United States' appellee's submission, para. 506 (quoting Appellate Body Report, *US – Anti-Dumping and Countervailing Duties (China)*, para. 355).

[211] *Ibid.*

governmental authority".[212] The United States further notes that the Panel recalled the Appellate Body's finding in *US – Anti-Dumping and Countervailing Duties (China)* that "evidence that a government exercises meaningful control … may serve, in certain circumstances, as evidence [of] governmental authority".[213] Thus, the United States maintains that the Panel correctly understood the Appellate Body's findings in *US – Anti-Dumping and Countervailing Duties (China)*, and did not err in its decision to examine whether the NMDC was "meaningfully controlled" by the GOI.

2.163 The United States recalls that the Panel noted that, in addition to the GOI's near-total ownership of the NMDC, the USDOC's determination was "also based on the NMDC being 'governed by' the GOI".[214] Thus, the Panel found that evidence on the administrative record before the USDOC supported the determination that the NMDC was "governed by" the GOI, and referred in particular to evidence that the GOI was heavily involved in the selection of the directors of the NMDC, and to evidence that the NMDC was under the "administrative control" of the GOI.[215]

2.164 Regarding the distinction drawn by India between "chief executives" and "directors", and between "appointment" and "nomination" of directors, the United States asserts that the more relevant distinction to be drawn is between the government having the formal right to appoint board members, like any shareholder with a significant stake in an entity, and the government actually exercising that right in a given situation.

2.165 The United States notes India's arguments that "shareholding and appointment of directors are merely two sides of the same coin", as "the right to appoint directors inheres in shareholders"[216], and that the GOI does not control the NMDC, in spite of the nearly 100% government ownership, because the GOI "only appoints 2 of the 13 directors".[217] The United States claims that India's assertions are contradictory, and contends that the GOI's influence over the naming of all 13 directors suggests a significant degree of "control" that extends well beyond its formal right to appoint two directors. The United States explains that "the GOI *in fact* plays a role in appointing all nine of the directors appointed by shareholders", while the remaining four directors are appointed by those nine board members in whose appointment the GOI already played an active role.[218]

---

[212] United States' appellee's submission, para. 515 (quoting Panel Report, para. 7.80).

[213] United States' appellee's submission, para. 515 (quoting Panel Report, para. 7.80, in turn quoting Appellate Body Report, *US – Anti-Dumping and Countervailing Duties (China)*, para. 318).

[214] United States' appellee's submission, para. 517 (quoting Panel Report, para. 7.81).

[215] United States' appellee's submission, para. 518 (referring to Panel Report, paras. 7.82-7.88).

[216] United States' appellee's submission, para. 520 (quoting India's appellant's submission, para. 291).

[217] United States' appellee's submission, para. 520 (quoting India's appellant's submission, para 295). (emphasis omitted by the United States)

[218] United States' appellee's submission, para. 522. (emphasis original)

The United States adds that the Panel considered India's arguments and rejected them.

2.166 In the view of the United States, the Panel correctly found that the GOI's involvement in the selection of the NMDC's directors, together with the statement on the website of the NMDC website that the latter was under the "administrative control" of the government, constitutes evidence of "meaningful control".[219] The United States adds that the Panel's conclusion is consistent with the Appellate Body report in *US – Anti-Dumping and Countervailing Duties (China)*.

2.2.2.2 Article 11 of the DSU

2.167 The United States contends that India has failed to establish that the Panel acted inconsistently with its obligations under Article 11 of the DSU, with respect to the Panel's assessment of the USDOC's determination that the NMDC is a "public body".

2.168 First, with respect to the Panel's treatment of an alleged admission made by the United States before the panel in *US – Anti-Dumping and Countervailing Duties (China)*, the United States argues that India "is simply incorrect as a matter of fact" in claiming that the United States admitted that the USDOC considered shareholding of the GOI as the sole factor without reference to any more factors, when it found the NMDC to be a public body.[220] In support of its contention, the United States quotes the statement of the panel in that dispute referred to by India: "The United States further notes that in a subsequent countervailing duty administrative review of *Hot-Rolled Carbon Steel Flat Products from India*, the USDOC found that a 98 per cent government-owned mining company *governed by the Ministry of Steel* was a public body, without reference to any more factors".[221] The United States points out therefore that the panel in that dispute noted the USDOC's finding that the NMDC was "governed by the Ministry of Steel".[222] The United States submits, therefore, that India's assertion that the United States even made the admission that India describes has no basis whatsoever in fact. In any event, the United States argues, India has failed to explain why this alleged assertion is so material to its case that the Panel's failure to address this evidence has a bearing on the objectivity of the Panel's assessment. Nor has India explained why the Panel should have accorded greater weight to this evidence than to the USDOC's determination.

---

[219] United States' appellee's submission, paras. 522 and 523 (referring to Panel Report, paras. 7.83 and 7.87).

[220] United States' appellee's submission, para. 529.

[221] United States' appellee's submission, para. 529 (quoting Panel Report, *US – Anti-Dumping and Countervailing Duties (China)*, para. 8.39 (fn omitted)). (emphasis added by the United States)

[222] United States' appellee's submission, para. 529 (quoting Panel Report, *US – Anti-Dumping and Countervailing Duties (China)*, para. 8.39).

2.169 Second, the United States maintains that the Panel did not rely on *ex post* rationalizations provided by the United States in the Panel proceedings. Contrary to India's argument, the USDOC explained that its "public body" determination was partly based on the NMDC being "governed by" the GOI, and the United States demonstrated in its submissions to the Panel that the USDOC considered various pieces of information in its "public body" determination.[223] Thus, the determination that the NMDC is "governed by" the GOI, contained in the USDOC's final determination, was supported by evidence discussed in other documents on the administrative record of the USDOC.[224] The Panel correctly found that the United States did not present new reasons and new evidence in support of the USDOC's determination[225], but was relying on the USDOC's final determination and the evidence on the administrative record. In this regard, the United States highlights the Appellate Body's finding in *US – Countervailing Duty Investigation on DRAMS* that the SCM Agreement "does not require the agency to cite or discuss *every* piece of supporting record evidence for each fact in the final determination".[226] The United States argues, therefore, that the Panel properly took into account the rationalization provided by the USDOC and evidence that was part of the USDOC evaluation process at the time of the its determination.

2.170 Third, the United States disagrees with India's claim that the Panel disregarded material evidence or drew "inferences and connections contrary to the evidence on record".[227] The United States notes India's argument that an objective assessment of the facts in the underlying investigation would have led the Panel to discard "administrative control" as a relevant factor in the USDOC's determination given that "the United States specifically admitted that 'administrative control' was not used in its determinations".[228] The United States disagrees to having made such an admission, and explains that the USDOC did not determine that the NMDC is under the "administrative control" of the GOI but, rather, that the NMDC is "governed by" the GOI. However, that determination was supported by evidence on the administrative record of the USDOC that the NMDC is under the "administrative control" of the GOI. According to the United States, the Panel addressed India's argument and did not consider the United States to have admitted that the USDOC did not rely on

---

[223] United States' appellee's submission, para. 536 (referring to United States' first written submission to the Panel, paras. 381-383; and second written submission to the Panel, paras. 104 and 105).

[224] United States' appellee's submission, para. 539 (referring to 2004 AR Preliminary Results; 2004 GOI Verification Report (Panel Exhibit USA-66); and 2007 AR Issues and Decision Memorandum).

[225] United States' appellee's submission, para. 539 (referring to Panel Report, fn 245 to para. 7.82).

[226] United States' appellee's submission, para. 543 (quoting Appellate Body Report, *US – Countervailing Duty Investigation on DRAMS*, para. 164 (emphasis original; fn omitted)).

[227] United States' appellee's submission, para. 545 (quoting India's appellant's submission, para. 278).

[228] United States' appellee's submission, para. 547 (referring to India's appellant's submission, paras. 267 and 270).

"administrative control" in its determination. Furthermore, the United States contends that India is "merely recast[ing] its arguments before the panel under the guise of an Article 11 claim", contrary to the Appellate Body's findings in *EC – Fasteners (China)*.[229]

2.171 Finally, regarding India's claim that the Panel ruled on a matter that was not before it by making a finding on the implication of the status of the NMDC as a *Miniratna* or *Navratna* company, the United States submits that "India appears to misunderstand what the panel did".[230] According to the United States, the Panel considered India's arguments but did not find the evidence provided by India to be relevant. The Panel's finding was, according to the United States, "directly responsive" to India's contention that the "USDOC ought to have considered [the] 'Miniratna' or 'Navratna' status of NMDC as being relevant evidence".[231] The United States further argues that, to the extent that India considered the Panel to have exceeded its terms of reference by making a finding on the status of the NMDC as a *Miniratna* or *Navratna* company, it should have requested reversal of the Panel's legal conclusion on this basis, "rather than inventing a new basis for an Article 11 claim".[232]

2.2.2.3 Completion of the legal analysis

2.172 The United States submits that the Appellate Body should reject India's appeal of the Panel's findings in respect of the USDOC's determination that the NMDC is a "public body". Thus, it would not be necessary for the Appellate Body to complete the legal analysis, as India requests. Nevertheless, in the event the Appellate Body reverses or modifies the Panel's interpretation of Article 1.1(a)(1) of the SCM Agreement, and/or reverses the Panel's finding that the USDOC was correct in determining the NMDC to be a public body, the United States considers that it would be possible for the Appellate Body to complete the legal analysis, as there would not appear to be any dispute about the facts on the Panel record. On this basis, the United States requests the Appellate Body to find that the evidence on the administrative record of the USDOC would support a finding that the NMDC is a public body.[233]

2.173 The United States contests India's claim that the USDOC's "public body" determination was based solely on a finding that the GOI owns over 98% of the NMDC[234], arguing that the claim does not reflect the full extent of the USDOC's analysis. To the contrary, the United States submits that the following evidence

---

229 United States' appellee's submission, para. 549 (quoting Appellate Body Report, *EC – Fasteners (China)*, para. 442).

230 United States' appellee's submission, para. 554.

231 United States' appellee's submission, para. 555 (quoting India's appellant's submission, para. 282).

232 United States' appellee's submission, para. 562.

233 United States' appellee's submission, para. 566.

234 United States' appellee's submission, para. 567 (referring to India's appellant's submission, paras. 285, 334, and 335).

on the record indicates that the NMDC is a public body because it is owned and controlled by the GOI and has the authority to perform GOI functions.

2.174 The United States recalls that the USDOC determined the NMDC to be a public body on the basis of: (i) the GOI's 98% ownership of the NMDC; and (ii) the NMDC being "governed by" the GOI's Ministry of Steel. Hence, the United States maintains that the USDOC's determination was not based solely on ownership, but also on an analysis of the control that the government has over the NMDC. Furthermore, the United States recalls India's argument that the Appellate Body found, in *US – Anti-Dumping and Countervailing Duties (China)*, that a "public body" must have the authority to perform government functions. The United States contends that, because the NMDC is exploiting public resources on behalf of the GOI (the owner of the resources), the NMDC is performing a government function in India. This is because in India, it is a function of the government to arrange for the exploitation of public assets, in this case iron ore, and the GOI specifically established the NMDC to perform part of this function – i.e. developing all minerals other than coal, petroleum oil, and atomic minerals. In support of its position, the United States cites evidence showing that an official from the Indian Ministry of Steel identified the NMDC as a "strategic company" that was monitored and reviewed by the GOI because it provided a specific service to the Indian public.[235]

2.175 Finally, the Unites States notes that the Appellate Body would not be precluded from finding that evidence on the record supports a finding that the NMDC is a public body based on a legal standard different from the one applied by the USDOC. In this respect, the United States submits that, in *US – Anti-Dumping and Countervailing Duties (China)*, the Appellate Body found that the evidence on record supported a finding that the SOCBs were public bodies, in spite of having rejected the interpretation adopted by the panel and the USDOC in that dispute.

2.2.3 Financial contribution

2.2.3.1 Captive mining rights

2.176 The United States submits that India's claim with respect to the Panel's finding under Article 1.1(a)(1)(iii) of the SCM Agreement is flawed because it mischaracterizes the Panel's finding, misunderstands the Appellate Body's finding in *US – Softwood Lumber IV*, and is contrary to the text of Article 1.1(a)(1)(iii). The United States contends that the Panel did not err in finding that the GOI provides minerals in accordance with Article 1.1(a)(1)(iii) of the SCM Agreement.

2.177 The United States argues that India incorrectly described the Panel's finding when it stated that the Panel improperly adopted a "but for" test instead

[235] United States' appellee's submission, para. 572 (referring to 2004 GOI Verification Report, p. 9).

of the Appellate Body's "reasonably proximate relationship" test in *US – Softwood Lumber IV*. According to the United States, in conducting a "reasonably proximate relationship" test, the Panel considered both the fact that the GOI has direct control over the availability of the relevant minerals and that the "GOI's grant of the rights to mine those minerals essentially made those minerals available to, and placed them at the disposal of, the beneficiaries of those rights."[236] Moreover, the United States argues, the Panel was careful to consider that this provision was more than a "but for" relationship when it stated that the grant of a mining lease "is more than a mere 'general governmental act' that simply facilitates the mining operation".[237]

2.178 The United States notes India's argument that the grant of mining rights does not constitute a provision of minerals by the government, because significant efforts, risks, and investment have to be undertaken by the miner to actually make the mineral available. The United States maintains that this requirement is nowhere found in the text of SCM Agreement or the Appellate Body report in *US – Softwood Lumber IV*. The United States argues that the Appellate Body, by focusing on the consequence of the transaction in that dispute, indicated that "making available timber is the *raison d'être* of the stumpage arrangements".[238] The United States considers that, analogous to the ruling in that dispute, making available iron ore and coal is the *raison d'être* of the GOI's mining leases. Moreover, in *US – Softwood Lumber IV*, the Appellate Body found that the concept of "making available" or "putting at the disposal of" requires there to be a "reasonably proximate relationship" between the action of the government providing the good or service, on the one hand, and the use or enjoyment of the good or service by the recipient, on the other hand. Just as in *US – Softwood Lumber IV*, the United States argues, there also exists a "reasonably proximate relationship" between the grant of mining rights and the availability of the mined iron ore or coal, such that the GOI provides the minerals in accordance with Article 1.1(a)(1)(iii).

2.179 The United States points to evidence considered by the USDOC that Indian state governments own all of the minerals in India, and the mining leases are approved by the central government. The United States also observes that, in return for the right to mine the iron ore and coal from public land, the miners pay only for the iron ore and coal that they extract from the ground. As the United States put it, whether the GOI mines and sells the iron ore and coal itself, or sells the mining rights to the iron ore and coal in the ground so that someone else may extract those minerals, the purpose of the transaction is to provide the government-owned iron ore and coal to certain enterprises for use. The United States adds that, from the point of view of the recipient, the objective of the

---

[236] United States' appellee's submission, para. 366 (quoting Panel Report, para. 7.238).

[237] *Ibid.*

[238] United States' appellee's submission, para. 367 (quoting Appellate Body Report, *US – Softwood Lumber IV*, para. 75).

transaction, whether to purchase directly iron ore and coal from the GOI or to obtain the mining rights from the GOI to extract those minerals itself, is to obtain the iron ore and coal. In the United States' view, "[w]hen a government gives a company the right to take a government-owned good, such as iron ore and coal from government lands, the government is 'providing' the goods within the meaning of Article 1.1(a)(1)(iii) of the SCM Agreement."[239]

2.180 The United States considers that the interpretation advanced by India would weaken the disciplines of the SCM Agreement, since it would allow governments to provide *in situ* minerals to specific industries as long as the government structured the transaction as the sale of rights to the mineral instead of the sale of the mineral itself. This, the United States argues, would allow a government to provide minerals for less than adequate remuneration or for free, without being subject to the disciplines of the SCM Agreement. The United States therefore requests the Appellate Body to reject India's claim in respect of Article 1.1(a)(1)(iii) of the SCM Agreement and to decline India's request to complete the legal analysis.

2.181 The United States also urges rejection of India's appeal of the Panel's finding under Article 11 of the DSU. According to the United States, India is incorrect to argue that the Panel refused to evaluate its arguments. Rather, the United States argues, the Panel expressly examined India's argument that, because of the amount of work required by the mining entity to extract the iron ore and coal once the lease has been granted, the grant of the mining lease by the GOI is too remote. The United States further considers that the Panel was not required to reference the evidence supplied by India as to the alleged cost breakdown between the government and the leaseholder because it "was not legally relevant".[240] The United States further considers that India's Article 11 challenge cannot be made simply as a subsidiary claim to what is in reality a disagreement on an issue of law or legal interpretation. For this reason, the United States argues, India's claim under Article 11 is not appropriate and should be dismissed.

2.2.3.2 SDF loans

2.182 The United States argues that India's appeal of the Panel's finding under Article 1.1(a)(1)(i) of the SCM Agreement rests on a fundamental misunderstanding of the record in the underlying proceeding. According to the United States, the Panel correctly found that the distribution of the SDF funds in the form of loans was a direct transfer of funds because the decision-making regarding the issuance, terms, and waivers of SDF loans was done by the SDF Managing Committee, a governmental body. Contrary to India's assertions, the United States maintains, the Panel determined that the SDF Managing

239 United States' appellee's submission, para. 371.
240 United States' appellee's submission, para. 361 (referring to Panel Report, para. 6.133).

Committee "was 'directly' involved in the issuance of SDF loans", because there was record evidence demonstrating that the SDF Managing Committee "made the decision whether or not loans should be issued, and on what terms".[241]

2.183 As the United States maintains, the Appellate Body has interpreted Article 1.1(a)(1)(i) to mean that any government practice the effect of which is to improve the financial position of the recipient may constitute a direct transfer of funds. The United States refers to the Appellate Body's statement in *US – Large Civil Aircraft (2nd complaint)* that "[t]he direct transfer of funds in subparagraph (i) therefore captures conduct on the part of the government by which money, financial resources, and/or financial claims are made available to a recipient."[242] The United States also points to other panel and Appellate Body findings that, before any determination can be made pursuant to one of the subparagraphs of Article 1.1(a)(1), a measure must be properly characterized according to its design, operation, and effects.[243] In this dispute, the Panel correctly looked to the design, operation, and effects of SDF loans, and found: that SDF levies are collected by the JPC; that the funds, once collected, are remitted to the SDF; and that the funds are held by the SDF and disposed of pursuant to the instructions of the SDF Managing Committee. The United States argues, therefore, that the Panel's finding is consistent with the text of the SCM Agreement, and with past interpretations of Article 1.1(a)(1)(i).

2.184 The United States maintains that India's argument that a "direct transfer" cannot involve an "intermediary entity" draws artificial distinctions that have no basis in the SCM Agreement or in the record evidence that was before the USDOC. Moreover, India's argument assumes a different structure for the SDF than exists on the record. According to the United States, it is the SDF Managing Committee, not the JPC, that decides what happens with the levies remitted to the SDF. The United States argues that India "presents the transfer of funds to steel companies as a discrete and isolated action performed by the JPC, wholly divorced from the decision by the SDF Managing Committee that the funds should be transferred and on what terms".[244] The United States further observes that Article 1.1(a)(1)(i) requires that a government practice "involve" the direct transfer of funds. Therefore, the government practice does not need to constitute such a transfer in and of itself, but it only needs to involve or include such a transfer. Thus, the United States argues, "even if the JPC were viewed as formally transferring the funds, the decision by the SDF Managing Committee to transfer the funds and on what terms would also be a practice involving the direct transfer of funds."[245]

---

[241] United States' appellee's submission, para. 400 (quoting Panel Report, para. 7.293).

[242] United States' appellee's submission, para. 402 (quoting Appellate Body Report, *US – Large Civil Aircraft (2nd Complaint)*, para. 614).

[243] United States' appellee's submission, para. 402 (referring to Appellate Body Report, *US – Large Civil Aircraft (2nd Complaint)*, para. 586; and Panel Report, *Japan – DRAMs (Korea)*, para. 7.444).

[244] United States' appellee's submission, para. 405.

[245] United States' appellee's submission, para. 406.

2.185 The United States also maintains that India is wrong to suggest that the Panel's findings render inutile Article 1.1(a)(1)(iv) of the SCM Agreement. The difference between subparagraph (i) and subparagraph (iv), the United States argues, is whether the government is providing a financial contribution covered under Article 1.1(a)(1)(i), or a private body has been entrusted or directed to do so under Article 1.1(a)(1)(iv). In the United States' view, the SDF Managing Committee did not entrust or direct the JPC to provide loans within the meaning of Article 1.1(a)(1)(iv), but rather itself made all decisions regarding the issuance, terms, and waivers of the SDF loans. While the JPC administered the distribution of these funds after the SDF made its decisions, the United States argues, its role was ministerial. This is because "the JPC had no authority to issue SDF loans absent a decision by the SDF Managing Committee"; "[t]hus, the JPC was not entrusted or directed to make loans using funds over which it otherwise had authority."[246] In the United States' view, India again artificially isolates the various actions involved such that the presence of any "intermediary" would preclude the application of Article 1.1(a)(1)(i).

2.186 The United States further notes that, while the JPC was not found by the USDOC to be the "public body" that made the financial contribution, the United States does not agree with India that the JPC is a "private body". To the contrary, the JPC is a constituent committee of the SDF programme, formed by the GOI through the issuance of an administrative order, "for the purpose of giving effect to the provisions of" the Iron and Steel (Control) Order, 1956.[247] The United States therefore argues that the JPC operated under the supervision of the GOI, both through the supervision of the SDF Managing Committee, as well as periodic administrative orders issued by the Ministry of Steel. The United States further submits that information that was before the USDOC during the original investigation "also indicated that the JPC was not acting in an independent capacity".[248]

2.187 The United States argues that neither the text of the SCM Agreement nor Appellate Body findings support India's contention that any direct transfer of funds must be accomplished through the transfer of ownership of the relevant funds from the government to the recipient. India's interpretation narrows the scope of Article 1.1(a)(1)(i), such that significant government action could be shielded from WTO subsidies disciplines. In the circumstances of this case, where a government can and does decide whether and on what terms certain funds will be made available to private entities, the United States considers that those transfers are covered by Article 1.1(a)(1)(i) of the SCM Agreement. Accordingly, the United States contends, the Panel correctly found that "there is

[246] United States' appellee's submission, para. 409.

[247] United States' appellee's submission, para. 411 (referring to United States' first written submission to the Panel, para. 531; and 2001 GOI Supplemental Questionnaire Response (Panel Exhibit USA-75), internal Exhibit 22, Ministry of Steel Notification of 1971).

[248] United States' appellee's submission, para. 411 (referring to, *inter alia*, United States' first written submission to the Panel, para. 532).

nothing in the text of Article 1.1(a)(1)(i) to suggest that the relevant government or public body must have title over the funds being transferred, or that there must be a charge on the public account, in order for a direct 'transfer' of funds to occur."[249]

2.188 In addition, the United States argues, the SDF levies operates as a tax. The United States points to evidence that was before the USDOC purportedly showing that, under the direction of the SDF Managing Committee, the JPC determined the amounts to be levied and sequestered the resulting funds, and the SDF Managing Committee thereafter determined the redistribution of those funds to steel producing entities and steel-related projects in accordance with the GOI's goals for the steel sector. According to the United States, Indian steel producers did not determine the amounts to be collected from consumers and remitted to the SDF. In addition, Indian steel producers did not own or control the funds that had been collected, either individually, or through association with the JPC. Accordingly, the United States contends, the SDF Managing Committee was in full control of these funds once they had been levied and sequestered, and determined their ultimate allocation and use. The United States adds that the Supreme Court decision cited by India, in which the Court found that the SDF levy is not a tax, is a domestic judicial interpretation of a municipal law and, therefore, not binding for purposes of WTO dispute settlement proceedings. The United States therefore concludes that, as the USDOC and the Panel found, the SDF loans constitute a direct transfer of funds under Article 1.1(a)(1)(i) of the SCM Agreement. For these reasons, the United States requests the Appellate Body to reject India's appeal of the Panel's interpretation and application of Article 1.1(a)(1)(i), and to uphold the Panel's finding in this regard.

2.2.4 Benefit – "As such" claims

2.189 The United States submits that the Panel correctly found that Section 351.511(a)(2)(i)-(iv) of the US Regulations, setting forth the US benchmarking mechanism, is not inconsistent with Article 14(d) of the SCM Agreement. The United States therefore requests the Appellate Body to reject India's claim that the US benchmarking mechanism is "as such" inconsistent with Article 14(d). Moreover, the United States considers that India's claims concerning the USDOC's determinations of benefit in respect of the provision of iron ore by the NMDC, and of captive mining rights by the GOI, are contingent on India's "as such" claims against the US benchmarking mechanism. Therefore, the United States further requests the Appellate Body to also reject these "as applied" claims. Finally, the United States requests the Appellate Body to reject the claims raised by India under Article 11 of the DSU.

[249] United States' appellee's submission, para. 413 (quoting Panel Report, para. 7.294).

2.2.4.1 Assessment of the adequacy of remuneration for government-provided goods required under Article 14(d) of the SCM Agreement

2.190 First, the United States contends that the Panel correctly rejected India's claim that the US benchmarking mechanism is inconsistent with Article 14(d) of the SCM Agreement because it does not require that the adequacy of remuneration for government-provided goods be assessed from the perspective of the government provider prior to assessing whether a benefit has been conferred from the perspective of the recipient. India's claim that the first sentence of Article 14(d) requires an assessment of the adequacy of remuneration from the perspective of the government provider contradicts the "core approach" to "benefit" under the SCM Agreement.[250] Moreover, India's arguments weigh in favour of a cost-to-government approach to assessing benefit, which has been rejected by the Appellate Body in prior disputes.[251]

2.191 The United States takes issue with India's argument that the term "unless" in Article 14(d) does not imply that a benefit is conferred each and every time the remuneration for government-provided goods is inadequate from the perspective of the recipient. India's interpretation contravenes the text of Article 14(d) and, in particular, the title and chapeau of Article 14. The title of Article 14 states that the provision concerns "Calculation of the Amount of a Subsidy *in Terms of the Benefit to the Recipient*".[252] Moreover, the chapeau of Article 14 makes clear that Members must provide in their laws or regulations for a methodology that allows their investigating authorities to calculate "the benefit to the recipient". Yet India, by contrast, argues for a methodology of calculating benefit based on "cost to government", which, according to the United States, is a proposition that has already been considered and rejected by the Appellate Body.[253]

2.192 The United States contends that, contrary to India's assertions on appeal, the Panel's conclusion that adequacy of remuneration under Article 14(d) need not be assessed before determining benefit does not suffer from inherent contradictions. First, the United States considers that there is no contradiction between, on the one hand, the Panel's finding that the terms "benefit" and "remuneration" in Article 14(d) refer to "different notions" and, on the other hand, the Panel's conclusion that a finding of inadequate remuneration necessarily results in a finding of benefit. The United States submits that there is

---

[250] United States' appellee's submission, para. 35.

[251] United States' appellee's submission, para. 35 (referring to Appellate Body Report, *Canada – Aircraft*, paras. 154 and 155).

[252] United States' appellee's submission, para. 43 (referring to Panel Report, para. 7.34). (emphasis added by the United States)

[253] United States' appellee's submission, para. 36 (referring to India's first written submission to the Panel; and Appellate Body Report, *Canada – Aircraft*, paras. 154 and 155).

nothing contradictory about different terms being connected through a single analysis.[254]

2.193 Second, the United States considers that there is no contradiction between, on the one hand, the Panel's finding that the term "remuneration" relates to the sum that is paid for the good provided by the government and, on the other hand, the Panel's finding that, under Article 14(d), the adequacy of remuneration for government-provided goods is to be assessed from the perspective of the potential recipient of a benefit. In this regard, the United States submits that it does not follow that because the SCM Agreement defines the type of financial contribution by reference to the action of a granting authority – i.e. "the provision of goods made by a government" – the benefit standard for that type of financial contribution is likewise to be determined by reference to the provider, rather than the recipient, of the relevant good.[255]

2.194 Third, the United States submits that the fact that a competitor's price is adopted to determine both the "adequacy of remuneration" and the amount of "benefit" conferred is not, as India asserts, irreconcilable with the Panel's finding that the use of the same standard for assessing the adequacy of remuneration and benefit will result in circularity. Noting the Panel's finding that the circularity that India had alleged would result only if the adequacy of remuneration, on the one hand, and benefit, on the other hand, are assessed separately, the United States submits that India has misread the Panel's findings.[256]

2.195 Finally, the United States asserts that India's argument that the adequacy of remuneration must be assessed from the perspective of the government provider prior to assessing benefit to the recipient is inconsistent with Article 1.1 of the SCM Agreement. Although India suggests that an investigating authority must assess the price-setting behavior of the government in addition to assessing the issues of financial contribution and of benefit, Article 1.1 states that "a subsidy shall be deemed to exist" where there is "a financial contribution by a government or any public body" and "a benefit" is thereby conferred. There is no additional requirement that focusses on the cost to government.

2.196 For these reasons, the United States requests the Appellate Body to uphold the Panel's finding that the US benchmarking mechanism is consistent with Article 14(d) of the SCM Agreement, because Article 14(d) does not require an assessment of the adequacy of remuneration received by the government provider of goods prior to determining the quantum of benefit to the recipient.

---

254 United States' appellee's submission, paras. 45-49.

255 United States' appellee's submission, paras. 51 and 52.

256 United States' appellee's submission, paras. 53 and 54.

2.2.4.2 Exclusion of government prices as benchmarks under the US benchmarking mechanism

2.197 The United States requests the Appellate Body to reject India's claim that the Panel erred in finding that government transactions can be presumptively rejected in assessing the adequacy of remuneration for government-provided goods under Article 14(d) of the SCM Agreement. The Panel correctly rejected India's claim that the US benchmarking mechanism is inconsistent with Article 14(d) of the SCM Agreement because it excludes the use of government prices as Tier I and II benchmarks. The United States asserts that India's claims are based on a flawed interpretation of Article 14(d), and are inconsistent with the Appellate Body's finding, in *US – Softwood Lumber IV*, that private prices are the preferred benchmark for assessing the adequacy of remuneration for government-provided goods. Moreover, as the Panel found, India had not established the factual premise of its claim that the US benchmarking mechanism excludes the use of government prices as Tier I and II benchmarks.[257] On this basis alone, the United States submits, the Appellate Body should reject India's claims on appeal.

2.198 The United States submits that India's assertion that the Panel found that an investigating authority must presumptively exclude government prices as benchmarks for assessing the adequacy of remuneration for government-provided goods is incorrect. Instead, the Panel found, and India did not dispute, that government prices are not "presumptively and conclusively" excluded from Tiers I and II of the US benchmarking mechanism in all cases. In this regard, Section 351.511(a)(2)(i) of the US Regulations specifies that prices from competitively run government auctions could be included in determining benchmarks for assessing the adequacy of remuneration for government-provided goods. The United States submits that the Panel found that an investigating authority "is not required to presume" that a government price reflects market principles or "prevailing market conditions" within the meaning of Article 14(d) of the SCM Agreement.[258]

2.199 Turning to India's contention that the Panel's interpretation of Article 14(d) is at odds with the first sentence of that provision, the United States considers that there is no apparent connection between the text of Article 14(d) and India's assertion that government prices must be presumed to be market driven. The benchmark analysis under Article 14(d) assesses whether a provision is made for less than adequate remuneration. India has not explained why the terms "shall not" and "unless" in the first sentence of Article 14(d) require an investigating authority to use government prices in determining market benchmarks for assessing the adequacy of remuneration for government-provided goods. As the Panel found, "it would be circular, and therefore

---

[257] United States' appellee's submission, para. 61 (referring to Panel Report, para. 7.38).

[258] United States' appellee's submission, paras. 71 (referring to Panel Report, para. 7.39) and 72.

uninformative, to include the government price for the good provided by the government in establishment of the market benchmark when assessing *whether such* governmental provision confers a benefit."[259]

2.200 The United States does not agree with India's reliance on the Appellate Body's finding that the text of Article 14(d) does not explicitly refer to a market undistorted by government intervention to support its argument that Article 14(d) does not permit prices set by governments to be disregarded as benchmarks for assessing the adequacy of remuneration for government-provided goods.[260] India does not explain how its position that government prices must presumptively be used for determining market benchmarks can be squared with the text of Article 14(d), or the Appellate Body's finding that "*private suppliers* in the country of provision are the *primary benchmark* that investigating authorities *must use* when determining whether goods have been provided by a government for less than adequate remuneration."[261] Moreover, India has ignored the Appellate Body's finding that, where in-country private prices are distorted, out-of-country benchmarks may be used for assessing the adequacy of remuneration for government-provided goods.[262]

2.201 Finally, the United States considers that the Panel correctly rejected India's argument that, because the Appellate Body found, in *US – Anti-Dumping and Countervailing Duties (China)*, that "government loans cannot be *ipso facto* rejected as non-commercial under Article 14(b)", it follows that government prices of goods cannot *ipso facto* be rejected as benchmarks under Article 14(d).[263] The Panel correctly found that the Appellate Body's finding in *US – Anti-Dumping and Countervailing Duties (China)* does not mean that government prices necessarily must be used as market benchmarks for assessing the adequacy of remuneration for government-provided goods.

2.202 For these reasons, the United States requests the Appellate Body to reject India's claims that the Panel erred in finding that the US benchmarking mechanism is not inconsistent with Article 14(d) of the SCM Agreement because it excludes the use of government prices as Tier I and II benchmarks.

---

259 United States' appellee's submission, para. 73 (quoting Panel Report, para. 7.39). (emphasis added by the United States)

260 United States' appellee's submission, para. 74 (referring to India's appellant's submission, para. 47, in turn referring to Appellate Body Report, *US – Softwood Lumber IV*, para. 87).

261 United States' appellee's submission, para. 74 (quoting Appellate Body Report, *US – Softwood Lumber IV*, para. 90). (emphasis added by the United States)

262 United States' appellee's submission, para. 74 (referring to Appellate Body Report, *US – Softwood Lumber IV*, para. 103).

263 United States' appellee's submission, para. 75 (referring to India's appellant's submission, para. 48, in turn referring to Appellate Body Report, *US – Anti-Dumping and Countervailing Duties (China)*, para. 479).

2.2.4.3 Use of world market prices under Tier II of the US benchmarking mechanism

2.203 The United States notes that India appeals the Panel's findings concerning the use of world market prices under Tier II of the US benchmarking mechanism on several grounds. First, India argues that the Panel acted inconsistently with Article 11 of the DSU by failing to evaluate India's claim that the US benchmarking mechanism permits the use of out-of-country benchmarks without first exhausting all possible sources of in-country benchmarks, and is therefore inconsistent with Article 14(d) of the SCM Agreement. Second, India argues that the Panel failed to make an objective assessment of the matter before it by failing to provide a basic rationale, as required under Article 12.7 of the DSU, for its finding that out-of-country benchmarks may be used by investigating authorities in situations other than where in-country private prices are distorted by governmental influence in the market. Third, India argues that the Panel incorrectly interpreted Article 14(d) of the SCM Agreement in finding that investigating authorities can use out-of-country benchmarks without first finding that the market is distorted by governmental interference or influence.[264] Fourth, India argues that the Panel acted inconsistently with Article 11 of the DSU, and erred in its application of Article 14(d) of the SCM Agreement, in rejecting India's claim that the US benchmarking mechanisms fails to require that Tier II benchmarks be adjusted to reflect prevailing market conditions in the country of provision, in accordance with the guideline prescribed in Article 14(d). The United States submits that India's claims are based on a misreading of the Panel Report, a misunderstanding of the measure at issue, and an incorrect interpretation of Article 14(d) of the SCM Agreement. The United States therefore requests the Appellate Body to reject India's claims.[265]

2.204 The United States considers as being without merit India's claim that the Panel acted inconsistently with Article 11 of the DSU by failing to evaluate India's claim that the US benchmarking mechanism permits the use of Tier II, out-of-country benchmark, without requiring that all possible sources of in-country benchmarks be exhausted first. A failure by a Panel to evaluate an argument raised by a party does not give rise to a violation of Article 11 of the DSU. In addition, an evaluation of India's claim would not have affected the Panel's "material findings" that Tier II of the US benchmarking mechanism is not inconsistent with Article 14(d) of the SCM Agreement, because India's assertion that Tier I benchmarks do not exhaust all possible sources of in-country benchmarks is factually inaccurate. The United States asserts in this regard that the nature and operation of the measure at issue demonstrates that, under Tier I of the US benchmarking mechanism, the USDOC is required to exhaust all available in-country benchmarks before turning to out-of-country

---

264 United States' appellee's submission, para. 78 (referring to India's appellant's submission, para 5).

265 United States' appellee's submission, paras. 79, 97, 102, 106, 107, and 121.

benchmarks under Tier II. Noting that the Panel, in fact, recorded India's argument that the US benchmarking mechanism "provides for the use of world market (Tier II) price benchmarks whenever Tier I in-country benchmarks are *not available*", the United States submits that it was uncontested that in-country benchmarks under Tier I of the US benchmarking mechanism are used whenever they are available.[266] The United States submits, therefore, that there was no need for the Panel to explain further this issue and that India has failed to demonstrate that the Panel acted inconsistently with Article 11 of the DSU.

2.205 The United States also considers as being without merit India's claim that the Panel acted inconsistently with Articles 11 and 12.7 of the DSU in finding that there could be "other situations" in which an investigating authority could resort to out-of-country benchmarks besides the situation where in-country private prices are distorted as a result of government intervention in the market. As an initial matter, India's claim under Article 11 should be rejected because it does not stand on its own but, instead, is simply a subsidiary claim to what is in reality a disagreement on an issue of law or legal interpretation.[267] Furthermore, the United States submits that India's claim is based on a misunderstanding of what the Panel actually found. Contrary to India's assertions on appeal, the Panel, in fact, defined the "other situations" in which out-of-country benchmarks may be used by an investigating authority as situations "in which the government is not a predominant provider" of the relevant good in question.[268] Moreover, the Panel did not purport to define the entire universe of scenarios in which out-of-country benchmarks can be used for assessing the adequacy of remuneration for government-provided goods. Therefore, the Panel did not find that the use of out-of-country benchmarks would be appropriate in any and all "other situations". The United States contends, therefore, that India's claims under Articles 11 and 12.7 of the DSU should be rejected by the Appellate Body.

2.206 With respect to India's claim that the Panel erred in its interpretation of Article 14(d) of the SCM Agreement in finding that investigating authorities can use out-of-country benchmarks without first finding that the market is distorted by governmental interference or influence, the United States submits that India's claim is based on an incorrect reading of the Appellate Body's findings in *US – Softwood Lumber IV* and *US – Anti-Dumping and Countervailing Duties (China)*. In this regard, the United States recalls that the Appellate Body's findings in *US – Softwood Lumber IV* were limited to the particular situation where in-country private prices are distorted by government predominance in the market.[269] Thus, India's argument that the circumstances permitting an

266 United States' appellee's submission, para. 97 (referring to Panel Report, para. 7.47). (emphasis original)

267 United States' appellee's submission, para. 99 (referring to Appellate Body Reports, *China – Rare Earths*, para. 5.173).

268 United States' appellee's submission, para. 101 (quoting Panel Report, para. 7.50).

269 United States' appellee's submission, para. 105 (referring to Appellate Body Report, *US – Softwood Lumber IV*, para. 99).

investigating authority to use out-of-country benchmarks must relate to governmental interference in the relevant market is in error.

2.207 The United States considers as being without merit India's claims that the Panel acted inconsistently with Article 11 of the DSU, and erred in its application of Article 14(d) of the SCM Agreement, in rejecting India's claim that the US benchmarking mechanism does not require that Tier II benchmarks be adjusted to reflect prevailing market conditions in the country of provision. Turning first to India's claim under Article 11 of the DSU, the United States does not agree with India's contention that the Panel was precluded from considering the language of the statute implemented by the US Regulations in assessing the consistency of Tier II of the US benchmarking mechanism with Article 14(d) of the SCM Agreement, and that the Panel, instead, should have restricted its assessment to the plain text of the US Regulations or "relevant domestic interpretive tools". According to the United States, the relevant statutory provision considered by the Panel is "exactly the type of context" that forms part of the "effective operationalization" of the US Regulations.[270] Indeed, the US Regulations, setting forth the US benchmarking mechanism, operates in connection with the statute that it implements. While India may disagree with the outcome of the Panel's conclusions, India has no basis to assert that the Panel did not rely on any evidence in reaching the finding challenged by India. The United States therefore requests the Appellate Body to reject India's claim under Article 11 of the DSU.[271]

2.208 Turning to India's claim that the Panel erred in its application of Article 14(d) of the SCM Agreement, the United States asserts that India has not contested the Panel's finding that the relevant US statute and regulations "require[] that the adequacy of remuneration must in all cases be assessed in relation to the prevailing market conditions in the country of provision".[272] Thus, India has not made out the factual premise underlying its claim. In any event, the United States explains that the relevant US statute on which the Panel relied in interpreting the US benchmarking mechanism gives effect to the guidelines in Article 14(d) of the SCM Agreement "nearly word-for-word".[273] Thus, the structure and operation of the US statute, and the implementing regulations setting forth the US benchmarking mechanism, are designed to ensure that the USDOC evaluates the adequacy of remuneration for government-provided goods in accordance with the guidelines prescribed by Article 14(d) of the SCM Agreement. The United States therefore requests the Appellate Body to reject India's claim that the Panel erred in its application of Article 14(d) in rejecting India's claim that the US benchmarking mechanism does not require that Tier II benchmarks be adjusted to reflect "prevailing market conditions" in the country

270 United States' appellee's submission, para. 110.

271 United States' appellee's submission, paras. 108-111.

272 United States' appellee's submission, para. 114 (quoting Panel Report, para. 7.51).

273 United States' appellee's submission, para. 116

of provision, in accordance with the guideline prescribed by Article 14(d) of the SCM Agreement.

2.2.4.4 The Panel's failure to assess two grounds of India's "as such" claim against the US benchmarking mechanism

2.209 The United States considers as being without merit India's claim that the Panel acted inconsistently with Article 11 of the DSU by failing to consider two of the six grounds underlying India's "as such" claim concerning the consistency of Section 351.511(a)(2)(i)-(iii) of the US Regulations with Article 14(d) of the SCM Agreement.[274] According to the United States, the Panel considered and rejected all of India's arguments. In any event, the United States recalls that a panel has no obligation under Article 11 of the DSU to address in its report every argument raised by a party.[275] The United States therefore requests the Appellate Body to reject India's claim under Article 11 of the DSU.

2.210 First, the United States disputes India's argument that the Panel failed to evaluate separately its claim that the US benchmarking mechanism is inconsistent with Article 14(d) of the SCM Agreement by mandating an affirmative finding of benefit without assessing whether the government price, or the price difference between the government price and the benchmark price, is in accordance with "commercial considerations". The United States submits that whether Article 14(d) requires an investigating authority to assess the adequacy of remuneration from the perspective of the government provider is akin to the issue of whether the pricing behavior of the government provider can be attributed to "commercial considerations". Therefore, the United States contends, having found that Article 14(d) does not require the adequacy of remuneration for government-provided goods to be assessed from the perspective of the government provider, the Panel correctly considered that "[t]he fact that the government price may have been set according to 'commercial considerations' is

---

[274] India alleges that these six grounds were as follows: (i) the US benchmarking mechanism is inconsistent with the first sentence of Article 14(d) because it fails to assess the adequacy of remuneration from the perspective of the government provider, before assessing whether there is a benefit to the recipient; (ii) the US benchmarking mechanism is inconsistent with the second sentence of Article 14(d) because it does not require a consideration of whether the difference between a government and a competitor's price is justified by "commercial considerations"; (iii) a government price that is "adequate" under Tier III will be deemed "less than adequate" merely based on the benchmark method under Tiers I or II; (iv) under Tiers I and II, all government prices are not considered as a "price" in relation to the prevailing market conditions; (v) world market prices prescribed under Tier II are not in relation to prevailing market conditions in the country of provision of goods; and (vi) Tiers II and III are inconsistent with Article 14(d) of the SCM Agreement since it prioritizes the Tier-II methodology above Tier-III. (India's appellant's submission, para. 19)

[275] United States' appellee's submission, para. 122 (referring to Appellate Body Reports, *China – Rare Earths*, para. 5.224).

then irrelevant", and found it therefore unnecessary to "examine India's 'commercial considerations' argument".[276]

2.211 Second, the United States disputes India's assertion that the Panel failed to evaluate its claim that the US benchmarking mechanism is inconsistent with Article 14(d) because a government price that is "adequate" under Tier III will nevertheless be found to be inadequate under Tiers I and II. The Panel fully considered India's arguments and accurately reflected these arguments in its Report. Having found that the adequacy of remuneration under Article 14(d) is to be assessed from the perspective of the recipient rather than the government provider of the relevant goods, the issue of whether an investigating authority would, in addition, need to undertake an analysis of the government provider's price-setting behavior was not legally relevant.[277] The Appellate Body should therefore reject India's claim under Article 11 of the DSU.

2.212 In the light of the foregoing, the United States requests the Appellate Body to decline India's requests to examine the claims that the Panel allegedly failed to examine, complete the legal analysis, and find that the US benchmarking mechanism is inconsistent with Article 14(d) of the SCM Agreement. Nevertheless, in the event that the Appellate Body finds that the Panel acted inconsistently with Article 11 of the DSU, and proceeds to complete the legal analysis, the United States requests the Appellate Body to find that the US benchmarking mechanism is consistent with Article 14(d) of the SCM Agreement. In support of this request, the United States puts forward the following arguments.

2.213 First, the United States disputes India's contention that the US benchmarking mechanism is inconsistent with Article 14(d) of the SCM Agreement because it mandates an affirmative finding of benefit merely because the government price in question is less than a benchmark price, without assessing whether the government price or the price difference, if any, is in accordance with "commercial considerations". For the United States, India's reliance on Article XVII of the GATT 1994 to support its claim is misplaced. Nothing in the text of Article 14(d) of the SCM Agreement supports India's argument that the term "in relation to prevailing market conditions", in Article 14(d), has the same meaning as the term "in accordance with commercial considerations" in Article XVII of the GATT 1994. The Appellate Body has cautioned against "assuming that the *same terms* in different agreements [have] the same meaning".[278] It therefore cannot be "assumed that *different terms* in different agreements [have] the same meaning".[279] Moreover, it is implausible to suggest, as India does, that the terms "prevailing market conditions" and

---

[276] United States' appellee's submission, para. 125 (quoting Panel Report, fn 195 to para. 7.33).

[277] United States' appellee's submission, paras. 132-140.

[278] United States' appellee's submission, para. 155 (referring to Appellate Body Report, *EC – Asbestos*, para. 89). (emphasis original)

[279] United States' appellee's submission, para. 155. (emphasis original)

"commercial considerations" should be given the same meaning simply because the negotiators of the SCM Agreement included the same list of factors in Article 14(d) that are found in Article XVII:1(b) of the GATT 1994. In the United States' view, had Members intended for benefit under Article 14(d) of the SCM Agreement to be calculated on the basis of "commercial considerations", the term "commercial considerations" would have been used explicitly in Article 14(d). Instead, Article 14(d) employs the term "prevailing market conditions".

2.214 The United States submits that India's reliance on alleged differences between subparagraphs (b) and (c) of Article 14 of the SCM Agreement, on the one hand, and, subparagraph (d) of Article 14, on the other hand, is also misplaced. India argues that, while under subparagraphs (b) and (c) of Article 14 an investigating authority must find the existence of a benefit "the moment there is a difference in the amounts being compared", Article 14(d), by contrast, employs a "much broader and more comprehensive framework".[280] India's claim, however, is inconsistent with the text of Article 14. In a similar manner to subparagraphs (b) and (c) of Article 14, the text of Article 14(d) provides that an investigating authority can find the existence of benefit once remuneration for government-provided goods is less than adequate. In this vein, a comparative analysis is envisaged under subparagraphs (b), (c), and (d) of Article 14.

2.215 The United States considers as being without merit India's claim that the US benchmarking mechanism is inconsistent with Article 14(d) because a government price that is "adequate" under Tier III of that mechanism will nevertheless be found to be inadequate on the basis of a comparison with benchmarks under Tiers I and II. In this regard, Article 14 contains no requirement that an investigating authority employ multiple methodologies for determining whether a financial contribution confers a benefit on a recipient. The requirement in Article 14 is that "any ... method" used by an investigating authority must be consistent with the guidelines listed in Article 14. As the Appellate Body has stated, "The reference to '*any*' method in the chapeau clearly implies that more than one method consistent with Article 14 is available to investigating authorities for purposes of calculating the benefit to the recipient."[281] Since India has not demonstrated that either Tier I or Tier II of the US benchmarking mechanism is inconsistent with Article 14(d), there is no basis for concluding that the United States has an obligation to apply its Tier III methodology in every investigation.

2.216 For these reasons, the United States requests the Appellate Body to reject India's claim that Section 351.511(a)(2)(i)-(iii) of the US Regulations is inconsistent with Article 14(d) of the SCM Agreement.

---

280 United States' appellee's submission, para. 150 (referring to India's appellant's submission, para. 131).

281 United States' appellee's submission, para. 170 (quoting Appellate Body Report, *US – Softwood Lumber IV*, para. 91 (emphasis original)).

2.2.4.5 Mandatory use of "as delivered" benchmarks under the US benchmarking mechanism

2.217 The United States submits that the Panel correctly found that the mandatory use of "as delivered" benchmarks under the US benchmarking mechanism is not inconsistent with Article 14(d) of the SCM Agreement. The United States therefore requests the Appellate Body to reject all of India's claims on appeal in relation to the Panel's findings on the use of "as delivered" benchmarks under the US benchmarking mechanism.

2.218 First, the United States submits that, contrary to India's assertion on appeal, the Panel did not act inconsistently with Article 11 of the DSU in assessing India's claim regarding the use of "as delivered" benchmarks under the US benchmarking mechanism. India argues in this regard that, by stating that India had conflated the term "prevailing market conditions" in Article 14(d) with the contractual terms and conditions of the government provision under investigation, the Panel altered India's claim and thereby acted inconsistently with its mandate under Article 11 of the DSU. The United States submits that India is attempting to amend, on appeal, the argument that India had made before the Panel. In this regard, India had argued before the Panel that "conditions of sale", within the meaning of Article 14(d) of the SCM Agreement, refer to the contractual terms of sale of the government transaction in question. For the United States, India's claim that the Panel acted inconsistently with Article 11 of the DSU is therefore devoid of any factual basis.[282]

2.219 The United States notes that India also requests the Appellate Body to find that the Panel acted inconsistently with Article 11 of the DSU by failing to apply the Panel's own interpretation of the terms "prevailing market conditions" and "conditions of sale" to the matter before it. In this regard, India notes that the Panel found that these terms refer to "general conditions of the relevant market, in the context of which market operators engage in sales transactions".[283] For India, the Panel should have applied this to assess whether the sale of a good in the country of provision generally on an *ex works* basis constitutes one of the "general conditions of the relevant market, in the context of which market operators engage in sales transactions". The United States asserts that India's claim is without merit. The question of whether the sale of goods generally on an *ex works* basis constitutes a "prevailing market condition" within the meaning of Article 14(d) was simply not put before the Panel. Thus, the Panel cannot be faulted under Article 11 of the DSU for failing to make an objective assessment of an argument that India had not presented. The United States thus requests the Appellate Body to reject India's claims under Article 11 of the DSU in relation to

---

282 United States' appellee's submission, paras. 181-185.

283 India's appellant's submission, para. 186 (quoting Panel Report, para. 7.60).

the Panel's findings concerning the mandatory use of "as delivered" benchmarks under the US benchmarking mechanism.[284]

2.220 The United States recalls India's claim that the Panel incorrectly rejected its arguments concerning the mandatory use of "as delivered" benchmarks "partly" on the basis of the Panel's understanding that government prices can *ipso facto* be rejected under Article 14(d) of the SCM Agreement. The United States submits that the Panel correctly found that comparing a government price to another government price is circular and uninformative because it does not indicate whether the government price is at, or below, the prevailing market conditions in the country of provision. Moreover, in the United States' view, the Panel correctly observed that the Appellate Body found, in *US – Softwood Lumber IV*, that private prices are the preferred benchmark for assessing the adequacy of remuneration for government-provided goods.[285]

2.221 The United States disagrees with India's claim that the Panel acted inconsistently with Articles 11 and 12.7 of the DSU by failing to provide reasoning for rejecting India's argument that the use of "as delivered" out-of-country benchmarks nullifies the comparative advantage of the country in which the good in question is provided. The United States submits that, contrary to India's assertion, the basis of the Panel's rejection of India's "as such" claim was not the fact that there existed an import transaction in the underlying investigation. Rather, the Panel found that, "to the extent that a delivered price benchmark relates to the prevailing market conditions in the country of provision, it will reflect any comparative advantage that such country might have."[286] The Panel then considered import transactions in India as illustrative of the general point that a benchmark set in relation to prevailing market conditions will reflect any comparative advantages in that country. In this regard, the Panel noted that the fact that a Member may source minerals locally does not mean that "as delivered" out-of-country prices do not reflect the prevailing market conditions in that Member's economy. The United States maintains, therefore, that the Panel provided ample explanation for its finding in accordance with its duties under both Articles 11 and 12.7 of the DSU.

2.222 According to the United States, the above explanation provided by the Panel also demonstrates that the Panel did not err in its interpretation and application of Article 14(d) of the SCM Agreement in rejecting India's argument concerning the countervailing of comparative advantages of the country of provision where "as delivered" out-of-country benchmarks are used to assess the adequacy of remuneration for government-provided goods. The United States adds that, if a benchmark price relates to prevailing market conditions in the country of provision, it will account for both supply and demand. In other words, supply and demand will be reflected in the price, as well as other factors an

---

[284] United States' appellee's submission, para. 189.

[285] United States' appellee's submission, paras. 190-192.

[286] United States' appellee's submission, para. 196 (quoting Panel Report, para. 7.62).

investigating authority will account for under the second sentence of Article 14(d). According to the United States, there is no additional requirement under Article 14(d) that an investigating authority must, as India asserts, undertake a comprehensive qualitative and quantitative analysis of a Member's alleged comparative advantage or of supply and demand.

2.223 The United States submits that India requests the Appellate Body to complete the legal analysis in accordance with a legal interpretation of Article 14(d) that was never before the Panel. In this regard, the United States asserts that India had argued in its submissions to the Panel that, under Article 14(d), the terms of sale of the government transaction in question must be presumed to reflect prevailing market conditions. On appeal, however, India asserts that the legal question that would be before the Appellate Body is whether the sale of a good generally in the market in question on an *ex works* or "as delivered" basis is a "prevailing market condition", within the meaning of Article 14(d). The United States submits that this legal question was never before the Panel, and that the Appellate Body should, therefore, reject India's request to complete the legal analysis. The United States further submits that, because the parties were not able to make submissions or to submit evidence in this regard, there are no undisputed facts on the record or factual findings by the Panel to demonstrate whether contractual terms of sale in India are generally *ex works* or "as delivered".

2.224 The above notwithstanding, should the Appellate Body decide to complete the legal analysis, the United States requests the Appellate Body to find that the mandatory use of "as delivered" benchmarks under the US benchmarking mechanism is consistent with Article 14(d). India's arguments are premised on its misplaced view that the adequacy of remuneration for government-provided goods under Article 14(d) is to be assessed from the perspective of the government provider. According to the United States, this is why India argues that, where the sale of the relevant good generally in the country of provision is not transacted on an "as delivered" basis, "transportation and other delivery charges are not part of the transaction price between the government provider and the beneficiary."[287] Moreover, India misreads both the text of Article 14(d) and the Appellate Body's findings in *US – Softwood Lumber IV* to the extent that India asserts that, in addition to assessing the adequacy of remuneration, an investigating authority is also required to engage in a comprehensive quantitative and qualitative analysis of supply and demand in order to ensure that it does not countervail an abstract concept of "comparative advantage". The United States emphasizes that Article 14(d) contains no such requirement.

2.225 The United States submits further that whether a subsidy exists does not depend on whether the terms of sale are *ex works* or "as delivered". An *ex works*

[287] United States' appellee's submission, para. 209 (quoting India's appellant's submission, para. 196 (emphases omitted)).

price does not include the cost incurred by the purchaser in obtaining a purchased input at its factory door. Thus, an *ex works* price is not reflective of "prevailing market conditions", within the meaning of Article 14(d), from the perspective of the recipient. Prevailing market conditions are such that a private purchaser (in making a purchasing decision) and a private seller (in setting a price at which to sell the good) would consider all of the costs associated with getting the relevant good to the factory in setting the market negotiated price. To accept India's interpretation would artificially isolate delivery costs from the price of a good and therefore shield it from the actual prevailing market conditions. Such an interpretation would not fulfil the purpose of Article 14(d), which is to assess whether the recipient is better off than it would have been absent that financial contribution.[288]

2.226 Turning to India's contention that the "sole objective of adjustments" under Section 351.511(a)(2)(iv) of the US Regulations "is to arbitrarily increase the benchmark price to a higher level so that benefit is established even in situations where no benefit is conferred"[289], the United States recalls that the purpose of the benefit calculation under Article 14(d) of the SCM Agreement is to assess whether a recipient is better off than it would have been absent the financial contribution. From that perspective, what matters is what alternative source and price the recipient would have in that market, and whether the price offered by the government for the relevant good is "better". The use of "as delivered" out-of-country prices as benchmarks (the constructed price reflecting the delivery of an internationally traded good to that market) provides a basis for determining whether the recipient is receiving any benefit from paying the price charged by a government provider.

2.227 Turning to India's contention that the use of "as delivered" out-of-country benchmarks countervails comparative advantages of the country of provision, the United States asserts that India has failed to provide any evidence of such an alleged comparative advantage or to further explain what this principle means. In any event, the United States considers, first, that India's reliance on the Appellate Body's findings, in *US – Softwood Lumber IV*, is misplaced. In *US – Softwood Lumber IV*, the benchmark at issue was an out-of-country benchmark, i.e. the price of the good in a country other than the Member (Canada) that provided the good in question. In this dispute, the benchmark price is not a price wholly within a foreign country but, instead, is either the actual or constructed price *in India* of an imported product. Therefore the prevailing market conditions, including any comparative advantages enjoyed by India, are already reflected in the benchmark price.[290]

---

[288] United States' appellee's submission, para. 211 (referring to Panel Report, *Canada – Aircraft*, para. 9.112).

[289] United States' appellee's submission, para. 221 (quoting India's appellant's submission, para. 201).

[290] United States' appellee's submission, paras. 224-230.

2.228 The United States therefore requests the Appellate Body to find that the use of "as delivered" benchmarks under the US benchmarking mechanism is not inconsistent with Article 14(d) of the SCM Agreement.

2.2.5 Benefit – "As applied" claims

2.2.5.1 The USDOC's determination that the NMDC provided iron ore for less than adequate remuneration

2.229 The United States disputes India's claims on appeal concerning the Panel's findings in relation to: (i) the *ex post* rationale put forward by the United States to justify the USDOC's rejection of certain domestic pricing information in determining Tier I benchmarks for assessing the adequacy of remuneration for iron ore provided by the NMDC; (ii) the USDOC's use of "as delivered" prices from Australia and Brazil as benchmarks for assessing the adequacy of remuneration for iron ore provided by the NMDC; and (iii) the USDOC's rejection of certain NMDC export prices as Tier II benchmarks in the 2006, 2007, and 2008 administrative reviews.

2.2.5.1.1 The Panel's findings concerning the USDOC's rejection of certain domestic pricing information

2.230 The United States considers that India's claim that the Panel acted inconsistently with Article 11 of the DSU by making findings on the *ex post* rationalizations put forward by the United States for the USDOC's rejection of certain domestic pricing information in determining Tier I benchmarks is predicated on the Panel having made findings in the first place. The only "findings" concerning the domestic pricing information at issue are contained in paragraphs 7.156-7.158 and 8.2.b.iii of the Panel Report. Specifically, in the "Conclusions and Recommendations" section of its Report, the Panel found that the United States acted inconsistently with "Article 14(d) of the SCM Agreement in connection with the USDOC's rejection of certain domestic pricing information when assessing benefit in respect of mining rights for iron ore."[291] Noting that the Panel provided no further findings or conclusions with respect to the domestic pricing information, or to the USDOC's reasons for rejecting them, the United States submits that the views provided by the Panel concerning the merits of the *ex post* rationalizations put forward by the United States are not "findings", but merely "considerations" that would not, upon adoption of the Report, become part of the DSB's recommendations and rulings. Thus, these considerations are "in a sense inherently moot and perhaps may be analogized to the considerations a panel would set out if it were to exercise its discretion to

[291] United States' appellee's submission, para. 235 (quoting Panel Report, para. 8.2.b.iii).

provide 'suggestions' under DSU Article 19.1". As there are no additional "findings" with respect to the domestic pricing information for the Appellate Body to modify, uphold, or reverse, the United States submits that the Appellate Body should decline to rule on India's claim under Article 11 of the DSU.[292]

2.231 The United States notes India's requests for the Appellate Body to examine the Panel's findings on the *ex post* rationalizations advanced by the United States for the USDOC's rejection of the domestic pricing information at issue, and to find that the Panel's findings are inconsistent with Articles 12.1, 12.4, 12.7, and 14 of the SCM Agreement. The United States requests the Appellate Body to reject India's requests as they are based on claims that were not before the Panel, a misreading of the SCM Agreement, or misrepresentations about the domestic pricing information at issue itself.

2.232 First, the United States argues that the Panel correctly found that the use of government prices as benchmarks is not required under Article 14(d) of the SCM Agreement. Recalling that the Appellate Body found, in *US – Softwood Lumber IV*, that private prices are the primary benchmark for assessing the adequacy of remuneration for government-provided goods, the United States submits that there is no requirement under Article 14(d) that an investigating authority use government prices as the basis for calculating a benchmark. Equally, there is no requirement under Article 14(d) that an investigating authority rely on pricing information that does not identify whether the entities concerned are private or government suppliers.

2.233 Second, the United States notes that India's claim that, in finding that the USDOC would have been entitled to reject the price quote submitted by Tata as a Tier I benchmark on the basis that it did not specify the exact percentage of iron ore content, the Panel erred in applying Articles 12.1, 12.4, 12.7, and 14 of the SCM Agreement. With respect to India's claims under Articles 12.1., 12.4, and 12.7, the United States submits that India did not claim before the Panel that the USDOC's failure to consider Tata's price quote was inconsistent with Articles 12.1, 12.4, and 12.7 of the SCM Agreement. In its panel request, for example, India only referred to Article 14(d) in connection with the availability of in-country benchmark information. As India did not raise these claims before the Panel, there are no findings in respect of Articles 12.1, 12.4, and 12.7 for the Appellate Body to uphold, reverse, or modify. On this basis, the United States submits that the Appellate Body should reject India's claim.

2.234 Turning to India's claim under Article 14(d), the United States recalls that it had argued before the Panel, and the Panel considered, that "the precise percentage of iron ore content is important in determining prices, because iron ore is priced per unit of iron content, and [the USDOC] made adjustments to reflect this."[293] Accordingly, using prices without taking the percentage of iron

---

292 United States' appellee's submission, paras. 233-236.

293 United States' appellee's submission, para. 248 (referring to Panel Report, para. 7.163).

ore content into consideration would unnecessarily distort the benefit calculation, particularly when the record contains other private market prices that do specify a precise content. For these reasons, the United States requests the Appellate Body to reject India's appeal under Article 14(d) in relation to the Panel's finding that the USDOC could reject the price quote submitted by Tata in determining market benchmarks, on the basis that this quote had not specified the precise percentage of iron ore content.

2.235 The United States notes India's appeal of the Panel's finding that an investigating authority is not required to determine price benchmarks on the basis of information that is not shown to pertain to actual transactions. The United States submits that India's claim is without merit as the Appellate Body has found that private prices are the primary benchmark for assessing the adequacy of remuneration for government-provided goods. Where price lists of actual transactions are not available, Indian exporters are not, as India claims, at the "mercy of the administering authority".[294] Nor is the administering authority at the "mercy" of the exporter. Pursuant to Article 14(d), the existence of actual sales means that the investigating authority must look at actual transaction data if such data is available. Accordingly, the Appellate Body should reject India's claim that, in finding that an investigating authority is not required to determine price benchmarks on the basis of information that is not shown to pertain to actual transactions, the Panel erred in interpreting Articles 12.1 and 14 of the SCM Agreement by placing an unreasonable burden on India.

2.236 The United States further notes India's claim that, in finding that the USDOC was not required to use the price quote submitted by Tata for the purpose of determining Tier I benchmarks because Tata had claimed confidentiality in respect of this price quote, the Panel erred in applying Articles 12.4, 12.1, and 14 of the SCM Agreement. The United States notes further India's claim that the price quote ought to have been used throughout the investigation to calculate the existence and amount of benefit allegedly obtained by Tata through the GOI's grand of captive mining right for iron ore. Moreover, the United States observes India's claim that this price quote should also have been used in the 2008 administrative review and the 2013 sunset review to calculate the benefit allegedly obtained by Tata through the provision of iron ore by the NMDC. The United States emphasizes that India did not raise any claims under Articles 12.1 and 12.4 in respect of the domestic pricing information at issue before the Panel. For this reason, the Appellate Body should reject India's claim. In any event, India's claim has no factual basis because the price quote submitted by Tata did not indicate the percentage of iron ore content, and, for this reason, the Panel was correct in finding that the price quote submitted by Tata could not be used as a benchmark. In addition, Tata had submitted the confidential price quote only in the context of the 2006 administrative review, but not in the context of the 2008 administrative review, or the 2013 sunset

[294] United States' appellee's submisson, para. 250 (quoting India's appellant's submission, para. 430).

review. The United States therefore maintains that the price quote in question would, in any event, not have been relevant for these determinations.[295]

2.2.5.1.2 The USDOC's use of "as delivered" prices from Australia and Brazil as benchmarks

2.237 Turning to India's claims concerning the Panel's findings in relation to the use of "as delivered" prices from Australia and Brazil as benchmarks for assessing the adequacy of remuneration in respect of iron ore provided by the NMDC, the United States requests the Appellate Body to reject India's claims that the Panel acted inconsistently with Article 11 of the DSU and erred in its interpretation and application of Article 14(d) of the SCM Agreement.

2.238 The United States notes India's claim that the Panel acted inconsistently with Article 11 of the DSU by relying on certain statements of NMDC officials to support its finding that Australian and Brazilian prices for iron ore, adjusted for delivery to steel producers in India, indicate what a steel producer in India would be "willing to pay", and thus necessarily relate to prevailing market conditions in India. First, the United States disputes India's contention that the Panel acted inconsistently with Article 11 by referring to statements on the record that the USDOC had itself not referred to in its determination in the underlying investigation. To the extent that India is arguing that a panel, in the context of trade remedy disputes, is not permitted to consider any evidence presented by the responding party unless that evidence is quoted in the determination of the investigating authority, India "misunderstands" the role of panels.[296] In any event, the United States notes that "the crux" of India's argument is that the Panel failed to attribute proper weight to record evidence, and maintains that a claim premised primarily on a party's disagreement with the panel's reasoning and weighing of evidence does not suffice to establish that the panel acted inconsistently with Article 11 of the DSU. The United States adds that the fact that a panel does not refer to specific evidence presented by a party in its report is not sufficient to establish that the panel has acted inconsistently with its duty under Article 11 of the DSU.[297]

2.239 The United States submits that, in any event, India has failed to explain what bearing the competing evidence offered by India would have on the objectivity of the Panel's factual assessment. First, the United States recalls India's argument that other evidence on the record suggests that NMDC officials must have been referring to *ex works* prices, rather than "as delivered" prices. However, in the light of competing evidence, India suggests only that the

---

[295] United States' appellee's submission, paras. 251-256.

[296] United States' appellee's submission, para. 285.

[297] United States' appellee's submission, para. 279 (referring to Appellate Body Reports, *China – Rare Earths*, para. 5.178; *EC – Fasteners (China)*, paras. 441 and 442; and *Brazil – Retreaded Tyres*, para. 202).

relevant statement made by NMDC officials "*could have been* a reference not to the delivered import prices, but rather the *ex-mines* or FOB prices of imported iron ore".[298] The fact that the Panel drew a different inference is not an error under Article 11 of the DSU.

2.240 Second, although India infers from the NMDC's description of its pricing methodology that the NMDC prices were f.o.b. and *ex mine*, and that the NMDC export price was "indirectly comparable to the Australian price", such inferences do not advance India's argument. Although the NMDC prices are expressed in f.o.b. and *ex mine* terms, the United States submits that, as a general matter, it is even more logical that these prices are set with all the delivery charges in mind (i.e. the ultimate cost to the purchaser).

2.241 Finally, the United States submits that India's assertions concerning certain evidence on the record are "misleading". For example, India asserts that the evidence on the record "highlights that the NMDC competes with local players as well and that therefore, its pricing policy had to account for the prices charged by other domestic suppliers".[299] Yet, there is virtually no evidence of any such domestic competition on the record. Throughout all of the reviews in which the Indian steel producers participated – with one exception – the record shows that Tata, Essar, and Ispat either purchased all of their ore from the NMDC or obtained their ore under government mining leases from their captive mines.[300] In the United States' view, the purchasing behavior of these companies, as reflected on the record, contradicts India's assertions.

2.242 For the United States, India has failed to establish that the Panel's failure to evaluate certain evidence is material to this dispute. Moreover, India has not demonstrated how such failure had a bearing on the objectivity of the Panel's assessment of the matter before it. The United States therefore requests the Appellate Body to reject India's claim that the Panel acted inconsistently with Article 11 of the DSU in relying on the evidence that it relied on to establish that the NMDC set its domestic prices based on what purchasers in India were willing to pay to import iron ore.[301]

2.243 Furthermore, the United States recalls India's claim that the Panel erred in its interpretation and application of Article 14(d) of the SCM Agreement in finding that the use of "as delivered" prices from Australia and Brazil as benchmarks in the NMDC investigation is consistent with Article 14(d). The United States maintains that India's claim in this respect is based on the same arguments that India advanced in relation to its "as such" claim against the

[298] United States' appellee's submission, para. 281 (quoting India's appellant's submission, para. 444). (emphasis added by the United States)

[299] United States' appellee's submission, para. 283 (quoting India's appellant's submission, para. 446).

[300] United States' appellee's submission, para. 283 (referring to 2006 AR Issues and Decision Memorandum (Panel Exhibit IND-33)).

[301] United States' appellee's submission, para. 288.

mandatory use of "as delivered" benchmarks under Section 351.511(a)(2)(iv) of the US Regulations. Noting that it has already responded to these arguments in addressing India's "as such" claim, the United States considers that these arguments lack merit, and therefore requests the Appellate Body to reject India's claim that the Panel erred in its interpretation and application of Article 14(d). In any event, according to the United States, India's arguments are based on an incorrect reading of Article 14(d) and of the Appellate Body's findings in *US – Softwood Lumber IV*. The United States asserts that Article 14(d) does not, as India argues, require an investigating authority to engage in a comprehensive qualitative and quantitative analysis of a country's supply-and-demand matrix in respect of a particular good in order to make a determination of whether a government provides goods for less than adequate remuneration. Instead, Article 14(d) requires an investigating authority to assess the adequacy of remuneration from the perspective of the recipient of government-provided goods, in relation to prevailing market conditions in the country of provision.

2.244 With regard to India's assertion that the Panel erred in its interpretation of Article 14(d) in rejecting India's argument that the use of "as delivered" prices from Australia and Brazil as benchmarks countervails India's comparative advantage in respect of iron ore, the United States observes that "the crux" of India's argument is that the USDOC did not engage in a comprehensive analysis of the iron ore market in India accounting for both import and domestic transactions of iron ore. The United States emphasizes that Article 14(d) does not require an investigating authority to undertake this analysis in calculating a benchmark for assessing the adequacy of remuneration for government-provided goods. In addition, in putting forward its claim, India has made several assertions concerning the nature of the Indian market for iron ore that are factually inaccurate. As an example, although India asserts that evidence on the record demonstrates that India's ports are too shallow to accommodate the importation of iron ore, this evidence is in "direct contradiction" with other record evidence of actual imports of iron ore from Brazil, as well as record evidence that the NMDC exports 30% of its iron ore to Japan, China, and Korea. The United States questions how a market would have the physical capabilities to export, yet not similarly have the facilities to import. Finally, a deficiency in India's arguments is that India has not identified any evidence of the alleged comparative advantage that India enjoys in respect of iron ore.[302]

2.245 For the reasons expressed above, the United States requests the Appellate Body to reject India's claim that the Panel erred in its interpretation and application of Article 14(d) in finding that the use of "as delivered" prices from Australia and Brazil as benchmarks to assess the adequacy of remuneration for iron ore provided by the NMDC is consistent with Article 14(d) of the SCM Agreement. The United States also requests the Appellate Body to reject India's related claim under Article 11 of the DSU.

302 United States' appellee's submission, paras. 292-295.

2.2.5.1.3 The USDOC's rejection of NMDC export prices as Tier II benchmarks

2.246 The United States disputes India's claims on appeal concerning the Panel's rejection of India's claim that the USDOC's exclusion of NMDC export prices from India to Japan as Tier II benchmarks in the 2006, 2007, and 2008 administrative reviews, for assessing the adequacy of remuneration for iron ore provided by the NMDC, is inconsistent with the chapeau of Article 14 of the SCM Agreement. Contrary to India's assertion, the Panel did not fail to assess whether the USDOC "adequately explained" its inconsistent treatment of the NMDC's export prices in the 2004 administrative review, on the one hand, and the subsequent reviews, on the other hand. Specifically, the Panel expressed its view that "[t]he obligation to 'adequately explain[]' conveys the sense of making clear or intelligible, and giving details of how the methodology was applied."[303] On this basis, the Panel examined the USDOC determination and correctly rejected India's claim that the USDOC's explanation for rejecting the NMDC export prices at issue is inconsistent with the requirements of the chapeau of Article 14. The United States requests the Appellate Body to reject India's claim that the Panel failed to assess objectively India's claim under the chapeau of Article 14. Consequently, the Appellate Body should also reject India's request for the Appellate Body to complete the legal analysis and find that the USDOC's explanation of the rejection of the NMDC's export prices at issue is inconsistent with the chapeau to Article 14. As regards India's claim that the Panel erred in its interpretation and application of Article 14(d) of the SCM Agreement in rejecting its claim concerning the USDOC's rejection of the NMDC's export prices at issue, the United States emphasizes that comparing the price of the entity under investigation with another price of that same entity would be circular, uninformative, and contrary to the requirements of Article 14(d) of the SCM Agreement.[304]

2.2.5.2 The USDOC's determination that the GOI provided iron ore for less than adequate remuneration through its grant of captive mining rights

2.247 The United States maintains that the Panel correctly found that the USDOC's methodology is consistent with Article 14(d) of the SCM Agreement. The United States asserts that India's argument is based on its view that remuneration should be assessed from the perspective of the government provider, and that this view, for reasons the United States previously explained, should be rejected. According to the United States, India has not established that the Panel erred in its legal interpretation of Article 14(d).

[303] United States' appellee's submission, para. 264 (quoting Panel Report, para. 7.191).
[304] United States' response to questioning at the oral hearing.

2.248 The United States also refers to India's assertion that remuneration cannot be "notional", as well as India's request for the Appellate Body to make findings in this respect. In the United States' view, it is not clear on what basis India requests such findings because the Panel found that, in the context of mining rights, the construction of a notional government price for the extracted minerals was "reasonable".[305] The United States points out that the Panel found that India did not challenge the calculations themselves, but only the fact that the basic methodology does not calculate benefit from the perspective of the government.[306] The United States therefore considers that India's claim that the USDOC's notional government price approach is inconsistent with Article 14(d) of the SCM Agreement is without merit and should be rejected.

2.249 In addition, the United States requests the Appellate Body to reject India's appeal of the Panel's finding that India's claims pertaining to "good faith" are outside the Panel's terms of reference. According to the United States, a panel's failure to consider claims not within its terms of reference does not amount to a violation of Article 11 of the DSU. A claim that a party is not acting in good faith is a serious one that should not be made lightly. However, India has "simply re-casted its arguments under Article 14 to argue that if there is a breach of Article 14 due to interpreting it in an 'unreasonable' manner, then the United States failed to act in good faith".[307] The United States notes, moreover, that the WTO Agreement does not call for a finding as to whether a breach of an agreement occurs in good faith; it requires panels to assess whether a measure is inconsistent with a WTO agreement. The United States asserts that the USDOC's actions were consistent with Article 14(d) in determining the benefit for goods sold for less than adequate remuneration based on the prevailing market conditions in the country of provision. Accordingly, the United States requests the Appellate Body to reject India's claim relating to "good faith" under Article 14(d) of the SCM Agreement.

2.2.5.3 The USDOC's determination that SDF loans conferred a benefit within the meaning of Article 14(b) of the SCM Agreement

2.250 The United States asserts that the Panel correctly found that the USDOC's benefit determination in respect of SDF loans was not inconsistent with Articles 1.1(b) and 14(b) of the SCM Agreement. The United States notes India's contention that the "deposits made by the participating steel producers to become eligible for the SDF program have to be accounted for in the benefit analysis."[308] According to the United States, India's assertion is incorrect, because the funds

---

305 United States' appellee's submission, para. 385 (quoting Panel Report, para. 7.260).
306 United States' appellee's submission, para. 385 (referring to Panel Report, para. 7.260).
307 United States' appellee's submission, para. 394.
308 United States' appellee's submission, para. 425 (quoting India's appellant's submission, para. 587).

remitted to the SDF were not deposits made by steel producers or producer levies, but rather were GOI-mandated price increases that were paid by consumers purchasing steel products. Moreover, the United States considers that the Panel correctly found that Article 14(b) "does not require the USDOC to take into account any alleged costs incurred by SDF loan recipients in obtaining SDF loans".[309] Article 14(b) provides that a benefit is conferred where there is a difference between the amount that the firm receiving the loan pays on the government loan and the amount the firm would pay on a comparable commercial loan that the firm could actually obtain on the market. In the United States' view, no other credits or adjustments are required by Article 14(b).

2.251 The United States also argues that Article 14 of the SCM Agreement provides flexibility to investigating authorities in applying a methodology to calculate the benefit of a subsidy. Furthermore, Article 14 contains no requirement that an investigating authority provide a credit when calculating the benefit of a subsidy to account for alleged costs associated with obtaining the subsidy. In the United States' view, India inappropriately relies on the word "comparable" in Article 14(b) to advance its flawed argument that the United States was required to provide a credit for an alleged "entry fee" to the fund. The United States maintains that the Panel correctly found that the USDOC's loan benchmark calculation did not need to include credits for any alleged costs to steel producers, and that the benchmark was therefore consistent with Article 14(b) of the SCM Agreement.

2.252 The United States also urges rejection of India's claim that the Panel did not fully account for a decision by the Supreme Court of India holding that the SDF levy did not constitute a tax, but rather consisted of steel producers' funds. The United States argues that the Panel is not required to make an explicit reference to all the evidence before it. Moreover, a domestic judicial interpretation of a municipal law for purposes of characterizing it under domestic law is not the same issue as a characterization of that law under WTO legal principles. In the United States' view, both the USDOC and the Panel considered the substance of the ruling and disagreed with the conclusion reached by the Supreme Court of India. Specifically, the USDOC examined the design and operation of the programme at issue and found that, contrary to the Court's ruling, the funds remitted to the SDF were not the Indian steel producers' own funds, but were funds collected from levies imposed on consumers who purchased certain steel products. The United States thus contends that the GOI set price increases that were to be added to certain steel products and were then remitted to the SDF. These price increases were paid by consumers purchasing these steel products. Consistent with Article 11 of the DSU, the Panel considered these facts and correctly found that the USDOC properly determined that the funds remitted to the SDF were not "the producers' own funds", but were instead funds "collected from consumers and always destined for the SDF", such that

[309] United States' appellee's submission, para. 426 (quoting Panel Report, para. 7.311).

steel producers would not have been able to use these funds or invest them to obtain interest.[310]

2.253 The United States also disagrees with India's argument that, because SDF loans were not open to all steel producers, participating steel producers were able to increase prices of their products so as to direct this additional element of price to create the SDF. The United States considers that India's argument is contrary to the record evidence. Moreover, the fact that SDF loans were limited to certain large, integrated steel producers, and not open to all steel producers in India, has no bearing on the question of whether or not the SDF levies were paid by consumers. The United States further asserts that, because the SDF funds consisted of GOI-mandated price increases that were paid by consumers purchasing steel products, they were no different from other types of involuntary taxes levied on individuals and enterprises. The United States thus submits that the Panel correctly found that India's characterization of these funds as the steel producer's "own funds" is incorrect, and that India's challenge under Article 11 of the DSU must be rejected.

2.2.6 Specificity

2.254 The United States submits that India's appeal regarding the Panel's finding under Articles 1.2 and 2.1(c) of the SCM Agreement is "without merit"[311] and requests the Appellate Body to reject India's claim. The United States asserts that India's further appeal of the Panel's finding under Article 2.4 of the SCM Agreement is based on India's view that the Panel improperly rejected its claim "solely" because such challenges under Article 2.4 are consequential to the Panel's finding under Article 2.1(c). According to the United States, India is of the mistaken view that these claims are the same. The United States maintains that, because India has not challenged the veracity of evidence and findings on the record, and has not provided any arguments independently supporting its claim, India has not shown a breach of Article 2.4. The United States therefore requests the Appellate Body to reject India's appeal under Article 2.4 of the SCM Agreement.

2.2.6.1 Discrimination in favour of "certain enterprises"

2.255 The United States argues that the Panel correctly rejected India's argument that, in order to make a finding of *de facto* specificity under Article 2.1(c) of the SCM Agreement, an investigating authority must establish that the programme in question discriminates between certain enterprises and other "similarly situated" enterprises. According to the United States, India fails to appreciate that, to the extent that the specificity analysis under Article 2.1(c)

[310] United States' appellee's submission, para. 422 (referring to Panel Report, para. 7.311).
[311] United States' appellee's submission, para. 303.

entails a comparison, it is between "certain enterprises" receiving the subsidy and the rest of the subsidizing Member's economy. The United States considers that this principle is recognized in WTO jurisprudence, where the Appellate Body has explained that whether a subsidy is specific to certain enterprises as compared to broadly available throughout a Member's economy is assessed on a case-by-case basis.[312] The United States therefore supports the Panel's finding that "Article 2.1 is not concerned with other enterprises, and whether or not such other enterprises have been discriminated against."[313] The United States further submits that India's approach would read the plain text out of the chapeau of Article 2.1, because it would leave no recourse for investigating authorities in instances where the term "certain enterprises" is defined as an industry or a single unique enterprise. Under India's view, "a subsidy that is provided to an entire industry could never be specific because there are no 'like' entities which would have been eligible for but did not receive the subsidy".[314]

2.256 The United States argues that India's approach would create an "easy means to circumvent the disciplines of the SCM Agreement".[315] For example, a grant that is expressly limited to iron ore users would be specific, but provision of iron ore to the same iron ore users would not. The United States adds that a government could then simply use its funds to purchase iron ore and then provide that iron ore to the users at a price that is reduced by exactly the same amount it would have otherwise provided as a grant. According to the United States, the same benefit would be provided to the same recipients. Under India's approach, simply changing the form of contribution would prevent finding that the contribution is a subsidy.

2.257 Regarding India's reliance on the Appellate Body report in *US – Large Civil Aircraft (2nd complaint)*, the United States considers that the relevant question for determining whether a financial contribution is granted in "disproportionately large" amounts to certain enterprises in that dispute was whether the actual distribution of a subsidy deviates materially from the expected distribution of that subsidy.[316] By contrast in this dispute, the USDOC determined that the NMDC's provision of high-grade iron ore was *de facto* specific to steel companies on the basis of the "use of a subsidy program by a limited number of certain enterprises", which is a different factor listed in Article 2.1(c) for purposes of the *de facto* specificity analysis. The United States submits that, where an investigating authority is examining whether "disproportionately large amounts" of the subsidy are being provided to certain enterprises under Article 2.1(c), this requires a comparison to determine the proportion of

---

312 United States' appellee's submission, para. 314 (referring to Panel Report, *US – Upland Cotton*, para. 7.1142).
313 United States' appellee's submission, para. 314 (quoting Panel Report, para. 7.121).
314 United States' appellee's submission, para. 316.
315 United States' appellee's submission, para. 317.
316 United States' appellee's submission, para. 318 (referring to Appellate Body Report, *US – Large Civil Aircraft (2nd complaint)*, para. 883).

subsidies received by different enterprises. By contrast, where the question before an investigating authority is whether the subsidy programme is being used by "a limited number of certain enterprises", the United States considers that there is no need to compare entities that might have been expected to receive a subsidy with those who actually received it. The relevant question, the United States notes, is whether the certain enterprises who receive the subsidy are a discrete segment of the economy.

2.2.6.2 The meaning of the phrase "limited number of certain enterprises"

2.258 The United States argues that the Panel also correctly rejected India's arguments that, under Article 2.1(c) of the SCM Agreement, an investigating authority must establish that only a "limited number" of certain enterprises within the set of certain enterprises eligible to use the subsidy programme actually received the subsidy. The United States submits that India's arguments seek to redraft Article 2.1(c). There is no connection between the notion "use … by" and India's argument that Article 2.1(c) distinguishes between "users" and "beneficiaries", nor has India explained why such a distinction would mean that Article 2.1(c) requires users to be a subset of potential beneficiaries. The United States also observes that India is attempting to read the phrase "limited number of users" into the text of Article 2.1(c) in place of the phrase "limited number of certain enterprises". Without this amendment, India would have no basis for arguing that there must be a "subset" of certain eligible enterprises receiving the subsidy. Similarly, although India contends that the term "certain enterprises" should be replaced by the word "persons", thereby rendering the provision to read "use of a subsidy program by a limited number of persons", the United States argues that this does not imply the comparative subset argument advanced by India.[317]

2.259 Thus, according to the United States, India has provided no reasons to reject the Panel's finding other than to argue that the Panel's interpretation would be incorrect if Article 2.1(c) were drafted differently. The United States maintains that India's proposed redrafting does not support India's understanding of Article 2.1(c), and is not supported by the actual text of Article 2.1(c). The United States therefore requests the Appellate Body to find that the Panel did not err in interpreting or applying the phrase "use of a subsidy programme by a limited number of certain enterprises" in interpreting Article 2.1(c) of the SCM Agreement.

2.2.6.3 Provision of goods and specificity

2.260 The United States argues that the Panel correctly interpreted Article 2.1(c) of the SCM Agreement in finding that any inherent limitations arising

[317] United States' appellee's submission, para. 327.

from a provision of goods cannot preclude a finding of *de facto* specificity. The United States notes that, on appeal, India maintains that "whole or parts of the treaty [will be] rendered redundant or ineffective if Article 2.1(c) is interpreted in a manner that permits a finding of *de facto* specificity based on the inherent limitations of the subsidized good".[318] The United States considers that India's concern is unfounded. The Panel did not find that the provision of goods that are inherently limited in utility will *ipso facto* be determined to be specific, but, rather, that inherent limitations are not a bar to a finding of specificity. Thus, under the Panel's interpretation, an investigating authority still must make a determination of specificity consistent with Article 2 of the SCM Agreement. The United States further notes that a determination of specificity in and of itself is not enough for an investigating authority to find that the provision of goods by a government amounts to a countervailable subsidy.

2.261 In the United States' view, the interpretation advanced by India would create a loophole in the subsidies disciplines. If investigating authorities were barred from making a determination of *de facto* specificity on the basis of inherent limitations on use, the provision of all goods, which could be said to be inherently limited, would be exempt from a finding of *de facto* specificity. The United States considers that there is no basis in the text of Article 2 for such an interpretation. Rather, previous panels have correctly found that, when a government provides a good that is of limited utility, it is all the more likely that a subsidy is conferred on certain enterprises.[319] In advancing interpretations that are at odds with both the text and context of the SCM Agreement, the United States argues, India seeks to carve out a loophole in the subsidies disciplines for its mining industry. The United States therefore requests the Appellate Body to reject India's appeal and uphold the Panel's findings under Article 2.1(c) of the SCM Agreement.

2.262 Finally, the United States maintains that India's claims under Article 11 of the DSU should be rejected. The United States recalls that a panel has no obligation under Article 11 to address every argument raised by a party and that the fact that a panel does not refer to specific evidence or arguments presented by a party is not sufficient to establish a panel's failure to make an objective assessment. The United States considers that India failed to demonstrate that the argument it had made in respect of the panel report in *US – Softwood Lumber IV* was so significant that, had the Panel addressed it, this would have materially altered the outcome of the Panel's analysis. The United States maintains that the Panel made clear that it did not consider India's arguments significant to its determination. Moreover, the United States notes that the Panel's finding was not

---

[318] United States' appellee's submission, para. 341 (referring to India's appellant's submission, para. 385).

[319] United States' appellee's submission, para. 344 (referring to United States' first written submission to the Panel, paras. 408-412, in turn referring to Panel Report, *US – Softwood Lumber IV*, para. 7.116).

based solely on *US – Softwood Lumber IV*, but also on its earlier findings rejecting India's arguments. In addition, the Panel did not rely on the panel report in *US – Softwood Lumber IV* to reject India's interpretation of Article 2.1(c), but rather to note that the panel in that dispute addressed a similar issue and reached "essentially the same conclusion".[320] Since the Panel had already reached its conclusion prior to addressing the panel's findings in *US – Softwood Lumber IV*, the United States submits that it would not have been useful to engage in an examination of India's alleged "cogent reasons", as those reasons were not material to the Panel's conclusion. The United States therefore requests the Appellate Body to reject India's claim under Article 11 of the DSU.[321]

2.2.7 Facts available

2.263 The United States requests that the Appellate Body dismiss India's appeal of the Panel's interpretation and application of Article 12.7 of the SCM Agreement in relation to India's "as such" and "as applied" claims. The United States argues that the Panel correctly interpreted Article 12.7 and did not err under Article 11 of the DSU by failing to address certain evidence for purposes of construing the meaning of the measure at issue, and that, in any event, such evidence does not support India's claim.

2.264 The United States further contends that India did not provide evidence or argumentation demonstrating how, in each of the instances of application, as well as in the 2013 sunset review, there is an inconsistency with Article 12.7. Thus, according to the United States, the Panel correctly found that India failed to establish a *prima facie* case in both of its "as applied" claims on appeal.

2.2.7.1 Interpretation of Article 12.7 of the SCM Agreement

2.265 The United States contends that the Panel correctly found that the text of Article 12.7 of the SCM Agreement "does not set out any express conditions" regarding the type of information that may be used for the application of facts available.[322] According to the United States, the Panel correctly took into account both the similarities between Article 12.7 of the SCM Agreement and Article 6.8 of the Anti-Dumping Agreement, as well as the absence in the SCM Agreement of an equivalent to Annex II to the Anti-Dumping Agreement.

---

[320] United States' appellee's submission, para. 338 (quoting Panel Report, para. 7.131).

[321] United States' appellee's submission, para. 339. The United States further argues that, although India had claimed in its Notice of Appeal that the Panel did not make an objective assessment of the matter before it "by limiting the circumstances in which negotiating history can be relied upon to interpret a treaty", India appears to have abandoned this claim. (*Ibid.*, para. 331 (quoting India's Notice of Appeal, para. 21)) The United States further notes that such a claim would have been, in any event, a matter of treaty interpretation. (*Ibid.*, para. 334)

[322] United States' appellee's submission, para. 437 (quoting Panel Report, para. 7.437).

2.266 The United States submits that the Panel's interpretation accords with the legal standard for Article 12.7 articulated by the Appellate Body in *Mexico – Anti-Dumping Measures on Rice*. In particular, the Panel found that "the Appellate Body very clearly did not apply the same standard" for Article 6.8 of the Anti-Dumping Agreement and for Article 12.7 of the SCM Agreement in *Mexico – Anti-Dumping Measures on Rice*, and further, the Panel found that the "absence of more detailed conditions" in the SCM Agreement informed the Appellate Body's finding in that case.[323] On that basis, as the Panel found, it would be improper to seek to import the standard under Article 6.8 of the Anti-Dumping Agreement, read in the light of its Annex II, into Article 12.7 of the SCM Agreement.

2.267 In the United States' view, the Appellate Body in *Mexico – Anti-Dumping Measures on Rice* expressly declined to rely on Annex II to the Anti-Dumping Agreement to determine the limits under Article 12.7. Rather than looking to Annex II to the Anti-Dumping Agreement to identify applicable conditions for Article 12.7 of the SCM Agreement, the Appellate Body looked instead to Article 12 of the SCM Agreement itself, while using Annex II only for context in the interpretation of Article 12.7. Further, the Appellate Body's finding that it would be "anomalous" if the use of facts available were "markedly different" in the SCM Agreement and the Anti-Dumping Agreement does not mean that the very same standard applies in each agreement. Rather, this statement recognizes that there is a difference between the standards, but that they should not be "markedly" different.

2.268 In respect of India's argument that "only facts that are most fitting or most appropriate, determined by way of an 'evaluative, comparative assessment' can be used", the United States responds that there is nothing in the text of the SCM Agreement or the Anti-Dumping Agreement to support this interpretation.[324] According to the United States, although this language appeared in the Appellate Body report in *Mexico – Anti-Dumping Measures on Rice*, it originated from the panel report in that case and was neither subject to appeal by the participants, nor did the Appellate Body explain its meaning. In any event, the United States submits that India fails to explain how its proposed principle of "comparative evaluation" to determine the "most fitting" information for a particular exporter could function when a respondent refuses to provide any information with regard to its sales in a particular period.

2.269 In the United States' view, nothing in Article 12.7 of the SCM Agreement speaks to which "facts available" should be selected, and, in particular, nothing prevents an investigating authority from selecting facts that are unfavourable to the interests of an interested party or interested Member. In any case, it is impossible to know whether the facts selected from the "facts available" are

[323] United States' appellee's submission, paras. 438 and 439 (quoting Panel Report, para. 7.439).

[324] United States' appellee's submission, paras. 446 and 447 (referring to India's appellant's submission, paras. 209 and 237).

more, or less, favourable to an interested party or interested Member, because the actual information against which this would be judged has not been provided to the investigating authority. The United States clarified at the oral hearing that, in its view, Article 12.7 is directed at obtaining the best information available and the most accurate information possible based on the facts available and taking into account all of the circumstances, but that this does not necessarily lead to the best result for the non-cooperating party.

2.270 Finally, in the light of India's argument that, "[f]rom a logical perspective ..., the Panel's so-called proper Article 12.7 standard is no different from the standard espoused by India", the United States questions how, if the two standards are similar or the same, India considers its appeal in this respect could lead to a reversal of the Panel's findings.[325]

2.2.7.2 The Panel's "as such" findings

2.271 The United States requests the Appellate Body to uphold the Panel's rejection of India's "as such" claim under Article 12.7 of the SCM Agreement. The United States argues that the Panel did not err in its appreciation of the ordinary meaning of the text of Section 1677e(b) of the US Statute and Section 351.308(a)-(c) of the US Regulations, and that, in any case, the evidence beyond the text does not support India's view that these laws preclude the United States from complying with Article 12.7.

2.272 In respect of a panel's examination of municipal law, the United States contends that the meaning of a challenged measure would be determined according to the domestic legal principles in the legal system of the Member maintaining that measure. WTO jurisprudence suggests that the starting point must be the measure on its face, and if its meaning is not clear on its face, further examination is required. The United States notes that this approach aligns with the approach to statutory interpretation under its own legal system.

2.273 Turning to the text of Section 1677e(b) of the US Statute and Section 351.308(a)-(c) of the US Regulations, the United States argues that it is plain that the use of an adverse inference in selecting from among the facts available is discretionary, and that an investigating authority must rely on facts in drawing adverse inferences and in making determinations. Further, the United States argues that other provisions of its law not challenged by India provide important context and support for the Panel's findings. In particular, pursuant to Section 351.308(d) of the US Regulations, when relying on secondary information[326] in

---

[325] United States' appellee's submission, para. 449 (quoting India's appellant's submission, para. 226).

[326] According to Section 351.308(c)(1) of the US Regulations the term "secondary information" may refer to:

> (1) Secondary information, such as information derived from:
>
> (i) The petition;

using an adverse inference, the investigating authority must, "'to the extent practicable, corroborate that information from independent sources that are reasonably at [its] disposal'", which means that the "probative value" of the information is examined.[327] Further, the United States notes that Section 351.308(e) states that the investigating authority "will not decline to consider information that is submitted by an interested party and is necessary to the determination", even if it does not meet all the requirements established by the USDOC, so long as certain conditions are met.[328] According to the United States, the Panel correctly found, having considered these provisions, that the "US measures do not allow for the application of facts available in a manner inconsistent with Article 12.7 of the SCM Agreement".[329]

2.274 In relation to India's argument that the Panel ignored material evidence regarding the interpretation of Section 1677e(b) of the US Statute and Section 351.308(a)-(c) of the US Regulations, the United States notes India's acceptance that the measure at issue is, on its face, "innocuous", and that India bears the burden to show that the measure is "as such" inconsistent with Article 12.7.[330] While India argues that the text is not a reliable basis on which to determine the meaning of Section 1677e(b) of the US Statute and Section 351.308(a)-(c) of the US Regulations, India may not base its claims on arguments relating to a US "practice" or "system" not reflected in the measure at issue. In this regard, the United States recalls India's clarification before the Panel that its challenge was limited to Section 1677e(b) of the US Statute and Section 351.308(a)-(c) of the US Regulations only, and that it did not challenge any "system" or "practice", which in any event did not appear in the Panel's terms of reference.

2.275 Further, the United States argues that the fact that the Panel did not refer to the evidence submitted by India is only indicative of the Panel not affording it the weight or significance India would have liked, and that this is not sufficient to establish a breach of Article 11 of the DSU. Rather, to succeed under Article 11, the burden on India is to demonstrate why the evidence not addressed in the Panel Report is so material to its case that the failure to address it has a bearing on the objectivity of the Panel's assessment. According to the United States, an analysis of this evidence demonstrates that India has failed to make this showing.

(ii) A final determination in a countervailing duty investigation or an antidumping investigation;

(iii) Any previous administrative review, new shipper review, expedited antidumping review, section 753 review, or section 762 review; ...

[327] United States' appellee's submission, para. 462 (quoting Section 351.308(d) of the US Regulations).

[328] United States' appellee's submission, para. 463 (quoting Section 351.308(e) of the US Regulations).

[329] United States' appellee's submission, para. 464 (referring to Panel Report, fn 742 to para. 7.445).

[330] United States' appellee's submission, para. 466 (quoting India's appellant's submission, paras. 232 and 239).

2.276 In the United States' view, the Statement of Administrative Action[331] pertaining to Section 1677e(b) of the US Statute and the legislative history of Section 351.308 of the US Regulations demonstrate that the measure at issue is discretionary. Further, the United States points to instances where the discretion has, in practice, been exercised without employing an adverse inference despite the non-cooperation of an interested party. In respect of the judicial decisions relied on by India, the United States firstly notes that Rhone Poulenc, Inc. v. The United States[332] pre-dates the adoption of commitments contained in the Uruguay Round agreements, as well as the measure at issue. In any event, this decision does not require, as a matter of law, the highest calculated rate from a prior determination to be applied, and further, other judicial decisions make clear that facts available may not be applied in a "punitive" manner, nor may reliable record evidence be disregarded.

2.277 Therefore, according to the United States, this review of the additional evidence cited by India demonstrates that India has not succeeded in showing how this evidence is so material that examination of it would have changed the outcome of the Panel's assessment. On the contrary, it supports the Panel's finding.

2.278 In respect of India's request that the Appellate Body complete the legal analysis under its alternative "as such" claim under Article 12.7, the United States contends that India has not demonstrated an inconsistency with Article 12.7 of the SCM Agreement, but simply repeats on appeal the arguments it made before the Panel, which the United States has rebutted.

2.2.7.3 The Panel's "as applied" findings

2.279 The United States requests the Appellate Body to uphold the Panel's finding that India failed to establish a *prima facie* case with regard to its "as applied" claim. The United States contends that India was required to demonstrate why each of the instances of application was inconsistent with Article 12.7, and, in any event, that the use of "facts available" to determine benefit in these instances was not inconsistent with Article 12.7 of the SCM Agreement.

2.280 At the outset, the United States emphasizes that India only challenged the application of the United States' measure.[333] Thus, in raising an "as applied" claim, India's burden was to demonstrate that each application of "facts available" was inconsistent with Article 12.7 of the SCM Agreement, including an identification of the specific instance of the application at issue, and an explanation of why that action was in error.[334] In the United States' view, the Panel found that India did not meet this burden on either element. The listing of

[331] Panel Exhibit IND-4.

[332] Rhone Poulenc, Inc. v. United States (Panel Exhibit IND-48).

[333] United States' appellee's submission, para. 482.

[334] United States' appellee's submission, para. 483 (referring to Panel Report, para. 7.7).

six groups of circumstances in which the highest non-*de minimis* subsidy rate was used was imprecise in challenging 230 programme-specific subsidy rates, and India failed to demonstrate how any of these applications were inconsistent with Article 12.7.

2.281 Further, the United States argues that the USDOC's use of "facts available" to determine benefit in the instances identified by India was not inconsistent with Article 12.7. First, recourse to the facts available in each instance was made only after the interested parties failed to provide necessary information or otherwise cooperate. Second, as "facts available", the USDOC sought to use other subsidy rates for the identical subsidy programme calculated for cooperating interested parties, and, where such information was unavailable, it sought next to use rates calculated for cooperating interested parties in similar or comparable subsidy programmes, and, finally, it resorted to rates calculated in another proceeding for a cooperating interested party that a non-cooperating interested party could have used. Third, the reliability and relevance of the subsidy rates selected were examined, to the extent practicable, prior to their use as "facts available". Thus, the United States contends that the "facts available" determinations reflected a reasoned analysis and were based on a factual foundation, and that India cannot point to any evidence on the Panel record that undermines the use of the subsidy rates selected as "facts available".[335]

2.282 Furthermore, the United States requests the Appellate Body to find that the Panel did not breach Article 11 of the DSU in finding that India failed to establish a *prima facie* case with respect to the 2013 sunset review.

2.283 As with India's other "as applied" claim under Article 12.7 relating to the application of the highest non-*de minimis* subsidy rates, the United States emphasizes that India bore the burden to identify the specific instances of the application of the measure at issue, and provide an explanation as to why that action was in error. This meant that, in order to make a *prima facie* case, India was required to explain the meaning of each claim and how or why the measure breached Article 12.7. According to the United States, the Panel correctly determined, on the basis of India's lack of argumentation, that "India had not even attempted"[336] to make out a *prima facie* case. In such circumstances, it would be an error for a panel to make India's case for it, and the failure to do so cannot be regarded as a breach of a panel's duty under Article 11 of the DSU.

2.284 Further, the United States contends that India did not furnish the 2013 sunset review to the Panel record. Moreover, India cited certain alleged information contained in this determination for the first time on appeal. Since new evidence may not be introduced on appeal, neither the United States as a participant nor the Appellate Body may engage with the substance of that document. In the United States' view, India's argument that the 2013 sunset

[335] United States' appellee's submission, paras. 489 and 490.
[336] United States' appellee's submission, para. 494.

review is a published and publicly available document is of no avail to India's position.

2.285 In respect of India's assertion that the matters challenged in the 2013 sunset review were clear because it simply repeated the violations of other administrative reviews, the United States contends that India's claims regarding the 2013 sunset review extend to companies and a review that were not the subject of other violations alleged by India in the dispute. Thus, India's argument that it merely avoided repeating the very same arguments to avoid duplication does not assist in clarifying its case in relation to the 2013 sunset review.

2.2.8 New subsidy allegations

2.286 The United States requests the Appellate Body to reject India's appeal on this issue. The United States underlines that: (i) the Panel did not err in its interpretation of Articles 11 and 21 of the SCM Agreement; and (ii) the Panel objectively assessed the matter before it, reasonably considered India's various claims, and provided a basic rationale for its findings, consistent with Articles 11 and 12.7 of the DSU.

2.287 As regards the relationship between Articles 11 and 21 of the SCM Agreement, the United States submits that the Panel was correct in rejecting India's attempt to import and apply the obligations contained in Article 11, 13, or 22 of the SCM Agreement to administrative review proceedings. In addition to the structure of the SCM Agreement separating the processes of investigation and review, the text of Articles 11.1, 13.1, 22.1, and 22.2 expressly limits the application of these provisions to original investigations, just as Articles 21.1 and 21.2 apply in the context of reviews. The United States relies on WTO jurisprudence in respect of the Anti-Dumping and SCM Agreements to argue that requirements found in provisions applicable to an anti-dumping or countervailing duty investigation will not automatically be read into those provisions expressly applying to proceedings that take place after the conclusion of an original investigation, such as administrative or sunset reviews.[337] In the United States' view, India's argument that Articles 11, 13, and 22 provide the manner in which new subsidies can be considered in a review under Article 21 conflates two different types of proceedings and lacks textual basis. In doing so, the United States argues, India also ignores the extensive procedural and evidentiary safeguards that the SCM Agreement provides for reviews through the incorporation of Article 12 into Article 21.

2.288 The United States adds that India's challenge of the Panel's findings is based on the erroneous proposition that an investigating authority may not levy

[337] United States' appellee's submission, para. 591 (referring to Appellate Body Reports, *US – Carbon Steel*, paras. 69-72; *US – Corrosion-Resistant Steel Sunset Review*, para. 152; and *US – Oil Country Tubular Goods Sunset Reviews*, paras. 294-300; and Panel Report, *US – Zeroing (EC)*, paras. 7.181-7.186).

countervailing duties pursuant to administrative reviews on subsidy programmes that were not examined in the original investigation. The United States argues that adopting India's approach would, in practice, require an investigating authority to conduct multiple investigations and administrative reviews simultaneously, even where the same Member, interested parties, and product are at issue. The United States points out that, if such a process were necessary simply because the subsidies identified in the review were not identical to those identified in the original investigation, it would create "an absurd result, whereby multiple investigations, reviews, and duty determinations would exist simultaneously with respect to a single product."[338]

2.289 In connection with India's claims under Articles 11 and 12.7 of the DSU, the United States asserts that the Panel objectively assessed the matter before it, as called for by Article 11, and provided a basic rationale for its findings, consistent with Article 12.7 of the DSU. Referring to the Appellate Body's statements that a claim under Article 11 "must stand by itself" and should not be made merely as a subsidiary argument or claim in support of a claim that the panel failed to apply correctly a provision of the covered agreements[339], the United States alleges that this is precisely what India has done. As the crux of India's complaint is that the Panel has misinterpreted Article 21 of the SCM Agreement as being exclusive of Article 11 of the SCM Agreement, this is a claim of legal error, and not a challenge to the Panel's objectivity. Hence, India's claim under Article 11 of the DSU should be rejected on that basis. The United States adds that India cannot impose on the Panel a particular legal analysis or order to its analysis. As regards Article 12.7 of the DSU, the United States posits that, although India may not agree with the Panel's basic rationale underpinning its findings under Articles 11, 13, and 22 of the SCM Agreement, the Panel Report reveals that this rationale was nonetheless provided. Therefore, India's claim under Article 12.7 of the DSU should also be rejected.

2.290 The United States further requests the Appellate Body to decline India's request for completion of the legal analysis, because India did not establish a *prima facie* case of inconsistency and because, in any event, there are not sufficient uncontested facts on the record or Panel findings on which the Appellate Body could base such an analysis.

2.291 With respect to India's claim under Article 11.1 of the SCM Agreement, the United States indicates that the USDOC's initiation of an examination into new subsidies was based on written requests submitted by the domestic industry in the relevant administrative reviews, which India placed on the Panel record. The United States submits that, even assuming that Article 11.1 applies in the context of an administrative review, India does not explain why these requests

[338] United States' appellee's submission, para. 594.

[339] United States' appellee's submission, para. 597 (referring to Appellate Body Reports, *China – Rare Earths*, para. 5.173; and *EC – Fasteners (China)*, para. 442).

would not satisfy the requirements of Article 11.1 of the SCM Agreement. As regards the new subsidies that were examined by the USDOC without a written request, the self-initiation by the USDOC of these additional subsidies would be covered by Article 11.6 of the SCM Agreement which, the United States stresses, is not an issue raised in this appeal.

2.292 Concerning India's claim under Article 13.1 of the SCM Agreement, the United States submits that India has not explained how Article 13.1 would apply in the context of a review proceeding when the provision on its face applies only to original investigations. In any event, the United States highlights that India does not cite to any record evidence, or explain why the evidence on record does not satisfy the requirements of Article 13.1.

2.293 In respect of India's claims under Articles 22.1 and 22.2 of the SCM Agreement, the United States avers that India's argument that the USDOC failed to provide public notice of the initiation of the administrative reviews in which new subsidies were being examined "is simply incorrect."[340] For each of its administrative reviews (2002, 2004, 2006, and 2007), the USDOC published a notice of initiation in the *United States Federal Register*, consistent with Article 22.1.[341] Furthermore, the GOI and interested parties were "notified" of newly alleged subsidies, because they received those allegations directly.[342] Regarding the content of the review proceeding being initiated, the United States notes that it made available to the public its new subsidy memoranda. Where new subsidies were not alleged and therefore the USDOC did not issue a new subsidy memorandum, any new subsidy programmes were notified to the GOI and interested parties through questionnaires issued by the USDOC, and were publicized in the preliminary and final review determinations.[343]

2.3 *Claims of Error by the United States – Other Appellant*

2.3.1 *Public Body*

2.294 While the United States agrees with the Panel's ultimate conclusions in this dispute, the United States considers that that it would be useful for the Appellate Body to clarify the Panel's interpretation of Article 1.1(a)(1) of the SCM Agreement. The United States submits that the Panel was correct to focus on the control exercised over the entities by the GOI. However, the United States requests the Appellate Body to find that a "public body" includes "an entity that

---

[340] United States' appellee's submission, para. 613.

[341] United States' appellee's submission, paras. 612 and 613 (referring to Panel Exhibits USA-47; USA-80; USA-81; and USA-82 (see table of Panel Exhibits at pp. 13-16 of this Report)).

[342] United States' appellee's submission, paras. 612 and 613 (referring to Panel Exhibits USA-69; USA-78; IND-15B; IND-24; IND-25; IND-26; and IND-27 (see table of Panel Exhibits at pp. 13-16 of this Report)).

[343] United States' appellee's submission, para. 614 (referring to India's appellant's submission, para. 655; and Panel Exhibits IND-17; IND-32; and IND-37 (see table of Panel Exhibits at pp. 13-16 of this Report)).

is controlled by the government such that the government can use that entity's resources as its own", irrespective of whether the entity also possesses governmental authority or exercises this authority in the performance of governmental functions. According to the United States, such an understanding follows from the interpretation of the term "public body" under customary rules of interpretation.

2.295 The United States agrees with the observation made by the Appellate Body in *US – Anti-Dumping and Countervailing Duties (China)* that the ordinary meaning of the term "public body" could be broad.[344] The United States considers, however, that, while the term "public body" in different contexts could denote a variety of entities, all of those entities would share the common characteristic of belonging to, or pertaining, to the community as a whole, and would therefore be owned or controlled by the community, or would be acting on its behalf. The United States further argues that to limit the term "public body" only to entities vested with or exercising governmental functions would restrict its meaning to a subset of those entities captured by dictionary definitions. In the United States' view, had the drafters of the SCM Agreement intended a narrower meaning restricting public bodies to only those entities exercising governmental authority, they might have used terms such as "governmental body", "public agency", "governmental agency", or "governmental authority".[345]

2.296 The United States contends that a contextual reading of the term "public body" supports the conclusion that the concept of "public body" within the meaning of Article 1.1(a)(1) of the SCM Agreement includes an entity controlled by the government such that the government can use that entity's resources as its own. The use of the distinct terms "a government" and "any public body" in the disjunctive phrase "by a government or any public body", suggests that the terms have distinct and different meanings. Therefore, the United States argues, the term "public body" should be interpreted as meaning something other than, or at least additional to, an entity that performs functions of a governmental character – i.e. to regulate, restrain, supervise, or control the conduct of private citizens.

2.297 The United States further argues that the word "any" before "public body", in Article 1.1(a)(1) refers to "public bodies" of "any" kind. Moreover, in the light of the broad range of entities that may constitute a "public body" pursuant to the dictionary definition of that term – i.e. an entity of, pertaining to, or belonging to a community – some entities that would correctly be deemed "public bodies" might be more akin to government agencies, while others might be corporations engaging in business activities.[346]

344 United States' other appellant's submission, para. 36 (referring to Appellate Body Report, *US – Anti-Dumping and Countervailing Duties (China)*, para. 285).

345 United States' other appellant's submission, para. 39.

346 United States' other appellant's submission, para. 46.

2.298 The United States argues that understanding the relationship of "government" and "public body" to be only one in which the government has authorized the "public body" to perform governmental acts – e.g. "to 'regulate', 'restrain', 'supervise' or 'control' the conduct of private citizens" – would mean that the terms "government" and "public body" "are not merely related, but that they are identical".[347] On the other hand, understanding the relationship to include control of a "public body" by "a government" (on behalf of the community it represents) gives meaning to both terms and avoids reducing the term "public body" to redundancy. The United States adds that the use of the term "government" in the SCM Agreement to refer to the phrase "a government or any public body within the territory of a Member" is a drafting technique, used so that the lengthy phrase need not be repeated throughout the SCM Agreement. The United States refers in this regard to the similar technique used in Article 2.1 of the SCM Agreement, which refers to "an enterprise or industry or group of enterprises or industries" as "certain enterprises", pointing out that the terms "enterprise" and "industry" also have different meanings, despite being referred to collectively as "certain enterprises".

2.299 The United States recalls the Appellate Body's finding in *US – Anti-Dumping and Countervailing Duties (China)* that "the performance of governmental functions, or the fact of being vested with, and exercising, the authority to perform such functions are core commonalities between government and public body".[348] According to the United States, relevant findings in *Korea – Commercial Vessels* and *US – Anti-Dumping and Countervailing Duties (China)* "suggest that government and any public body can share 'core commonalities' that do not result in the two terms effectively carrying the same meaning".[349] For the United States, the essential characteristics that are shared by the terms "government" and "public body" relate to "*whose* economic resources are being conveyed in the financial contribution" such that "a transfer by that entity is a transfer of the government's resources, the same as a transfer by the government itself".[350] The United States submits, therefore, that "it would be helpful for the Appellate Body to clarify whether it is *only* the possession or exercise of governmental authority that can distinguish a public body", or whether, as the United States argues, "a public body may *also* include an entity controlled by the government such that financial contributions made by the entity can be said to have been made on behalf of the government, *i.e.*, such that the government can use the entity's resources as its own".[351]

---

[347] United States' other appellant's submission, para. 49.

[348] United States' other appellant's submission, para. 51 (quoting Appellate Body Report, *US – Anti-Dumping and Countervailing Duties (China)*, para. 290).

[349] United States' other appellant's submission, para. 53 (referring to Panel Reports, *Korea – Commercial Vessels*, para. 7.50 and fn 43 thereto; and *US – Anti-Dumping and Countervailing Duties (China)*, para. 8.90).

[350] United States' other appellant's submission, para. 54. (emphasis original)

[351] United States' other appellant's submission, para. 52. (emphasis original)

2.300 The United States argues that the broad language used and multiple methods of conveying value described in Article 1.1(a)(1) of the SCM Agreement reveal an intention to capture within the meaning of "financial contribution" a broad array of transfers of value. The United States adds that entities controlled by the government "can convey value just as the government can, and the value conveyed can be precisely the same as that conveyed by the government".[352] Moreover, "[i]rrespective of the government's ownership stake, if the government, through whatever means, controls the entity such that it can use the entity's resources as its own, then a grant provided by the entity to a recipient is a conveyance of value by the Member".[353] The United States further claims that nothing in Article 1.1(a)(1) of the SCM Agreement suggests that a distinction should be drawn between transactions based on whether the entity or corporation is controlled by the government or is "vested with or exercising governmental authority".[354] Instead, the United States argues, if a conveyance is made of the government's own resources, a "financial contribution" has been made by the government.

2.301 The United States submits that the inclusion of government payments to a funding mechanism as a form of "financial control" under Article 1.1(a)(1)(iv) provides additional support for its interpretation of "public body". Specifically, if the government makes payments to such a funding mechanism, and then those funds are provided to recipients, there is the same conveyance of value from the Member even though nothing in the ordinary meaning of the term "funding mechanism" indicates that the funding mechanism is vested with or exercising governmental authority when it carries out this transfer.

2.302 The United States asserts that its view is further supported by the context provided by Article 1.1(a)(1)(iv) of the SCM Agreement. The United States claims that the term "public", as the opposite of "private" in Article 1.1(a)(1)(iv), could be defined as provided or owned by the State or a "public body" rather than an individual. Therefore, government ownership of an entity, when accompanied by the ability to control the entity's resources as its own, would be a relevant factor in considering whether an entity is a "public body" capable of providing subsidies on behalf of the government for purposes of Article 1.1(a)(1). Furthermore, the United States agrees with the Appellate Body's statement that "for a public body to be able to exercise its authority over a private body (direction), a public body must itself possess such authority, or ability to compel or command" and, "[s]imilarly, in order to be able to give responsibility to a private body (entrustment), it must itself be vested with such responsibility."[355] However, it does not necessarily follow that "all public

---

[352] United States' other appellant's submission, para. 58.

[353] United States' other appellant's submission, para. 60.

[354] United States' other appellant's submission, para. 61.

[355] United States' other appellant's submission, para. 69 (quoting Appellate Body Report, *US – Anti-Dumping and Countervailing Duties (China)*, para. 294).

bodies" must have this authority, as many organs of Member governments – including ministries, departments, and agencies – do not possess the legal authority to entrust or direct private bodies to carry out the functions identified in Article 1.1(a)(1)(i)-(iii), even if, in other respects, they may possess and exercise authority to "'regulate', 'restrain', 'supervise' or 'control' the conduct of private citizens".[356] The United States notes, moreover, that some ministries, departments, and agencies may not even have the authority to regulate, restrain, supervise, or control the conduct of private citizens. For the United States, the absence of authority to entrust or direct private bodies does not move these organs outside the category of government, and, in a similar manner, the absence of authority to entrust or direct private bodies should not, as a definitional matter, mean that an entity cannot be a "public body".[357]

2.303 The United States further contends that the term "government" in Article 1.1(a)(1)(iv) is used in the collective sense, and the reference to governmental functions in Article 1.1(a)(1)(iv) simply refers back to the functions described in subparagraphs (i) through (iii). Consequently, reading Article 1.1(a)(1)(iv) as requiring that the term "public body" be interpreted as meaning an entity vested with or exercising authority to perform governmental functions is circular. This is because an entity alleged to have taken one or more of the actions identified in Article 1.1(a)(1)(i)-(iii) necessarily possesses authority to perform such actions, and an entity's possession of such authority does not indicate whether it is a "public body". By contrast, the presence or absence of government control permits distinctions to be drawn between entities that are "public bodies" on the one hand, and those that are "private bodies" on the other, requiring a finding of entrustment or direction with respect to alleged financial contributions provided by the latter type of entity.

2.304 The United States further argues that the term "*organismo público*" in the Spanish version of Article 1.1(a)(1) of the SCM Agreement does not need to be interpreted in a manner identical to the term "*organismos públicos*" in the Spanish version of Article 9.1(a) of the Agreement on Agriculture. The United States submits that the same words are used in Article 1.1(a)(1) and Article 9.1(a) in only one of the three WTO languages – i.e. Spanish. Specifically, Article 9.1(a) of the Agreement on Agriculture refers to "governments or their agencies", "*les pouvoirs publics ou leurs organismes*", and "*los gobiernos o por organismos públicos*". By contrast, Article 1.1(a)(1) of the SCM Agreement refers to "a government or any public body within the territory of a Member", "*des pouvoirs publics ou de tout organisme public du ressort territorial d'un Membre*", and "*un gobierno o de cualquier organismo público en el territorio de un Miembro*". The United States submits that these differences in the terms used in English, French, and Spanish must be taken into account in the interpretive

[356] United States' other appellant's submission, para. 70 (quoting Appellate Body Report, *Canada – Dairy*, para. 97).

[357] United States' other appellant's submission, para. 70.

process. For these reasons, the United States contends, the Appellate Body's interpretation in *Canada – Dairy* of "government agency" (*organismo público*) in Article 9.1(a) of the Agreement on Agriculture should not dictate the interpretation of "public body" (*organismo público*) in Article 1.1(a)(1) of the SCM Agreement.[358]

2.305 Finally, the United States submits that the object and purpose of the SCM Agreement supports its interpretation. The United States recalls that the Appellate Body and panels have sought to ensure that the SCM Agreement is not interpreted rigidly or formalistically in a manner that would undermine its disciplines on trade-distorting subsidization. Thus, the interpretation advocated by the United States, whereby the term "public body" includes an entity controlled by the government such that the government can use the entity's resources as its own, preserves the strength and effectiveness of subsidies disciplines. The United States claims that, by emphasizing the possession or exercise of governmental authority, the Panel's interpretation could be read as removing a potentially broad range of subsidization from the disciplines of the SCM Agreement in a manner at odds with the object and purpose of the Agreement. The United States adds that a finding that an entity is a "public body" does not end the subsidy analysis; instead, it only means that there is the potential for a financial contribution that confers a benefit, and ensures that subsidizing governments are subject to the disciplines of the SCM Agreement even when making financial contributions through entities they control.

2.3.2 Cross-cumulation

2.306 The United States appeals the Panel's finding that Section 1677(7)(G) of the US Statute is inconsistent, "as such" and "as applied", with Articles 15.1, 15.2, 15.3, 15.4, and 15.5 of the SCM Agreement because it requires "cross-cumulation" – i.e. cumulative assessment of the effects on the domestic industry of subsidized imports with the effects of dumped, non-subsidized imports.[359] The United States argues that, in reaching this finding, the Panel erred in interpreting Article 15.3, as well as Articles 15.1, 15.2, 15.4, and 15.5 of the SCM Agreement as prohibiting cross-cumulation in countervailing duty investigations. The United States further argues that the Panel acted inconsistently with Article 11 of the DSU in finding that Section 1677(7)(G) "requires" such cross-cumulation.[360]

---

[358] United States' other appellant's submission, paras. 75-83 (referring to Appellate Body Report, *Canada – Dairy*, para. 97).

[359] United States' other appellant's submission, para. 92 (referring to Panel Report, paras. 7.356 and 7.369).

[360] United States' other appellant's submission, para. 92 (quoting Panel Report, paras. 7.322, 7.339, 7.340, and 7.358).

2.3.2.1 Interpretation of Article 15.3 and Articles 15.1, 15.2, 15.4, and 15.5 of the SCM Agreement

2.307 The United States maintains that the Panel erred in interpreting Article 15.3 of the SCM Agreement by imposing an obligation on WTO Members not to cumulate the effects of subsidized imports with dumped imports. According to the United States, Article 15.3 does not contain such an obligation, and the Panel's interpretation is not supported by the text of Article 15.3 read in the light of relevant context and the object and purpose of the SCM Agreement.

2.308 The United States recalls that, pursuant to Article 15.3, "[w]here imports of a product from more than one country are simultaneously subject to countervailing duty investigations, the investigating authorities may cumulatively assess the effects of such imports only if" certain conditions are met. The United States submits that Article 15.3 makes clear that the only imports subject to the requirement thereunder are imports of countries that "are simultaneously subject to countervailing duty investigations". Thus, "Article 15.3 is *silent* on the issue of whether cumulation of dumped and subsidized imports is permissible."[361] The United States contends that, as the Appellate Body found in *US – Oil Country Tubular Goods Sunset Reviews*, the silence of an agreement on the permissibility of a particular methodological approach does not indicate that the methodology is prohibited. In that dispute, the Appellate Body found that, although cumulative assessment of the effects of dumped imports was not expressly authorized in sunset reviews, it was permissible because it was consistent with the rationale behind cumulation in injury determinations.[362] The United States maintains that, following the same approach, the fact that Article 15.3 of the SCM Agreement does not specifically authorize an authority to cumulate the effects of subsidized imports with those of dumped imports does not, in itself, indicate that such cross-cumulation is prohibited by the SCM Agreement.

2.309 The United States argues that the context provided by the Anti-Dumping Agreement and Article VI of the GATT 1994 supports its interpretation of Article 15.3 as permitting cross-cumulation. The United States recalls that, in *EC – Tube or Pipe Fittings*, the Appellate Body found that Article 3.3 of the Anti-Dumping Agreement, which concerns cumulative assessment of the effects of dumped imports, "is premised on a recognition that the domestic industry faces the impact of the 'dumped imports' as a whole ... even though those dumped imports originate from various countries".[363] According to the United States, the Appellate Body's explanation regarding the important role cumulative

---

[361] United States' other appellant's submission, para. 102. (emphasis original)

[362] United States' other appellant's submission, para. 104 (referring to Appellate Body Report, *US – Oil Country Tubular Goods Sunset Reviews*, paras. 294-300).

[363] United States' other appellant's submission, para. 106 (quoting Appellate Body Report, *EC – Tube or Pipe Fittings*, para. 116).

assessment plays in the context of anti-dumping investigations applies with equal force to a situation in which subject imports are dumped and subsidized. This is because an analysis that focuses solely on the injurious effects of either dumped or subsidized imports alone, when both types of "unfairly traded imports" are injuring the domestic industry at the same time, would necessarily prevent the investigating authority from adequately taking into account the injurious effects of all unfairly traded imports.[364]

2.310 Turning to Article VI of the GATT 1994, the United States contends that the phrase "the effect of dumping or subsidization, as the case may be" in Article VI:6(a) indicates that cumulation of dumped and subsidized imports may be appropriate in a particular injury investigation. This is because a domestic industry will often be faced with both dumped and subsidized imports and, under such circumstances, it would be appropriate to interpret Article VI:6(a) as contemplating a cumulative analysis of injury, such that an injury investigation may involve an examination of the injurious effects of dumped and subsidized imports. Furthermore, the United States argues, the word "or", which joins the words "dumping" and "subsidization", and the phrase "as the case may be" reflect the fact that injury determinations can involve either or both unfair trade practices.

2.311 The United States contends that the Panel's interpretation, which prohibits cross-cumulation under Article 15.3 of the SCM Agreement, impairs the right afforded to Members under the SCM Agreement to countervail injurious subsidized imports. This is because, from the perspective of the domestic industry, the injury that has resulted from dumped and subsidized imports is "cumulative".[365] The United States maintains, therefore, that the treatment of these imports must be consistent under all applicable provisions of the WTO agreements.

2.312 The United States further contends that the Panel erred in finding that the consistent reference to "subsidized imports" in Articles 15.1, 15.2, 15.4, and 15.5 of the SCM Agreement limits the scope of the injury assessment to subsidized imports only.[366] According to the United States, this finding of the Panel was based in large part on the Panel's "flawed reasoning" with respect to Article 15.3.[367] The United States stresses that none of the provisions of Article 15 expressly prohibits the practice of cross-cumulation or otherwise addresses a situation in which both anti-dumping and countervailing duty investigations are occurring simultaneously. Rather, silence on the issue of cross-cumulation should not be read as a prohibition. Moreover, contrary to the Panel's finding[368],

---

[364] United States' other appellant's submission, para. 107.

[365] United States' other appellant's submission, para. 111.

[366] United States' other appellant's submission, para. 117 (referring to Panel Report, paras. 7.346 and 7.360).

[367] United States' other appellant's submission, para. 118.

[368] United States' other appellant's submission, para. 120 (referring to Panel Report, para. 7.361).

the United States' interpretation does not result in the inclusion of imports other than those found to be dumped or subsidized into the scope of an injury determination.

2.3.2.2 Article 11 of the DSU

2.313 The United States alleges that the Panel acted inconsistently with Article 11 of the DSU in finding that Section 1677(7)(G) of the US Statute "requires, in certain situations, the USITC to cumulate the effects of subsidized imports with the effects of dumped, non-subsidized imports".[369]

2.314 The United States maintains that, where a Member challenges another Member's legislation as such, Article 11 of the DSU requires a panel "to examine the meaning and scope of the municipal law at issue"[370], and "to conduct a detailed examination of that legislation in assessing its consistency with WTO law".[371] Furthermore, the meaning of a challenged measure would be determined according to the domestic legal principles in the legal system of the Member maintaining that measure. In the United States' view, legal instruments are interpreted according to the ordinary meaning of the text and, where the terms of a legal instrument are not clear on their face, additional evidence must be examined, including legislative history, judicial decisions, and application by an administering agency.[372]

2.315 According to the United States, "the statute on its face is not definitive" with respect to cross-cumulation.[373] At the oral hearing, the United States clarified that Section 1677(7)(G) permits cross-cumulation – i.e. the cumulation of subsidized and non-subsidized dumped imports – but does not require that such cumulation be performed in every injury analysis. Specifically, the measure uses the word "or" when it states that the USITC shall cumulate imports with respect to which petitions were filed or investigations initiated under Section 1671a (for countervailing duty investigations), *or* under Section 1673a (for anti-dumping investigations) of the US Statute on the same day. In the United States' view, the Panel was required to look beyond the text of Section 1677(7)(G) to explain how the word "or" should be read as an "and" in determining the meaning and scope of the measure.

2.316 However, the United States contends, the Panel failed to examine the text of the measure, or make any substantive findings on the US law at issue to support its conclusions. Rather, the Panel's analysis of Section 1677(7)(G)

---

[369] United States' other appellant's submission, para. 122 (quoting Panel Report, para. 7.340). See also Panel Report, paras. 7.322, 7.339, and 7.358.

[370] United States' other appellant's submission, para. 123 (quoting Appellate Body Report, *US – Countervailing and Anti-Dumping Measures (China)*, para. 4.98).

[371] United States' other appellant's submission, para. 123 (quoting Appellate Body Report, *US – Hot-Rolled Steel*, para. 200).

[372] United States' opening statement at the oral hearing.

[373] United States' other appellant's submission, para. 96.

merely consists of the "assertion" that this measure "requires" cross-cumulation, without reference to the US law or explanation describing how the Panel came to its conclusion.[374] Moreover, besides the text, India merely referred to the single instance of application at issue in this dispute. Thus, the United States argues, without any factual findings by the Panel and any additional evidence, the Appellate Body should refrain from completing the analysis regarding the interpretation of the US measure at issue in this dispute.[375]

2.317 On the basis of the above, the United States requests the Appellate Body to reverse the Panel's interpretation of Articles 15.1, 15.2, 15.3, 15.4, and 15.5 of the SCM Agreement and find, instead, that these provisions do not prohibit an investigating authority from cross-cumulating dumped and subsidized imports for purposes of determining injury in countervailing duty investigations. The United States also requests the Appellate Body to reverse the Panel's findings that Section 1677(7)(G) of the US Statute is inconsistent with Articles 15.1, 15.2, 15.3, 15.4, and 15.5 of the SCM Agreement.

2.4 *Arguments of India – Appellee*

2.4.1 *Public Body*

2.318 India requests the Appellate Body to reject the United States' request for clarifications with respect to the Panel's findings on the interpretation of the term "public body" in Article 1.1(a)(1) of the SCM Agreement. India notes that the United States requests the Appellate Body to clarify that, "where sufficient government control over an entity exists, ... it is not necessary also to find that the entity exercises 'governmental authority' [nor it is] necessary to find that the entity has 'the effective power to regulate, control or supervise individuals'".[376] India submits that the United States "attempts to reinforce the very same legal error committed by the Panel in interpreting and applying the term 'public body'".[377] According to India, the United States effectively seeks to substitute governmental control as a sufficient condition for the purposes of Article 1.1(a)(1), discarding the need to prove the existence of governmental authority to perform governmental functions – i.e. the effective power to regulate, control, or supervise individuals or otherwise restrain their conduct, through the exercise of lawful authority.

2.319 In addition, India notes that the United States also requests the Appellate Body to clarify that an entity that is controlled by the government, such that the government may use the entity's resources as its own, is a "public body" for

---

[374] United States' other appellant's submission, para. 127.

[375] United States' opening statement at the oral hearing.

[376] India's appellee's submission, para. 8 (quoting United States' other appellant's submission, para. 23).

[377] India's appellee's submission, para. 9.

purposes of the SCM Agreement.[378] However, India argues that this is not really a clarification of the Panel's findings, because neither did the Panel's legal interpretation of Article 1.1(a)(1) touch upon this issue nor did the Panel attempt to apply any such test to the facts of the case. India further alleges that the United States' request for a clarification has no relation with the Panel Report under challenge, as it neither caters to an issue covered in the Panel Report nor involves any legal interpretation developed by the Panel. Moreover, according to India, the United States does not request the Appellate Body to find that the USDOC was correct in determining that the NMDC was a "public body" on the basis of the test proposed by the United States. India argues, therefore, that the clarification sought by the United States "is only an academic point that bears no relation to resolving the dispute between the parties".[379]

2.320 Moreover, India contends, on an *arguendo* basis, that the United States' request for clarification is essentially a "concealed attempt" to overturn a previously adopted Appellate Body report, without providing "cogent reasons".[380] India submits that the principles to be applied in determining whether an entity is a "public body" have been settled in the adopted report of the Appellate Body in *US – Anti-Dumping and Countervailing Duties (China)*. India further recalls that the Appellate Body has observed, in past disputes, that ensuring security and predictability in the dispute settlement system implies that, absent cogent reasons, an adjudicatory body will resolve the same legal question in the same way in a subsequent case.[381] Accordingly, India argues that the Appellate Body's interpretation of the term "public body" in *US – Anti-Dumping and Countervailing Duties (China)* is dispositive to the case at hand, unless challenged for "cogent reasons".

2.321 According to India, the United States does not, at any point in its other appellant's submission, challenge the interpretation of the term "public body" contained in the Appellate Body report in *US – Anti-Dumping and Countervailing Duties (China)*. Nor does the United States contend that it is offering "cogent reasons" that justify reconsideration of the findings in that report. Instead, the United States only asserts that the term "public body" includes an entity that is controlled by the government, such that the government may use the entity's resources as its own. India submits that the word "includes" suggests that the United States is postulating an additional and alternative test to those contained in *US – Anti-Dumping and Countervailing Duties (China)*.

2.322 India submits that the United States' arguments that the dictionary definitions of the terms "public body", "*organisme public*", and "*organismo*

---

378 India's appellee's submission, para. 12 (referring to United States' other appellant's submission, paras. 6 and 25).

379 India's appellee's submission, para. 14.

380 India's appellee's submission, para. 7 and section II.C.

381 India's appellee's submission, para. 18 (referring to Appellate Body Reports, *US – Continued Zeroing*, para. 362; and *US – Stainless Steel (Mexico)*, paras. 160 and 161).

público" support a conclusion that a "public body" includes an entity controlled by the government have already been considered by the Appellate Body in *US – Anti-Dumping and Countervailing Duties (China)*. The Appellate Body found in that dispute that "the dictionary definitions suggest a 'broad range of potential meanings', 'including both entities that are vested with or exercise governmental authority and entities belonging to the community or nation'".[382] According to India, in the light of the Appellate Body's finding, one possible meaning for the term "public body" as adopted from the dictionary means that it only covers entities vested with or exercising governmental authority. India submits that the United States' conclusions based on dictionaries are, therefore, selective and narrow.

2.323 India further argues that each of the contextual references in the United States' other appellant's submission were raised by the United States in *US – Anti-Dumping and Countervailing Duties (China)* and that most of them were "categorically rejected" by the Appellate Body.[383] India acknowledges that the United States' argument that the term "*organismo público*" in the Spanish version of Article 1.1(a)(1) of the SCM Agreement does not need to be interpreted as having the same meaning as the term "*organismos públicos*" in the Spanish version of Article 9.1(a) of the Agreement of Agriculture was not rejected by the Appellate Body in *US – Anti-Dumping and Countervailing Duties (China)*. Nonetheless, India claims that the Appellate Body did find that the panel erred in accepting the United States' contention on this point, and ruled that a "public body" under Article 1.1(a)(1) must possess governmental authority to perform governmental functions. In India's view, this means that the aforementioned argument of the United States was also effectively rejected by the Appellate Body in *US – Anti-Dumping and Countervailing Duties (China)*.

2.324 India also admits that the United States' contextual reference to "financial contribution" and "payments to a funding mechanism" was not specifically evaluated in the earlier dispute by the Appellate Body. India notes that the United States considers that the term "financial contribution" is intended to cover anything of value being transferred from the government, including the resources of an entity controlled by the government. However, India submits that the United States' argument is "misplaced", because it ignores the concept of "entrusting or directing" a private body covered under Article 1.1(a)(1)(iv), which specifically caters to the situation noted by the United States.[384]

2.325 Finally, India submits that the United States' argument relating to the object and purpose of the SCM Agreement was also rejected by the Appellate Body in *US – Anti-Dumping and Countervailing Duties (China)*. India further recalls that, in that dispute, the Appellate Body specifically ruled that government shareholding

---

382 India's appellee's submission, para. 22 (quoting Appellate Body Report, *US – Anti-Dumping and Countervailing Duties (China)*, para. 285).

383 India's appellee's submission, para. 24.

384 India's appellee's submission, paras. 25 and 26.

in itself is insufficient to determine than an entity is a "public body". Yet, according to India, the United States seeks to make "control" a dispositive and determinative factor. In sum, India submits that the Appellate Body has rejected all of the United States' contentions regarding the interpretation of Article 1.1(a)(1) of the SCM Agreement, and reiterates the reasoning by the Appellate Body in *US – Anti-Dumping and Countervailing Duties (China).*

2.4.2 Cross-cumulation

2.326 India submits that, contrary to the United States' "misplaced" claims of error, the Panel neither erred in its interpretation of Articles 15.1 15.2, 15.3, 15.4, and 15.5 of the SCM Agreement, nor erred in finding that Section 1677(7)(G) of the US Statute is inconsistent with these provisions.[385] As a preliminary matter, India notes that the United States defines the term "cross-cumulation" as "the aggregation of the volume and effect of dumped and subsidized imports from all countries subject to simultaneous antidumping and countervailing duty investigations for purposes of assessing material injury".[386] India clarifies that its claim is not concerned with cumulation of subsidized imports with imports that are both dumped and subsidized; rather, its claim focuses on cumulation of subsidized imports with dumped *but non-subsidized* imports.

2.4.2.1 Interpretation of Article 15.3 and Articles 15.1, 15.2, 15.4, and 15.5 of the SCM Agreement

2.327 India argues that the United States mischaracterizes the Panel's finding by claiming that the Panel inferred a prohibition of cross-cumulation "from the mere silence" on this issue in Article 15.3 of the SCM Agreement.[387] Rather, in finding that subsidized imports cannot be cumulated with dumped but non-subsidized imports under Article 15.3 of the SCM Agreement, the Panel engaged in a comprehensive analysis of the text and context of Article 15.3, as well as the object and purpose of the SCM Agreement.

2.328 India maintains that Article 15.3 expressly restricts cumulation to only those imports from countries simultaneously subject to countervailing duty investigations, and the United States cannot ignore this express textual implication. Moreover, India highlights the consistent use of "subsidized imports" throughout the provisions under Article 15 of the SCM Agreement. In India's view, therefore, Article 15.3 cannot be construed as being silent on the

---

[385] India's appellee's submission, para. 33.

[386] India's appellee's submission, para. 34 (quoting United States' other appellant's submission, para. 93).

[387] India's appellee's submission, para. 38 (referring to United States' other appellant's submission, para. 105).

issue of cumulating subsidized imports with non-subsidized imports, but must be understood as prohibiting such cross-cumulation. In addition, the United States' position that Article 15.3 of the SCM Agreement permits cross-cumulation is premised on the logic that both subsidization and dumping cause the same type of injury. According to India, however, the injury analysis under the Anti-Dumping Agreement or the SCM Agreement is not intended to identify different types of injury, but rather to identify the factor causing injury. Thus, the analysis under the SCM Agreement is whether the injury is being caused by subsidization, rather than other factors, and the distinction between subsidized imports and non-subsidized imports cannot be "obliterated by the United States" simply because non-subsidized imports may be causing the same type of injury.[388]

2.329 India further argues that, even assuming, *arguendo*, that Article 15.3 were silent on the issue of cross-cumulation, such silence must be interpreted as prohibiting cross-cumulation. An interpretation to the contrary would mean that, while cumulation of subsidized imports is subject to several conditions, cumulation of subsidized imports with non-subsidized imports is entirely at the discretion of domestic investigating authorities. Such an interpretation, in India's view, is "anomalous" and "absurd".[389] Moreover, India emphasizes that silence in the text of a treaty provision, alone, cannot be dispositive, but must be construed in its context. If cross-cumulation were, as the United States argues, permitted under Article 15.3, an investigating authority would be assessing the volume and effect of subsidized and non-subsidized imports for purposes of its injury determination, and would be attributing effects of non-subsidized imports to subsidized imports. This, India argues, would render the non-attribution requirement under Article 15.5 of the SCM Agreement "redundant".[390]

2.330 India submits that the United States' reliance on the Appellate Body's findings in *US – Oil Country Tubular Goods Sunset Reviews* and *EC – Tube or Pipe Fittings* is misplaced for four reasons. First, in *US – Oil Country Tubular Goods Sunset Reviews*, the issue before the Appellate Body was whether cumulation is permissible in a sunset review of anti-dumping duties, given that both Articles 3.3 and 11.3 of the Anti-Dumping Agreement are silent on this issue and the concept of cumulation is not addressed in the latter provision. In contrast, the concept of cumulation is specifically addressed in Article 15.3. Second, India argues that the United States' attempt to rely on the object and purpose of the SCM Agreement when referring to the Appellate Body's findings in the above disputes is inapposite, because the SCM Agreement does not contain express statements regarding its object and purpose. In any event, India recalls the Appellate Body's finding that the objective of the provisions under Article 15 is to "delineate the framework and relevant disciplines for the

388 India's appellee's submission, para. 58.
389 India's appellee's submission, para. 45.
390 India's appellee's submission, para. 48.

authority's analysis in reaching a final determination on the injury caused by subject imports, and to ensure that the analysis and the conclusion drawn therefrom is robust".[391] This objective, in India's view, does not support the United States' position.

2.331 Third, India maintains that the Appellate Body's findings in both disputes concerned cumulative assessment of dumped imports, and that the issue of cross-cumulation did not arise. Fourth, India recalls that, according to the Appellate Body's findings in both disputes, the rationale for allowing cumulative assessment under Article 3.3 of the Anti-Dumping Agreement is based on the recognition that the domestic industry faces the impact of dumped imports as a whole, even though those imports originate from various sources. Contrary to the United States' assertion, India argues, this rationale does not mean that a prohibition on cross-cumulation would force WTO Members to conduct country-specific analyses in injury determinations.[392] Rather, Members may cumulatively assess dumped imports from all sources under Article 3.3 of the Anti-Dumping Agreement, or cumulatively assess subsidized imports from all sources under Article 15.3 of the SCM Agreement, as long as the conditions under each provision are respected.

2.332 India further contends that the United States' reliance on Article VI:6(a) of the GATT 1994 is similarly unjustifiable. India submits that, as the Panel correctly found, the word "or" in the clause "dumping or subsidization, as the case may be" in this provision indicates that the effects of dumping and subsidization are to be considered "separately".[393] India recalls the United States' argument that Article VI:6(a) permits cross-cumulation of the effects of dumped and subsidized imports because both are "unfairly traded" imports.[394] However, as the Panel rightly pointed out, the concept of "unfairly traded" imports is not found in Article VI:6(a) of the GATT 1994. Moreover, India submits that Article VI:6(a) is silent on "fairly traded imports" and that, following the United States' logic in interpreting Article 15.3 of the SCM Agreement, this silence would mean that Article VI:6(a) also permits Members to cumulate the effects of fairly traded imports with those of unfairly traded imports. Such a result, India contends, leads to "absurdity".[395] India additionally contends that Article VI:6(a) does not address the issue of cumulation. Rather, the issue of cumulation must be analysed according to the disciplines under Article 15 of the SCM Agreement.

---

[391] India's appellee's submission, para. 54 (quoting Appellate Body Report, *China – GOES*, para. 153).

[392] India's appellee's submission, para. 57 (referring to United States' other appellant's submission, para. 111).

[393] India's appellee's submission, para. 62 (quoting Panel Report, para. 7.348).

[394] India's appellee's submission, para. 50 (quoting United States' other appellant's submission, para. 114).

[395] India's appellee's submission, para. 51.

2.333 Finally, India alleges that the United States has failed to raise any independent claim of error with regard to the Panel's interpretation of Articles 15.1, 15.2, 15.4, and 15.5 of the SCM Agreement. In India's view, the United States has failed to explain why the Panel erred in interpreting the term "subsidized imports" as excluding dumped, but non-subsidized, imports from the scope of an injury determination under the above provisions. The United States has also failed to identify any error in the Panel's finding that, by cumulatively assessing the effects of subsidized and non-subsidized imports, the United States acted inconsistently with Article 15.5 for failing to ensure that injury caused by factors other than the subsidized imports are not attributed to such imports.

2.4.2.2 Article 11 of the DSU

2.334 India asserts that the United States' challenge of the Panel's examination of the US law at issue – Section 1677(7)(G) of the US Statute – is "mischievous".[396] India recalls that the text of the measure uses the word "shall", which is mandatory in nature, and clearly states that all imports from countries covered by anti-dumping or countervailing duty investigations initiated on the same day must be cumulatively assessed. India emphasizes that the United States never contested this understanding of the measure during the Panel proceedings. India further recalls that it referred to the application of this measure in the underlying countervailing duty investigation at issue. It was also undisputed that, in that investigation, the USITC cumulatively assessed imports from 11 countries, even though imports from six of these countries were subject to anti-dumping duty investigations alone.

2.335 India maintains that the interpretation and understanding of the US law at issue "is a matter of fact"[397], and that the Panel was entitled to reach its conclusion on the basis of the evidence submitted by India when the United States did not challenge such evidence. Thus, if the United States had intended to challenge the Panel's factual finding regarding the interpretation of the measure, it should have raised such a challenge before the Panel. Not having done so, the United States cannot be permitted to raise indirectly a factual issue in the form of a claim under Article 11 of the DSU on appeal.

2.336 India contends that, as the Appellate Body has "repeatedly held", it will not lightly interfere with the manner in which a panel has weighed the evidence.[398] Moreover, to the extent that the text of the measure at issue is self-evident, and given that the United States never contested India's understanding, no additional explanation by the Panel was required. India recalls that, in several disputes, the Appellate Body has found that the production of the text of a

---

[396] India's appellee's submission, para. 69.

[397] India's appellee's submission, para. 71 (referring to Appellate Body Report, *India – Patents (US)*, para. 66; and Panel Report, *US – Section 301 Trade Act*, para. 7.18).

[398] India's appellee's submission, para. 72 (referring to Appellate Body Report, *Dominican Republic – Import and Sale of Cigarettes*, para. 111).

measure, alone, may be considered adequate to establish a *prima facie* case.[399] India further recalls that, only when the text of the measure is unclear will there be a need to resort to materials that go beyond the text.[400]

2.337 On the basis of the above, India requests the Appellate Body to reject the United States' appeal of the Panel's finding that Section 1677(7)(G) of the US Statute is inconsistent, "as such" and "as applied", with Articles 15.1, 15.2, 15.3, 15.4, and 15.5 of the SCM Agreement.

2.5 Arguments of the Third Participants

2.5.1 Australia

2.338 Australia recalls the Appellate Body's finding in *US – Anti-Dumping and Countervailing Duties (China)* that a public body is "an entity that possesses, exercises, or is vested with governmental authority".[401] Australia further recalls the Appellate Body's finding that "evidence that a government exercises meaningful control over an entity and its conduct may serve, in certain circumstances, as evidence that the relevant entity possesses governmental authority and exercises such authority in the performance of governmental functions".[402] Australia submits that the Appellate Body in that dispute did not go on to consider what might constitute "meaningful control", and in which circumstances it may serve as evidence that an entity possesses governmental authority. Instead, the Appellate Body simply found that majority shareholding was an insufficient basis for a finding that an entity is a "public body". For Australia, this means that determining what characteristics might evince "meaningful control" was left to subsequent disputes.[403]

2.339 Australia supports the Panel's approach to the relevance of "meaningful control" in the inquiry of whether an entity is a "public body", and considers that approach to be consistent with the Appellate Body's guidance on the issue. Australia submits, as the Panel properly found, that government shareholding, combined with other factors indicating the existence of such control, would be sufficient to establish "meaningful control".

2.340 Australia emphasizes that the Appellate Body's statement that a "public body" must be an entity that possesses, exercises, or is vested with governmental authority should not be cited in isolation from the Appellate Body's subsequent

---

[399] India's appellee's submission, para. 73 (referring to Appellate Body Reports, *US – Oil Country Tubular Goods Sunset Reviews*, para. 263; *US – Carbon Steel*, para. 157; *Chile – Price Band System (Article 21.5 –Argentina)*, para. 135; and *Mexico – Anti-Dumping Measures on Rice*, para. 269).

[400] India's appellee's submission, para. 73 (referring to Appellate Body Report, *US – Carbon Steel*, para. 157).

[401] Australia's third participant's submission, para. 9 (quoting Appellate Body Report, *US – Anti-Dumping and Countervailing Duties (China)*, para. 317).

[402] Australia's third participant's submission, para. 10 (quoting Appellate Body Report, *US – Anti-Dumping and Countervailing Duties (China)*, para. 318).

[403] Australia's third participant's submission, para. 11.

statements on this matter. Australia further asserts that the Appellate Body's finding in any individual case may provide guidance regarding the interpretation of Article 1.1(a)(1) of the SCM Agreement, adding that such guidance must be capable of practical application by investigating authorities in different contexts. Australia therefore cautions against a too narrow application of the notion of "governmental authority", and maintains that "a case by case analysis is unavoidable".[404]

2.5.2 Canada

2.341 In Canada's view, the Panel's finding that the USDOC properly determined the NMDC to be a "public body" is correct. Canada maintains that the indicia identified by the Panel in reviewing the USDOC's determination, combined with government ownership, are sufficient for a proper determination that the NMDC is a public body.

2.342 Canada nevertheless supports the United States' request that the Appellate Body clarify the interpretation of "public body" given by the Panel. Canada submits that "an entity controlled by a government, for example through whole or majority ownership or shareholding, should constitute a 'public body' within the meaning of Article 1.1(a)(1)" of the SCM Agreement.[405] According to Canada, this interpretation is consistent with the ordinary meaning of the term "public body", the context of Article 1.1(a)(1), and the object and purpose of the SCM Agreement. Moreover, it also ensures that the disciplines of the SCM Agreement are given a broad enough scope in terms of entities to which they apply.

2.343 Canada submits that an investigating authority may, in appropriate circumstances, use prices other than in-country private prices as benchmarks for assessing the adequacy of remuneration for government-provided goods. Such prices may include those constructed on the basis of production costs or world market prices.[406] Canada highlights, however, the statement of the Appellate Body in *US – Softwood Lumber IV* that, where an investigating authority relies on out-of-country benchmarks, it must proceed in a way that ensures that "the resulting benchmark relates or refers to, or is connected with, prevailing market conditions in the country of provision, and must reflect price, quality, availability, marketability, transportation and other conditions of purchase or sale".[407]

2.344 With regard to the use of "as delivered" out-of-country benchmarks to assess the adequacy of remuneration in respect of iron ore provided by the

---

[404] Australia's third participant's submission, para. 25.

[405] Canada's third participant's submission, para. 4.

[406] Canada's third participant's submission, para. 22 (referring to Appellate Body Report, *US – Softwood Lumber IV*, para. 106).

[407] Canada's third participant's submission, para. 23 (quoting Appellate Body Report, *US – Softwood Lumber IV*, para. 106).

NMDC, Canada does not take a position as to whether the USDOC was entitled to use such prices in the underlying countervailing duty investigation at issue. Canada contends, however, that "the presence of actual transactions between exporters in the benchmark country and purchasers in the country of provision, as well as relevant statements made by market participants, may support the use of out-of-country benchmarks on an as delivered basis."[408]

2.345 Canada submits that there is no obligation in Article 2.1 of the SCM Agreement to compare enterprises that receive a subsidy with other similarly situated entities to establish specificity. In Canada's view, Article 2.1 is not a non-discrimination obligation. Canada states that it agrees with the Panel that what makes a subsidy specific pursuant to Article 2.1 is that it is provided only to an enterprise, an industry, or group thereof, that represents a sufficiently discrete segment of the economy. This determination, Canada adds, "does not involve or require the establishment of sub-groups or pairs of similarly-situated entities, resulting in a comparison of subsidy recipients versus similarly-situated eligible companies that do not receive the subsidy".[409] Such an interpretation, Canada maintains, is not supported by the text of Article 2.1.

2.346 Canada considers that the Panel's finding in this dispute is also consistent with the panel's finding in *US – Softwood Lumber IV*, which stated that "Article 2 speaks of the use by a limited number of certain enterprises or the predominant use by certain enterprises, not of the use by a limited number of certain *eligible* enterprises".[410] While acknowledging that a comparison may be required under Article 2.1(c) to determine *de facto* specificity, Canada considers that India mischaracterizes the nature of the comparative analysis that is required. According to Canada, the requirement for comparison in Article 2.1(c) is expressed through the relational concepts in the second and third of the four factors listed in the second sentence, because these factors entail a comparison between sub-groupings of recipients of the same subsidy. Canada does not consider, however, that the first factor of Article 2.1(c) involves a comparison with entities that do not receive the subsidy. In Canada's view, the text of Article 2.1 of the SCM Agreement makes it clear that, where a subsidy is limited to "certain enterprises", it is specific.

2.347 Canada submits that it is possible for an investigating authority to draw adverse inferences in a manner consistent with Article 12.7 of the SCM Agreement when using the "facts available". In Canada's view, the choice of unfavourable facts may be justified where an interested party is aware of the evidence on the record and where it withholds necessary information. This is because it may be inferred that, if it had more favourable information, the interested party could have provided it to the investigating authority in its own

[408] Canada's third participant's submission, para. 24.
[409] Canada's third participant's submission, para. 31.
[410] Canada's third participant's submission, para. 32 (quoting Panel Report, *US – Softwood Lumber IV*, para. 7.116 (emphasis original)).

best interest. Canada submits that, while an investigating authority must carry out its task in a reasonable and objective way, it must also have discretion in deciding what is necessary to conduct its investigation effectively. In that regard, it should be borne in mind that the frequency and extent of gaps in the record and the need for those gaps to be filled by drawing inferences that may be adverse will depend largely on the conduct of the interested party in question. In Canada's view, a reasonable and objective investigating authority may find that a party should not benefit from a lack of cooperation and use facts on the record in a way that is not favourable to that party.

2.348 Finally, Canada states that, subject to the protection of due process rights for interested parties, neither Article 21.1 nor Article 21.2 of the SCM Agreement limits the review of the need for continued imposition of the duty to the consideration of previously examined subsidization.[411]

2.5.3 China

2.349 China submits that, in finding that the USDOC correctly determined the NMDC to be a "public body", the Panel erred in its interpretation and application of Article 1.1(a)(1) of the SCM Agreement, and failed to make an objective assessment of the matter before it, as required under Article 11 of the DSU. China therefore agrees with India that the Appellate Body should reverse the Panel's finding upholding the USDOC's determination that the NMDC is a "public body", and that the Appellate Body should also complete the legal analysis and find that the USDOC's determination is inconsistent with the Article 1.1(a)(1) of the SCM Agreement. Furthermore, China submits that the Appellate Body should reject the United States' request to clarify the legal standard adopted in *US – Anti-Dumping and Countervailing Duties (China)*.

2.350 China argues that the Panel's interpretation and application of Article 1.1(a)(1) of the SCM Agreement would be tantamount to reversing the Appellate Body's interpretation in *US – Anti-Dumping and Countervailing Duties (China)*. China submits that the Panel correctly noted the Appellate Body's statement in *US – Anti-Dumping and Countervailing Duties (China)* that "evidence that a government exercises meaningful control over an entity and its conduct may serve, in certain circumstances, as evidence that the relevant entity possesses governmental authority and exercises such authority in the performance of governmental functions".[412] However, the Panel went on to find on the basis of that statement that "a combination of government shareholding plus other factors indicative of control may suffice" for purposes of establishing that an entity is a public body.[413] According to China, the Panel "took a single sentence out of the Appellate Body's holding and improperly elevated it into a stand-alone

---

[411] Canada's opening statement at the oral hearing.
[412] China's third participant's submission, para. 69 (quoting Panel Report, para. 7.80).
[413] China's third participant's submission, para. 69 (quoting Panel Report, para. 7.81).

standard".[414] More specifically, the Panel "latched on to the term 'meaningful control'", and "improperly equated the mere 'existence' of what the Panel considers to constitute 'meaningful control' with the 'exercise' of 'meaningful control'".[415] China submits that it is evident from the Appellate Body's finding that "the subject of the 'control' has to be the 'entity' *and* its 'conduct'".[416] Moreover, the Appellate Body "expressly declined to make 'meaningful control' a hard and fast rule", and emphasized that only "in certain circumstances" "may" the exercise of meaningful control serve as evidence of governmental authority.[417]

2.351 China further argues that "meaningful control" is only one piece of possible evidence that is relevant to a "public body" determination, and that there could well be other evidence rebutting the existence of governmental authority. As the Appellate Body found, an investigating authority must "give due consideration to all relevant characteristics of the entity" and "avoid focusing exclusively or unduly on any single characteristic".[418] China submits that the Panel reduced these requirements to a "simple test", disregarding whether there were "manifold" indicia of control, or whether such control has been exercised in a meaningful way.[419]

2.352 China alleges that the evidence cited by the Panel does not support its finding that control is "meaningful". The Panel's finding, that government ownership and government involvement in the selection of the board of directors of the entity prove "meaningful control", "requires several logical leaps".[420] China agrees with India that "shareholding and appointing directors are merely two sides of the same coin"[421], and submits that one key aspect of a shareholder's rights is its voting right, which includes the right to elect the board of directors. Moreover, the Panel's reasoning leads to "absurd results"[422], because a government-owned entity, or even an entity in which a government holds a non-controlling but substantial percentage of shares, will always be held to be a public body, unless its government shareholder waives altogether the right to elect directors and any other shareholders' rights. The Panel's approach thus implies that any exercise of rights inherent to government ownership and control would be sufficient to determine that an entity is a public body. In China's view,

---

414 China's third participant's submission, para. 69.

415 China's third participant's submission, paras. 76 and 77.

416 China's third participant's submission, paras. 77 and 78 (quoting Appellate Body Report, *US – Anti-Dumping and Countervailing Duties (China)*, para. 318). (emphasis original)

417 China's third participant's submission, para. 78.

418 China's third participant's submission, para. 79 (quoting Appellate Body Report, *US – Anti-Dumping and Countervailing Duties (China)*, para. 319).

419 China's third participant's submission, para. 80 (referring to Appellate Body Report, *US – Anti-Dumping and Countervailing Duties (China)*, para. 319).

420 China's third participant's submission, para. 81.

421 China's third participant's submission, para. 82 (quoting India's appellant's submission, para. 291).

422 China's third participant's submission, para. 83.

the Panel's approach cannot be reconciled with the Appellate Body's interpretation in *US – Anti-Dumping and Countervailing Duties (China)* that neither government ownership nor control can in itself be sufficient to establish that an entity is a public body.

2.353 With respect to the United States' request that the Appellate Body clarify the legal standard adopted in *US – Anti-Dumping and Countervailing Duties (China)*, China "finds it puzzling" that the United States asks for clarification on certain aspects of the Panel's analysis so as to make that analysis consistent with an interpretation that was neither applied by the Panel nor by the USDOC.[423] China notes that the Panel "explicitly disclaimed any reliance" on the interpretation proposed by the United States that a "public body" should be defined as an entity that is controlled by the government such that the government can use that entity's resources as its own.[424] For China, the United States' request is of no apparent utility for the ultimate purpose of prompt dispute settlement.

2.354 China argues that the arguments of the United States before the Panel, and the interpretation that it advocates for in this appeal, show that the United States is requesting the Appellate Body to "reverse itself".[425] The United States argued before the Panel that India's "public body" claims were based "on an erroneous interpretation".[426] According to China, by "erroneous interpretation" the United States was referring to the Appellate Body's interpretation in *US – Anti-Dumping and Countervailing Duties (China)*. In China's view, "it is not possible to clarify an 'erroneous' interpretation".[427]

2.355 China notes the United States' request for clarification that "where sufficient government control over an entity exists [...] it is not necessary also to find that the entity exercises 'governmental authority'".[428] Thus, China contends that the United States is asking the Appellate Body to reject "the cornerstone" of its interpretation and adopt instead the "control-based theory" of the United States.[429] In China's opinion, the "new" control-based standard differs in no meaningful way from the "old" control-based standard advocated by the United States and rejected by the Appellate Body in *US – Anti-Dumping and Countervailing Duties (China)*.[430] China recalls that the United States argued in that case that entities controlled by the government are "public bodies", and that government ownership is indicative of control. In this dispute, the United States

---

[423] China's third participant's submission, para. 98.

[424] China's third participant's submission, para. 97 (referring to Panel Report, fn 260 to para. 7.89).

[425] China's third participant's submission, para. 99.

[426] China's third participant's submission, para. 100 (referring to United States' first written submission to the Panel, section IV.A.1).

[427] China's third participant's submission, para. 100.

[428] China's third participant's submission, para. 101 (quoting United States' other appellant's submission, para. 23).

[429] China's third participant's submission, para. 102.

[430] China's third participant's submission, para. 103.

explains that "government control of an entity – and therefore its resources – is central to the proper interpretation of 'public body,' for in such a situation, when the entity transfers resources, it is transferring the government's resources".[431] However, the government's ability to use an entity's resources as its own is the necessary result of government ownership or control over the entity. China contends, therefore, that the United States' control-based standard is inconsistent with the legal standard adopted by the Appellate Body in *US – Anti-Dumping and Countervailing Duties (China)*.

2.356 China argues that the Panel acted inconsistently with Article 11 of the DSU in its assessment of the USDOC's findings that the NMDC is a "public body". In support of its contention, China submits that: (i) the USDOC's determinations do not reflect the legal standard articulated by the Appellate Body in *US – Anti-Dumping and Countervailing Duties (China)*; and that (ii) the Panel's review of the USDOC determinations is based on *ex post facto* explanations.

2.357 China asserts that "[i]t is evident on the face of the USDOC's public body determinations that the USDOC applied the same ownership/control test that was rejected by the Appellate Body in *US – Antidumping and Countervailing Duties (China)*".[432] China submits that the USDOC "expressly confirmed" this in the 2007 administrative review.[433] Moreover, the USDOC "explicitly disavowed" any obligation to look beyond government ownership.[434] In support of this assertion, China quotes the USDOC's statement in the 2007 administrative review that "[i]t is the [USDOC's] *practice* that majority ownership of an input supplier qualifies it as a government authority".[435]

2.358 China also submits that the USDOC explained, in the 2007 AR Issues and Decision Memorandum[436], that information regarding the composition of the board of directors of the NMDC "only bolsters" its prior determinations that the NMDC is a public body.[437] Therefore, the USDOC did not apply the legal standard articulated by the Appellate Body in *US – Anti-Dumping and Countervailing Duties (China).* China also observes that the determinations at issue predate the aforementioned Appellate Body report and that the United States expressly represented to the Panel that the USDOC "applied *a simple*

[431] China's third participant's submission, para. 104 (quoting United States' other appellant's submission, para. 40).

[432] China's third participant's submission, para. 20.

[433] China's third participant's submission, para. 25 (referring to 2007 AR Issues and Decision Memorandum, Analysis of Comment 10, pp. 43-45).

[434] China's third participant's submission, para. 26.

[435] China's third participant's submission, para. 26 (quoting 2007 AR Issues and Decision Memorandum, Analysis of Comment 10, pp. 43-45). (emphasis added by China)

[436] See *supra*, fn 70.

[437] China's third participant's submission, para. 26 (referring to 2007 AR Issues and Decision Memorandum, Analysis of Comment 10, pp. 43-45).

control test in the determinations at issue in this dispute".[438] Hence, China maintains that, by its own admission, the USDOC's entire rationale for the "public body" finding was majority government ownership.

2.359 China contends that the Panel ought to have assessed the consistency of the USDOC's finding with Article 1.1(a)(1) of the SCM Agreement on the basis of the USDOC's own explanations. Instead, the Panel relied on *ex post facto* explanations submitted by the United States and on the Panel's *de novo* consideration of the evidence on the record. China submits that, under Article 11 of the DSU, a panel reviewing an investigating authority's determinations is required to carry out an "'in-depth' examination of the 'explanations given by the authority in its published report'", and abstain from conducting a *de novo* review.[439] China argues, therefore, that the Panel acted inconsistently with its obligations under Article 11 of the DSU.

2.360 China notes that the USDOC's "public body" analysis is "extremely brief" and that, in the 2004 administrative review, the USDOC's entire rationale was limited to a single sentence.[440] Thus, the USDOC determined the NMDC to be a "public body" because it "is a mining company governed by the GOI's Ministry of Steel and that the GOI holds 98 percent of its shares".[441] China submits that the Panel attached great significance to the USDOC's statement that the NMDC was "governed by" the GOI, in spite of the fact that the USDOC provided no explanation for this statement in its determinations. China recalls the United States' explanations to the Panel that the USDOC's determination that the NMDC was "governed by" the GOI was based on: (i) evidence on the record demonstrating the GOI's heavy involvement in the selection of the NMDC's board of directors; and (ii) the statement posted on the NMDC's own website that the latter was under the "administrative control" of the GOI. In China's opinion, these constitute *ex post facto* explanations.

2.361 With respect to the GOI's involvement in the appointment of the NMDC's board of directors, China contends that, although the 2004 GOI Verification Report was cited in the preliminary determination of the 2004 administrative review, the USDOC never discussed how this fact supported the factual finding that the NMDC was "governed by" the GOI, or its relevance to the legal issue being investigated. Nevertheless, the Panel concluded that government involvement in the selection of the board of directors was "'extremely relevant' to the issue of 'meaningful control'", despite the lack of explanation in the determination.[442] Regarding the statement from the website of the NMDC that the latter was under the "administrative control" of the GOI, China observes that

---

[438] China's third participant's submission, para. 27 (quoting United States' response to Panel question No. 42). (emphasis added by China)

[439] China's third participant's submission, para. 30 (quoting Appellate Body Report, *US – Softwood Lumber VI (Article 21.5 – Canada)*, para. 93).

[440] China's third participant's submission, para. 31.

[441] China's third participant's submission, para. 31 (quoting Panel Report, para. 7.81).

[442] China's third participant's submission, para. 38.

the United States admitted before the Panel that this term was not used in any of the USDOC's determinations. Yet, the Panel found the said statement to be providing additional support for a finding that an entity is under the "meaningful control" of the government, despite there being no evidence that it was providing any support for the USDOC's determinations.

2.362 According to China, the Panel's findings suggest that, if an investigating authority's rationalization is not clear (i.e. not reasoned and adequate), it is appropriate for a Member, through the course of dispute settlement, to explain that rationalization on an *ex post basis*. In China's opinion, such an approach is "flatly inconsistent" with the Appellate Body's finding that an investigating authority must "provide a reasoned and adequate explanation for its conclusions".[443] China also claims that the Panel's approach would allow, and in fact encourage, investigating authorities to use vague and broad language in their determinations in order to maintain maximum flexibility in the case that they are called upon later to defend those determinations in dispute settlement.

2.363 China further notes that the Panel made no mention of the United States' "express acknowledgment"[444] that the USDOC had applied a "simple control" test in the determination at issue. Instead, relying on the United States' *ex post facto* explanations, the Panel found that the USDOC's findings "effectively amounted to a determination that the NMDC was under the *'meaningful control'* of the GOI".[445] China maintains that this finding by the Panel was based principally on the GOI's involvement in the selection of directors for the NMDC. However, the USDOC's determination relied on government ownership, and the information regarding the GOI's involvement in the board of directors served only to corroborate the USDOC's finding that the NMDC was a public body. Therefore, China contends that the Panel engaged in a *de novo* review, by "attributing weight to the evidence cited by the United States in a manner evidently contrary to the weight attributed to that evidence by the USDOC itself".[446]

2.364 In relation to the Panel's "as such" finding under Article 12.7 of the SCM Agreement, China submits that the core interpretative issue is whether Article 12.7 imposes similar disciplines to those in Article 6.8 of the Anti-Dumping Agreement, read in the light of its Annex II. In China's view, the Ministerial Declaration on Dispute Settlement Pursuant to the Agreement on Implementation of Article VI of the General Agreement on Tariffs and Trade 1994 or Part V of the Agreement on Subsidies and Countervailing Measures constitutes context for interpreting Article 12.7 of the SCM Agreement, and

[443] China's third participant's submission, para. 43 (quoting Appellate Body Report, *Japan – DRAMs (Korea)*, para. 159).

[444] China's third participant's submission, para. 36.

[445] China's third participant's submission, para. 36 (quoting Panel Report, para. 7.89). (emphasis original)

[446] China's third participant's submission, para. 39.

supports a reading that it should be interpreted in a manner consistent with Article 6.8 of the Anti-Dumping Agreement.[447] Further, China argues that the approach of the Appellate Body in *Mexico – Anti-Dumping Measures on Rice* supports the view that the limitations imposed by Article 12.7 on the use of the "facts available" and the limitations imposed by Article 6.8 of the Anti-Dumping Agreement, read in the light of its Annex II, are one and the same. China finds additional support for this view in the panel reports in *China – Broiler Products*, *China – GOES*, and *China – Autos (US)*.

2.365 In any event, China argues that, even if the standards in Annex II to the Anti-Dumping Agreement do not apply to Article 12.7 of the SCM Agreement, the requirement set out in the Appellate Body report in *US – Softwood Lumber VI (Article 21.5 – Canada)*, that an investigating authority must provide a reasoned and adequate explanation for a determination under Article 12.7, leads to the same conclusion.[448] In particular, China argues that an investigating authority would need to engage in a comparative evaluation of the available evidence and select the most appropriate information in order to be able to provide a "reasoned and adequate explanation" of its determination under Article 12.7.

2.366 In respect of the Panel's "as applied" finding on the use of the highest non-*de minimis* subsidy rate, China submits that the USDOC always uses the highest rate when resorting to the facts available, whereas Article 12.7 does not permit a determination to be based on the worst information available.[449] In China's view, the evidence submitted by India suggests that adverse inferences were used to punish non-cooperation by applying the highest non-*de minimis* subsidy rate. For instance, China points to one Panel exhibit that suggests that the policy objective of using adverse inferences is "to effectuate the purpose of the facts available rule to induce respondents to provide the [USDOC] with complete and accurate information in a timely manner".[450] In China's view, the approach of "punishing" non-cooperation through adverse inferences was rejected by the panel in *China – GOES* and is inconsistent with the obligation in Article 12.7 to engage in an evaluative, comparative assessment to select the most fitting facts available.

2.367 China submits that the United States' appeal of the Panel's finding on cross-cumulation "has no merit and should be rejected".[451] China maintains that

---

[447] China's third participant's submission, para. 127 (referring to Ministerial Declaration on Dispute Settlement Pursuant to the Agreement on Implementation of Article VI of the General Agreement on Tariffs and Trade 1994 or Part V of the Agreement on Subsidies and Countervailing Measures, adopted by the Trade Negotiations Committee on 15 December 1993).

[448] China's third participant's submission, paras. 143 and 146 (quoting Appellate Body Report, *US – Softwood Lumber VI (Article 21.5 – Canada)*, para. 93).

[449] China's third participant's submission, paras. 148 and 149.

[450] China's third participant's submission, paras. 152 and 153 (quoting 2006 AR Issues and Decision Memorandum, p. 7).

[451] China's third participant's submission, para. 156.

the Panel correctly interpreted Article 15.3, as well as Articles 15.1, 15.2, 15.4, and 15.5 of the SCM Agreement. China recalls the United States' argument that Article 15.3 is silent on the issue of cumulative assessment in cases where there are simultaneous anti-dumping and countervailing duty investigations[452], and contends that such an interpretation would lead to "absurd results".[453] China notes that Article 15.3 does not address the situation in which multiple countervailing duty investigations are not initiated simultaneously. Thus, following the United States' logic, an investigating authority would be free to cumulatively assess the effects of imports in asynchronous countervailing duty investigations without having to fulfil the conditions laid down in Article 15.3 with regard to cumulative assessment.

2.368 China further maintains that the United States' interpretation does not comport with the immediate context of Article 15.3 – i.e. Articles 15.1, 15.2, 15.4, and 15.5 of the SCM Agreement. China contends that these provisions consistently refer to "subsidized imports", rather than "unfairly traded" imports, which is a term that has no basis in the covered agreements.[454] Furthermore, Article 15.5 of the SCM Agreement prohibits an authority from attributing to the subsidized imports the injury caused by factors "other than the subsidized imports", and dumped imports are one of such factors. In addition, China notes that the United States has no response to the Panel's detailed analysis regarding Articles 15.1, 15.2, 15.4, and 15.5 of the SCM Agreement. In China's view, therefore, the "silence" in Article 15.3 asserted by the United States must be understood in its context, and cannot be interpreted to allow cross-cumulation.

2.369 China argues that, contrary to the United States' assertion[455], Article VI:6(a) of the GATT 1994 does not speak to the permissibility of cross-cumulation. Rather, the conjunction "or" between "dumping" and "subsidization" suggests that the effects thereof are to be considered separately. Moreover, the ordinary meaning of the phrase "as the case may be" indicates that it is used when referring to one of two alternatives. China recalls that, pursuant to the General Interpretative Note to Annex 1A Incorporating the GATT into the WTO Agreement, in the event of conflict between a provision of the GATT 1994 and a provision of another agreement in Annex 1A, the latter prevails. Thus, China contends, even if Article VI:6(a) of the GATT 1994 were to be understood as permitting cross-cumulation, it would conflict with Article 15.3 of the SCM Agreement, and the latter should prevail.

2.370 Finally, China submits that the meaning and scope of Section 1677(7)(G) of the US Statute is "crystal clear" on its face.[456] By using the term "shall", China

452 China's third participant's submission, para. 167 (referring to United States' other appellant's submission, paras. 101 and 102).
453 China's third participant's submission, para. 168.
454 China's third participant's submission, para. 175 (referring to Panel Report, para. 7.346).
455 China's third participant's submission, para. 170 (referring to United States' other appellant's submission, para. 110).
456 China's third participant's submission, para. 160.

argues, this measure requires the USITC to engage in "cross-cumulation" when certain conditions are met. Given that the text of the measure itself suffices to clarify the scope and meaning of the measure, China submits that it was not necessary for the Panel to provide further reasoning for the conclusion it reached. China further contends that the United States has not provided any explanation for its assertion that "the statute on its face is not definitive".[457] China highlights that the United States had not asserted that the USITC had foregone cross-cumulation in any investigation where the conditions set out in the statute were met. For these reasons, China submits that the United States has failed to establish that the Panel acted inconsistently with Article 11 of the DSU.

2.5.4 European Union

2.371 The European Union notes that the requirements set out in Article 6.2 of the DSU for panel requests serve not only to define the scope of a dispute, but also to meet the requirements of due process. In respect of the fourth requirement in Article 6.2 of the DSU, namely, to provide a brief summary of the legal basis of the complaint, it is not enough that the "legal basis of the complaint" is summarily identified; such summary must also be "sufficient to present the problem clearly".[458] According to the European Union, the Appellate Body has clarified that, pursuant to this requirement, the summary must explain succinctly how or why the measure at issue is considered by the complaining Member to be violating the WTO obligation in question. An assessment of compliance with this requirement obliges a panel to scrutinize carefully the panel request, read as a whole, in the light of attendant circumstances, and on the basis of the language used. The European Union argues, therefore, that a party's submissions during the panel proceedings cannot cure a defect in a panel request, and the ability of a respondent to defend itself does not mean that a panel request complies with Article 6.2 of the DSU.

2.372 The European Union contends that an "objective reader" would have understood the language in India's panel request to mean that there was a violation of Article 11 of the SCM Agreement because the investigations were not initiated or conducted to determine the effects of new subsidies included in the administrative reviews.[459] According to the European Union, the requirement about the sufficiency of the evidence to initiate a review in accordance with Article 11.2 of the SCM Agreement is different from the claim that no investigation was initiated. Thus, India failed to present the problem clearly in its panel request.

---

[457] China's third participant's submission, para. 162 (quoting United States' other appellant's submission, paras. 126).

[458] European Union's third participant's submission, para. 132 (quoting Appellate Body Report, *Korea – Dairy*, para. 120).

[459] European Union's third participant's submission, para. 139.

2.373 With respect to the term "public body" in Article 1.1(a)(1) of the SCM Agreement, the European Union recalls that the Appellate Body report in *US – Anti-Dumping and Countervailing Duties (China)* was unconditionally accepted by the parties to that dispute, as required by Article 17.14 of the DSU, and is therefore now part of the *acquis* of the WTO dispute settlement. In the view of the European Union, this implies that, in the absence of cogent reasons, the same legal question will be resolved in the same way in a subsequent case. However, the European Union cautions against considering any one particular statement out of the context of the whole of the Appellate Body's analysis.

2.374 Regarding India's argument that a "public body" must always be able to entrust or direct a "private body", the European Union does not consider that such a capacity is an essential characteristic of a public body. The European Union argues that the Appellate Body did not directly address the question of whether or not a public body *must always* have the capacity to be the *source* of entrustment or direction, and it did not make any finding to that effect. Instead, the Appellate Body merely concluded that the capacity to entrust or direct a private body is a "common"[460] characteristic of both the government, in the narrow sense, and a "public body". Hence, it is possible that "common" means "frequent", as opposed to India's apparent understanding that it means "shared".[461] According to the European Union, the Appellate Body was making the point that "a public body, unlike a private body, *could be* the *source* of governmental authority *expressed in terms of entrustment or direction*, and this observation supported the Appellate Body's analysis".[462] The European Union also submits that the Appellate Body should take into account the "serious difficulties" that an investigating authority might encounter in obtaining evidence demonstrating that a particular public body would have the lawful authority, without acting *ultra vires*, to entrust or direct a private body.[463]

2.375 The European Union disagrees with India that the Panel substituted the standard articulated by the Appellate Body in *US – Anti-Dumping and Countervailing Duties (China)* with a standard of "meaningful control". In the opinion of the European Union, the Panel's findings are based on the Appellate Body's findings in that dispute.

2.376 The European Union recalls India's claim that the Panel refused to consider an alleged admission by the United States in *US – Anti-Dumping and Countervailing Duties (China)* that the USDOC found a mining company in which the government owned 98% of the shares, and which was governed by India's Ministry of Steel, to be a public body, without reference to any more factors. The European Union, however, does not see any additional admission in

---

[460] European Union's third participant's submission, para. 25 (quoting Appellate Body Report, *US – Anti-Dumping and Countervailing Duties (China)*, para. 294).

[461] European Union's third participant's submission, para. 25.

[462] European Union's third participant's submission, para. 26. (emphases original)

[463] European Union's third participant's submission, para. 30.

that statement, noting that the Panel relied on the same fact as stated in the alleged admission in reaching its finding. Therefore, the European Union considers that the Appellate Body should reject India's argument, without it being necessary to consider the circumstances in which "admissions" in current or past DSU proceedings might have specific legal consequences.[464]

2.377 With respect to India's arguments that the Panel engaged in *ex post* rationalization, the European Union submits that a measure may be defended by referring not only to the text of the measure at issue, but also to supporting documents (such as an issues and decisions memorandum), as well as, depending on the circumstances, the record itself. The European Union further submits that it would be impossible for an investigating authority to "lift the entire record into the text of the measure at issue".[465] Finally, the European Union disagrees with India's submission that shareholding and directorships are be equated. The European Union considers that the appointment of directors is an additional indicator, "over and above shareholding", to be taken into account together with other factors when inquiring into whether an entity is a public body.[466]

2.378 Turning to the issue of financial contribution, the European Union agrees with the United States that the grant of mining rights for iron ore and coal does amount to the "provision" of a good within the meaning of Article 1.1(a)(1)(iii) of the SCM Agreement. In the European Union's view, India has not established any meaningful distinction between the facts of *US – Softwood Lumber IV* and the facts of this case. Furthermore, the European Union considers that the rights in question are akin to intellectual property rights and therefore caught by the term "goods or services" in Article 1.1(a)(1)(iii). In the same way, the European Union notes, the Appellate Body has found that Article 1.1(a)(1)(iii) may also capture a lease of land and the right to exclusive use of a runway.[467]

2.379 The European Union further considers that, with respect to the SDF loans, India has not identified any legal error in the Panel Report. The European Union contends that Article 1.1(a)(1)(i) does not provide that there must always be a "direct" transfer between a government or public body and a recipient, but "merely that there must be a government practice that involves (and in this sense 'implies' or 'entails') a direct transfer".[468] The European Union agrees with the Panel that the flow of funds from the JPC to the recipient, following a decision of the SDF Managing Committee, may be characterized as a direct transfer, and that the overall mechanism may be characterized as a government practice that involves a direct transfer. In addition, there may be some overlap between

---

464 European Union's third participant's submission, para. 32.

465 European Union's third participant's submission, para. 33.

466 European Union's third participant's submission, para. 34.

467 European Union's third participant's submission, para. 41 (referring to Appellate Body Report, *EC and certain member States – Large Civil Aircraft*, para. 967).

468 European Union's third participant's submission, para. 37.

subparagraphs (i) and (iv). The European Union argues that allowing for such flexibility is an appropriate approach to the interpretation and application of these provisions. The European Union also does not consider that there is complete overlap between subparagraphs (i) and (iv), since subparagraph (iv) would continue to cover the case of entrustment or direction in which the initial source of the funds plays no role in the analysis. In addition, its view that the role of the SDF Managing Committee, as decision maker, is even stronger than the role that would be played by the government in the case of entrustment or direction. The European Union thus considers that, just because the fact pattern might be reasonably classified under subparagraph (iv), this does not invalidate the analysis under subparagraph (i).

2.380 The European Union addresses interpretative issues concerning Article 14(d) of the SCM Agreement that arise from India's appeal of the Panel's findings in relation to India's "as such" claim against the US benchmarking mechanism. First, the European Union contends that India's argument that Article 14(d) of the SCM Agreement requires the adequacy of remuneration for government-provided goods to be assessed from the perspective of the government provider is fundamentally flawed. Contrary to India's assertion on appeal, the perspective of the government provider is not dispositive in determining the existence of "benefit" under Article 1.1(b) of the SCM Agreement, or its amount, in accordance with Article 14(d) of the SCM Agreement. Instead, under Article 14(d), the adequacy of remuneration for government-provided goods must be assessed by applying the "market standard", i.e. "whether the recipient of the financial contribution ... is 'better off' in comparison with what such a recipient would have paid in that marketplace, absent the financial contribution".[469]

2.381 With regard to India's claims concerning the use of government prices as benchmarks for assessing the adequacy of remuneration for government-provided goods under Article 14(d), the European Union recalls the Appellate Body's statement, in *Canada – Aircraft*, that whether a "benefit" within the meaning of the SCM Agreement exists should be assessed by reference to what the recipient would have obtained from the market, absent the government's financial contribution.[470] The government price at issue therefore does not form part of the "prevailing market conditions" under Article 14(d). However, the fact of government intervention in the market in question does not imply that there are no "market" conditions in the sense of Article 14(d), or that independent operators' prices in that market must be disregarded. Rather, "[o]nly those government interventions that distort prices" should be considered as a basis for

---

469 European Union's third participant's submission, para. 86.

470 European Union's third participant's submission, para. 94 (referring to Appellate Body Report, *Canada – Aircraft*, para. 157).

finding that "market" conditions do not exist.[471] The European Union submits that, "whereas the government price in question cannot form part of the relevant counterfactual to determine the existence or quantum of 'benefit', the existence of other government prices for the same or a similar good or service cannot be disregarded automatically".[472] The assessment as to whether the use of those government prices would render the Article 14(d) circular has to be made on a case-by-case basis.

2.382 Turning to the use of out-of-country benchmarks for the purpose of assessing the adequacy of remuneration for government-provided goods, the European Union submits that the use of out-of-country benchmarks to determine the existence and quantum of benefit is not prohibited under the SCM Agreement. This is confirmed by the Appellate Body's finding, in *US – Softwood Lumber IV*, that Article 14(d) does not require the use of private prices in the country of provision as benchmarks in every situation. Rather, Article 14(d) "requires that the method selected for calculating the benefit must relate or refer to, or be connected with, the prevailing market conditions in the country of provision, and must reflect price, quality, availability, marketability, transportation and other conditions of purchase or sale, as required by Article 14(d)".[473] Further, the European Union observes the finding of the panel, in *US – Anti-Dumping and Countervailing Duties (China)*, that the use of a benchmark other than in-country private prices was, in that case, made necessary by the fact that the relevant market in the country of provision was distorted, and that in such a situation "Article 14(d) require[s] an investigating authority to do its best to identify a benchmark that approximates the market conditions that *would* prevail in the absence of the distortion."[474] Thus, the use of out-of-country benchmarks when in-country benchmarks are not appropriate would not appear to be inconsistent with Article 14(d) of the SCM Agreement.[475]

2.383 Turning to India's claim concerning the mandatory use of "as delivered" benchmarks under the US benchmarking mechanism, the European Union submits that, once the proper benchmark price has been identified, the comparison required to determine the existence and amount of benefit has to be made at the same level of trade. If a government price is set on an *ex works* basis, and the benchmark is set on an "as delivered" basis, it would not be inconsistent with either Article 14(d) or Articles 19.3 and 19.4 of the SCM Agreement to adjust the government price and the benchmark price in order to make a comparison between delivered prices. In the European Union's view,

---

[471] European Union's third participant's submission, para. 97 (referring to Appellate Body Report, *US – Softwood Lumber IV*, para. 93).

[472] European Union's third participant's submission, para. 98.

[473] European Union's third participant's submission, para. 103 (quoting Appellate Body Report, *US – Softwood Lumber IV*, paras. 87 and 96).

[474] European Union's third participant's submission, para. 104 (quoting Panel Report, *US – Anti-Dumping and Countervailing Duties (China)*, para. 10.187).

[475] European Union's third participant's submission, paras. 105 and 106.

such an adjustment would not seek to reproduce the "conditions of sale" in the country of provision in accordance with Article 14(d). Rather, such adjustments would ensure that, once the benchmark price has been found, the comparison between the government price and that benchmark price is properly made at the same level of trade. In addition, the European Union contends that, where the product in question is not available in the Indian market but for the provision of goods that is the subject of the investigation, and the Indian customer would therefore have to purchase the product from somewhere else and pay a delivered price, if India intervenes to secure the production and provision of the product in India at a cheaper delivered price, then the difference between the two prices constitutes a benefit. The European Union further submits that it may be appropriate to compare government and benchmark prices on an "as delivered" basis in other situations where in-country prices are not available, such as where in-country prices are distorted.[476]

2.384 The European Union does not consider that the Panel erred in its analysis of *de facto* specificity. According to the European Union, if the government chooses a form of measure that is inherently *de facto* specific, "that does not provide an excuse for it to avoid the disciplines of the SCM Agreement".[477] The European Union notes that, if the text of legislation explicitly limited access to a subsidy to enterprises using iron ore, this would be covered by Article 2.1(a). Similarly, if the access to the subsidy is limited to such enterprises, then this is clearly a *de facto* specific subsidy, even if there were no such legislative text. The European Union further considers that the first factor of Article 2.1(c) can also capture instances in which the users of the subsidy programme do not form a subset of certain enterprises. Moreover, the European Union argues that subsidies for an entire sector, as opposed to one firm within a sector, are normally far more likely to be of particular concern to trading partners. The European Union considers that India's argument, that such subsidies fall outside the scope of the SCM Agreement as long as the programme is not explicitly written down, "is highly implausible and would create a substantial breach in the disciplines of the SCM Agreement".[478]

2.385 The European Union argues that whether a WTO Member has acted inconsistently with Article 12.7 of the SCM Agreement through the use of certain inferences depends on a specific examination of all the surrounding facts and procedural context, thus making such claims more amenable to resolution on an "as applied" basis rather than on an "as such" basis. In the European Union's view, inferences are a routine and necessary part of all economic law determinations, and that how attenuated an inference may be is a function of all the surrounding facts and consequences, including the procedural context, such as whether questions have been properly put to the interested parties and the

---

476 European Union's third participant's submission, paras. 112-116.
477 European Union's third participant's submission, para. 44.
478 European Union's third participant's submission, para. 47.

opportunity afforded to respond and comment. Thus, the more uncooperative a party, the more attenuated and extensive the inferences that it may be reasonable to draw. Although an inference drawn from a fact or the procedural context may be "adverse" to an interested party, it is impossible to know so, since such inferences are drawn where information representing the real situation of the interested party is missing. The European Union adds that an investigating authority must draw the inference that best fits the facts on the record, rather than an inference solely on the basis that it may be "adverse" to an interested party.

2.386 According to the European Union, the measure at issue is not inconsistent with Article 12.7 of the SCM Agreement because it does not prevent the investigating authority from conforming with the legal standard set out in *Mexico – Anti-Dumping Measures on Rice*, namely, by not precluding all substantiated facts on the record from being taken into account, and by not permitting the use of "facts available" that do not reasonably replace the missing information. Further, the Panel was correct to find that India failed to make a *prima facie* case under its "as applied" claims.

2.387 With regard to the new subsidy allegations, the European Union observes that the US administrative reviews subject of this claim combined both a prospective element (i.e. the rate of duty to be applied going forward), and a retrospective element (i.e. the amount of duty to be finally collected with respect to the past). According to the European Union, the prospective elements of the administrative reviews are subject to the disciplines of Article 21 of the SCM Agreement, while the retrospective elements are subject to Article 19.3 of the SCM Agreement.

2.388 The European Union does not agree with India that Article 11 applies to review investigations initiated pursuant to Article 21.2 of the SCM Agreement. At the same time, the European Union notes that the SCM Agreement is not based on an absolute definitional distinction between the term "investigation" and the term "review". The two terms are not defined in the SCM Agreement, and the European Union considers it "simply wrong" to posit that any provision using the term "investigation" is necessarily limited to original investigations.[479]

2.389 While acknowledging that new subsidies could be brought within the scope of reviews, the European Union emphasizes that Members should not be permitted to use the instrument of Article 21.2 administrative review proceedings in so broad a manner as to circumvent the disciplines governing original investigations, as set out in Article 11. The European Union suggests that, if the original subsidy and the alleged new subsidy are very different, then

[479] European Union's third participant's submission, para. 66.

it may be that the assessment of such new subsidies calls for the initiation of an Article 11 investigation.[480]

2.390 For the European Union, the consultation obligation prescribed in Article 13.1 of the SCM Agreement must apply with respect to each new subsidy. This means that, if the same subsidy or subsidy programme that was the subject of an original investigation is subsequently the subject of a review investigation, there is no obligation to re-consult. However, if a new subsidy is brought within the scope of a review investigation, either following a request from the applicant or in special circumstances by the investigating authority, because there is positive evidence warranting the initiation of the review investigation also with respect to such new subsidy, then the obligation of prior consultation in Article 13.1 applies.

2.391 With regard to the United States' appeal of the Panel's finding on cross-cumulation, the European Union submits that Article 15.3 of the SCM Agreement exhaustively regulates cumulation of imports from different countries in the same countervailing investigations and subjects such cumulation to a very specific set of circumstances. Because no other situations are foreseen, the consequence should be that cross-cumulation is not permitted. The European Union further submits that the term "subsidized imports" appears several times in Article 15 of the SCM Agreement and should be interpreted as referring to imports with respect to which the investigating authority has found subsidization.

2.392 The European Union recalls the Appellate Body's finding, in *EC – Tube or Pipe Fittings*, that a cumulative analysis under Article 3.3 of the Anti-Dumping Agreement is premised on a recognition that the domestic industry may be injured by the total impact of the dumped imports from various countries. This finding indicates that cumulation of imports makes sense in the context of the investigations of the same phenomenon, be it dumping or subsidization, so as to determine the total impact of the imports at issue. Moreover, the same distinction between the two phenomena – dumping and subsidization – is also contained in Article VI:6(a) of the GATT 1994. In the European Union's view, therefore, the use of the terms "or" and "as the case may be" indicates that the two phenomena should not be mixed when determining the effects of each phenomenon.

2.393 Furthermore, the European Union observes that the Panel's analysis of Section 1677(7)(G) of the US Statute "is very succinct", and submits that the Panel could have elaborated further its findings with respect to the meaning of the US measure.[481] Nonetheless, in the European Union's view, although the

---

[480] European Union's third participant's submission, para. 71. The European Union provided examples of situations in which the original subsidies may be deemed to be very different, such as those involving different regional levels, different granting authorities, different types of financial contributions, different calculations of benefit, etc.

[481] European Union's third participant's submission, para. 120.

United States raises a claim under Article 11 of the DSU, the United States is not making an argument that the Panel misinterpreted the meaning of the measure at issue, but is taking issue with the lack of basic rationale behind the Panel's finding. The European Union maintains, therefore, that the United States "appears to confuse" the allegation that the Panel acted inconsistently with Article 11 of the DSU with the allegation that the Panel failed to provide a basic rationale for its finding under Article 12.7 of the DSU.[482]

2.5.5 Saudi Arabia

2.394 Saudi Arabia submits that governmental authority is the defining characteristic of any public body, and no other factor is dispositive.[483] Saudi Arabia argues that the defining element of "governmental authority" is the power to command or compel a private body, and that the defining elements of the term "government" – i.e. "the effective power to regulate, control, or supervise individuals, or otherwise restrain their conduct", also define a "public body".[484] Saudi Arabia further submits that the existence of government ownership or control of an entity does not establish governmental authority, and that possessing or exercising governmental authority is distinct from, and not interchangeable with, the notion of being owned or controlled by the government.

2.395 According to Saudi Arabia, a government-owned or -controlled entity might be a public body, but only where the government has delegated to the entity the ability to control or govern the actions of a private body.[485] Saudi Arabia contends that the government's delegation of authority, not its ownership or control, thus dictates the entity's status as a public body. Thus, in the view of Saudi Arabia, an investigating authority inquiring into whether an entity is a "public body" is required, in every case: (i) to undertake an objective evaluation of all evidence related to governmental authority without undue emphasis on any single factor, such as state ownership or control; and (ii) to ensure that positive evidence supports its determination that an entity possesses, exercises, or is vested with governmental authority. An investigating authority basing its determination solely on evidence of government ownership or control would fail to meet these requirements. Saudi Arabia maintains that a "public body" determination requires a case-by-case basis approach, and that a "formulaic

---

[482] *Ibid.*

[483] Saudi Arabia's third participant's submission, para. 15 (quoting Appellate Body Report, *US – Anti-Dumping and Countervailing Duties (China)*, paras. 317, 318, and 346).

[484] Saudi Arabia's third participant's submission, para. 17 (quoting Appellate Body Report, *US – Anti-Dumping and Countervailing Duties (China)*, para. 290).

[485] Saudi Arabia's third participant's submission, para. 20 (referring to Appellate Body Report, *US – Anti-Dumping and Countervailing Duties (China)*, para. 294).

reliance on evidence of ownership and control would be inconsistent with that requirement".[486]

2.396 On the issue of financial contribution, Saudi Arabia submits that the "granting of intangible extraction rights" is not the provision of "goods" or "services" under Article 1.1(a)(1)(iii) of the SCM Agreement.[487] In Saudi Arabia's view, extraction rights are not tangible items because the quantity and value of resources at issue are unknown when the government grants the right to extract them. Saudi Arabia adds that whether an extraction right will produce any tangible good is speculative, and will depend on the quantities of extractable resources actually available and the actions of the rights-holder, including its business decision to begin extraction, the investments made in order to extract the resources, and the specific skills required to make such extraction possible. According to Saudi Arabia, panel and Appellate Body findings support the distinction between goods and intangible extraction rights. In *US – Softwood Lumber IV*, the Appellate Body agreed that the Canadian stumpage programmes "provide goods" under Article 1.1(a)(1)(iii) of the SCM Agreement "for reasons that demonstrate why intangible extraction rights, by themselves, are not goods: the resource in question was manifest and quantifiable".[488] Saudi Arabia also notes the Appellate Body's reasoning that governmental acts do not constitute the provision of a good unless the government has control over the availability of the good in question, and there is a reasonably proximate relationship between the government action and the enjoyment of the tangible goods by the recipient. According to Saudi Arabia, neither of these requirements is met where the government grants only the intangible right to extract unknown quantities of unseen materials. The reasoning in *US – Softwood Lumber IV*, therefore, supports the conclusion that the granting of extraction rights alone cannot constitute the provision of a good under Article 1.1(a)(1)(iii). Saudi Arabia adds that this provision cannot be interpreted so widely as to include items that are neither goods nor services, such as intangible assets.

2.397 Saudi Arabia also argues that the granting of a right to exploit a nation's natural resources is a sovereign function that the Panel should distinguish from the government's actual provision of those resources. In Saudi Arabia's view, a determination that the granting of intangible extraction rights alone constitutes a financial contribution would infringe upon the public international law principle that each State enjoys permanent sovereignty over its natural resources (PSNR). Saudi Arabia adds that the principle of PSNR is recognized by the International Court of Justice as an established principle of customary international law. In Saudi Arabia's view, an expansive interpretation of financial contribution to cover intangible extraction rights would undermine the principle of PSNR by discouraging developing country policies related to sustainable development.

486 Saudi Arabia's third participant's submission, para. 27.

487 Saudi Arabia's third participant's submission, para. 37.

488 Saudi Arabia's third participant's submission, para. 39.

Saudi Arabia explains its view that subjecting Members' essential resource development policies to SCM Agreement disciplines would undermine the certainty of control over sovereign development that PSNR is intended to ensure. Saudi Arabia urges the Appellate Body to recognize that the SCM Agreement should be interpreted in a manner that provides Members with the autonomy to use their natural resources both for sustainable development needs and the welfare of future generations.

2.398 Saudi Arabia contends that the use of benchmarks other than in-country prices for the determination of benefit is permissible only in "very limited" circumstances, that is, where such prices are "distorted". Moreover, an investigating authority must ensure that any alternative benchmark "reflects prevailing market conditions and does not offset a Member's comparative advantages". In this respect, Saudi Arabia contends that a domestic, cost-based benchmark is more accurate than international or third-country prices.[489] Saudi Arabia advances five arguments in this regard.

2.399 First, Saudi Arabia refers to the language in Article 14(d) of the SCM Agreement that adequacy of remuneration "shall" be determined in relation to "prevailing market conditions ... in the country of provision". In Saudi Arabia's view, this demonstrates the primacy of domestic market conditions as the proper benchmark. Second, Saudi Arabia submits that Article 14(d) establishes domestic market prices as the principal standard for determining whether, and to what extent, a benefit is conferred by the provision of a good, because "price" is foremost among the "prevailing market conditions" enumerated in Article 14(d). Third, Saudi Arabia submits that, in order to reject in-country benchmarks when determining whether a government-provided good confers a benefit, an investigating authority must establish domestic price distortion, based on all available evidence. Evidence of government involvement in the relevant domestic market, alone, does not automatically establish distortion. Nor can distortion be assumed on the basis that the government is the predominant home market supplier. Fourth, Saudi Arabia submits that external benchmarks should be avoided because they are inherently incapable of reflecting prevailing in-country market conditions. The use of external benchmarks is impermissible when used to offset differences in comparative advantages between countries.[490] Further, such benchmarks should not be permitted unless an exhaustive application of the standard provided in Article 14(d) demonstrates that no other value based on "prevailing market conditions" in the country of provision is available, and no alternative in-country values are available. Finally, Saudi Arabia contends that in-country, cost-based benchmarks are preferable to external benchmarks, because they are tailored to the circumstances of the country, industry, and enterprises concerned, and therefore can reflect the

---

489 Saudi Arabia's third participant's submission, para. 2. (fn omitted)

490 Saudi Arabia's third participant's submission, para. 10 (referring to Appellate Body Report, *US – Softwood Lumber IV*, para. 109).

prevailing market conditions in the country of provision with little or no adjustment. Saudi Arabia argues that such benchmarks are more likely to be consistent with the requirement that the benefit analysis under the SCM Agreement may not nullify a country's comparative advantage.[491]

2.400 In respect of India's claim regarding the USDOC's benefit determination for captive mining rights, Saudi Arabia contends that the granting of extraction rights cannot constitute a benefit, because the granting of extraction rights does not constitute the provision of a good or service within the meaning of Article 1.1(a)(1)(iii) of the SCM Agreement. While an authority has some latitude in the methodology employed pursuant to the guidelines under Article 14(d), it may not act outside the clear and mandatory parameters that they establish. Accordingly, Saudi Arabia contends that, because extraction rights are not a "good or service", an investigating authority may not determine the existence of any benefit conferred by the granting of such rights by reference to "adequacy of remuneration".

2.401 Saudi Arabia submits that investigating authorities may not find *de facto* specificity under Article 2.1(c) of the SCM Agreement based solely on the inherent characteristics of a good or service. The notion of "inherent specificity", Saudi Arabia argues, "is inconsistent with the text and intent of the SCM Agreement".[492] According to Saudi Arabia, authorities may not avoid the obligations of Article 2.1(c) by simply noting that a good's inherent characteristics render it useable by only certain enterprises. This, Saudi Arabia argues, "would amount to an irrebuttable presumption, without regard to the factors that authorities must examine under Article 2.1(c)".[493] In Saudi Arabia's view, many natural resources are not amenable to such an analysis because they are used by an indefinite number of industries. Saudi Arabia also contends that the Panel's interpretation of *de facto* specificity could render redundant the requisite determination under Article 2. Saudi Arabia further argues that "inherent specificity" penalizes less diversified economies in violation of the requirement under Article 2.1(c) that a *de facto* specificity determination take account of the exporting Member's economic diversification. Saudi Arabia contends that, when a Member's economy is dependent upon a single natural resource, an investigating authority should not find that the Member's provision of that resource is *de facto* specific due to the good's inherently limited uses. According to Saudi Arabia, such a finding "would result in precisely the type of *per se* rule that the diversification requirement of Article 2.1(c) prohibits".[494]

[491] Saudi Arabia's third participant's submission, paras. 8-13.
[492] Saudi Arabia's third participant's submission, para. 32.
[493] Saudi Arabia's third participant's submission, para. 33.
[494] Saudi Arabia's third participant's submission, para. 35.

3. ISSUES RAISED IN THIS APPEAL

3.1 The following issues are raised in this appeal:

a. with respect to the Panel's findings under Article 1.1(a)(1) of the SCM Agreement, whether the Panel erred in its interpretation and application of the term "public body" in Article 1.1(a)(1) of the SCM Agreement in determining that the NMDC is a public body;

b. with respect to the Panel's findings regarding financial contribution under Article 1.1(a)(1)(i) and (iii) of the SCM Agreement:

   i. whether the Panel erred in rejecting India's claim that the USDOC's determination that the GOI provided goods through the grant of mining rights of iron ore and coal is inconsistent with Article 1.1(a)(1)(iii) of the SCM Agreement; and

   ii. whether the Panel erred in rejecting India's claim that the USDOC's determination that the SDF Managing Committee provided direct transfers of funds is inconsistent with Article 1.1(a)(1)(i) of the SCM Agreement;

c. with respect to the Panel's "as such" findings, under Article 14(d) of the SCM Agreement, concerning the US benchmarking mechanism for the calculation of benefit set forth in Section 351.511(a)(2)(i)-(iv) of the US Regulations:

   i. whether the Panel erred in rejecting India's claim that the US benchmarking mechanism is inconsistent with Article 14(d) of the SCM Agreement because it fails to require investigating authorities to assess the adequacy of remuneration from the perspective of the government provider before assessing whether a benefit has been conferred on the recipient;

   ii. whether the Panel erred in rejecting India's claim that the US benchmarking mechanism is inconsistent with Article 14(d) of the SCM Agreement because it excludes the use of government prices in determining price benchmarks;

   iii. whether the Panel erred in rejecting India's claim that the use of "world market prices" as Tier II benchmarks under the US benchmarking mechanism is inconsistent with Article 14(d) of the SCM Agreement; and

   iv. whether the Panel erred in rejecting India's claim that the mandatory use of "as delivered" prices under the US benchmarking mechanism is inconsistent with Article 14(d) of the SCM Agreement;

d. with respect to the Panel's "as applied" findings regarding benefit under Article 14 of the SCM Agreement:

   i. whether the Panel's alternative findings on the *ex post* rationales, put forward by the United States to justify the USDOC's failure to consider certain domestic pricing information in assessing whether the NMDC provided iron ore for less than adequate remuneration, are inconsistent with Articles 12 and 14(d) of the SCM Agreement;

ii. whether the Panel erred in rejecting India's claims that the USDOC's exclusion of the NMDC's export prices in determining a Tier II benchmark is inconsistent with Article 14(d) and the chapeau of Article 14 of the SCM Agreement;

iii. whether the Panel erred in rejecting India's claim that the USDOC's use of "as delivered" prices from Australia and Brazil in assessing the adequacy of remuneration for iron ore provided by the NMDC is inconsistent with Article 14(d) of the SCM Agreement;

iv. whether the Panel erred in rejecting India's claim that the USDOC's construction of government prices of iron ore and coal is inconsistent with Articles 1.1(b) and 14(d) of the SCM Agreement; and

v. whether the Panel erred in rejecting India's claim as it relates to the USDOC's determination that loans provided under the SDF conferred a benefit within the meaning of Articles 1.1(b) and 14(b) of the SCM Agreement;

e. with respect to the Panel's findings regarding specificity under Article 2.1(c) of the SCM Agreement:

i. whether the Panel erred in finding that there was no obligation on the USDOC to establish that only a "limited number" within the set of "certain enterprises" actually used the subsidy programme;

ii. whether the Panel erred in rejecting India's argument that specificity must be established on the basis of discrimination in favour of "certain enterprises" against a broader category of other, similarly situated entities; and

iii. whether the Panel erred in rejecting India's argument that, if the inherent characteristics of the subsidized good limit the possible use of the subsidy to a certain industry, the subsidy will not be specific unless access to this subsidy is further limited to a subset of this industry;

f. with respect to the Panel's findings regarding the use of "facts available" under Article 12.7 of the SCM Agreement:

i. whether the Panel erred in its interpretation of Article 12.7 of the SCM Agreement in finding that it does not require an investigating authority to engage in a comparative evaluation of all available evidence with a view to selecting the best information;

ii. whether the Panel erred in its application of Article 12.7 of the SCM Agreement in finding that India failed to establish a *prima facie* case that Section 1677e(b) of the US Statute and Section 351.308(a)-(c) of the US Regulations are inconsistent "as such" with Article 12.7 of the SCM Agreement; and

iii. whether the Panel erred in its application of Article 12.7 of the SCM Agreement in finding that India failed to establish a *prima facie* case that the use of an alleged "rule" on selecting the highest non-*de minimis* subsidy rates, either in general or "as applied" in the instances identified by India, is inconsistent with Article 12.7 of the SCM Agreement;

g. with respect to the Panel's findings regarding the examination of new subsidy allegations in administrative reviews, whether the Panel erred in rejecting India's claims that the USDOC's examination of new subsidy allegations in administrative reviews related to the imports at issue is inconsistent with Articles 11.1, 13.1, 21.1, 21.2, 22.1, and 22.2 of the SCM Agreement;

h. with respect to the Panel's findings regarding "cross-cumulation", whether the Panel erred in finding that Article 15.3, and Articles 15.1, 15.2, 15.4, and 15.5, of the SCM Agreement do not authorize investigating authorities to assess cumulatively the effects of imports that are not subject to simultaneous countervailing duty investigations with the effects of imports that are subject to countervailing duty investigations;

i. with respect to the issues identified in paragraphs 3.1.a through 3.1.h, whether the Panel failed to make an objective assessment of the matter before it, and therefore acted inconsistently with Article 11 of the DSU; and

j. with respect to the issues identified in paragraphs 3.1.c and 3.1.g above, whether the Panel failed to provide a basic rationale for its findings, and therefore acted inconsistently with Article 12.7 of the DSU.

4. ANALYSIS OF THE APPELLATE BODY

4.1 Article 1.1(a)(1) of the SCM Agreement – Public body

4.1.1 Introduction

4.1 Before the Panel, India claimed that the US Department of Commerce (USDOC) "improperly focused" on the Government of India's (GOI's) 98% shareholding in the National Mineral Development Corporation (NMDC) in determining whether that entity constitutes a "public body" within the meaning of Article 1.1(a)(1) of the SCM Agreement. India argued that "an entity only constitutes a public body if it performs a governmental function, and has the powers and authority to perform that function."[495]

4.2 The Panel observed that India's arguments "rely heavily" on the findings of the Appellate Body in *US – Anti-Dumping and Countervailing Duties*

[495] Panel Report, para. 7.68 (referring to India's first written submission to the Panel, para. 222).

(China).[496] The Panel recalled that it was required under Article 11 of the DSU to make its own objective assessment of the matter before it, adding, however, that the Appellate Body had previously affirmed that it was not only appropriate, but also expected from panels, that they follow the Appellate Body's conclusions in earlier disputes "especially where the issues are the same".[497] Quoting from the findings of the Appellate Body in *US – Anti-Dumping and Countervailing Duties (China)*, the Panel said that it understood the Appellate Body to have found that "the critical consideration in identifying a public body is the question of governmental authority, i.e. the authority to perform governmental functions", and that the relevant entity must therefore be shown to have been "vested with" governmental authority, "or to have actually exercised such authority through the performance of governmental functions".[498] The Panel further recalled that, in order to determine whether an entity has governmental authority, an investigating authority must "evaluate the core features of the entity and its relationship to government".[499] The Panel added that government "control of the entity is relevant if that control is 'meaningful'."[500]

4.3 Turning to the USDOC's determination that the NMDC is a public body, the Panel noted that the USDOC had found that "the NMDC is a mining company governed by the GOI's Ministry of Steel and that the GOI holds 98 percent of its shares."[501] For the Panel, this indicated that the USDOC had "looked to" the question of control of the NMDC, in addition to considering evidence of ownership.[502] The Panel agreed with the Appellate Body that, "in certain circumstances, a body may be found to be public in nature when it is subject to 'meaningful control' by governmental, and therefore public, authorities."[503] The Panel explained that it would therefore examine "whether the USDOC's determination amounts to a proper finding that the NMDC is subject to 'meaningful control' by the GOI".[504]

4.4 Based on its analysis, the Panel concluded that the USDOC's determination, when viewed in the light of the record evidence, "effectively amounted" to a finding that the NMDC was under the "meaningful control" of the GOI.[505] The Panel therefore rejected India's claim that the USDOC's public

---

496 Panel Report, paras. 7.68 and 7.79.

497 Panel Report, para. 7.79 (quoting Appellate Body Report, *US – Continued Zeroing*, para. 362 (fn omitted)).

498 Panel Report, para. 7.80.

499 *Ibid.*

500 *Ibid.*

501 Panel Report, para. 7.81 (quoting 2004 AR Preliminary Results (Panel Exhibit IND-17), p. 1516).

502 Panel Report, para. 7.81.

503 *Ibid.*

504 *Ibid.*

505 Panel Report, para. 7.89.

body determination in the underlying investigation is inconsistent with Article 1.1(a)(1) of the SCM Agreement.[506]

4.5 On appeal, India argues that the Panel erred in its interpretation and application of Article 1.1(a)(1) of the SCM Agreement, and failed to make an objective assessment of the matter before it as required under Article 11 of the DSU. India requests that we reverse the Panel's finding, complete the legal analysis, and find that the USDOC acted inconsistently with Article 1.1(a)(1) of the SCM Agreement in determining that the NMDC is a public body.

4.6 The United States counters that the Panel interpreted and applied Article 1.1(a)(1) of the SCM Agreement in a manner consistent with the interpretation given by the Appellate Body in *US – Anti-Dumping and Countervailing Duties (China)*, and argues that India has not established that the Panel failed to make an objective assessment of the matter before it, as required by Article 11 of the DSU. In its other appeal, the United States argues that, "where sufficient government control over an entity exists, such as that found by the Panel relating to NMDC, it is not necessary also to find that the entity exercises 'governmental authority'".[507] The United States therefore requests that we clarify that "an entity that is controlled by the government, such that the government may use the entity's resources as its own", is a public body within the meaning of the SCM Agreement, "irrespective of whether the entity also possesses 'governmental authority' or exercises this authority in the performance of governmental functions".[508] Should we reverse or modify the Panel's findings under Article 1.1(a)(1) of the SCM Agreement, the United States requests that we complete the legal analysis and find that the evidence on the administrative record of the USDOC would support a finding that the NMDC is a public body.

4.7 We begin by addressing the participants' arguments regarding the legal standard to be applied in determining whether an entity is or is not a public body within the meaning of Article 1.1(a)(1) of the SCM Agreement. Thereafter, we address India's claim that the Panel erred in its analysis of the USDOC's determination that the NMDC is a public body.

4.1.2 *The legal standard for determining whether an entity is a public body under Article 1.1(a)(1) of the SCM Agreement*

4.8 Article 1.1 of the SCM Agreement stipulates that a "subsidy" shall be deemed to exist if there is a "financial contribution by a government or any public body" and "a benefit is thereby conferred".[509]

---

[506] *Ibid.*

[507] United States' other appellant's submission, para. 23.

[508] United States' other appellant's submission, para. 6.

[509] Articles 1.1(a)(2) and 1.1(b) of the SCM Agreement stipulate that a subsidy shall also be deemed to exist if there is any form of income or price support in the sense of Article XVI of the GATT 1994

4.9 Regarding the meaning of the term "public body", the Appellate Body found, in *US – Anti-Dumping and Countervailing Duties (China)*, that a "public body within the meaning of Article 1.1(a)(1) of the SCM Agreement must be an entity that possesses, exercises or is vested with governmental authority."[510] In determining whether or not a specific entity is a public body, it may be relevant to consider "whether the functions or conduct are of a kind that are ordinarily classified as governmental in the legal order of the relevant Member."[511] The Appellate Body stated that the classification and functions of entities within WTO Members generally may also bear on the question of what features are normally exhibited by public bodies.[512] The Appellate Body added that "just as no two governments are exactly alike, the precise contours and characteristics of a public body are bound to differ from entity to entity, State to State, and case to case."[513] The Appellate Body explained that, in some cases, such as when a statute or other legal instrument expressly vests authority in the entity concerned, determining that such entity is a public body is a straightforward exercise. In other cases, the picture may be more mixed, and the challenge more complex.[514]

4.10 The Appellate Body further stressed that the absence of an express statutory delegation of governmental authority does not necessarily preclude a determination that a particular entity is a public body.[515] Instead, there are different ways in which a government could be understood to vest an entity with "governmental authority", and therefore different types of evidence may be relevant in this regard. The Appellate Body stated that evidence that "an entity is, in fact, exercising governmental functions may serve as evidence that it possesses or has been vested with governmental authority".[516] The Appellate Body added that "evidence that a government exercises meaningful control over an entity and its conduct may serve, in certain circumstances, as evidence that the relevant entity possesses governmental authority and exercises such authority in the performance of governmental functions."[517] The Appellate Body stressed, however, that "the existence of mere formal links between an entity and government in the narrow sense is unlikely to suffice to establish the necessary possession of governmental authority".[518] Instead, "[a]n investigating authority

---

and a benefit is thereby conferred. This dispute does not raise the issue of subsidies granted in the form of income or price support.

[510] Appellate Body Report, *US – Anti-Dumping and Countervailing Duties (China)*, para. 317.

[511] Appellate Body Report, *US – Anti-Dumping and Countervailing Duties (China)*, para. 297.

[512] *Ibid.*

[513] Appellate Body Report, *US – Anti-Dumping and Countervailing Duties (China)*, para. 317.

[514] Appellate Body Report, *US – Anti-Dumping and Countervailing Duties (China)*, para. 318.

[515] Appellate Body Report, *US – Anti-Dumping and Countervailing Duties (China)*, para. 318. As the Appellate Body observed, "[w]hat matters is *whether* an entity is vested with authority to exercise governmental functions, rather than *how* that is achieved". (*Ibid.* (emphasis original))

[516] Appellate Body Report, *US – Anti-Dumping and Countervailing Duties (China)*, para. 318.

[517] *Ibid.*

[518] Appellate Body Report, *US – Anti-Dumping and Countervailing Duties (China)*, para. 318. The Appellate Body also explained that panels and investigating authorities are called upon, in all instances, "to engage in a careful evaluation of the entity in question and to identify its common

must, in making its determination, evaluate and give due consideration to all relevant characteristics of the entity and, in reaching its ultimate determination as to how that entity should be characterized, avoid focusing exclusively or unduly on any single characteristic without affording due consideration to others that may be relevant".[519] Thus, the mere ownership or control over an entity by a government, without more, is not sufficient to establish that the entity is a public body.

4.1.2.1 Arguments by the participants

4.11 India contends that the Panel erred in its interpretation of Article 1.1(a)(1) of the SCM Agreement when it construed the term "public body" to mean any entity that is "meaningfully controlled" by a government. India maintains instead that the key characteristic of a public body is that it exercises authority vested in it by the government for performing governmental functions. For India, this means that, for an entity to be a "public body" within the meaning of Article 1.1(a)(1), it must have the power to regulate, control, or supervise individuals or otherwise restrain their conduct[520], and must also be able to give responsibility to, or exercise authority over, a "private body".[521]

4.12 For its part, the United States refers to the Panel's interpretation of the term "public body"[522], and submits that "it would be helpful for the Appellate Body to clarify whether it is *only* the possession or exercise of governmental authority that can distinguish a public body", or whether, as the United States argues, "a public body may *also* include an entity controlled by the government such that financial contributions made by the entity can be said to have been made on behalf of the government, i.e., such that the government can use the entity's resources as its own."[523]

4.1.2.2 Preliminary issue raised by India

4.13 We note, as a preliminary matter, India's contention that the United States' request for the Appellate Body to clarify the meaning of Article 1.1(a)(1) of the SCM Agreement should be rejected because, in seeking such a

---

features and relationship with government" (*Ibid.*, para. 319), and that the "mere fact that a government is the majority shareholder of an entity does not demonstrate that the government exercises meaningful control over the conduct of that entity" (*Ibid.*, para. 318).

519 Appellate Body Report, *US – Anti-Dumping and Countervailing Duties (China)*, para. 319. (fn omitted)

520 See India's appellant's submission, para. 307.

521 India's appellant's submission, para. 310.

522 United States' other appellant's submission, para. 2 (referring to Panel Report, para. 7.80). As a basis for its request for clarification, the United States also refers to India's argument that for an entity to be a public body, it must have the power to regulate, control, or supervise individuals or otherwise restrain their conduct, and must also be able to give responsibility to, or exercise authority over a private body. (*Ibid.* (referring to India's appellant's submission, para. 318))

523 United States' other appellant's submission, para. 52. (emphasis original)

clarification, the United States is not challenging "issues of law covered in the panel report and legal interpretations developed by the panel".[524] India further contends that the United States' request for clarification is essentially an attempt to overturn a previously adopted Appellate Body report, without providing "cogent reasons"[525], and argues that the principles to be applied in determining whether an entity is a public body have been settled in the adopted report of the Appellate Body in *US – Anti-Dumping and Countervailing Duties (China)*.

4.14 In response, the United States submits that it does not request that the Appellate Body overturn its interpretation of the term "public body" in *US – Anti-Dumping and Countervailing Duties (China)*.[526] The United States recalls that the Appellate Body did not, in that dispute, reject every aspect of the United States' arguments. Instead, the Appellate Body found, for example, that a government's "meaningful control" over an entity may provide a sufficient basis to find that an entity is a public body within the meaning of Article 1.1(a)(1) of the SCM Agreement.[527] The United States further points out that it has not appealed the Panel's reiteration of the Appellate Body's finding, in *US – Anti-Dumping and Countervailing Duties (China)*, that government ownership, taken alone, does not demonstrate that an entity is a public body.

4.15 The Appellate Body is required under Article 17.12 of the DSU to address each of the legal issues raised in the appellate proceedings. As we see it, the United States has appealed a "legal interpretation" developed by the Panel in the sense of Article 17.6 of the DSU. We therefore consider that the United States' request for clarification falls within the ambit of the appeal, and disagree with India to the extent that it suggests otherwise.[528]

4.16 We now proceed to review the arguments of India and the United States regarding the Panel's articulation of the standard to be applied in determining whether an entity is or is not a "public body" within the meaning of Article 1.1(a)(1) of the SCM Agreement.

4.1.2.3 The interpretation of the term "public body"

4.17 India argues that it follows from the Appellate Body's reasoning in *Canada – Dairy* and in *US – Anti-Dumping and Countervailing Duties (China)* that, in order to be a public body, an entity must have the power to regulate, control, or supervise individuals, or otherwise restrain conduct of others.[529] In

---

[524] India's appellee's submission, para. 13 (quoting Article 17.6 of the DSU).

[525] India's appellee's submission, para. 7 and section II.C.

[526] United States' opening statement at the oral hearing.

[527] *Ibid.*

[528] We recall that, in previous disputes, the Appellate Body has addressed panel statements that do not constitute a legal finding or conclusion. (See e.g. Appellate Body Report, *EC and certain member States – Large Civil Aircraft*, paras. 930-936)

[529] See India's appellant's submission, para. 308 (referring to Appellate Body Reports, *Canada – Dairy*, para. 101; and *US – Anti-Dumping and Countervailing Duties (China)*, para. 290). See also India's appellant's submission, para. 318.

US – Anti-Dumping and Countervailing Duties (China), the Appellate Body emphasized that "being vested with governmental authority is the key feature of a public body"[530] and that a public body within the meaning of Article 1.1(a)(1) of the SCM Agreement "must be an entity that possesses, exercises or is vested with governmental authority".[531] Although certain entities that are found to constitute public bodies may possess the power to regulate, we do not see why an entity would necessarily have to possess this characteristic in order to be found to be vested with governmental authority or exercising a governmental function and therefore to constitute a public body.[532]

4.18 We also do not consider that it follows from the Appellate Body's reasoning in *US – Anti-Dumping and Countervailing Duties (China)* that, in order to be a public body, the relevant entity must have the power to entrust or direct private bodies to carry out the functions identified in Article 1.1(a)(1)(i)-(iii) of the SCM Agreement.[533] The Appellate Body did not find in *US – Anti-Dumping and Countervailing Duties (China)* that an entity must have the power to "entrust" or "direct" a private body to carry out functions identified in Article 1.1(a)(1)(i)-(iii) in order to constitute a public body exercising governmental functions.

4.19 That said, we note that the terminology advocated by the United States – "a public body may also include an entity controlled by the government … such that the government may use the entity's resources as its own"[534] – is difficult to reconcile with that used by the Appellate Body in *US – Anti-Dumping and Countervailing Duties (China)*. In that dispute, the Appellate Body emphasized that a public body within the meaning of Article 1.1(a)(1) of the SCM Agreement "must be an entity that possesses, exercises or is vested with governmental authority."[535]

4.20 Consistent with the Appellate Body's interpretation, a government's exercise of "meaningful control" over an entity and its conduct, including control such that the government can use the entity's resources as its own, may certainly be relevant evidence for purposes of determining whether a particular entity constitutes a public body. Similarly, government ownership of an entity, while not a decisive criterion, may serve, in conjunction with other elements, as

---

[530] Appellate Body Report, *US – Anti-Dumping and Countervailing Duties (China)*, para. 310.

[531] Appellate Body Report, *US – Anti-Dumping and Countervailing Duties (China)*, para. 317.

[532] See Appellate Body Report, *US – Anti-Dumping and Countervailing Duties (China)*, para. 318.

[533] Appellate Body Report, *US – Anti-Dumping and Countervailing Duties (China)*, para. 318. The Appellate Body explicitly recognized in that case that the "same entity may possess certain features suggesting it is a public body, and others that suggest that it is a private body". (*Ibid.* (referring to Panel Report, *US – Countervailing Duty Investigation on DRAMS*, fn 29 to para. 7.8))

[534] United States' other appellant's submission, para. 52.

[535] Appellate Body Report, *US – Anti-Dumping and Countervailing Duties (China)*, para. 317. The Appellate Body added that an entity's "sustained and systematic practice" of exercising governmental functions "may serve as evidence that it possesses or has been vested with governmental authority". (*Ibid.*, para. 318)

evidence.[536] Significantly, however, in its consideration of evidence, an investigating authority must "avoid focusing exclusively or unduly on any single characteristic without affording due consideration to others that may be relevant".[537]

4.21 The United States argues that the use of the term "government" to refer to the phrase "a government or any public body within the territory of a Member" is a drafting technique, used so that the lengthy phrase need not be repeated throughout the SCM Agreement.[538] The United States refers in this regard to the similar technique used in Article 2.1 of the SCM Agreement, which refers to "an enterprise or industry or group of enterprises or industries" as "certain enterprises", pointing out that the terms "enterprise" and "industry" also have different meanings, despite being referred to collectively as "certain enterprises".[539]

4.22 While the Appellate Body disagreed with the panel in *US – Anti-Dumping and Countervailing Duties (China)* that the use of the collective term "government" was "*merely* a device to simplify the drafting"[540], it did *not* reject the proposition that the term "government" was used in the SCM Agreement as a shorthand for "a government or any public body" and, thus, may well have been employed as a drafting device. Instead, the Appellate Body disagreed with the proposition that the collective expression "government" does not have any interpretative significance.[541] To the contrary, the term "government" is relevant context for interpreting the meaning of the phrase "or any public body".

4.23 We note that the United States agrees with the Appellate Body's finding in *US – Anti-Dumping and Countervailing Duties (China)* that, "for a public body to be able to exercise its authority over a private body (direction), a public body must itself possess such authority, or ability to compel or command", and, "[s]imilarly, in order to be able to give responsibility to a private body (entrustment), it must itself be vested with such responsibility."[542] However, according to the United States, it does not necessarily follow from this that "all public bodies" must have this authority. The United States points out, for

[536] See Appellate Body Report, *US – Anti-Dumping and Countervailing Duties (China)*, para. 310.

[537] Appellate Body Report, *US – Anti-Dumping and Countervailing Duties (China)*, para. 319. The Appellate Body explained that, in some cases, such as when a statute or other legal instrument expressly vests authority in the entity concerned, determining that such entity is a public body is a straightforward exercise. In other cases, the picture may be more mixed, and the challenge more complex. (*Ibid.*, para. 318)

[538] United States' other appellant's submission, para. 50 (referring to Panel Report, *US – Anti-Dumping and Countervailing Duties (China)*, para. 8.66).

[539] United States' other appellant's submission, para. 50.

[540] Appellate Body Report, *US – Anti-Dumping and Countervailing Duties (China)*, para. 289 (quoting Panel Report, *US – Anti-Dumping and Countervailing Duties (China)*, para. 8.66). (emphasis added)

[541] Appellate Body Report, *US – Anti-Dumping and Countervailing Duties (China)*, para. 289.

[542] United States' other appellant's submission, para. 69 (quoting Appellate Body Report, *US – Anti-Dumping and Countervailing Duties (China)*, para. 294).

example, that many organs of Member governments – including ministries, departments, and agencies – do not possess the legal authority to entrust or direct private bodies to carry out the functions identified in Article 1.1(a)(1)(i)-(iii), even if, in other respects, they may possess and exercise authority to "'regulate', 'restrain', 'supervise' or 'control' the conduct of private citizens".[543] For the United States, the absence of authority to entrust or direct private bodies "does not move" these organs outside the category of government, and, in a similar manner, the absence of authority to entrust or direct private bodies should not, as a definitional matter, mean that an entity cannot be a "public body".[544]

4.24 The United States also contends that the reference to governmental functions in Article 1.1(a)(1)(iv) cannot be understood as relating to the authority to "'regulate, control, supervise or restrain' the conduct of others", as that language "simply refers back" to the functions described in subparagraphs (i) through (iii).[545] Consequently, reading Article 1.1(a)(1)(iv) as requiring that the term "public body" be interpreted as meaning an entity vested with or exercising authority to perform governmental functions is "circular".[546] The United States adds that an entity alleged to have taken one or more of the actions identified in Article 1.1(a)(1)(i)-(iii) necessarily possesses – at least allegedly – authority to perform such actions. Thus, an entity's possession of such authority does not indicate that the entity is a "public body" or a "private body" – or part of "a government" for that matter.[547] By contrast, for the United States, the presence or absence of governmental control does permit distinctions to be drawn between entities that are "public bodies", on the one hand, and those that are "private bodies", on the other hand, and thus requiring a finding of entrustment or direction with respect to alleged financial contributions provided by the latter type of entity.[548] We agree that the types of conduct listed in Article 1.1(a)(1)(i) and (iii) could be carried out by a government, by a public body, as well as by private bodies.[549] However, as explained above, it is only through "a proper evaluation of the core features of the entity concerned, and its relationship with the government in the narrow sense", that panels and investigating authorities will be in a position to determine whether conduct falling within the scope of Article 1.1(a)(1) is that of a public body.[550]

---

543 United States' other appellant's submission, para. 70 (quoting Appellate Body Report, *Canada – Dairy*, para. 97.

544 United States' other appellant's submission, para. 70.

545 United States' other appellant's submission, para. 72.

546 United States' other appellant's submission, para. 73.

547 *Ibid.*

548 United States' other appellant's submission, para. 74.

549 See Appellate Body Report, *US – Anti-Dumping and Countervailing Duties (China)*, para. 296.

550 Appellate Body Report, *US – Anti-Dumping and Countervailing Duties (China)*, para. 317. In addition, due consideration should be given to "all relevant characteristics of the entity" and investigating authorities should therefore avoid focusing exclusively or unduly on any single characteristic without affording due consideration to others that may be relevant". (*Ibid.*, para. 319)

4.25 The United States further argues that the term "*organismo público*" in the Spanish version of Article 1.1(a)(1) of the SCM Agreement does not need to be interpreted in a manner identical to the term "*organismos públicos*" in the Spanish version of Article 9.1(a) of the Agreement on Agriculture. The United States submits that the same words are used in Article 1.1(a)(1) and Article 9.1(a) in only one of the three WTO languages – i.e. Spanish. The United States further argues that Article 9.1(a) of the Agreement on Agriculture refers to "governments or their agencies", "*les pouvoirs publics ou leurs organismes*", and "*los gobiernos o por organismos públicos*". By contrast, Article 1.1(a)(1) of the SCM Agreement refers to "a government or any public body within the territory of a Member", "*des pouvoirs publics ou de tout organisme public du ressort territorial d'un Membre*", and "*un gobierno o de cualquier organismo público en el territorio de un Miembro*". The United States submits that these differences in the terms used – in English, French, and Spanish – must be taken into account in the interpretative process. For these reasons, the United States contends, the Appellate Body's interpretation in *Canada – Dairy* of "government agency" (*organismo público*) in Article 9.1(a) of the Agreement on Agriculture should not dictate the interpretation of "public body" (*organismo público*) in Article 1.1(a)(1) of the SCM Agreement.[551] Arguments based on different language versions of Article 9.1 and Article 1.1(a)(1) were also raised in *US – Anti-Dumping and Countervailing Duties (China)*.[552]

4.26 With regard to the significance of the Appellate Body's findings in *Canada – Dairy*, we agree with the United States that the meaning of the term "government agency" in Article 9.1(a) of the Agreement on Agriculture must be interpreted in the light of the substantive obligations of the agreement where that term is located. In the light of differences in the text, context, rationale, and object of Article 9.1(a) of the Agreement on Agriculture and Article 1.1 of the SCM Agreement, we do not read the Appellate Body's interpretation of Article 9.1(a) in *Canada – Dairy* to be determinative of its interpretation of the term "public body" in Article 1.1(a)(1) of the SCM Agreement. The Appellate Body noted, moreover, that "specific terms may not have identical meanings in every covered agreement", adding that, "[w]here the ordinary meaning of the term is broad enough to allow for different interpretations, and the context as well as the object and purpose of the relevant agreements point in different directions, the meaning of a term used in different places of the covered agreements may differ."[553]

4.27 As noted, the United States submits that the object and purpose of the SCM Agreement supports an interpretation of the term "public body" as "including an entity controlled by the government such that the government can

[551] United States' other appellant's submission, paras. 75-84 (referring to Appellate Body Report, *Canada – Dairy*, para. 97).

[552] Appellate Body Report, *US – Anti-Dumping and Countervailing Duties (China)*, paras. 328-332.

[553] Appellate Body Report, *US – Anti-Dumping and Countervailing Duties (China)*, para. 330.

use the entity's resources as its own, without the additional requirement that the entity must be vested with authority from the government to perform governmental functions".[554] The United States argues that the Appellate Body and panels have sought to ensure that the SCM Agreement is not interpreted rigidly or formalistically in a manner that would undermine its disciplines on trade-distorting subsidization. Thus, the interpretation advocated by the United States "preserves the strength and effectiveness of subsidy disciplines".[555] The United States claims that, by emphasizing the possession or exercise of "governmental authority", the Panel's interpretation could be read as removing a potentially broad range of subsidization from the disciplines of the SCM Agreement in a manner that is at odds with the object and purpose of the Agreement. The United States adds that a finding that an entity is a "public body" does not end the subsidy analysis; instead, it only means that "there is the potential for a financial contribution that confers a benefit", and ensures that "subsidizing governments are subject to the disciplines of the SCM Agreement even when making financial contributions through entities they control".[556]

4.28 We note that the Appellate Body addressed similar arguments made by the United States in *US – Anti-Dumping and Countervailing Duties (China)*. There, it found that "considerations of the object and purpose of the *SCM Agreement* do not favour either a broad or a narrow interpretation of the term 'public body'."[557] The Appellate Body therefore disagreed with the panel's finding in that case that "interpreting 'any public body' to mean any entity that is controlled by the government best serves the object and purpose of the *SCM Agreement*."[558] However, the Appellate Body emphasized that "entities that are considered not to be public bodies are not, thereby, immediately excluded from the *SCM Agreement*'s disciplines or from the reach of investigating authorities in a countervailing duty investigation" because they still would be subject to scrutiny under Article 1.1(a)(1)(iv) as to whether they are private bodies entrusted by or directed by the government.[559] As the Appellate Body saw it, however, "too broad an interpretation of the term 'public body' could ... risk upsetting the delicate balance embodied in the *SCM Agreement* because it could serve as a license for investigating authorities to dispense with an analysis of entrustment and direction [under subparagraph (iv)] and instead find entities with any connection to government to be public bodies."[560] As we see it, the same considerations apply here.

4.29 In sum, as the Appellate Body has explained, the term "public body" in Article 1.1(a)(1) of the SCM Agreement means "an entity that possesses,

[554] United States' other appellant's submission, para. 85.
[555] United States' other appellant's submission, para. 88.
[556] United States' other appellant's submission, para. 91.
[557] Appellate Body Report, *US – Anti-Dumping and Countervailing Duties (China)*, para. 303.
[558] *Ibid.*
[559] *Ibid.*
[560] *Ibid.*

exercises or is vested with governmental authority".[561] Whether the conduct of an entity is that of a public body must in each case be determined on its own merits, with due regard being had to the core characteristics and functions of the relevant entity, its relationship with the government, and the legal and economic environment prevailing in the country in which the investigated entity operates. For example, evidence regarding the scope and content of government policies relating to the sector in which the investigated entity operates may inform the question of whether the conduct of an entity is that of a public body. The absence of an express statutory delegation of governmental authority does not necessarily preclude a determination that a particular entity is a public body.[562] Instead, there are different ways in which a government could be understood to vest an entity with "governmental authority", and therefore different types of evidence may be relevant in this regard.[563] In order properly to characterize an entity as a public body in a particular case, it may be relevant to consider "whether the functions or conduct [of the entity] are of a kind that are ordinarily classified as governmental in the legal order of the relevant Member", and the classification and functions of entities within WTO Members generally.[564] In the same way that "no two governments are exactly alike, the precise contours and characteristics of a public body are bound to differ from entity to entity, State to State, and case to case".[565]

4.30 Having addressed the participants' arguments as they pertain to the meaning of the term "public body" under Article 1.1(a)(1) of the SCM Agreement, we turn to examine whether, as India contends, the Panel erred in its analysis of the USDOC's determination that the NMDC is a public body.

4.1.3 Whether the Panel erred in its analysis of the USDOC's determination that the NMDC is a public body

4.31 India argues that the Panel erred in its interpretation when it construed the term "public body" to mean any entity that is "meaningfully controlled" by a government. India further submits that, as a result of its erroneous interpretation of Article 1.1(a)(1) of the SCM Agreement, the Panel erred, in its application of that provision to the determinations made by the USDOC in the underlying investigation, by failing to examine if the USDOC had considered whether the NMDC: (i) was vested with the power and authority to perform governmental functions; (ii) had the power and authority to direct or entrust a private body;

---

561 Appellate Body Report, *US – Anti-Dumping and Countervailing Duties (China)*, para. 317.

562 As the Appellate Body observed, "[w]hat matters is *whether* an entity is vested with authority to exercise governmental functions, rather than *how* that is achieved." (Appellate Body Report, *US – Anti-Dumping and Countervailing Duties (China)*, para. 318 (emphasis original))

563 For instance, "[e]vidence that an entity is, in fact, exercising governmental functions may serve as evidence that it possesses or has been vested with governmental authority". (Appellate Body Report, *US – Anti-Dumping and Countervailing Duties (China)*, para. 318)

564 Appellate Body Report, *US – Anti-Dumping and Countervailing Duties (China)*, para. 297.

565 Appellate Body Report, *US – Anti-Dumping and Countervailing Duties (China)*, para. 317.

and (iii) was in fact exercising governmental functions. In addition, India argues that the Panel wrongly relied on the United States' assertion that the NMDC was "governed by the Ministry of Steel"[566], without assessing whether the USDOC had provided an adequate explanation as to whether the GOI exercises meaningful control over the conduct of the NMDC.

4.32 In describing the standard to be applied under Article 1.1(a)(1), the Panel quoted from the Appellate Body report in *US – Anti-Dumping and Countervailing Duties (China)*, stating that the relevant entity must be shown to have been "vested with" governmental authority, "*or* to have actually exercised such authority through the performance of governmental functions".[567] The Panel observed that, in order to determine whether an entity possesses those characteristics, an investigating authority must "evaluate the core features of the entity and its relationship to government".[568] The Panel expressed the view that "[g]overnmental control of the entity is relevant if that control is 'meaningful'."[569] Noting the Appellate Body's statement that "evidence that a government exercises meaningful control over an entity and its conduct may serve, in certain circumstances, as evidence that the relevant entity possesses governmental authority and exercises such authority in the performance of governmental functions", the Panel said that it agreed with the Appellate Body that "'meaningful control' may not be established on the basis of government shareholding alone but [that] a combination of government shareholding plus other factors indicative of control may suffice."[570] On this basis, the Panel considered that determining whether the USDOC's public body determination was in conformity with Article 1.1(a)(1) of the SCM Agreement required it to examine "whether the USDOC's determination amounts to a proper finding that the NMDC is subject to 'meaningful control' by the GOI."[571]

4.33 The Panel observed that the USDOC had determined that "the NMDC is a mining company governed by the GOI's Ministry of Steel and that the GOI holds 98 percent of its shares."[572] For the Panel, this indicated that the USDOC had "looked to" the question of control of the NMDC, in addition to considering evidence of ownership.[573] Referring to arguments made by the United States before the Panel, the Panel noted the United States' explanation that the USDOC's determination that the NMDC is "governed by" the GOI was based on record evidence demonstrating that: (i) the GOI was "heavily involved" in the

---

566 India's appellant's submission, para. 323 (quoting Panel Report, para. 7.82).

567 Panel Report, para. 7.80 (referring to Appellate Body Report, *US – Anti-Dumping and Countervailing Duties (China)*, para. 310). (emphasis added)

568 Panel Report, para. 7.80 (referring to Appellate Body Report, *US – Anti-Dumping and Countervailing Duties (China)*, para. 317).

569 Panel Report, para. 7.80.

570 Panel Report, para. 7.81.

571 *Ibid.*

572 Panel Report, para. 7.81 (quoting 2004 AR Preliminary Results, p. 1516).

573 Panel Report, para. 7.81.

selection of directors of the NMDC; and (ii) the NMDC is under the "administrative control" of the GOI.[574] The Panel observed that the United States also referred to evidence in the 2007 administrative review that the GOI had reported in a questionnaire response that it had appointed two directors and "had approval power over an additional seven out of 13 total directors".[575]

4.34 The Panel then proceeded to characterize "government involvement in the appointment of an entity's directors" as "extremely relevant to the issue of whether that entity is *meaningfully controlled* by the government".[576] The Panel explained that this is because such involvement indicates that "the relationship between the government and that entity is closer than it would be if the government simply held a shareholding in that entity."[577] The Panel described such government involvement in the appointment and nomination of directors as "*meaningful*".[578]

4.35 The Panel noted, in this regard, that GOI officials had informed the USDOC at verification for the 2004 administrative review that "the NMDC's chairman, or managing director, and four functional directors are full-time directors selected by a Board that is part of the GOI."[579] GOI officials had also informed the USDOC that there were "two part-time directors from, and appointed by, the Ministry of Steel".[580] In addition, the Panel noted that the USDOC had stated in its Issues and Decision Memorandum for the 2007 administrative review that, "with regard to the NMDC's 13 board members, information from the GOI indicates that it directly appoints two members and approves the appointments of an additional seven members."[581] The Panel also attached significance to record evidence indicating that the "NMDC is under the administrative control of the Ministry of Steel & Mines, Department of Steel Government of India"[582], which suggested to the Panel that the relationship between that entity and the government was "very different from the relationship that would normally prevail between a private body and the government"[583] and that this, in the Panel's view, provided "additional support

---

[574] Panel Report, para. 7.82 (referring to United States' second written submission to the Panel, paras. 104 and 105).

[575] Panel Report, para. 7.82.

[576] Panel Report, para. 7.85. (emphasis added)

[577] Panel Report, para. 7.85.

[578] Panel Report, para. 7.85. (emphasis added)

[579] Panel Report, para. 7.83 (referring to 2004 GOI Verification Report (Panel Exhibit USA-66), pp. 5-6).

[580] Panel Report, para. 7.83 (referring to 2004 GOI Verification Report, pp. 5-6).

[581] Panel Report, para. 7.83 (quoting 2007 AR Issues and Decision Memorandum (Panel Exhibit IND-38), Analysis of Comment 10, internal p. 45).

[582] Panel Report, para. 7.87 (referring to 2004 New Subsidy Allegations (Essar) (Panel Exhibit USA-69), Exhibit 6 attached thereto, "NMDC at a Glance", internal p. 2).

[583] Panel Report, para. 7.87.

for a finding that an entity is under the '*meaningful control*' of the government".[584]

4.36 We believe that the Panel, in grappling with the case-by-case nature of public body determinations, correctly articulated the appropriate standard when it observed that "evidence that a government *exercises* meaningful control over an entity and its *conduct* may serve, in certain circumstances, as evidence that the relevant entity possesses governmental authority and exercises such authority in the performance of governmental functions."[585] However, the Panel erred in its substantive interpretation of Article 1.1(a)(1) by construing the term "public body" to mean *any* entity that is "meaningfully controlled" by a government. Consequently, the Panel erred in its application of Article 1.1(a)(1) to the USDOC's public body determination in the underlying investigation, in effect treating the GOI's ability to control the NMDC as determinative for purposes of establishing whether the NMDC constitutes a public body. Moreover, the Panel failed properly to consider whether the USDOC had adequately explained and supported, in its written determination, the basis for its finding that the NMDC is a public body.

4.37 As noted above, the Appellate Body has explained that the term public body in Article 1.1(a)(1) of the SCM Agreement means "an entity that possesses, exercises or is vested with governmental authority".[586] The *substantive legal question* to be answered is therefore whether one or more of these characteristics exist in a particular case. This *substantive standard* should not be confused with the *evidentiary standard* required to establish that an entity is a public body within the meaning of the SCM Agreement. Although the Panel quoted extensively from the Appellate Body report in *US – Anti-Dumping and Countervailing Duties (China)*, it appears to have blurred the distinction drawn by the Appellate Body in that report between the *existence* of control by a government over an entity, on the one hand, and "meaningful control", on the other hand. Thus, the Panel did not analyse, in our view, the question of whether the GOI in fact *exercised* control over the NMDC and its conduct. Nor did the Panel assess whether the USDOC had properly established that the NMDC "possesses, exercises or is vested with governmental authority", and is therefore a public body.

4.38 Regarding the Panel's treatment of evidence on the administrative record of the USDOC, we note that the Panel attached significance to record evidence indicating that the "NMDC is under the administrative control of the Ministry of Steel & Mines, Department of Steel Government of India"[587], which suggested

---

584 Panel Report, para. 7.87. (emphasis added)

585 Panel Report, para. 7.80 (quoting Appellate Body Report, *US – Anti-Dumping and Countervailing Duties (China)*, para. 318). (emphasis added)

586 Appellate Body Report, *US – Anti-Dumping and Countervailing Duties (China)*, para. 317

587 Panel Report, para. 7.87 (referring to 2004 New Subsidy Allegations, Exhibit 6 attached thereto, "NMDC at a Glance", internal p. 2).

to the Panel that the relationship between that entity and the government was "very different from the relationship that would normally prevail between a private body and the government"[588] and, in the Panel's view, provided "additional support for a finding that an entity is under the '*meaningful control*' of the government".[589] The United States had explained, however, in response to a question posed by the Panel, that:

> ... the term "administrative control" was used by NMDC in its website description of the company, and was not used in [the USDOC's] determinations. [The USDOC] applied a simple control test in the determinations at issue in this dispute, because this was the standard WTO panels and the Appellate Body up to that time had indicated was appropriate. However, as stated in the US first written submission, [the USDOC] nevertheless discussed in its determinations a variety of evidence regarding the relationship between the GOI and NMDC, all of which would support a finding that the government controlled NMDC such that it could use that entity's resources as its own.[590]

4.39 Thus, in attaching significance to evidence on the administrative record of the USDOC indicating that the NMDC was under the "administrative control" of the GOI, the Panel appears to have focused on *ex post* explanations provided by the United States to the Panel, rather than on the reasoning provided by the USDOC in its written determinations.[591]

4.40 At the same time, the Panel did not, in our view, give proper consideration to India's argument that the USDOC failed to consider evidence before it regarding the NMDC's status as a *Miniratna* or *Navratna* company. According to India, the evidence before the USDOC pointed to a "lack of government control" over the NMDC, and showed "that government directions or policies have not influenced the transactions or pricing of the products sold by" the NMDC.[592] We note, for example, that, in response to a question posed by the USDOC, the GOI had explained:

> [NMDC] is a Mini RATNA Category 1 Company, which gives it, enhanced autonomy with regard to investment decisions and personnel matters. NMDC is operating in a commercial, market driven de-regulated environment and conducts its operations and businesses on commercial principles. It enjoys freedom in its day-to-day operations. Except for certain personnel related matters and

588 Panel Report, para. 7.87.

589 Panel Report, para. 7.87. (emphasis added)

590 United States' response to Panel question No. 42(b), para. 10 (referring to United States' first written submission to the Panel, paras. 381-383).

591 In any event, simple control of an entity by a government, without more, is not sufficient, however, to establish that an entity is a public body.

592 India's appellant's submission, para. 281.

> investment decisions over specified limits it takes its own decisions with the approval of its Board. All commercial matters are dealt with by the company on its own.[593]

4.41 Instead of considering the relevance of the USDOC's failure to evaluate this evidence, the Panel assessed India's contention that the NMDC "enjoyed a 'significant amount of autonomy' from the GOI, as a result of having been granted either 'Miniratna' or 'Navratna' status during the relevant review periods" in the light of two exhibits provided by India to the Panel.[594] The Panel observed that these exhibits referred to the GOI "[t]urning selected public sector enterprises into global giants", and explained that "greater autonomy" was granted in order "to make the public sector more efficient and competitive".[595] The Panel's failure to consider whether the *USDOC* properly assessed the implications of the status of the NMDC in the legal order of India is troubling, particularly considering that the Panel appears to have taken into account evidence on the USDOC's record that was cited by the United States at the Panel stage, but that was not cited or explained in the USDOC's decisions.[596]

4.42 The Panel reviewed some indicia of control by the GOI (such as shareholding and the GOI's involvement in the selection of directors), but did not address the question of whether there was evidence that the NMDC was performing governmental functions on behalf of the GOI. As the Appellate Body explained in *US – Anti-Dumping and Countervailing Duties (China)*, "the precise contours and characteristics of a public body are bound to differ from entity to entity, State to State, and case to case"[597]; so too will the nature and amount of evidence and analysis that is sufficient to establish that an entity possesses governmental authority or effectively exercises such authority in the performance of governmental functions.

4.43 As noted above, the question of whether the conduct of an entity is that of a public body must in each case be determined on its own merits, with due regard being had to the core characteristics and functions of the relevant entity,

---

[593] 2005 GOI Supplemental Questionnaire Response for 2004 AR (Panel Exhibit IND-58), internal p. 4, response to question 2a. (See also India's appellant's submission, para. 279 and fn 236 thereto)

[594] Panel Report, para. 7.88 (referring to India's second written submission to the Panel, para. 138; and DPE Guidelines, Chapter IX: Navratna/Miniratna Status of PSUs, section 1, "Turning selected public sector enterprises into global giants – grant of autonomy" (Panel Exhibit IND-72-1(2)); and DPE Guidelines, Chapter IX: Navratna/Miniratna Status of PSUs, section 5, "Financial and operational autonomy for profit making public sector enterprises – Mini-Ratnas" (Panel Exhibit IND-72-2(1)).

[595] Panel Report, para. 7.88 (quoting DPE Guidelines, Chapter IX: Navratna/Miniratna Status of PSUs, section 5, "Financial and operational autonomy for profit making public sector enterprises – Mini-Ratnas" (Panel Exhibit IND-72-2(1)).

[596] Moreover, regarding the evidence on the USDOC's record concerning *Miniratna* or *Navratna* status, the Panel said that to the extent that "public sector enterprises" were at issue, the grant of a greater degree of autonomy was not "necessarily at odds" with a determination that such enterprises constitute public bodies. (Panel Report, para. 7.88)

[597] Appellate Body Report, *US – Anti-Dumping and Countervailing Duties (China)*, para. 317.

its relationship with the government, and the legal and economic environment prevailing in the country in which the investigated entity operates. The Panel failed to evaluate whether the USDOC had properly considered the relationship between the NMDC and the GOI within the Indian legal order, or the extent to which the GOI in fact "exercised" meaningful control over the NMDC as an entity and over its *conduct*. Instead, the Panel examined evidence that would, in our view, more properly be seen as evidence of mere "formal indicia of control", such as the GOI's ownership interest in the NMDC, the GOI's power to appoint and nominate directors, and the reference on the NMDC's website indicating that the NMDC is under "administrative control" of the GOI. Those indicia, insofar as they were discussed by the USDOC in its determinations, are certainly relevant to the question at issue. Yet, without further evidence and analysis, they do not provide a sufficient basis for a finding that the NMDC is a public body.

4.44 Moreover, as explained above, the Panel took into account evidence from the USDOC record that was cited by the United States at the Panel stage but was not cited or explained in the USDOC determinations. At the same time, the Panel overlooked evidence on the record from subsequent administrative reviews that would have been relevant to assessing the relationship between the government and the NMDC and, in particular, the degree of control by the GOI and the degree of autonomy enjoyed by the NMDC.

4.45 India argues that "shareholding and appointing directors are merely two sides of the same coin."[598] We disagree with India that the power to appoint or nominate directors is nothing more than a corollary of shareholding. Although the two concepts are related, a government's power to appoint directors to the board of an entity, and the issue of whether those directors are independent, would seem to be distinct factors in assessing whether an entity is a public body.

4.46 Finally, we note that the Panel referred to the Appellate Body's analysis, in *US – Anti-Dumping and Countervailing Duties (China)*, of the USDOC's public body determination in the off-the-road (OTR) tires investigation.[599] Rather than acknowledging that the Appellate Body's review of the USDOC's public body determination in respect of state-owned commercial banks (SOCBs) in the OTR tires investigation was based on an analysis of the USDOC's substantive and detailed consideration of "the facts and circumstances of the Chinese banking system"[600], the Panel suggested that the Appellate Body had

---

[598] India's appellant's submission, para. 291. China similarly argues that, under the Panel's rationale, "a government-owned entity, or even an entity in which a government holds a non-controlling but substantial percentage of shares, will always be held to be a public body, unless its government shareholder waives altogether the right to elect directors and any other shareholders' rights." (China's third participant's submission, para. 83)

[599] Panel Report, para. 7.85 (referring to Appellate Body Report, *US – Anti-Dumping and Countervailing Duties (China)*, para. 350).

[600] The Appellate Body remarked, for example, that the USDOC had discussed "extensive evidence" in its determinations in Countervailing Duty Investigation of Coated Free Sheet from the People's Republic of China concerning the relationship between the government and the SOCBs, including

"implicitly accepted that an investigating authority's determination that certain entities constitute public bodies could be based on evidence indicating that the chief executives of those entities were 'government appointed', and 'the party retain[ed] significant influence in their choice'."[601] We disagree with the Panel that the Appellate Body "implicitly accepted" that an investigating authority's public body determination can rely exclusively on a single aspect of the entity's relationship with a government, namely, on the issue of whether an entity is controlled by a government in the sense that the chief executives of the entity are "government appointed".[602]

4.47 For all these reasons, we consider that the Panel erred in its application of Article 1.1(a)(1) of the SCM Agreement in its analysis of the USDOC's determination that the NMDC is a public body, and we consequently *reverse* the Panel's finding, in paragraphs 7.89 and 8.3.c.i of the Panel Report, rejecting India's claim that the USDOC's determination that the NMDC is a public body is inconsistent with Article 1.1(a)(1) of the SCM Agreement. Having done so, we do not consider it necessary to rule on India's claims that the Panel acted inconsistently with Article 11 of the DSU in its review of the evidence underlying the USDOC's public body determination by relying on an *ex post* rationalization provided by the United States of the USDOC's public body determination, and by disregarding certain evidence regarding the GOI's involvement in the appointment of directors of the NMDC. India's allegations of error under Article 11 of the DSU are, as we see it, linked to issues that we have already dealt with in reviewing the Panel's application of Article 1.1(a)(1) of the SCM Agreement.

4.48 This brings us to the question of whether we can complete the legal analysis of whether or not the USDOC's determination that the NMDC is a public body is inconsistent with the United States' obligations under Article 1.1(a)(1) of the SCM Agreement.

4.49 India requests that we complete the legal analysis and find that the USDOC's determination that the NMDC is a public body is inconsistent with Article 1.1(a)(1) of the SCM Agreement and, consequently, that the imposition of countervailing duties based on the NMDC programme in the 2004, 2006, and 2007 administrative reviews, and the "mere reiterations in the 2008 AR and the

---

evidence that "the SOCBs are meaningfully controlled by the government in the exercise of their functions" and evidence that SOCBs "effectively exercise certain governmental functions". (Appellate Body Report, *US – Anti-Dumping and Countervailing Duties (China)*, para. 355) The Appellate Body concluded that "the USDOC's public body determination in respect of SOCBs was supported by evidence on the record that these SOCBs exercise governmental functions on behalf of the Chinese Government", and found that China had not established that the USDOC's public body determination in respect of SOCBs was inconsistent with Article 1.1(a)(1) of the SCM Agreement. (*Ibid.*)

[601] Panel Report, para. 7.85.

[602] Panel Report, para. 7.85 (quoting Appellate Body Report, *US – Anti-Dumping and Countervailing Duties (China)*, para. 350).

2013 Sunset Review", are inconsistent with Article 1.1(a)(1) of the SCM Agreement.[603] In support of its request, India points to facts that it considers demonstrate that the USDOC "only paid attention to the ownership of shares" and "failed to observe that there is no government involvement in the functioning of the board of directors".[604] India refers to: the statement in the Issues and Decision Memorandum for the 2007 administrative review that "[a]nalyzing additional factors is not necessary absent information that calls into question whether government ownership does not mean government control"[605]; the *ex post facto* nature of the arguments advanced by the United States to support its explanation of the meaning of the term "governed by" in the context of the "USDOC's determinations under challenge"[606]; and the USDOC's having "completely overlooked the 'miniratna' and 'navratna' status of NMDC".[607]

4.50 In response, the United States argues that, in the event that we were to reverse or modify the Panel's findings under Article 1.1(a)(1), then we should complete the legal analysis and conclude that the USDOC did not err in determining that the NMDC is a public body within the meaning of Article 1.1(a)(1) of the SCM Agreement. Referring to the Appellate Body report in *US – Anti-Dumping and Countervailing Duties (China)*, the United States observes that the legal order of the relevant Member may be a relevant consideration for determining whether or not a specific entity is a public body[608], and submits that, "in the legal order of India, the NMDC performs a government function."[609]

4.51 As we have indicated above, in reviewing the Panel's analysis of the USDOC's determinations at issue, it does not appear that the USDOC provided a reasoned and adequate explanation of the basis for its determination that the NMDC is a public body within the meaning of Article 1.1(a)(1) of the SCM Agreement, as clarified by the Appellate Body.[610]

4.52 As noted by the Panel, the USDOC determined that "the NMDC is a mining company governed by the GOI's Ministry of Steel and that the GOI holds 98 percent of its shares".[611] We agree with the Panel that this language in the

[603] India's appellant's submission, para. 289.
[604] India's appellant's submission, para. 287.
[605] India's appellant's submission, para. 285 (quoting 2007 AR Issues and Decision Memorandum, Analysis of Comment 10, internal p. 45).
[606] India's appellant's submission, paras. 286 and 287.
[607] India's appellant's submission, para. 288.
[608] United States' appellee's submission, para. 571 (quoting Appellate Body Report, *US – Anti-Dumping and Countervailing Duties (China)*, para. 297).
[609] United States' appellee's submission, para. 571.
[610] We have stated that a panel must examine whether the conclusions reached by the investigating authority are reasoned and adequate, and that such an examination must be critical, and be based on the information contained on the record and the explanations given by the authority in its published report. (See Appellate Body Report, *US – Tyres (China)*, para. 123) Thus, there must be, in the investigating authority's determinations, an explanation of how the evidence on the record supports its factual findings.
[611] Panel Report, para. 7.81 (quoting 2004 AR Preliminary Results, p. 1516).

USDOC's 2004 administrative review determination indicates that the USDOC's public body determination "[was] not based solely on the GOI's shareholding in NMDC".[612] However, as the Appellate Body reasoned in *US – Anti-Dumping and Countervailing Duties (China)*, a determination of whether a particular conduct is that of a public body "must be made by evaluating the core features of the entity and its relationship to government" and "must focus on evidence relevant to the question of whether the entity is vested with or exercises governmental authority."[613] The USDOC does not appear to have addressed these questions in its determinations. It would also seem that the USDOC did not evaluate the relationship between the NMDC and the GOI within the Indian legal order, and the extent to which the GOI in fact "exercised" meaningful control over the NMDC and over its *conduct*.

4.53 In the 2007 administrative review proceedings, the USDOC stated that "majority ownership of an input supplier qualifies it as a government authority within the meaning of [Section 1677(5)(D)(i)) of Title 19 of the *United States Code*]" and that "[a]nalyzing additional factors is not necessary absent information that calls into question whether government ownership does not mean government control."[614] As we see it, these statements suggest that factors beyond government shareholding and the GOI's power to appoint directors were not considered by the USDOC. We also note that, in response to Panel question No. 42, the United States explained that the term "administrative control" was used by the "NMDC in its website description of the company, and was not used in [the USDOC's] determinations." Instead, the United States stated that the USDOC "applied a simple control test in the determinations at issue in this dispute, because this was the standard WTO panels and the Appellate Body up to that time had indicated was appropriate".[615]

4.54 In sum, the USDOC did not evaluate the relationship between the NMDC and the GOI within the Indian legal order, and the extent to which the GOI in fact "exercised" meaningful control over the NMDC and over its *conduct* in order to conclude properly that the NMDC is a public body within the meaning of Article 1.1(a)(1) of the SCM Agreement. Instead, the USDOC examined

---

612 Panel Report, para. 7.81. The Panel quoted from the USDOC's Issues and Decision Memorandum for the 2007 administrative review:

> The information on the record of the instant review only further bolsters the [USDOC's] prior determinations that the NMDC is a GOI authority capable of providing a financial contribution within the meaning of section 771(5)(D)(iii) of the Act. For example, with regard to the NMDC's 13 board members, information from the GOI indicates that it directly appoints two members and approves the appointments of an additional seven members.

(*Ibid.*, para. 7.83 (quoting 2007 AR Issues and Decision Memorandum, Analysis of Comment 10, internal p. 45))

613 Appellate Body Report, *US – Anti-Dumping and Countervailing Duties (China)*, para. 345.

614 2007 AR Issues and Decision Memorandum, Analysis of Comment 10, internal p. 45.

615 United States' response to Panel question No. 42(b), para. 10 (referring to United States' first written submission to the Panel, paras. 381-383).

evidence which, in our view, would be seen more appropriately as evidence of "formal indicia of control" such as the GOI's ownership interest in the NMDC and the GOI's power to appoint or nominate directors. These factors are certainly relevant but do not provide a sufficient basis for a determination that an entity is a public body that possesses, exercises, or is vested with governmental authority. Moreover, the USDOC did not refer in its determinations to evidence contained on the USDOC's administrative record that was referred to by the United States in the Panel proceedings as well as on appeal. Nor did the USDOC discuss in its determinations evidence on record regarding the NMDC's status as a *Miniratna* or *Navratna* company that could have been relevant to the question of whether the USDOC's determinations contain a sufficient and adequate evaluation of the relationship between the GOI and the NMDC, and, in particular, the degree of control exercised by the GOI over the *conduct* of the NMDC and the degree of autonomy enjoyed by the NMDC.

4.55 For all these reasons, we conclude that the USDOC did not provide a reasoned and adequate explanation of the basis for its finding that the NMDC is a public body within the meaning of Article 1.1(a)(1) of the SCM Agreement, as interpreted by the Appellate Body. We therefore *find* that the USDOC's determination that the NMDC is a public body is inconsistent with Article 1.1(a)(1) of the SCM Agreement.

4.2 The Panel's Preliminary Ruling on its Terms of Reference

4.56 India requests us to reverse the Panel's finding that certain claims raised by India before the Panel were outside the Panel's terms of reference. In particular, India refers to its claims that the USDOC acted inconsistently with Articles 11.1, 11.2, and 11.9 of the SCM Agreement by initiating, and failing to terminate, an investigation into the NMDC and the Target Plus Scheme (TPS) programmes, despite insufficient evidence in the written application of the domestic industry on the existence, amount, and nature of the subsidies.

4.57 In respect of these claims, the Panel held that, "by clearly and only stating that an investigation was *not* initiated or conducted, India's panel request precludes claims relating to the alleged initiation of an investigation, or the manner in which an investigation was conducted, being included in the scope of the dispute."[616] On that basis, the Panel concluded that, in respect of these claims, India's panel request did not comply with the requirement in Article 6.2 of the DSU to "provide a brief summary of the legal basis of the complaint sufficient to present the problem clearly", and accordingly found these claims to be not within the Panel's terms of reference.[617]

4.58 On appeal, India raises two claims with respect to this finding of the Panel. First, India alleges that the Panel acted inconsistently with Article 11 of

[616] Panel Report, para. 1.34. (emphasis original)

[617] Panel Report, para. 1.43.

the DSU by failing to consider India's argument that the term "initiated" in the panel request should be construed in the light of footnote 37 of the SCM Agreement and, further, by failing to follow previous panel and Appellate Body reports without offering cogent reasons. Second, India alleges that the Panel also acted inconsistently with Article 6.2 of the DSU in finding that the above claims raised by India were not within the Panel's terms of reference, because India had complied with the requirement of Article 6.2 to present the problem clearly in its request for the establishment of a panel.

4.59 India requests us to assess this claim on appeal only in the event that we find that the United States did not act inconsistently with Article 1.1(a)(1), or Articles 1.2 and 2 of the SCM Agreement, in respect of sales of iron ore by the NMDC. As we have found in the previous section that the USDOC's determination that the NMDC is a public body is inconsistent with Article 1.1(a)(1) of the SCM Agreement, we are not called upon to assess India's claim on appeal.

4.3 Article 1.1(a)(1) of the SCM Agreement – Financial Contribution

4.3.1 Captive mining rights

4.60 India appeals the Panel's rejection of India's claim that the USDOC's determination that the GOI provided goods through the grant of mining rights for iron ore and coal is inconsistent with Article 1.1(a)(1)(iii) of the SCM Agreement. Below, we summarize the Panel's findings before proceeding to analyse India's claims on appeal.

4.3.1.1 The Panel's findings

4.61 India asserted before the Panel that a grant of mining rights for iron ore and coal by the GOI cannot be considered a provision of goods within the meaning of Article 1.1(a)(1)(iii) of the SCM Agreement, due to the intervening acts of non-government entities.[618] India submitted that, given the uncertainty inherent in mining activities, as well as the need for significant intervention through private conduct in extracting the minerals, the link between the grant of mining rights by the government and the actual iron ore or coal extracted is too remote to fulfil the "reasonably proximate relationship" standard applied by the Appellate Body in *US – Softwood Lumber IV*.[619]

4.62 Pointing to the Appellate Body's reasoning in *US – Softwood Lumber IV*, the Panel considered that, in certain circumstances, a government may provide goods constituting a financial contribution "by making them available through

[618] Panel Report, para. 7.223 (referring to India's first written submission to the Panel, para. 365).
[619] Panel Report, para. 7.226 (referring to India's first written submission to the Panel, para. 369).

the grant of extraction rights".[620] The Panel was not persuaded by India's argument that, due to the uncertainties involved in mining operations, and because of the amount of work required by the mining entity in extracting the iron ore and coal, the grant of mining rights by the GOI is too remote from the extracted minerals to be treated as the provision of a good within the meaning of Article 1.1(a)(1)(iii). In the Panel's view, India's approach "lacks legal certainty", for it would lead to different results depending on the complexity of the process required to extract the relevant mineral, or to the uncertainty regarding the amount of minerals to be extracted.[621]

4.63 The Panel also considered that India's approach was at odds with the meaning of the term "provides", defined by the Appellate Body in *US – Softwood Lumber IV* as "make available" or "put at the disposal of".[622] The Panel explained that, given the GOI's direct control over the availability of the relevant minerals, the GOI's grant of rights to mine them essentially made those minerals available to, and placed them at the disposal of, the beneficiaries of those rights. Because the grant of the right to mine allows the beneficiary to extract government-owned minerals from the ground, and then use those minerals for its own purposes, the Panel considered that the GOI's grant of the right to mine is "reasonably proximate" to the use or enjoyment of the minerals by the mining entity to constitute a provision of a good within the meaning of Article 1.1(a)(1)(iii) of the SCM Agreement.[623]

4.64 The Panel acknowledged the doubts expressed by the panel in *US – Softwood Lumber IV* about treating the grant of certain exploration rights as the provision of a good under Article 1.1(a)(1)(iii). The Panel considered, however, that the panel's statements in *US – Softwood Lumber IV* were *obiter dicta* and that they referred to a possibly relevant difference between rights of extraction and rights of exploration. According to the Panel, the grant of mining licences differs from reconnaissance permits or prospecting licences because it involves the right to extract minerals from known sites, rather than the right to explore or prospect for minerals and, if anything is found, to extract them.[624] By acquiring mining rights, steel companies have paid for the right to extract minerals from known sites, which is more than "the right to explore a particular site and the chance of finding something".[625] The Panel also cited evidence on the USDOC's

---

620 Panel Report, para. 7.235.

621 Panel Report, para. 7.237.

622 Panel Report, para. 7.238 (quoting Appellate Body Report, *US – Softwood Lumber IV*, para. 69 (fns omitted)).

623 Panel Report, para. 7.238.

624 Panel Report, para. 7.240 and fn 431 thereto (referring to National Mineral Policy, Report of the High Level Committee (December 2006) (Hoda Report), internal p. 2, attached to 2006 New Subsidy Allegations (Tata) (Panel Exhibit USA-71)).

625 Panel Report, para. 7.240 (quoting Panel Report, *US – Softwood Lumber IV*, fn 99 to para. 7.18).

record that miners pay royalties under the relevant mining leases per unit of extracted mineral.[626]

4.65 On these grounds, the Panel rejected India's claim that the USDOC's determination that the GOI provided goods through the grant of mining rights for iron ore and coal is inconsistent with Article 1.1(a)(1)(iii) of the SCM Agreement.[627]

4.3.1.2 Whether the GOI's grant of mining rights constitutes a provision of goods within the meaning of Article 1.1(a)(1)(iii) of the SCM Agreement

4.66 India principally contends that Article 1.1(a)(1)(iii) of the SCM Agreement does not cover grants for which the beneficiaries have to engage in significant intervening acts to make a good available for use or enjoyment. India recalls the Appellate Body's finding in *US – Softwood Lumber IV* that only governmental actions that bear a "reasonably proximate connection" to the use or enjoyment of the goods in question could be covered under Article 1.1(a)(1)(iii).[628] In India's view, specific action undertaken by the government or public body must be "providing" the "goods" such that the governmental action itself, rather than the intervening acts of non-government bodies, directly results in the provision of the goods. India contends that the grant of mining rights is a situation where the government does not really "provide" the mineral in question, because "significant efforts, risks and investment have to be undertaken by the miner to actually make the mineral available for use or enjoyment".[629] India contends that, unlike the Appellate Body's conclusion in *US – Softwood Lumber IV* that the right to harvest standing timber is not severable from standing timber, the grant of mining rights and the provision of the mineral itself is severed by a series of significant actions performed by the beneficiary at its own risk and cost.

4.67 The United States submits that the Panel correctly understood and applied the "reasonably proximate relationship" test articulated by the Appellate Body in *US – Softwood Lumber IV*. The United States maintains that India's argument, that the grant of mining rights does not constitute a provision of goods due to significant efforts, risks, and investment undertaken by the miner, is not found in the SCM Agreement or the Appellate Body report in *US – Softwood Lumber IV*. The United States further considers that, analogous to the ruling in *US –*

---

[626] Panel Report, para. 7.240 (referring to 2007 Tata Questionnaire Response for 2006 AR (Panel Exhibit IND-65), internal pp. 12 and 16; and United States' first written submission to the Panel, para. 494).

[627] Panel Report, para. 7.241.

[628] India's appellant's submission, para. 491 (referring to Appellate Body Report, *US – Softwood Lumber IV*, para. 71; and India's second written submission to the Panel, para. 215).

[629] India's appellant's submission, para. 495.

Softwood Lumber IV, there exists a reasonably proximate relationship between the grant of mining rights and the availability of the mined iron ore or coal, such that the GOI provides the minerals in accordance with Article 1.1(a)(1)(iii). Whether the GOI itself mines and sells the iron ore and coal, or sells the mining rights to the iron ore and coal in the ground so that someone else may extract those minerals, the purpose of the transaction is to provide the government-owned iron ore and coal to certain enterprises for use. In the United States' view, "[w]hen a government gives a company the right to take a government-owned good, such as iron ore and coal from government lands, the government is 'providing' the goods within the meaning of Article 1.1(a)(1)(iii) of the SCM Agreement."[630] Finally, the United States considers that the interpretation advanced by India would weaken the disciplines of the SCM Agreement where governments structure transactions as the sale of rights to the mineral instead of the sale of the mineral itself.

4.68 India's appeal thus addresses the question of whether the GOI's grant of mining rights for iron ore and coal constitutes a provision of goods within the meaning of Article 1.1(a)(1)(iii) of the SCM Agreement. The Appellate Body previously considered the meaning of elements of Article 1.1(a)(1)(iii) in *US – Softwood Lumber IV*. That dispute involved the examination of what were referred to as "stumpage arrangements", which gave private entities a right to enter onto government lands, cut standing timber, and enjoy exclusive rights over the timber that is harvested.[631] On appeal in that dispute, the Appellate Body addressed Canada's contention that stumpage arrangements do not "provide" standing timber, but rather an intangible right to harvest. Canada maintained that it would not be appropriate to understand the term "provides" as to "make available", as the panel had done, because it would capture "any circumstance in which a government action makes possible a later receipt of services and ... every property law in a jurisdiction".[632] The Appellate Body rejected Canada's argument as follows:

> [W]e do not see how the general governmental acts referred to by Canada would necessarily fall within the concept of a government "making available" services or goods. In our view, such actions would be too remote from the concept of "making available" or "putting at the disposal of", which requires there to be a reasonably proximate relationship between the action of the government providing the good or service on the one hand, and the use or enjoyment of the good or service by the recipient on the

---

[630] United States' appellee's submission, para. 371.

[631] Appellate Body Report, *US – Softwood Lumber IV*, para. 75 (referring to Panel Report, *US – Softwood Lumber IV*, paras. 7.14 and 7.15).

[632] Appellate Body Report, *US – Softwood Lumber IV*, para. 70 (quoting Canada's other appellant's submission, para. 54).

other. Indeed, a government must have some control over the *availability* of a specific thing being "made available".[633]

4.69 In *US – Softwood Lumber IV*, the Appellate Body considered that the term "provides" means "to make available" or "to put at the disposal of". Not every governmental act, even if it could be argued to make available a particular good or service, or to put a particular good or service at the disposal of a beneficiary, will necessarily constitute a provision of that good or service. Rather, as the Appellate Body explained, there must exist a "reasonably proximate relationship" between the governmental action of providing a good or service, and the use or enjoyment of that good or service by a beneficiary. As noted, the Panel in this dispute agreed with these findings and considered that, "in certain circumstances, a government might properly be determined to have provided goods by making them available through the grant of extraction rights".[634]

4.70 India does not challenge the Panel's reliance on the "reasonably proximate relationship" standard in assessing whether the GOI's grant of mining rights provided a financial contribution in the form of iron ore and coal.[635] Rather, India takes issue with the manner in which the Panel "emasculat[ed]"[636] or "dilute[d]"[637] that standard when applying it. India maintained before the Panel that, due to the uncertainties involved in mining operations, and because of the amount of work required by the mining entity in extracting the iron ore and coal, the grant of mining rights by the GOI is too remote from the extracted minerals to be treated as the provision of goods within the meaning of Article 1.1(a)(1)(iii).[638] On appeal, India adds that a grant of mining rights cannot result in the provision of the extracted mineral because "significant efforts, risks and investment have to be undertaken by the miner to actually make the mineral available for use or enjoyment".[639] We therefore understand India to argue that the extraction process undertaken by Indian steel producers, due to its complexity and uncertainty, was a significant intervening act that undermined any reasonably proximate relationship between the GOI's grant of mining rights and the final goods consisting of extracted iron ore and coal.

4.71 The Panel put forward two rationales in rejecting India's claim. First, the Panel stated that India's approach "lacks legal certainty"[640] because it would lead to different results depending on the complexity of the process required to extract the relevant mineral, or the uncertainty regarding the amount of mineral to be extracted. Second, the Panel considered "[m]ore fundamentally" that

---

633 Appellate Body Report, *US – Softwood Lumber IV*, para. 71. (emphasis original)
634 Panel Report, para. 7.235.
635 India's response to questioning at the oral hearing.
636 India's appellant's submission, paras. 497 and 502.
637 India's appellant's submission, paras. 502 and 503.
638 Panel Report, para. 7.236.
639 India's appellant's submission, para. 495.
640 Panel Report, para. 7.237.

India's approach is at odds with the meaning of the term "provides" in Article 1.1(a)(1)(iii), which the Appellate Body had defined in *US – Softwood Lumber IV* as "make available" or "put at the disposal of".[641]

4.72 We disagree with the Panel's suggestion that the considerations described by India ought to be rejected because they "lack legal certainty". Rather, it is precisely an examination of the complexity and uncertainty of the mining rights arrangement that the Panel was called upon to consider in assessing whether there is a reasonably proximate relationship between the grant of mining rights and the final extracted goods. This suggestion is all the more surprising given that the Panel, in fact, went on to make such an assessment when it examined the complexity and uncertainty concerning the extraction of iron ore and coal in respect of the mining rights that were granted. Relying on the Appellate Body's reasoning in *US – Softwood Lumber IV*, the Panel considered there to be a difference between a "'general governmental act' that simply facilitates the mining operation", and a "grant of the right to mine [that] allows the beneficiary to extract government-owned minerals from the ground, and then use those minerals for its own purposes".[642] The Panel also pointed to a distinction that could be drawn between the mining rights at issue in this case, which involve "the right to extract minerals from known sites", as opposed to exploration rights, which involve "the right to explore or prospect, and, if anything is found, extract it".[643] The Panel noted that the USDOC's determinations at issue concern the grant of mining rights, and not reconnaissance permits or prospecting licences.[644] In addition, the Panel observed that the mining rights at issue involved the payment of royalties that were tied to the amount of extracted material. The Panel specifically cited a response by Tata Steel Limited (Tata) to the USDOC as part of the 2006 administrative review, which showed that Tata made royalty payments for extracted iron ore and coal that were calculated on the basis of the extracted material, and noted that India had not disputed the United States' assertion that this evidence is proof that miners pay a per unit extraction fee.[645]

4.73 The Panel therefore appears to have relied on several features of the mining rights in rendering its conclusion regarding the proximate nature of the link with the final extracted goods, including as it relates to the nature and certainty of the extraction results as reflected in the terms of the mining rights. We consider that the foregoing considerations by the Panel substantiate a conclusion that there is a reasonably proximate relationship between the GOI's

641 Panel Report, para. 7.238 (quoting Appellate Body Report, *US – Softwood Lumber IV*, para. 69 (fns omitted)).

642 Panel Report, para. 7.238.

643 Panel Report, para. 7.240.

644 Panel Report, fn 431 to para. 7.240 (referring to Hoda Report, internal p. 2, attached to 2006 New Subsidy Allegations (Tata)).

645 Panel Report, para. 7.240 and fn 433 thereto (referring to 2007 Tata Questionnaire Response for 2006 AR, internal pp. 12 and 16; and United States' first written submission to the Panel, para. 494).

grant of mining rights and the final goods consisting of extracted iron ore and coal.

4.74 India contends that the circumstances of this case are not analogous to those in *US – Softwood Lumber IV* because, in that case, the Appellate Body was examining the connection between a right to harvest standing timber and the standing timber itself. As India argues, that situation differs from a grant of mining rights, for which any connection with extracted iron ore and coal "is 'severed' by a series of significant actions performed by the beneficiary at its own risk and cost".[646] Although India is correct to point out that the good at issue in *US – Softwood Lumber IV* was standing timber, and not felled trees, the Appellate Body nevertheless observed in that dispute that rights over felled trees "crystallize as a natural and inevitable consequence of the harvesters' exercise of their harvesting rights", and thus that "making available timber is the *raison d'être* of the stumpage arrangements".[647] We do not see that this reasoning supports India's view that the grant of mining rights is "severable" from the extracted minerals. Like the right to harvest standing timber, the mining rights put iron ore and coal deposits at the disposal of steel companies, which allowed them exclusively to make use of those resources. We further recall the distinction drawn by the Panel between the mining rights at issue in this dispute, which permit the right to extract minerals from known sites, and more tenuous arrangements such as exploration rights.[648] Indeed, rights over extracted iron ore and coal follow as a natural and inevitable consequence of the steel companies' exercise of their mining rights, which suggests that making available iron ore and coal is the *raison d'être* of the mining rights. This, in our view, supports the Panel's conclusion that the government's grant of mining rights is reasonably proximate to the use or enjoyment of the minerals by the beneficiaries of those rights.

4.75 India further contends that the Panel's approach would permit other governmental acts, such as the granting of a business licence, to constitute a provision of goods, since, but for the governmental action, the mining company would not have been able to access the mineral in the first place.[649] Taking into account the considerations reflected in the Panel's assessment, we disagree. The captive mining rights at issue allowed beneficiary steel companies an exclusive right to mine iron ore or coal for their own use in the production of steel. Thus, unlike some of the "general governmental acts" to which India refers, the governmental act of granting these mining rights has a reasonably proximate relationship with the output in the sense that it is provided expressly to enable the beneficiary to extract for its use or enjoyment what was previously a government-controlled mineral, in this case, iron ore or coal.

---

[646] India's appellant's submission, para. 499.
[647] Appellate Body Report, *US – Softwood Lumber IV*, para. 75. (fn omitted)
[648] Panel Report, para. 7.240.
[649] India's appellant's submission, para. 496.

4.3.1.3 Whether the Panel acted inconsistently with Article 11 of the DSU

4.76 India also asserts a claim under Article 11 of the DSU. India points to evidence on the Panel record showing that the royalty payments constituted only 9.03% of the final cost of the extracted minerals, and argues that this fact is "highly relevant" in assessing whether there is a reasonably proximate relationship between the grant of the mining rights and the use of the extracted material.[650] In India's view, this "presents an accurate image of how insufficient the government grant of mining rights in itself is".[651] During the interim review stage, India asked the Panel to include this fact in its Report. The Panel declined, stating that it did not consider this issue "necessary for, or relevant to, the Panel's findings".[652] On this basis, India now argues on appeal that the Panel acted inconsistently with Article 11 of the DSU "by refusing to evaluate India's explanation as to its relevance and ultimately rejecting this fact as irrelevant".[653]

4.77 Article 11 of the DSU provides, in relevant part:

> *Function of Panels*
>
> The function of panels is to assist the DSB in discharging its responsibilities under this Understanding and the covered agreements. Accordingly, a panel should make an objective assessment of the matter before it, including an objective assessment of the facts of the case and the applicability of and conformity with the relevant covered agreements, and make such other findings as will assist the DSB in making the recommendations or in giving the rulings provided for in the covered agreements.

4.78 As the Appellate Body has observed, Article 11 of the DSU requires a panel to "consider all the evidence presented to it, assess its credibility, determine its weight, and ensure that its factual findings have a proper basis in that evidence".[654] Panels may not "make affirmative findings that lack a basis in the evidence contained in the panel record".[655] Within these parameters, "it is generally within the discretion of the Panel to decide which evidence it chooses

---

650 India's appellant's submission, para. 489.

651 India's appellant's submission, para. 488.

652 Panel Report, para. 6.133.

653 India's appellant's submission, para. 489.

654 Appellate Body Reports, *China – Rare Earths*, para. 5.178 (referring to Appellate Body Reports, *Brazil – Retreaded Tyres*, para. 185; *EC – Hormones*, paras. 132 and 133; *Australia – Salmon*, para. 266; *EC – Asbestos*, para. 161; *EC – Bed Linen (Article 21.5 – India)*, paras. 170, 177, and 181; *EC – Sardines*, para. 299; *EC – Tube or Pipe Fittings*, para. 125; *Japan – Apples*, para. 221; *Japan – Agricultural Products II*, paras. 141 and 142; *Korea – Alcoholic Beverages*, paras. 161 and 162; *Korea – Dairy*, para. 138; *US – Carbon Steel*, para. 142; *US – Gambling*, para. 363; *US – Oil Country Tubular Goods Sunset Reviews*, para. 313; and *EC – Selected Customs Matters*, para. 258).

655 Appellate Body Report, *US – Carbon Steel*, para. 142 (referring to Appellate Body Report, *US – Wheat Gluten*, paras. 161 and 162).

to utilize in making findings"[656], and the mere fact that a panel did not explicitly refer to each and every piece of evidence in its reasoning is insufficient to establish a claim of violation under Article 11.[657] Rather, an appellant must explain why such evidence is so material to its case that the panel's failure to address explicitly and rely upon the evidence has a bearing on the objectivity of the panel's factual assessment.[658]

4.79 The Appellate Body has also considered it unacceptable for an appellant simply to recast factual arguments that it made before the panel in the guise of an Article 11 claim.[659] Instead, an appellant must identify specific errors regarding the objectivity of the panel's assessment[660], and "it is incumbent on a participant raising a claim under Article 11 on appeal to explain *why* the alleged error *meets* the standard of review under that provision".[661] Indeed, a claim that a panel has failed to conduct the "objective assessment of the matter before it" required by Article 11 of the DSU is "a very serious allegation"[662], and the Appellate Body will not "interfere lightly" with a panel's fact-finding authority.[663] Rather, for a claim under Article 11 to succeed, the Appellate Body "must be satisfied that the panel has exceeded the bounds of its discretion, as the trier of facts".[664] We stress that "not every error allegedly committed by a panel amounts to a violation of Article 11 of the DSU"[665], but only those that are so material that, "taken together or singly"[666], they undermine the objectivity of the panel's assessment of the matter before it.[667]

4.80 Turning to the issue before us, we consider that the fact that India does not agree with a conclusion the Panel reached regarding the evidence does not mean that the Panel committed an error amounting to a violation of Article 11 of the DSU. In this dispute, the Panel considered the fact that "the royalty paid for

---

[656] Appellate Body Report, *EC – Hormones*, para. 135. The Appellate Body has also stated that a panel "must base its findings on a sufficient *evidentiary* basis on the record" (Appellate Body Report, *EC – Fasteners (China)*, para. 441 (emphasis added; fn omitted)); "may not ... 'appl[y] a double standard of proof'" (Appellate Body Report, *US – Upland Cotton (Article 21.5 – Brazil)*, para. 293 (fn omitted)); and its treatment of the evidence must not lack "even-handedness" (*Ibid.*, para. 292).

[657] Appellate Body Reports, *EC – Fasteners (China)*, paras. 441 and 442; *Brazil – Retreaded Tyres*, para. 202.

[658] Appellate Body Report, *EC – Fasteners (China)*, para. 442.

[659] *Ibid.*

[660] *Ibid.*

[661] Appellate Body Reports, *China – Rare Earths*, paras. 5.178 (quoting Appellate Body Report, *EC – Fasteners (China)*, para. 442 (emphasis original)).

[662] Appellate Body Reports, *China – Rare Earths*, para. 5.227 (quoting Appellate Body Report, *EC – Poultry*, para. 133).

[663] Appellate Body Reports, *EC – Sardines*, para. 299 (quoting Appellate Body Report, *US – Wheat Gluten*, para. 151); *US – Carbon Steel*, para. 142.

[664] Appellate Body Report, *US – Wheat Gluten*, para. 151.

[665] Appellate Body Report, *EC – Fasteners (China)*, para. 442.

[666] Appellate Body Report, *EC and certain member States – Large Civil Aircraft*, para. 1318. See also Appellate Body Report, *EC – Fasteners (China)*, para. 499.

[667] Appellate Body Reports, *China – Rare Earths*, para. 5.179.

the grant accounts for only a certain percentage of the costs borne by the miner"[668] and stated that it did not consider it to be "necessary" or "relevant" to its findings.[669] This demonstrates that the Panel considered this evidence but disagreed with India as to its significance. We also do not see that the evidence to which India refers negates the significance of other features of the mining rights that the Panel relied upon in reaching its conclusion that there was a reasonably proximate relationship between the grant of those mining rights and the extracted goods in the form of iron ore and coal. We therefore *reject* India's claim that the Panel acted inconsistently with Article 11 of the DSU.

4.81 For the above reasons, we *uphold* the Panel's finding, in paragraphs 7.241 and 8.3.d.i of the Panel Report, rejecting India's claim that the USDOC's determination that the GOI provided goods through the grant of mining rights for iron ore and coal is inconsistent with Article 1.1(a)(1)(iii) of the SCM Agreement.

4.3.2 SDF loans

4.82 India appeals the Panel's rejection of India's claim that the USDOC's determination that the Steel Development Fund (SDF) Managing Committee provided direct transfers of funds is inconsistent with Article 1.1(a)(1)(i) of the SCM Agreement. Below, we summarize the Panel's findings and the issues appealed. We then address the interpretation of Article 1.1(a)(1)(i) before turning to consider the Panel's analysis as challenged by India on appeal.

4.3.2.1 The Panel's findings

4.83 India asserted before the Panel that SDF loans were not transferred to the borrowers by the SDF Managing Committee, which the USDOC had found constituted a public body, but were rather disbursed by the Joint Plant Committee (JPC), which was not found to be a public body. India therefore maintained that, because the SDF Managing Committee did not disburse the loans, and because the funding for the loans was not owned or sourced by the government, the loans could not be considered "direct transfers" of funds within the meaning of Article 1.1(a)(1)(i) of the SCM Agreement.[670]

4.84 The Panel noted the USDOC's observations that the SDF Managing Committee handles all decisions regarding the issuance, terms, and waivers of SDF loans, that it considers and grants the ultimate approval on loan proposals put forth by the JPC, and that the JPC handles the day-to-day affairs of the SDF, such as overseeing and administering the SDF loans.[671] The Panel also noted that

[668] Panel Report, para. 6.131.
[669] Panel Report, para. 6.133.
[670] Panel Report, para. 7.290.
[671] Panel Report, para. 7.291 (referring to 2001 Investigation Verification Report of GOI Responses (Panel Exhibit USA-74), p. 3).

India did not deny that the SDF Managing Committee is the decision-maker regarding the issuance, terms, and waivers of the SDF loans. The Panel also took note, however, of India's contentions that the disbursement and collection of funds is the responsibility of the JPC, that the authority to operate the fund is vested only in the JPC, and that the function of management and operation of the corpus of the SDF is with the JPC. The Panel also referred to India's assertions that the SDF loan agreements were executed between the JPC and the member steel plants, that the recitals to these agreements clearly provide that the JPC was constituted with the power to maintain and disburse loans out of the SDF, and that the issuance and administration of loans under the SDF programme is supervised by the JPC.[672]

4.85 The Panel considered that, although the JPC formally administers the disbursement and collection of funds, and the day-to-day operations of the SDF, the USDOC could reasonably have determined that the SDF Managing Committee was directly involved in the issuance of SDF loans. According to the Panel, evidence on the USDOC's record indicates that the SDF Managing Committee made the decision whether or not loans should be issued, and on what terms. Because disbursements were made only following an affirmative decision by the SDF Managing Committee as to the issuance, terms, and conditions of the loans, the Panel reasoned, the SDF Managing Committee was "directly" involved in the provision of SDF loans.[673]

4.86 Regarding the issue of whether or not the USDOC could reasonably have found that the SDF Managing Committee "transferred" the relevant funds, the Panel stated that there is nothing in the text of Article 1.1(a)(1)(i) to suggest that the relevant government or public body must have title over the funds being transferred, or that there must be a charge on the public account, in order for a direct "transfer" of funds to occur.[674] The Panel noted that SDF levies are collected by the JPC and that, once the funds are remitted to the SDF, they are no longer held by either the steel producers or the JPC. Rather, the Panel considered that those funds are held by the SDF and disposed of pursuant to the instructions of the SDF Managing Committee. The Panel reasoned that, even though the SDF Managing Committee may not have taken title over the funds, or imposed a charge on the public account when releasing those funds as loans, the SDF Managing Committee was instrumental due to its role as decision-maker regarding the issuance, terms, and waivers of SDF loans.[675] The Panel further noted that, even if the SDF Managing Committee could not be said to have transferred funds to the SDF loan beneficiaries, at the very least, the SDF Managing Committee "made available" those funds once it provided the

[672] Panel Report, para. 7.292.
[673] Panel Report, para. 7.293.
[674] Panel Report, para. 7.294.
[675] Panel Report, para. 7.295.

requisite loan authorizations.[676] The Panel therefore rejected India's claim that the USDOC's determination that the SDF Managing Committee provided direct transfers of funds is inconsistent with Article 1.1(a)(1)(i) of the SCM Agreement.

4.3.2.2 India's claims on appeal

4.87 India challenges the Panel's finding in several respects. India argues that Article 1.1(a)(1)(i) of the SCM Agreement covers only transfers of funds that are direct, which means that the action and its consequence must be immediately linked without involving any intermediary or intervening agency.[677] India considers that allowing transfers of funds under Article 1.1(a)(1)(i) by means of an intermediary or intervening agency would render Article 1.1(a)(1)(iv) inutile. India further argues that, because the JPC formally administers the disbursement and collection of funds, it is the JPC, not the SDF Managing Committee, that transfers the funds. There is therefore no direct link between the government practice of the SDF Managing Committee and the transfer of funds to the loan beneficiaries because the JPC acted as an intervening entity between the actions of the SDF Managing Committee and those beneficiaries. India further contends that a "transfer" of funds within the meaning of Article 1.1(a)(1)(i) refers only to situations in which the funds are drawn from government resources or result in a charge on the public account. India argues that, because the loan funds were garnered for the SDF only through the JPC, the SDF funds were not government funds. India argues that, while there was a dispute between the parties about whether the SDF consists of "consumer funds" or "producer funds", it was never established that "the SDF funds are actually owned by the government in any way or that release of these funds results in a charge on the public account."[678] India also points to a decision of the Supreme Court of India, which, in its view, confirms that the SDF funds did not consist of government funds or tax revenue. India considers that the role played by the SDF Managing Committee in issuing the SDF loans does not establish a direct transfer of funds within the meaning of Article 1.1(a)(1)(i).

---

676 Panel Report, para. 7.296 (quoting Appellate Body Report, *US – Large Civil Aircraft (2nd complaint)*, para. 614).

677 In its Notice of Appeal, India also stated that the Panel erred because it did not make an objective assessment of the matter when it failed to conduct a proper interpretation of Article 1.1(a)(1)(i) of the SCM Agreement. (India's Notice of Appeal, para. 46) In its appellant's submission, India argued that the Panel did not conduct a proper interpretation in accordance with Articles 31 to 33 of the Vienna Convention of the Law on Treaties (done at Vienna, 23 May 1969, UN Treaty Series, Vol. 1155, p. 331), but did not indicate that it was presenting a claim under Article 11 of the DSU, or explain how the Panel's analysis amounted to a failure to make an objective assessment of the matter under that provision. (See India's appellant's submission, paras. 548 and 549) In response to questioning at the oral hearing, India confirmed that it was not raising this issue as a separate claim under Article 11 of the DSU.

678 India's appellant's submission, para. 572.

4.88 The United States argues that the Panel correctly found that the distribution of the SDF funds in the form of loans was a direct transfer of funds because the decision-making regarding the issuance, terms, and waivers of SDF loans was done by the SDF Managing Committee, a government body. According to the United States, the Panel correctly interpreted and applied Article 1.1(a)(1)(i) by looking to the design, operation, and effects of the SDF loan programme, and finding that: (i) SDF levies are collected by the JPC; (ii) the funds, once collected, are remitted to the SDF; and (iii) the funds are held by the SDF and disposed of pursuant to the instructions of the SDF Managing Committee. The United States maintains that India's argument that a direct transfer cannot involve an "intermediary entity" assumes a different structure for the SDF than exists on the record. According to the United States, it is the SDF Managing Committee, not the JPC, that decides what happens with the levies remitted to the SDF. Article 1.1(a)(1)(i) requires that a government practice "involve" the direct transfer of funds, which, the United States argues, means that the government practice does not need to constitute such a transfer in and of itself. The United States also disagrees with India that the SDF loans are indirect transfers covered by Article 1.1(a)(1)(iv) of the SCM Agreement. According to the United States, the JPC does not resemble a private body because it operates under the supervision of the SDF Managing Committee, and does not have the authority to issue SDF loans and was therefore not entrusted or directed to do so.

4.3.2.3 Article 1.1(a)(1)(i) of the SCM Agreement

4.89 India's appeal thus addresses the question of whether the SDF loans constitute a financial contribution within the meaning of Article 1.1(a)(1)(i) of the SCM Agreement. Article 1.1(a)(1)(i) provides for the existence of a financial contribution where "a government practice involves a direct transfer of funds". We first note that this provision concerns transfers of "funds", which are identified parenthetically as consisting of, for example, grants, loans, and equity infusions. This relates to *what* is to be transferred, which the Appellate Body has explained encompasses, not only money, but also financial resources and other financial claims more generally.[679] We further note that there must be a "transfer" of funds, which signifies a conveyance of something from one person or entity to another.[680] Importantly, however, the term "transfer" is further modified by the adjective "direct", which indicates something occurring immediately, without intermediaries or interference.[681] The phrase "a direct

[679] See Appellate Body Report, *Japan – DRAMs (Korea)*, para. 250.

[680] Relevant definitions of the term "transfer" are "[c]onveyance of property, esp. of stocks or shares, from one person to another"; "[t]he action of transferring or fact of being transferred; conveyance or removal from one place, person, etc., to another". (*Shorter Oxford English Dictionary*, 6th edn, A. Stevenson (ed.) (Oxford University Press, 2007), Vol. 2, p. 3321)

[681] Relevant definitions of the term "direct" are "[s]traight, undeviating in course, not circuitous or crooked"; "[p]roceeding immediately from consequent to antecedent, from cause to effect"; "[e]xisting or occurring without intermediaries or intervention; immediate, uninterrupted". (*Shorter*

transfer of funds" therefore suggests that what is at issue is the *manner* or *method* by which the funds are conveyed. These terms thus indicate a certain immediacy to the conveyance. What is not evident from the language of this provision, however, is precisely under what circumstances a "transfer" may be considered to be "direct". It may be, for instance, that the term "direct" refers to the immediacy of the link between the parties to the transfer, the immediacy of the mechanism by which the transfer is effectuated, and/or possibly on some other basis.

4.90 We further note that Article 1.1(a)(1)(i) provides that a financial contribution exists where a "government practice involves" a direct transfer of funds. A "government practice" denotes action, potentially customary, by a government or public body.[682] The reference to "practice" of a government also arises in the context of Article 1.1(a)(1)(iv), which notes that any practice arising from the entrustment or direction of a private body to carry out the functions in the other subparagraphs of Article 1.1(a)(1) must not "differ[] from practices normally followed by governments". This supports an understanding of a government practice as evincing conduct that is potentially customary or usual in nature or manner. The term "involves" signifies to affect, include, or entail something.[683] The use of the word "involves" thus suggests that the government practice need not consist, or be comprised, solely of the transfer of funds, but may be a broader set of conduct in which such a transfer is implicated or included. The term also appears to introduce an element suggesting a lack of immediacy to the extent that it does not prescribe that a government must necessarily make the direct transfer of funds, but only that there be a "government practice" that "involves" the direct transfer of funds.

4.91 We find relevant context in the language of Article 1.1(a)(1)(iii) that relates to financial contributions where "a government provides goods or services". We have discussed above the Appellate Body's guidance on the meaning of the term "provides", focusing on the provision of goods. We have noted that the meaning of the term "provides" is "to make available" or "to put at the disposal of", although not every governmental act that makes available a particular good, or that puts a particular good at the disposal of a beneficiary, will necessarily constitute a provision of that good. Nevertheless, by specifying that it is the "government" that "provides" the goods, the phrase emphasizes the

---

Oxford English Dictionary, 6th edn, A. Stevenson (ed.) (Oxford University Press, 2007), Vol. 1, p. 691)

682 Relevant definitions of the term "practice" are "habitual doing or carrying out *of* something; usual or customary action or performance"; "custom; a habit; a habitual action"; "action *of* doing something; performance, operation; method of action or working". (*Shorter Oxford English Dictionary*, 6th edn, A. Stevenson (ed.) (Oxford University Press, 2007), Vol. 2, p. 2311) Throughout this section we use the term "government" to mean either a government or a public body.

683 Relevant definitions of the term "involve" are "[i]nclude, contain, comprehend"; "[c]ontain implicitly; include as essential; imply, call for, entail"; "[a]ffect; concern directly". (*Shorter Oxford English Dictionary*, 6th edn, A. Stevenson (ed.) (Oxford University Press, 2007), Vol. 1, p. 1427)

pivotal role served by the action taken by the government in making available a particular good, or in putting a particular good at the disposal of a beneficiary. We therefore see contextual significance in the fact that subparagraph (iii) refers to a "government" that "provides", whereas subparagraph (i) refers to a "government practice" that "involves". In our view, when juxtaposing these terms, it becomes apparent that this latter language suggests a potentially broadened framework for examining the government's role in respect of a direct transfer of funds under Article 1.1(a)(1)(i).[684]

4.92 Having considered the various terms of Article 1.1(a)(1)(i) together, we note that there is a tension between elements of the provision that alternatively appear to narrow and broaden the scope of coverage as it relates to the parties to the transfer, and the nature of the transfer itself. Thus, as we have noted, the meaning of the term "direct" in relation to a "transfer of funds" suggests the immediacy of the conveyance of funds, which in turn points to the existence of a close nexus concerning, for instance, the parties to, and/or the actions relating to, the transfer of the funds. At the same time, we have noted that any such immediacy is mitigated by the context provided by a "government practice" that "involves" the direct transfer of funds. These latter terms suggest a more attenuated role for a government or public body for purposes of Article 1.1(a)(1)(i) than what would otherwise have been understood through an examination of the phrase "direct transfer of funds" in isolation. We therefore consider that Article 1.1(a)(1)(i) does not rigidly prescribe the scope of its coverage. Rather, the provision reflects a balance of different considerations to be taken into account when assessing whether a particular transfer of funds constitutes a financial contribution.

4.93 As noted, India argues that Article 1.1(a)(1)(i) covers only transfers of funds that are direct, which means that the action and its consequence must be immediately linked without involving any intermediary or intervening agency. In India's view, where the governmental action consists of decision-making on the issuance or terms of the transfer, and this action precedes the actual transfer of the funds by an intermediary, "this is not a government practice that involves the direct transfer of funds".[685] India argues that this is supported by the fact that Article 1.1(a)(1)(iv) is intended to cover indirect transfers, that is, transfers involving an intermediary or intervening agency. To read Article 1.1(a)(1)(i) as also including indirect transfers would, in India's view, render Article 1.1(a)(1)(iv) inutile.

4.94 We have noted that the use of the term "direct" in Article 1.1(a)(1)(i) suggests a certain immediacy in the conveyance of funds, which in turn points to

[684] We note in this respect that, in *US – Large Civil Aircraft (2nd complaint)*, the Appellate Body considered that subparagraph (i) "captures conduct on the part of the government by which money, financial resources, and/or financial claims are made available to a recipient". (Appellate Body Report, *US – Large Civil Aircraft (2nd complaint)*, para. 614)

[685] India's appellant's submission, para. 552.

the existence of a close nexus concerning, for instance, the parties to, and/or the actions relating to, the transfer of the funds. However, we have also noted that the requirement that "a government practice involves" suggests a more attenuated role for a government or public body for purposes of Article 1.1(a)(1)(i) than what would otherwise have been understood through an examination of the phrase "direct transfer of funds" in isolation. We therefore believe that India places undue emphasis on the word "direct" in subparagraph (i), and does not attribute sufficient relevance to the term "a government practice involves" that is also found in that provision. In the light of these interpretative considerations, we do not consider that the fact that a government effects a transfer through an intermediary necessarily negates a finding of financial contribution under Article 1.1(a)(1)(i). Indeed, it would seem that a conveyance of funds through an intermediary might still, depending on the circumstances relating to the nature and role of the intermediary, exhibit sufficient indicia of directness in order to establish that "a government practice involves a direct transfer of funds".

4.95 We also do not consider that the foregoing interpretation of the scope of Article 1.1(a)(1)(i) renders Article 1.1(a)(1)(iv) inutile. Depending on the nature of the involvement of an intermediary in the transfer of an alleged subsidy, the outcome may differ under subparagraph (i) and subparagraph (iv). For instance, there may be circumstances where the intermediary acts as "entrusted" or "directed" by the government. In yet other circumstances, the intermediary may not have been accorded sufficient entrustment or direction in order to effect the type of financial contribution contemplated under Article 1.1(a)(1)(iv), but may yet still qualify under Article 1.1(a)(1)(i). We therefore do not consider that the scope of Article 1.1(a)(1)(iv) dictates a reading of the term "direct" in Article 1.1(a)(1)(i) to exclude all government transfers conducted through an intermediary. At the same time, we recognize that an assessment of the role and involvement of any intermediaries in the relationship between the government and the recipient would clearly be important in assessing whether a government practice involves a direct transfer of funds within the meaning of Article 1.1(a)(1)(i), or the entrustment or direction of a private body within the meaning of Article 1.1(a)(1)(iv).

4.96 India further contends that the term "transfer" means that the rights or interest in the resources is terminated with the transferor and simultaneously created with the transferee. India thus maintains that a "transfer of funds" within the meaning of Article 1.1(a)(1)(i) refers only to situations in which the funds are drawn from government resources or result in a "charge on the public account".[686] We again note that Article 1.1(a)(1)(i) relates to a "government practice" that "involves" a direct transfer of funds. Thus, while we would agree

[686] India's appellant's submission, para. 567. India considers that such a view is supported by the preparatory work of the group that negotiated the SCM Agreement, which included statements referring to a link between subsidies and the taxation function of government. (*Ibid.*, paras. 568-571)

that a "transfer" indicates that funds are moved from a transferor to a transferee, we do not consider that Article 1.1(a)(1)(i) prescribes that the resources must necessarily be drawn from government resources or result in a charge on the public account. Moreover, an interpretation that limits the scope of subparagraph (i) to funds drawn from government resources or charged on the public account would accord little relevance to the fact that subparagraph (i) refers only to a "government practice" that "involves" direct transfers of funds. Following the interpretation developed above, we consider that, if there is a government practice that involves a transfer of financial resources exhibiting sufficient indicia of directness, we do not see that such a transfer must necessarily emanate from government title or possession over such resources. Indeed, there may be limited situations in which a government is able to exercise control over resources pooled from non-government contributors in such a manner that its decision to transfer those resources could qualify as a financial contribution under Article 1.1(a)(1)(i) of the SCM Agreement.[687]

4.3.2.4 Whether SDF loans constitute direct transfers of funds within the meaning of Article 1.1(a)(1)(i) of the SCM Agreement

4.97 Taking the foregoing considerations into account, we now turn to the Panel's analysis of the particular circumstances of this case. We note that the USDOC found that the SDF Managing Committee was a public body, but did not make such a finding with respect to the JPC.[688] We further note the Panel's finding that the JPC administers the disbursement and collection of funds and the day-to-day operations of the SDF, but that the SDF Managing Committee makes all decisions regarding the issuance, terms, and waivers regarding SDF loans.[689] The Panel stated that, although the JPC may have formally disbursed the funds, such disbursements were made only following an affirmative decision by the

---

[687] In the context of agricultural subsidies, the Appellate Body has found that the existence of subsidy payments "financed by virtue of governmental action", within the meaning of Article 9.1(c) of the Agriculture Agreement, covers circumstances where there is a non-government intermediary involved in a subsidy programme. As the Appellate Body stated, even if the government does not fund the payments itself, it may nevertheless play a sufficiently important part in the process by which a private party funds "payments" such that the requisite nexus exists between the "governmental action" and the "financing". (Appellate Body Report, *Canada – Dairy (Article 21.5 – New Zealand and US II)*, para. 133) We further note that Article 9.1(c) provides that payments may be financed by governmental action "whether or not a charge on the public account is involved". The Appellate Body has remarked that this is borne out by the fact that the text indicates that "financing" need only be "by virtue of governmental action", rather than "by government" itself. Article 9.1(c) therefore contemplates that "payments may be financed by virtue of governmental action even though significant aspects of the financing might not involve government." (*Ibid.*, para. 132 (quoting Appellate Body Report, *Canada – Dairy (Article 21.5 – New Zealand and US)*, para. 114))

[688] Panel Report, para. 7.291.

[689] Panel Report, para. 7.293.

SDF Managing Committee.[690] Thus, the Panel considered that, notwithstanding the JPC's role in administering the disbursement and collection of funds, the SDF Managing Committee made all decisions regarding the issuance of those loans, the terms on which they were approved, and any waiver conditions. The Panel therefore concluded that the SDF Managing Committee was directly involved in the provision of the SDF loans.[691]

4.98 As we discussed above, we do not consider that the fact that a government effects a transfer through an intermediary necessarily excludes such funds from the scope of, and thereby negates a finding of financial contribution under, Article 1.1(a)(1)(i). To be sure, the role of the JPC in administering the SDF is significant in the sense that it handles the day-to-day operations of the SDF, and is responsible for the collection of steel levies comprising the SDF as well as the disbursement of loans under the SDF. At the same time, the JPC had no authority to make any decisions regarding the issuance of those loans, the terms on which they were approved, or any waiver conditions. In essence, no major decision regarding SDF loans can be made, and no loans can be extended, by the JPC alone. Rather, all such decisions, including the terms of repayment and waivers, require the approval of the SDF Managing Committee. Thus, although the SDF Managing Committee and the JPC are distinct entities serving different functions with respect to the SDF loans, we do not see that the relationship between the SDF Managing Committee and the loan beneficiaries is undermined by the nature of the involvement of the JPC. In these particular circumstances, the Panel appears to have had a credible basis to conclude that, notwithstanding the JPC's role as an intermediary administrator of the SDF, the role of the SDF Managing Committee in making critical decisions regarding the issuance and terms of the SDF loans supports a finding that the actions of the SDF Managing Committee involve a direct transfer of funds within the meaning of Article 1.1(a)(1)(i).

4.99 The Panel also considered India's argument that the SDF loans could not result in a direct transfer of funds because the funds were neither owned by, nor sourced from, the government.[692] The Panel remarked that there is nothing in the text of Article 1.1(a)(1)(i) to suggest that the relevant government or public body must have title over the funds being transferred, or that there must be a charge on the public account, in order for a direct transfer of funds to occur.[693] In addition, the Panel noted that steel levies were collected by the JPC and that the GOI had itself asserted that, once the levies were collected, they were remitted to the SDF.[694] The Panel therefore considered that the collected steel levies were

[690] Panel Report, para. 7.293 (referring to 2001 AR Issues and Decision Memorandum (Panel Exhibit IND-7), Analysis of Comment 1, pp. 9-10).
[691] Panel Report, para. 7.293.
[692] Panel Report, para. 7.290.
[693] Panel Report, para. 7.294.
[694] Panel Report, para. 7.295 (quoting 2001 GOI Supplemental Questionnaire Response (Panel Exhibit USA-75), p. 3).

held by the SDF, and disposed of pursuant to the instructions of the SDF Managing Committee. On that basis, the Panel concluded as follows:

> Even though the SDF Managing Committee may not have taken title over the funds, or imposed a charge on the public account when releasing those funds as loans, the SDF Managing Committee was instrumental (because of its role as decision-maker regarding the issuance, terms and waivers of SDF loans) in "transfer[ring]" those funds from the SDF to the loan beneficiaries.[695]

4.100 As we have previously noted, we do not consider that Article 1.1(a)(1)(i) requires that a transfer necessarily emanate from government title or possession over the transferred resources. In the circumstances of this case, the Panel appears to have reached the conclusion that, regardless of the source of the resources used to fund the SDF loans, those funds were held in an account and could only be issued as loans on terms and conditions as decided by the SDF Managing Committee. For this reason, the Panel concluded that the SDF Managing Committee was, due to its role as decision-maker regarding the issuance, terms, and waivers of SDF loans, instrumental in transferring those funds to the beneficiaries. In these circumstances, we do not consider that the Panel erred in concluding that the actions of the SDF Managing Committee involve a direct transfer of funds within the meaning of Article 1.1(a)(1)(i).

4.101 We further note, however, that implicit in India's claim is also the contention that, because the funds contributed to the SDF consist of steel levies set and collected by the participating steel companies that are also the loan beneficiaries, the funds cannot be considered government resources capable of constituting a financial contribution. To put this argument differently, we understand India to contend that, because the funding for the loans is essentially drawn from the very entities that receive the loans, there is an inherent circularity to the scheme that indicates that the resources were never the government's to give. The Panel made reference to this issue when it noted that the parties had argued extensively over the question of whether the steel levies are imposed on consumers pursuant to a government mandate, such that they may be similar to government taxation, or rather are voluntary contributions made by the steel producers.[696] For purposes of its financial contribution analysis, however, the Panel did not address these arguments of the parties.[697] Rather, the Panel concluded that, regardless of the source of the SDF funds, they were held in an account and could only be issued as loans on terms and conditions as decided by the SDF Managing Committee.

---

[695] Panel Report, para. 7.295.

[696] *Ibid.*

[697] We note that the Panel subsequently addressed aspects of the SDF funding arrangements in assessing India's claim concerning the USDOC's finding of "benefit" in respect of the SDF loans. See *infra*, Section 4.4.2.3.

4.102 It does not appear to us that the question of whether there is an inherent circularity to the SDF loan scheme alters the outcome of the financial contribution analysis. Even if one were to accept India's contention that the SDF loans consisted of voluntary contributions from steel producers, this would not have a bearing on the assessment of whether, as part of the overall scheme, there is a government practice that involves a direct transfer of funds. As the Appellate Body affirmed in *US – Large Civil Aircraft (2nd complaint)*, the primary focus of Article 1.1(a)(1) is "on the action taken by the government or a public body".[698] Thus, we consider that, even if the issuance of SDF loans forms only part of an overall SDF loan scheme funded by the eventual loan recipients, it was nevertheless proper for the Panel to focus on the role of the SDF Managing Committee vis-à-vis the JPC in assessing whether it constituted a government practice that involves a direct transfer of funds.

4.103 For the foregoing reasons, we *uphold* the Panel's finding, in paragraphs 7.297 and 8.3.e.ii(1) of the Panel Report, rejecting India's claim that the USDOC's determination that the SDF Managing Committee provided direct transfers of funds is inconsistent with Article 1.1(a)(1)(i) of the SCM Agreement.

4.4 Article 14 of the SCM Agreement – Benefit

4.4.1 "As such" claims under Article 14(d) of the SCM Agreement

4.4.1.1 Introduction

4.104 Before the Panel, India claimed that the US benchmarking mechanism – as set forth in Section 351.511(a)(2)(i)-(iv) of the *United States Code of Federal Regulations*, Title 19, Volume 3, Chapter III, Part 351 (US Regulations) – is inconsistent "as such" with Article 14(d) of the SCM Agreement because: (i) it does not require in all cases an assessment of the "adequacy of remuneration" for government-provided goods from the perspective of the government provider, prior to an assessment of whether a benefit has been conferred on a recipient; (ii) it excludes the use of government prices as benchmarks; (iii) it permits the use of out-of-country benchmarks in circumstances not permitted by Article 14(d) of the SCM Agreement; and (iv) it mandates the use of "as delivered" prices as benchmarks. The first three of these claims relate to Section 351.511(a)(2)(i)-(iii), while the fourth relates to Section 351.511(a)(2)(iv) of the US Regulations.

4.105 The Panel rejected all of India's "as such" claims against the US benchmarking mechanism. On appeal, India submits that, in rejecting its claims outlined above, the Panel erred in its interpretation and application of Article 14(d) of the SCM Agreement, and acted inconsistently with Articles 11 and 12.7 of the DSU. Below, we provide an overview of the measure at issue, namely,

---

698 Appellate Body Report, *US – Large Civil Aircraft (2nd complaint)*, para. 613.

Section 351.511(a)(2)(i)-(iv) of the US Regulations, before examining India's appeal of the Panel's findings under Article 14 of the SCM Agreement.

4.106 Section 351.511(a)(2)(i)-(iv) of the US Regulations provides as follows:

> § 351.511 Provision of goods or services.
>
> (a) Benefit— ...
>
> (2) *"Adequate Remuneration" defined*—
>
> (i) *In general*. The Secretary will normally seek to measure the adequacy of remuneration by comparing the government price to a market-determined price for the good or service resulting from actual transactions in the country in question. Such a price could include prices stemming from actual transactions between private parties, actual imports, or, in certain circumstances, actual sales from competitively run government auctions. In choosing such transactions or sales, the Secretary will consider product similarity; quantities sold, imported, or auctioned; and other factors affecting comparability.
>
> (ii) *Actual market-determined price unavailable*. If there is no useable market-determined price with which to make the comparison under paragraph (a)(2)(i) of this section, the Secretary will seek to measure the adequacy of remuneration by comparing the government price to a world market price where it is reasonable to conclude that such price would be available to purchasers in the country in question. Where there is more than one commercially available world market price, the Secretary will average such prices to the extent practicable, making due allowance for factors affecting comparability.
>
> (iii) *World market price unavailable*. If there is no world market price available to purchasers in the country in question, the Secretary will normally measure the adequacy of remuneration by assessing whether the government price is consistent with market principles.
>
> (iv) *Use of delivered prices*. In measuring the adequacy of remuneration under Paragraph (a)(2)(i) or (a)(2)(ii) of this section, the Secretary will adjust the comparison price to reflect the price that a firm actually paid or would pay if it imported the product. This adjustment will include delivery charges and import duties.

4.107 Section 351.511(a)(2)(i)-(iii) of the US Regulations prescribes a three-tiered benchmark approach for assessing whether a government has provided goods for less than adequate remuneration. Tier I of the US benchmarking mechanism requires the USDOC to compare the government price under investigation to a market-determined price of actual transactions in the country in question. Under Tier I, an in-country market-determined price could include prices stemming from: (i) actual transactions between private parties; (ii) actual imports; or (iii) in certain circumstances, actual sales from competitively run government auctions. Section 351.511(a)(2)(i) provides that, in selecting Tier I benchmarks, the USDOC will consider product similarity, quantities sold, imported, or auctioned, and other factors affecting comparability.

4.108 Tier II of the US benchmarking mechanism becomes relevant in situations where actual in-country market-determined prices are not available or usable. Section 351.511(a)(2)(ii) provides that the USDOC may compare the government price under investigation to a world market price where it is reasonable to conclude that the latter would be available to purchasers in the country in question. Where there is more than one commercially available world market price, the USDOC will average such prices where practicable, making due allowance for factors affecting comparability.

4.109 Tier III of the US benchmarking mechanism addresses situations where market-determined prices from actual transactions in the country in question, or world market prices, are not available to purchasers in the country in question. Section 351.511(a)(2)(iii) provides that the USDOC will normally measure the adequacy of remuneration by assessing whether the government price under investigation is consistent with market principles.

4.110 Finally, Section 351.511(a)(2)(iv) of the US Regulations applies where the USDOC uses a Tier I or Tier II benchmark for the purpose of assessing the adequacy of remuneration for government-provided goods. Pursuant to Section 351.511(a)(2)(iv), when Tier I or Tier II benchmarks are used, the USDOC is required to ensure that these prices reflect the price that a firm has actually paid or would pay if it imported the product. Such adjustments will include delivery charges and import duties.

4.4.1.2 Whether Article 14(d) of the SCM Agreement requires separate analyses of "adequacy of remuneration" and of "benefit"

4.111 We turn to India's claim that the Panel erred in finding that Article 14(d) of the SCM Agreement does not require an assessment of the adequacy of remuneration for government-provided goods from the perspective of the government provider, prior to an assessment of whether a benefit has been conferred on a recipient. We set forth below the relevant findings of the Panel.

4.4.1.2.1 The Panel's findings

4.112 Before the Panel, India asserted that Article 14(d) of the SCM Agreement prescribes a two-step analysis pursuant to which the adequacy of remuneration for government-provided goods must first be assessed from the perspective of the government provider before benefit is assessed from the perspective of the recipient. India contended that the US benchmarking mechanism is inconsistent with Article 14(d) because it contains a preference for determining benefit by comparing the government price in question with Tier I or Tier II benchmarks, and only provides for a Tier III analysis of the adequacy of remuneration from the perspective of the government provider when Tier I and Tier II benchmarks are unavailable. Thus, India submitted that, to the extent that the adequacy of remuneration is not evaluated, in every case, from the perspective of the government provider, the US benchmarking mechanism is inconsistent with the two-step analysis prescribed by Article 14(d).[699]

4.113 In addressing India's claim, the Panel first examined whether, as argued by India, the adequacy of remuneration is a threshold issue under Article 14(d), separate and distinct from the issue of benefit under the same provision. The Panel noted that the first sentence of Article 14(d) provides that the governmental provision of a good "shall not be considered as conferring a benefit unless the provision is made for less than adequate remuneration". In the Panel's view, the term "unless" establishes a clear textual connection between the existence of benefit, on the one hand, and the adequacy of remuneration, on the other hand. Thus, the Panel considered that, although the terms "remuneration" and "benefit" are different, they are nevertheless connected by the concept of "adequacy". In other words, a given amount of "remuneration" may be considered to confer a "benefit" if it is not adequate. According to the Panel, there is nothing in the text of Article 14(d) to suggest that the question of the adequacy of remuneration is a separate threshold issue, such that the question of benefit arises only – as a separate and subsequent matter – after the question of adequacy of remuneration has been resolved. Thus, the Panel considered that assessing the adequacy of remuneration for government-provided goods is part of the process of determining whether a benefit exists.[700]

4.114 The Panel then addressed India's argument that, under Article 14(d) of the SCM Agreement, the adequacy of remuneration for government-provided goods must be assessed from the perspective of the government provider, rather than the recipient. The Panel considered that India's argument was predicated on the premise that, under Article 14(d), the adequacy of remuneration, on the one hand, and benefit, on the other hand, should be assessed separately. According to the Panel, since benefit is established from the perspective of the recipient, and because the adequacy of remuneration forms part of the assessment of benefit, the adequacy of remuneration must also be established from the perspective of the recipient.[701]

4.115 The Panel also relied on the title of Article 14, which "explains that Article 14 is concerned with the 'Calculation of the Amount of a Subsidy in Terms of the Benefit to the Recipient'".[702] The Panel considered that it would be "incongruous" to find that the United States acted inconsistently with Article 14(d) by calculating benefit in terms of benefit to the recipient simply because it

---

699 Panel Report, para. 7.17. (fns omitted)
700 Panel Report, paras. 7.26-7.28.
701 Panel Report, paras. 7.29 and 7.30.
702 Panel Report, para. 7.34.

did not first, as a separate matter, determine the adequacy of remuneration from the perspective of the government provider of the good in question.[703]

4.116 For these reasons, the Panel rejected India's claim that the US benchmarking mechanism, as set forth in Section 351.511(a)(2)(i)-(iii) of the US Regulations, is inconsistent with Article 14(d) of the SCM Agreement because it fails to require that the adequacy of remuneration be assessed from the perspective of the government provider before assessing benefit to the recipient.[704]

4.4.1.2.2 Assessing whether remuneration is "less than adequate" within the meaning of Article 14(d) of the SCM Agreement

4.117 On appeal, India claims that, in finding that Article 14(d) of the SCM Agreement does not require an assessment of the adequacy of remuneration from the perspective of the government provider, prior to an assessment of whether a benefit has been conferred on a recipient, the Panel erred in its interpretation of Article 14(d). India requests the Appellate Body to reverse the Panel's finding, and to find instead that Article 14(d) first requires an assessment of the adequacy of remuneration actually received by the government provider of goods before assessing the benefit conferred on the recipient. In addition, India further requests the Appellate Body to find that the US benchmarking mechanism, as reflected in Section 351.511(a)(2)(i)-(iii) of the US Regulations, is inconsistent with a proper interpretation of Article 14(d).

4.118 India interprets Article 14(d) of the SCM Agreement as requiring a two-step analysis for assessing benefit. First, an investigating authority is required to assess whether the remuneration received by a government provider for the good in question is, from the perspective of the government provider, "less than adequate" within the meaning of Article 14(d). Second, if the remuneration is found to be less than adequate, the investigating authority is required to assess whether a benefit has been conferred on the recipient.

4.119 Noting that the first sentence of Article 14(d) refers to the terms "benefit" and "remuneration", India submits that the fact that separate terms are used implies that, conceptually, "benefit" and "remuneration" are not the same. Moreover, the presence of the term "unless" in the first sentence of Article 14(d), preceded by the phrase "shall not be considered as conferring a benefit", implies that, without establishing that the government provided the good in question for less than adequate remuneration, there can be no benefit conferred on a recipient. In India's view, this does not suggest, however, that inadequacy of remuneration must always result in a finding of benefit. In other words, under

[703] *Ibid.*
[704] Panel Report, para. 7.35.

Article 14(d), a determination that a government has provided goods for less than adequate remuneration is necessary, but not always sufficient, to establish that a benefit has been conferred on a recipient. India submits that, in finding that a determination of inadequate remuneration necessarily results in a finding of benefit, the Panel incorrectly interpreted the first sentence of Article 14(d).

4.120 India considers further that, in finding that the adequacy of remuneration must be assessed from the perspective of the recipient, rather than the government provider of the good in question, the Panel erred in its interpretation of Article 14(d) of the SCM Agreement. India observes that, used as a verb, "remunerate" means "pay (someone) for services rendered or work done", while, used as a noun, "remuneration" means "money paid for work or a service".[705] India further argues that, because the first sentence of Article 14(d) refers to "*the provision* of goods or services ... *by a government*", the adequacy of remuneration for government-provided goods must be assessed from the perspective of the government provider.[706] Moreover, India submits that, because "benefit" under Article 14(d) is determined from the perspective of the recipient of the goods, it is "logical" that the adequacy of remuneration should be assessed from the perspective of the provider of the goods.[707]

4.121 The United States responds that the Panel correctly found that Article 14(d) of the SCM Agreement does not require that the adequacy of remuneration be assessed from the perspective of the government provider, prior to assessing whether a benefit has been conferred on a recipient. According to the United States, India's interpretation of Article 14(d) contravenes the text of that provision, as well as the title and chapeau of Article 14. The United States notes in this regard that the chapeau of Article 14 makes clear that Members must provide in their laws or regulations for a methodology that allows their investigating authorities to calculate "the benefit to the recipient". In the United States' view, India argues for a methodology of calculating benefit based on "cost to government".[708] According to the United States, this standard for assessing benefit has already been considered and rejected by the Appellate Body.[709]

4.122 At the outset, we note that Article 1.1 of the SCM Agreement identifies a "benefit" as one of the constituent elements of a subsidy.[710] The term "benefit"

---

[705] India's appellant's submission, para. 28 (quoting *Oxford Dictionary of English*, 3rd edn, A. Stevenson (ed.) (Oxford University Press, 2010), p. 1503).

[706] India's appellant's submission, para. 29. (emphasis added by India)

[707] India's appellant's submission, para. 31.

[708] United States' appellee's submission, para. 56 (referring to India's first written submission to the Panel, para. 27).

[709] United States' appellee's submission, paras. 55 and 56 (referring to Appellate Body Report, *Canada – Aircraft*, paras. 154 and 155).

[710] Appellate Body Reports, *Brazil – Aircraft*, para. 157; *US – Softwood Lumber IV*, para. 51. According to Article 1.1 of the SCM Agreement, "a subsidy shall be deemed to exist" when: (i)

appears in Article 1.1(b), as well as Article 14, of the SCM Agreement. While the former provision is concerned with the existence of a "benefit", the latter provision is, in the context of Part V of the SCM Agreement, concerned with the calculation of its amount. The determination of the mere existence, as opposed to the amount, of benefit conferred by a financial contribution does not, however, call for different interpretations of the term "benefit".[711] Indeed, the explicit textual reference to Article 1.1 in the chapeau of Article 14 indicates that "benefit" is used in the same sense in Article 14 as it is in Article 1.1.[712]

4.123 The Appellate Body has established the following basic propositions concerning the concept of "benefit" under the SCM Agreement. First, the term "benefit" clearly encompasses some form of advantage[713], and the notion of "benefit" is concerned with "benefit to the recipient" and not with "cost to government".[714] Second, the term "benefit" implies a comparison, since there can be no "benefit" to the recipient unless the "financial contribution" makes the recipient "better off" than it would otherwise have been, absent that contribution.[715] Third, in undertaking the comparative analysis required by the term "benefit", the marketplace provides the appropriate basis for comparison. This is so because the trade-distorting potential of a "financial contribution" can be identified only by determining whether the recipient has received that "financial contribution" on terms more favourable than those available in the market.[716]

4.124 We observe that Article 14 of the SCM Agreement is entitled: "Calculation of the Amount of a Subsidy in Terms of the Benefit to the Recipient". Through each of its subparagraphs, Article 14 establishes guidelines for determining whether certain financial contributions – equity investments, loans, loan guarantees, the provision of goods or services by a government, and the purchase of goods by a government – confer a benefit on their recipients.[717] The Appellate Body has stated that "[a] 'benefit' arises under *each* of these guidelines if the recipient has received a 'financial contribution' on terms more favourable than those available to the recipient in the market."[718]

"there is a financial contribution by a government or any public body"; and (ii) "a benefit is thereby conferred".

711 Appellate Body Reports, *Canada – Renewable Energy / Canada – Feed-in Tariff Program*, para. 5.165.

712 Appellate Body Report, *Canada – Aircraft*, para. 155.

713 Appellate Body Report, *Canada – Aircraft*, para. 153.

714 Appellate Body Report, *Canada – Aircraft*, para. 154.

715 Appellate Body Report, *Canada – Aircraft*, para. 157.

716 *Ibid.*

717 Article 14(a) prescribes guidelines in respect of government-provided equity capital; Article 14(b) prescribes guidelines in respect of government-provided loans; Article 14(c) prescribes guidelines in respect of government-provided loan guarantees; and Article 14(d) prescribes guidelines in respect of government-provided goods or services, or purchases of goods.

718 Appellate Body Report, *Canada – Aircraft*, para. 158. (emphasis added)

4.125 India argues that the use of two distinct terms in the first sentence of Article 14(d), namely, "benefit" and "remuneration", implies that these terms are conceptually distinct. We agree that the terms "benefit" and "remuneration" are distinct terms. However, this does not necessarily mean that they must, as India argues, be separately assessed for the purposes of Article 14(d). We also consider that the term "unless", in the first sentence of Article 14(d), preceded by the phrase "shall not be considered as conferring a benefit", implies that, without establishing that the government provided the good in question for less than adequate remuneration, there can be no benefit conferred on a recipient. The term "unless", as used in Article 14(d), thus makes clear that it is only in a specific circumstance that the provision of goods by a government confers a benefit on a recipient. In this regard, Article 14(d) prescribes that the provision of goods by a government shall not be considered as conferring a benefit "unless", i.e. "except if"[719], "the provision is made for less than adequate remuneration". We therefore read the term "unless" as expressly linking the concepts of "benefit" and "remuneration" such that, under Article 14(d), a showing that "remuneration" is "less than adequate" is consonant with a finding of "benefit".

4.126 In the light of the above, we consider that Article 14(d) of the SCM Agreement establishes the adequacy of remuneration as the lens through which "benefit", within the meaning of that provision, must be assessed. Thus, Article 14(d) prescribes a unitary assessment in which a determination of benefit is reached *through* an analysis of the adequacy of remuneration for government-provided goods. Accordingly, we consider that, contrary to India's assertions, separate analyses of "benefit" and "remuneration" are not required under Article 14(d) of the SCM Agreement.

4.127 India also claims that the Panel erred in finding that, under Article 14(d), the adequacy of remuneration is to be assessed from the perspective of the recipient, rather than the government provider of the good in question. In India's view, the ordinary meaning of the term "remuneration", in the context of Article 14(d), "inherently refers to the government provider".[720] Moreover, noting the reference to "the provision of goods or services ... by a government" in the first sentence of Article 14(d), India considers this to be supportive of its contention that the adequacy of remuneration must be assessed from the perspective of the government provider, rather than the recipient of the good in question.

4.128 Although the concept of "remuneration" reflects a payment for goods or services that could be viewed from the perspective of either the person providing or receiving the payment, other interpretative elements lead us to consider that this assessment must properly be conducted from the perspective of the recipient. First, the title of Article 14 of the SCM Agreement – "Calculation of

[719] *Shorter Oxford English Dictionary*, 6th edn, A. Stevenson (ed.) (Oxford University Press, 2007), Vol. 2, p. 3446.

[720] India's appellant's submission, para. 31.

the Amount of a Subsidy in Terms of the Benefit to the Recipient" – suggests that the adequacy of the "remuneration" paid in exchange for goods or services is, under Article 14(d), to be examined from the perspective of the recipient, rather than the government provider. In addition, the text of the second sentence of Article 14(d) prescribes how the adequacy of remuneration is to be determined, namely, in relation to prevailing market conditions in the country of provision. As the Appellate Body has stated, a benefit arises under *each* of the subparagraphs of Article 14 if the recipient has received a "financial contribution" on terms more favourable than those that are available to the recipient in the market.[721] It follows that, as the Panel found, "[o]nce it is established that the price paid to the government provider is less than the price that would be required by the market", the government price in question is inadequate, and a benefit is thereby conferred.[722]

4.129 In the light of the foregoing considerations, we consider that Article 14(d) of the SCM Agreement does not require separate analyses of the adequacy of remuneration and of benefit, and does not require that the adequacy of remuneration be assessed from the perspective of the government provider. Consequently, we *uphold* the Panel's finding, in paragraph 7.35 of the Panel Report, rejecting India's claim that the US benchmarking mechanism is inconsistent with Article 14(d) of the SCM Agreement because it fails to require investigating authorities to assess the adequacy of remuneration from the perspective of the government provider before assessing whether a benefit has been conferred on the recipient.

4.4.1.2.3 The Panel's alleged failure to assess two grounds of India's "as such" claim against the US benchmarking mechanism

4.130 India claims that the Panel acted inconsistently with Article 11 of the DSU by failing to assess, separately, two grounds of India's "as such" claim against Section 351.511(a)(2)(i)-(iii) of the US Regulations.

4.131 India recalls that it had submitted six "different grounds" before the Panel in support of its claim that the "tiered approach" prescribed by the US benchmarking mechanism is inconsistent with Article 14(d) of the SCM Agreement.[723] India submits that the Panel failed to assess two of these

---

[721] Appellate Body Report, *Canada – Aircraft*, para. 158.

[722] Panel Report, para. 7.33.

[723] India alleges that these six grounds were as follows:

(i) the US benchmarking mechanism is inconsistent with the first sentence of Article 14(d) because it fails to assess the adequacy of remuneration from the perspective of the government provider, before assessing whether there is a benefit to the recipient;

(ii) the US benchmarking mechanism is inconsistent with the second sentence of Article 14(d) because it does not require a consideration of whether the

grounds, namely, that the US benchmarking mechanism is inconsistent with Article 14(d) of the SCM Agreement because: (i) it does not require an assessment of whether the difference between a government price and a benchmark price is justified by "commercial considerations"; and (ii) a government price that is "adequate" under Tier III of the US benchmarking mechanism will be deemed "less than adequate" merely based on a comparison with Tier I or Tier II benchmarks.

4.132 India notes that the Panel rejected the above two grounds on the basis of its rejection of another ground for India's claim, namely, that Article 14(d) of the SCM Agreement requires that the adequacy of remuneration for government-provided goods be assessed from the perspective of the government provider, prior to assessing whether a benefit has been conferred on a recipient. India submits that the above two grounds that the Panel failed to assess were focused on different aspects of Article 14(d). India requests the Appellate Body to find that, by failing to examine separately the above two grounds of India's "as such" claim, the Panel acted inconsistently with Article 11 of the DSU.

4.133 We recall that, under Article 11 of the DSU, a panel has the discretion to address only those arguments that it deems necessary to resolve a particular claim. Thus, the fact that a particular argument relating to a claim is not specifically addressed does not, in and of itself, lead to the conclusion that a panel has failed to conduct an objective assessment of the matter before it, in accordance with Article 11 of the DSU.[724]

4.134 Turning to the first ground, India argued that a government price in accordance with "commercial considerations" cannot constitute remuneration that is "less than adequate" within the meaning of Article 14(d) of the SCM Agreement. This ground is, in our view, premised on India's view that the adequacy of remuneration under Article 14(d) must be assessed from the perspective of the government provider and, more specifically, whether the government provider has set the price at issue in accordance with "commercial considerations". Turning to the second ground, India argued that a government

---

difference between a government and a competitor's price is justified by "commercial considerations";

(iii) a government price that is "adequate" under Tier III will be deemed "less than adequate" merely based on the benchmark method under Tiers I or II;

(iv) under Tiers I and II, all government prices are not considered as a "price" in relation to the prevailing market conditions;

(v) world market prices prescribed under Tier II are not in relation to prevailing market conditions in the country of provision of goods; and

(vi) Tiers II and III are inconsistent with Article 14(d) since the US benchmarking mechanism prioritizes the Tier II methodology above Tier III.

(India's appellant's submission, para. 19)

[724] Appellate Body Reports, *China – Rare Earths*, para. 5.224 (referring to Appellate Body Report, *EC – Fasteners (China)*, para. 511, in turn referring to Appellate Body Report, *EC – Poultry*, para. 135).

price that is "adequate" under the Tier III methodology will be rejected on the basis of the application of Tier I and Tier II benchmarks. India therefore maintained that reliance on Tier I and Tier II benchmarks is inconsistent with Article 14(d) because those benchmarks, unlike the Tier III methodology, do not start with an assessment of the "adequacy" of remuneration from the perspective of the government provider. This ground for India's claim is also, in our view, premised on India's view that Article 14(d) of the SCM Agreement requires an assessment of the adequacy of remuneration from the perspective of the government provider, prior to an assessment of benefit from the perspective of the recipient.

4.135 Above, we have upheld the Panel's finding that Article 14(d) of the SCM Agreement does not require that the adequacy of remuneration be assessed from the perspective of the government provider, prior to an assessment of whether a benefit has been conferred on a recipient. The Panel correctly found that, "[o]nce it is established that the price paid to the government provider is less than the price that would be required by the market, assessed in relation to prevailing market conditions, the remuneration afforded by the government price is inadequate, and a benefit is conferred."[725] Because the two grounds that India claims the Panel failed to evaluate are premised on an interpretation of Article 14(d) that the Panel correctly rejected, we do not consider that it was necessary for the Panel separately to evaluate them.

4.136 Accordingly, we *reject* India's claim that the Panel acted inconsistently with Article 11 of the DSU by failing to address separately two of the six grounds for its claim that Section 351.511(a)(2)(i)-(iii) is inconsistent with Article 14(d) of the SCM Agreement.

4.4.1.3 India's claims concerning the use of benchmarks under the US benchmarking mechanism

4.137 Before the Panel, India advanced two main claims concerning the selection of benchmarks under the US benchmarking mechanism. In this regard, India claimed that the US benchmarking mechanism is inconsistent with Article 14(d) of the SCM Agreement because: (i) it excludes the use of government prices as Tier I benchmarks; and (ii) it allows for the use of Tier II benchmarks in circumstances not permitted by Article 14(d). The Panel rejected India's claims. India submits that the Panel's findings are based on an erroneous interpretation of Article 14(d) of the SCM Agreement. In addition, India asserts that, in addressing the claims before it, the Panel acted inconsistently with Articles 11 and 12.7 of the DSU.

4.138 In addressing India's appeal, we first describe the relevant Panel findings under Article 14(d) of the SCM Agreement, followed by a summary of India's

[725] Panel Report, para. 7.33. (fn omitted)

claims on appeal. We then provide an interpretation of Article 14(d) as it relates to the identification of an appropriate benchmark for calculating benefit, before turning to address India's claims on appeal.

4.4.1.3.1 The Panel's findings

4.139 The Panel first considered India's claim that the US benchmarking mechanism is inconsistent with Article 14(d) of the SCM Agreement because it excludes the use of government prices as benchmarks. The Panel observed that India did not dispute that government prices are not excluded from the US benchmarking mechanism in all cases. The Panel therefore considered that the factual premise of India's claim was "undermined".[726] The Panel further considered that it would be circular, and therefore uninformative, to include the government price for the good in question in the establishment of the market benchmark when assessing whether such governmental provision confers a benefit. Recalling that benefit is assessed in relation to the market, the Panel considered that, since governments may set prices in order to pursue public policy objectives, rather than market-based profit maximization, there is no basis for requiring investigating authorities to treat government prices as being representative of "prevailing market conditions" within the meaning of the second sentence of Article 14(d) of the SCM Agreement. According to the Panel, private prices are the "primary benchmark" for assessing whether a government has provided goods for "less than adequate" remuneration within the meaning of Article 14(d).[727]

4.140 The Panel also rejected India's argument that the government price may be rejected as a benchmark only in situations where the government is the sole or dominant provider of the good in question. The Panel considered that the fact that a government is not dominant in its domestic market does not mean, as India argued, that the government's prices are likely to reflect market principles, and therefore be indicative of prevailing market conditions. Instead, for the Panel, it means that those government prices, which in any event need not be presumed to reflect market principles – because the government's pricing may be determined by policy objectives other than profit-maximization – would likely not have distorted *private* prices in that market, enabling those *private* prices to serve as benchmarks for the purposes of Article 14(d) of the SCM Agreement. The Panel therefore rejected India's claim that the US benchmarking mechanism is inconsistent with Article 14(d) because it excludes the use of government prices as benchmarks.[728]

4.141 The Panel then turned to consider India's claim that the US benchmarking mechanism is inconsistent with Article 14(d) of the SCM Agreement because it

[726] Panel Report, para. 7.38.
[727] Panel Report, paras. 7.40 and 7.41 (referring to Appellate Body Report, *US – Softwood Lumber IV*, para. 90).
[728] Panel Report, paras. 7.42 and 7.46.

provides for the use of Tier II world market prices as benchmarks whenever Tier I in-country prices are not available. The Panel was not persuaded by India's reliance on the Appellate Body's findings, in *US – Softwood Lumber IV*, to support its contention that Article 14(d) permits an investigating authority to resort to out-of-country benchmarks only where the market in the country of provision is distorted due to the predominant role of the government in the market. The Panel considered that the Appellate Body's findings were necessarily confined to the situation where the government provider of goods plays a predominant role in the market. According to the Panel, this does not mean, however, that the reasoning underlying the Appellate Body's findings does not apply in situations in which the government is not a predominant provider.[729]

4.142 Finally, the Panel considered India's claim that the US benchmarking mechanism is inconsistent with Article 14(d) of the SCM Agreement because it does not require that Tier II benchmarks relate to the prevailing market conditions in the country of provision. Noting that the overarching statutory provision implemented by the US benchmarking mechanism requires that the adequacy of remuneration must, in all cases, be assessed in relation to the prevailing market conditions in the country of provision, the Panel considered that, "in law", Tier II benchmarks applied pursuant to the US benchmarking mechanism must also relate to the prevailing market conditions in the country of provision.[730] The Panel therefore rejected India's claim that the use of Tier II benchmarks under the US benchmarking mechanism is inconsistent with Article 14(d) of the SCM Agreement.[731]

4.4.1.3.2 India's claims on appeal

4.143 On appeal, India presents two principal interpretative claims concerning the Panel's assessment of what may serve as a proper benchmark for the purposes of Article 14(d) of the SCM Agreement. First, India claims that, in finding that Article 14(d) permits investigating authorities presumptively to reject government prices as potential benchmarks, the Panel erred in its interpretation of that provision. India requests the Appellate Body to reverse this finding of the Panel, as well as the Panel's conclusion that the US benchmarking mechanism is not inconsistent with Article 14(d). India further requests the Appellate Body to find, instead, that the US benchmarking mechanism is inconsistent with that provision because it presumptively excludes, as benchmarks, government prices that do not emanate from competitively run government auctions.

4.144 Second, India requests the Appellate Body to reverse the Panel's finding that the use of world market prices as Tier II benchmarks under the US

729 Panel Report, paras. 7.49 and 7.50.
730 Panel Report, para. 7.51.
731 *Ibid.*

benchmarking mechanism is consistent with Article 14(d) of the SCM Agreement, and to find, instead, that the US benchmarking mechanism is inconsistent with Article 14(d) because: (i) it requires the use of out-of-country benchmarks without first establishing that the market in question is distorted by governmental intervention in that market; (ii) it requires the use of out-of-country benchmarks without first exhausting all possible sources of in-country benchmarks; and (iii) it does not require that Tier II benchmarks be adjusted to reflect prevailing market conditions in the country of provision.

4.145 India also presents several claims under Articles 11 and 12.7 of the DSU. First, India claims that the Panel acted inconsistently with Article 11 of the DSU by failing to record and assess its claim that Tier II of the US benchmarking mechanism is inconsistent with Article 14(d) of the SCM Agreement because it permits the use of out-of-country benchmarks without requiring the exhaustion of all possible sources of in-country benchmarks. Second, India claims that, in finding that Article 14(d) permits recourse to out-of-country benchmarks in situations in which the government is not a predominant provider, the Panel failed to provide a basic rationale for its rulings and thereby acted inconsistently with Articles 11 and 12.7 of the DSU. Third, India claims that, in relying on the parent legislation implemented by the US benchmarking mechanism to reject India's claim that Tier II of the US benchmarking mechanism does not require adjustments to out-of-country benchmarks, the Panel acted inconsistently with its duty under Article 11 of the DSU.

4.146 After setting out our interpretation of Article 14(d) of the SCM Agreement as it relates to the selection of a proper benchmark, we address each of India's discrete claims on appeal.

4.4.1.3.3 Interpretation of the guidelines prescribed under Article 14(d) of the SCM Agreement for selecting benchmarks

4.147 The chapeau of Article 14 of the SCM Agreement indicates that each of its subparagraphs establishes "guidelines" for determining whether a government-provided financial contribution confers a benefit on a recipient. The Appellate Body has found that the term "guidelines" suggests that Article 14 provides the framework within which the calculation of benefit is to be performed, although the precise detailed method of calculation is not determined, and that these guidelines should not be interpreted as rigid rules that purport to contemplate every conceivable factual circumstance.[732]

4.148 Turning to the first sentence of Article 14(d) of the SCM Agreement, we have explained in the previous section that a determination of "benefit" is reached through an analysis of whether a government provides goods for "less

---

[732] Appellate Body Report, *US – Softwood Lumber IV*, para. 92. (fn omitted)

than adequate" remuneration. An analysis of whether remuneration is "less than adequate" and, thus, confers a benefit, implies a comparative exercise. In this regard, we note that the Appellate Body has found that the term "benefit" implies a comparison since there can be no benefit to the recipient unless the "financial contribution" makes the recipient "better off" than it would otherwise have been, absent that contribution.[733] Thus, a determination of whether remuneration is "less than adequate" within the meaning of Article 14(d) involves the selection of a comparator – i.e. a benchmark price – with which to compare the government price for the good in question. If the result of this comparison is that the government price is less than the benchmark price, the difference between the two prices reflects the benefit conferred under Article 14(d).

4.149 The second sentence of Article 14(d) of the SCM Agreement prescribes that the adequacy of remuneration for a government-provided good or service "shall be determined in relation to prevailing market conditions for the good or service in question in the country of provision or purchase". Prevailing market conditions in the country of provision is thus the standard for assessing the adequacy of remuneration. In *US – Softwood Lumber IV*, the Appellate Body remarked that the meaning of the phrase "in relation to", in the second sentence of Article 14(d), is not limited to "in comparison with". Instead, the Appellate Body considered that the phrase "in relation to" connotes a broader sense of "relation, connection, reference" to prevailing market conditions in the country of provision.[734] Article 14(d) thus sets out critical elements that guide the assessment of the adequacy of remuneration for government-provided goods. In particular, the second sentence of Article 14(d) requires that such an assessment be made "in relation to prevailing market conditions", and that such conditions are those existing "in the country of provision".

4.150 In looking at the term "prevailing market conditions", we first note that the term "conditions" refers to characteristics or qualities.[735] Importantly, such characteristics or qualities are modified by the term "market". In *US – Upland Cotton*, the Appellate Body endorsed the panel's finding that the meaning of the term "market", in the context of Article 6.3(c) of the SCM Agreement, is "'a place ... with a demand for a commodity or service'; 'a geographical area of demand for commodities or services'; 'the area of economic activity in which buyers and sellers come together and the forces of supply and demand affect prices'".[736] We note that the "market conditions" are further modified by the

[733] Appellate Body Report, *Canada – Aircraft*, para. 157.

[734] Appellate Body Report, *US – Softwood Lumber IV*, para. 89. (fn omitted)

[735] Relevant definitions of the term "condition" are "[n]ature, character, quality; a characteristic, an attribute". (*Shorter Oxford English Dictionary*, 6th edn, A. Stevenson (ed.) (Oxford University Press, 2007), Vol. 1, p. 483)

[736] Appellate Body Report, *US – Upland Cotton*, para. 404 (quoting Panel Report, *US – Upland Cotton*, para. 7.1236). Although the Appellate Body considered the term "market" in the context of Article 6.3(c), we consider that such a meaning would apply equally in the context of Article 14(d).

word "prevailing", which means "predominant", or "generally accepted".[737] Taken together, these terms suggest that "prevailing market conditions", in the context of Article 14(d) of the SCM Agreement, consist of generally accepted characteristics of an area of economic activity in which the forces of supply and demand interact to determine market prices.

4.151 We consider it important to emphasize the market orientation of the inquiry under Article 14(d) of the SCM Agreement. As the Appellate Body stated in *EC and certain member States – Large Civil Aircraft*, the language found in the second sentence of Article 14(d) "highlights that a proper market benchmark is derived from an examination of the conditions pursuant to which the goods or services at issue would, *under market conditions*, be exchanged".[738] Because Article 14(d) requires that the assessment of the adequacy of remuneration for a government-provided good must be made in relation to *prevailing market conditions in the country of provision*, it follows that any benchmark for conducting such an assessment must consist of market-determined prices for the same or similar goods that relate or refer to, or are connected with, the prevailing market conditions for the good in question in the country of provision.[739] Proper benchmark prices would normally emanate from the market for the good in question in the country of provision. To the extent that such in-country prices are market determined, they would necessarily have the requisite connection with the prevailing market conditions in the country of provision that is prescribed by the second sentence of Article 14(d). In our view, such in-country prices could emanate from a variety of potential sources, including private or government-related entities.[740]

4.152 Investigating authorities bear the responsibility to conduct the necessary analysis in order to determine, on the basis of information supplied by petitioners and respondents in a countervailing duty investigation, whether proposed benchmark prices are market determined such that they can be used to determine whether remuneration is less than adequate. The chapeau of Article 14 requires investigating authorities to explain adequately, consistent with the guidelines set out in Article 14, the application of the methodology applied to calculate the amount of benefit that is conferred by a government-provided financial contribution. We note, moreover, that Article VI:3 of the GATT 1994 has been interpreted to impose certain requirements on investigating authorities. The Appellate Body has stated that, "under Article VI:3 of the GATT 1994,

[737] Relevant definitions of the term "prevailing" include "predominant in extent or amount; generally current or accepted". (*Shorter Oxford English Dictionary*, 6th edn, A. Stevenson (ed.) (Oxford University Press, 2007), Vol. 2, p. 2340)

[738] Appellate Body Report, *EC and certain member States – Large Civil Aircraft*, para. 975. (emphasis added)

[739] Appellate Body Report, *US – Softwood Lumber IV*, para. 89.

[740] We use the term "government-related entities" to refer to all government bodies (whether national or regional), public bodies, and any other government-owned entities for which there has not been a "public body" determination.

investigating authorities, before imposing countervailing duties, must ascertain the precise amount of a subsidy attributed to the imported products under investigation."[741] The Appellate Body has further explained that the obligation under Article VI:3 "encompasses a requirement to conduct a sufficiently diligent 'investigation' into, and solicitation of, relevant facts, and to base its determination on positive evidence in the record".[742] As we see it, the obligation under Article 14 of the SCM Agreement to calculate the amount of a subsidy in terms of the benefit to the recipient encompasses the same requirement.

4.153 What an investigating authority must do in conducting the necessary analysis for the purpose of arriving at a proper benchmark, however, will vary depending upon the circumstances of the case, the characteristics of the market being examined, and the nature, quantity, and quality of the information supplied by petitioners and respondents, including such additional information an investigating authority seeks so that it may base its determination on positive evidence on the record.[743] In all cases, in arriving at a proper benchmark, an investigating authority must explain the basis for its conclusions.

4.154 We recognize that, depending on the circumstances, some types of prices may, from an evidentiary standpoint, be more easily found to constitute market-determined prices in the country of provision. In this regard, the Appellate Body has considered that the *primary* benchmark, and therefore the *starting point* of the analysis in determining a benchmark for the purposes of Article 14(d) of the SCM Agreement, is the prices at which the same or similar goods are sold by private suppliers in arm's-length transactions in the country of provision. This is so because "private prices in the market of provision will *generally* represent an appropriate measure of the 'adequacy of remuneration' for the provision of goods."[744] This should not be read to suggest that there is, in the abstract, a hierarchy between different types of in-country prices that can be relied upon in arriving at a proper benchmark. We emphasize that whether a price may be relied upon for benchmarking purposes under Article 14(d) is not a function of its source but, rather, whether it is a market-determined price reflective of prevailing market conditions in the country of provision. Accordingly, while the prices at which the same or similar goods are sold by private suppliers in the country of provision may serve as a starting point of analysis, this does not mean that, having found such prices, the analysis must necessarily end there. For example, prices on record of government-related entities other than the entity providing the financial contribution at issue also need to be considered to assess whether they are market determined and can

---

741 Appellate Body Report, *US – Countervailing Measures on Certain EC Products*, para. 139. (fn omitted)

742 Appellate Body Report, *US – Anti-Dumping and Countervailing Duties (China)*, para. 602.

743 We also consider that, to the extent that an investigating authority has recourse to facts available in conducting the necessary analysis for the purpose of arriving at a proper benchmark, any such recourse must conform to the requirements under Article 12.7 of the SCM Agreement.

744 Appellate Body Report, *US – Softwood Lumber IV*, para. 90. (emphasis added)

therefore form part of a proper benchmark. Article 14(d) establishes no legal presumption that in-country prices from any particular source can be discarded in a benchmark analysis. Rather, Article 14(d) requires an analysis of the market in the country of provision to determine whether particular in-country prices can be relied upon in arriving at a proper benchmark.

4.155 Although the benchmark analysis begins with a consideration of in-country prices for the good in question, it would not be appropriate to rely on such prices when they are not market determined. Proposed in-country prices will not be reflective of prevailing market conditions in the country of provision when they deviate from a market-determined price as a result of governmental intervention in the market. In *US – Softwood Lumber IV*, the Appellate Body recognized that a government, in its role as a provider of a good, may distort in-country private prices for that good by setting an artificially low price with which the prices of private providers in the market align.[745] The ability of a government provider to have such an influence on in-country private prices presupposes that it has sufficient market power to do so.[746] The Appellate Body reasoned that, in such a situation, "there may be little difference, if any, between the government price and the private prices" in the country of provision.[747] In other words, "the government's role in providing the financial contribution [may be] so predominant that it effectively determines the price at which private suppliers sell the same or similar goods, so that the comparison contemplated by Article 14 would become circular."[748] Because this would lead to a calculation of benefit that was artificially low, or even zero, the Appellate Body reasoned that the right of Members to countervail subsidies could be undermined or circumvented in such a scenario. The Appellate Body considered that Article 14(d) "ensures that the provision's purposes are not frustrated in such situations" by permitting investigating authorities to use an alternative benchmark to in-country private prices.[749]

4.156 The Appellate Body has emphasized that, although a government's predominant role as a supplier in the market makes it "likely" that private prices will be distorted, the distortion of in-country private prices must be established "on a case-by-case basis, according to the particular facts underlying each countervailing duty investigation".[750] In *US – Anti-Dumping and Countervailing Duties (China)*, the Appellate Body emphasized that "an investigating authority cannot, based simply on a finding that the government is the predominant supplier of the relevant goods, refuse to consider evidence relating to factors

[745] Appellate Body Report, *US – Softwood Lumber IV*, para. 100.

[746] Appellate Body Report, *US – Anti-Dumping and Countervailing Duties (China)*, para. 444.

[747] Appellate Body Report, *US – Softwood Lumber IV*, para. 100.

[748] Appellate Body Report, *US – Softwood Lumber IV*, para. 93. (fn omitted)

[749] Appellate Body Report, *US – Softwood Lumber IV*, para. 101.

[750] Appellate Body Report, *US – Anti-Dumping and Countervailing Duties (China)*, para. 453 (quoting Appellate Body Report, *US – Softwood Lumber IV*, para. 102).

other than government market share."[751] It clarified that its reasoning in *US – Softwood Lumber IV* excluded the application of a *per se* rule, according to which an investigating authority could properly conclude in every case, and regardless of any other evidence, that the fact that the government is the predominant supplier means that private prices are distorted.[752] The Appellate Body has therefore cautioned against equating the concepts of price distortion and government predominance, and has highlighted that the link between the two concepts is an evidentiary one. Thus, there does not exist "a threshold above which the fact that the government is the predominant supplier in the market alone becomes sufficient to establish price distortion, but clearly, the more predominant a government's role in the market is, the more *likely* this role will result in the distortion of private prices."[753]

4.157 In conducting the necessary analysis to determine whether proposed in-country prices can be relied upon in arriving at a proper benchmark, an investigating authority may be called upon to examine various aspects of the relevant market.[754] We further recognize that there may be circumstances in which investigating authorities cannot verify necessary market or pricing information. As we have stated previously, what an investigating authority must do in conducting the necessary analysis for the purpose of arriving at a proper benchmark will vary depending upon the circumstances of the case, the characteristics of the market being examined, and the nature, quantity, and quality of the information supplied by petitioners and respondents, including such additional information an investigating authority seeks so that it may base its determination on positive evidence on the record. In any event, investigating authorities have a responsibility to explain the basis for their conclusions in arriving at a proper benchmark for the purposes of Article 14(d) of the SCM Agreement.

---

[751] Appellate Body Report, *US – Anti-Dumping and Countervailing Duties (China)*, para. 446.

[752] Appellate Body Report, *US – Anti-Dumping and Countervailing Duties (China)*, para. 443 (referring to Appellate Body Report, *US – Softwood Lumber IV*, para. 100).

[753] Appellate Body Report, *US – Anti-Dumping and Countervailing Duties (China)*, para. 444. (emphasis original) The panel in *US – Softwood Lumber IV* considered that it would not be possible to use in-country prices as a benchmark: (i) where the government is the only supplier of the particular goods in the country; and (ii) where the government administratively controls all of the prices for those goods in the country. The panel reasoned that, in these situations, the "only remaining possibility would appear to be the construction of some sort of a proxy for, or estimate of, the market price for the good in that country". (Appellate Body Report, *US – Softwood Lumber IV*, para. 98 (quoting Panel Report, *US – Softwood Lumber IV*, para. 7.57)) On appeal, the Appellate Body limited itself to considering only the situation of government predominance in the market as a provider of goods because it was "the only one raised on appeal". (*Ibid.*, para. 99)

[754] This examination may involve an assessment of the structure of the relevant market, including the type of entities operating in that market, their respective market share, as well as any entry barriers. It could also require assessing the behaviour of the entities operating in that market in order to determine whether the government itself, or acting through government-related entities, exerts market power so as to distort in-country prices.

4.158 The analysis referred to above may lead an investigating authority to conclude that in-country prices cannot be relied on in determining a benchmark for the purposes of Article 14(d) of the SCM Agreement, and that an alternative benchmark should be employed. We recall that, in *US – Softwood Lumber IV*, the Appellate Body considered the question of what types of alternative benchmarks could be relied on in a manner consistent with Article 14(d). The Appellate Body considered that alternative methods for determining the adequacy of remuneration "could include proxies that take into account prices for similar goods quoted on world markets, or proxies constructed on the basis of production costs".[755] The Appellate Body reiterated, however, that where an investigating authority proceeds in this manner, "it is under an obligation to ensure that the resulting benchmark relates or refers to, or is connected with, prevailing market conditions in the country of provision, and must reflect price, quality, availability, marketability, transportation and other conditions of purchase or sale, as required by Article 14(d)."[756] In doing so, the Appellate Body underscored the importance of making appropriate adjustments to ensure that alternative benchmarks reflect prevailing market conditions in the country of provision.[757] In any event, the Appellate Body stated that it would not be assessing various alternative benchmarks but rather only the specific alternative benchmark that had been employed by the United States in that case, namely, out-of-country prices for the good in question.[758] The Appellate Body thus clarified that it was making no findings on the WTO-consistency of alternative benchmarks "in the abstract".[759]

4.159 On the basis of the foregoing, we do not consider that there is any prescribed preference for the use of particular alternative benchmarks over others. In our view, it would be difficult to assess the appropriateness of one alternative over another in the abstract. As the Appellate Body has stated, an assessment of the consistency of an alternative method for determining benefit with Article 14(d) of the SCM Agreement "will depend on how any such method is applied in a particular case".[760] We emphasize, however, that the alternative benchmark ultimately determined by an investigating authority for the purposes of Article 14(d) must, in accordance with the second sentence of that provision, relate or refer to, or be connected with, "prevailing market conditions" in the country of provision.

4.160 With these considerations in mind, we turn now to examine India's claims on appeal.

755 Appellate Body Report, *US – Softwood Lumber IV*, para. 106.
756 *Ibid.*
757 Appellate Body Report, *US – Softwood Lumber IV*, para. 108.
758 Appellate Body Report, *US – Softwood Lumber IV*, para. 107.
759 Appellate Body Report, *US – Softwood Lumber IV*, para. 106.
760 *Ibid.*

4.4.1.3.4 Government-related prices under Tier I of the US benchmarking mechanism

4.161 We begin with India's claim concerning the alleged exclusion of government prices as benchmarks under the US benchmarking mechanism. Before the Panel, India argued that the US benchmarking mechanism is inconsistent with Article 14(d) of the SCM Agreement because, under Tier I of that mechanism, the United States simply rejects government prices that do no emanate from competitively run government auctions. According to India, the Panel found that "government transactions and prices can be presumptively and conclusively ignored in the assessment of 'prevailing market conditions' under Article 14(d)".[761] India submits that, in making this finding, the Panel erred in its interpretation of Article 14(d) of the SCM Agreement.

4.162 India notes that the first sentence of Article 14(d) of the SCM Agreement states that the provision of goods by a government is not to be considered as conferring a benefit unless proved otherwise. India contends that the direct implication of this is that investigating authorities are not permitted to reject presumptively the government price under challenge as not being market driven. India submits that, contrary to Article 14(d), the Panel simply assumed that all government prices are *ipso facto* presumed to cater to public policy objectives and, hence, can be disregarded as benchmarks.

4.163 India further submits that Article 14(d) of the SCM Agreement is concerned with the market on an "as is" basis, and therefore does not permit government prices to be disregarded in the analysis of benefit. In this regard, India relies on the Appellate Body's finding, in *US – Softwood Lumber IV*, that the term "market conditions" in Article 14(d) does not refer to a market undistorted by the government's financial contribution.[762] In addition, India submits that the Panel's interpretation of Article 14(d) fails to account for the implications of the Appellate Body's finding, in *US – Anti-Dumping and Countervailing Duties (China)*, that government loans cannot *ipso facto* be rejected as "non-commercial".[763] For India, this means that there is no presumption that government prices are *ipso facto* unusable as benchmarks, and investigating authorities are required to establish whether government presence or influence in the relevant market causes distortions that render the relevant government prices unusable.

4.164 In response, the United States observes that the Panel found, and India did not dispute, that government prices are not "presumptively and conclusively"

---

[761] India's appellant's submission, para. 42.

[762] India's appellant's submission, para. 47 (referring to Appellate Body Report, *US – Softwood Lumber IV*, para. 87).

[763] India's appellant's submission, para. 48 (referring to Appellate Body Report, *US – Anti-Dumping and Countervailing Duties (China)*, para. 479).

excluded as benchmarks under the US benchmarking mechanism in all cases.[764] As India has not established the factual premise of its claim that the US benchmarking mechanism excludes the use of government prices as benchmarks[765], the United States submits that, on this basis alone, India's claim on appeal should be dismissed. The United States adds that, in any event, there is no apparent connection between the text of Article 14(d) and India's assertion that government prices must be presumed to be market driven. Noting that the benchmark analysis under Article 14(d) assesses whether a government's provision of goods is made for less than adequate remuneration, the United States contends that India has not explained why the terms "shall not" and "unless" in the first sentence of Article 14(d) require an investigating authority to use government prices in determining market benchmarks. The United States submits that the Panel correctly found that "it would be circular, and therefore uninformative, to include the government price for the good provided by the government in the establishment of the market benchmark when assessing *whether such* governmental provision confers a benefit."[766]

4.165 In addition, the United States contends that India has not explained how the presumptive use of government prices for the purpose of determining benchmarks can be squared with the Appellate Body's finding that the prices of "*private suppliers* in the country of provision are the *primary benchmark* that investigating authorities *must use* when determining whether goods have been provided by a government for less than adequate remuneration."[767] The United States further contends that the Panel correctly rejected India's reliance on the Appellate Body's finding, in *US – Anti-Dumping and Countervailing Duties (China)*, that "government loans cannot be *ipso facto* rejected as non-commercial under Article 14(b)".[768] In the United States' view, the Panel correctly found that the Appellate Body's finding does not mean that government prices must be used as market benchmarks for the purposes of Article 14(d) of the SCM Agreement.

4.166 We note that, both before the Panel and on appeal, India has not been consistent in articulating *which* government prices ought to be included in a market benchmark for the purposes of Article 14(d) of the SCM Agreement.[769]

---

[764] United States' appellee's submission, para. 71 (quoting India's appellant's submission, para. 42).

[765] United States' appellee's submission, para. 61 (referring to Panel Report, para. 7.38).

[766] United States' appellee's submission, para. 73 (quoting Panel Report, para. 7.39). (emphasis added by the United States)

[767] United States' appellee's submission, para. 74 (quoting Appellate Body Report, *US – Softwood Lumber IV*, para. 90). (emphasis added by the United States)

[768] United States' appellee's submission, para. 75 (quoting India's appellant's submission, para. 48, in turn referring to Appellate Body Report, *US – Anti-Dumping and Countervailing Duties (China)*, para. 479).

[769] For instance, in its first written submission to the Panel, India referred at certain points to the exclusion of "the government price in question" from the benchmark, while at other points, to "government players" in the market. (India's first written submission to the Panel, paras. 74 and 75) Similarly, in its appellant's submission, India refers at one point to the "government price under

Certainly, it is inherently circular to require that the very government price that investigating authorities are seeking to test against the market be used as the market benchmark for the purposes of Article 14(d). In response to questioning at the oral hearing, India clarified that its reference to "government prices" means government prices other than the financial contribution at issue. In the light of this clarification, we proceed with our analysis by examining whether Article 14(d) requires the use of such prices as benchmarks. We further note that, because some of the prices to which the participants refer may be those set by entities that have not been found to be a government or public body, and may, for example, consist of state-owned enterprises for which there is no determination as to whether or not they are public bodies within the meaning of Article 1.1(a)(1) of the SCM Agreement, we refer below in our analysis to "government-related prices" other than the financial contribution at issue.[770]

4.167 As we have explained above, Article 14(d) establishes that the benchmark for conducting an assessment of the adequacy of remuneration consists of market-determined prices for the same or similar goods in the country of provision – i.e. prices that relate or refer to, or are connected with, the prevailing market conditions in the country of provision.[771] As we have also explained, whether a price may be relied on for benchmarking purposes under Article 14(d) is not a function of its source but, rather, whether it is determined to be reflective of prevailing market conditions in the country of provision.

4.168 Hence, we agree with the proposition that government-related prices on record other than the financial contribution at issue need to be considered in determining a proper benchmark for the purposes of Article 14(d), provided that such prices relate or refer to, or are connected with, the prevailing market conditions in the country of provision. As we have said, because Article 14(d) establishes no legal presumption that in-country prices from any particular source can be discarded in a benchmark analysis, a determination of a benchmark for the purposes of Article 14(d) cannot, at the outset, exclude consideration of any potential in-country prices, including government-related prices other than the financial contribution at issue.

4.169 In the course of examining India's claim, the Panel found that "investigating authorities should [not] be required to treat government prices as being representative of 'prevailing market conditions' within the meaning of the second sentence" of Article 14(d) of the SCM Agreement.[772] The Panel gave

---

challenge" (India's appellant's submission, para. 46), while at other points to "government prices" more generally (*Ibid.*, para. 55).

[770] This formulation is intended to capture prices other than the financial contribution at issue which are provided by other government-related entities. As previously explained, we use the term "government-related entities" to refer to all government bodies (whether national or regional), public bodies, and any other government-owned entities for which there has not been a "public body" determination.

[771] Appellate Body Report, *US – Softwood Lumber IV*, para. 89.

[772] Panel Report, para. 7.39.

three reasons in support of this finding. First, the Panel considered that it would be circular, and therefore uninformative, to include the government price for the good provided by the government in the establishment of the market benchmark when assessing whether such governmental provision confers a benefit. We do not consider that investigating authorities are required to consider the use of the very government price under challenge – in other words, the financial contribution at issue – as a benchmark for the purposes of Article 14(d) of the SCM Agreement. However, as we have noted, Article 14(d) requires the use of market-determined government-related prices other than the financial contribution at issue in determining a proper benchmark.

4.170 The second reason that the Panel gave for its finding was that, because benefit is assessed in relation to the market, and "[s]ince governments may set prices in order to pursue public policy objectives, rather than market-based profit maximization, [there is] no basis ... to include government prices when determining market benchmarks in the context of Article 14(d)."[773] In our view, the fact that governments *may* set prices in pursuit of public policy objectives, rather than market-based profit maximization, does not permit a general inference that there is "no basis ... to include government prices" in determining a benchmark for the purposes of Article 14(d) of the SCM Agreement. In particular, we consider the Panel's statement to be erroneous in respect of government-related prices that have the requisite nexus with prevailing market conditions in the country of provision. Thus, we disagree with the Panel's conclusion to the extent that it suggests that Article 14(d) does not require the consideration of government-related prices simply because governments may set prices in pursuit of public policy objectives.

4.171 The third reason that the Panel gave for its finding was that, because in-country private prices are the primary benchmark for assessing whether a government's provision of goods is made for less than adequate remuneration, Article 14(d) of the SCM Agreement does not require investigating authorities to consider government prices in determining a benchmark. In making this finding, the Panel considered its approach as being consistent with the Appellate Body's findings in *US – Softwood Lumber IV*. In particular, the Panel relied on the Appellate Body's finding that in-country private prices "are the primary benchmark that investigating authorities must use when determining whether goods have been provided by a government for less than adequate remuneration".[774]

4.172 As we have found above, the second sentence of Article 14(d) of the SCM Agreement clearly establishes that the benchmark for assessing the adequacy of remuneration for government-provided goods is a price that relates or refers to, or is connected with, prevailing market conditions in the country of provision. Private prices and government-related prices can both reflect

---

773 *Ibid.*

774 Panel Report, para. 7.40 (quoting Appellate Body Report, *US – Softwood Lumber IV*, para. 90).

prevailing market conditions in the country of provision. The proposition that in-country private prices are the primary benchmark reflects only the fact that such prices may, as recognized by the Appellate Body, serve as a starting point for determining a benchmark.[775] This does not mean, however, that government-related prices that reflect prevailing market conditions in the country of provision cannot be relied upon, together with in-country private prices, to determine a benchmark for the purposes of Article 14(d). We therefore consider that the Appellate Body's finding in *US – Softwood Lumber IV* does not stand for the proposition that Article 14(d) permits an investigation authority to refuse to consider whether government-related prices reflect prevailing market conditions in the country of provision.

4.173 In the light of the above, we consider that the Panel's finding is in error to the extent that it may be read as suggesting that Article 14(d) does not require investigating authorities to consider any in-country government-related prices in determining a benchmark for assessing benefit under Article 14(d) of the SCM Agreement.

4.174 We recall that the Panel found that "[t]he factual premise for India's claim" was undermined because "India [did] not dispute the United States' assertion that government prices are not excluded from the benchmarking mechanism in all cases."[776] Perhaps, for this reason, the Panel never engaged in an assessment of whether the US Regulation at issue, as India claims, excludes consideration of government prices other than those from competitively run government auctions.

4.175 Section 351.511(a)(2)(i) of the US Regulations provides:

> (i) *In general.* The Secretary will normally seek to measure the adequacy of remuneration by comparing the government price to a market-determined price for the good or service resulting from actual transactions in the country in question. Such a price could include prices stemming from actual transactions between private parties, actual imports, or, in certain circumstances, actual sales from competitively run government auctions. In choosing such transactions or sales, the Secretary will consider product similarity; quantities sold, imported, or auctioned; and other factors affecting comparability.

4.176 Tier I of the US benchmarking mechanism thus prescribes that the USDOC will normally measure the adequacy of remuneration by comparing the government price to a "market-determined price" that results from "actual transactions" in the country in question. According to Section 351.511(a)(2)(i), such a price "could include" a price based on actual transactions between private parties, actual imports, or, in certain circumstances, actual sales from

[775] Appellate Body Report, *US – Softwood Lumber IV*, para. 90.
[776] Panel Report, para. 7.38.

competitively run government auctions. To us, the fact that Tier I prices "could include" an illustrative list of sample transactions suggests that other types of transactions, including government-related prices other than government auction prices, may constitute a Tier I benchmark.[777] Indeed, we consider that Section 351.511(a)(2)(i), on its face, requires consideration of all market-determined in-country prices.

4.177 To the extent that Section 351.511(a)(2)(i) does not exclude that government-related prices other than the financial contribution at issue can be used as Tier I benchmarks, the premise of India's claim that government-related prices are necessarily excluded as benchmarks under the US benchmarking mechanism has not been established. Accordingly, although we have expressed above concerns about the Panel's interpretation of Article 14(d) of the SCM Agreement, we ultimately *uphold*, albeit for different reasons, the Panel's finding, in paragraph 7.46 of the Panel Report, rejecting India's claim that the US benchmarking mechanism is inconsistent "as such" with Article 14(d) of the SCM Agreement because it excludes the use of government prices as benchmarks.

4.4.1.3.5 World market prices under Tier II of the US benchmarking mechanism

4.178 We turn now to India's claims concerning the use of world market prices under Tier II of the US benchmarking mechanism. We begin with India's claim concerning the Panel's finding that Article 14(d) of the SCM Agreement permits the use of out-of-country benchmarks in situations in which the government is not a predominant provider of the good in question. Next, we consider India's claim concerning the Panel's finding that the US benchmarking mechanism requires that Tier II benchmarks reflect prevailing market conditions in the country of provision.

4.4.1.3.5.1 Whether the Panel erred in finding that Article 14(d) of the SCM Agreement permits the use of out-of-country benchmarks in situations in which the government is not a predominant provider of the good in question

4.179 India claims that the Panel erred in finding that Article 14(d) of the SCM Agreement permits the use of out-of-country benchmarks in situations in which the government is not a predominant provider of the good in question. India

---

777 In response to questioning at the oral hearing, the United States agreed with this reading of the US Regulations.

submits that, in making this finding, the Panel erred in its interpretation of Article 14(d). India adds that, in finding that Article 14(d) permits the use of out-of-country benchmarks in "other situations", the Panel failed to provide basic guidelines to determine what these "other situations" are, and therefore failed to provide a basic rationale for its findings.[778] India submits that, for these reasons, the Panel acted inconsistently with Articles 11 and 12.7 of the DSU. We begin our analysis with India's claim under Article 14(d) of the SCM Agreement.

4.180 According to India, the Appellate Body did not endorse, in *US – Softwood Lumber IV*, the use of out-of-country benchmarks in circumstances unrelated to governmental intervention in the relevant market. India notes that the panel in that dispute considered that out-of-country benchmarks may be used in the following situations: (i) where the government is the sole provider of the good in question; and (ii) where the government administratively controls all of the prices for the good in question. India notes further that, on appeal, the Appellate Body identified a third situation, namely, where in-country prices are distorted as a result of the predominant role played by the government as a provider of the relevant good. India emphasizes that all of the situations identified by the panel and the Appellate Body in *US – Softwood Lumber IV* involve governmental intervention in the market to varying degrees.[779] For India, this means that the circumstances in which Article 14(d) permits the use of out-of-country benchmarks "ought to be something akin to governmental predominance in the market".[780]

4.181 India notes further that, in *US – Anti-Dumping and Countervailing Duties (China)*, the Appellate Body found that the "very limited" circumstance in which an investigating authority may use a benchmark other than private prices of the goods in question in the country of provision is "when it has been established that those private prices are distorted, because of the predominant role of the government in the market as a provider of the same or similar goods".[781] Thus, Article 14(d) of the SCM Agreement does not permit investigating authorities to use out-of-country benchmarks simply because a limited set of in-country benchmarks are unavailable.

4.182 The United States responds that the Panel correctly interpreted Article 14(d) of the SCM Agreement as permitting investigating authorities to use out-of-country benchmarks without first finding that the in-country market is distorted by governmental intervention. The United States submits that India's claim is based on an incorrect reading of the Appellate Body's findings in *US – Softwood Lumber IV* and *US – Anti-Dumping and Countervailing Duties*

778 India's appellant's submission, para. 64.

779 India's appellant's submission, paras. 66 and 67.

780 India's appellant's submission, para. 68.

781 India's appellant's submission, para. 69 (quoting Appellate Body Report, *US – Anti-Dumping and Countervailing Duties (China)*, para. 439, in turn quoting Appellate Body Report, *US – Softwood Lumber IV*, paras. 102 and 103).

(China). Moreover, the United States submits that the Appellate Body's findings in *US – Softwood Lumber IV* were limited to the particular situation where in-country private prices are distorted by government predominance in the market.[782] Thus, India's argument that the circumstances permitting an investigating authority to use out-of-country benchmarks must relate to governmental intervention in the relevant market is in error.

4.183 As we see it, India's claim does not concern whether Article 14(d) of the SCM Agreement permits the use of out-of-country prices as benchmarks. It is common ground between the participants that Article 14(d) permits the use of out-of-country benchmarks, and does so in situations where in-country prices are distorted by governmental intervention in the market. The participants, however, dispute whether Article 14(d) permits the use of out-of-country benchmarks in other circumstances.

4.184 We note, as did the Panel, that, in examining the situations in which Article 14(d) of the SCM Agreement permits the use of alternative benchmarks to in-country prices, the Appellate Body, in *US – Softwood Lumber IV*, expressly limited itself to considering only the situation of government predominance in the market as a provider of goods because it was "the only one raised on appeal".[783] In the light of this statement, we do not consider that the Appellate Body foreclosed the possibility that Article 14(d) permits the use of alternative benchmarks in situations where the government is not a predominant provider of the good in question. We therefore agree with the Panel that the Appellate Body's findings in *US – Softwood Lumber IV* are necessarily circumscribed by the facts of that case.

4.185 With regard to India's reliance on the Appellate Body's findings in *US – Anti-Dumping and Countervailing Duties (China)*, we note that the issue in that dispute was whether the USDOC had, inconsistently with Article 14(d) of the SCM Agreement, relied solely on evidence of predominant government market share as a basis for concluding that in-country prices were distorted and, therefore, could not be used in determining a benchmark. The Appellate Body found that "an investigating authority cannot, based simply on a finding that the government is the predominant supplier of the relevant goods, refuse to consider evidence relating to factors other than government market share."[784] In our view, the Appellate Body's findings under Article 14(d) of the SCM Agreement in that dispute were made in the context of examining a claim in which it was alleged that an investigating authority had not properly found that in-country prices were distorted by governmental intervention in the market as a basis for resorting to out-of-country prices for the purpose of determining a benchmark. We do not see any findings made by the Appellate Body in *US – Anti-Dumping and*

---

[782] United States' appellee's submission, para. 105 (referring to Appellate Body Report, *US – Softwood Lumber IV*, para. 99).

[783] Panel Report, para. 7.50 (quoting Appellate Body Report, *US – Softwood Lumber IV*, para. 99).

[784] Appellate Body Report, *US – Anti-Dumping and Countervailing Duties (China)*, para. 446.

Countervailing Duties (China) that indicate that the Appellate Body was foreclosing the possibility that there could be situations other than price distortion due to government predominance as a provider in the market, in which Article 14(d) permits the use of out-of-country prices for the purpose of determining a benchmark.

4.186 In the light of the Appellate Body's findings in *US – Softwood Lumber IV* and *US – Anti-Dumping and Countervailing Duties (China)*, we are not persuaded by India's assertion that the Appellate Body has established that the only situation in which out-of-country prices may be used to determine a benchmark is where in-country prices are distorted by governmental intervention in the market. While the Appellate Body has clarified that recourse to out-of-country prices is exceptional, the Appellate Body has not, in previous disputes, addressed the issue of whether there are other circumstances in which Article 14(d) permits the use of out-of-country prices and, if so, what those other circumstances are.

4.187 We note that, in rejecting India's claim, the Panel expressed the view that, although the Appellate Body's findings in *US – Softwood Lumber IV* are limited to the facts of that dispute, "this does not mean that the reasoning underlying the Appellate Body's findings in that case cannot apply, with equal force, in other situations, in which the government is not a predominant provider."[785]

4.188 In *US – Softwood Lumber IV*, the Appellate Body interpreted Article 14(d) of the SCM Agreement, in accordance with its text, context, and object and purpose, and established that Article 14(d) does not require the use of in-country prices for benchmarking purposes in every case. First, the Appellate Body interpreted the phrase "in relation to" in the second sentence of Article 14(d) and found that this phrase does not denote a rigid comparison, but rather implies a broader sense of "relation, connection, reference".[786] Thus, the Appellate Body reasoned that the use of the phrase "in relation to" in Article 14(d) suggests that the drafters did not intend to exclude any possibility of using as a benchmark something other than in-country prices.[787] Second, the Appellate Body noted that the chapeau of Article 14 of the SCM Agreement requires that "any" method used by investigating authorities to calculate the benefit to the recipient shall be provided for in a WTO Member's legislation or regulations, and it requires that its application be transparent and adequately explained. In the Appellate Body's view, the reference to "any" method clearly implies that more than one method consistent with Article 14 is available to investigating authorities for purposes of calculating the benefit to the recipient. The Appellate Body found that the context provided by the chapeau of Article 14 does not suggest that in-country prices, whenever available, have to be used exclusively

---

785 Panel Report, para. 7.50.

786 Appellate Body Report, *US – Softwood Lumber IV*, para. 89.

787 *Ibid.*

as a benchmark for the purposes of Article 14(d).[788] Third, the Appellate Body considered that, given the objective of Article 14 – the calculation of the amount of a subsidy in terms of the benefit to the recipient – an interpretation of Article 14(d) that required in-country prices to be used as benchmarks in all cases would frustrate the objective of Article 14 in "situations in which there is no way of telling whether the recipient is 'better off' absent the financial contribution".[789] Fourth, the Appellate Body found that such a restrictive interpretation of Article 14 frustrates the object and purpose of the SCM Agreement, "which includes disciplining the use of subsidies and countervailing measures while, at the same time, enabling WTO Members whose domestic industries are harmed by subsidized imports to use such remedies".[790]

4.189 In our view, the rationale underpinning the Appellate Body's findings in *US – Softwood Lumber IV* is that, properly interpreted in the light of its context and object and purpose, Article 14(d) of the SCM Agreement does not prohibit the use of alternative benchmarks in situations where in-country prices cannot properly be used as a basis for determining a benchmark. Thus, contrary to what India asserts, we do not consider that in-country prices may not be used to determine a benchmark only where such prices are distorted as a result of governmental intervention in the market. Indeed, there may be other circumstances where an investigating authority would not be required to use in-country prices to determine a benchmark for the purposes of Article 14(d), for example, where information pertaining to in-country prices cannot be verified so as to determine whether they are market determined in accordance with the second sentence of Article 14(d). As we see it, to find that an investigating authority is precluded from using alternative benchmarks in these situations would be contrary to a proper interpretation of Article 14(d).

4.190 This does not suggest that an investigating authority may have easy recourse to out-of-country prices. We have found that, in accordance with the second sentence of Article 14(d), the benchmark required for the purposes of that provision consists of market-determined prices that reflect prevailing market conditions in the country of provision. We have emphasized above that the analysis of prices within the country of provision does not, at the outset, exclude prices from any particular source, including government-related prices other than the financial contribution at issue. Moreover, we have considered that the obligation under Article 14 to calculate the amount of subsidy in terms of the benefit to the recipient encompasses a requirement to conduct a sufficiently diligent investigation into, and solicitation of, relevant facts, and to base a determination on positive evidence on the record. To our minds, it is only once an investigating authority has properly complied with its obligation to

[788] Appellate Body Report, *US – Softwood Lumber IV*, para. 91.

[789] Appellate Body Report, *US – Softwood Lumber IV*, para. 93. (emphasis omitted)

[790] Appellate Body Report, *US – Softwood Lumber IV*, para. 95 (referring to Appellate Body Report, *US – Carbon Steel*, paras. 73 and 74).

investigate whether there are in-country prices that reflect prevailing market conditions in the country of provision that it may, consistently with Article 14(d) of the SCM Agreement, use alternative benchmarks. Finally, where an investigating authority considers that it must have recourse to a benchmark other than in-country prices, it must explain its basis for doing so.

4.191 In the light of the foregoing considerations, we therefore consider that the Panel did not err in finding that Article 14(d) of the SCM Agreement permits the use of out-of-country benchmarks in situations other than where the government is a predominant provider of the good in question.

4.192 We turn now to India's claim that, by finding that Article 14(d) of the SCM Agreement permits investigating authorities to use out-of-country benchmarks in "other situations", the Panel failed to provide a basic rationale for its finding as required by Article 12.7 of the DSU, "read with" Article 11 of the DSU.[791]

4.193 The United States submits that India's claim under Article 11 should be rejected because it is subsidiary to India's claim that the Panel erred in its legal interpretation of Article 14(d) of the SCM Agreement.[792] Moreover, in response to India's claim under Article 12.7 of the DSU, the United States submits that, contrary to India's assertions on appeal, the Panel, in fact, defined the "other situations" in which out-of-country benchmarks may be used by an investigating authority as situations "in which the government is not a predominant provider" of the good in question.[793] In addition, the United States submits that the Panel did not find that the use of out-of-country benchmarks would be appropriate in any and all "other situations" because the Panel did not purport to define the entire universe of scenarios in which out-of-country benchmarks can be used.

4.194 Turning first to India's claim under Article 12.7 of the DSU, we note that the Appellate Body has considered that the term "basic rationale" in that provision establishes a minimum standard for the reasoning that panels must provide in support of their findings and recommendations.[794] Thus, panels must set forth explanations and reasons sufficient to disclose the essential, or fundamental, justification for those findings and recommendations. Moreover, whether a panel has articulated a basic rationale for its findings must be determined on a case-by-case basis. Fundamentally, Article 12.7 of the DSU does not require panels to expound at length on the reasons for their findings and recommendations. In this regard, the Appellate Body has considered that "a panel's 'basic rationale' might be found in reasoning that is set out in other

[791] India's appellant's submission, para. 64.

[792] United States' appellee's submission, para. 99 (referring to Appellate Body Reports, *China – Rare Earths*, para. 5.173).

[793] United States' appellee's submission, para. 101 (quoting Panel Report, para. 7.50).

[794] Appellate Body Report, *Mexico – Corn Syrup (Article 21.5 – US)*, para. 106.

documents, such as in previous panel or Appellate Body reports – provided that such reasoning is quoted or, at a minimum, incorporated by reference."[795]

4.195 As we see it, the Panel provided a basic rationale for its finding by incorporating by reference the reasoning set forth in the Appellate Body report in *US – Softwood Lumber IV*. As we have found above, the reasoning in that report supports the Panel's finding that Article 14(d) permits the use of out-of-country benchmarks in situations in which the government is not a predominant provider of the relevant good. Accordingly, we do not consider that the Panel acted inconsistently with the standard under Article 12.7 of the DSU. We therefore *reject* India's claim that the Panel acted inconsistently with Article 12.7 of the DSU.

4.196 Turning to India's claim that the Panel also failed to fulfil its duty under Article 11 of the DSU, we recall that a claim under Article 11 must be clearly articulated and substantiated with specific arguments, and must not be ambiguous, vague, or subsidiary to another alleged violation.[796] As we see it, India has not articulated or substantiated a claim under Article 11 of the DSU independent of its claim under Article 12.7 of the DSU. We therefore do not consider this claim of India under Article 11 of the DSU.

4.197 India also makes a separate claim under Article 11 of the DSU in which it alleges that the Panel understood India's argument concerning the use of out-of-country prices under the US benchmarking mechanism in a narrow manner, and ignored India's argument that the measure at issue effectively permits the USDOC to use out-of-country benchmarks without exhausting all possible sources of in-country benchmarks.

4.198 The United States responds that an evaluation of this argument would not have affected the Panel's "material findings" that Tier II of the US benchmarking mechanism is not inconsistent with Article 14(d) of the SCM Agreement, because India's assertion that Tier I benchmarks do not exhaust all possible sources of in-country benchmarks is factually inaccurate.[797] Noting that the Panel, in fact, recorded India's argument that the US benchmarking mechanism "provides for the use of world market (Tier II) price benchmarks whenever Tier I in-country benchmarks *are not available*", the United States submits that it was uncontested that in-country benchmarks under Tier I of the US benchmarking mechanism are used whenever they are available.[798] The United States submits that there was, therefore, no need for the Panel to explain further this issue and that India has failed to demonstrate that the Panel acted inconsistently with Article 11 of the DSU.

---

[795] Appellate Body Report, *Mexico – Corn Syrup (Article 21.5 – US)*, para. 109.

[796] Appellate Body Reports, *US – Steel Safeguards*, para. 498; *Australia – Apples*, para. 406; *US – Anti-Dumping and Countervailing Duties (China)*, para. 337; *EC – Fasteners (China)*, para. 499.

[797] United States' appellee's submission, para. 92.

[798] United States' appellee's submission, para. 97 (quoting Panel Report, para. 7.47). (emphasis added by the United States)

4.199 In our view, India's claim that the US benchmarking mechanism does not require the exhaustion of all possible sources of in-country benchmarks is not materially different from its claim that the US benchmarking mechanism excludes the use of government prices in determining in-country benchmarks for the purpose of Article 14(d) of the SCM Agreement. The Panel addressed this latter claim. Moreover, we have found above that, on its face, Section 351.511(a)(2)(i) of the US Regulations requires consideration of all market-determined in-country prices. Thus, we read this provision as requiring the USDOC to exhaust all possible sources of in-country prices in determining a benchmark for the purpose of Article 14(d) of the SCM Agreement. We therefore *reject* this claim of India under Article 11 of the DSU.

4.4.1.3.5.2 Whether the Panel erred in finding that the US benchmarking mechanism requires adjustments to Tier II benchmarks

4.200 We turn now to India's appeal of the Panel's rejection of India's claim that Section 351.511(a)(2)(ii) of the US Regulations is inconsistent "as such" with Article 14(d) of the SCM Agreement because it does not require that Tier II benchmarks, consisting of world market prices, be adjusted to reflect prevailing market conditions in the country of provision.

4.201 In examining India's claim, the Panel observed that the overarching statutory provision implemented by the US Regulations setting forth the US benchmarking mechanism requires that the adequacy of remuneration for government-provided goods must, in all cases, be assessed in relation to the prevailing market conditions in the country of provision. The Panel considered that, "in law", Tier II benchmarks applied pursuant to the implementing regulation – i.e. Section 351.511(a)(2)(ii) of the US Regulations – must also relate to the prevailing market conditions in the country of provision.[799] The Panel therefore rejected India's claim that Section 351.511(a)(2)(ii) of the US Regulations is inconsistent "as such" with Article 14(d) of the SCM Agreement because it fails to require that Tier II benchmarks be adjusted to reflect prevailing market conditions in the country of provision.[800]

4.202 India claims on appeal that the Panel, in rejecting its claim, acted inconsistently with Article 11 of the DSU, and erred in its application of Article 14(d) of the SCM Agreement.[801] India requests the Appellate Body to reverse the Panel's finding above, and to find that the US benchmarking mechanism does not require that Tier II benchmarks be adjusted to reflect prevailing market

[799] Panel Report, para. 7.51.
[800] *Ibid.*
[801] India's appellant's submission, para. 77.

conditions in the country of provision.[802] We begin with India's claim under Article 11 of the DSU.

4.203 India notes that the Panel rejected its claim on the basis that the overarching statutory provision implemented by the US Regulations requires that the adequacy of remuneration must be assessed in relation to the prevailing market conditions in the country of provision. Noting that the specific measure challenged by India is the US Regulations, rather than the parent legislation that they implement, India submits that the Panel ignored the plain text and meaning of the specific measure at issue, and simply accepted the United States' assertions about the parent legislation. These assertions, India maintains, lack a sufficient evidentiary basis.[803] For these reasons, India claims that the Panel acted inconsistently with its duty under Article 11 of the DSU.

4.204 The United States responds that the Panel was not precluded from considering the language of the statute implemented by the US Regulations in assessing the consistency of these regulations with Article 14(d) of the SCM Agreement. According to the United States, the relevant statutory provision considered by the Panel is "exactly the type of context" that forms part of the "effective operationalization" of the US Regulations.[804] The United States explains that the US Regulations, setting forth the US benchmarking mechanism, operates in connection with the statute that they implement. The United States submits that, while India may disagree with the outcome of the Panel's conclusions, India has no basis to assert that the Panel did not rely on any evidence in reaching the finding challenged by India.[805]

4.205 As we see it, the Panel examined the overarching legislation at issue to elucidate the meaning of Section 351.511(a)(2)(ii) of the US Regulations, and to evaluate its consistency with Article 14(d) of the SCM Agreement. We do not consider that a panel acts inconsistently with Article 11 of the DSU merely because it seeks to determine the meaning of a municipal law by reference to the legislative framework within which that municipal law is situated. The Appellate Body has considered that, "in ascertaining the meaning of municipal law, a panel should undertake a holistic assessment of all relevant elements".[806] To us, in examining a municipal law in the form of an implementing regulation, "relevant elements" that may assist a panel in ascertaining the meaning of that regulation include the overarching legislation that it implements. We therefore *reject* India's claim under Article 11 of the DSU.

4.206 Turning to India's claim under Article 14(d) of the SCM Agreement, India contends that the Panel erred in its application of that provision because, in India's view, neither the US Regulations, nor the overarching statutory provision

---

[802] India's appellant's submission, para. 95.

[803] India's appellant's submission, paras. 79-84.

[804] United States' appellee's submission, para. 110.

[805] United States' appellee's submission, paras. 108-111.

[806] Appellate Body Report, *US – Countervailing and Anti-Dumping Measures (China)*, para. 4.101.

that they implement, mandates the need to make adjustments to Tier II benchmarks.[807] India recalls the Appellate Body's finding that, where proxies such as prices for similar goods quoted on world markets are used as benchmarks under Article 14(d), investigating authorities are under an obligation to ensure that the resulting benchmark relates or refers to, or is connected with, prevailing market conditions in the country of provision.[808] India emphasizes that, because market conditions are not presumed to be the same inside and outside the country of provision, Members are mandated to make necessary adjustments to ensure that out-of-country benchmarks reflect prevailing market conditions in the country of provision. According to India, the Appellate Body in *US – Softwood Lumber IV* acknowledged that it may be close to impossible to adjust out-of-country benchmarks to reflect prevailing market conditions in the country of provision.[809]

4.207 In response, the United States asserts that India has not contested the Panel's finding that the overarching legislation implemented by the US Regulations "require[s] that the adequacy of remuneration must in all cases be assessed in relation to the prevailing market conditions in the country of provision".[810] Thus, India has not made out the factual premise underlying its claim. In any event, the United States explains that the relevant US statute on which the Panel relied in interpreting the US benchmarking mechanism gives effect to the guidelines in Article 14(d) of the SCM Agreement "nearly word-for-word".[811] Thus, according to the United States, the structure and operation of the US statute, and the implementing regulations setting forth the US benchmarking mechanism, are designed to ensure that the USDOC evaluates the adequacy of remuneration for government-provided goods in accordance with the guidelines prescribed by Article 14(d) of the SCM Agreement.[812]

4.208 We recall that the Appellate Body has emphasized that, where an investigating authority uses alternative benchmarks for the purpose of assessing the adequacy of remuneration, "it is under an obligation to ensure that the resulting benchmark relates or refers to, or is connected with, prevailing market conditions in the country of provision, and must reflect price, quality, availability, marketability, transportation and other conditions of purchase or sale, as required by Article 14(d)."[813]

---

807 India's appellant's submission, paras. 91 and 92.

808 India's appellant's submission, para. 87 (referring to Appellate Body Report, *US – Softwood Lumber IV*, paras. 106 and 120).

809 India's appellant's submission, paras. 71 and 73 (referring to Appellate Body Report, *US – Softwood Lumber IV*, para. 108).

810 United States' appellee's submission, para. 114 (quoting Panel Report, para. 7.51).

811 United States' appellee's submission, para. 116.

812 United States' appellee's submission, paras. 113-116.

813 Appellate Body Report, *US – Softwood Lumber IV*, para. 106.

4.209 The text of the relevant provision of the US Statute[814] implemented by the US Regulations setting forth the US benchmarking mechanism provides as follows:

> [Where goods or services are provided], the adequacy of remuneration shall be determined in relation to prevailing market conditions for the good or service being provided or the goods being purchased in the country which is subject to the investigation or review. Prevailing market conditions include price, quality, availability, marketability, transportation, and other conditions of purchase or sale.[815]

4.210 Moreover, the text of Section 351.511(a)(2)(ii) of the US Regulations prescribes the use of Tier II benchmarks in the following terms:

> (ii) *Actual market-determined price unavailable.* If there is no useable market-determined price with which to make the comparison under paragraph (a)(2)(i) of this section, the Secretary will seek to measure the adequacy of remuneration by comparing the government price to a world market price where it is reasonable to conclude that such price would be available to purchasers in the country in question. Where there is more than one commercially available world market price, the Secretary will average such prices to the extent practicable, making due allowance for factors affecting comparability.

4.211 We note that, pursuant to Section 351.511(a)(2)(ii) of the US Regulations, the USDOC is required, in selecting Tier II prices for use as benchmarks, to make "due allowance *for factors affecting comparability*".[816] In our view, the illustrative list of "prevailing market conditions" parenthetically identified in the second sentence of Article 14(d) – "price, quality, availability, marketability, transportation and other conditions of purchase or sale" – are all factors that may affect the comparability of a benchmark price with the financial contribution at issue. Thus, we consider that the text of Section 351.511(a)(2)(ii) of the US Regulations does not prohibit, and indeed requires, the USDOC to make, where necessary, adjustments to world market prices in order to ensure that they reflect prevailing market conditions in the country of provision, in accordance with the requirements of Article 14(d) of the SCM Agreement.

4.212 We are not persuaded by India's argument on appeal that there is insufficient evidence to suggest that the overarching legislation implemented by the US Regulations mandates the need to make adjustments to Tier II

[814] *United States Code*, Title 19, Chapter 4, Subtitle IV.

[815] Countervailable subsidy – Benefit conferred, US Statute, Section 1677(5)(E) (Panel Exhibit USA-4).

[816] US Regulations, Section 351.511(a)(2)(ii). (emphasis added)

benchmarks.[817] In the absence of compelling evidence to the contrary, we see nothing on the face of the overarching legislation or the implementing regulation that permits the conclusion that the USDOC is not mandated to make adjustments to Tier II benchmarks where necessary. We therefore consider that the Panel did not err under Article 14(d) of the SCM Agreement in rejecting India's claim that the US benchmarking mechanism "as such" provides for the use of Tier II benchmarks that do not reflect prevailing market conditions in the country of provision.

4.213 For the reasons expressed above, we *uphold* the Panel's finding, in paragraph 7.52 of the Panel Report, rejecting India's claim that the use of "world market prices" as Tier II benchmarks provided for in Section 351.511(a)(2)(ii) is inconsistent "as such" with Article 14(d) of the SCM Agreement.

4.4.1.4 India's claims concerning the mandatory use of "as delivered" prices under the US benchmarking mechanism

4.214 We turn now to examine India's claims concerning the mandatory use of "as delivered" prices under the US benchmarking mechanism. India appeals the Panel's rejection of India's claim that the use of "as delivered" prices, provided for in Section 351.511(a)(2)(iv) of the US Regulations, is inconsistent with Article 14(d) of the SCM Agreement. India submits that, in reaching this finding, the Panel erred in its interpretation and application of Article 14(d) of the SCM Agreement, and acted inconsistently with Articles 11 and 12.7 of the DSU.[818] We begin our analysis with a brief overview of the measure at issue, namely, Section 351.511(a)(2)(iv) of the US Regulations.

4.215 Section 351.511(a)(2)(iv) of the US Regulations, provides as follows:

> (iv) *Use of delivered prices*. In measuring the adequacy of remuneration under Paragraph (a)(2)(i) or (a)(2)(ii) of this section, the Secretary will adjust the comparison price to reflect the price that a firm actually paid or would pay if it imported the product. This adjustment will include delivery charges and import duties.

4.216 Section 351.511(a)(2)(iv) applies where the USDOC uses, as a benchmark, Tier I or Tier II prices for the purpose of determining whether goods have been provided by a government for less than adequate remuneration.[819]

---

817 India's appellant's submission, para. 91.

818 India's appellant's submission, para. 162.

819 We recall that a Tier I price consists of "a market-determined price for the good or service resulting from actual transactions in the country in question. Such a price could include prices stemming from actual transactions between private parties, actual imports, or, in certain circumstances, actual sales from competitively run government auctions." (US Regulations, Section 351.511(a)(2)(i)) We recall further that a Tier II price consists of "a world market price where it is reasonable to conclude that such price would be available to purchasers in the country in question". (US Regulations, Section 351.511(a)(2)(ii))

Pursuant to Section 351.511(a)(2)(iv), the USDOC is required, when using Tier I or Tier II prices, to adjust these prices to reflect the price that a firm actually paid or would pay if it imported the product. Section 351.511(a)(2)(iv) provides that such adjustments "will include" delivery charges and import duties.

4.217 The adjustments required by Section 351.511(a)(2)(iv) apply not only to the Tier I or Tier II benchmarks, but also to the relevant government price with which such benchmarks are compared in order to determine whether that government price constitutes less than adequate remuneration. In this regard, the Panel noted that "India [had] expressly accepted the United States' contention that the delivered price adjustment is made to both the government price and the Tier I or II benchmark."[820]

4.4.1.4.1 The Panel's findings

4.218 At the outset of its analysis, the Panel considered India's contention to be that the mandatory use of "as delivered" benchmarks is inconsistent with the requirement under Article 14(d) of the SCM Agreement that the adequacy of remuneration be determined in relation to prevailing market conditions in the country of provision. More specifically, the Panel understood India's claim to be that, in cases where the "government price in question" does not include delivery charges, such as where the government provider sells the good in question on an *ex works* basis, the use of "as delivered" benchmarks results in a determination of the adequacy of remuneration that, contrary to Article 14(d), does not relate to prevailing market conditions in the country of provision.[821]

4.219 The Panel considered India's argument to be "flawed" because, in the Panel's view, India had conflated the term "prevailing market conditions", within the meaning of the second sentence of Article 14(d) of the SCM Agreement, with the contractual terms and conditions of the government provision under investigation.[822] According to the Panel, market benchmarks that relate to the "prevailing market conditions" in the country of provision need not mirror the contractual terms on which the government provider sells its goods because "government prices are not an indicator of prevailing market conditions".[823] The Panel agreed with the United States that the terms "prevailing market conditions" and "conditions of sale" in the second sentence of Article 14(d) do not relate to the specific contractual terms on which the government provides goods. Instead, these terms relate to the general conditions of the relevant market, in the context of which market operators engage in sales transactions.[824]

4.220 The Panel then addressed India's argument that the mandatory use of "as delivered" benchmarks is inconsistent with Article 14(d) of the SCM

[820] Panel Report, fn 215 to para. 7.59.
[821] Panel Report, para. 7.59.
[822] Panel Report, para. 7.60.
[823] Panel Report, para. 7.60. (fn omitted)
[824] Panel Report, para. 7.60.

Agreement because it nullifies the comparative advantage of the country of provision in terms of being able to provide the good in question locally. The Panel considered that, to the extent that an "as delivered" benchmark relates to the prevailing market conditions in the country of provision, it will reflect any comparative advantage that such country might have. The Panel explained that "import transactions occur even in situations where minerals may be sourced locally, and such import transactions necessarily relate to prevailing market conditions in India because they are made by entities in India operating subject to Indian market conditions." In the light of these considerations, the Panel rejected India's argument that the mandatory use of "as delivered" benchmarks nullifies the comparative advantage of the country of provision in terms of being able to provide the good in question locally.[825]

4.221 For these reasons, the Panel rejected India's claim that Section 351.511(a)(2)(iv) of the US Regulations is "as such" inconsistent with Article 14(d) of the SCM Agreement.[826]

4.4.1.4.2 India's claims on appeal

4.222 India presents two claims on appeal under Article 14(d) of the SCM Agreement. First, India asserts that the Panel's rejection of its claim was "partly" based on the Panel's finding that government prices can *ipso facto* be considered as not reflecting "prevailing market conditions" within the meaning of Article 14(d).[827] In India's view, this reflects an erroneous interpretation of Article 14(d).[828] Second, India challenges the Panel's rejection of its claim that the mandatory use of "as delivered" benchmarks results in the countervailing of the comparative advantage of the country of provision. India submits that the premise on which the Panel rejected its claim, namely, that import transactions necessarily reflect prevailing market conditions in the country of provision, reflects an erroneous interpretation and application of Article 14(d).[829]

4.223 In connection with the above, India also claims that the Panel acted inconsistently with Articles 11 and 12.7 of the DSU. First, India asserts that, in finding that India had conflated the term "prevailing market conditions" with the contractual terms and conditions of the government provision under investigation, the Panel altered India's claim, engaged in an assessment of a matter that was not before it, and thereby acted inconsistently with its duty under Article 11 of the DSU.[830] Second, India asserts that, in rejecting its claim that the mandatory use of "as delivered" benchmarks is inconsistent with the requirement that the adequacy of remuneration be determined in relation to prevailing market

---

825 Panel Report, para. 7.62.
826 Panel Report, para. 7.63.
827 India's appellant's submission, para. 180.
828 India's appellant's submission, paras. 180 and 181.
829 India's appellant's submission, paras. 185 and 189.
830 India's appellant's submission, paras. 168 and 174.

conditions in the country of provision, the Panel failed to apply its own interpretation of Article 14(d) of the SCM Agreement to the measure at issue, and therefore acted inconsistently with its duty under Article 11 of the DSU.[831] Third, India asserts that, in rejecting its claim that the mandatory use of "as delivered" benchmarks is inconsistent with Article 14(d) because it results in the countervailing of a comparative advantage of the country of provision, the Panel failed to provide a "basic rationale" for its findings, and thereby acted inconsistently with its mandate under Article 12.7 of the DSU "read with" Article 11 of the DSU.[832]

4.224 India requests the Appellate Body to reverse the Panel's finding that the mandatory use of "as delivered" benchmarks, provided for in Section 351.511(a)(2)(iv) of the US Regulations, is not inconsistent with Article 14(d) of the SCM Agreement. India further requests the Appellate Body to complete the legal analysis and find that Section 351.511(a)(2)(iv) of the US Regulations is inconsistent with Article 14(d) of the SCM Agreement.[833]

4.4.1.4.3 The Panel's analysis of India's claims regarding Section 351.511(a)(2)(iv) of the US Regulations

4.225 Before the Panel, India's claim that Section 351.511(a)(2)(iv) of the US Regulations is inconsistent with Article 14(d) of the SCM Agreement appears to have rested on two grounds. First, India asserted that the mandatory use of "as delivered" benchmarks is inconsistent with the requirement under Article 14(d) that the adequacy of remuneration be determined in relation to prevailing market conditions in the country of provision. Second, India asserted that the mandatory use of "as delivered" benchmarks is inconsistent with Article 14(d) because it results in the countervailing of a comparative advantage of the country of provision. We examine in turn India's claims on appeal as they relate to these two grounds as considered by the Panel.

4.226 India asserts that, in rejecting its argument that the mandatory use of "as delivered" benchmarks is inconsistent with the requirement that the adequacy of remuneration be determined in relation to prevailing market conditions in the country of provision, the Panel erred in its interpretation of Article 14(d). According to India, the Panel's rejection of this argument was "partly" based on the Panel's erroneous interpretation that government prices are *ipso facto* not an indicator of "prevailing market conditions" within the meaning of Article 14(d).[834] India notes that it has appealed this interpretation of the Panel in the context of its claim regarding the exclusion of government prices under the US

[831] India's appellant's submission, paras. 175, 176, and 178.
[832] India's appellant's submission, para. 184.
[833] India's appellant's submission, para. 205.
[834] India's appellant's submission, para. 180

benchmarking mechanism. India submits that, for the same reasons, the Panel erred in rejecting its claim on the basis that government prices are not an indicator of "prevailing market conditions" within the meaning of Article 14(d) of the SCM Agreement.[835]

4.227 The United States observes that the finding of the Panel challenged by India was made in the context of examining India's argument that the measure at issue is inconsistent with Article 14(d) of the SCM Agreement because it does not require the USDOC to consider the terms and conditions of the government transaction under investigation as being reflective of "prevailing market conditions" in the country of provision. The United States submits that the Panel correctly found that comparing a government price to another government price is circular and uninformative because it does not indicate whether the government price is at, or below, the prevailing market conditions in the country of provision. Moreover, in the United States' view, the Panel correctly observed that the Appellate Body found in *US – Softwood Lumber IV* that private prices are the preferred benchmark for assessing the adequacy of remuneration for government-provided goods.[836]

4.228 At the outset of its analysis, the Panel considered India's claim to be that the mandatory use of "as delivered" benchmarks is inconsistent with Article 14(d) of the SCM Agreement because such benchmarks will not relate to prevailing market conditions in the country of provision in cases where the "government price in question" does not include delivery charges.[837] The Panel found India's argument to be "flawed" because, in the Panel's view, India had conflated "the 'prevailing market conditions' referred to in the second sentence of Article 14(d) with the contractual terms and conditions of the government provision under investigation".[838] Recalling that the adequacy of remuneration is, under Article 14(d), to be assessed from the perspective of the recipient using market benchmarks that relate to the prevailing market conditions in the country of provision, the Panel considered that "such market benchmarks need [not] mirror the contractual terms on which the government provider sells its good, since government prices are not an indicator of the prevailing market conditions" in the country of provision.[839]

4.229 It appears that India takes issue with the Panel's statement that "government prices are not an indicator of the prevailing market conditions" in the country of provision. We, too, express concern with the Panel's statement to the extent that it may be read as suggesting that Article 14(d) of the SCM Agreement establishes a legal presumption that government prices cannot reflect prevailing market conditions in the country of provision. We have found above,

[835] *Ibid.*
[836] United States' appellee's submission, paras. 190-192.
[837] Panel Report, para. 7.59.
[838] Panel Report, para. 7.60.
[839] Panel Report, para. 7.60. (fn omitted)

in relation to India's claim that the US benchmarking mechanism excludes the use of government prices for the purpose of determining benchmarks, that Article 14(d) establishes no such legal presumption. We therefore disagree with the Panel's statement.

4.230 Having said that, we do not consider that the above statement formed the central basis upon which the Panel rejected India's claim. Rather, the Panel dismissed India's claim on the basis of its understanding of what India had argued, namely, that the mandatory use of "as delivered" benchmarks is inconsistent with Article 14(d) because such benchmarks will not relate to prevailing market conditions in the country of provision in cases where the "government price in question" does not include delivery charges.[840] In this regard, we recall that the Panel considered that the terms "prevailing market conditions" and "conditions of sale", in the second sentence of Article 14(d) of the SCM Agreement, do not relate to the specific contractual terms on which the government provides goods but, rather, "relate to the general conditions of the relevant market, in the context of which market operators engage in sales transactions".[841] On appeal, India has not challenged this finding of the Panel.

4.231 India has, however, also presented two separate claims under Article 11 of the DSU. First, India asserts that the Panel misconstrued its argument and thereby acted inconsistently with its duty under Article 11 of the DSU. According to India, its case before the Panel was that the term "conditions of sale", within the meaning of Article 14(d) of the SCM Agreement, refers to the "general or common stipulation"[842] present in contracts for the provision of the relevant goods in the country of provision. India thus submits that, in finding that India had conflated the term "prevailing market conditions", within the meaning of Article 14(d), with the contractual terms and conditions of the government provision under investigation, the Panel altered India's claim, engaged in an assessment of a matter that was not before it, and thereby acted inconsistently with its duty under Article 11 of the DSU.[843]

4.232 In response, the United States submits that India is attempting to amend, on appeal, the argument that India had made before the Panel. According to the United States, India had argued before the Panel that the term "conditions of sale", within the meaning of Article 14(d) of the SCM Agreement, refer to the contractual terms of sale of the government transaction in question. For the United States, India's claim that the Panel acted inconsistently with Article 11 of the DSU is therefore devoid of any factual basis.[844]

---

840 Panel Report, para. 7.59.

841 Panel Report, para. 7.60.

842 India's appellant's submission, para. 168 (quoting India's first written submission to the Panel, para. 88).

843 India's appellant's submission, paras. 168 and 174.

844 United States' appellee's submission, paras. 181-185.

4.233 We note that the Appellate Body has emphasized that a panel must consider the claims and arguments of the parties to a dispute in order to comply with the obligation under Article 11 of the DSU to make an objective assessment of the matter before it. At the same time, the Appellate Body has clarified that it is not necessary for a panel to "refer explicitly to every argument made by the parties"[845] or "consider each and every argument put forward by the parties in support of their respective cases, so long as it completes an objective assessment".[846]

4.234 We recall that, according to India, its case before the Panel was that the term "conditions of sale", within the meaning of Article 14(d) of the SCM Agreement, refers to the "general or common stipulation"[847] present in contracts for the provision of the relevant goods in the country of provision. Thus, for India, its case before the Panel did not focus on the terms and conditions of the government provision under investigation. By contrast, the Panel understood India to have argued that the terms "prevailing market conditions" and "conditions of sale", within the meaning of Article 14(d) of the SCM Agreement, relate to the specific contractual terms on which the government provides goods.[848]

4.235 We note that the relevant part of India's panel request – which established the Panel's jurisdiction by defining the precise claims at issue in the dispute[849] – states:

> *Even if the government price is at ex-factory level, ocean freight, delivery charges and import duties are included in the benchmark price to arrive at delivered prices.* In measuring the adequacy of remuneration for the provision of goods, it is inappropriate to mandatorily include delivery charges and import duties.[850]

4.236 It seems to us that India's case before the Panel was that Section 351.511(a)(2)(iv) of the US Regulations is inconsistent with Article 14(d) of the SCM Agreement because it mandates the USDOC to use "as delivered" benchmarks to determine the adequacy of remuneration, even in cases where the government price in question is an *ex works* price. India's claim was necessarily premised on its view that the use of "as delivered" benchmarks in cases where the government price at issue is an *ex works* price means that such benchmarks will not, contrary to Article 14(d), relate to prevailing market conditions in the

[845] Appellate Body Reports, *EC – Seal Products*, para. 5.288 (quoting Appellate Body Report, *US – Upland Cotton*, para. 446).

[846] Appellate Body Reports, *EC – Seal Products*, para. 5.288 (quoting Appellate Body Report, *Dominican Republic – Import and Sale of Cigarettes*, para. 125).

[847] India's appellant's submission, para. 168 (quoting India's first written submission to the Panel, para. 88).

[848] Panel Report, para. 7.60.

[849] See Appellate Body Report, *Brazil – Desiccated Coconut*, p. 22, DSR 1997:I, p. 186.

[850] India's panel request, para. 7. (emphasis added)

country of provision. As noted above, the Panel evaluated this claim and found that the terms "prevailing market conditions" and "conditions of sale", in the second sentence of Article 14(d) of the SCM Agreement, do not relate to the specific contractual terms on which the government provides goods but, rather, "relate to the general conditions of the relevant market, in the context of which market operators engage in sales transactions".[851]

4.237 In the light of the above, we do not agree with India that "[t]he entire focus" of its claim was that a determination of the adequacy of remuneration in relation to prevailing market conditions in the country of provision requires an "evaluation of the *terms of sale of the goods* in question in *the country of provision* as a whole".[852] In the light of India's panel request and its submissions to the Panel, we consider that it was reasonable, and in accordance with its duty under Article 11 of the DSU, for the Panel to have understood India's claim in the way that it did. We therefore *reject* India's claim that the Panel acted inconsistently with Article 11 of the DSU in this regard.

4.238 Turning to India's second claim under Article 11 of the DSU, India submits that the Panel acted inconsistently with that provision by failing to apply its own interpretation of Article 14(d) of the SCM Agreement to its assessment of India's claim. Noting that, in the course of rejecting India's claim, the Panel interpreted Article 14(d) and found that the terms "prevailing market conditions" and "conditions of sale" relate to "the general conditions of the relevant market, in the context of which market operators engage in sales transactions"[853], India asserts that the Panel did not, however, make a finding on whether the sale of a good in the market generally on an *ex works* basis constitutes one of such "general conditions". India argues that a finding on this specific issue would have "materially affected"[854] the Panel's decision to reject India's claim. This is because, if the fact that a given good in the market is being sold generally on an *ex works* basis constitutes one of the "general conditions" referred to by the Panel, then, determining the adequacy of remuneration on an "as delivered" basis, in every case, would result in disregarding "prevailing market conditions" where the good in question is generally sold on an *ex works* basis in the country of provision. Thus, India submits that the Panel failed to assess the claim that was before it and, therefore, acted inconsistently with Article 11 of the DSU.

4.239 The United States responds that India's claim is without merit because the question of whether the sale of goods generally on an *ex works* basis constitutes a "prevailing market condition", within the meaning of Article 14(d), was not put before the Panel. In the United States' view, the Panel cannot be faulted under Article 11 of the DSU for failing to make an objective assessment of an argument that India had not presented to the Panel. The United States thus

851 Panel Report, para. 7.60.
852 India's appellant's submission, para. 173. (emphasis original)
853 India's appellant's submission, para. 176 (quoting Panel Report, para. 7.60).
854 India's appellant's submission, para. 176.

requests the Appellate Body to reject India's claim under Article 11 of the DSU.[855]

4.240 As we see it, the crux of India's claim is that, having interpreted the terms "prevailing market conditions" and "conditions of sale" as relating to "the general conditions of the relevant market, in the context of which market operators engage in sales transactions"[856], the Panel was required to apply this interpretation of Article 14(d) to the measure at issue, namely, Section 351.511(a)(2)(iv) of the US Regulations. For India, this means that the Panel was required to make a finding on whether the sale of a good in the market generally on an *ex works* basis constitutes one of such "general conditions" and, if so, whether Section 351.511(a)(2)(iv) of the US Regulations allows for the consideration of such "general conditions".[857]

4.241 We have found above that it was reasonable, and in accordance with its duty under Article 11 of the DSU, for the Panel to have understood India's claim in the way that it did. We therefore do not consider that the question of whether the sale of a good in the country of provision generally on an *ex works* basis constitutes a "prevailing market condition" within the meaning of Article 14(d) of the SCM Agreement was before the Panel. Consequently, we *reject* India's claim that the Panel acted inconsistently with Article 11 of the DSU.

4.242 In any event, we note that India argues that, had the Panel evaluated the question of whether the sale of a good in the market generally on an *ex works* basis constitutes a "prevailing market condition" within the meaning of Article 14(d) of the SCM Agreement, this would have "materially affected"[858] the Panel's decision to reject India's claim.

4.243 We recall that the term "prevailing market conditions" in Article 14(d) of the SCM Agreement describes the generally accepted characteristics of an area of economic activity in which the forces of supply and demand interact to determine market prices. We therefore agree with the Panel's finding that the terms "prevailing market conditions" and "conditions of sale", in the second sentence of Article 14(d) of the SCM Agreement, do not relate to the specific contractual terms on which the government provides goods but, rather, "relate to the general conditions of the relevant market, in the context of which market operators engage in sales transactions".[859]

4.244 As we see it, the requirement under Article 14(d) of the SCM Agreement that the adequacy of remuneration be determined in relation to prevailing market conditions in the country of provision ensures that the comparison undertaken, for the purposes of Article 14(d), is a meaningful one that does not overstate or understate the calculation of benefit. In this regard, the inclusive list of

[855] United States' appellee's submission, para. 189.
[856] India's appellant's submission, para. 176 (referring to Panel Report, para. 7.60).
[857] India's appellant's submission, para. 176.
[858] *Ibid.*
[859] Panel Report, para. 7.60.

prevailing market conditions identified in the second sentence of Article 14(d) – price, quality, availability, marketability, transportation and other conditions of purchase or sale – describe factors that may affect the comparability of the financial contribution at issue with a benchmark. Thus, if a proposed benchmark does not reflect prevailing market conditions in the country of provision, adjustments in the light of the factors listed in the second sentence of Article 14(d) are necessary to ensure comparability and, by extension, a meaningful benefit comparison.

4.245 In our view, an assessment of "prevailing market conditions", within the meaning of Article 14(d) of the SCM Agreement, necessarily involves an analysis of the market generally, rather than isolated transactions in that market. It is only through such an analysis that a conclusion can be drawn as to the conditions that are "prevailing" in the market in the country of provision. Moreover, we consider that "prevailing market conditions", within the meaning of Article 14(d), cannot be assessed solely from the perspective of the providers of the relevant good in question. As we see it, an understanding of "prevailing market conditions" as referring solely to the conditions set by the providers of the good in question stands in tension with the proposition that a government-provided financial contribution confers a benefit if the "'financial contribution' makes the *recipient* 'better off' than it would otherwise have been, absent that contribution".[860] Thus, a determination of the adequacy of remuneration in relation to prevailing market conditions in the country of provision must capture the full cost to the recipient of receiving the government-provided good in question.

4.246 In considering the extent to which delivery charges for the good in question must be accounted for in assessing the prevailing market conditions for that good, we find it significant that the term "transportation" is explicitly listed among the "prevailing market conditions" illustratively identified in the second sentence of Article 14(d) of the SCM Agreement. To us, this confirms that the costs associated with the transportation of the good in question is a factor that must be accounted for in determining, in accordance with Article 14(d), the adequacy of remuneration in relation to prevailing market conditions in the country of provision. In our view, the use of *ex works* prices for the purpose of a benefit comparison under Article 14(d) of the SCM Agreement would not capture the full cost to the recipient of receiving the government-provided good in question, and would therefore fail to assess whether the financial contribution at issue makes the recipient better off than it would otherwise have been absent that contribution.

4.247 The considerations expressed above suggest that, where a good is sold in the market generally on an *ex works* basis, it would be necessary to make adjustments to ensure that the prices compared for the purposes of Article 14(d)

[860] Appellate Body Report, *Canada – Aircraft*, para. 157. (emphasis added)

of the SCM Agreement reflect the prevailing market conditions in the country of provision, including the generally applicable delivery charges for that good. As we see it, such adjustments serve two purposes. First, they ensure that the comparison undertaken, for the purposes of Article 14(d), is a meaningful one that does not overstate or understate the calculation of benefit. Second, they ensure, by capturing the full cost to the recipient of receiving the government-provided good in question, a determination of benefit that responds to the question of whether the financial contribution at issue makes the *recipient* better off than it would otherwise have been absent that contribution.

4.248 To us, the fact that delivery charges are not generally paid directly to the providers of the good in question in the country of provision does not mean that the benefit comparison under Article 14(d) of the SCM Agreement must be conducted at an *ex works* level. India's insistence that a benefit comparison should be conducted at an *ex works* level where delivery charges are not generally paid directly to the providers of the good in question seems informed by India's view that Article 14(d) requires that the adequacy of remuneration be assessed from the perspective of the provider, rather than the recipient of the good in question. We have rejected this interpretation, and have found, instead, that Article 14(d) requires that the adequacy of remuneration be assessed from the perspective of the recipient so that an assessment can be made as to whether the financial contribution at issue makes that recipient better off than it would otherwise have been absent that contribution. We therefore do not agree with India's assertion that, had the Panel evaluated the question of whether the sale of a good in the market generally on an *ex works* basis constitutes a "prevailing market condition" within the meaning of Article 14(d) of the SCM Agreement, this would have "materially affected"[861] the Panel's decision to reject India's claim.

4.249 Having said that, we have considered above that it is only by analysing the market in the country of provision generally, rather than isolated transactions in that market, that a conclusion can be drawn as to the conditions that are "prevailing" in that market. It follows that, insofar as adjustments for delivery charges are required to undertake a proper assessment of benefit in the context of Article 14(d), any such adjustments must reflect the generally applicable delivery charges for the good in question in the country of provision. For example, in cases where the incidence of imports of the good in question are minimal in relation to domestic transactions for that good, it may not be appropriate to compare a benchmark price, adjusted to reflect international delivery charges, with the government price, adjusted to reflect local delivery charges. This is because, in this specific scenario, such imports may only reflect isolated transactions in the market and, therefore, international delivery charges may not be representative of the generally applicable delivery charges for the good in question in the country of provision. In such a case, the methodology

[861] India's appellant's submission, para. 176.

used by an investigating authority to calculate "benefit", within the meaning of Article 14(d), must allow for adjustments to the benchmark price to reflect delivery charges that more closely approximate the generally applicable delivery charges for the good in question in the country of provision.

4.250 It appears to us that India's concern with Section 351.511(a)(2)(iv) of the US Regulations is not so much that it mandates a benefit comparison at an "as delivered" level. Rather, India's concern appears to be that, in cases where the USDOC uses as a benchmark an actual import price under Tier I of the US benchmarking mechanism, or a world market price under Tier II of that mechanism, the assessment of benefit will always reflect a comparison between a government price adjusted to reflect local delivery charges, and a benchmark price adjusted to reflect international delivery charges. India therefore suggests that, on its face, the US benchmarking mechanism precludes adjustments to Tier I or Tier II benchmarks to reflect anything other than the international cost of delivery of the good in question.

4.251 Turning to the measure at issue, we note that Section 351.511(a)(2)(iv) of the US Regulations requires the USDOC to adjust Tier I and Tier II benchmarks to reflect the price that a firm actually paid or would pay if it imported the product. As the Regulation states, such adjustment "will include delivery charges and import duties". We note that, in selecting Tier I prices for use as benchmarks, the USDOC is required to consider "product similarity; quantities sold, imported, or auctioned; *and other factors affecting comparability*".[862] Similarly, in selecting Tier II prices for use as benchmarks, the USDOC is required to make "due allowance *for factors affecting comparability*".[863] As we see it, the extent to which international delivery charges are generally applicable, or "prevailing", in the country of provision is a factor affecting comparability of the financial contribution at issue with a benchmark. Thus, contrary to what India asserts, we do not consider that the US benchmarking mechanism, on its face, precludes adjustments to Tier I or Tier II benchmarks to reflect, in a given case, delivery charges that approximate the generally applicable delivery charges in the country of provision – e.g. local delivery charges.

4.252 It remains for us to consider India's claims as they relate to the Panel's finding rejecting India's argument that the use of "as delivered" out-of-country prices as benchmarks under the US benchmarking mechanism nullifies the comparative advantage of the country of provision in terms of being able to provide the goods in question locally. India submits that, in rejecting this argument, the Panel erred in its application of Article 14(d) of the SCM Agreement, and acted inconsistently with Articles 11 and 12.7 of the DSU.

4.253 In addressing India's argument that the use of "as delivered" benchmarks "nullifies the comparative advantage of the country of provision in terms of

[862] US Regulations, Section 351.511(a)(2)(i). (emphasis added)
[863] US Regulations, Section 351.511(a)(2)(ii). (emphasis added)

being able to provide the goods in question locally"[864], the Panel, relying on the Appellate Body's findings in *US – Softwood Lumber IV*, considered that, "[t]o the extent that a delivered price benchmark relates to the prevailing market conditions in the country of provision, it will reflect any comparative advantage that such country might have."[865] The Panel explained further that "import transactions occur even in situations where minerals may be sourced locally, and such import transactions necessarily relate to prevailing market conditions in India because they are made by entities in India operating subject to Indian market conditions."[866] In the light of these considerations, the Panel rejected India's argument that the mandatory use of "as delivered" benchmarks nullifies the comparative advantage of the country of provision in terms of being able to provide the good in question locally.[867]

4.254 Turning first to India's claim under Article 14(d) of the SCM Agreement, India submits that the "underlying premise"[868] on which the Panel rejected its argument is that import transactions necessarily reflect prevailing market conditions in the country of provision. According to India, the Panel conflated the term "prevailing market conditions" with the existence of import transactions. Yet, as the Panel itself recognized, "prevailing market conditions" relate to the general conditions of the relevant market, in the context of which market operators engage in sales transactions. Noting that the Appellate Body has considered that Article 14(d) demands an examination of the entire market, accounting for both sides of the transaction – i.e. supply and demand – India submits that the Panel's premise places a disproportionate emphasis on import transactions. However, where there is domestic supply for the good in question, as well as one or more import transactions for that good, the "prevailing market conditions" in the country of provision can only be determined by comprehensively accounting for both types of transactions. India submits that the measure under challenge forecloses any such examination. For India, the premise on which the Panel rejected its argument is "fundamentally flawed" and "ignores the ordinary understanding of Article 14(d)".[869]

4.255 The United States responds that, contrary to India's assertion on appeal, the basis of the Panel's rejection of India's argument was that, "[t]o the extent that a delivered price benchmark relates to the prevailing market conditions in the country of provision, it will reflect any comparative advantage that such country might have."[870] The United States adds that, if a benchmark price relates to prevailing market conditions in the country of provision, considerations of

---

864 Panel Report, para. 7.62 (quoting India's first written submission to the Panel, para. 97).

865 Panel Report, para. 7.62 (referring to Appellate Body Report, *US – Softwood Lumber IV*, para. 109).

866 Panel Report, para. 7.62.

867 *Ibid.*

868 India's appellant's submission, para. 185.

869 India's appellant's submission, para. 189.

870 United States' appellee's submission, para. 196 (quoting Panel Report, para. 7.62).

supply and demand will be reflected in the price, as well as other factors an investigating authority will account for in accordance with the second sentence of Article 14(d). According to the United States, there is no additional requirement under Article 14(d) that an investigating authority must, as India asserts, undertake a comprehensive qualitative and quantitative analysis of a Member's alleged comparative advantage or of supply and demand.

4.256 We recall that, in *US – Softwood Lumber IV*, the Appellate Body remarked that the countervailing of differences in comparative advantages between countries would not be consonant with the very purpose of levying countervailing duties.[871] It appears that, for India, a country enjoys a comparative advantage where it has the ability to supply domestic demand for the good in question. Thus, in India's view, if the good in question can be supplied locally, then the use of "as delivered" out-of-country benchmarks countervails a comparative advantage of the country of provision by creating a hypothetical situation where the good in question is non-existent in the country of provision. It is on the basis of this notion of "comparative advantage" that India challenges the use of "as delivered" out-of-country benchmarks under the US benchmarking mechanism.[872]

4.257 We have difficulties with India's notion of "comparative advantage". We do not consider that, in every situation where local supply of a good in the country of provision is sufficient to cater to local demand the country of provision enjoys a comparative advantage "in terms of being able to provide the goods in question locally".[873] The existence of minimal or even zero import transactions in respect of a particular good does not, as India seems to suggest, *ipso facto* mean that a country enjoys a comparative advantage in respect of that good. The lack of import transactions could also, conceivably, be a result of the government providing the good in question for less than adequate remuneration. In such circumstances, the levying of countervailing measures may not countervail a "comparative advantage" of the country of provision but, rather, a subsidy, which is permitted under the SCM Agreement.

4.258 In any event, in examining the Panel's findings challenged by India, we do not agree that the basis on which the Panel rejected India's argument was, as India asserts, that import transactions *necessarily* reflect prevailing market conditions in the country of provision. Instead, the Panel considered that, "[t]o *the extent that* a delivered price benchmark relates to the prevailing market conditions in the country of provision, it will reflect any comparative advantage that such country might have."[874] In other words, the Panel considered that, insofar as "as delivered" out-of-country benchmarks relate to prevailing market conditions in the country of provision, these conditions already reflect any

---

[871] Appellate Body Report, *US – Softwood Lumber IV*, para. 109.

[872] India's appellant's submission, para. 203.

[873] India's appellant's submission, para. 204.

[874] Panel Report, para. 7.62. (emphasis added)

comparative advantage enjoyed by the country of provision. The basis for the Panel's rejection of India's argument was, in our view, in accordance with the Appellate Body's guidance in *US – Softwood Lumber IV*. In this regard, the Appellate Body considered that, although the countervailing of comparative advantages between countries would not be in accordance with the very purpose of levying countervailing duties, any comparative advantage would be reflected in the prevailing market conditions in the country of provision and, therefore, would have to be taken into account and reflected in the adjustments made to any method used for the determination of adequacy of remuneration if it is to relate or refer to, or be connected with, prevailing market conditions in the market of provision.[875]

4.259 It seems to us that India's contention before the Panel, and now on appeal, is that the US benchmarking mechanism precludes adjustments to Tier I, actual import prices, or Tier II, world market prices, to ensure that such benchmarks reflect prevailing market conditions in the country of provision, including the generally applicable delivery charges for the good in question. We have found above, however, that the US Regulations, on their face, do not preclude the USDOC from making such adjustments, where necessary, to Tier I and Tier II benchmarks.

4.260 In the light of the above, we do not consider that the Panel erred in its interpretation and application of Article 14(d) of the SCM Agreement in rejecting India's claim that the mandatory use of "as delivered" out-of-country benchmarks results in the countervailing of comparative advantages of the country of provision.

4.261 Finally, India claims that, in rejecting its argument concerning the countervailing of a comparative advantage of the country of provision through the use of "as delivered" out-of-country benchmarks, the Panel failed to provide a "basic rationale" for its findings, and thereby acted inconsistently with its mandate under Article 12.7 of the DSU "read with" Article 11 of the DSU. India notes that the Panel rejected this argument based on the alleged existence of an import transaction in the underlying investigation, which, in the Panel's view, meant that import transactions necessarily relate to prevailing market conditions in India. India maintains that the Panel failed to provide a basic rationale to justify its rejection of India's claim concerning the countervailing of "comparative advantages" and, therefore, acted inconsistently with its mandate under Article 12.7 of the DSU "read with" Article 11 of the DSU.

4.262 As we see it, the premise of India's claims under Articles 11 and 12.7 of the DSU is that the Panel rejected India's argument on the basis that import transactions *necessarily* reflect prevailing market conditions in the country of provision. We have found above, however, that the Panel did not reject India's argument on that basis. Instead, the Panel considered that, insofar as

[875] Appellate Body Report, *US – Softwood Lumber*, para. 109.

"as delivered" out-of-country benchmarks relate to prevailing market conditions in the country of provision, these conditions will necessarily reflect any comparative advantage enjoyed by the country of provision. Moreover, the Panel provided a basic rationale for its finding by incorporating by reference the guidance of the Appellate Body in *US – Softwood Lumber IV*. We therefore *reject* India's claims that the Panel acted inconsistently with Articles 11 and 12.7 of the DSU in this regard.

4.263 In the light of the foregoing considerations, we *uphold*, albeit for different reasons, the Panel's finding, in paragraph 7.63 of the Panel Report, rejecting India's claim that the mandatory use of "as delivered" benchmarks provided for in Section 351.511(a)(2)(iv) of the US Regulations is inconsistent "as such" with Article 14(d) of the SCM Agreement.

4.4.2 "As applied" claims under Article 14(d) of the SCM Agreement

4.264 We turn now to India's "as applied" claims under Article 14(d) of the SCM Agreement. India appeals the Panel's findings in relation to the USDOC's determinations of benefit in the countervailing duty investigation concerning: (i) the provision of iron ore by the NMDC; and (ii) the provision of captive mining rights for iron ore and coal by the GOI. We begin our analysis with India's claims in respect of the USDOC's determination of benefit in the countervailing duty investigation concerning the provision of iron ore by the NMDC.

4.4.2.1 India's claims concerning the provision of iron ore by the NMDC

4.265 Before the Panel, India claimed that the USDOC's determination that the NMDC provided iron ore for less than adequate remuneration is inconsistent with Articles 1.1(b) and 14(d) of the SCM Agreement because, *inter alia*: (i) the USDOC failed to consider and apply certain domestic pricing information as Tier I benchmarks; (ii) the USDOC excluded the NMDC's export prices from the Tier II, world benchmark price; and (iii) the USDOC used, as benchmarks, prices from Australia and Brazil that were adjusted to reflect international delivery charges to India.[876] The Panel rejected all except one of India's claims, namely, that the United States acted inconsistently with Articles 1.1(b) and 14(d) of the SCM Agreement because the United States had put forward *ex post* rationales to justify the USDOC's failure to consider certain domestic pricing information submitted by the GOI and Tata for the purpose of determining a potential Tier I benchmark.[877]

4.266 On appeal, India claims that, in reaching its findings, the Panel erred in its interpretation and application of Article 14(d), the chapeau of Article 14, and

[876] Panel Report, para. 7.141.
[877] Panel Report, paras. 7.158 and 8.2.a.ii.

Articles 12.1, 12.4, and 12.7, of the SCM Agreement. Moreover, India claims that the Panel acted inconsistently with its duty under Article 11 of the DSU.

4.267 India's claims of error relate to the Panel's findings concerning: (i) the *ex post* rationales put forward by the United States to justify the USDOC's failure to consider certain domestic pricing information for the purpose of determining a Tier I benchmark; (ii) the USDOC's rejection of certain NMDC export prices in determining a Tier II benchmark in the 2006, 2007, and 2008 administrative reviews; and (iii) the USDOC's use of "as delivered" prices from Australia and Brazil as benchmarks. In addressing India's appeal, we examine the Panel's findings on these issues in turn. Thus, we begin with India's claims concerning the *ex post* rationales put forward by the United States to justify the USDOC's failure to consider certain domestic pricing information for the purpose of determining a Tier I benchmark.

4.4.2.1.1 India's claims concerning the USDOC's failure to consider certain domestic pricing information for the purpose of determining a Tier I benchmark

4.268 Before the Panel, India claimed that the USDOC's failure to consider certain domestic pricing information in determining a Tier I benchmark for assessing whether the NMDC provided iron ore for less than adequate remuneration is inconsistent with Article 14(d) of the SCM Agreement. This domestic pricing information consisted of: (i) price charts that were compiled by the Mine Owners/Goa Mineral Ore Exporters Association and submitted to the USDOC by the GOI and Tata; and (ii) a letter submitted by Tata to the USDOC in which a private iron ore supplier quotes existing and revised prices for sales of high-grade iron ore to Tata.[878]

4.269 The Panel found that the United States' explanation of why the USDOC rejected the domestic pricing information at issue constitutes *ex post* rationales that the Panel was bound not to consider in evaluating India's claim. Moreover, the Panel recalled that private domestic prices are the "primary benchmark" for assessing benefit under Article 14(d) of the SCM Agreement, and found that India had established a *prima facie* case in support of its claim which had not been rebutted by any contemporaneous rationale or justification in the USDOC's determinations. The Panel therefore found that the USDOC's failure to consider the domestic pricing information at issue is inconsistent with Article 14(d), and therefore Article 1.1(b), of the SCM Agreement.[879]

4.270 The above notwithstanding, the Panel stated that it would review the *ex post* rationales advanced by the United States in order to facilitate

[878] Panel Report, para. 7.148 (referring to Panel Exhibits IND-61; IND-67; and IND-70).
[879] Panel Report, paras. 7.148-7.158.

implementation of a DSB recommendation by the United States and completion of the analysis in the event that the Appellate Body reversed its finding. First, the Panel agreed with the United States' assertion that the USDOC would have been entitled to reject, as potential benchmarks, pricing information of government-owned entities.[880] In this regard, the Panel considered that Article 14(d) of the SCM Agreement does not require an investigating authority to rely on government prices when determining market benchmarks. Second, the Panel agreed with the United States' assertion that the USDOC would not have been required to determine price benchmarks on the basis of pricing information that pertained to unidentified entities. Third, in relation to the United States' assertion that the USDOC would have been entitled to reject the domestic pricing information because such information was not shown to pertain to actual transactions, the Panel considered that Members have sufficient discretion under Article 14(d) to require actual transaction data for the purpose of determining a benchmark. However, the Panel found that, in the absence of any compelling explanation to the contrary, there was no reason why the domestic pricing information at issue should not have been treated as actual transaction prices. Fourth, the Panel agreed with the United States' contention that the USDOC would have been entitled to reject the price quote submitted by Tata on the basis that it did not specify the exact percentage of iron ore content. Finally, the Panel agreed with the United States' assertion that the price quote provided by Tata could not be used in determining a Tier I benchmark because it is a proprietary document containing confidential information that is easily susceptible, through reverse calculation, to disclosure. The Panel therefore saw no basis to consider that the USDOC should have used the Tata price quote for the purpose of determining a Tier I benchmark to assess the NMDC's sales to purchasers other than Tata.[881]

4.271 On appeal, India claims that, by examining the *ex post* rationales put forward by the United States, the Panel assessed a matter that was not before it, and thereby acted inconsistently with its duty under Article 11 of the DSU. India argues that a panel can examine only information contained on the record and the explanations given by the investigating authority in its published report, and that the *ex post* rationales put forward by the United States therefore fell outside the Panel's jurisdiction.[882] India therefore requests the Appellate Body to declare moot the Panel's findings and observations in respect of these *ex post* rationales. In the event that the Appellate Body declines this request, India further requests the Appellate Body to examine the findings made by the Panel on the merits of the *ex post* rationales, and find that, in making these findings, the Panel erred in

[880] Panel Report, para. 7.160.

[881] Panel Report, paras. 7.160-7.165.

[882] India's appellant's submission, paras. 416 and 417 (referring to Appellate Body Reports, *US – Tyres (China)*, para. 329; and *US – Wheat Gluten*, para. 162).

its interpretation and application of Articles 12.1, 12.4, 12.7, and 14 of the SCM Agreement.[883]

4.272 The United States responds that the views provided by the Panel concerning the merits of the *ex post* rationales put forward by the United States are not "findings", but merely "considerations" that would not, upon adoption of the Report, become part of the DSB's recommendations and rulings.[884] Thus, the United States contends that these considerations are "in a sense inherently moot and perhaps may be analogized to the considerations a panel would set out were it to exercise its discretion to provide 'suggestions' under Article 19.1 of the DSU".[885] As there are no additional "findings" with respect to the domestic pricing information for the Appellate Body to modify, uphold, or reverse, the United States requests the Appellate Body to decline to rule on India's claim under Article 11 of the DSU.

4.273 We agree with India that, in principle, a panel must review the conduct of an investigating authority in the light of information contained on the record and the explanations given by the investigating authority in its published report. To us, however, this is precisely what the Panel did when it reviewed the relevant determinations of the USDOC and found that "there is no reference to the domestic price data at issue in the USDOC's preliminary or final determinations, or in any other contemporaneous USDOC document".[886] It is on this basis that the Panel considered that "India's *prima facie* case [was] not rebutted by any contemporaneous rationale or justification in the USDOC's determinations".[887] Having found that the explanation put forward by the United States for the USDOC's rejection of the domestic pricing information constitutes *ex post* rationales, and that India's case had not been rebutted by any contemporaneous rationale in the USDOC's determinations, the Panel found that the United States acted inconsistently with Articles 14(d) and 1.1(b) of the SCM Agreement. As we see it, any findings made by the Panel thereafter on the domestic pricing information at issue are *alternative* findings to the Panel's findings that the United States had not properly rebutted India's case, and therefore acted inconsistently with Articles 14(d) and 1.1(b) of the SCM Agreement.

4.274 India seems to suggest that the Panel was precluded from examining, *in the alternative*, the merits of the *ex post* rationales put forward by the United States. In our view, although the Panel was certainly not *required* to assess these *ex post* rationales, we do not consider that the Panel was precluded from doing so. In particular, we do not consider that a panel acts inconsistently with its duty under Article 11 of the DSU merely because it makes *alternative* findings that might become relevant in the event that the Appellate Body reverses other

---

883 India's appellant's submission, paras. 412-423.

884 United States' appellee's submission, para. 235.

885 United States' appellee's submission, para. 236.

886 Panel Report, para. 7.154.

887 Panel Report, para. 7.158.

findings made by that panel. As the Appellate Body has noted, "[i]t is not unprecedented for panels to make alternative findings, and indeed this may be useful in resolving a dispute, particularly when, on appeal, the Appellate Body reverses other findings made by a panel."[888] Moreover, to the extent that such alternative findings concern issues of law or legal interpretations, they may fall within the scope of appellate review under Article 17.6 of the DSU. In the light of the foregoing considerations, we do not consider that the Panel acted inconsistently with Article 11 of the DSU by making alternative findings on the *ex post* rationales put forward by the United States, and we *reject* India's claims in this regard.

4.275 India further requests that we examine the Panel's alternative findings on the *ex post* rationales put forward by the United States, and find that they reflect an erroneous interpretation and application of Articles 12.1, 12.4, 12.7, and 14 of the SCM Agreement.[889] As noted, the Panel found that the United States put forward *ex post* rationales to justify the USDOC's failure to consider the domestic pricing information at issue, and that, because India's case had not been rebutted by any contemporaneous rationale in the USDOC's determinations, the United States acted inconsistently with Articles 14(d) and 1.1(b) of the SCM Agreement. As we have explained, we consider that the Panel's findings on the merits of these *ex post* rationales are alternative findings, and that their relevance in this dispute is conditioned on the prospect that the Panel's finding that the United States acted inconsistently with Articles 14(d) and 1.1(b) of the SCM Agreement would be found on appeal to be in error. Nevertheless, the United States has neither appealed the Panel's finding that the United States put forward impermissible *ex post* rationales to justify the USDOC's rejection of the domestic pricing information at issue, nor the Panel's finding that the United States acted inconsistently with Articles 14(d) and 1.1(b) of the SCM Agreement. Because these findings by the Panel remain undisturbed, we decline to review the Panel's alternative findings, in paragraphs 7.160-7.165 of the Panel Report, and *declare* them moot and of no legal effect.

4.4.2.1.2 India's claims concerning the exclusion of the NMDC's export prices as Tier II benchmarks

4.276 We turn now to examine India's claims concerning the exclusion of the NMDC's export prices from the determination of a Tier II benchmark for assessing whether the NMDC provided iron ore for less than adequate remuneration.

4.277 In its preliminary determination for the 2006 administrative review concerning the provision of iron ore by the NMDC, the USDOC continued to

---

[888] Appellate Body Reports, *China – Auto Parts*, para. 208. (fns omitted)

[889] India's appellant's submission, paras. 423 and 435.

apply, as a Tier II benchmark, the prices reflected in the Tex Report[890] that it had applied in previous reviews.[891] Thus, the USDOC applied a benchmark based, in part, on the NMDC's export prices from the Tex Report, just as the USDOC had done in the 2004 administrative review. However, in its subsequent Issues and Decision Memorandum for the 2006 administrative review, the USDOC explained that it had revised the benchmark used in its preliminary determination by excluding the NMDC's export prices from the Tex Report. The USDOC explained that it did so because the NMDC's export prices at issue pertain to "the very government provider" that was the subject of the investigation, namely, the NMDC.[892]

4.278 Before the Panel, India claimed that the exclusion of the NMDC's export prices from the determination of a Tier II benchmark is inconsistent with Article 14(d), as well as the chapeau of Article 14 of the SCM Agreement. In examining India's claim under Article 14(d) of the SCM Agreement, the Panel recalled that it had already found, in the context of India's "as such" claim against the US benchmarking mechanism, that Article 14(d) does not require an investigating authority to rely on a government's domestic prices when determining market benchmarks, because a government may set prices on the basis of public policy considerations rather than market principles. In the Panel's view, "the same risk arises" in respect of a government's export pricing.[893] In this regard, the Panel explained that, "[f]or example, a government might provide goods to export customers for less than adequate remuneration in order to promote domestic production and employment."[894] For this reason, the Panel rejected India's claim that the USDOC should have used the NMDC's export prices for the purpose of determining a Tier II benchmark in the 2006, 2007, and 2008 administrative reviews.

4.279 Turning to India's claim under the chapeau of Article 14 of the SCM Agreement, the Panel considered that the requirement in the chapeau of Article 14 that the application of a benefit methodology be "transparent" conveys the sense that such application should be set out in a manner that it can be "easily understood or discerned".[895] The Panel considered further that the obligation to "adequately explain[]" conveys the sense of making clear or intelligible, and

---

[890] 2007 GOI Questionnaire Response for 2006 AR (Panel Exhibit IND-59), internal p. 6; and Tex Reports of 2006 and 2007 iron ore prices from foreign suppliers paid by purchasers in Japan, Supplemental questionnaire responses of Essar Steel Ltd., dated 14 November 2007 (Panel Exhibit USA-118) and dated 21 November 2008 (Panel Exhibit USA-119) (referred herein jointly as "Tex Report").

[891] Panel Report, para. 7.192 (referring to 2006 AR Preliminary Results (Panel Exhibit IND-32), p. 1587).

[892] Panel Report, para. 7.192 (referring to 2006 AR Issues and Decision Memorandum (Panel Exhibit IND-33), Analysis of Comment 2, internal p. 33).

[893] Panel Report, para. 7.189.

[894] *Ibid.*

[895] Panel Report, para. 7.191.

giving details of how the methodology was applied.[896] The Panel also agreed with the United States that the adequacy of an investigating authority's explanation should be assessed on a case-by-case basis.[897] Noting that the USDOC had explained that the NMDC's export prices were rejected because they pertain to the "very government provider ... at issue"[898], the Panel considered that "the USDOC's explanation of its change in approach in respect of the NMDC's export prices is clear and intelligible, and is easily understood and discerned."[899] Accordingly, the Panel rejected India's claim that the USDOC's explanation of why the NMDC's export prices were excluded from the determination of a Tier II benchmark is inconsistent with the requirements of the chapeau of Article 14 of the SCM Agreement.

4.280 India appeals the Panel's findings rejecting its claims that the USDOC's exclusion of the NMDC's export prices from India to Japan in determining a Tier II benchmark in the 2006, 2007, and 2008 administrative reviews is inconsistent with Article 14(d) and the chapeau of Article 14 of the SCM Agreement. We begin with India's claims under Article 14(d) before turning to India's claim under the chapeau of Article 14.

4.281 India submits that the Panel's finding that government prices can be presumptively rejected as benchmarks under Article 14(d) of the SCM Agreement led the Panel to reject India's claim concerning the USDOC's exclusion of the NMDC's export prices from the determination of a Tier II benchmark. India submits that, because the Panel, in considering India's "as such" claim, erred in finding that government prices can be presumptively rejected in determining benchmarks for the purposes of Article 14(d), the Panel's finding rejecting India's claim concerning the exclusion of the NMDC's export prices from the determination of a Tier II benchmark is also in error. India therefore requests the Appellate Body to find that the Panel erred in its interpretation and application of Article 14(d) in finding that the rejection of the NMDC's export prices as a Tier II benchmark is consistent with that provision.[900]

4.282 As regards India's claim concerning the USDOC's exclusion of the NMDC's export prices to Japan, the United States emphasizes that comparing the price of the entity under investigation with another price of that same entity would be circular, uninformative, and contrary to the requirements of Article 14(d) of the SCM Agreement.[901]

---

[896] *Ibid.*

[897] Panel Report, para. 7.191 (referring to United States' response to Panel question No. 104, para. 60).

[898] Panel Report, para. 7.192 (referring to 2006 AR Issues and Decision Memorandum, Analysis of Comment 2, internal p. 33).

[899] Panel Report, para. 7.192.

[900] India's appellant's submission, paras. 45, 55, and 56.

[901] United States' response to questioning at the oral hearing.

4.283 At the outset, we wish to highlight that India's present claims concern the issue of whether the export prices of the provider of the financial contribution under investigation can be used in determining a world market price and assessing, by reference to that world market price, whether the financial contribution at issue represents "less than adequate remuneration" within the meaning of Article 14(d) of the SCM Agreement. In examining India's "as such" claims against the US benchmarking mechanism, we have stated that proper benchmark prices would normally emanate from the market for the good in question in the country of provision. Thus, in determining a benchmark for the purposes of Article 14(d), an investigating authority must first consider in-country prices, that is, the prices of the same or similar goods on the market in the country of provision. We have also stated that it is only once an investigating authority has properly complied with its obligation to investigate whether there are market-determined in-country prices that reflect prevailing market conditions in the country of provision that it may, consistently with Article 14(d), use alternative benchmarks for the purposes of Article 14(d). In addition, we have emphasized that, where an investigating authority considers that it must have recourse to a benchmark other than in-country prices, it must explain its basis for doing so.

4.284 We note that a "world market price" is an *alternative* benchmark that investigating authorities may, in certain circumstances, have recourse to for the purposes of Article 14(d) of the SCM Agreement. In this regard, we recall that, in *US – Softwood Lumber IV*, the Appellate Body examined the question of what types of alternative benchmarks could be relied on in a manner consistent with Article 14(d), and considered that alternative methods for determining the adequacy of remuneration "could include proxies that take into account prices for similar goods quoted on world markets, or proxies constructed on the basis of production costs".[902] The Appellate Body reiterated, however, that, where an investigating authority proceeds in this manner, "it is under an obligation to ensure that the resulting benchmark relates or refers to, or is connected with, prevailing market conditions in the country of provision, and must reflect price, quality, availability, marketability, transportation and other conditions of purchase or sale, as required by Article 14(d)."[903] In our view, it follows that any price that is used for the purpose of determining an alternative benchmark must approximate prevailing market conditions in the country of provision. We note, in this connection, that the Appellate Body has underscored the importance of making appropriate adjustments to ensure that alternative benchmarks reflect prevailing market conditions in the country of provision.[904]

4.285 Turning more specifically to India's claim concerning the USDOC's exclusion of the NMDC's export prices in determining a Tier II benchmark, we

902 Appellate Body Report, *US – Softwood Lumber IV*, para. 106.
903 *Ibid.*
904 Appellate Body Report, *US – Softwood Lumber IV*, para. 108.

consider that, because an export price would normally relate to prevailing market conditions in the export market, rather than the market in the country of provision, such a price is not *per se* an in-country price. In this regard, the Appellate Body has considered that it cannot be presumed that market conditions prevailing in one Member relate or refer to, or are connected with, market conditions prevailing in another Member.[905]

4.286 We note that, in rejecting India's claim, the Panel recalled that, in the context of examining India's "as such" claim against the US benchmarking mechanism, it had already found that Article 14(d) of the SCM Agreement does not require an investigating authority to rely on a government's domestic prices when determining market benchmarks because "a government may set prices on the basis of public policy considerations rather than market principles."[906] Moreover, in explaining how this logic applies to the export pricing philosophy of a government provider of a particular good, the Panel considered that "[f]or example, a government might provide goods to export customers for less than adequate remuneration in order to promote domestic production and employment."[907]

4.287 In addressing India's appeal of the Panel's findings on its "as such" claim against the US benchmarking mechanism, we considered that the fact that governments *may* set prices in pursuit of public policy objectives, rather than market-based profit maximization, does not permit a general inference that government-related prices other than the financial contribution at issue may be presumptively discarded in determining a benchmark for the purpose of Article 14(d) of the SCM Agreement. We therefore disagreed with the Panel's conclusion to the extent that it suggests that Article 14(d) does not require the consideration of government-related prices simply because governments may set prices in pursuit of public policy objectives. In examining India's claim that the USDOC's exclusion of the NMDC's export prices from the determination of a Tier II benchmark is inconsistent with Article 14(d), the Panel appears to have made the same error. In particular, we do not consider that the fact that a government provider *may* set its export prices in pursuit of public policy objectives, rather than market-based profit maximization, permits a *per se* conclusion that Article 14(d) does not require the consideration of any export prices of government providers for the purpose of determining an alternative benchmark. As we see it, the Panel's reasoning would necessarily be erroneous in respect of export prices that approximate prevailing market conditions in the country of provision, and can therefore serve as a basis for determining an alternative benchmark. While there may be reasons to exclude an export price of a government provider in determining an alternative benchmark, we are not persuaded that an investigating authority can *presume* that the export price set by

[905] *Ibid.*
[906] Panel Report, para. 7.189.
[907] *Ibid.*

a government provider is inherently unreliable. This must be proven on the basis of evidence that an investigating authority must examine so that it may base its determination on positive evidence on the record.

4.288 On the basis of the Panel's interpretation of Article 14(d) of the SCM Agreement, the Panel rejected India's claim that the USDOC should have used the NMDC's export prices to determine a Tier II benchmark in the 2006, 2007, and 2008 administrative reviews. As stated above, we do not agree with the Panel's interpretation to the extent that it suggests that Article 14(d) of the SCM Agreement does not require investigating authorities to consider prices of government-related entities in determining a proper benchmark simply because governments may set prices in pursuit of public policy objectives. At this stage of our analysis, we are not saying that the export prices at issue should have been used by the USDOC in determining a Tier II benchmark. Rather, we consider that the basis for the Panel's rejection of India's claim, as explained above, constitutes legal error. On that basis, we *reverse* the Panel's finding, in paragraph 7.189 of the Panel Report, rejecting India's claim that the USDOC should have used the NMDC's export prices to determine a Tier II benchmark in the 2006, 2007, and 2008 administrative reviews.

4.289 In the light of the above, it remains for us to consider whether we can complete the legal analysis and determine, by reference to the USDOC's determination, whether the USDOC properly excluded the NMDC's export prices from its determination of a Tier II benchmark. In order to complete the analysis, the panel's factual findings and the undisputed facts on the panel record must provide us with a sufficient basis for our own analysis.[908]

4.290 We note that, in excluding the NMDC's export prices from its determination of a Tier II benchmark in the 2006, 2007, and 2008 administrative reviews, the USDOC explained that "[b]ecause [the NMDC export prices] pertain to the very government provider of the goods at issue, we would not *normally* use these prices for comparison purposes under [Tier I or Tier II] where other more appropriate benchmark data are available."[909] First, by stating that it would not "normally" use the export prices of the government provider under investigation in determining a Tier II benchmark, the USDOC appears to acknowledge that it is not precluded from using such prices in determining a Tier II benchmark. In any event, the USDOC excluded the NMDC's export prices from the determination of a Tier II benchmark because, in its view, other benchmark data were "more appropriate" given that the NMDC's export prices at

[908] See e.g. Appellate Body Reports, *Canada – Periodicals*, p. 24, DSR 1997:I, p. 469; *EC – Poultry*, para. 156; *EC – Hormones*, para. 222; *US – Shrimp*, paras. 123 and 124; *Japan – Agricultural Products II*, para. 112; *US – FSC*, para. 133; *Australia – Salmon*, paras. 117 and 118; *US – Lamb*, paras. 150 and 172; *US – Section 211 Appropriations Act*, para. 352; *EC and certain member States – Large Civil Aircraft*, paras. 1174-1178; *US – Large Civil Aircraft (2nd complaint)*, paras. 1272-1274; and *US – Countervailing and Anti-Dumping Measures (China)*, para. 4.124.

[909] 2007 AR Issues and Decision Memorandum, Analysis of Comment 11, internal p. 50. (emphasis added)

issue emanated from the very government provider under investigation. We would expect an investigating authority, in selecting an alternative benchmark for the purposes of Article 14(d) of the SCM Agreement, to approach export prices of the very government provider under investigation with caution. Yet, the USDOC did not explain why, in this instance, it was excluding prices that it had previously used, in the 2004 administrative review, in determining a Tier II benchmark. We have stated that a panel must examine whether the conclusions reached by the investigating authority are reasoned and adequate, and that such an examination must be critical, and be based on the information contained in the record and the explanations given by the authority in its published report.[910] We do not see that the USDOC provided in its determination a reasoned and adequate explanation as to why the benchmark data that it relied on, namely, world market prices from Australia and Brazil, is more appropriate than the benchmark data that it had previously relied on but subsequently excluded, namely, the NMDC's export prices at issue. Consequently, we *find* that the USDOC's exclusion of these prices is inconsistent with Article 14(d) of the SCM Agreement.

4.291 We note that India also asserts on appeal that the Panel erred in rejecting its claim that the USDOC, contrary to the requirements of the chapeau of Article 14 of the SCM Agreement, failed to "adequately explain" its inconsistent treatment of the NMDC's export prices in the 2004 administrative review, on the one hand, and in the 2006, 2007, and 2008 administrative reviews, on the other hand.[911] In our view, India's claim under the chapeau of Article 14 is essentially resolved by our consideration of India's claim under Article 14(d). For the reasons set out above, we consider that, contrary to what the Panel found, the USDOC's exclusion of the NMDC's export prices at issue from its determination of a Tier II benchmark is not adequately explained for the purpose of the chapeau of Article 14. We therefore also *reverse* the Panel's finding, in paragraph 7.192 of the Panel Report, rejecting India's claim that the USDOC's explanation of the exclusion of the NMDC's export prices is inconsistent with the requirements of the chapeau of Article 14 of the SCM Agreement, and *find* that the USDOC's exclusion of these prices is inconsistent with the chapeau of Article 14 of the SCM Agreement.

---

[910] Appellate Body Report, *US – Tyres (China)*, para. 123.

[911] India's appellant's submission, para. 463. Although India claims on appeal that the Panel failed to "objectively assess" its claim against the requirements of the chapeau of Article 14, it seems to us that, ultimately, India's claim relates to the Panel's application of the requirements of the chapeau of Article 14 of the SCM Agreement to the facts. In this regard, India asserts that "the Panel committed a legal error in applying the requirements of the chapeau of Article 14 to the facts of the dispute." (*Ibid.*, para. 464) We therefore examine India's claim as a challenge to the Panel's application of the legal standard under the chapeau of Article 14 and, accordingly, there is no basis to consider separately whether the Panel, in assessing India's claim under the chapeau of Article 14, acted inconsistently with Article 11 of the DSU.

4.4.2.1.3 India's claims concerning the use of "as delivered" prices from Australia and Brazil as benchmarks

4.292 We turn now to consider India's claims concerning the USDOC's use of "as delivered" prices from Australia and Brazil as benchmarks for assessing whether the NMDC provided iron ore for less than adequate remuneration. Before the Panel, India claimed that the USDOC's use of these prices as benchmarks is inconsistent with Article 14(d) of the SCM Agreement. First, India claimed that the use of such benchmarks is inconsistent with the requirement under Article 14(d) that the adequacy of remuneration be assessed in relation to "prevailing market conditions" in the country of provision.[912] Second, India asserted that the use of such benchmarks is inconsistent with Article 14(d) because it nullifies the comparative advantage that India enjoys in terms of being able to source iron ore locally for Indian steel makers.[913] The Panel rejected India's claims. On appeal, India claims that, in reaching its findings, the Panel erred in its interpretation and application of Article 14(d) of the SCM Agreement, and acted inconsistently with its duty under Article 11 of the DSU.[914]

4.293 In addressing India's appeal, we first provide a summary of the Panel's findings before reviewing these findings in the light of the participants' arguments on appeal.

4.4.2.1.3.1 The Panel's findings

4.294 In addressing India's claims, the Panel first considered whether, as India argued, benchmarks for assessing whether the NMDC provided iron ore for less than adequate remuneration should have been set at an *ex mine* level, rather than at an "as delivered" level. The Panel considered that India's argument was based on its "as such" claim that the mandatory use of "as delivered" prices, under Section 351.511(a)(2)(iv) of the US Regulations, is inconsistent with Article 14(d) of the SCM Agreement. Noting that it had rejected this claim on the basis that market benchmarks that relate to the "prevailing market conditions" in the country of provision need not mirror the contractual terms on which the government provider sells its goods, the Panel also rejected India's claim that the USDOC acted inconsistently with Article 14(d) of the SCM Agreement by using benchmark prices set at the delivered level, despite the fact that prices were set by the NMDC at the *ex mine* level.[915]

4.295 The Panel then assessed whether, as argued by India, the "as delivered" prices from Brazil and Australia did not reflect "prevailing market conditions" in

---

912 India's first written submission to the Panel, paras. 310 and 311.
913 India's first written submission to the Panel, paras. 305-309.
914 India's appellant's submission, paras. 448 and 449.
915 Panel Report, para. 7.173.

India, as required by Article 14(d) of the SCM Agreement. The Panel observed that the Brazilian price used by the USDOC was based on an actual transaction in which an Indian steel producer purchased iron ore from a Brazilian mine on a delivered basis. The Panel considered that, because the transaction was made by an Indian steel producer established in India, the transaction necessarily related to the prevailing market conditions in India. Thus, the Panel found that the Brazilian price, including delivery charges, reflects and relates to the prevailing market conditions in India, as required by Article 14(d).[916]

4.296 In addition, the Panel observed that, in the course of the countervailing duty investigation, NMDC officials had explained that the NMDC sets its domestic prices in the light of competition from Australia and Brazil, and therefore in the light of how much an Indian steel producer would be willing to pay to import iron ore from mines in those countries. On the basis that such prices indicate what an Indian steel producer would be "willing to pay" to import iron ore from Australia and Brazil, the Panel rejected India's assertion that Australian and Brazilian prices, adjusted for delivery to steel producers in India, do not relate to the prevailing market conditions in India.[917]

4.297 Finally, the Panel considered India's argument that the USDOC's use of the "as delivered" prices from Australia and Brazil as benchmarks countervailed India's comparative advantage in respect of iron ore. Noting India's statement that "the comparative advantage for [a country with natural resources] lies in the fact that users of the natural resources can procure it without having to suffer the costs and risks associated with their import from a different country", the Panel considered that India's argument regarding comparative advantage was based on the existence of iron ore in India.[918] In the light of record evidence that Indian steel producers actually imported iron ore from overseas, and that the NMDC set its domestic prices in the light of import competition, the Panel considered that there was no factual basis for the argument that India's comparative advantage was such that users of iron ore had no need to engage in import transactions. Accordingly, the Panel rejected India's argument that the "as delivered" benchmarks applied by the USDOC nullified India's comparative advantage.[919]

4.298 For these reasons, the Panel rejected India's claim that the use of "as delivered" prices from Australia and Brazil as benchmarks for assessing whether the NMDC provided iron ore for less than adequate remuneration is inconsistent with Article 14(d) of the SCM Agreement.

---

[916] Panel Report, para. 7.181.

[917] Panel Report, para. 7.182.

[918] Panel Report, para. 7.184 (quoting India's first written submission to the Panel, para. 305).

[919] Panel Report, para. 7.185.

4.4.2.1.3.2 India's claims on appeal

4.299 On appeal, India asserts that, in rejecting its claims, the Panel erred in its interpretation and application of Article 14(d), and acted inconsistently with its duty under Article 11 of the DSU. In addressing India's claims on appeal, we begin with India's claims under Article 14(d) of the SCM Agreement. We then turn to examine India's claim under Article 11 of the DSU.

4.300 First, India contends that the Panel erred in its interpretation and application of Article 14(d) of the SCM Agreement in finding that the "as delivered" prices from Australia and Brazil reflect the "prevailing market conditions" in India. In India's view, the term "prevailing market conditions" refers to the conditions prevailing in the market in general, as opposed to isolated acts of individual players in the market in question. Thus, the assessment of "prevailing market conditions" for countries having both import and domestic transactions for a particular good will depend on a qualitative and quantitative analysis of both types of transactions. India asserts that the mere fact that one steel producer procured iron ore from Brazil in one isolated transaction in which it paid an "as delivered" price for the iron ore cannot be expanded into the generic conditions applicable to the market in India. Similarly, contends India, the Panel's reliance on a statement by NMDC officials that the NMDC allegedly prices iron ore based on what steel producers are willing to pay to import does not mean that all suppliers of iron ore in the market behaved in such a manner. India asserts that evidence on the record shows that there were other domestic suppliers of iron ore in India, and that iron ore was not being supplied on an "as delivered" basis. Thus, India argues that the Panel's reliance on "isolated import transactions" involving payment for iron ore on an "as delivered" basis to establish that these transactions reflect the "prevailing market conditions" in India was based on an incorrect understanding of the term "prevailing market conditions" in Article 14(d) of the SCM Agreement.[920]

4.301 The United States responds that India's arguments are based on an incorrect reading of Article 14(d) of the SCM Agreement and of the Appellate Body's findings in *US – Softwood Lumber IV*. The United States asserts that Article 14(d) does not, as India argues, require an investigating authority to engage in a comprehensive qualitative and quantitative analysis of a country's supply-and-demand matrix in respect of a particular good in order to determine whether a government provides goods for less than adequate remuneration. Instead, Article 14(d) requires an investigating authority to assess the adequacy of remuneration from the perspective of the recipient of government-provided goods, in relation to the prevailing market conditions in the country of provision.[921]

---

[920] India's appellant's submission, paras. 452-454.
[921] United States' appellee's submission, para. 290.

4.302 We recall that, in the context of examining India's "as such" claims concerning the mandatory use of "as delivered" prices under Section 351.511(a)(2)(iv) of the US Regulations, we have considered above the extent to which *ex works* prices can be used for the purpose of a benefit comparison under Article 14(d) of the SCM Agreement. First, we considered that an understanding of the term "prevailing market conditions" as referring solely to the conditions set by the providers of the good in question stands in tension with the well-established proposition that a financial contribution provided by a government confers a benefit if it makes the recipient "better off" than it would otherwise have been absent that contribution.[922] Thus, we considered that a determination of the adequacy of remuneration in relation to prevailing market conditions in the country of provision must capture the full cost to the recipient of receiving the government-provided good in question. In addition, we observed that the term "transportation" is explicitly listed among the "prevailing market conditions" illustratively identified in the second sentence of Article 14(d), and considered this as confirming that the costs associated with the transportation of the good in question is a factor that must be accounted for in determining, in accordance with Article 14(d), the adequacy of remuneration in relation to prevailing market conditions in the country of provision. We therefore considered that the use of *ex works* prices for the purpose of a benefit comparison under Article 14(d) would not capture the full cost to the recipient of receiving the government-provided good in question, and would, therefore, fail to assess whether the financial contribution at issue makes the recipient better off than it would otherwise have been absent that contribution.

4.303 In the light of these considerations concerning the use of *ex works* prices for the purposes of a benefit analysis under Article 14(d) of the SCM Agreement, we disagree with India to the extent that India suggests that the USDOC was required to use *ex works* prices in assessing whether the NMDC provided iron ore for less than adequate remuneration.

4.304 Although we have found that the USDOC was not required to undertake a benefit comparison at an *ex works* level, we must consider whether, as India argues, the Panel erred in finding that the "as delivered" prices from Australia and Brazil that the USDOC used as benchmarks reflect the prevailing market conditions in India. India's contention is that the Panel erred in its interpretation of Article 14(d) of the SCM Agreement to the extent that it relied on "isolated transactions" to establish that "as delivered" prices from Australia and Brazil reflect "prevailing market conditions" in India. The crux of India's claim is that "prevailing market conditions", within the meaning of Article 14(d) of the SCM Agreement, refers to the conditions prevailing in the market in general, as opposed to isolated acts of individual players in the market in question.

922 Appellate Body Report, *Canada – Aircraft*, para. 157.

4.305 In the context of examining India's "as such" claim against the use of "as delivered" prices under Section 351.511(a)(2)(iv) of the US Regulations, we have considered that an assessment of "prevailing market conditions", within the meaning of Article 14(d) of the SCM Agreement, necessarily involves an analysis of the market generally, because it is only through such an analysis that a conclusion can be drawn as to the conditions that are "prevailing" in that market. Moreover, we have considered that, insofar as adjustments for delivery charges are required to undertake a proper assessment of benefit in the context of Article 14(d), any such adjustments must reflect the generally applicable delivery charges for the good in question in the country of provision. As an example, we have noted that, where the incidence of imports of the good in question are minimal in relation to domestic transactions for that good, it may not be appropriate to compare a benchmark price, adjusted to reflect international delivery charges, with the government price, adjusted to reflect local delivery charges, because, in this specific scenario, international delivery charges may not reflect the generally applicable delivery charges for the good in question in the country of provision. We have considered further that, in such a case, an investigating authority may need to make adjustments to the benchmark price to reflect delivery charges that approximate the generally applicable delivery charges for the relevant good in the country of provision.

4.306 The foregoing considerations suggest that, in order to assess the adequacy of remuneration in relation to prevailing market conditions in the country of provision, as required by Article 14(d) of the SCM Agreement, it may be necessary for an investigating authority to seek, and engage with, evidence concerning the prevailing market conditions for the good in question, including the generally applicable delivery charges for that good. As we have stated, investigating authorities bear the responsibility to conduct the necessary analysis in order to determine, on the basis of information supplied by petitioners and respondents in a countervailing duty investigation, whether proposed benchmark prices are market determined and are, therefore, reflective of prevailing market conditions in the country of provision such that they can be used to determine whether remuneration is less than adequate. An assessment of "prevailing market conditions", within the meaning of Article 14(d) of the SCM Agreement, necessarily involves an analysis of the market generally in order to draw a conclusion concerning the conditions that are "prevailing" in that market.

4.307 India faults the Panel for relying on "isolated transactions" in order to establish that the "as delivered" prices from Australia and Brazil – reflecting import duties and ocean freight to India – relate to the prevailing market conditions for iron ore in India. It seems to us that India's contention is that international delivery charges are not representative of "prevailing market conditions" for iron ore in India. We must thus consider the evidence that the Panel relied on in finding that the "as delivered" prices at issue reflect the prevailing market conditions for iron ore in India.

4.308 With regard to the "as delivered" Brazilian price, we recall that the Panel observed that this price was based on an actual transaction in which an Indian steel producer purchased iron ore from a Brazilian mine on a delivered basis. The Panel considered that, because the transaction was made by an Indian steel producer established in India, the transaction necessarily related to the prevailing market conditions in India. Thus, in the Panel's view, the Brazilian price, including international delivery charges, reflects and relates to the prevailing market conditions in India, consistent with the requirements of Article 14(d).[923]

4.309 On appeal, India asserts that the mere fact that one steel producer procured iron ore from Brazil in one isolated transaction in which it paid an "as delivered" price cannot be expanded into the general conditions applicable to the market in India. We see merit in India's argument that an isolated import transaction for a good may not necessarily reflect the prevailing market conditions for that good in the country of provision. In our view, the fact that an importer has paid a price, inclusive of international delivery charges, for a particular good may, as an evidentiary matter, provide some indication as to the generally applicable delivery charges for that good in the country of provision. However, we do not consider that it can be inferred, without more, that a single, isolated import transaction for a particular good reflects or relates to prevailing market conditions for that good in the country of provision.

4.310 Turning to the "as delivered" prices from Australia and Brazil more generally, we recall that the Panel referred to evidence on the record and observed that, in the course of the countervailing duty investigation, NMDC officials had explained that the NMDC sets its domestic prices in the light of competition from Australia and Brazil, and therefore in the light of how much an Indian steel producer would be willing to pay to import iron ore from mines in those countries. The Panel considered that, because the "as delivered" prices at issue indicate what an Indian steel producer would be "willing to pay" to import iron ore from Australia and Brazil, they necessarily relate to the prevailing market conditions in India.[924]

4.311 At the outset, we have several concerns with the Panel's reliance on the statement referred to above as a basis for rejecting India's claims. First, we note that the statement on which the Panel relied in rejecting India's claims under Article 14(d) of the SCM Agreement is not referred to in the USDOC's determinations but, rather, is contained in a document on the administrative record of the USDOC.[925] We have stated that a panel must examine whether the conclusions reached by the investigating authority are reasoned and adequate, and that such an examination must be critical, and be based on the information contained on the record and the explanations given by the authority in its published report.[926] Thus, there must be, in the investigating authority's determinations, an explanation of how the evidence on the record supports its

923 Panel Report, para. 7.181.
924 Panel Report, para. 7.182.
925 2004 GOI Verification Report (Panel Exhibit USA-114), pp. 6-7.
926 Appellate Body Report, *US – Tyres (China)*, para. 123.

factual findings. Yet, we do not see that the USDOC's determination contains a reference to the statement relied on by the Panel, or an explanation of how that statement supports the conclusion that "as delivered" prices from Australia and Brazil relate to prevailing market conditions in India. We are troubled that the Panel appears to have based its assessment of India's claims under Article 14(d) on evidence found on the administrative record of the USDOC, rather than on the reasoning provided by the USDOC in its written determination.

4.312 Second, it is not clear to us that the statement relied on by the Panel permits the inference that the Panel ultimately drew. As stated above, the Panel relied on a statement by NMDC officials that, in setting the price for iron ore in the domestic market, the "NMDC reviews the negotiated international price when determining how much the purchaser would be willing to pay to import".[927] It was not disputed before the Panel, and the participants do not dispute on appeal, that the reference to the "negotiated international price" is not a reference to a price inclusive of international delivery charges, but rather a reference to prices in the Tex Report which do not reflect the cost of international delivery. Indeed, in using the "as delivered" price from Australia as a benchmark, the USDOC adjusted this price, as reported in the Tex Report, to reflect the cost of international delivery to India. Thus, the statement relied on by the Panel does not, in our view, *necessarily* permit an inference that the NMDC's domestic prices were set based on international prices inclusive of international delivery charges.

4.313 In any event, we have considered that an assessment of "prevailing market conditions" within the meaning of Article 14(d) of the SCM Agreement necessarily involves an analysis of the market generally, rather than isolated transactions in that market. As we have explained, it is only through such an analysis that a conclusion can be drawn as to the conditions that are "prevailing" in the market of the country of provision. Thus, insofar as adjustments for delivery charges are required to undertake a proper assessment of benefit in the context of Article 14(d), any such adjustments must reflect the generally applicable delivery charges for the good in question in the country of provision. We note that the statement relied on by the Panel focusses solely on the NMDC. We consider that, without further explanation and substantiation, evidence focusing on one provider of the good in question in the country of provision may not be sufficient to establish the prevailing market conditions for that good.

4.314 In the light of the foregoing considerations, we do not consider that the Panel properly concluded that the "as delivered" prices from Australia and Brazil reflect prevailing market conditions in India. We therefore consider that, in rejecting India's claim under Article 14(d) of the SCM Agreement, the Panel erred in its application of that provision. Consequently, we *reverse* the Panel's findings, in paragraphs 7.183 and 7.185 of the Panel Report, rejecting India's

[927] Panel Report, para. 7.182 (quoting 2004 GOI Verification Report, pp. 6-7).

claim that the USDOC's use of "as delivered" prices from Australia and Brazil in assessing whether the NMDC provided iron ore for less than adequate remuneration is inconsistent with Article 14(d) of the SCM Agreement.

4.315 We must thus consider whether we can complete the legal analysis and determine whether there is a sufficient basis in the USDOC's determination to sustain a finding that the "as delivered" prices from Australia and Brazil reflect prevailing market conditions, including the generally applicable delivery charges, for iron ore in India.

4.316 We have found above that, in rejecting India's claims, the Panel appears to have focused its analysis on evidence found on the administrative record of the USDOC, rather than on the reasoning provided by the USDOC in its written determination. Upon our own examination of the USDOC's determination, it appears that the USDOC considered that a world market price, such as the "as delivered" prices from Australia and Brazil, which is "available to purchasers in the country in question", is "necessarily inclusive of related costs, including shipping".[928] We do not see that the USDOC provided in its determination a reasoned and adequate explanation for concluding that world market prices from Australia and Brazil, adjusted to reflect the cost of international delivery to India, relate to the "prevailing market conditions" for iron ore in India. As we have found above, an analysis of prevailing market conditions in the country of provision requires an analysis of the market generally in order to draw a conclusion about the conditions prevailing in that market. It does not appear from the USDOC's determination that the USDOC properly determined that the "as delivered" prices at issue relate to prevailing market conditions in India.

4.317 In the light of the foregoing considerations, we consider that the USDOC did not provide a reasoned and adequate explanation of the basis for its use of "as delivered" prices from Australia and Brazil as benchmarks for assessing whether the NMDC provided iron ore for less than adequate remuneration. We therefore *find* that the USDOC's use of these prices as benchmarks in assessing whether the NMDC provided iron ore for less than adequate remuneration is inconsistent with Article 14(d) of the SCM Agreement.

4.318 India further claims on appeal that, by relying on an isolated statement by NMDC officials on the record as a basis for rejecting India's claims under Article 14(d) of the SCM Agreement, the Panel justified the USDOC's determination on a basis that the USDOC itself had not referred to, disregarded material evidence on the record, and thereby acted inconsistently with its duty under Article 11 of the DSU.[929]

4.319 As we see it, India's claim under Article 11 of the DSU implicates issues that we have already considered in reviewing the Panel's findings under Article 14(d) of the SCM Agreement. As we have found that the Panel erred in its

[928] 2007 AR Issues and Decision Memorandum, Analysis of Comment 13, internal p. 55.

[929] India's appellant's submission, para. 448.

application of Article 14(d) of the SCM Agreement in rejecting India's claims, we decline to further examine India's claim under Article 11 of the DSU.

4.320 Finally, India requests, if we find that the USDOC's use of "as delivered" prices from Australia and Brazil as benchmarks is inconsistent with Article 14(d) of the SCM Agreement, that we also find inconsistent with Article 14(d) the USDOC's determination that the GOI provided iron ore and coal for less than adequate remuneration through its provision of captive mining rights.[930]

4.321 As regards the GOI's provision of iron ore, we note that, in calculating benefit, the USDOC used as a Tier II benchmark the same "as delivered" Australian price that it used for assessing whether the NMDC provided iron ore for less than adequate remuneration.[931] We have found above that the USDOC did not provide, in its determination, a reasoned and adequate explanation of the basis for its use of this benchmark price, and that, therefore, the USDOC's use of this benchmark is inconsistent with Article 14(d). It follows that, for the same reasons, the USDOC's use of this benchmark in calculating benefit in the context of the GOI's provision of iron ore through the grant of captive mining rights is also inconsistent with Article 14(d). However, because the Panel already found that the use of this benchmark in respect of the provision of iron ore through captive mining rights is inconsistent with Article 14(d) on other grounds, which were not appealed by the United States, we do not disturb this finding of the Panel.[932]

4.322 Turning to the GOI's provision of coal, we note that, in calculating benefit, the USDOC used a Tier I benchmark based on actual "as delivered" prices paid by an Indian company for importing coal from a private supplier in Australia. India argues that *as a consequence* of finding that the USDOC's use of "as delivered" prices for iron ore from Australia and Brazil as benchmarks is inconsistent with Article 14(d) of the SCM Agreement, we must also find that the USDOC's use of actual "as delivered" import prices for coal from Australia is also inconsistent with Article 14(d). Yet, we do not see that our findings on the USDOC's use of "as delivered" prices for iron ore have this consequence. The benchmark used to assess benefit in the context of the GOI's provision of coal through the grant of captive mining rights is different than the benchmark used to assess benefit in respect of the GOI's or the NMDC's provision of iron ore.[933]

930 India's appellant's submission, paras. 459 and 460.

931 The USDOC compared this Tier II benchmark with a constructed government price in order to determine whether the GOI provided iron ore for less than adequate remuneration. In the next subsection, we address India's challenge to the Panel's findings concerning the USDOC's use of a constructed government price for iron ore and coal.

932 The Panel found that the use of this Tier II benchmark for the purpose of determining whether the GOI's provision of captive mining rights for iron ore conferred a benefit is inconsistent with Article 14(d) of the SCM Agreement on the basis that the USDOC had failed to consider certain domestic pricing information for iron ore as a Tier I benchmark. (See Panel Report, para. 7.158)

933 In addition, we note that India has not provided us with specific arguments on the actual "as delivered" import prices for coal from Australia that the USDOC used as a Tier I benchmark.

There is thus no basis for India's consequential request as it relates to the benchmark used by the USDOC for assessing whether the GOI provided coal for less than adequate remuneration through its grant of captive mining rights. We therefore decline India's request.

4.4.2.2 India's claims concerning captive mining rights for iron ore and coal

4.323 We now turn to India's appeal of the Panel's rejection of India's claim that the USDOC's use of a methodology to construct a government price for iron ore and coal is inconsistent with Articles 1.1(b) and 14(d) of the SCM Agreement. In respect of grants of mining rights for iron ore and coal, the USDOC determined benefit by constructing government prices, and then comparing those prices with Tier I and Tier II benchmarks. The USDOC constructed the government prices by calculating royalties paid to the GOI for mining rights, and then adding per unit operational mining costs associated with the extraction of iron ore and coal.[934] Below, we summarize the Panel's findings before addressing India's claims on appeal.

4.4.2.2.1 The Panel's findings

4.324 India argued before the Panel that, because the GOI provided only the rights to mine minerals, rather than the extracted minerals themselves, the USDOC violated Articles 1.1(b) and 14(d) of the SCM Agreement by applying a methodology for determining benefit that compared a constructed government price for extracted minerals to benchmark prices. India submitted that the costs incurred by an Indian miner in extracting the mineral and the reasonable profit, if any, that a miner may obtain upon using and selling such extracted mineral cannot form part of the "remuneration" to be received by the GOI.[935] According to India, the USDOC should have assessed the adequacy of the remuneration for the GOI before assessing whether there was any benefit to the recipient. India contended that the USDOC should have assessed the adequacy of remuneration for the GOI by analysing the royalty rate charged by the GOI in comparison to royalty rates in other countries.[936]

4.325 The Panel considered that India's claim against the USDOC's constructed price methodology was premised on two arguments that the Panel had already rejected. First, because it had found that the grant of mining rights constituted a

---

[934] The Panel stated that the USDOC constructed government prices "by calculating a per unit price for the captive mining fees paid to GOI, and then adding per unit operational mining costs, which consisted of materials, labour, depreciation, overhead, and royalties". (Panel Report, para. 7.254) In response to questioning at the oral hearing, the participants clarified that payments to the GOI consisted solely of royalties, and that such payments were not separately factored into the constructed costs associated with extraction.

[935] Panel Report, para. 7.256.

[936] Panel Report, para. 7.257.

provision of goods within the meaning of Article 1.1(a)(1)(iii) of the SCM Agreement, the Panel rejected India's argument that the steel producers were provided only the right to mine minerals, rather than the extracted minerals themselves. Second, on the basis of its rejection of India's contention that adequacy of remuneration should be assessed from the perspective of the government, the Panel considered that the USDOC was entitled to assess adequacy of remuneration from the perspective of the recipient using a benchmarking methodology. The Panel concluded that, since the USDOC needed a government price for the provided good against which to compare the relevant benchmarks, it was reasonable for the USDOC to construct a government price for the extracted minerals. The Panel therefore rejected India's claim that such methodology is inconsistent with Articles 1.1(b) and 14(d) of the SCM Agreement.[937]

4.326 The Panel further noted that India had also alleged that the USDOC's use of a constructed price methodology is inconsistent with the principle of good faith. The Panel agreed with the United States that India's good faith claim fell outside the Panel's terms of reference since it was not included in India's panel request.[938]

4.4.2.2.2 The Panel's use of a methodology to construct government prices for iron ore and coal

4.327 India principally contends on appeal that the Panel erred under Article 14(d) of the SCM Agreement by endorsing the USDOC's constructed price methodology. India considers that, because the GOI provided mining rights and received royalties in return, the "remuneration" under Article 14(d) cannot consist of anything other than the actual amount received by the GOI. India maintains that the methodology used by the USDOC to determine benefit is erroneous and that, instead, the USDOC should have determined whether the government price was set in accordance with market principles. India also claims that the Panel acted inconsistently with Article 11 of the DSU in refusing to assess its claim that the USDOC's methodology is not in accordance with a good faith interpretation of Article 14(d).

4.328 The United States maintains that India's claim is based on the view that remuneration should be assessed from the perspective of the government provider. The United States points out that the Panel found that India did not

---

937 Panel Report, para. 7.260.

938 Panel Report, para. 7.261. We note that the Panel then went on to evaluate India's challenge against certain aspects of the Tier I and Tier II price benchmarks with which the constructed government prices for iron ore and coal were compared. In doing so, the Panel upheld India's claim under Article 14(d) regarding the USDOC's rejection of certain domestic price information when assessing benefit in respect of the provision of iron ore, but rejected India's claim relating to benefit in respect of the provision of coal. (*Ibid.*, para. 7.265)

challenge the calculations themselves, but only the fact that the basic methodology does not calculate benefit from the perspective of the government. In addition, the United States requests the Appellate Body to reject India's appeal of the Panel's finding that India's claims pertaining to "good faith" were outside the Panel's terms of reference. According to the United States, a panel's failure to consider claims not within its terms of reference does not amount to a violation of Article 11 of the DSU. Moreover, the United States notes that a claim that a party is not acting in good faith is a serious one that should not be made lightly, and that the WTO agreements do not call for a finding as to whether a breach occurs in good faith.

4.329 India's appeal raises the question of whether the USDOC's use of a methodology to construct government prices for iron ore and coal is consistent with Article 14(d) of the SCM Agreement. As noted, India claims that the Panel erred in its interpretation and application of Article 14(d) and acted inconsistently with Article 11 of the DSU.

4.330 We first observe that much of India's claim appears founded on its contention that the adequacy of remuneration must first be assessed from the perspective of the government provider, before assessing whether a benefit has been conferred on a recipient. On this basis, India maintains that, should the Appellate Body agree with India's "as such" claim regarding what it means to assess adequacy of remuneration, then "as a logical consequence the Panel's findings in respect of the determination of benefit for the iron ore and coal mining programs in paragraphs 7.260-7.261 of the Panel Report must also be reversed."[939] India further asserts that, because the only payment received by the GOI consisted of royalties paid in return for the grant of mining rights, it is only the "adequacy" of this "remuneration" that can be examined under Article 14(d). We have upheld the Panel's findings that Article 14(d) of the SCM Agreement does not require separate analyses of the adequacy of remuneration and of benefit, and that Article 14(d) does not require that the adequacy of remuneration be assessed from the perspective of the government provider. For this reason, we do not agree with India's contention that the Panel erred in its interpretation of Article 14(d) in respect of grants of mining rights by not first evaluating the adequacy of remuneration from the perspective of the government provider.

4.331 Additionally, however, India's claim under Article 14(d) is premised on its view that, because the financial contribution at issue consists only of the GOI's grants of mining rights – i.e. what the GOI actually provided to the recipients, and what the GOI was actually paid for – the analysis must necessarily be limited to any benefit arising from the grant of the mining rights, and not the final extracted material in the form of iron ore and coal. India observes that the extraction of iron ore and coal is performed by Indian miners,

939 India's appellant's submission, para. 510.

and any profit associated with that extraction accrues to those miners. Accordingly, in India's view, such elements of the transaction do not "devolve on the GOI and cannot form part of the 'remuneration' to be assessed under Article 14(d) of the SCM Agreement".[940]

4.332 Above we have stated that the Panel was correct to conclude that there is a reasonably proximate relationship between the GOI's grant of mining rights and the final goods consisting of extracted iron ore and coal. On this basis, we have upheld the Panel's rejection of India's claim that the United States acted inconsistently with Article 1.1(a)(1)(iii) of the SCM Agreement by determining that the GOI provided goods through the grant of mining rights for iron ore and coal. We recall that the Appellate Body has underscored that, in the context of a benefit analysis, the use of the term "guidelines" in Article 14 should not be interpreted as "rigid rules", and that this conveys a certain degree of flexibility in the analysis under Article 14(d).[941] Having concluded, in respect of a grant of mining rights, that it was proper to consider that the provided good consists of the extracted minerals, we consider that it is permissible for an investigating authority in a benefit calculation to construct a price on the basis of any fees and royalties paid for the mining rights plus the cost plus profit of the extraction process. As we understand it, this is what the USDOC did when it calculated the royalties for the mining rights and then added operational mining costs associated with the extraction of the iron ore and coal. Once an investigating authority arrives at such a price, it would then be compared with a benchmark consisting of a market-determined price for iron ore or coal. We note that, in this case, India has not challenged the manner in which the USDOC actually constructed the government prices for iron ore and coal.[942] Accordingly, in the circumstances of this case, we do not consider that the Panel erred in finding that the USDOC did not act inconsistently with Article 14(d) in constructing government prices for iron ore and coal.

4.333 Finally, we note India's claim that the Panel committed legal error under Article 11 of the DSU in refusing to assess India's claim that the USDOC's methodology is not in accordance with a good faith interpretation of Article 14(d). As we have noted above, the Panel rejected India's allegation because it agreed with the United States that it was outside the Panel's terms of reference.[943] India responds on appeal that, "under customary rules of international law and treaty interpretation, a good faith obligation flows through the text of [the] entire treaty including each and every article of a treaty, which is the subject matter of interpretation before a Panel."[944] India therefore appears to

940 India's appellant's submission, para. 516.

941 Appellate Body Report, *US – Anti-Dumping and Countervailing Duty (China)*, para. 483 (quoting Appellate Body Report, *US – Softwood Lumber IV*, para. 92).

942 Panel Report, para. 7.260.

943 Panel Report, para. 7.261.

944 India's appellant's submission, para. 522.

argue that the Panel was wrong to dismiss India's good faith argument because it forms part of a panel's duty when engaging in treaty interpretation.

4.334 Having reviewed the participants' submissions before the Panel, we do not see that India, as it maintains on appeal, framed its good faith arguments in the context of treaty interpretation. Before the Panel, India drew a distinction between the principle of good faith as it informs treaty interpretation, and the exercise of good faith by a Member in the performance of its treaty obligations.[945] India made clear that it was referring to the latter context when it argued that the United States had breached its commitment to act in good faith and not to abuse the rights and privileges granted to it under the SCM Agreement.[946] As noted, the Panel concluded that this claim was not contained in India's request for panel establishment and was therefore outside the Panel's terms of reference.[947] We do not see that India presented arguments relating to the principle of good faith in treaty interpretation, which would have formed part of its broader claim that the Panel erred in its interpretation of Article 14(d). Rather, we consider that India presented arguments that would have related to a distinct legal claim that the United States had breached the international law principle of good faith in performing its treaty obligations. In our view, the Panel was warranted in rejecting this claim as not falling within its terms of reference.[948] Accordingly, we also *reject* India's claim that the Panel acted inconsistently with Article 11 of the DSU in this regard.

4.335 For the foregoing reasons, we *uphold* the Panel's finding, in paragraph 7.260 of the Panel Report, rejecting India's claim that the USDOC's construction of government prices for iron ore and coal is inconsistent with Articles 1.1(b) and 14(d) of the SCM Agreement.

4.4.2.3 India's claims concerning SDF loans

4.336 India appeals the Panel's rejection of India's claim that the USDOC's determination that SDF loans confer a benefit is inconsistent with Articles 1.1(b) and 14(b) of the SCM Agreement. Below we summarize the Panel's findings before addressing India's claims on appeal.

---

945 India's first written submission to the Panel, para. 320.

946 India's first written submission to the Panel, paras. 397 and 400.

947 Panel Report, para. 7.261 (referring to India's panel request, WT/DS436/3). In addition, India asked the Panel during the interim review to reconsider its finding that India's "good faith" claim was outside the Panel's terms of reference. The Panel declined by affirming that the claim, as defined by India's panel request, was not within the Panel's terms of reference and that India's allegation of nullification or impairment did not amount to an allegation of violation of the principle of "good faith". (*Ibid.*, para. 6.142)

948 We note that India has not claimed that the Panel breached Article 6.2 of the DSU in not assessing this claim.

4.4.2.3.1 The Panel's findings

4.337 India argued before the Panel that the USDOC acted inconsistently with the chapeau and subparagraph (b) of Article 14 of the SCM Agreement by not adequately explaining how the benchmark it used, consisting of prime lending rates of the Reserve Bank of India, properly reflected the interest on a "comparable commercial loan". India submitted that the prime lending rates used by the USDOC are interest rates for banks, rather than rates for loans actually disbursed. India also argued that the USDOC's determination of benefit is inconsistent with the chapeau of Article 14 and Article 14(b) because the USDOC did not take into account the costs incurred by steel producers to participate in the SDF loan programme, or provide any explanation of its treatment of such costs. India submitted that the USDOC also acted inconsistently with Article 1.1(b) by finding benefit, even though the price controls under the SDF actually made producers worse off.

4.338 The Panel considered that the chapeau of Article 14 requires that the application of the "method used by the investigating authority to calculate the benefit to the recipient ... to each particular case shall be transparent and adequately explained".[949] According to the Panel, the requirement that the application of a benefit methodology be "transparent" conveys the sense that such application should be set out in such a fashion that it can be easily understood or discerned. The Panel added that the obligation to "adequately explain" conveys the sense of making clear or intelligible, and giving details of how the methodology was applied. The Panel considered that the adequacy of an investigating authority's explanation should be assessed on a case-by-case basis. The Panel did not consider that, in explaining that it would determine benefit by comparing SDF loan rates with prime lending rates, the USDOC was also required by the chapeau of Article 14 to indicate the reasons why it chose to determine benefit on that basis. In the Panel's view, the USDOC's explanation was such that the application of its benefit methodology was clear and intelligible, and could be easily understood and discerned.[950]

4.339 Regarding the USDOC's obligations under Article 14(b), the Panel agreed with the Appellate Body that "Article 14(b) does not preclude the possibility of using as benchmarks interest rates on commercial loans that are not actually available in the market where the firm is located, such as, for instance, loans in other markets or constructed proxies."[951] According to the Panel, the USDOC was not prevented from applying the prime lending rates simply because they did not represent rates that SDF loan recipients could actually obtain. The Panel considered that India's approach to Article 14(b) would be excessively

[949] Panel Report, para. 7.308.
[950] Panel Report, para. 7.309.
[951] Panel Report, para. 7.310 (quoting Appellate Body Report, *US – Anti-Dumping and Countervailing Duties (China)*, para. 480).

formalistic, and would ignore the flexibility found in the Article 14(b) guideline.[952]

4.340 The Panel then addressed India's argument that the USDOC violated the chapeau of Article 14 and Article 14(b) by failing to account for the costs incurred by steel producers in participating in the SDF loan programme. The Panel noted India's contention that the USDOC's analysis failed to account for various expenses and charges associated with steel producer participation in the SDF loan programme and that, by contributing their own funds, steel producers also lose the interest that they could otherwise obtain on these funds if they were invested elsewhere. The Panel did not agree that SDF levies could be treated as the producers' own funds. Rather, the Panel noted that SDF levies are collected from consumers through an addition to the steel producers' *ex works* prices and then remitted directly to the SDF. Since the levies are collected from consumers and always destined for the SDF, the Panel reasoned that steel producers would not be able to obtain interest by investing these funds elsewhere.[953]

4.341 The Panel also stated that, as a legal matter, investigating authorities are not required to take account of the costs incurred by recipients in participating in the programme under which the loans are provided. According to the Panel, Article 14(b) provides for a comparison "between the amount that the firm receiving the loan pays on the government loan and the amount the firm would pay on a comparable commercial loan", and that the benefit "shall" be the difference between those amounts.[954] The Panel considered that the focus of Article 14(b) is therefore on the difference between the amounts paid "on" the relevant loans, and that there is no reference in Article 14(b) to the amount of any cost incurred in obtaining the loans. The Panel further observed that, while Article 14(c) provides that the amount of benefit in respect of loan guarantees shall be "adjusted for any differences in fees", there is no such requirement in Article 14(b). The Panel therefore concluded that Article 14(b) does not require the USDOC to take into account the costs incurred by SDF loan recipients in obtaining SDF loans.[955]

4.342 Finally, the Panel stated that the basis for India's Article 1.1(b) claim is essentially the same as the basis for India's Article 14(b) claim. The Panel considered that Article 14 contains guidelines for calculating the benefit to the recipient under Article 1.1(b). The Panel explained that, since India had failed to establish that the USDOC's failure to take account of costs incurred by SDF loan recipients is inconsistent with the Article 14(b), India's claim under Article 1.1(b) must also fail. In other words, the Panel concluded, by complying with the Article 14(b) guideline in respect of loan recipients' costs, the USDOC

---

952 Panel Report, para. 7.310.
953 Panel Report, para. 7.311.
954 *Ibid.*
955 *Ibid.*

necessarily complied with Article 1.1(b) of the SCM Agreement in respect of that same matter.

4.4.2.3.2 Whether the SDF loans confer a benefit within the meaning of Article 14(b) of the SCM Agreement

4.343 India's appeal focuses on the question of whether the prime lending rates, against which the terms of SDF loans were compared, constitute a "comparable commercial loan" within the meaning of Article 14(b) of the SCM Agreement. India argues that, under a proper understanding of the term "comparable commercial loan" in Article 14(b), the benchmark to be chosen must have a "similar structure" as the loan under challenge.[956] India observes that the decision of the Supreme Court of India that it had introduced before the Panel categorically states that "steel producers who did not contribute to the SDF program in the first place cannot obtain the SDF loans."[957] In particular, India maintains that, because the steel producers that benefit from the loans also first contribute the funds to the SDF loan programme, the USDOC was required to use benchmark loans that have a similar entry fee. As India contends, "the presence of an entry deposit into a loan program significantly affects the rate at which loans would later be disbursed using the same funds", such that "commercial players would expect a lower rate of interest".[958]

4.344 The United States considers that the Panel correctly found that Article 14(b) does not require the USDOC to take into account any alleged costs incurred by SDF loan recipients in obtaining SDF loans. Article 14(b) provides that a benefit is conferred where there is a difference between the amount that the firm receiving the loan pays on the government loan and the amount the firm would pay on a comparable commercial loan that the firm could actually obtain on the market. In the United States' view, no other credits or adjustments are required by Article 14(b). The United States also argues that Article 14 of the SCM Agreement provides flexibility to investigating authorities in applying a methodology to calculate the benefit of a subsidy. Furthermore, Article 14 contains no requirement that an investigating authority provide a credit when calculating the benefit of a subsidy to account for alleged costs associated with obtaining the subsidy.

4.345 The Appellate Body has stated that a benchmark for purposes of Article 14(b) consists of a "comparable commercial loan", and that such a benchmark

---

956 India's appellant's submission, para. 589.

957 India's appellant's submission, para. 589 (referring to 2006 AR Issues and Decision Memorandum, Analysis of Comment 31; and referring further to Supreme Court of India, Tata Iron and Steel Co. Ltd. v. Collector of Central Excise, Jamshedpur (2002) 8 SCC, pp. 338-351 (Panel Exhibit IND-54B)).

958 India's appellant's submission, para. 590.

loan "should have as many elements as possible in common with the investigated loan to be comparable".[959] According to the Appellate Body, "selecting a benchmark under Article 14(b) involves a progressive search for a comparable commercial loan, starting with the commercial loan that is closest to the investigated loan (a loan to the same borrower that is nearly identical to the investigated loan in terms of timing, structure, maturity, size and currency) and moving to less similar commercial loans while adjusting them to ensure comparability with the investigated loan."[960] The Appellate Body has further relied on the use of the conditional tense in Article 14(b) to explain that, in the absence of an actual comparable commercial loan that is available on the market, an investigating authority should be allowed to use a proxy for what "would" have been paid on a comparable commercial loan that "could" have been obtained on the market.[961] The Appellate Body remarked that the further away an investigating authority moves from the ideal benchmark of an identical or nearly identical loan, the more adjustments will be necessary to ensure that the benchmark loan approximates the "comparable commercial loan which the firm could actually obtain on the market" specified in Article 14(b). Finally, we note that the Appellate Body has stated that a certain degree of flexibility applies under Article 14(b) in the selection of benchmarks, so that such selection can ensure a meaningful comparison for the determination of benefit. At the same time, when an investigating authority resorts to a benchmark loan in another currency or to a proxy, it must ensure that such benchmark is adjusted so that it approximates the "comparable commercial loan", and that any such method, as well as how it approximates a "comparable commercial loan", must be transparent and adequately explained.[962]

4.346 The Panel evaluated whether Article 14(b) requires that a benchmark loan take into account costs incurred by beneficiaries under a loan programme. The Panel stated as follows:

> As a legal matter, we do not consider that investigating authorities are required to take account of the costs incurred by recipients in participating in the scheme under which the loans are provided. We note in this regard that the text of Article 14(b) provides for a comparison "between the amount that the firm receiving the loan pays on the government loan and the amount the firm would pay on a comparable commercial loan". Article 14(b) states that the benefit "shall" be the difference between those amounts. The focus of Article 14(b) is therefore on the difference between the amounts paid "on" the relevant loans. There is no reference in Article 14(b)

---

959 Appellate Body Report, *US – Anti-Dumping and Countervailing Duties (China)*, para. 476.

960 Appellate Body Report, *US – Anti-Dumping and Countervailing Duties (China)*, para. 486.

961 Appellate Body Report, *US – Anti-Dumping and Countervailing Duties (China)*, para. 487. (emphasis omitted)

962 Appellate Body Report, *US – Anti-Dumping and Countervailing Duties (China)*, para. 489.

> to the amount of any cost incurred in obtaining the loans. Furthermore, while Article 14(c) provides that the amount of benefit in respect of loan guarantees shall be "adjusted for any differences in fees", there is no such requirement in Article 14(b). Accordingly, Article 14(b) does not require the USDOC to take into account the costs incurred by SDF loan recipients in obtaining SDF loans.[963]

4.347 As we see it, a proper assessment under Article 14(b) examines what the total cost of the investigated loan is to the loan recipient, and whether there is a difference between that and the total cost of a comparable commercial loan. The distinction that the Panel draws between costs associated with the interest or repayment terms of a loan, and other costs arising from entry or administrative charges, does not seem to reflect accurately the cost of the relevant loans from the perspective of the recipient. Moreover, depending on the manner in which a particular commercial loan is structured, the costs associated with obtaining a loan could be significant and should be factored into a market assessment of that loan. In this respect, failing to take into account a cost that potentially alters a commercial actor's valuation of a loan simply because it does not relate to interest or repayment terms appears unduly artificial and contrary to the requirements of Article 14(b). Thus, we do not agree with the Panel's conclusion that investigating authorities are not required to take account of the costs incurred by recipients in participating in the programme under which the loans are provided.

4.348 We understand India to argue that, in evaluating the structure of the SDF loans, one cannot simply focus on the interest rates attached to the loans, because Indian steel producers must first pay amounts into the fund that are derived from increased levies on steel products. As India explained before the Panel, Indian steel producers "contributed their own funds to the SDF Program and as a result, lost the interest that they could otherwise obtain on their own funds had it been invested elsewhere".[964] We consider this argument to be consistent with the Appellate Body's understanding that Article 14(b) entails a "progressive search" for a comparable loan that begins with the commercial loan that is "closest" to the investigated loan and moves to "less similar" commercial loans.[965] In examining whether the particular terms of a loan programme are in accordance with market terms, a benchmark must be selected that ensures that there are sufficient similarities between the investigated loan and the benchmark "as to make that comparison worthy or meaningful".[966] To the extent that the terms associated with a loan programme are determined by the conditions of funding for the programme, such terms should also be taken into account if a

---

963 Panel Report, para. 7.311.

964 Panel Report, para. 7.311 (quoting India's first written submission to the Panel, para. 477).

965 Appellate Body Report, *US – Anti-Dumping and Countervailing Duties (China)*, para. 486.

966 Appellate Body Report, *US – Anti-Dumping and Countervailing Duties (China)*, para. 476.

failure to do so would render the comparison meaningless. India makes precisely this point when it argues that the interest rates of SDF loans are necessarily lower due to the fact that beneficiaries of SDF loans also have to contribute to the fund.

4.349 For the foregoing reasons, we consider that the Panel improperly excluded consideration of a borrower's costs in assessing the cost of a loan programme to the recipient for purposes of a benchmark analysis, and that the Panel therefore erred in finding that Article 14(b) does not require the USDOC to take into account the costs incurred by SDF loan recipients in obtaining SDF loans. This error led the Panel, in turn, to err in rejecting India's claim regarding the USDOC's determination that the SDF loans conferred a benefit. Moreover, because the Panel's finding regarding India's claim was based on an understanding of Article 14(b) that we have found to be in error, we need not separately consider India's claim that the Panel acted inconsistently with Article 11 of the DSU by disregarding the significance of certain evidence. Consequently, we *reverse* the Panel's finding, in paragraph 7.313 of the Panel Report, rejecting India's claim as it relates to the USDOC's determination that loans provided under the SDF conferred a benefit within the meaning of Articles 1.1(b) and 14(b) of the SCM Agreement.[967]

4.350 It remains for us to consider whether we can complete the legal analysis and determine whether it was proper for the USDOC to have conducted its benefit analysis in respect of SDF loans by comparing them with a benchmark consisting of prime lending rates in India. In order to complete the legal analysis, the Panel's factual findings and the undisputed facts on the Panel record must provide us with a sufficient basis for our own analysis.[968]

4.351 We start with the Panel's explanation that, in its view, SDF levies are not producer funds, but "were rather collected from consumers, through an addition to the steel producers' ex-works prices, and then remitted directly to the SDF".[969] The Panel stated that, "[s]ince the levies were collected from consumers and always destined for the SDF, steel producers would not have been able to obtain interest by investing those funds elsewhere."[970] As support for this proposition, the Panel refers to its earlier discussion, in the context of its financial contribution analysis, where it relied on a GOI statement that, once collected, the

---

[967] See also Panel Report, para. 8.3.e.iii.

[968] See e.g. Appellate Body Reports, *US – Gasoline*, p. 19, DSR 1996:I, p. 18; *Canada – Periodicals*, p. 24, DSR 1997:I, p. 469; *EC – Poultry*, para. 156; *EC – Hormones*, para. 222; *US – Shrimp*, paras. 123 and 124; *Japan – Agricultural Products II*, para. 112; *US – FSC*, para. 133; *Australia – Salmon*, paras. 117 and 118; *US – Lamb*, paras. 150 and 172; *US – Section 211 Appropriations Act*, para. 352; *EC and certain member States – Large Civil Aircraft*, paras. 1174-1178; *US – Large Civil Aircraft (2nd complaint)*, paras. 1272-1274; and *US – Countervailing and Anti-Dumping Measures (China)*, para. 4.124.

[969] Panel Report, para. 7.311. (fn omitted)

[970] Panel Report, para. 7.311.

steel levies are "remitted to the Fund".[971] Although the statement to which the Panel refers indeed confirms that the steel levies, once collected, are remitted to the SDF, it does not appear to provide any indication as to the source of the funds. Accordingly, we do not see how the piece of evidence to which the Panel refers supports the conclusion reached by the Panel that the steel levies necessarily consist of consumer funds.

4.352 We note, moreover, that the Panel did not refer at any point in its analysis to the USDOC's own reasoning as it pertains to the question of whether participating steel companies incur entry costs in the funding and allocation of SDF loans. In its determination during the 2006 administrative review, the USDOC made various statements that generated, in our view, an uncertain basis for a finding that there were, or were not, entry costs associated with SDF loans. In its preliminary determination, for instance, the USDOC stated that "companies that contributed to the fund are eligible to take out long-term loans at advantageous rates."[972] The USDOC further concluded that "[s]teel producers collected this price increase, which was paid by steel consumers in India, and these additional funds were then placed into the SDF as a source of concessional financing for the Indian steel industry."[973] These statements suggest that steel producers are contributing funds derived from steel levies imposed on consumers that they possibly could employ otherwise in the absence of the SDF. The USDOC's statements that steel producers "collected" the funds, and "contributed" them to the SDF, possibly indicate that making such contributions might have represented an opportunity cost for participation in the SDF loan programme. In conducting its financial contribution analysis, however, the USDOC stated that, "rather than constituting the steel producers' own funds, the SDF levies, as noted by petitioners, are analogous to tax revenues collected from consumers as mandated by the GOI."[974] Although the USDOC made this statement in the context of refuting the argument that the funds could not constitute a financial contribution because they are provided by steel producers, and not the GOI, it still reflects a view that the SDF loans are derived from consumers and therefore do not represent producer funds. In the light of the above, we are concerned that the Panel did not refer to, or seek to reconcile, these seemingly disparate statements in the USDOC's underlying determinations that may have been assessed in the context of the USDOC's selection of a benchmark loan.

4.353 We have stated that a panel must examine whether the conclusions reached by the investigating authority are reasoned and adequate, and that such an examination must be critical, and be based on the information contained in

---

[971] Panel Report, para. 7.295 (quoting 2001 GOI Supplemental Questionnaire Response (Panel Exhibit USA-75), p. 3) and fn 526 to para. 7.311.

[972] 2006 AR Preliminary Results, p. 1589.

[973] 2006 AR Preliminary Results, p. 1590.

[974] 2006 AR Issues and Decision Memorandum, Analysis of Comment 31, internal p. 78.

the record and the explanations given by the authority in its published report.[975] We do not see that the Panel did so in this case. Moreover, we have noted considerable disagreement between the parties, and conflicting indications in the USDOC and Panel records, regarding the question of whether, and to what extent, entry costs for steel companies affected the terms on which the SDF Managing Committee issues SDF loans. We therefore do not consider that we have a basis upon which to assess whether the prime lending rates on which the USDOC relied constitute a "comparable commercial loan" within the meaning of Article 14(b) of the SCM Agreement. We therefore *find* that we are unable to complete the legal analysis in this regard.

4.5 Article 2 of the SCM Agreement – Specificity

4.354 India appeals, under Articles 1.2 and 2.1 of the SCM Agreement, aspects of the Panel's analysis in respect of the USDOC's determination that the sale of iron ore by the NMDC is specific within the meaning of Article 2.1(c). Below, we summarize the Panel's findings before proceeding to analyse India's claims on appeal.

4.5.1 The Panel's findings

4.355 Before the Panel, India argued that the USDOC's determination of *de facto* specificity is inconsistent with Articles 2.1(c) and 2.4 of the SCM Agreement because the USDOC: (i) failed to show that the subsidy discriminated in favour of "certain enterprises" over a comparative set of other, similarly situated enterprises; (ii) based its determination of specificity on limitations inherent in the nature of the product; (iii) failed to establish that the subsidy was used by a limited number of certain enterprises; (iv) failed to examine the mandatory factors listed in Article 2.1(c); and (v) failed to determine *de facto* specificity on the basis of positive evidence.

4.356 Before addressing India's claims, the Panel turned to two preliminary arguments raised by the parties. First, the Panel rejected the United States' argument that subparagraphs (a) and (c) of Article 2.1 of the SCM Agreement are "merely definitional provisions, devoid of any legal obligations".[976] In accordance with Article 2.4 of the SCM Agreement, a "determination" of specificity must be clearly substantiated on the basis of positive evidence. Such determination, which is made explicitly or implicitly every time a subsidy is found to fall within the scope of the SCM Agreement, is either consistent, or inconsistent, with the principles set forth in subparagraphs (a) through (c) of Article 2.1. The Panel considered that, in *US – Anti-Dumping and Countervailing Duties (China)*, the Appellate Body endorsed the position that

[975] See Appellate Body Report, *US – Tyres (China)*, para. 123.

[976] Panel Report, para. 7.116 (referring to United States' first written submission to the Panel, para. 389).

Article 2.1 contains legal obligations by upholding the panel's finding that the United States had not acted inconsistently with its obligations under Article 2.1(a).[977] Second, the Panel disagreed with India's argument that the USDOC should have examined specificity under subparagraphs (a) and (b) of Article 2.1 before applying Article 2.1(c). Recalling that the Appellate Body has established that the subparagraphs of Article 2.1 need not be applied sequentially in all cases, the Panel considered that, in the present case, the USDOC was entitled to proceed directly to examine the provision of iron ore by the NMDC under Article 2.1(c).[978]

4.357 The Panel rejected India's argument that a subsidy can be specific under Article 2 of the SCM Agreement only if it discriminates in favour of "certain enterprises" against a broader category of other, similarly situated entities. In the Panel's view, subparagraphs (a) and (c) of Article 2.1 both focus on "the existence of a restriction on access to the subsidy, in the sense that the subsidy is available to certain enterprises, industries, or groups of enterprises or industries, but not to others".[979] Once access to the subsidy is shown to be limited to certain enterprises, either *de jure* or *de facto*, the subsidy is specific. For the Panel, Article 2.1 provides "no requirement to show that the subsidy is at the same time *not* available to other, *undefined* – but similarly situated – entities".[980]

4.358 The Panel further indicated that Article 2 is not concerned with the identity or nature of the excluded entities. In this regard, Article 2 contains no reference to the notion of "discrimination". The Panel referred to the Appellate Body's finding, in *US – Anti-Dumping and Countervailing Duties (China)* that "the principles set forth in Articles 2.1(a) and (b) concern the issue of whether the 'conduct or instruments of the granting authority discriminate or not'."[981] The Panel considered that the Appellate Body's use of the term "discriminate" does not suggest that Article 2.1 should be interpreted as requiring that, having determined that access to a subsidy is limited to certain enterprises, an investigating authority must also determine that access is denied to other, similarly situated entities. The Panel also observed that, under India's approach, specificity could not be established where the "certain enterprises" represent the totality of an industry. In such cases, the "similarly situated" entities and the "certain enterprises" would be the same, such that it would not be possible to establish that similarly situated entities were excluded from the subsidy. In the

---

[977] Panel Report, para. 7.118 (referring to Appellate Body Report, *US – Anti-Dumping and Countervailing Duties (China)*, para. 401).

[978] Panel Report, para. 7.119 (referring to Appellate Body Report, *US – Anti-Dumping and Countervailing Duties (China)*, para. 371).

[979] Panel Report, para. 7.121.

[980] Panel Report, para. 7.121. (emphasis original)

[981] Panel Report, para. 7.124 (quoting Appellate Body Report, *US – Anti-Dumping and Countervailing Duties (China)*, para. 367).

Panel's view, India's approach is clearly at odds with the language of Article 2.1 of the SCM Agreement.[982]

4.359 Next, the Panel turned to examine India's argument that specificity should not be established in cases where, because of the nature of the subsidized product, the use of that product is necessarily restricted to a limited number of entities. India argued that this would occur in all cases where the government is involved in providing raw materials. In support of its argument, India stated that the negotiating history of Article 2 shows that there was no consensus among the negotiating members on the issue of determining specificity based solely on the inherent characteristics of the goods.[983]

4.360 The Panel rejected India's argument on two grounds. First, the Panel did not consider that the negotiating history necessarily indicates that the "negotiators could not agree to include a provision concerning specificity based on the inherent characteristics of goods."[984] In the Panel's view, such negotiating history may also suggest that the negotiators addressed the issue, and concluded that no such provision was necessary. Second, the Panel found that, if access to a subsidy is limited by virtue of the fact that only certain enterprises may use the subsidized product, the subsidy is specific. The Panel relied on the reasoning provided by the panel in *US – Softwood Lumber IV* that had addressed a similar argument raised by Canada.[985] Third, the Panel also rejected India's argument that the USDOC needed to prove that the subsidy programme was being used by only a limited number of users within the set of "certain enterprises" that constitute the beneficiaries. For the Panel, India's argument is based on a proposed distinction between "users" and "beneficiaries" that is not provided for in Article 2.1. Subparagraphs (a) and (c) of this provision are concerned with situations where access to a subsidy is limited to the same category of "certain enterprises". Under Article 2.1(c), an authority may determine that a subsidy is specific by relying on the fact that the number of "certain enterprises" using the subsidy is limited.[986]

4.361 Next, the Panel turned to examine India's argument that the USDOC had failed to examine the mandatory factors listed in Article 2.1(c) of the SCM Agreement. The Panel began by indicating that "Article 2.1(c) expressly requires that, in the context of a determination of *de facto* specificity, 'account shall be taken' of the extent of diversification of the relevant economy and the length of time that the relevant programme has been in operation."[987] After reviewing the USDOC's determinations, the Panel failed to find any information indicating that the USDOC actually took those two factors into account. Accordingly, the Panel

982 Panel Report, para. 7.125.
983 Panel Report, para. 7.129.
984 Panel Report, para. 7.130.
985 Panel Report, para. 7.131 (referring to Panel Report, *US – Softwood Lumber IV*, para. 7.116).
986 Panel Report, para. 7.135.
987 Panel Report, para. 7.136.

found that the USDOC failed to comply with the Article 2.1(c) requirement to take those factors into account when determining whether the provision of goods by the NMDC is *de facto* specific.

4.362 Finally, the Panel rejected India's argument that the USDOC acted inconsistently with Article 2.4 of the SCM Agreement because there was no evidentiary basis for its finding that the NMDC made iron ore available only to users of iron ore, or that only users of iron ore purchased from the NMDC. The Panel reached this conclusion after examining evidence submitted by the United States that established that many of the companies listed in the NMDC's customer base are indeed concerned with the iron and steel business. Accordingly, the Panel found that there is no factual basis for claiming that the USDOC's *de facto* specificity was not based on positive evidence.[988]

4.5.2 India's challenge to the Panel's finding regarding de facto specificity

4.363 In the present dispute, the factor on which the USDOC based its specificity finding, and which is the subject of India's appeal, concerns the "use of a subsidy programme by a limited number of certain enterprises". We note that, as part of its challenge before the Panel, India also argued that the USDOC failed to consider the factors set out in the last sentence of Article 2.1(c) of the SCM Agreement relating to the diversification of the relevant economy and the duration of the relevant subsidy programme. The Panel found that the USDOC failed to comply with Article 2.1(c) by not taking those factors into account in determining that the provision of goods by the NMDC is *de facto* specific.[989] The United States has not appealed this finding. For its part, India challenges on appeal discrete findings in which the Panel rejected India's arguments other than those relating to the last sentence of Article 2.1(c). The following analysis therefore does not concern the Panel's conclusion, in paragraph 7.136 of the Panel Report, that the USDOC acted inconsistently with Article 2.1(c) of the SCM Agreement by failing to take account of the factors in the last sentence of that provision in its determination of *de facto* specificity regarding the NMDC.

4.364 India addresses three aspects of the Panel's analysis concerning *de facto* specificity under Article 2.1(c). First, India submits that the Panel erred in interpreting the phrase "limited number of certain enterprises" set out in Article 2.1(c) because it failed to recognize that the "limited number" of users of the subsidy must form a subset of enterprises within a broader group of "certain enterprises".[990] Second, India argues that the Panel erred in finding that Article 2.1(c) did not require an examination of whether the subsidy programme discriminates between "certain enterprises" and other, "similarly situated"

---

[988] Panel Report, para. 7.140.
[989] Panel Report, para. 7.136.
[990] India's appellant's submission, para. 370 et seq.

enterprises.[991] Third, India argues that the Panel erred in finding that a government provision of goods can be *de facto* specific, merely based on the inherent limitations of the goods provided.[992]

4.365 The Appellate Body has provided guidance regarding the inquiry required under Article 2 of the SCM Agreement. In *US – Anti-Dumping and Countervailing Duties (China)*, the Appellate Body observed that "[t]he chapeau [of Article 2.1] frames the central inquiry as a determination as to whether a subsidy is specific to 'certain enterprises' within the jurisdiction of the granting authority".[993] The chapeau of Article 2.1 further defines the term "certain enterprises" as "an enterprise or industry or group of enterprises or industries". The ordinary meanings of the terms "group" and "certain" do not indicate any numerical threshold pointing to a minimum or maximum number of things required in order to qualify as a "group" or "certain". These definitions suggest rather that the relevant enterprises must be "known and particularized", but not necessarily "explicitly identified", and that they may have "some mutual or common relation or purpose", or "degree of similarity".[994] The Appellate Body has acknowledged, however, that "any determination of whether a number of enterprises or industries constitute 'certain enterprises' can only be made on a case-by-case basis."[995]

4.366 In examining whether a subsidy is specific, "the 'principles' set out in subparagraphs (a) through (c) [of Article 2.1] 'shall apply'".[996] Subparagraphs (a) and (b) of Article 2.1 set forth the principles applicable to, respectively, a determination of *de jure* specificity and non-specificity. Article 2.1(a) establishes that a subsidy is specific if the granting authority, or the legislation pursuant to which the granting authority operates, explicitly limits access to that subsidy to eligible enterprises or industries. Article 2.1(b), in turn, sets out that specificity shall not exist if the granting authority, or the legislation pursuant to which the granting authority operates, establishes objective criteria or conditions governing the eligibility for, and the amount of, the subsidy.[997] Article 2.1(c) relates to the determination of *de facto* specificity. This provision states that, if, notwithstanding any appearance of non-specificity resulting from the application of the principles laid down in subparagraphs (a) and (b), there are reasons to believe that the subsidy may in fact be specific, other factors set out in subparagraph (c) may be considered.

---

991 India's appellant's submission, para. 351 et seq.

992 India's appellant's submission, para. 380 et seq.

993 Appellate Body Report, *US – Anti-Dumping and Countervailing Duties (China)*, para. 366.

994 Appellate Body Report, *US – Anti-Dumping and Countervailing Duties (China)*, para. 373 (quoting *Shorter Oxford English Dictionary*, 6th edn, A. Stevenson (ed.) (Oxford University Press, 2007), Vol. 1, pp. 375 and 1167, respectively).

995 Appellate Body Report, *US – Anti-Dumping and Countervailing Duties (China)*, para. 373 (quoting Panel Report, *US – Upland Cotton*, para. 7.1142).

996 Appellate Body Report, *US – Anti-Dumping and Countervailing Duties (China)*, para. 366.

997 Appellate Body Report, *US – Anti-Dumping and Countervailing Duties (China)*, para. 367.

4.367 With respect to the structure of Article 2.1, the Appellate Body has observed that the use of the term "principles" in this provision – instead of, for example, "rules" – suggests that subparagraphs (a) through (c) are to be considered within an analytical framework that accords appropriate weight to each principle.[998] The Appellate Body has also indicated that "a proper understanding of specificity under Article 2.1 must allow for the concurrent application of these principles to the various legal and factual aspects of a subsidy in any given case."[999] The Appellate Body has further explained that the application of one of the subparagraphs of Article 2.1 may not, by itself, be determinative in arriving at a conclusion that a particular subsidy is or is not specific.[1000] The Appellate Body has therefore cautioned against "examining specificity on the basis of the application of a particular subparagraph of Article 2.1, when the potential for application of other subparagraphs is warranted in the light of the nature and content of measures challenged in a particular case".[1001] The Appellate Body has also envisaged, however, that, although the analysis will ordinarily proceed in a sequential order, an investigating authority or panel could examine and establish that a given subsidy is specific under only one of the subparagraphs of Article 2.1 when the circumstances of the case so require.[1002]

4.368 In *US – Anti-Dumping and Countervailing Duties (China)*, the Appellate Body observed that subparagraphs (a) and (b) of Article 2.1 identify certain common elements in the analysis of the specificity of a subsidy, such as "the eligibility requirements imposed by 'the granting authority, or the legislation pursuant to which the granting authority operates'".[1003] In this regard, subparagraphs (a) and (b) of Article 2.1 set out indicators of eligibility for a subsidy. Article 2.1(c) further specifies that, "if ... there are reasons to believe that the subsidy may in fact be specific", application of the factors under Article 2.1(c) to factual features of a challenged subsidy may be warranted. The provision further specifies that this is the case even "notwithstanding any appearance of non-specificity resulting from the application of the principles laid down in subparagraphs (a) and (b)".[1004]

4.369 Article 2.1(c) thus points to certain indicia that investigating authorities and panels may evaluate in determining whether, despite not being *de jure* specific, a subsidy may be specific in fact. The focus of this provision is therefore on *de facto* circumstances surrounding the use of a subsidy. Article

[998] Appellate Body Report, *US – Anti-Dumping and Countervailing Duties (China)*, para. 366.
[999] Appellate Body Report, *US – Anti-Dumping and Countervailing Duties (China)*, para. 371.
[1000] Appellate Body Report, *US – Anti-Dumping and Countervailing Duties (China)*, para. 366.
[1001] Appellate Body Report, *US – Anti-Dumping and Countervailing Duties (China)*, para. 371.
[1002] See Appellate Body Reports, *US – Anti-Dumping and Countervailing Duties (China)*, para. 371; *EC and certain member States – Large Civil Aircraft*, para. 945; and *US – Large Civil Aircraft (2nd complaint)*, para. 873.
[1003] Appellate Body Report, *US – Anti-Dumping and Countervailing Duties (China)*, para. 368.
[1004] The Appellate Body has pointed out that "[a] finding of non-specificity under subparagraphs (a) and (b) does not provide license to a panel to refrain from examining claims made under subparagraph (c)". (Appellate Body Report, *US – Large Civil Aircraft (2nd complaint)*, para. 793)

2.1(c) identifies four factors for consideration in determining whether a subsidy is *de facto* specific: (i) use of a subsidy programme by a limited number of certain enterprises; (ii) predominant use by certain enterprises; (iii) the granting of disproportionately large amounts of subsidy to certain enterprises; and (iv) the manner in which discretion has been exercised by the granting authority in the decision to grant a subsidy. Subparagraph (c) adds that, in examining these factors, diversification of the relevant economy and the duration of the relevant subsidy programme shall be taken into account. In *US – Large Civil Aircraft (2nd complaint)*, the Appellate Body considered that these elements define the terrain for assessing whether subsidies are specific in fact, and that the elements that are relevant to the analysis under Article 2.1(c) will be a function of what reasons there are to believe that the subsidy may in fact be specific. An investigating authority or panel must therefore "remain open to the applicability of each of the elements set out in Article 2.1(c), and to the possibility that a conclusion in respect of specificity in fact may, depending on the circumstances of the case, rely on an assessment of one, several, or all of those elements".[1005]

4.370 Having set out the above framework for understanding the requirement of specificity, we now turn to consider India's claims as they relate to the first factor set out in Article 2.1(c).

4.5.2.1 Use of a subsidy programme by a limited number of certain enterprises

4.371 India claims that the Panel erred in its interpretation of the first factor under Article 2.1(c) of the SCM Agreement. India observes that the term "limited number" is preceded by "use ... by", and that Article 2.1(c) therefore focuses on the users of the subsidy programme being limited in number. India further notes that the term "limited number" is followed by "of certain enterprises", and that the use of the word "of" denotes a "sub-set – super-set" relationship between "limited number" and "certain enterprises".[1006] Thus, in India's view, the "limited number" of users must be understood as forming a subset of "certain enterprises". India submits that, in rejecting its claim, the Panel ignored these and other textual elements, and therefore concluded that the relevant category for its assessment was that of "certain enterprises". India considers that, when properly interpreted, an assessment under the first factor of Article 2.1(c) "is to be performed on the users of the program within the category of 'certain enterprises'".[1007] India states that the "certain enterprises" in this case are users of iron ore. As a result, Article 2.1(c) required the USDOC to demonstrate that the alleged subsidy programme is being used by a limited number of entities within the set of "users of iron ore". In India's view, the

[1005] Appellate Body Report, *US – Large Civil Aircraft (2nd complaint)*, para. 878.
[1006] India's appellant's submission, para. 371.
[1007] India's appellant's submission, para. 376.

USDOC did not do so, and its determination is therefore not justified under Article 2.1(c).

4.372 The United States responds that the Panel correctly rejected India's argument that an investigating authority must establish that only a limited number of enterprises within a set of certain enterprises eligible to use the subsidy programme actually receive the subsidy. The United States submits that India is seeking to redraft Article 2.1(c), but that its argument is not supported by the text of Article 2.1(c). The United States therefore requests the Appellate Body to find that the Panel did not err in interpreting or applying the phrase "use of a subsidy programme by a limited number of certain enterprises" in Article 2.1(c) of the SCM Agreement.

4.373 We recall that Article 2.1(c) identifies factors that investigating authorities and panels are to evaluate in assessing whether, despite not seemingly *de jure* specific, a subsidy may still be specific in fact. This suggests that, while *de jure* and *de facto* analyses are both focused on whether a subsidy is specific, they do so from somewhat different perspectives. While a *de jure* analysis examines concrete evidence relating to *explicit limitations on access*, a *de facto* analysis focuses on *indicia* of the allocation or use of a subsidy that support a finding of specificity. The aim of this latter inquiry, by virtue of the fact that it discerns the existence of specificity through *de facto* considerations, and does so notwithstanding any appearance of non-specificity that might arise from a *de jure* analysis, is to identify evidence of allocation or use that provides an investigating authority or panel sufficient assurance as to the existence of specificity. In this way, the second sentence of Article 2.1(c) lists particular factors regarding allocation or use of a subsidy, such as the use of a subsidy programme by either a limited number of, or through predominant use by, certain enterprises, the granting of disproportionately large amounts of subsidy to certain enterprises, or the manner in which discretion has been exercised in the decision to grant a subsidy.[1008]

4.374 On the basis of this general understanding, we examine the first factor in Article 2.1(c), namely, the use of a subsidy programme by a limited number of certain enterprises. The word "use" refers to the action of using or employing something.[1009] In this context, what is used or employed is "a subsidy programme". Moreover, the term "use" reveals the type of evidence that is examined in the inquiry mandated by the first factor under Article 2.1(c). Contrary to a *de jure* analysis that examines whether a granting authority, or the legislation pursuant to which it operates, *explicitly limits access* to a subsidy, the focus under the first factor of Article 2.1(c) is on a quantitative assessment of the

[1008] We recall that Article 2.1(c) requires that, in examining these factors, diversification of the relevant economy and the duration of the relevant subsidy programme also be taken into account.

[1009] The term "use" is defined as "the action of using something; the fact or state of being used; application or conversion to some purpose". (*Shorter Oxford English Dictionary*, 6th edn, A. Stevenson (ed.) (Oxford University Press, 2007), Vol. 2, p. 3484)

entities that *actually use* a subsidy programme and, in particular, on whether such *use* is shared by a "limited number of certain enterprises".

4.375 We also note that the use of the term "limited number" bears certain similarities with the text of Article 2.1 more generally. For example, the concept of limitation is contained in Article 2.1(c), as well as in Article 2.1(a), which addresses the situation "[w]here the granting authority, or the legislation ... explicitly *limits* access to a subsidy".[1010] The common use of words derived from the verb "to limit" in these circumstances, whether *de jure* or *de facto*, centres on the existence of limitations in the access to, or the number of enterprises or industries that use, such subsidy.[1011] The references to such limitations, however, operate somewhat differently under these two principles. In order to fall within subparagraph (a), such limitations must be found explicitly in, for example, the legal instruments of a government authority. Subparagraph (c), in turn, indicates an examination of the factors listed in that provision that focus on *de facto*, instead of *de jure*, considerations. Under the first factor of subparagraph (c), the analysis focuses on whether the users of the subsidy programme are limited in number.

4.376 We have previously discussed the definition in Article 2.1 of the term "certain enterprises", highlighting that it suggests that relevant enterprises must be "known and particularized" but not necessarily "explicitly identified".[1012] This indicates that the meaning of "certain enterprises", which serves as both text and context in the chapeau and each of the subparagraphs of Article 2.1, does not itself entail a precise identification or quantification exercise. When this term is viewed in conjunction with the term "limited number" in Article 2.1(c), however, this would seem to suggest greater specification by requiring a more quantitative assessment of the users of a subsidy programme. As we understand it, this is consistent with a *de facto* exercise, which aims to identify evidence of allocation or use that provides an investigating authority or panel sufficient assurance as to the existence of specificity.

4.377 We note that the word "of" in the phrase "by a limited number of certain enterprises" may, on its face, give rise to different understandings as to the relationship between "a limited number" and "certain enterprises". Although the phrase could be read to suggest that the use of the subsidy programme must be limited to a number of enterprises that form part of a broader group of "certain enterprises"[1013], we consider the better reading to be that the term "limited

---

[1010] Emphasis added.

[1011] In this regard, we note that, in the context of regional specificity under Article 2.2, a positive determination of specificity also hinges on whether a subsidy is *limited* to certain enterprises. In that context, those enterprises must be located within a designated geographical region.

[1012] Appellate Body Report, *US – Anti-Dumping and Countervailing Duties (China)*, para. 373 (quoting *Shorter Oxford English Dictionary*, 6th edn, A. Stevenson (ed.) (Oxford University Press, 2007), Vol. 1, p. 375)

[1013] See India's appellant's submission, para. 371 (quoting *The Oxford English Dictionary*, 3rd edn, A. Stevenson (ed.) (Oxford University Press, 2010), p. 1230).

number" reflects a quantity of "certain enterprises" that must be found to have used the subsidy programme in order to indicate the existence of *de facto* specificity.[1014] Such a reading is more compatible with our contextual understanding of the term "certain enterprises" and its relationship to the term "limited number", the latter of which serves to determine whether the former, known and particularized enterprises or industries can be quantitatively assessed as limited in number. In our view, the word "certain" appears to indicate a more qualitative particularization of enterprises, industries, or groups thereof, whereas the term "limited number", in the context of Article 2.1(c), suggests an inquiry into whether the enterprises or industries so particularized constitute a quantitatively limited group.

4.378 Based on the foregoing, we do not disagree with India's view that the use of the term "limited number" after the terms "use ... by" indicates that this factor focuses on the "*users of the program being limited in number*".[1015] This does not answer, however, whether the limited number of users must form a subset of certain enterprises. India contends that the use of the term "of" between "limited number" and "certain enterprises" denotes a "sub-set – super-set" relationship between these two terms.[1016] We do not agree; rather, we consider that a proper interpretation of the two terms, joined by the use of the word "of", is that "limited number" is meant to convey a finite and limited quantity of "certain enterprises". Put another way, these terms indicate that a limited quantity of enterprises or industries qualifying as "certain enterprises" must be found to have used the subsidy programme, without requiring that the limited quantity represent a subset of some larger grouping of "certain enterprises". Such a reading is also compatible with our contextual understanding of the term "certain enterprises" and its relationship to the term "limited number", the latter of which serves to determine whether the known and particularized enterprises or industries can be quantitatively assessed as limited in number.

4.379 We also take note of the United States' argument that India's interpretation could lead to the result that, notwithstanding evidence that the users of a subsidy are limited to a unique industry or even a single enterprise qualifying as "certain enterprises", this would leave an investigating authority with no recourse in determining specificity.[1017] Such an interpretation cannot be sustained in the light of the clear focus of Article 2.1 on identifying whether a subsidy is limited to "certain enterprises". For these reasons, we consider that the phrase "use of a subsidy programme by a limited number of certain enterprises" seeks to examine evidence that the "certain enterprises" using a subsidy

---

[1014] We note that the word "of" can be used to connect two nouns "of which the former is a collective term, a classificatory word, a quantitative or numeral word, or the name of something having component parts, and the latter is the substance or elements of which this consists". (*Shorter Oxford English Dictionary*, 6th edn, A. Stevenson (ed.) (Oxford University Press, 2007), Vol. 2, p. 1985)

[1015] India's appellant's submission, para. 370. (emphasis original)

[1016] India's appellant's submission, para. 371.

[1017] United States' appellee's submission, para. 315.

programme are limited in number, and does not denote that the actual recipients must form a subset of "certain enterprises".

4.380 For the foregoing reasons, we *uphold* the Panel's finding, in paragraph 7.135 of the Panel Report, that there was no obligation on the USDOC to establish that only a "limited number" within the set of "certain enterprises" actually used the subsidy programme.[1018]

4.5.2.2 Whether the first factor of Article 2.1(c) requires a finding of discrimination between "certain enterprises" and other, similarly situated enterprises

4.381 India claims that the Panel erred in finding that Article 2.1(c) of the SCM Agreement does not require an examination of whether the subsidy programme *de facto* discriminates between "certain enterprises" and other "similarly situated" enterprises. India submits that the Panel's findings are contradictory. On the one hand, the Panel recognized that "the specificity determination under both Articles 2.1(a) and 2.1(c) is about '... existence of a restriction on access to the subsidy, in the sense that the subsidy is available to [certain enterprises], but not to others'."[1019] On the other hand, the Panel held that "the test of 'specificity' is not about 'discrimination'."[1020] India considers that the fact that a subsidy is being given to some but not others is exactly how one would normally define discrimination. India further submits that these "other" entities that are denied the subsidy would have to be "like" the "certain enterprises" that are granted the subsidy, and that this is supported by the text and context of Article 2.1. India considers that the Appellate Body report in *US – Large Civil Aircraft (2nd complaint)* supports its view because it contains an analysis of whether or not there is *de facto* discrimination.

4.382 The United States argues that the Panel correctly rejected India's argument that Article 2.1(c) of the SCM Agreement requires a showing of discrimination between certain enterprises and other, similarly situated enterprises. According to the United States, India fails to appreciate that, to the extent that the specificity analysis under Article 2.1(c) entails a comparison, it is between certain enterprises receiving the subsidy and the rest of the subsidizing Member's economy. The United States therefore supports the Panel's finding that "Article 2.1 is not concerned with other enterprises, and whether or not such

---

[1018] India further requests that, to the extent we accept India's claim that the Panel acted inconsistently with Article 2.1(c), we also find that the Panel acted inconsistently with Article 2.4 of the SCM Agreement, which requires that specificity determinations be clearly substantiated on the basis of positive evidence. (India's appellant's submission, para. 378) Because the condition for India's request in respect of Article 2.4 is not met, we also reject India's request in this regard.

[1019] India's appellant's submission, para. 351.

[1020] India's appellant's submission, para. 353.

other enterprises have been discriminated against."[1021] The United States further submits that India's approach would read the plain text out of the chapeau of Article 2.1, because it would leave no recourse for investigating authorities in instances where the term "certain enterprises" is defined as an industry or a single unique enterprise. The United States also considers that India's reliance on the Appellate Body report in *US – Large Civil Aircraft (2nd complaint)* is misplaced, since that case dealt with whether a financial contribution was granted in disproportionately large amounts to certain enterprises, which is a different factor under Article 2.1(c) than the factor at issue in this dispute.

4.383 India seeks to introduce the notion that, in order for a subsidy to be specific, the recipients and some category of non-recipients of the subsidy must be "like" or "similarly situated". This contention, India argues, is supported by the text and context of Article 2.1, which would be rendered meaningless if the "others" that were allegedly denied the subsidy would not have had access to it anyway.[1022]

4.384 In addressing India's arguments, we recall the Appellate Body's observation that "[t]he chapeau [of Article 2.1] frames the central inquiry as a determination as to whether a subsidy is specific to 'certain enterprises' within the jurisdiction of the granting authority."[1023] This indicates that, whether the inquiry is focusing on the *de jure* or *de facto* elements of a subsidy programme, determining that access to, or the actual allocation or use of, a subsidy is limited requires showing that the subsidy is available only to certain enterprises within the jurisdiction of the granting authority. We do not see a textual basis in Article 2.1(c), and specifically in the terms "certain" and "limited number", for a requirement to identify which enterprises or industries are "similarly situated" prior to then having to assess whether only a subset of those "similarly situated" have *de facto* access to, or are otherwise eligible for, the subsidy. As the Appellate Body has explained, eligibility is key to a consideration of *de jure* specificity under subparagraphs (a) and (b) of Article 2.1 of the SCM Agreement: "Article 2.1(a) describes limitations on eligibility that favour certain enterprises, whereas Article 2.1(b) describes criteria or conditions that guard against selective eligibility."[1024] We do not see that this focus on the eligibility of subsidy recipients, however, conveys a comparative assessment of subsidy recipients with some category of "others" that are similarly situated. The fact that a specificity inquiry may, in certain circumstances, proceed from subparagraphs (a) and (b) to subparagraph (c) illustrates a scenario in which the subsidy in question may be *de jure* explicitly accessible to all enterprises or industries. It is then the function of the inquiry under subparagraph (c) to

---

[1021] United States' appellee's submission, para. 314 (quoting Panel Report, para. 7.121).
[1022] India's appellant's submission, para. 357.
[1023] Appellate Body Report, *US – Anti-Dumping and Countervailing Duties (China)*, para. 366.
[1024] Appellate Body Report, *US – Anti-Dumping and Countervailing Duties (China)*, para. 367.

determine whether, for example, only a limited number of certain enterprises, in fact, have access to the subsidy.

4.385 India maintains that the provisions are "meaningless" without confining the "others" to enterprises that are "like" or "similarly situated", but India has not explained why this would be so. The Panel stated that a positive determination that a subsidy is specific under the first factor set out in Article 2.1(c) would require showing that "the subsidy is available to certain enterprises, industries, or groups of enterprises or industries, but not to others."[1025] Contrary to India's position, we do not see that the reference to "others" compels an understanding that the focus of the analysis should be on comparing the treatment accorded to the recipients of the subsidy and other, similarly situated enterprises that also have access to the subsidy. As the Panel observed, what matters for the inquiry called for by subparagraph (a) and the first factor in subparagraph (c) is the existence of a limitation on access to, or use of, the subsidy.[1026]

4.386 India has not explained why trade distortion potentially resulting from the selective distribution of subsidies would be more likely to result where the set of subsidy recipients constitutes a subset of similarly situated enterprises, rather than a subset of the economy as a whole. The United States further observes that India's position is problematic because, if, for example, users of a subsidy were limited to a single industry qualifying as "certain enterprises", the allocation would still not be considered *de facto* specific because it was not provided to a subset of that industry. The fact that a *de facto* analysis of a subsidy granted to a single industry would not, in India's view, indicate the existence of specificity is difficult to square with the aim of determining whether a subsidy is specific to "certain enterprises" under Article 2.1.

4.387 India relies on the Appellate Body's reasoning in *US – Large Civil Aircraft (2nd complaint)* to support its position. In particular, India points to the Appellate Body's statement that the inquiry under Article 2.1(c) "requires a panel to examine the reasons as to why the actual allocation of 'amounts of subsidy' differs from an allocation that would be expected to result if the subsidy were administered in accordance with the conditions for eligibility for that subsidy".[1027] India argues that this reasoning indicates a comparative approach between the expected and actual allocations of a subsidy, which, in India's view, supports its position that the specificity analysis requires a comparison between subsidy recipients and other, "similarly situated" enterprises. India notes that, even when there is a *de facto* disparity in the way a subsidy is allocated, the Appellate Body has considered that this requires a further examination of factors

---

1025 Panel Report, para. 7.121.

1026 We note that the Panel similarly pointed out that what matters for the inquiry called for by subparagraphs (a) and (c) of Article 2.1 is "the existence of a restriction on access to the subsidy". (Panel Report, para. 7.121)

1027 India's appellant's submission, para. 358 (quoting Appellate Body Report, *US – Large Civil Aircraft (2nd complaint)*, para. 877).

that would explain or justify why a subset of entities *de facto* benefits from the subsidy. According to India, this examination is an analysis of whether or not there is *de facto* discrimination.[1028]

4.388 We recall that, in *US – Large Civil Aircraft (2nd complaint)*, the Appellate Body specifically analysed the third factor listed in Article 2.1(c) relating to whether there had been a "granting of disproportionately large amounts of subsidy to certain enterprises". In that case, the Appellate Body examined the particular situation in which the panel had made a *de jure* finding of non-specificity, but then proceeded to analyse whether there was evidence of *de facto* specificity.[1029] The Appellate Body underscored that the third factor in Article 2.1(c) reflects a relational concept, requiring a determination as to whether the actual allocation of the subsidy to certain enterprises is too large relative to what the allocation would have been if the subsidy were administered in accordance with the conditions for eligibility for that subsidy as assessed under subparagraphs (a) and (b).[1030] The Appellate Body stated that, where a disparity exists between those allocations, the reasons for that disparity must be examined so as ultimately to determine whether there has been a granting of disproportionately large amounts of subsidy to certain enterprises.

4.389 In our view, the Appellate Body's analysis in *US – Large Civil Aircraft (2nd complaint)* was particular to the third factor in Article 2.1(c) and the circumstances of that case. The Appellate Body further noted that the language of the third factor necessarily involves a "relational concept" that assesses whether the actual allocation of the subsidy is too large relative to what the allocation would have been if administered in accordance with the conditions for eligibility for that subsidy.[1031] We do not see that an investigating authority or a panel could assess whether "amounts of subsidy" that were granted were "disproportionately large" without having some benchmark, perhaps informed by who was expected to receive that subsidy, against which to compare those granted amounts. This suggests that different considerations inform an assessment under the first and third factors of Article 2.1(c).[1032] We therefore do not consider that the Appellate Body's reasoning in *US – Large Civil Aircraft (2nd complaint)* concerning the third factor of Article 2.1(c) is apt in assessing whether the first factor entails an assessment of whether there has been

[1028] India's appellant's submission, para. 361.

[1029] Appellate Body Report, *US – Large Civil Aircraft (2nd complaint)*, paras. 875 and 876.

[1030] Appellate Body Report, *US – Large Civil Aircraft (2nd complaint)*, para. 879.

[1031] *Ibid.*

[1032] The Appellate Body's consideration of the third factor was also informed by the mandatory factors in the last sentence of Article 2.1(c) relating to the diversification of the relevant economy and the duration of the industrial revenue bond programme. (Appellate Body Report, *US – Large Civil Aircraft (2nd complaint)*, paras. 884 and 888) As we have noted, the Panel in this dispute found that the USDOC failed to consider the factors set out in the last sentence of Article 2.1(c) relating to the diversification of the relevant economy and the duration of the relevant subsidy programme, which formed the basis for the Panel's finding that the USDOC acted inconsistently with Article 2.1(c) of the SCM Agreement. (Panel Report, para. 7.136)

discrimination between a limited number of subsidy users representing a subset of "certain enterprises".

4.390 For the foregoing reasons, we *uphold* the Panel's finding, in paragraph 7.126 of the Panel Report, rejecting India's argument that specificity must be established on the basis of discrimination in favour of "certain enterprises" against a broader category of other, similarly situated entities.[1033]

4.5.2.3 Provisions of goods and findings of specificity

4.391 India claims that the Panel's analysis is in error because it allowed for a finding that a government provision of goods can be *de facto* specific based merely on the inherent limitations on use of the goods provided. In India's view, the Panel's interpretation creates redundancy in the SCM Agreement, given that it permits the authority to find "specificity" as a matter of course, diluting the requirements in Articles 1.2 and 2.1. In particular, India contends that, under the Panel's interpretation, "[i]f an authority is permitted to determine *de facto* specificity based on the inherent characteristics of the goods provided by a government, all government provisions of goods that amount to a subsidy under Article 1.1(a)(1)(iii) would *ipso facto* be *de facto* specific in every case."[1034] The Panel's interpretation thus renders Article 2.1(c) inutile in the context of the subsidy programmes covered by Article 1.1(a)(1)(iii) of the SCM Agreement. India further argues that the negotiating history of Article 2 indicates that there was no consensus among the negotiators on the issue of determining specificity based solely on the inherent limitations of the goods, and that Article 2.1(c) of the SCM Agreement cannot be interpreted in a manner that would indirectly incorporate into the treaty what the negotiators could not agree on.

4.392 The United States argues that the Panel correctly interpreted Article 2.1(c) of the SCM Agreement in finding that any inherent limitations arising from a provision of goods cannot preclude a finding of *de facto* specificity. The United States considers that India's concern regarding the Panel's finding is unfounded. The Panel did not find that the provision of goods that are inherently limited in utility will *ipso facto* be determined to be specific, but, rather, that inherent limitations are not a bar to a finding of specificity. Thus, under the Panel's interpretation, an investigating authority still must make a determination of specificity consistent with Article 2 of the SCM Agreement. The United States adds that the interpretation advanced by India would create a loophole in the subsidies disciplines because it would mean that the provision of all goods would be exempt from a finding of *de facto* specificity. The United States

---

[1033] India further requests that, to the extent we accept India's claim that the Panel acted inconsistently with Article 2.1(c), we also find that the Panel acted inconsistently with Article 2.4 of the SCM Agreement, which requires that specificity determinations be clearly substantiated on the basis of positive evidence. (India's appellant's submission, para. 368) Because the condition for India's request in respect of Article 2.4 is not met, we also reject India's request in this regard.

[1034] India's appellant's submission, para. 388. (emphasis omitted)

considers that there is no basis in the text of Article 2 for such an interpretation. Rather, previous panels have correctly found that, when a government provides a good that is of limited utility, it is all the more likely that a subsidy is conferred on certain enterprises.

4.393 We begin with India's contention that, where a subsidy consists of the provision of a good within the meaning of Article 1.1(a)(1)(iii), the subsidy will necessarily be used by a subset of the economy that qualifies as "certain enterprises", and therefore will always be specific within the meaning of Article 2.1(c). We recall that, in *US – Anti-Dumping and Countervailing Duties (China)*, the Appellate Body stated that the term "certain enterprises" set out in Article 2.1 refers to "a single enterprise or industry or a class of enterprises or industries that are known and particularized".[1035] This would suggest that, anytime the financial contribution at issue consists of a discrete transfer of value from the government to a class of recipients, and the nature of the transfer makes the class of recipients more likely to be identified and circumscribed, this in turn makes it more likely that an investigating authority or panel may reach a conclusion that the subsidy is specific. So it may be that, in respect of a provision of goods, there is a greater likelihood of a finding of specificity in instances where the input good is used by only a circumscribed group of entities and/or industries. At the same time, we are not persuaded that *every* provision of goods with limitations inherent in the characteristics of the goods will necessarily lead to a finding of specificity.[1036]

4.394 We further note that the inutility to which India refers is not borne of a redundancy in the substantive obligations set out in Articles 1.1(a)(1)(iii) and 2.1(c), but rather of a redundancy in *outcome* to the extent that India argues that an affirmative determination in the former necessarily results in an affirmative determination with regard to the latter. However, we recall that the analyses under Articles 1.1(a)(1)(iii) and 2.1(c) focus on different legal questions, neither of which is itself capable of rendering a determination of a specific subsidy, which requires findings of financial contribution, benefit, and specificity. Thus, even if there are circumstances for which, by virtue of the nature of the government transfer, there is a greater likelihood that an analysis in respect of Article 1.1(a)(1)(iii) and of 2.1(c) will both lead to affirmative outcomes, the legal reasoning and conclusions required under each provision remain distinct. The Appellate Body has noted, "[a]n interpreter is not free to adopt a reading that would result in reducing whole clauses or paragraphs of a treaty to

---

[1035] Appellate Body Report, *US – Anti-Dumping and Countervailing Duties (China)*, para. 373.

[1036] The Panel noted examples cited by the panel in *US – Softwood Lumber IV* for which the provision of certain natural resources, such as oil, gas, and water, would not be rendered automatically specific because they may be used by an indefinite number of industries. (Panel Report, paras. 7.131 and 7.132 (referring to Panel Report, *US – Softwood Lumber IV*, para. 7.116)) Although India maintains that such examples may not always be provided to an indefinite number of industries, we do not exclude that there may be circumstances in which the provision of resources is sufficiently broadly available so as to be considered non-specific.

redundancy or inutility."[1037] It is not clear to us that the potential for simultaneous affirmative determinations under financial contribution and specificity analyses can be characterized as reducing whole clauses or paragraphs of the treaty to redundancy or inutility.

4.395 Finally, we take note of India's argument that the negotiating history supports its position that an affirmative finding of *de facto* specificity will not be reached merely based on the inherent limitations of the goods in question, and that this must be taken into account in accordance with Article 32 of the Vienna Convention of the Law on Treaties.[1038] On appeal, India reiterates the argument it made before the Panel that the negotiating history of Article 2 of the SCM Agreement indicates that there was no consensus among the negotiating members on the issue of determining specificity based solely on the inherent limitations of the goods. Consequently, India emphasizes that "Article 2.1(c) of the SCM Agreement cannot be interpreted in a manner that would indirectly incorporate into the treaty what the negotiators could not originally agree on."[1039] India places particular reliance on a footnote in the Second Cartland Draft[1040] of September 1990, which states: "It remains for signatories to address the issue of limited access as a result of the inherent characteristics of goods, services or extraction or harvesting rights provided by a government."[1041] India argues that this footnote makes clear that the negotiators had not addressed the issue in the Second Cartland Draft and that, by removing the footnote in the final text, there had been no consensus.

4.396 We consider it difficult to draw a conclusion about the consensus, or lack thereof, of the negotiators from the removal of the footnote identified by India. It is possible that the deletion of the footnote could suggest, as India argues, that the negotiators were unable to reach a consensus. Equally as plausible, however, is the possibility that the negotiators removed the footnote because they were

---

[1037] Appellate Body Report, *US – Gasoline*, p. 23, DSR 1996:I, p. 21. (fn omitted)

[1038] Done at Vienna, 23 May 1969, UN Treaty Series, Vol. 1155, p. 331. In its Notice of Appeal, India also states that the Panel erred because it did not make an objective assessment of the matter before it by limiting the circumstances in which negotiating history can be relied upon to interpret a treaty. (India's Notice of Appeal, para. 21) In its appellant's submission, India argues that Article 32 of the Vienna Convention of the Law on Treaties also allows for the use of negotiating history as supplementary means of interpretation. However, India has not indicated that it is presenting a claim under Article 11 of the DSU, and has not presented arguments that would explain how the Panel's analysis amounted to a failure to make an objective assessment of the matter under that provision. (See India's appellant's submission, paras. 392 and 399; and United States' appellee's submission, paras. 333 and 334) In response to questioning at the oral hearing, India explained that it considers these arguments to be covered by its substantive claim regarding the interpretation of Article 2.1(c). For these reasons, we do not address this issue separately from our consideration of India's argument regarding the significance of the negotiating history to which it refers.

[1039] India's appellant's submission, para. 397.

[1040] The Second Cartland Draft contains draft text by the Chairman covering the Framework for Negotiations and was circulated in the Negotiating Group on Subsidies and Countervailing Measures in September 1990 as document MTN.GNG/NG10/W/38/Rev.1.

[1041] India's appellant's submission, para. 395 (quoting Second Cartland Draft, fn to Article 4).

satisfied that the issue was addressed by the existing text.[1042] We therefore do not consider that the negotiating history to which India refers is helpful in understanding whether and how the specificity requirement applies uniquely to subsidies limited by the inherent characteristics of goods.

4.397 India additionally maintains that the Panel failed to record and evaluate the "cogent reasons" offered by India for not following the panel's finding in *US – Softwood Lumber IV*, and that this is inconsistent with the Panel's mandate under Article 11 of the DSU.[1043] We recall that a panel does not fall into error under Article 11 of the DSU simply because it fails to address every argument of a party.[1044] Furthermore, we agree with the United States' argument that, despite India's position to the contrary, the Panel's conclusion did not depend on the reasoning cited in *US – Softwood Lumber IV*. As the United States points out, the Panel, after providing reasoning in rejecting India's claim, further stated that only the reasoning of the panel in *US – Softwood Lumber IV* was "consistent with [the Panel's] approach outlined above".[1045] In these circumstances, we do not consider that the Panel acted inconsistently with its obligation to conduct an objective assessment of the matter under Article 11 of the DSU, and we therefore *reject* India's claim in this regard.

4.398 For the foregoing reasons, we *uphold* the finding of the Panel, in paragraph 7.133 of the Panel Report, rejecting India's argument that, if the inherent characteristics of the subsidized good limit the possible use of the subsidy to a certain industry, the subsidy will not be specific unless access to this subsidy is further limited to a subset of this industry.

4.6 Article 12.7 of the SCM Agreement

4.399 India requests us to reverse the Panel's finding rejecting India's claim that the measure at issue, Section 1677e(b) of the US Statute and Section 351.308(a)-(c) of the US Regulations, is inconsistent "as such" and "as applied" with Article 12.7 of the SCM Agreement. India submits that, in respect of its "as such" claim, the Panel erred in its interpretation by finding that Article 12.7 does not require investigating authorities to engage in a comparative evaluation of all available evidence with a view to selecting the best information. Alternatively, even if the Panel's interpretation is upheld, India submits that the Panel nevertheless acted inconsistently with Article 11 of the DSU by failing to take into account relevant evidence on the meaning of the measure at issue.

[1042] The Panel made a similar point when it suggested that the deletion of the footnote "may suggest that negotiators addressed the issue, and concluded that no such provision was necessary". (Panel Report, para. 7.130)

[1043] India's appellant's submission, para. 382.

[1044] Appellate Body Report, *EC – Fasteners (China)*, para. 511 (referring to Appellate Body Report, *EC – Poultry*, para. 135).

[1045] Panel Report, para. 7.132.

4.400 In respect of its "as applied" claims, India argues that the Panel erred by applying an incorrect legal standard under Article 12.7 of the SCM Agreement in its evaluation of the USDOC's use of the highest non-*de minimis* subsidy rates in the instances identified by India. Alternatively, assuming that the Panel applied the correct legal standard under Article 12.7, India argues that the Panel erred in applying an "unnecessary burden of proof" by requiring India to demonstrate how each specific application of the measure breached the legal standard for Article 12.7.[1046] India also claims that the Panel acted inconsistently with Article 11 of the DSU in finding that India had failed to make a *prima facie* case in respect of its claim that the 2013 sunset review violated Article 12.7 of the SCM Agreement.

4.401 India further requests the Appellate Body to complete the legal analysis in relation to its "as such" and "as applied" claims regarding Article 12.7 of the SCM Agreement.

4.402 In the light of the contingent nature of a number of these claims, we begin by examining whether the Panel erred in its interpretation of Article 12.7. We then turn to India's claim that the Panel erred under Article 11 of the DSU in ascertaining the meaning of the measure at issue. We then evaluate India's claims relating to the Panel's finding on the use of the highest non-*de minimis* subsidy rates, before turning to India's challenge under Article 11 of the DSU relating to the 2013 sunset review.

4.6.1 India's claim that the Panel erred in its interpretation of Article 12.7 of the SCM Agreement

4.403 India requests us to find that the Panel erred in its interpretation of Article 12.7 of the SCM Agreement. In particular, India appeals the Panel's statement that investigating authorities are not required, under Article 12.7 of the SCM Agreement, to engage in a comparative evaluation of all available evidence with a view to selecting the best information, or, in other words, the most fitting or most appropriate information available.

4.404 Before the Panel, India referred to the standard articulated by the panel, and quoted with approval by the Appellate Body, in *Mexico – Anti-Dumping Measures on Rice* in relation to Article 6.8 of the Anti-Dumping Agreement, and argued that Article 12.7 requires an investigating authority to employ the best information available, after engaging in an evaluative, comparative assessment of the evidence available.[1047] According to India, Article 12.7 cannot be interpreted as granting the right to draw adverse consequences or inferences in all cases of non-cooperation, because this would not involve a process of

---

[1046] India's appellant's submission, paras. 602-607.

[1047] India's first written submission to the Panel, paras. 162-164 (referring to Appellate Body Report, *Mexico – Anti-Dumping Measures on Rice*, para. 289; and Panel Report, *Mexico – Anti-Dumping Measures on Rice*, para. 7.166).

"comparative evaluation", and would not lead to the use of the "best information" on which to base a determination under Article 12.7.

4.405 For its part, the United States contended before the Panel that the ordinary meaning of the term "facts available" does not speak to which facts should be selected by an investigating authority invoking Article 12.7. Rather, according to the United States, Article 12.7 merely provides that an investigating authority, when faced with a situation in which necessary information has not been supplied, may apply those facts that are otherwise available, which may include facts that are less favourable to an interested party or Member. For the United States, Article 12.7 does not prohibit the use of adverse inferences in selecting from amongst the "facts available". The United States also stated that inferences cannot be drawn that contradict verifiable facts, or that aim merely to punish an uncooperative party. Rather, the United States claimed that, where more relevant or reliable information is available on the record, the USDOC applies such information in making its determinations based upon the facts available.

4.6.1.1 The Panel's findings

4.406 The Panel began by noting that the text of Article 12.7 of the SCM Agreement does not contain any express conditions for determining which and what type of "facts available" should be used by an investigating authority.[1048] However, the Panel also noted that the Appellate Body, in *Mexico – Anti-Dumping Measures on Rice*, found there to be "certain limits" upon an investigating authority's recourse to Article 12.7, and, in particular, referred to the Appellate Body's consideration of the due process context of Article 12.[1049] The Panel then cited the Appellate Body's statement on the function of Article 12.7, namely, to permit "the use of facts on record solely for the purpose of replacing information that may be missing, in order to arrive at an accurate subsidization or injury determination"[1050], before quoting its finding on the legal standard for Article 12.7:

> [R]ecourse to facts available does not permit an investigating authority to use any information in whatever way it chooses. First, such recourse is not a licence to rely on only part of the evidence provided. To the extent possible, an investigating authority using the "facts available" in a countervailing duty investigation must

---

[1048] Panel Report, para. 7.437. The Panel also noted that the provision refers to the available "facts", and thus agreed with the panel's findings in *China – GOES* that determinations made under Article 12.7 must have a factual foundation. (*Ibid.*, para. 7.437 (referring to Panel Report, *China – GOES*, para. 7.296))

[1049] Panel Report, para. 7.438 (referring to Appellate Body Report, *Mexico – Anti-Dumping Measures on Rice*, paras. 292-294).

[1050] Panel Report, fn 729 to para. 7.438 (quoting Appellate Body Report, *Mexico – Anti-Dumping Measures on Rice*, para. 293).

> take into account all the substantiated facts provided by an interested party, even if those facts may not constitute the complete information requested of that party. Secondly, the "facts available" to the agency are generally limited to those that may reasonably replace the information that an interested party failed to provide. In certain circumstances, this may include information from secondary sources.[1051]

4.407 In sum, the Panel considered that:

> [T]he standard in Article 12.7 of the SCM Agreement requires that all substantiated facts on the record be taken into account, that "facts available" determinations have a factual foundation, and that "facts available" be generally limited to those facts that may reasonably replace the missing information.[1052]

4.408 The Panel stated that India's argument, contending that Article 12.7 requires the use of the "best information available" after an "evaluative, comparative assessment", sought "to import into the standard under Article 12.7 the specific requirements the Appellate Body found applicable under Article 6.8 of the [Anti-Dumping] Agreement read in light of Annex II of that Agreement".[1053] The Panel found that this would be inappropriate, since, in its view, the Appellate Body in *Mexico – Anti-Dumping Measures on Rice* "did not apply that same standard in respect of its findings pursuant to Article 12.7 of the SCM Agreement, noting expressly the lack of an equivalent to Annex II of the [Anti-Dumping] Agreement in the SCM Agreement".[1054] In that context, the Panel made the specific statement that is subject to appeal by India:

> [W]e reject India's assertion that the findings of the panel in *Mexico – Anti-Dumping Measures on Rice* establish that Article 12.7 of the SCM Agreement requires that investigating authorities engage in a comparative evaluation of all available evidence with a view to selecting the *best* information, i.e. the most fitting or most appropriate information available.[1055]

4.409 The Panel also appeared to consider that it may be permissible to use an adverse inference in resorting to the "facts available", but only where it is used in a manner consistent with this legal standard for Article 12.7.[1056] The Panel cited the panel report in *EC – Countervailing Measures on DRAM Chips* as

---

[1051] Panel Report, para. 7.438 (quoting Appellate Body Report, *Mexico – Anti-Dumping Measures on Rice*, para. 294).

[1052] Panel Report, para. 7.441.

[1053] Panel Report, para. 7.439.

[1054] Panel Report, para. 7.439 (referring to Appellate Body Report, *Mexico – Anti-Dumping Measures on Rice*, para. 290).

[1055] Panel Report, para. 7.439. (emphasis original) See also India's appellant's submission, paras. 210 and 227.

[1056] Panel Report, para. 7.442.

support for its position that, in certain circumstances, an investigating authority may draw an adverse inference from non-cooperation in selecting from and assessing "facts available".[1057] However, the Panel also understood the panel report in *EC – Countervailing Measures on DRAM Chips* to stand for the proposition that Article 12.7 does not allow investigating authorities to punish non-cooperation, particularly in the absence of a factual foundation.[1058] In respect of India's argument that Article 12.7 of the SCM Agreement does not grant the right to draw adverse inferences or consequences in all cases of non-cooperation, the Panel sought to distinguish the case at hand from that before the panel in *China – GOES*. In particular, the Panel stated that the panel in *China – GOES* was faced with "speculative 'adverse inferences'" that were "devoid of any factual foundation", whereas "the 'adverse inferences' envisaged in Sections 1677e(b) and 351.308(a)-(e) ... properly rest on factual foundations."[1059]

4.6.1.2 Interpretation of Article 12.7 of the SCM Agreement

4.410 The participants do not dispute that the Appellate Body's interpretation of Article 12.7 of the SCM Agreement in *Mexico – Anti-Dumping Measures on Rice* represents the applicable legal standard.[1060] However, they disagree on whether Article 12.7 necessarily requires a comparative evaluation of all available evidence with a view to selecting the best information.

4.411 India claims that the Panel erred in its interpretation of Article 12.7 of the SCM Agreement by finding that investigating authorities are not required to engage in a comparative evaluation of all available evidence with a view to selecting the best information, or, in other words, the most fitting or most appropriate information available. India argues that the Panel misconstrued the legal standard articulated by the Appellate Body in *Mexico – Anti-Dumping Measures on Rice*, contending that, although the Appellate Body identified textual differences between Article 12.7 of the SCM Agreement and Article 6.8 of the Anti-Dumping Agreement, it nonetheless found both provisions to appear in the same context and fulfil the same objective, and that they could not be interpreted in a markedly different manner. Thus, in India's view, the Appellate

---

[1057] Panel Report, para. 7.443 (referring to Panel Report, *EC – Countervailing Measures on DRAM Chips*, paras. 7.60, 7.61, 7.80, and 7.143).

[1058] Panel Report, para. 7.443 (referring to Panel Report, *EC – Countervailing Measures on DRAM Chips*, paras. 7.60, 7.61, 7.80, and 7.143).

[1059] Panel Report, para. 7.444 (referring to Panel Report, *China – GOES*, para. 7.302).

[1060] India's and United States' responses to questioning at the oral hearing; United States' appellee's submission, paras. 436-445; India's appellant's submission, para. 208. We also note that the participants agree that Article 12.7 cannot be used by an investigating authority to punish non-cooperating parties by choosing adverse facts for that purpose. (United States' response to questioning at the oral hearing; United States' response to Panel question No. 76, para. 130; India's appellant's submission, para. 237)

Body applied the same standard in that case for both provisions. Since the Appellate Body agreed with the panel's articulation of the legal standard for Article 6.8 of the Anti-Dumping Agreement in that case, this same standard should also apply in respect of Article 12.7 of the SCM Agreement in the present case.[1061]

4.412 According to India, contrary to the Panel's reasoning, the omission to include, in the SCM Agreement, an equivalent to Annex II to the Anti-Dumping Agreement, does not mean that the "general standards" under Article 12.7 of the SCM Agreement and Article 6.8 of the Anti-Dumping Agreement are different.[1062] India points to the fact that the first sentence of both provisions is identical. In addition, India contends that Annex II to the Anti-Dumping Agreement does not prescribe any substantive standard by which an investigating authority is required to determine what type of information can be used to replace the missing information. Therefore, the absence, in the SCM Agreement, of something similar to Annex II to the Anti-Dumping Agreement does not mean that Article 12.7 of the SCM Agreement imposes a standard that is markedly different from that prescribed under Article 6.8 of the Anti-Dumping Agreement in determining those "facts available" on which to base a determination.

4.413 For its part, the United States argues, on appeal, that the Panel's interpretation of Article 12.7 is consistent with its text, and accords with the legal standard articulated by the Appellate Body in *Mexico – Anti-Dumping Measures on Rice*. In the United States' view, the ordinary meaning of the term "facts available" does not speak to which facts should be selected, and India's purported requirement of a "comparative evaluation" is not supported by the text of the SCM Agreement. In any case, the United States argues that it cannot be concluded that the panel's finding in *Mexico – Anti-Dumping Measures on Rice* on Article 6.8 of the Anti-Dumping Agreement should be extrapolated beyond the particular factual circumstances of that case.

4.414 According to the United States, the Panel correctly found that the Appellate Body in *Mexico – Anti-Dumping Measures on Rice* did not articulate the same standard for Article 6.8 of the Anti-Dumping Agreement, read in the light of its Annex II, and Article 12.7 of the SCM Agreement. Thus, in the United States' view, the Appellate Body's approach in that case should not be read as identifying conditions in Annex II to the Anti-Dumping Agreement applicable to Article 12.7 of the SCM Agreement. Rather, the Appellate Body relied upon Annex II only for context in interpreting Article 12.7. While the title of Annex II to the Anti-Dumping Agreement provides context that suggests that an investigating authority is trying to arrive at the best information available

---

[1061] India's appellant's submission, paras. 216-218 (referring to Appellate Body Report, *Mexico – Anti-Dumping Measures on Rice*, paras. 295, 297, and 298; and Panel Report, *Mexico – Anti-Dumping Measures on Rice*, para. 7.242).

[1062] India's appellant's submission, para. 220.

under Article 12.7, paragraph 7 of Annex II also suggests that recourse to the "facts available" does not necessarily lead to the best result, and that it could lead to an adverse result because the necessary information is not available.[1063] The United States adds that Article 12.7 cannot be used to punish non-cooperation.[1064]

4.415 Our analysis commences with the text of Article 12.7 of the SCM Agreement, construed within its immediate context and in the light of the object and purpose of the SCM Agreement. Thereafter, we turn to the further context of the other covered agreements, in particular Annex II to the Anti-Dumping Agreement.[1065] Article 12.7 of the SCM Agreement states:

Article 12

Evidence

...

> 12.7 In cases in which any interested Member or interested party refuses access to, or otherwise does not provide, necessary information within a reasonable period or significantly impedes the investigation, preliminary and final determinations, affirmative or negative, may be made on the basis of the facts available.

4.416 First, we note that Article 12.7 of the SCM Agreement limits use of the "facts available" to instances where an interested Member or interested party "refuses access to, or otherwise does not provide, necessary information within a reasonable period or significantly impedes the investigation".[1066] This sets the parameters within which an investigating authority makes a determination on the basis of the "facts available", namely, in a context of missing "necessary information". It is the absence of this particular information that the use of the "facts available" is designed to mitigate.[1067] This suggests that the process of identifying the "facts available" should be limited to identifying replacements for the "necessary information" that is missing from the record. In this regard, the use of the term "necessary" to qualify the term "information" carries significance. It is meant to ensure that Article 12.7 is not directed at mitigating the absence of "any" or "unnecessary" information, but is rather concerned with

---

[1063] United States' response to questioning at the oral hearing.

[1064] United States' response to questioning at the oral hearing.

[1065] Appellate Body Reports, *US – Clove Cigarettes*, fn 274 to para. 100; *EC – Asbestos*, paras. 88 and 89; and *EC – Chicken Cuts*, para. 193. We also note that this was the approach of the Appellate Body in *Mexico – Anti-Dumping Measures on Rice* with respect to interpreting Article 12.7 of the SCM Agreement. (See Appellate Body Report, *Mexico – Anti-Dumping Measures on Rice*, para. 295)

[1066] See Appellate Body Report, *Japan – DRAMs (Korea)*, para. 235; and Panel Report, *US – Anti-Dumping and Countervailing Duties (China)*, para. 16.9.

[1067] Appellate Body Report, *Mexico – Anti-Dumping Measures on Rice*, para. 291.

overcoming the absence of information required to complete a determination. In that vein, the Appellate Body has held that Article 12.7 "permits the use of facts on record solely for the purpose of replacing information that may be missing, in order to arrive at an accurate subsidization or injury determination".[1068] Accordingly, there has to be a connection between the "necessary information" that is missing and the particular "facts available" on which a determination under Article 12.7 is based. For this reason, the Appellate Body in *Mexico – Anti-Dumping Measures on Rice* stated that an investigating authority must use those "facts available" that "*reasonably replace* the information that an interested party failed to provide"[1069], with a view to arriving at an accurate determination.[1070]

4.417 It is also clear from the text of the provision that determinations made under Article 12.7 must be based on available "facts". "The" facts "available" refers to those facts that are in the possession of the investigating authority and on its written record.[1071] This may include, for instance, facts contained in the application of the domestic industry that led to the initiation of the investigation[1072], or facts contained in information requested by, and submitted to, the investigating authority by other interested parties or interested Members.[1073] Thus, "the facts available" in Article 12.7 refers to pieces of information that can be used as evidence and that are on the written record of the investigating authority.[1074] As determinations made under Article 12.7 are to be made on the basis of the "facts available", they cannot be made on the basis of non-factual assumptions or speculation.[1075]

4.418 In our view, this understanding is confirmed by the immediate context of Article 12.7. First, we consider that the title of Article 12, namely, "Evidence", situates recourse to the "facts available" under Article 12.7 within a broader process of identifying and gathering evidence for the countervailing duty investigation.[1076] In Article 11.2 of the SCM Agreement, the term "sufficient

---

[1068] Appellate Body Report, *Mexico – Anti-Dumping Measures on Rice*, para. 293.

[1069] Appellate Body Report, *Mexico – Anti-Dumping Measures on Rice*, para. 294. (emphasis added)

[1070] Appellate Body Report, *Mexico – Anti-Dumping Measures on Rice*, para. 293.

[1071] Article 12.2 of the SCM Agreement.

[1072] Articles 11.2 and 11.3 of the SCM Agreement.

[1073] Articles 12.1 and 12.5 of the SCM Agreement.

[1074] The term "facts" can connote items of information used or useable as evidence. (Oxford English Dictionary online, <http://www.oed.com/view/Entry/67478>)

[1075] Panel Report, *China – GOES*, para. 7.302. We also note that, pursuant to Article 2.4 of the SCM Agreement, "[a]ny determination of specificity under the provisions of this Article shall be clearly substantiated on the basis of *positive evidence*" (emphasis added), and pursuant to Article 15.1 of the SCM Agreement, "[a] determination of injury for purposes of Article VI of GATT 1994 shall be based on *positive evidence*" (emphasis added). In our view, these requirements relating to the need for determinations to be based on "positive evidence" support our understanding that determinations may not be made on the basis of non-factual assumptions or speculation.

[1076] The term "evidence" refers to something directed at proving or disproving the existence of an alleged fact. (*Shorter Oxford English Dictionary*, 6th edn, A. Stevenson (ed.) (Oxford University Press, 2007), Vol. 1, p. 880)

evidence" is juxtaposed against the phrase "[s]imple assertion, unsubstantiated by relevant evidence". This indicates that the function of "evidence" is to substantiate assertions by interested parties. Article 12.5 of the SCM Agreement, which provides that "the authorities shall during the course of an investigation satisfy themselves as to the accuracy of the information supplied by interested Members or interested parties upon which their findings are based", gives a similar indication on the process of identifying and gathering evidence.[1077] In the light of this context, we consider that the task of ascertaining which "facts available" reasonably replace the missing "necessary information" under Article 12.7 calls for a process of reasoning and evaluation. In our view, it would not be possible to identify whether replacements for the missing "necessary information" are "reasonable", and thus constitute the "evidence" on which to ground a determination, without engaging in such a process.

4.419 We further consider that, as part of the process of reasoning and evaluating which "facts available" reasonably replace the missing information, all substantiated facts on the record must be taken into account.[1078] It would frustrate the function of Article 12.7, namely, to "replac[e] information that may be missing, in order to arrive at an accurate subsidization or injury determination", if certain substantiated facts were arbitrarily excluded from consideration.[1079] In addition, we note that the participants agree that Article 12.7 should not be used to punish non-cooperating parties by choosing adverse facts for that purpose.[1080] Rather, the participants agreed at the oral hearing that the function of Article 12.7 is to replace the missing "necessary information" with a view to arriving at an accurate determination.

4.420 In the process of reasoning and evaluating which "facts available" constitute reasonable replacements for the missing "necessary information", an investigating authority may be called upon to draw inferences from the evidence before it in order to reach a conclusion. As the Appellate Body has recognized, albeit in another – yet similar – context, the drawing of an inference to reach a conclusion on the veracity of evidence, including from the refusal to provide information, is "an ordinary aspect of the task of all panels to determine the relevant facts of any dispute involving any covered agreement".[1081]

[1077] We note that Article 12.5 includes the qualification "[e]xcept in circumstances provided for in paragraph 7". In this regard, we note that it would not be possible for an investigating authority to "satisfy themselves as to the accuracy of the information" in circumstances where an interested party or Member refuses access to, or otherwise does not provide, such information.

[1078] Appellate Body Report, *Mexico – Anti-Dumping Measures on Rice*, para. 294.

[1079] Appellate Body Report, *Mexico – Anti-Dumping Measures on Rice*, para. 293. In this connection, we note the statement of the Appellate Body that Article 12.7 does not provide "a licence to rely on only part of the evidence provided", and that an investigating authority should "take into account all the substantiated facts provided by an interested party, even if those facts may not constitute the complete information requested of that party". (*Ibid.*, para. 294)

[1080] United States' response to questioning at the oral hearing; United States' response to Panel question No. 76, para. 130; India's appellant's submission, para. 237.

[1081] Appellate Body Report, *Canada – Aircraft*, para. 202.

4.421 Further, we note that the extent of the evaluation of the "facts available" that is required, and the form it may take, depend on the particular circumstances of a given case, including the nature, quality, and amount of the evidence on the record, and the particular determinations to be made in the course of an investigation. Similarly, whereas the explanation and analysis provided in a published report must be sufficient to allow a panel to assess whether the "facts available" employed by the investigating authority are reasonable replacements for the missing "necessary information", their nature and extent will necessarily vary from determination to determination.

4.422 We also consider that Articles 12.4 and 12.11 shed light on the meaning of Article 12.7. This is because these provisions recognize some potential reasons why the "necessary information" referred to in Article 12.7 may not be provided, namely, confidentiality and resource constraints. This is implicit in the requirement for investigating authorities to protect confidentiality and to provide any assistance practicable, in particular to small companies, in the provision of information. In our view, the context provided by these provisions suggests that the manner or procedural circumstances in which information is missing can be relevant to an investigating authority's use of "facts available" under Article 12.7. In particular, Article 12.11 requires an investigating authority to take "due account of any difficulties experienced by interested parties", which includes interested parties that have not provided the "necessary information" referred to in Article 12.7. The kinds of "difficulties", or lack thereof, experienced by interested parties to be taken into account by an investigating authority in having recourse to Article 12.7 could relate, *inter alia*, to the nature and availability of the evidence being sought, the adequacy of protection accorded by an investigating authority to the confidentiality of information, the time period provided in which to respond, and the extent or number of opportunities to respond, including in relation to the essential facts under consideration as provided in Article 12.8. Whether and how such procedural circumstances should be taken into account by an investigating authority, and any appropriate inferences that may be drawn, will necessarily depend on the particularities of a given investigation. We recall, however, that determinations under Article 12.7 must be made on the basis of "facts" that reasonably replace the "necessary information" that is missing, and thus cannot be made on the basis of procedural circumstances alone.

4.423 Additional context for the interpretation of Article 12.7 of the SCM Agreement is provided by Article 6.8 of the Anti-Dumping Agreement and its associated Annex II.[1082] The Appellate Body noted in *Mexico – Anti-Dumping Measures on Rice* both textual similarities and differences between Article 12.7 of the SCM Agreement and Article 6.8 of the Anti-Dumping Agreement. On the one hand, as a difference, the Appellate Body noted the absence of an equivalent, in the SCM Agreement, to Annex II to the Anti-Dumping

[1082] Annex II is entitled "Best Information Available in Terms of paragraph 8 of Article 6".

Agreement.[1083] On the other hand, as similarities, the Appellate Body noted first that both provisions "permit[] an investigating authority, under certain circumstances, to fill in gaps in the information necessary to arrive at a conclusion as to subsidization (or dumping) and injury".[1084] Further, the Appellate Body noted that both provisions use the term "facts available" to denote what may replace the missing "necessary information", and both provisions appear within the context of disciplines on the identification and collection of evidence.[1085] Thus, while Annex II to the Anti-Dumping Agreement does not form part of the SCM Agreement, it has been found by the Appellate Body to be relevant context for the interpretation of Article 12.7, which is almost identically worded to Article 6.8 of the Anti-Dumping Agreement. In particular, the similarities between these provisions led the Appellate Body to state that its understanding of the limitations of an investigating authority's use of "facts available" in Article 12.7:

> ... is further supported by the similar, limited recourse to "facts available" permitted under Annex II to the *Anti-Dumping Agreement*. Indeed, in our view, it would be anomalous if Article 12.7 of the *SCM Agreement* were to permit the use of "facts available" in countervailing duty investigations in a manner markedly different from that in anti-dumping investigations.[1086]

4.424 As regards the nature of the "facts available" that may form the basis of determinations under Article 12.7, the title of Annex II, "Best Information Available in Terms of Paragraph 8 of Article 6", supports our understanding that these facts must be limited to those that reasonably replace the missing "necessary information".[1087] In respect of the process for ascertaining which "facts available" to use, we note that the Appellate Body in *Mexico – Anti-Dumping Measures on Rice* quoted from and agreed with the panel's explanation in respect of Article 6.8 of the Anti-Dumping Agreement that "[d]etermining that something is 'best' inevitably requires ... an evaluative, comparative assessment", and that the nature of this standard depends on the "particular circumstances" of a given case.[1088] This supports our understanding of Article 12.7, namely, that ascertaining the reasonable replacements for the missing "necessary information" involves a process of reasoning and evaluation. As with Article 6.8 of the Anti-Dumping Agreement, this in turn calls for a consideration of all substantiated facts on the record.

[1083] Appellate Body Report, *Mexico – Anti-Dumping Measures on Rice*, para. 290.

[1084] Appellate Body Report, *Mexico – Anti-Dumping Measures on Rice*, para. 291.

[1085] Appellate Body Report, *Mexico – Anti-Dumping Measures on Rice*, paras. 291 and 292 (quoting Appellate Body Report, *EC – Tube or Pipe Fittings*, para. 138, in turn quoting Appellate Body Report, *EC – Bed Linen (Article 21.5 – India)*, para. 136).

[1086] Appellate Body Report, *Mexico – Anti-Dumping Measures on Rice*, para. 295.

[1087] Appellate Body Report, *Mexico – Anti-Dumping Measures on Rice*, para. 294.

[1088] Appellate Body Report, *Mexico – Anti-Dumping Measures on Rice*, para. 289 (quoting Panel Report, *Mexico – Anti-Dumping Measures on Rice*, para. 7.166).

4.425 We find further support for this understanding in the references in paragraph 7 of Annex II to exercising "special circumspection" when relying on information from secondary sources, and to, where practicable, "check[ing] the information from other independent sources", both of which are indicative of a process of reasoning and evaluation.[1089] The final sentence of paragraph 7 of Annex II to the Anti-Dumping Agreement is also relevant to the interpretation of Article 12.7 of the SCM Agreement, particularly in respect of the measure at issue. It states that:

> It is clear, however, that if an interested party does not cooperate and thus relevant information is being withheld from the authorities, this situation could lead to a result which is less favourable to the party than if the party did cooperate.

4.426 This clause acknowledges that non-cooperation could lead to an outcome that is less favourable for the non-cooperating party. It describes what could occur as a result of a non-cooperating party's failure to supply or otherwise withhold relevant information and the investigating authority's use of the "facts available" on the record. The juxtaposition between the "result" and the "situation" of non-cooperation in this clause confirms our understanding that the non-cooperation of a party is not itself the "basis" for replacing the "necessary information". Rather, non-cooperation creates a situation in which a less favourable result becomes possible due to the selection of a replacement for an unknown fact. Annex II to the Anti-Dumping Agreement thus provides contextual support for our understanding that the procedural circumstances in which information is missing are relevant to an investigating authority's use of "facts available" under Article 12.7 of the SCM Agreement. In this regard, we note that paragraph 1 of Annex II makes a connection between the "awareness" of an interested party, and the ability for an investigating authority to have recourse to the "facts available". This suggests that the knowledge of a non-cooperating party of the consequences of failing to provide information can be taken into account by an investigating authority, along with other procedural circumstances in which information is missing, in ascertaining those "facts available" on which to base a determination and in explaining the selection of facts. Having said that, where there are several "facts available" from which to choose, an investigating authority must nevertheless evaluate and reason which of the "facts available" reasonably replace the missing "necessary information", with a view to arriving at an accurate determination.

[1089] In this regard, we note the statement of the Appellate Body that these elements of paragraph 7 of Annex II suggest that an investigating authority "should ascertain for itself the *reliability* and *accuracy* of such information by checking it, where practicable, against information contained in other independent sources at its disposal, including material submitted by interested parties". (Appellate Body Report, *Mexico – Anti-Dumping Measures on Rice* para. 289 (emphasis added))

4.6.1.3 Evaluation of India's claim of error

4.427 With these considerations in mind, we turn to assess India's claim on appeal that the Panel erred in its interpretation of Article 12.7 of the SCM Agreement. We recall that India takes issue with the Panel's statement that investigating authorities are not required under Article 12.7 to engage in a comparative evaluation of all available evidence with a view to selecting the best information, or in other words, the most fitting or most appropriate information available.

4.428 We begin with an assessment, in general terms, of whether the Panel's approach to Article 12.7 of the SCM Agreement comports with the Appellate Body's findings in *Mexico – Anti-Dumping Measures on Rice* as discussed above, before turning to India's specific allegation of error. The Panel first noted that Article 12.7 refers to the available "facts", and thus determinations made under its auspices must have a factual foundation.[1090] We find this statement to be unobjectionable. In particular, we have found that, as determinations made under Article 12.7 are to be on the basis of the "facts available", they may not be made on the basis of non-factual assumptions or speculation.

4.429 Second, the Panel noted the Appellate Body's consideration in *Mexico – Anti-Dumping Measures on Rice* of the due process context of Article 12, before citing the Appellate Body's finding in that case that an investigating authority having recourse to Article 12.7 must take into account all the substantiated facts provided by an interested party, and that it must generally limit itself to those facts that reasonably replace the information that an interested party failed to provide.[1091] In the light of these considerations, the Panel articulated its understanding of Article 12.7 in the following terms:

> [T]he standard in Article 12.7 of the SCM Agreement requires that all substantiated facts on the record be taken into account, that "facts available" determinations have a factual foundation, and that "facts available" be generally limited to those facts that may reasonably replace the missing information.[1092]

4.430 In our view, this articulation comports with the interpretation of Article 12.7 by the Appellate Body in *Mexico – Anti-Dumping Measures on Rice* and as set out above. However, we note further that the Appellate Body in that case enunciated the standard for Article 12.7 in the light of its function, namely, to facilitate "arriv[ing] at an *accurate* ... determination".[1093] It is in view of this

---

[1090] Panel Report, para. 7.437 (referring to Panel Report, *China – GOES*, para. 7.296).

[1091] Panel Report, para. 7.438 (referring to Appellate Body Report, *Mexico – Anti-Dumping Measures on Rice*, paras. 292-294).

[1092] Panel Report, para. 7.441.

[1093] Appellate Body Report, *Mexico – Anti-Dumping Measures on Rice*, para. 293. (emphasis added)

function that an investigating authority is generally limited to those facts that may reasonably replace the missing information under Article 12.7.[1094]

4.431 We note that the Panel referenced this function of Article 12.7.[1095] However, the Panel appears to have misunderstood this function in rejecting, without further clarification, India's proposition that Article 12.7 requires a comparative evaluation of all available evidence with a view to identifying the best information, or in other words, the most fitting or appropriate information on the record. Rather, as we explain above, we would expect that a process of reasoning and evaluation in respect of the "facts available" on the record flows from the legal standard for Article 12.7, although the degree and nature of the reasoning and evaluation required will depend on the circumstances of a particular case. Where there are several "facts available" from which to choose, it would seem to follow naturally that the process of reasoning and evaluation would involve a degree of comparison.

4.432 The Panel's reasoning for rejecting India's proposition is founded on the role of Annex II to the Anti-Dumping Agreement in the interpretation of Article 12.7 of the SCM Agreement. In our view, the Panel correctly considered that Annex II to the Anti-Dumping Agreement should not be "imported" into the SCM Agreement, of which it is not a part.[1096] The Panel also correctly noted the Appellate Body's statement in *Mexico – Anti-Dumping Measures on Rice* that the lack of an equivalent, in the SCM Agreement, to Annex II to the Anti-Dumping Agreement gives rise to "important textual differences".[1097] However, the Panel appears to have misread the significance of such "differences" to the interpretation of Article 12.7 of the SCM Agreement. It relied on the lack of an equivalent, in the SCM Agreement, to Annex II to the Anti-Dumping Agreement for differentiating between the *legal standards* under Article 12.7 of the SCM Agreement and Article 6.8 of the Anti-Dumping Agreement. The Appellate Body, however, clarified in *Mexico – Anti-Dumping Measures on Rice* that the absence of an equivalent, in the SCM Agreement, to Annex II to the Anti-Dumping Agreement does not mean that "no such conditions exist in the *SCM Agreement*".[1098] Instead, the Appellate Body used Article 6.8 of the Anti-Dumping Agreement and its Annex II as context to inform the meaning of Article 12.7 of the SCM Agreement.[1099] It found that it would be "anomalous if Article 12.7 of the *SCM Agreement* were to permit the use of 'facts available' in

[1094] Appellate Body Report, *Mexico – Anti-Dumping Measures on Rice*, para. 294.

[1095] Panel Report, fn 729 to para. 7.438 (quoting Appellate Body Report, *Mexico – Anti-Dumping Measures on Rice*, para. 293).

[1096] Panel Report, para. 7.439.

[1097] Panel Report, fn 731 to para. 7.439 (quoting Appellate Body Report, *Mexico – Anti-Dumping Measures on Rice*, para. 290).

[1098] Appellate Body Report, *Mexico – Anti-Dumping Measures on Rice*, para. 291.

[1099] Appellate Body Report, *Mexico – Anti-Dumping Measures on Rice*, para. 295.

countervailing duty investigations in a manner markedly different from that in anti-dumping investigations".[1100]

4.433 In the light of these general observations regarding the Panel's interpretation of Article 12.7, we now turn to India's specific allegation of error. India alleges that the Panel erred in rejecting its proposition that "the findings of the panel in *Mexico – Anti-Dumping Measures on Rice* establish that Article 12.7 of the SCM Agreement requires that investigating authorities engage in a comparative evaluation of all available evidence with a view to selecting the *best* information, i.e. the most fitting or most appropriate information available."[1101] According to India, Article 12.7 includes "an 'obligation of conduct' to engage in a comparative evaluation of all the available evidence, prior to making this determination".[1102] As we understand it, India argues that Article 12.7 requires a comparative evaluation of all available evidence as a necessary pre-requisite to the making of a determination under Article 12.7.

4.434 We consider India's conception of the evaluation that flows from the legal standard for Article 12.7 to be too rigid. Rather, as we have set out above, the extent to which an "evaluation" of the "facts available" is required under Article 12.7, and the form it should take, depend on the particular circumstances of a given case, including the quantity and quality of the available facts on the record, and the types of determinations to be made in a given investigation. In this regard, we recall that the Appellate Body expressed agreement with the standard articulated by the panel in *Mexico – Anti-Dumping Measures on Rice*, including the proposition that "for the conditions of Article 6.8 of the [Anti-Dumping] Agreement and Annex II to be complied with, there can be no better information available to be used in the *particular circumstances*."[1103] Thus, we do not agree with India that the Appellate Body's finding in *Mexico – Anti-Dumping Measures on Rice* stands for the proposition that a "comparative evaluation" is a necessary pre-requisite to making a determination in every instance in which an investigating authority has recourse to the "facts available". Conceivably, there may be circumstances where the kind of "comparative evaluation" envisaged by India is not practicable. For instance, a comparative approach to the evaluation required would not be feasible where there is only one set of reliable information on the record that is relevant to a particular issue and may thus serve as a factual basis for a determination. Thus, we do not accept India's argument that Article 12.7 of the SCM Agreement requires a comparative evaluation of the "facts available" in every case.

[1100] *Ibid.*

[1101] Panel Report, para. 7.439. (emphasis original) See also India's appellant's submission, paras. 210 and 227.

[1102] India's first written submission to the Panel, para. 163.

[1103] Appellate Body Report, *Mexico – Anti-Dumping Measures on Rice*, para. 289 (quoting Panel Report, *Mexico – Anti-Dumping Measures on Rice*, para. 7.166). (emphasis added)

4.435 Turning to the specific statement of the Panel articulating the legal standard of Article 12.7 that is appealed by India, we observe that it is somewhat ambiguous and open to different readings.[1104] On the one hand, it could be read to reject the proposition that Article 12.7 requires, in every case, the kind of "comparative evaluation" referred to in *Mexico – Anti-Dumping Measures on Rice*. When read in this way, we would agree with the statement of the Panel, because, as we have explained above, the extent and nature of the evaluation required will depend on the particular circumstances of a given case. On the other hand, the Panel's statement could be read to expressly exclude, in all instances, a "comparative evaluation" and the use of the "best information" from the legal standard for Article 12.7 of the SCM Agreement. When read in this way, we would disagree with the statement. This is because, as we have explained above, an investigating authority would generally be expected to engage in a process of reasoning and evaluation with regard to the facts on the record as an incident of conforming to the legal standard for Article 12.7, i.e. to ascertain those "facts available" that reasonably replace the missing "necessary information", with a view to arriving at an accurate determination. Where there are several "facts available" from which to choose, it would seem to follow naturally that the process of reasoning and evaluation would involve a degree of comparison. Thus, to the extent that the Panel Report can be read to exclude, in all instances, a comparative evaluation of all available evidence with a view to selecting the best information from the legal standard for Article 12.7 of the SCM Agreement, we *modify* the Panel's finding. We instead *find* that Article 12.7 requires an investigating authority to use "facts available" that reasonably replace the missing "necessary information", with a view to arriving at an accurate determination, which calls for a process of evaluation of available evidence, the extent and nature of which depends on the particular circumstances of a given case.

4.6.2 Whether the Panel erred under Article 11 of the DSU in ascertaining the meaning of Section 1677e(b) of the US Statute and Section 351.308(a)-(c) of the US Regulations

4.436 We turn now to India's alternative claim that the Panel acted inconsistently with Article 11 of the DSU in ascertaining the meaning of the measure at issue, namely, Section 1677e(b) of the US Statute and Section 351.308(a)-(c) of the US Regulations. In particular, India requests us to reverse the Panel's finding that India failed to make a *prima facie* case that the measure at issue is inconsistent with Article 12.7 of the SCM Agreement, on the basis that the Panel erred in applying a legal standard for construing municipal law that is limited to the text of the measure, thus leading to a further error of

[1104] Panel Report, para. 7.439.

disregarding evidence on the record beyond the text of the measure. We begin with a brief overview of the parties' arguments before the Panel, as relevant to India's claim on appeal.[1105]

4.437 The parties agreed before the Panel that the measure is, on the face of its text, permissive in nature.[1106] However, India first submitted before the Panel that discretionary measures are nonetheless capable of being challenged "as such" under WTO jurisprudence, and advanced an argument that appeared to presume that the measure is discretionary. India argued that the evidence it submitted of judicial decisions and the Statement of Administrative Action demonstrate that the measure allows an investigating authority to draw the inference contemplated by the measure solely because that inference is adverse to the party concerned, and not because it is the most appropriate or fitting information available. As an alternative, India submitted that, assuming the Panel were to find that discretionary measures are not capable of being challenged "as such", the measure should be construed as mandatory notwithstanding its text, and advanced a second argument on that premise. In order to demonstrate under this second argument that the measure is *de facto* mandatory, India submitted evidence of judicial decisions, the Statement of Administrative Action, and quantitative and qualitative material on the application of the measure, such as determinations of the USDOC and a datasheet synthesizing aspects of hundreds of determinations. In presenting this evidence, India emphasized that it was not challenging a "practice" or "approach" of the investigating authority as a discrete "measure", but rather submitted evidence relating to the application of the measure as proof of the *de facto* mandatory nature of the measure itself.[1107]

4.438 In response, the United States contested India's characterization of the measure as *de facto* mandatory. In rebutting India's claim, the United States cited evidence relating to the legislative history of the measure, suggesting that the mandatory application of the measure was considered and consciously rejected by its drafters. The United States also produced evidence of instances where the investigating authority had exercised discretion not to apply the measure, or to apply the measure in a manner that does not result in drawing worst possible inferences. Further, the United States argued that India's reliance on evidence of the practice of the investigating authority in applying the measure is unfounded because India did not challenge a "practice" as a "measure", and the alleged "practice" is not reflected in the measure itself. In relation to the operation of the measure, the United States drew the Panel's attention to Section 1677e(c) of the US Statute and Section 351.308(e) of the US Regulations. These provisions

[1105] We note that the evidence referred to in this section is discussed and referenced in more detail in section 4.6.3 below.

[1106] India's first written submission to the Panel, para. 167; United States' first written submission to the Panel, paras. 161-163.

[1107] India's second written submission to the Panel, para. 89.

provide, respectively, where the use of an "adverse inference" includes reliance on "secondary information", this must be corroborated where practicable, and that consideration of information that is submitted by an interested party and is necessary to the determination that is timely, verified, and can be used without undue difficulty will not be declined. For the United States, these provisions demonstrate that the measure is not applied in a mechanistic fashion, but rather that it is possible under the measure to obtain the best, or most fitting and appropriate, information as the "facts available" on which to base a determination, including those facts selected based upon an adverse inference.

4.6.2.1 The Panel's findings

4.439 We note that the Panel's analysis in the Panel Report is limited to the text of the measure itself.[1108] In response to India's request following the circulation of the Interim Report that the Panel reference and evaluate India's evidence beyond the text of the measure pointing to its mandatory operation in practice[1109], the Panel stated:

> ... India's alternative argument at issue relates to whether discretionary measures may be found WTO inconsistent. We have explained at footnote 597 (footnote 722 of the Final Report) that our examination is limited to the US provisions "as such", and not the USDOC's "approach" as a "measure", because India's claims related to the US law "as such". In addition, we have found that the measure at issue is not inconsistent with Article 12.7 of the SCM Agreement. Consequently, as explained at footnote 617 (footnote 742 of the Final Report), we need not address whether the United States' measure at issue is not mandatory and thus cannot breach the United States' obligations under the WTO covered agreements.[1110]

4.440 Footnote 722 to paragraph 7.435 of the Panel Report states:

> The United States submitted that India cannot challenge the USDOC's "approach" to making determinations "as such" because (i) such claim is not within the Panel's terms of reference, and (ii) India has not identified the USDOC's "approach" as a "measure" of general and prospective application that may be challenged "as such". (United States' first written submission, paras. 196-203; and second written submission, para. 121) India clarified that India does not challenge the USDOC's "practice" or "approach" as a "measure", and recalled that India's claims relate to US law "as such", i.e. Sections 1677e(b) and 351.308 (India's second written

[1108] Panel Report, para. 7.442.

[1109] India's comments on the Interim Panel Report, paras. 110 and 113-115.

[1110] Panel Report, para. 6.158.

submission, para. 89) Thus, our examination is limited to the US provisions "as such". We need not and do not examine the USDOC's "approach" as a "measure".

4.441 Footnote 742 to paragraph 7.445 of the Panel Report states, in turn:

> Taking this view [that India has not established a *prima facie* case of inconsistency with Article 12.7], we need not and do not address the United States' argument that the US provisions at issue are not mandatory in nature and thus cannot breach the United States' obligations under the WTO Agreements.[1111]

4.6.2.2 Evaluation of India's claim of error under Article 11 of the DSU

4.442 India requests us to find that the Panel erred under Article 11 of the DSU in applying an incorrect legal standard for construing municipal law in WTO dispute settlement and, consequently, erred in disregarding material evidence on the Panel record. First, India submits that, although the Panel was correct in starting its analysis of the measure by considering its text, the Panel was also required to consider domestic interpretative tools to ensure that it developed an understanding of the measure that is not different to the way it is actually understood and applied by the USDOC. Second, India alleges that the Panel failed to consider the evidence it submitted on the "real understanding of the [measure], as is understood and applied by the USDOC", including evidence of judicial decisions, the Statement of Administrative Action, and quantitative and qualitative material on the application of the measure.[1112] In India's view, this evidence demonstrates the existence of a system created to punish non-cooperation by drawing adverse inferences in every case of non-cooperation, and is thus clearly material to its claim.

4.443 For its part, the United States submits on appeal that India's allegation falls far short of the standard for establishing a breach of Article 11 of the DSU. Rather, the United States argues that the Panel did not err in its appreciation of the ordinary meaning of the text. The United States notes that the meaning of a challenged measure must be determined according to the domestic legal principles in the legal system of the Member maintaining that measure, and that, under US law, a court's statutory interpretation must begin with the ordinary meaning of the text of the statute or regulation, taking account of a federal agency's administrative practice where the text of the statute is ambiguous. The United States further argues that India may not base its claims on arguments relating to a "practice" or "system" that is not reflected in the challenged measure, and that, to the extent India's arguments do not relate to the measure itself, any such claims were outside the Panel's terms of reference and the scope

[1111] Fn reference omitted.

[1112] India's appellant's submission, para. 232.

of the present appeal. Moreover, the United States submits that the fact that the Panel did not refer in its Panel Report to the evidence submitted by India is only indicative of the Panel not affording it the weight or significance India would have liked, and is not sufficient to establish a breach of Article 11 of the DSU. Rather, in the United States' view, an assessment of the evidence beyond the text of the measure supports the Panel's assessment, thus demonstrating that the objectivity of the Panel's assessment was not impaired.

4.444 Before turning to evaluate India's claim before us, we recall the standard articulated by the Appellate Body concerning a panel's duty under Article 11 of the DSU. We have addressed this standard above.[1113] We recall that India claims that the Panel failed to fulfil the standard required of it under Article 11 of the DSU, first, by making an error of law in applying an incorrect legal standard in construing municipal law, and second, as a consequence of that error, by failing to take into account certain evidence.[1114] In view of India's claim, we supplement the above overview of the standard articulated by the Appellate Body regarding a panel's duty under Article 11 of the DSU with the following considerations relating in particular to a panel's obligations in construing municipal law, and in examining the evidence placed on the panel record.

4.445 With regard to the construction of municipal law, the Appellate Body explained in *US – Hot-Rolled Steel* that, "[a]lthough it is not the role of panels or the Appellate Body to interpret a Member's domestic legislation as such, it is permissible, indeed essential, to conduct a detailed examination of that legislation in assessing its consistency with WTO law".[1115] As part of their duties under Article 11 of the DSU, panels have the obligation to examine the meaning and content of the municipal law at issue in order to make an objective assessment of the matter before it, including an objective assessment of the facts of the case and the applicability and conformity with the covered agreements. This obligation under Article 11 means that panels must conduct their own objective and independent assessment of the meaning of municipal law, instead of deferring to a party's characterization of such law.[1116]

4.446 In respect of the types and threshold of evidence that may be required to prove a particular construction of municipal law, the Appellate Body in *US – Corrosion-Resistant Steel Sunset Review* explained that, "[i]f the meaning and content of the measure are clear on its face, then the consistency of the measure as such can be assessed on that basis alone. If, however, the meaning ... is not evident on its face, further examination is required."[1117] The Appellate Body clarified in *US – Carbon Steel* that "[t]he nature and extent of the evidence

---

1113 See *supra*, section 4.3.1.3.

1114 India's appellant's submission, paras. 229 and 230.

1115 Appellate Body Report, *US – Hot-Rolled Steel*, para. 200.

1116 Appellate Body Report, *India – Patents (US)*, para. 66.

1117 Appellate Body Report, *US – Corrosion-Resistant Steel Sunset Review*, para. 168.

required to satisfy the burden of proof will vary from case to case."[1118] Thus, whereas in some cases the text of the relevant legislation may suffice to clarify the content and meaning of the relevant legal instruments, in other cases the complainant will also need to support its understanding of the content and meaning of such legal instruments with evidence beyond the text of the instrument, such as evidence of consistent application of such laws, pronouncements of domestic courts on the meanings of such laws, the opinions of legal experts, and the writings of recognized scholars.[1119] In that regard, the Appellate Body stated in *US – Countervailing and Anti-Dumping Duties (China)* that, "in ascertaining the meaning of municipal law, a panel should undertake a holistic assessment of all relevant elements, starting with the text of the law and including, but not limited to, relevant practices of administering agencies" or legal interpretations of municipal law "given by a domestic court".[1120] In respect of the burden of proof, the Appellate Body in *US – Carbon Steel* also clarified that "[t]he party asserting that another party's municipal law, as such, is inconsistent with relevant treaty obligations bears the burden of introducing evidence as to the scope and meaning of such law to substantiate that assertion."[1121]

4.447 More generally, with regard to a panel's duty under Article 11 of the DSU concerning the examination of evidence, the Appellate Body has found that "in view of the distinction between the respective roles of the Appellate Body and panels, ... we will not interfere lightly with the panel's exercise of its discretion."[1122] Moreover, the Appellate Body will not interfere lightly with a panel's fact-finding authority, and will not base a finding of inconsistency under Article 11 simply on the conclusion that it might have reached a different factual finding.[1123] In other words, not every error allegedly committed by a panel amounts to a violation of Article 11 of the DSU[1124], but only those that are so material that, taken together or singly, they undermine the objectivity of the panel's assessment of the matter before it.[1125] Accordingly, it is insufficient for an appellant simply to disagree with a statement or to assert that it is not supported by evidence. Indeed, the Appellate Body has held that panels are not required to accord to factual evidence of the parties the same meaning and weight as do the parties.[1126] Instead, for a claim to succeed under Article 11, the

---

[1118] Appellate Body Report, *US – Carbon Steel*, para. 157.

[1119] Appellate Body Reports, *US – Countervailing and Anti-Dumping Measures (China)*, para. 4.101; *US – Carbon Steel*, para. 157.

[1120] Appellate Body Report, *US – Countervailing and Anti-Dumping Duties (China)*, para. 4.101.

[1121] Appellate Body Report, *US – Carbon Steel*, para. 157 (referring to Appellate Body Report, *US – Wool Shirts and Blouses*, p. 14, DSR 1997:I, p. 335).

[1122] Appellate Body Report, *US – Wheat Gluten*, para. 151. (fn omitted)

[1123] Appellate Body Report, *Philippines – Distilled Spirits*, para. 136.

[1124] Appellate Body Report, *EC – Fasteners (China)*, para. 442.

[1125] Appellate Body Reports, *EC – Fasteners (China)*, para. 499; *EC and certain member States – Large Civil Aircraft*, para. 1318.

[1126] Appellate Body Report, *Australia – Salmon*, para. 267.

Appellate Body must be satisfied that the panel has exceeded its authority as initial trier of facts.

4.448 As the initial trier of facts, a panel must provide reasoned and adequate explanations and coherent reasoning[1127], and must base its finding on a sufficient evidentiary basis.[1128] Moreover, a participant claiming that a panel disregarded certain evidence must explain why the evidence is so material to its case that the panel's failure to address such evidence has a bearing on the objectivity of the panel's assessment.[1129] In *Brazil – Retreaded Tyres*, the Appellate Body further clarified that "[a] panel enjoys discretion in assessing whether a given piece of evidence is relevant for its reasoning, and is not required to discuss, in its report, each and every piece of evidence."[1130] The Appellate Body, however, has found fault with panels that have deliberately disregarded evidence that was relevant to one of the parties.[1131]

4.449 With these considerations in mind, we turn to whether the Panel discharged its duty under Article 11 of the DSU in its consideration of the measure at issue. India submits that, although the Panel was correct in starting its analysis of the measure by considering its text, the Panel failed to consider the evidence submitted beyond the text of the measure in ascertaining its meaning.

4.450 As we have recounted above, the Appellate Body has described it as "essential" that a panel "conduct a detailed examination of [domestic] legislation in assessing its consistency with WTO law".[1132] Further, the Appellate Body has stated that:

> [t]he party asserting that another party's municipal law, as such, is inconsistent with relevant treaty obligations bears the burden of introducing evidence as to the scope and meaning of such law to substantiate that assertion. Such evidence will typically be produced in the form of the text of the relevant legislation or legal instruments, which may be supported, as appropriate, by evidence of the consistent application of such laws, the pronouncements of domestic courts on the meaning of such laws, the opinions of legal experts and the writings of recognized scholars.[1133]

4.451 Where a party seeks to support its argument on the construction of a measure with evidence beyond its text, "a panel should undertake a holistic assessment of all relevant elements, starting with the text of the law and

[1127] Appellate Body Report, *US – Upland Cotton (Article 21.5 – Brazil)*, fn 618 to para. 293.

[1128] See Appellate Body Report, *US – Carbon Steel*, para. 142. (fn omitted)

[1129] Appellate Body Report, *EC – Fasteners (China)*, para. 442.

[1130] Appellate Body Report, *Brazil – Retreaded Tyres*, para. 202. (fns omitted)

[1131] See Appellate Body Reports, *EC – Hormones*, para. 133; and *US/Canada – Continued Suspension*, para. 615.

[1132] Appellate Body Report, *US – Hot-Rolled Steel*, para. 200. (fn omitted)

[1133] Appellate Body Report, *US – Carbon Steel*, para. 157. (fn omitted)

including, but not limited to, relevant practices of administering agencies" or "domestic court ruling[s]".[1134]

4.452 In the case at hand, India submitted evidence to support its argument that the measure should be construed as mandatory in the form of judicial decisions, the Statement of Administrative Action, and quantitative and qualitative material on the application of the measure. In India's view, this evidence demonstrated the "real understanding of the [measure], as is understood and applied by the USDOC".[1135] In rebutting these claims, the United States also submitted evidence beyond the text of the measure. In particular, it produced a document on the legislative history of the measure, suggesting that the mandatory application of the measure was considered and consciously rejected by its drafters, in addition to evidence of instances in which it argued that the investigating authority had exercised discretion not to apply the measure, or to apply the measure in a manner that does not result in drawing the worst possible inferences.[1136] Thus, the United States contended that the measure is, properly construed, discretionary in nature. Further, the United States argued that the alleged "practice" in applying the measure is not reflected in the measure itself, and thus cannot be used as evidence in its construction.[1137]

4.453 It was in this evidentiary context that the Panel was called upon to undertake an assessment of the meaning of the measure at issue in order to evaluate whether it is inconsistent "as such" with Article 12.7 of the SCM Agreement. In this regard, we recall that the Panel's assessment of the measure was limited to reproducing excerpts of its text and making some rather cursory observations.[1138] The Panel did not explain the legal standard it applied in its construction of the measure at issue. The Panel's discussion of India's claim that the measure is, properly construed, mandatory in nature, is confined to the statements extracted above, including that "our examination is limited to the US provisions 'as such', and not the USDOC's 'approach' as a 'measure'", and that, having found no inconsistency on the basis of the text of the measure, "we need not and do not address the United States' argument that the US provisions at issue are not mandatory in nature".[1139] Beyond these statements, there is no discussion or explanation in the Panel Report as to why the Panel omitted to consider or address the evidence beyond the text of the measure that had been submitted to it.

4.454 We recall that the Appellate Body explained in *US – Hot-Rolled Steel* that it is "essential" for a panel "to conduct a detailed examination of ... legislation in

[1134] Appellate Body Report, *US – Countervailing and Anti-Dumping Measures (China)*, para. 4.101.
[1135] India's appellant's submission, para. 232.
[1136] United States' first written submission to the Panel, paras. 167 and 168; second written submission to the Panel, para. 123; appellee's submission, paras. 473-476.
[1137] United States' first written submission to the Panel, paras. 196-210.
[1138] Panel Report, para. 7.442.
[1139] Panel Report, para. 6.158 and fn 742 to para. 7.445.

assessing its consistency with WTO law".[1140] In our view, in order to conduct a "detailed examination" of the measure at issue, and to engage in an "objective assessment of the matter", it is incumbent on a panel to engage in a thorough analysis of the measure on its face and to address evidence submitted by a party that the alleged inconsistency with the covered agreements arises from a particular manner in which a measure is applied. While a review of such evidence may ultimately reveal that it is not particularly relevant, that it lacks probative value, or that it is not of a nature or significance to establish a *prima facie* case, this can only be determined after its probative value has been reviewed and assessed. In the case at hand, India argued that the evidence it presented demonstrated the existence of a system created to punish non-cooperation by drawing adverse inferences in every case of non-cooperation, which is not apparent from the plain language on the face of the measure, and was pivotal to India's claim. Indeed, in view of India's claim, both parties engaged in elaborate and meaningful argumentation before the Panel and submitted substantial evidence throughout the Panel proceedings in relation to the meaning of the measure at issue.[1141] In the circumstances of this case, a "detailed examination" of the measure at issue called for the Panel to consider and address the measure on its face and the evidence submitted beyond its text.

4.455 We recall that the United States submits that the omission of the Panel to refer to the evidence presented by India is not sufficient to establish a violation of Article 11 of the DSU, and shows only that the Panel did not attribute to it the weight or significance that India would have liked. We note, however, that the Panel responded to India's request that it consider the evidence presented by India beyond the text of the measure by stating that its "examination is limited to the US provisions 'as such'", and that it "need not and do[es] not examine the USDOC's 'approach' as a 'measure'".[1142] It is implicit from the context in which the Panel made this statement, namely, in response to India's request that it address the evidence beyond the text of the measure, that the Panel considered it unnecessary to consider evidence concerning the application of the measure. The Panel also stated that it "need not and do[es] not address the United States' argument that the US provisions at issue are not mandatory in nature".[1143] The United States' argument in this regard was in rebuttal to India's argument that the measure is mandatory. The Panel's statement therefore seems to indicate that it also declined to address the argumentation and evidence provided by India on the allegedly mandatory nature of the measure. These statements of the Panel suggest to us that, rather than considering the evidence and declining to ascribe

---

[1140] Appellate Body Report, *US – Hot-Rolled Steel*, para. 200.

[1141] United States' first written submission to the Panel, paras. 167, 168, 196, and 204-207; United States' second written submission to the Panel, paras. 120, 123, and 124; India's first written submission to the Panel, paras. 178-188; India's second written submission to the Panel, paras. 93-96.

[1142] Panel Report, paras. 6.158 and fn 722 to para. 7.435.

[1143] Panel Report, fn 742 to para. 7.445.

it probative value, the Panel in fact did not consider evidence submitted by the parties beyond the text of the measure at issue.[1144]

4.456 Thus, we *find* that the Panel failed to comply with its duty under Article 11 of the DSU to make an objective assessment of the matter before it by disregarding the evidence submitted by the parties beyond the text of the measure at issue. Consequently, we *reverse* the Panel's finding, in paragraphs 7.445 and 8.3.h of the Panel Report, that India failed to establish a *prima facie* case that Section 1677e(b) of the US Statute and Section 351.308(a)-(c) of the US Regulations are inconsistent "as such" with Article 12.7 of the SCM Agreement.

4.6.3 Completion of the legal analysis of whether the measure at issue is "as such" inconsistent with Article 12.7 of the SCM Agreement

4.6.3.1 Introduction

4.457 We have developed above our interpretation of Article 12.7 of the SCM Agreement and we have modified the Panel's finding relating to the interpretation of Article 12.7 accordingly. We have also found that the Panel erred under Article 11 of the DSU in failing to take into account evidence beyond the text of the measure at issue, and have consequently reversed the Panel's finding that India failed to establish a *prima facie* case that the measure at issue is "as such" inconsistent with Article 12.7 of the SCM Agreement. India requests, on either basis, that we complete the legal analysis and find that the measure at issue is "as such" inconsistent with Article 12.7 of the SCM Agreement. We thus turn to consider whether we are in a position to complete the legal analysis.

4.458 Before the Panel, India presented two alternative claims alleging that the measure at issue is inconsistent with Article 12.7 of the SCM Agreement. First, India submitted that drawing an inference that is adverse to the interests of a non-cooperating party is not permitted under Article 12.7. In particular, India alleged that the measure at issue authorizes an investigating authority to draw the inference contemplated by the measure solely because it is adverse to the party concerned, and not because it is the most appropriate or fitting information available. Second, in the alternative, India submitted that, although the measure at issue states that an inference that is adverse to the interests of a non-cooperating party may be drawn, it more accurately means, in reality, that in all cases of a finding that a party has not cooperated to the best of its ability, the USDOC necessarily draws such an inference by imposing the highest possible

[1144] We note that the Appellate Body has "not, as yet, been required to pronounce generally upon the continuing relevance or significance of the mandatory/discretionary distinction" in respect of "as such" claims. (Appellate Body Report, *US – Corrosion-Resistant Steel Sunset Review*, para. 93 (fn omitted))

margin against that party. India submitted that such inferences are drawn without examining all of the evidence or engaging in a comparative assessment of such evidence to utilize the most appropriate or fitting information.

4.459 At the outset, we note that, on a number of occasions, the Appellate Body has completed the legal analysis with a view to facilitating the prompt settlement and effective resolution of the dispute.[1145] In previous disputes, the Appellate Body has completed the legal analysis when sufficient factual findings by the panel and undisputed facts on the panel record allowed it to do so.[1146]

4.460 In the present case, it is the Panel's omission to take into account, weigh, and assess certain evidence beyond the text of the measure at issue that gave rise to our finding of error under Article 11 of the DSU. It would thus be inappropriate to seek to complete the legal analysis on the basis of the Panel's findings on the meaning of the measure on its face. Rather, where a party alleges that the meaning of a challenged measure diverges in practice from the understanding that might appear warranted when its plain text is read in isolation, a holistic assessment of the measure calls for consideration of all relevant elements of evidence submitted by the parties.[1147] As discussed above, this may include evidence on the consistent application of the measure, the pronouncements of domestic courts on its meaning, the opinions of legal experts and the writings of recognized scholars.[1148] Certainly, it may be the case that particular practices or approaches developed in the application of the measure are distinct from the measure itself and are accordingly not relevant to its construction. However, this may only be determined after having regard to the relevant evidence. This cannot be determined if evidence on the application of a measure is disregarded in the first instance.

4.461 Although the Panel's findings on the meaning of the measure do not provide a basis for completing the analysis as they were reached on a flawed approach, we nonetheless see no inherent impediments to engaging with the evidence submitted by the parties to the Panel. By and large, the participants do not dispute the veracity or factual existence of the relevant documents submitted as evidence, including judicial decisions, the Statement of Administrative Action, the legislative history of the measure, and quantitative and qualitative

[1145] See e.g. Appellate Body Reports, *Australia – Salmon*, paras. 117-136; *US – Wheat Gluten*, paras. 80-92; and *Canada – Aircraft (Article 21.5 – Brazil)*, paras. 43-52.

[1146] See e.g. Appellate Body Reports, *US – Gasoline*, p. 19, DSR 1996:I, p. 18; *Canada – Periodicals*, p. 24, DSR 1997:I, p. 469; *EC – Poultry*, para. 156; *EC – Hormones*, para. 222; *US – Shrimp*, paras. 123 and 124; *Japan – Agricultural Products II*, para. 112; *US – FSC*, para. 133; *Australia – Salmon*, paras. 117 and 118; *US – Lamb*, paras. 150 and 172; *US – Section 211 Appropriations Act*, para. 352; *EC and certain member States – Large Civil Aircraft*, paras. 1174-1178; and *US – Large Civil Aircraft (2nd complaint)*, paras. 1272-1274.

[1147] Appellate Body Report, *US – Countervailing and Anti-Dumping Measures (China)*, para. 4.101.

[1148] Appellate Body Report, *US – Carbon Steel*, para. 157.

material on the application of the measure.[1149] Rather, the participants dispute the conclusions or inferences drawn from each other's evidence, such as the appropriate relevance, meaning, and probative value to be ascribed to such evidence, including through the submission of rebuttal evidence. Further, we recall that the issue under consideration was addressed by both parties in each of their first and second written submissions to the Panel, all of which included evidence that engaged and rebutted their respective positions.[1150] This suggests that the parties availed themselves of the opportunity to submit evidence, including supplementary evidence, on the meaning of the measure at issue. We thus proceed to examine whether we are in a position to complete the legal analysis on the basis of the uncontested evidence on the meaning and scope of the measure at issue on the Panel record.

4.462 This task is to be performed on the basis of a construction of the measure that takes into account all relevant elements pursuant to the correct legal standard for construing municipal law in WTO dispute settlement. Thus, in assessing the consistency of the measure at issue, we will engage in a holistic assessment of all relevant elements, beginning with an examination of the text of the measure at issue, before turning to the other elements of evidence on its meaning submitted by the parties.

4.6.3.2 The text of Section 1677e(b) of the US Statute and Section 351.308(a)-(c) of the US Regulations

4.463 India has presented two alternative claims in its request for finding that the measure is "as such" inconsistent with Article 12.7 of the SCM Agreement. Under its first claim, India submits that the very grant of an authorization in the text of the measure to draw an inference that is adverse to the interests of non-cooperating parties, merely on the basis of their non-cooperation, is inconsistent with Article 12.7. This is because, in India's view, the use of an "inference that is adverse to the interests" of a non-cooperating party pursuant to the measure involves non-factual speculation as to the motivation behind the omission to cooperate, and represents a "punitive application" of the "facts available"

[1149] In particular, in its written submissions to the Panel, the United States did not dispute the facts submitted by India, but rather the inferences to be drawn from them. (United States' first written submission to the Panel, paras. 167, 168, and 204-207; second written submission to the Panel, paras. 120, 123, and 124) Similarly, while India contested the United States' characterization of some of the facts submitted by the United States, it did not contest the veracity or accuracy of those underlying facts. (India's opening statement at the first Panel meeting, para. 27; second written submission to the Panel, paras. 93-96)

[1150] United States' first written submission to the Panel, paras. 167, 168, 196, and 204-207; United States' second written submission to the Panel, paras. 120, 123, and 124; India's first written submission to the Panel, paras. 173, 174, 186, and 187; India's second written submission to the Panel, paras. 93-96.

standard.[1151] In the alternative, India submits that the text of Sections 1677e(b) and 351.308(a)-(c) is "innocuous"[1152], but that evidence beyond the text of the measure establishes the inconsistency of the measure with Article 12.7 of the SCM Agreement. Under this claim, we understand that India does not take issue with the plain text of the measure *per se*, but rather with the manner in which it is interpreted and applied in practice.

4.464 India's first claim calls on us to assess whether, pursuant to the authorization contained in the text of the measure, the investigating authority is required to act inconsistently with Article 12.7. We begin by extracting the text of the measure, including the additional elements referred to by the United States.[1153]

4.465 In particular, Section 1677e(a)-(c) of the US Statute provides that:

> § 1677e. Determinations on basis of facts available
>
> (a) In general
>
> If—
>
> (1) necessary information is not available on the record, or
>
> (2) an interested party or any other person—
>
> (A) withholds information that has been requested by the administering authority or the Commission under this subtitle,
>
> (B) fails to provide such information by the deadlines for submission of the information or in the form and manner requested, subject to subsections (c)(1) and (e) of section 1677m of this title,
>
> (C) significantly impedes a proceeding under this subtitle, or

[1151] India's first written submission to the Panel, paras. 172 and 524; response to questioning at the oral hearing.

[1152] India's appellant's submission, paras. 232 and 239.

[1153] United States' first written submission to the Panel, para. 171 (referring to Determinations on basis of facts available, *United States Code*, Title 19, Chapter 4, Subtitle IV, Section 1677e (Panel Exhibit USA-12) and Determinations on the basis of the facts available, *United States Code of Federal Regulations*, Title 19, Vol. 3, Chapter III, Part 351, Section 351.308 (Panel Exhibit USA-13)); United States' appellee's submission, para. 461; Panel Report, fn 736 to para. 7.442. India challenges Section 1677e(b) of the US Statute and Section 351.308(a)-(c) of the US Regulations. The United States additionally refers to subparagraphs (a) and (c) of Section 1677e of the US Statute and subparagraphs (d) and (e) of Section 351.308 of the US Regulations as elements relevant to understanding the measure.

(D) provides such information but the information cannot be verified as provided in section 1677m(i) of this title,

the administering authority and the Commission shall, subject to section 1677m(d) of this title, use the facts otherwise available in reaching the applicable determination under this subtitle.

(b) Adverse inferences

If the administering authority or the Commission (as the case may be) finds that an interested party has failed to cooperate by not acting to the best of its ability to comply with a request for information from the administering authority or the Commission, the administering authority or the Commission (as the case may be), in reaching the applicable determination under this subtitle, may use an inference that is adverse to the interests of that party in selecting from among the facts otherwise available. Such adverse inference may include reliance on information derived from—

(1) the petition,

(2) a final determination in the investigation under this subtitle,

(3) any previous review under section 1675 of this title or determination under section 1675b of this title, or

(4) any other information placed on the record.

(c) Corroboration of secondary information

When the administering authority or the Commission relies on secondary information rather than on information obtained in the course of an investigation or review, the administering authority or the Commission, as the case may be, shall, to the extent practicable, corroborate that information from independent sources that are reasonably at their disposal.

4.466 Additionally, Section 351.308(a)-(e) of the US Regulations provides:

(a) *Introduction.* The Secretary may make determinations on the basis of the facts available whenever necessary information is not available on the record, an interested party or any other person withholds or fails to provide information requested in a timely manner and in the form required or significantly impedes a proceeding, or the Secretary is unable to verify submitted information. If the Secretary finds that an interested party "has failed to cooperate by not acting to the best of its ability to comply with a request for information," the Secretary may use an inference that is adverse to the interests of that party in selecting from among the facts otherwise available. This section lists some of the sources of information upon which the Secretary may base an adverse inference and explains the actions the Secretary will take with respect to corroboration of information.

(b) *In general*. The Secretary may make a determination under the Act and this part based on the facts otherwise available in accordance with section 776(a) of the Act.

(c) *Adverse inferences*. For purposes of section 776(b) of the Act, an adverse inference may include reliance on:

(1) Secondary information, such as information derived from:

(i) The petition;

(ii) A final determination in a countervailing duty investigation or an antidumping investigation;

(iii) Any previous administrative review, new shipper review, expedited antidumping review, section 753 review, or section 762 review; or

(2) Any other information placed on the record.

(d) *Corroboration of secondary information*. Under section 776(c) of the Act, when the Secretary relies on secondary information, the Secretary will, to the extent practicable, corroborate that information from independent sources that are reasonably at the Secretary's disposal. Independent sources may include, but are not limited to, published price lists, official import statistics and customs data, and information obtained from interested parties during the instant investigation or review. Corroborate means that the Secretary will examine whether the secondary information to be used has probative value. The fact that corroboration may not be practicable in a given circumstance will not prevent the Secretary from applying an adverse inference as appropriate and using the secondary information in question.

(e) *Use of certain information*. In reaching a determination under the Act and this part, the Secretary will not decline to consider information that is submitted by an interested party and is necessary to the determination but does not meet all the applicable requirements established by the Secretary if the conditions listed under section 782(e) of the Act are met.

4.467 We begin by noting that determinations under the measure at issue, as specified in Section 351.308(a) of the US Regulations, must be made "on the basis of the *facts* available".[1154] We further note that Section 1677e(b) of the US Statute stipulates that an inference used pursuant to the measure may include reliance on information derived from the petition, from a final determination, from any previous review under Section 1675 or determination under Section 1675b, or from any other information placed on the record. Moreover, Section 351.308(a)-(e) of the US Regulations lists the types of information on which an inference may be based, such as information derived from the written application of the domestic industry (petition), final determinations in a countervailing duty investigation or anti-dumping investigation, and any previous administrative review. From these aspects of the measure on its face, we understand that determinations made under its auspices must have a factual foundation. This comports with the requirement of Article 12.7 that determinations must be based on facts and may not be made on the basis of non-factual assumptions or speculation.

4.468 The use of the inference contemplated by the measure is part of a process of "selecting from among the facts otherwise available" on which to base such a determination.[1155] In this regard, we recall our finding that, as part of the process of reasoning and evaluating which "facts available" constitute reasonable replacements for the missing "necessary information", an investigating authority may use inferences. Further, as part of the process of reasoning and evaluating which "facts available" constitute reasonable replacements, the procedural circumstances in which information is missing, including the non-cooperation of an interested party, may be taken into account. We note, however, that the use of inferences in order to select adverse facts that punish non-cooperation would lead to an inaccurate determination and thus not accord with Article 12.7. Further, as we have considered above, procedural circumstances and any resulting inferences may not alone form the basis of a determination. Rather, determinations pursuant to Article 12.7 must be made on the basis of "facts" that reasonably replace the "necessary information" that is missing.

4.469 India claims that Article 12.7 prohibits the grant of the authorization to use an inference that is "adverse to the interests" of a non-cooperating party in the measure. In our view, however, the authorization to use an inference that is "adverse to the interests" of a non-cooperating party is not necessarily inconsistent with Article 12.7. As we see it, the permissibility of using an inference derived from the procedural circumstances in which information is missing, as part of selecting from the "facts available", depends on whether such use comports with the legal standard for Article 12.7. This is to be determined in the light of the particular circumstances of a given case. In this regard, we note that India claims that, pursuant to the measure, the inference is used in a

[1154] Emphasis added.

[1155] See *supra*, paras. 4.465 and 4.466.

mechanical or reflexive manner in all cases of non-cooperation. On its face, however, and without prejudice to our consideration in the next section of the other evidence submitted by the parties on the meaning of the measure, the measure is framed in permissive terms. In particular, it states that the investigating authority "*may* use an inference that is adverse to the interests of that party".[1156] We consider that, in the light of this permissive framing of the text of the measure, the use of the inference is capable of being limited to those instances where it accords with the legal standard for Article 12.7 of the SCM Agreement. At the same time, the explanation provided by the investigating authority in its published report must be sufficient to allow a panel to assess whether the "facts available" employed by the investigating authority resulted from a process of reasoning and analysis, including an assessment of whether the use of an inference comports with the legal standard of Article 12.7 we have set out above.

4.470 For the foregoing reasons, we do not consider that the measure at issue, on its face, requires the investigating authority to act inconsistently with Article 12.7.

4.6.3.3 Other evidence relating to the meaning and construction of Section 1677e(b) of the US Statute and Section 351.308(a)-(c) of the US Regulations

4.471 India submits in the alternative that, notwithstanding the innocuous appearances in the text of the measure, the evidence it submitted to the Panel record beyond the text of the measure on its meaning demonstrates the existence of a system created to punish non-cooperation by drawing adverse inferences in every case of non-cooperation so as to penalize the non-cooperating party. According to India, this evidence demonstrates that the investigating authority assumes in all cases of non-cooperation that the worst possible information is appropriate. This necessarily precludes the investigating authority from taking into account all of the substantiated facts on the record and from identifying reasonable replacements for the missing information. The United States, by contrast, submits that India cannot base its claims on arguments relating to a "practice" that is not reflected in the measure at issue, and that, in any event, the evidence relied upon by India does not sustain its claim. The United States also points to other evidence on the application of the measure in practice that, in its view, demonstrates that the measure need not be applied in all cases of non-cooperation to select the worst possible information.

4.472 We recall that the Panel was required to examine the evidence submitted by the parties on the meaning of the measure pursuant to the correct legal standard for construing municipal law in WTO dispute settlement. As the

[1156] Emphasis added. See *supra*, paras. 4.465 and 4.466.

Appellate Body has held, a "panel should undertake a holistic assessment of all relevant elements."[1157]

4.473 In the present case, we note that the Panel did not make findings on the meaning of the measure that took into account the evidence submitted by the parties beyond its text. We therefore cannot rely on findings by the Panel in considering the completion of the legal analysis. However, we recall that the parties submitted evidence to the Panel beyond the text of the measure to support their arguments in respect of its meaning. The participants do not, by and large, dispute the factual existence or content of the relevant documents submitted in this regard, including judicial decisions, the Statement of Administrative Action, the legislative history of the measure, and quantitative and qualitative material on the application of the measure. Rather, the participants disagree on the appropriate relevance, meaning, and probative value to be ascribed to these documents. In particular, the participants contest whether it can be established from this evidence that the measure requires the drawing of an adverse inference and the use of the worst possible information in making a determination on the "facts available" in every case of non-cooperation, notwithstanding the discretionary nature of the measure on its face. We thus assess the extent to which this evidence sustains this proposition. In doing so, we examine the legal value, relevance, and import of the judicial decisions, the Statement of Administrative Action, the legislative history of the measure, and the quantitative and qualitative material on the application of the measure, including the determinations of the USDOC and a datasheet synthesizing aspects of hundreds of determinations submitted by India and extracts of cases and determinations submitted by the United States, as relevant to the completion analysis. We note, however, that the absence of pertinent findings or consideration in the Panel Report magnifies the complexity of our assessment, and may make it more difficult for us to resolve ambiguities. We begin with the judicial decisions submitted to the Panel record, and then turn to the Statement of Administrative Action and the legislative history of the measure, before considering the quantitative and qualitative material on the application of the measure in practice.

4.474 Turning first to the judicial decisions referred to by India, we observe that these suggest that the measure should be understood as a discretionary measure rather than a binding requirement to apply adverse inferences in all cases of non-cooperation.[1158] In particular, the court in Hyosung Corporation v. United States stated "it is within Commerce's *discretion* to presume that the highest prior

[1157] Appellate Body Report, *US – Countervailing and Anti-Dumping Measures (China)*, para. 4.101. This may include, *inter alia*, the "consistent application of such laws, pronouncements of domestic courts on the meanings of such laws, the opinions of legal experts, and the writings of recognized scholars". (Appellate Body Report, *US – Carbon Steel*, para. 157)

[1158] Hyosung Corporation v. United States (Panel Exhibit IND-47), p. 7; Essar Steel Ltd v. United States (Panel Exhibit IND-49B), p. 1274; Mueller Comercial de Mexico v. United States (Panel Exhibit IND-49A), p. 1368.

margin reflects the current margins"[1159], and the court in Essar Steel Ltd v. United States referred to the USDOC's "power", "authority", and "ability" to have recourse to the measure.[1160] In this regard, we recall that the participants do not contest that the measure is, on its face, discretionary in nature.[1161]

4.475 The cases of Mueller Comercial de Mexico v. United States and Essar Steel Ltd v. United States point to a role for the objective of inducing cooperation in applying the measure.[1162] For instance, the court in Essar Steel Ltd v. United States stated that "[a]n appropriate decision based on adverse facts is 'a reasonably accurate estimate of the respondent's actual rate, albeit with some built-in increase intended as a deterrent to non-compliance'."[1163] In contrast, the case of Rhone Poulenc, Inc. v. United States[1164] points to accuracy as the goal for applying the inference in the measure. It stated that "determining current margins as accurately as possible" is the "basic purpose of the statute", and described the compliance function of the measure as an unintended consequence.[1165]

4.476 The cases of Mueller Comercial de Mexico v. United States and Rhone Poulenc, Inc. v. United States suggest that, in applying the measure, the investigating authority has developed a "practice" of presuming that the highest prior non-*de minimis* subsidy rate constitutes the best information of current margins in instances of non-cooperation.[1166] In this regard, we recall that India clarified that it did not challenge the "practice" of the USDOC in the application of the measure "as such", but rather sought to rely on such a "practice" to shed light on the meaning of the instruments challenged as the "measure".[1167] The court in Rhone Poulenc, Inc. v. United States referred to the "agency's presumption" of applying the "highest prior margin [as] the most probative evidence of current margins" where an interested party fails to respond to a request for information.[1168] The court in Mueller Comercial de Mexico v. United States referred to the USDOC's "usual practice ... to assign an uncooperative respondent the highest overall rate from any segment of the proceeding as [adverse facts available]."[1169] These cases also suggest that this presumption is

[1159] Hyosung Corporation v. United States, p. 7. (emphasis added; internal citations omitted)

[1160] Essar Steel Ltd v. United States, pp. 1274, 1276, and 1278.

[1161] India's appellant's submission, paras. 232 and 239; India's first written submission to the Panel, para. 167; India's opening statement at the second Panel meeting, para. 21; United States' appellee's submission, para. 452.

[1162] Mueller Comercial de Mexico v. United States, p. 1365; Essar Steel Ltd v. United States, p. 1276.

[1163] Essar Steel Ltd v. United States, p. 1276. (internal citation omitted)

[1164] Panel Exhibit IND-48.

[1165] Rhone Poulenc, Inc. v. United States, p. 1191.

[1166] Mueller Comercial de Mexico v. United States, p. 1371; Rhone Poulenc, Inc. v. United States, pp. 1190-1191.

[1167] India's second written submission to the Panel, para. 89.

[1168] Rhone Poulenc, Inc. v. United States, pp. 1190-1191.

[1169] Mueller Comercial de Mexico v. United States, p. 1366. (fn omitted)

"rebuttable" and the USDOC may "depart" from it and, further, that the "practice" of the investigating authority is based on the discretion afforded by the measure, rather than being required by it.[1170] For instance, the court in Rhone Poulenc, Inc. v. United States stated that the measure "*allows* the agency to make such a presumption".[1171] Further, the "practice" appears to be subject to rules and disciplines separate from the measure itself.[1172] The court in Mueller Comercial de Mexico v. United States found that "any decision to abandon the application of this rate in favor of the highest transaction specific rate for another respondent in a previous review must be fully explained and based on substantial evidence", or would otherwise be "arbitrary".[1173]

4.477 These aspects suggest that the "practice" of presumptively applying the highest prior non-*de minimis* subsidy rate does not form an integral part of the measure itself, and is not necessarily applied in all instances of non-cooperation. Thus, the judicial decisions referred to by India do not appear to support the proposition that the measure at issue is mandatory in requiring the use of the worst possible information in all cases of non-cooperation.

4.478 We turn next to the Statement of Administrative Action, submitted by India as evidence of a binding statutory interpretation of the measure to the Panel, and a document submitted by the United States on the legislative history of Section 351.308 of the US Regulations. Our review of the Statement of Administrative Action suggests that, in applying the measure, investigating authorities "must make their determinations based on all evidence of record, weighing the record evidence to determine that which is most probative of the issue under consideration".[1174] This suggests that, in a determination pursuant to the measure at issue, investigating authorities are required to take into account all substantiated facts to identify the most probative evidence on which to base their determination. Our review of the document on the legislative history of Section 351.308 of the US Regulations suggests that the measure provides authority to the USDOC rather than requiring the drawing of adverse inferences in all instances of non-cooperation.[1175] In response to proposals that the regulations be framed in a mandatory manner, the document states that "[t]he Department does not agree that the imposition of adverse inferences is mandatory".[1176] In our view, therefore, the Statement of Administrative Action and the legislative history of the measure do not support India's proposition that the measure is mandatorily applied in all cases of non-cooperation without

1170 Rhone Poulenc, Inc. v. United States, pp. 1190-1191; Mueller Comercial de Mexico v. United States, pp. 1368-1371.

1171 Rhone Poulenc, Inc. v. United States, p. 1190. (emphasis added)

1172 Mueller Comercial de Mexico v. United States, pp. 1368-1371.

1173 Mueller Comercial de Mexico v. United States, p. 1371.

1174 Statement of Administrative Action, p. 131.

1175 Final Rule on Antidumping and Countervailing Duties (Panel Exhibit USA-14), p. 27340.

1176 Final Rule on Antidumping and Countervailing Duties, p. 27340.

examining all evidence or engaging in a comparative assessment of such evidence to use the most appropriate or fitting information.

4.479 Finally, we turn to consider the evidence submitted to the Panel record in relation to particular instances of application of the measure. We recall that India submitted documents to the Panel record in order to establish that the measure had been applied in many instances routinely and mechanically to always draw the worst possible inference.[1177] We further recall that such "worst possible inferences" include determinations that a subsidy is specific, or that an exporter benefited from an alleged programme, as well as applying the highest prior non-*de minimis* subsidy rates.[1178] India contends that this evidence represents a consistent and systematic application of the measure, which contributes to proving the existence, as part of the measure, of a system created to punish non-cooperation by drawing adverse inferences in every case of non-cooperation.

4.480 We recall, however, that our review above of the judicial decisions referred to by India suggests that any "practice" of the investigating authority in applying the measure is not required by the measure, but is rather developed pursuant to the discretion afforded by the measure. The "practice" also appears to be distinct and separate from the measure at issue.[1179] It is therefore not clear to us why a number of instances of the application of the measure should, in this case, conclusively establish the meaning of the measure at issue in general, which in this case is confined to Section 1677e(b) of the US Statute and Section 351.308(a)-(c) of the US Regulations.[1180] In any event, we note that the United States placed a number of cases on the Panel record where the "worst possible inference" was not applied in instances of non-cooperation. On their face, these instances appear to demonstrate that, in cases of non-cooperation, it is possible for an investigating authority to use facts other than those reflected by the worst possible inference.[1181] For example, where there is information on the record that

[1177] See Table of relevant USDOC determinations regarding the application of "adverse facts available" provisions in administrative reviews (Panel Exhibit IND-71).

[1178] India's appellant's submission, para. 231.

[1179] We recall that one court found that "any decision to abandon the application of this rate in favor of the highest transaction specific rate for another respondent in a previous review must be fully explained and based on substantial evidence", or would otherwise be "arbitrary". (Mueller Comercial de Mexico v. United States, p. 1371)

[1180] In this regard, we recall that India expressly clarified that it did not challenge the "practice" of the USDOC in the application of the measure "as such". (India's second written submission to the Panel, para. 89)

[1181] We agree with India (see India's second written submission to the Panel, para. 95) that one of the instances provided by the United States does not fully support the United States' claim (namely, USDOC, Final Affirmative Countervailing Duty Determination: Certain Cut-to-Length Carbon-Quality Steel Plate from Indonesia, *United States Federal Register*, Vol. 64, No. 249 (29 December 1999), pp. 73155-73164 (Panel Exhibit USA-15), p. 73162) because the USDOC does not appear to have ultimately relied on non-adverse information in that instance. However, that instance does demonstrate that reliance on non-adverse information is not necessarily impermissible. In respect of two of the other instances submitted by the United States, however, and contrary to India's

may not represent the worst possible inference but could nonetheless lead to a "more precise subsidy rate", it may be used as the basis for a determination notwithstanding the non-cooperation of a party[1182], and "[w]here circumstances indicate that the information is not appropriate as [adverse facts available]", the USDOC's practice in the application of the measure suggests that it "will not use it".[1183]

4.481 On the basis of our review of the "practice" in the application of the measure, we are not convinced by India's assertion that the measure requires the USDOC to draw the worst possible inference in all cases of non-cooperation, or to assume that those "facts available" with adverse consequences are the only facts that it may use. In the absence of pertinent findings or consideration by the Panel, our review of the evidence concerning the application of the measure suggests that, even if the "practice" in respect of its application were relevant to ascertaining its meaning in this case, it does not conclusively support the proposition advanced by India. Based on our review of the "practice" in the application of the measure, we are unable to resolve the ambiguities raised by the participants on how the measure operates in practice. Rather, it appears that, under the measure at issue, the investigating authority has the authority not to use an inference that is adverse to a non-cooperating party in selecting from the facts otherwise available, or to limit its use of such an inference to circumstances where its use accords with the requirements of Article 12.7. In particular, we note in this respect that the judicial decisions and the legislative history on the Panel record reviewed above suggest that the measure need not be applied in all instances of non-cooperation, as does the plain language of the measure, which we recall the participants agree is discretionary.[1184]

4.482 Thus, our review of the judicial decisions, the Statement of Administrative Action, the legislative history of the measure, and the quantitative and qualitative material on the application of the measure submitted to the Panel record does not reveal an "as such" inconsistency of Section 1677e(b) of the US Statute and Section 351.308(a)-(c) of the US Regulations with Article 12.7 of the SCM Agreement. In particular, having reviewed these

---

submissions, we consider that these support the United States' claim that adverse inferences are not always drawn to apply the worst possible result in all cases. (USDOC, Issues and Decision Memorandum: Final Determination in the Countervailing Duty Investigation of Stainless Steel Bar From Italy (C-475-830), 15 January 2002, pp. 1 and 15-19 (Panel Exhibit USA-17), pp. 18-19; USDOC, Issues and Decision Memorandum: Final Results of Countervailing Duty Administrative Review: Certain In-shell Pistachios from the Islamic Republic of Iran (C-507-501), 6 September 2005 (Panel Exhibit USA-19), p. 8)

[1182] USDOC, Issues and Decision Memorandum: Final Determination in the Countervailing Duty Investigation of Stainless Steel Bar From Italy (C-475-830), 15 January 2002, pp. 1 and 15-19 (Panel Exhibit USA-17), p. 18.

[1183] 2006 AR Issues and Decision Memorandum, internal p. 8.

[1184] India's appellant's submission, paras. 232 and 239; India's first written submission to the Panel, para. 167; India's opening statement at the second Panel meeting, para. 21; United States' appellee's submission, para. 452.

documents, we do not consider that they establish conclusively that the measure requires the USDOC to act inconsistently with the obligations of Article 12.7 reflexively in all cases of non-cooperation.

4.6.3.4 Conclusion

4.483 In the light of the above review of the evidence, we do not consider that India's claim that Section 1677e(b) of the US Statute and Section 351.308(a)-(c) of the US Regulations are "as such" inconsistent with Article 12.7 of the SCM Agreement is sustained. Our review of the text of the measure on its face reveals its discretionary nature and does not identify elements requiring an investigating authority to engage in conduct inconsistent with Article 12.7 of the SCM Agreement. Further, in the absence of any consideration or findings by the Panel, having reviewed the judicial decisions, the Statement of Administrative Action, the legislative history of the measure, and quantitative and qualitative material on the application of the measure, we find that they do not establish conclusively that the measure requires an investigating authority to consistently apply inferences in a manner that would not comport with Article 12.7 in all cases of non-cooperation. Where inferences are drawn, this evidence of the use of "adverse inferences" does not establish conclusively that the measure at issue cannot be applied in a manner that comports with Article 12.7. We therefore complete the legal analysis and *find* that India has not established that Section 1677e(b) of the US Statute and Section 351.308(a)-(c) of the US Regulations are "as such" inconsistent with Article 12.7 of the SCM Agreement. We emphasize, however, that this does not mean that the measure is not susceptible to being applied in a manner inconsistent with Article 12.7. We also make no findings on the consistency of any distinct and separate "practice" of the investigating authority in the application of the measure, since this was not subject to an "as such" challenge by India.[1185]

*4.6.4 The consistency of the measure with Article 12.7 of the SCM Agreement "as applied" – Use of the highest non-*de minimis *subsidy rate*

4.484 India requests us to reverse the Panel's finding that India failed to establish a *prima facie* case that the USDOC's "rule"[1186] of using the highest

[1185] India's second written submission to the Panel, para. 89.

[1186] We note that India referred to this alleged methodology or practice as a "rule" before the Panel. (India's first written submission to the Panel, para. 526) The Panel adopted this terminology in the Panel Report to refer to the matter under challenge by India for the sake of convenience, noting that the United States did not challenge the use of this term. (Panel Report, para. 7.447 and fn 745 thereto) Further, the United States has not contested the use of the term "rule" on appeal, albeit describing it as the USDOC's "typical approach". (United States' appellee's submission, para. 485 and fn 612 thereto) On that basis, we also use the term "rule" for the sake of convenience, without prejudice to its existence, scope, or nature.

non-*de minimis* subsidy rate in the instances identified by India is inconsistent with Article 12.7 of the SCM Agreement. India makes this request on two alternative grounds. India contends, pursuant to the first ground, that the Panel applied an incorrect interpretation of Article 12.7 in assessing its claim. The claim on this ground is thus contingent upon us reversing the Panel's interpretation of Article 12.7 of the SCM Agreement. In the alternative, India contends, pursuant to its second ground, that the Panel erred by imposing an "unnecessary burden of proof" on India.[1187] Since we have only modified the Panel's interpretation of Article 12.7, we confine our analysis to this second ground of India's claim on appeal.

4.6.4.1 Whether the Panel applied an "unnecessary burden of proof" in respect of India's claim on the use of highest non-*de minimis* subsidy rates

4.485 India submits that the Panel erred in requiring it to establish how, in each instance of the use of the highest non-*de minimis* subsidy rate, the use of such rate does not reasonably replace the missing information, or is otherwise inconsistent with Article 12.7 of the SCM Agreement. India requests that we find that the very application of the "rule" in the instances identified by India is sufficient to demonstrate an "as applied" violation of Article 12.7 of the SCM Agreement. The United States, by contrast, submits that India needed to demonstrate an inconsistency with Article 12.7 on a case-by-case basis, and in any event, that the investigating authority's use of the "facts available" was not inconsistent with Article 12.7.

4.486 We turn first to the parties' arguments before the Panel, before setting out the claims and arguments of the participants on appeal, and evaluating India's claim of error. India argued before the Panel that the investigating authority had applied what it termed the following "rule" to determine the subsidy rate in a number of instances:

- Where data is available, the highest above *de minimis* subsidy rate calculated for an identical program from any segment of the investigation in question (i.e. the original investigation or any of the administrative reviews);
- Absent such a rate, where data is available, the highest above *de minimis* subsidy rate calculated for a similar program from any segment of the investigation in question (i.e. the original investigation or any of the administrative reviews);
- Absent the above, the highest above *de minimis* subsidy rate calculated for any program in any countervailing duty

[1187] India's appellant's submission, paras. 602-607.

> investigation involving the same country, so long as the industry in question could have used the programs for which the said rates were calculated.[1188]

4.487 India argued that this "rule" is inconsistent with Article 12.7 because it disallows the United States from engaging in an evaluative, comparative assessment in order to select the most fitting or most appropriate information available. Rather, in India's view, this "rule" was "mechanistic" and was used to "punish" non-cooperating parties.[1189] India maintained that using the facts available standard in a punitive manner so as to draw adverse inferences against a non-cooperating party is inconsistent with Article 12.7.

4.488 The United States contended that, contrary to India's assertions, the USDOC's benefit determination in each case reflects a reasoned analysis and is based upon a factual foundation, and that the rates it used reflect the actual subsidy practices of the central and state governments in India as reflected in the actual experience of companies in India. In the United States' view, where a company refuses to provide information, it is reasonable to conclude that the company has benefitted from the subsidy programme under investigation at least as much as the cooperating company in the same industry who received the higher benefit amount. This justifies recourse to the higher calculated rate for the particular subsidy programme at issue, unless information on the record indicates that such a rate is inaccurate or inappropriate.

4.489 The Panel firstly assessed the "rule" identified by India, and made a number of observations in relation to its nature and operation:

> The USDOC methodology explicitly requires that the investigating authority's determination have a factual foundation. First, it mandates that the investigating authority use subsidy rates previously calculated for a subsidy programme. Such rates, in our view, are by definition facts. Second, by requiring the investigating authority to use such subsidy rates in a progressive fashion – i.e. first using those calculated for the identical programme, then using those calculated for similar programmes, and only in the absence of either of these two using those calculated for any programme in any CVD proceeding involving the same country – we consider that the investigating authority is directed, in selecting "facts available", to use those facts which most reasonably replace the missing information, in light of all substantiated facts on record. In other words, pursuant to this alleged "rule", the USDOC is required to replace unknown facts with the most relevant known facts, and only move on to other

[1188] India's first written submission to the Panel, para. 526.

[1189] India's first written submission to the Panel, para. 528.

known facts, in diminishing degrees of relevance, when more closely relevant facts are not available.[1190]

4.490 Based on these observations on the nature and operation of the "rule", the Panel considered that the "rule" appeared on its face to be consistent with Article 12.7 of the SCM Agreement. Thus, the application of the "rule" in a given instance would not, in and of itself, demonstrate a violation of Article 12.7 of the SCM Agreement. Rather, the Panel considered that whether selecting information pursuant to the "rule" does not reasonably replace the missing information can only be determined on a case-by-case basis, and that India did not explain how each specific use of information pursuant to the "rule" is inconsistent with Article 12.7.[1191]

4.6.4.2 Evaluation of India's claim

4.491 India appeals the Panel's finding that it was required to establish how, in each instance of the use of the highest non-*de minimis* subsidy rate, the use of such a rate does not reasonably replace the missing information, or is otherwise inconsistent with Article 12.7 of the SCM Agreement. In India's view, this represents an "unnecessary burden of proof".[1192] India's argument is premised on the "rule" being necessarily inconsistent with Article 12.7 of the SCM Agreement. In particular, India submits that the fact that the USDOC starts with applying the highest non-*de minimis* rate, pursuant to the "rule", is *ipso facto* a violation of Article 12.7. In India's view, the rationale for applying the highest rate is to penalize non-cooperation. Moreover, the presumptive and conclusive manner in which the highest rate is applied demonstrates that it is not a reasonable replacement for the missing information. This being the case, India contends that it does not need to further show why each of the instances in the underlying investigation does not represent a reasonable replacement for the missing information.

4.492 For its part, the United States submits that the Panel correctly concluded that India failed to make a *prima facie* case, because for no challenged instance of application did India explain how the information used as facts available did not reasonably replace the missing information. In the United States' view, India needed to demonstrate an inconsistency with Article 12.7 on a case-by-case basis, and India failed to demonstrate that these applications were inconsistent with Article 12.7. In any event, the United States argues that the investigating authority's use of facts available was not inconsistent with Article 12.7. In particular, before using "facts available", the USDOC examined the reliability and relevance of such information to the extent practicable. The United States asserts that India can point to no evidence on the record that undermines the subsidy rates that were applied as facts available.

1190 Panel Report, para. 7.448.
1191 Panel Report, para. 7.449.
1192 India's appellant's submission, paras. 602-607.

4.493 India's claim on appeal calls for us to evaluate the adequacy of the burden of proof applied by the Panel in respect of India's claim regarding the use of highest non-*de minimis* subsidy rates. In general terms, the Appellate Body has considered that a complaining party must establish a *prima facie* case of inconsistency with a provision of a covered agreement to discharge its burden of proof[1193], and that the nature and scope of arguments and evidence required will necessarily vary from measure to measure, provision to provision, and case to case.[1194]

4.494 As a preliminary matter, we observe that the Panel does not appear to have analysed and discussed the existence or scope of the "rule" alleged by India to have been applied in a number of instances.[1195] Rather, the Panel seems to have presumed that the "rule" existed and extended to all of the about 230 instances identified by India, before turning to whether the "rule" is *per se* consistent with Article 12.7.[1196] We view this as problematic, not least because the United States appears to have identified at least one instance challenged by India where the "rule" itself was not applied in the manner described by India and in the Panel Report.[1197] The existence and scope of the "rule", and, for instance, the extent to which it is applied reflexively or contains exceptions, derogations or elements beyond those specified by India, would appear to us to constitute threshold matters for the Panel to resolve in the light of the claim presented by India.[1198] Further, in evaluating India's claim, we would have expected the Panel to assess whether India had sufficiently identified the

[1193] Appellate Body Report, *EC – Hormones*, para. 98 (referring to Appellate Body Report, *US – Wool Shirts and Blouses*, p. 14, DSR 1997:I, p. 335).

[1194] Appellate Body Report, *Chile – Price Band System (Article 21.5 – Argentina)*, para. 134 (referring to Appellate Body Reports, *US – Wool Shirts and Blouses*, p. 14, DSR 1997:I, p. 335; and *US – Carbon Steel*, para. 157).

[1195] Panel Report, paras. 7.447-7.449.

[1196] Panel Report, para. 7.448. In particular, the Panel framed India's challenge as "effectively" an "as such" claim, and proceeded immediately to assess the consistency of the "rule" as if it were an "as such" claim. Although the Panel stated that it only used the term "rule" "for the sake of convenience", its approach to evaluating India's claim presumes that the "rule" exists and was applied in each instance pleaded by India. (*Ibid.*, fn 745 to para. 7.447)

[1197] United States' first written submission to the Panel, para. 207 and fn 332 thereto (referring to the USDOC's calculation of benefit in respect of Essar's Certain Export Promotion Capital Goods Scheme licences in 2007 Issues and Decision Memorandum, internal pp. 8 and 44). We note that the application of the measure in respect of Essar's EPCGS licences is one of the instances of application referred to by India under this claim. (India's first written submission to the Panel, para. 527 and fn 540 thereto)

[1198] As one example, we note that India's and the Panel's framing of the "rule" omit one particular element that appears to have been applicable to at least some of the instances listed by India, namely, a corroboration element. (See 2006 AR Issues and Decision Memorandum, internal p. 8; and India's first written submission to the Panel, para. 527 and fns 537 and 539 thereto) Pursuant to this element, as set out in the citation provided by India, the USDOC "will satisfy itself that the secondary information to be used has probative value" by examining, to the extent practicable, "the reliability and relevance of the information to be used", such that "[w]here circumstances indicate that the information is not appropriate as [adverse facts available], the Department will not use it." (2006 AR Issues and Decision Memorandum, internal p. 8)

particular instances of application that it claimed were inconsistent with Article 12.7. In this regard, we observe that India's identification of the scope of its "as applied" claim before the Panel was quite limited, and it is not clear to us from its Report how the Panel arrived at the figure of 230 instances of application. However, we note that, pursuant to India's claim on appeal, we are not called upon to assess the Panel's findings on whether India discharged its burden of proof, for instance by establishing the existence and application of a "rule" that is "as such" inconsistent with Article 12.7 and was applied in all of the instances referred to by India. Rather, India's claim on appeal calls on us to assess whether the Panel erred in the burden of proof it applied.

4.495 We note that India brought a claim in relation to a number of instances of application of the measure, and requested the Panel to find that each specific application resulted in a breach of Article 12.7 of the SCM Agreement.[1199] The Panel, in turn, considered that India would need to explain how each specific application of the measure breached the legal standard for Article 12.7, or in the Panel's terms, "how each specific use of [the highest non-*de minimis* subsidy rate] does not, in each instance, reasonably replace the missing information, or is otherwise inconsistent with Article 12.7 of the SCM Agreement."[1200] In the light of the "as applied" nature of India's claim, we agree with the Panel that India was required to explain how each specific application of the measure breached the legal standard for Article 12.7. In this connection, we also note that each application of the measure challenged by India was mediated through a determination of the investigating authority. We thus consider that India was required to show for each determination where the alleged "rule", or the highest non-*de minimis* subsidy rate calculated in previous determinations, was applied, that the explanation provided in such determinations did not reveal why the selection of information was inconsistent with Article 12.7. Accordingly, we disagree with India that it did not need to show why, in each of the claimed instances of inconsistency, the information selected was inconsistent with Article 12.7.[1201] In particular, we fail to see how India could have made a *prima facie* case for its specific "as applied" claims without demonstrating that each impugned application was inconsistent with Article 12.7 of the SCM Agreement, as required by the Panel, regardless of whether this were demonstrated through the application of a necessarily inconsistent "rule" or through some other approach pursued by India.

4.496 For the foregoing reasons, we consider that the Panel did not err in the burden of proof it imposed in respect of India's "as applied" claim regarding the use of highest non-*de minimis* subsidy rates. Consequently, we *uphold* the Panel's finding, in paragraph 7.450 of the Panel Report, that India failed to

---

[1199] India's first written submission to the Panel, paras. 527 and 528; appellant's submission, paras. 592-594.

[1200] Panel Report, para. 7.449.

[1201] India's appellant's submission, para. 606.

establish a *prima facie* case of inconsistency with Article 12.7 of the SCM Agreement.

4.6.5 *Whether the Panel acted inconsistently with its obligations under Article 11 of the DSU in finding that India had failed to make a prima facie case in respect of its claim that the 2013 sunset review violated Article 12.7 of the SCM Agreement*

4.497 India requests us to reverse the Panel's finding that it failed to make a *prima facie* case in respect of its claim that the 2013 sunset review is inconsistent with Article 12.7 of the SCM Agreement. India further requests us to complete the legal analysis in respect of that claim. India submits that the Panel acted inconsistently with Article 11 of the DSU because it assessed India's claim without due regard to the evidence and legal arguments submitted by India.

4.498 India's argument before the Panel regarding the 2013 sunset review consisted of the following paragraph in its first written submission:

> On a similar note, in its recent 2013 Sunset review determination, the United States assumed, without any sort of factual foundation, that Tata, Ispat, Essar and SAIL all benefitted from close to 92 different programs. Therefore, for substantially the same reasons as enunciated above, the entire set of findings in the 2013 Sunset review determination is inconsistent with Article 12.7 of the SCM Agreement.[1202]

4.499 The United States argued that the 2013 sunset review was not listed in the panel request, and was therefore outside the Panel's terms of reference.[1203] India responded that the 2013 sunset review was covered by virtue of the reference in the panel request to "all the amendments, implementing acts, or any other related measure in connection with the measures referred herein".[1204]

4.500 The Panel agreed with India that the 2013 sunset review was within its terms of reference.[1205] Turning to the substantive aspect of India's claim, the Panel understood India's claim to be that the USDOC's "applications of 'facts available' [in the 2013 sunset review] are inconsistent with Article 12.7 of the SCM Agreement, because the USDOC assumed facts and applied 'facts

[1202] India's first written submission to the Panel, para. 576. We note that India did not expand on this argument substantively in its second written submission to the Panel. (See India's second written submission to the Panel, para. 280)

[1203] United States' first written submission to the Panel, paras. 274-283.

[1204] India's response to the United States' requests for preliminary rulings, para. 28 (referring to India's panel request, para. 5).

[1205] Panel Report, para. 1.41.

available' in a punitive fashion."[1206] The Panel then found that India had failed to make a *prima facie* case of inconsistency with Article 12.7 for the following reasons:

> We note that the presentation of India's Article 12.7 claims relating to these 92 instances of alleged improper application of facts available is limited to a single paragraph in its first written submission, with no further development of any substantive argument in subsequent submissions. Moreover, India did not adduce any evidence in support of its claims in its first written submission, or subsequently. India did not even specify the instances of alleged application of "facts available" or the particular subsidy programmes at issue. As a result, we are unable to evaluate India's claims, or to assess the consistency with Article 12.7 of any use of facts available by USDOC in the context of the 2013 sunset review.[1207]

4.501 Thus, the Panel concluded that India failed to establish a *prima facie* case that the determinations of the USDOC in the 2013 sunset review are inconsistent with Article 12.7 of the SCM Agreement.[1208]

4.6.5.1 Evaluation of India's claim

4.502 India submits on appeal that the Panel failed to fulfil its obligation under Article 11 of the DSU to make an objective assessment of the matter before it in rejecting India's "as applied" claim against the 2013 sunset review. First, India argues that, since its claim challenged every single finding in the 2013 sunset review, the alleged non-identification of the instances is not a material defect in its first written submission to the Panel. Second, India argues that there was no need to set out detailed argumentation in relation to its claim relating to the 2013 sunset review. This is because, in India's view, the 2013 sunset review simply repeated the same errors that India had already argued in relation to earlier determinations. Further, since the Panel agreed with India in respect of some of those errors in earlier determinations, India considers it "anomalous" for the Panel to then reject some of those claims as repeated in respect of the 2013 sunset review.[1209]

4.503 According to the United States, in making a *prima facie* case, a party must do more than identify a measure and identify a claim. It must explain the meaning of each and how or why the measure breaches an obligation. In the United States' view, India did not even attempt this. Further, in relation to India's omission to place the document containing the 2013 sunset review on the Panel

---

[1206] Panel Report, para. 7.478. (fn omitted)
[1207] Panel Report, para. 7.479. (fn omitted)
[1208] Panel Report, para. 7.480.
[1209] India's appellant's submission, para. 612.

record, the United States argues that India is seeking to have the Appellate Body reach a conclusion that the Panel failed to make an objective assessment by considering information in a document India failed to present to the Panel. The United States also contests India's assertion that the 2013 sunset review merely repeats the claimed inconsistencies of earlier determinations by pointing out that the 2013 sunset review covered companies and previous determinations on which India had brought no separate claims.

4.504 India's request on appeal calls on us to assess whether the Panel failed objectively to assess the matter before it under Article 11 of the DSU in determining that India did not establish a *prima facie* case in respect of its claim that the 2013 sunset review is inconsistent with Article 12.7 of the SCM Agreement.

4.505 We note that the Appellate Body has previously stated that "a *prima facie* case is one which, in the absence of effective refutation by the defending party, requires a panel, as a matter of law, to rule in favour of the complaining party presenting the *prima facie* case."[1210] The extent and nature of evidence required to establish such a presumption will necessarily vary from measure to measure, provision to provision, and case to case.[1211] A *prima facie* case involves not just adducing sufficient evidence, but also involves accompanying that evidence with sufficient legal argumentation.[1212] Where a party has not presented sufficient legal argumentation, a panel cannot "make the case" for a party to the dispute. However, where arguments have been "affirmatively *raised*", it is incumbent on panels to "fully scrutinize such evidence and argumentation".[1213] Thus, there is a positive duty on panels under Article 11 of the DSU to assess and weigh the evidence and seek further information if necessary to determine whether the evidence presented by a party satisfies the burden of proof in a given case.[1214]

4.506 With regard to the sufficiency of the legal argumentation provided by India in support of its claim, we recall that India's argument was contained in a single paragraph in its first written submission. A plain reading of India's claim on its face appears to reveal a number of ambiguities. First, the substance of India's argument is vague, insofar as India stated "[o]n a similar note" and "for substantially the same reasons as enunciated above", without making any reference to which particular reasons or arguments it sought to rely upon in making its claim. While India's argument was part of its broader claim relating to Article 12.7 of the SCM Agreement, it is unclear whether "substantially the same reasons as enunciated above" refers to the reasons contained in India's "as such" claim, or whether it refers to India's first "as applied" claim relating to the application of a particular "rule", or whether it refers to the general reasoning

---

1210 Appellate Body Report, *EC – Hormones*, para. 104.

1211 Appellate Body Report, *US – Wool Shirts and Blouses*, p. 14, DSR 1997:1, p. 335. (fn omitted)

1212 Appellate Body Report, *US – Gambling*, para. 140.

1213 Appellate Body Report, *EC – Fasteners (China)*, para. 566. (emphasis original)

1214 Appellate Body Report, *US – Continued Zeroing*, para. 347. (fn omitted)

contained in its other "as applied" claims. Further, although India asserted that the United States "assumed, without any sort of factual foundation" the existence of subsidization and benefit, India provided no further explanation, justification, or evidence in respect of this assertion. India did not point to any specific instances of flawed reasoning or omissions by the investigating authority.

4.507 According to India, these ambiguities are clarified by reference to the document containing the 2013 sunset review. In particular, India argues that the 2013 sunset review simply cited all the prior determinations made in the same investigation in the previous years, and that it challenged every single finding in that document. However, without this document having been placed on the Panel record, as clarified by India at the oral hearing, we fail to see how it could assist in elucidating India's legal argumentation in this dispute.

4.508 Moreover, the failure to submit this document to the Panel record diminishes the sufficiency of the evidence provided to support India's claim. In this regard, we recall that, where arguments have been affirmatively raised, panels are under a duty under Article 11 of the DSU to seek further information if necessary to determine whether the evidence presented by a participant satisfies the burden of proof in a given case.[1215] In this case, however, it is apparent from the ambiguities in India's claim that evidence and arguments were not sufficiently and affirmatively raised to activate a panel's duty to seek further information.

4.509 For the foregoing reasons, we *reject* India's claim that the Panel acted inconsistently with Article 11 of the DSU.

4.7 New Subsidy Allegations

4.7.1 Introduction

4.510 India contends that the Panel erred in rejecting India's claims that the examination by the USDOC of new subsidy[1216] allegations in administrative reviews related to the imports at issue is inconsistent with Articles 11.1, 13.1, 21.1, 21.2, 22.1, and 22.2 of the SCM Agreement. India presents two main arguments in support of its contention. First, India argues that the Panel erred in interpreting the relationship between Articles 11 and 21 of the SCM Agreement. Second, India alleges that the Panel breached its duties under Articles 11 and 12.7 of the DSU to conduct an objective assessment of the matter before it and to provide a "basic rationale" for its findings. Consequently, India requests us to reverse the Panel's finding rejecting India's claims under Articles 11.1, 13.1, 22.1, and 22.2 of the SCM Agreement, and further requests us to complete the legal analysis in respect of these claims.

[1215] Appellate Body Reports, *EC – Fasteners (China)*, para. 566; *US – Continued Zeroing*, para. 347.

[1216] The Panel explained that the term "new subsidy" was used by India to refer to subsidy programmes not formally examined in the original investigation, but included and examined in subsequent reviews. (See Panel Report, para. 7.481) We also use this term in this Report.

4.511 India does not challenge the Panel's finding that an investigating authority may examine new subsidy allegations in the conduct of an administrative review pursuant to Article 21 of the SCM Agreement.[1217] Furthermore, India does not challenge the precise considerations that the USDOC took into account in deciding to examine each of the new subsidy allegations at issue. Rather, India's position on appeal is that, where any Article 21 review is conducted and involves the examination of new subsidy allegations, such examination must comply with the requirements set out in Articles 11, 13, and 22 of the SCM Agreement.[1218] Bearing in mind the nature and scope of India's appeal, we summarize below the Panel's findings that are the subject of India's appeal before turning to our analysis of India's claims.

4.7.2 The Panel's findings

4.512 Before the Panel, India claimed that, in investigating certain new subsidy allegations in annual administrative reviews, the USDOC circumvented the obligations of Articles 11.1, 11.2, 11.9, 13.1, 22.1, and 22.2 of the SCM Agreement, and inappropriately expanded the scope of a review contrary to Articles 21.1 and 21.2 of the SCM Agreement.[1219] In particular, India contended that Article 21 is not intended to govern the imposition of duties *per se*, and does not cover a new examination into the existence, degree, and effect of newly alleged subsidies. Thus, India submitted that the United States was not permitted to expand the scope of a review under Articles 21.1 and 21.2 so as to initiate new investigations against new subsidies.[1220]

4.513 The Panel highlighted certain undisputed facts in connection with India's claim. First, the Panel noted that the US measures at issue were administrative review determinations and the underlying proceedings, which the United States acknowledged, were conducted under Article 21 of the SCM Agreement. Second, the Panel observed that the examination of the new subsidy allegations involved the same product at issue as in the original investigation. Third, the Panel noted that India's arguments pointed to "no obligation in the text of Article 21 that was breached by the USDOC in its examination of the new subsidy allegations in administrative reviews".[1221] Nor did India raise any issue relating to whether the new subsidy allegations involved a financial contribution, which confers a benefit and is considered to be specific.[1222] Fourth, the Panel clarified that its reference to Article 11.1 of the SCM Agreement was limited to India's claim under this provision regarding the alleged failure to initiate an

[1217] India's response to questioning at the oral hearing.

[1218] India's appellant's submission, para. 643.

[1219] Panel Report, para. 7.490 (referring to India's first written submission to the Panel, paras. 596, 597, and 623).

[1220] Panel Report, para. 7.492 (referring to India's first written submission to the Panel, para. 623).

[1221] Panel Report, para. 7.500. (fn omitted)

[1222] Panel Report, fn 836 to para. 7.500.

investigation into new subsidies. The Panel recalled its preliminary ruling that India's claims relating to the initiation of an investigation despite the insufficiency of evidence under Articles 11.1, 11.2, and 11.9 of the SCM Agreement fell outside the Panel's terms of reference.[1223]

4.514 The Panel thereafter framed the issue before it in the following terms: whether the USDOC was entitled, under Articles 21.1 and 21.2 of the SCM Agreement, to consider new subsidy allegations in the administrative reviews at issue; or whether, as India argued, new subsidy allegations could only be considered in the context of an investigation initiated under Article 11.1 of the SCM Agreement, and undertaken consistently with Articles 13.1, 22.1, and 22.2 of the SCM Agreement. The Panel therefore considered that, if the USDOC was authorized to examine new subsidy allegations under Articles 21.1 and 21.2, the Panel need not consider further India's claims. Conversely, if it found that the USDOC was not authorized to consider new subsidy allegations in administrative reviews, the Panel would go on to examine whether the USDOC acted consistently with Articles 11.1, 13.1, 22.1, and 22.2 in the investigation and reviews at issue. The Panel observed that this was the first time that a panel had addressed this question.[1224]

4.515 The Panel considered that there is nothing in the text of Article 21.1 that could be understood necessarily to relate the term "subsidization" in this provision to specific subsidy programmes or limit the meaning of this term to previously examined subsidization – i.e. subsidization under programmes formally examined and found to constitute countervailable subsidies in the original investigation. In the Panel's view, nothing in Article 21.1 suggests that the term "subsidization" may not cover newly alleged subsidy programmes as well. Similarly, the Panel considered that nothing in the text of Article 21.2 limited the review of the need for continued imposition of the duty to consideration of previously examined subsidization. For the Panel, consideration of the "need for the continued imposition of the duty" pursuant to Article 21.2 could refer to both consideration in the light of subsidy programmes formally examined in the original investigation and consideration in the light of subsidy programmes identified in new allegations in the context of a review. According to the Panel, new subsidy allegations are relevant to the investigating authority's consideration of the need for continued imposition of the duty with respect to the particular subsidized imports, as continued imposition of the duty may be necessary in the light of new subsidization, even if previously examined subsidization has expired.[1225]

4.516 The Panel considered its reasoning to be consistent with the understanding of the panel in *US – Carbon Steel*. In the context of sunset reviews, that panel found that Article 21.3 of the SCM Agreement requires an

[1223] *Ibid.*
[1224] Panel Report, para. 7.501.
[1225] Panel Report, para. 7.503.

investigating authority to engage in an inherently prospective analysis of whether subsidization is likely to continue or recur should the countervailing duty be revoked, and that, in doing so, it may well consider, *inter alia*, "any new subsidy programmes introduced after the imposition of the original [countervailing duty]".[1226]

4.517 The Panel did not agree with India's assertion that reviews under Article 21 of the SCM Agreement are aimed only at correcting or re-examining determinations relating to subsidization and injury that already exist. While noting that India's argument appeared to rest on the view that the focus of the review under Article 21 is the original determination, the Panel held that Article 21.2 clearly establishes that what is to be reviewed is "the need for the continued imposition of the duty", and not the original determination. Therefore, the question to be answered in the review under Article 21.2 is whether the continued imposition of the countervailing duty is justified. The Panel found that nothing in the text of Article 21.1 or 21.2 limits an investigating authority to consider only whether the original basis for the measure is sufficient to justify its continued existence.[1227]

4.518 The Panel took note of the reference in Article 21.2 to the possibility of continued imposition of the duty if it "is necessary to offset subsidization, whether the injury would be likely to continue or recur if the duty were removed or varied, or both". The Panel understood this to mean that, if a subsidy programme, found in the original investigation to be countervailable, was decreased (in terms of the benefit) or was terminated, interested exporting parties could request that the countervailing duty imposed on the basis of that programme be reduced or terminated. Likewise, it seemed "only logical and fair" that, if there was an allegation that new subsidy programmes benefitted the product that was the subject of the countervailing duty and were countervailable, interested domestic parties could request that the duty level be amended, and possibly increased, to take such new subsidies into account.[1228] In order to do so, it would be necessary for the investigating authority to determine that such programmes are in fact countervailable subsidies benefitting imports of the same product, as well as the amount of such subsidies. As the Panel understood it, "that is precisely what the USDOC undertook to do with respect to the new subsidy allegations at issue here."[1229]

[1226] Panel Report, para. 7.504 (quoting Panel Report, *US – Carbon Steel*, para. 8.96). The Panel noted that, in its report, the Appellate Body quoted this passage, but stated that "it [was] *not* called upon, in [the] particular appeal, to review the Panel's [] *interpretation* of Article 21.3 and the obligations it sets forth with respect to the determination to be made in a sunset review." (*Ibid.*, fn 839 to para. 7.504 (quoting Appellate Body Report, *US – Carbon Steel*, para. 138 (emphasis original)))

[1227] Panel Report, para. 7.505.

[1228] Panel Report, para. 7.506.

[1229] Panel Report, para. 7.506. The Panel noted that, pursuant to Article 21.4 of the SCM Agreement, the evidentiary and procedural requirements of Article 12 of the SCM Agreement apply to reviews

4.519 The Panel concluded that the USDOC was entitled, under Articles 21.1 and 21.2 of the SCM Agreement, to examine new subsidy allegations in the administrative reviews at issue. Consequently, the Panel determined that it need not consider further and separately, India's claims under Articles 11.1, 13.1, 22.1, and 22.2 of the SCM Agreement.[1230] Therefore, the Panel rejected India's claims that the examination by the USDOC of new subsidy allegations in administrative reviews related to the imports at issue is inconsistent with Articles 11.1, 13.1, 21.1, 21.2, 22.1, and 22.2 of the SCM Agreement.

4.520 During the interim review, India requested the Panel to clarify whether the Panel had exercised judicial economy with regard to India's claims under Articles 11.1, 13.1, 22.1, and 22.2 of the SCM Agreement. India also requested that the Panel make a specific finding on whether the USDOC had complied with these provisions. India argued that its claims under these provisions were entirely independent from India's other claims relating to new subsidy allegations.[1231] The Panel decided "not to accommodate India's request".[1232] The Panel clarified that it had not exercised judicial economy with regard to India's claims under Articles 11.1, 13.1, 22.1, and 22.2 of the SCM Agreement. Rather, the Panel reiterated its explanation that, as the USDOC was entitled, under Articles 21.1 and 21.2 of the SCM Agreement, to examine new subsidy allegations in the administrative reviews at issue, there was no need to examine the provisions that regulate original investigations.

4.7.3 Review of the Panel's analysis of India's claims under Articles 11.1, 13.1, 21.1, 21.2, 22.1, and 22.2 of the SCM Agreement

4.521 India's appeal calls for us to review the Panel's analysis regarding whether the requirements set out in certain provisions of the SCM Agreement apply to an investigating authority's examination of new subsidy allegations in the conduct of an administrative review. Hence, we will first examine whether an administrative review conducted pursuant to Article 21.2 of the SCM Agreement is subject to the requirements set out in Articles 11.1, 13.1, 22.1, and 22.2 of the SCM Agreement, before addressing the circumstances under which an investigating authority may examine new subsidy allegations in the conduct of an administrative review. Thereafter, we address India's claims that the Panel erred in rejecting India's claims under Articles 11.1, 13.1, 22.1, and 22.2 of the SCM Agreement, and that the Panel acted inconsistently with Articles 11 and 12.7 of the DSU.

---

carried out under Article 21 of the SCM Agreement. However, India had not raised any claim under Article 12 in the context of the examination of new subsidy allegations in administrative reviews. (*Ibid.*, fn 842 to para. 7.506)

[1230] Panel Report, para. 7.507.

[1231] Panel Report, para. 6.166.

[1232] Panel Report, para. 6.168.

4.7.3.1 Applicability of Articles 11, 13, 21, and 22 of the SCM Agreement to the examination of new subsidy allegations in administrative reviews

4.522 We begin by observing that Articles 11, 13, 21, and 22 are all contained in Part V of the SCM Agreement, which addresses countervailing measures. We recall the Appellate Body's statement that Part V of the SCM Agreement is aimed at striking a balance between the right to impose countervailing duties to offset subsidization that is causing injury, and the obligations disciplining the use of countervailing measures that Members must respect.[1233]

4.523 The Appellate Body has determined that the applicable provision covering administrative reviews is Article 21 of the SCM Agreement[1234], which provides, in relevant part, as follows:

> *Article 21*
>
> *Duration and Review of Countervailing Duties and Undertakings*
>
> 21.1 A countervailing duty shall remain in force only as long as and to the extent necessary to counteract subsidization which is causing injury.
>
> 21.2 The authorities shall review the need for the continued imposition of the duty, where warranted, on their own initiative or, provided that a reasonable period of time has elapsed since the imposition of the definitive countervailing duty, upon request by any interested party which submits positive information substantiating the need for a review. Interested parties shall have the right to request the authorities to examine whether the continued imposition of the duty is necessary to offset subsidization, whether the injury would be likely to continue or recur if the duty were removed or varied, or both. If, as a result of the review under this paragraph, the authorities determine that the countervailing duty is no longer warranted, it shall be terminated immediately. A countervailing duty shall remain in force only as long as and to the extent necessary to counteract subsidization which is causing injury.
>
> ...

[1233] Appellate Body Report, *US – Carbon Steel*, para. 74.
[1234] Appellate Body Report, *US – Lead and Bismuth II*, para. 53.

> 21.4 The provisions of Article 12 regarding evidence and procedure shall apply to any review carried out under this Article. Any such review shall be carried out expeditiously and shall normally be concluded within 12 months of the date of initiation of the review.

4.524 The Appellate Body has explained that Article 21.1 sets out a general rule that, after the imposition of a countervailing duty, the continued application of that duty is subject to certain disciplines. These disciplines "relate to the *duration* of the countervailing duty ('only as long as ... necessary'), its *magnitude* ('only ... to the extent necessary'), and its *purpose* ('to counteract subsidization which is causing injury')".[1235] Hence, the focus of the inquiry under Article 21 "is on the amount of time that a duty may *remain* in force, rather than the circumstances under which that duty initially *entered into* force".[1236]

4.525 While the general rule of Article 21.1 "underlines the requirement for periodic review of countervailing duties and highlights the factors that must inform such reviews"[1237], Article 21.2 provides a review mechanism to ensure that Members comply with the rule set out in Article 21.1.[1238] The first sentence of Article 21.2 provides that the authorities shall review the need for the continued imposition of the duty: (i) where warranted, on their own initiative; or (ii) provided that a reasonable period of time has elapsed since the imposition of the definitive countervailing duty, upon request by any interested party that submits positive information substantiating the need for a review. The Appellate Body has emphasized that Article 21.2 sets out requirements for a "rigorous review" and that the determination to be made following such review must be a "meaningful" one.[1239]

4.526 Whereas Articles 21.1 and 21.2 govern the conduct of administrative reviews, Article 11 sets out a number of evidentiary requirements that must be satisfied in order to initiate a countervailing duty investigation.[1240] Past panels and the Appellate Body have referred to the investigation conducted pursuant to Article 11 as the "original investigation".[1241] Article 11.1 provides for the manner in which an original investigation is to be initiated. It states that "an investigation to determine the existence, degree and effect of any alleged subsidy shall be initiated upon a written application by or on behalf of the domestic industry."

[1235] Appellate Body Report, *US – Carbon Steel*, para. 70. (emphasis original)

[1236] Panel Report, *Japan – DRAMs (Korea)*, para. 7.350. (emphasis original)

[1237] Appellate Body Report, *US – Carbon Steel*, para. 70.

[1238] Appellate Body Report, *US – Lead and Bismuth II*, para. 53.

[1239] Appellate Body Report, *US – Carbon Steel*, para. 71 (referring to Appellate Body Report, *US – Lead and Bismuth II*, para. 61).

[1240] Appellate Body Report, *US – Carbon Steel*, para. 115.

[1241] See e.g. Appellate Body Reports, *US – Lead and Bismuth II*, para. 63; *US – Carbon Steel*, paras. 83 and 88; and Panel Report, *US – Carbon Steel*, paras. 8.95 and 8.96.

4.527 We recall that Article 21.2 mandates authorities to "review the need for the continued imposition of the duty". It further provides that interested parties shall have the right to request the authorities to examine whether continued imposition of the duty is necessary to offset subsidization, and/or "whether the injury would be likely to continue or recur if the duty were removed or varied, or both". As the Appellate Body found in *Mexico – Anti-Dumping Measures on Rice*, these conditions are "exhaustive" and Members are not allowed to condition the right of interested parties to an administrative review upon requirements other than those set out in Article 21.2.[1242] Additionally, while Article 21.4 imposes the evidentiary rules in Article 12 of the SCM Agreement to reviews conducted pursuant to Article 21, nothing in the language of Articles 11 and 21 expressly imports the requirements of Article 11 to the conduct of administrative reviews under Article 21.[1243]

4.528 We also note certain distinctions between the mandate that an investigating authority has in conducting an original investigation pursuant to Article 11, and the mandate it has in conducting an administrative review pursuant to Article 21.2. As the Appellate Body in *US – Lead and Bismuth II* stated:

> We believe that it is important to distinguish between the original investigation leading to the imposition of countervailing duties and the administrative review. In an original investigation, the investigating authority must establish that *all* conditions set out in the *SCM Agreement* for the imposition of countervailing duties are fulfilled. In an administrative review, however, the investigating authority must address those issues which have been raised before it by the interested parties or, in the case of an investigation conducted on its own initiative, those issues which warranted the examination.[1244]

4.529 Furthermore, we recall that the Appellate Body has discussed the differences between the inquiries under Articles 11 and 21, albeit in the context of sunset reviews conducted pursuant to Article 21.3 of the SCM Agreement. In *US – Carbon Steel*, the Appellate Body explained that:

[1242] Appellate Body Report, *Mexico – Anti-Dumping Measures on Rice*, para. 315.

[1243] In *US – Carbon Steel*, the Appellate Body noted the following regarding the applicability of Article 11 requirements to sunset reviews conducted pursuant to Article 21.3:

> Given that the requirements of Articles 11 and 12 are placed consecutively in the Agreement, and the fact that both Articles expressly set out obligations in relation to *investigations*, we read the express reference in Article 21.4 to Article 12, but not to Article 11, as an indication that the drafters intended that the obligations in Article 12, but not those in Article 11, would apply to reviews carried out under Article 21.3.

(Appellate Body Report, *US – Carbon Steel*, para. 72 (emphasis original) See also para. 116)

[1244] Appellate Body Report, *US – Lead and Bismuth II*, para. 63. (emphasis original)

> ... original investigations and sunset reviews are distinct processes with different purposes. The nature of the determination to be made in a sunset review differs in certain essential respects from the nature of the determination to be made in an original investigation. For example, in a sunset review, the authorities are called upon to focus their inquiry on what would happen if an existing countervailing duty were to be removed. In contrast, in an original investigation, the authorities must investigate the existence, degree and effect of any alleged subsidy in order to determine whether a subsidy exists and whether such subsidy is causing injury to the domestic industry so as to warrant the imposition of a countervailing duty. These qualitative differences may also explain the absence of a requirement to apply a specific *de minimis* standard in a sunset review.[1245]

4.530 Article 21.2 mandates authorities to "review the need for the continued imposition of the duty" and, in particular, to examine "whether the continued imposition of the duty is necessary to offset subsidization". Article 21.2 also gives investigating authorities the power to determine "whether the injury would be likely to continue or recur if the duty were removed or varied, or both". Hence, Article 21.2 appears to call for a present and retrospective analysis as it relates to the necessity and impact of the duty prior to and during the administrative review, as well as a prospective analysis focusing on the likely future consequences of the maintenance, changing, or removal of the duty. This differs in scope from a review under Article 21.3, which is an exclusively prospective analysis that focuses on the future consequences of the removal of the duty. Both provisions, however, bear a similar prospective focus. To the extent that the prospective focus of a review under Article 21.2 is similar to that under Article 21.3, this would suggest that the requirements set out in Article 11 of the SCM Agreement would not apply to administrative reviews conducted pursuant to Article 21.2 of the SCM Agreement.

4.531 Turning to Article 13 of the SCM Agreement, we observe that it sets out the consultations requirements that an investigating authority must abide by in the conduct of investigations. Specifically, Article 13.1 states:

> As soon as possible after an application under Article 11 is accepted, and in any event before the initiation of any investigation, Members the products of which may be subject to such investigation shall be invited for consultations with the aim of clarifying the situation as to the matters referred to in paragraph 2 of Article 11 and arriving at a mutually agreed solution.

[1245] Appellate Body Report, *US – Carbon Steel*, para. 87.

4.532 We note that Article 13.1 refers expressly to the investigations conducted pursuant to Article 11 and makes it mandatory for an investigating authority to provide an opportunity for consultations with the Member whose products may be subject to the Article 11 investigation. Conversely, neither Article 13 nor Article 21 makes explicit reference to the other.[1246] Furthermore, the Appellate Body has emphasized that the use of the word "investigation" in Article 11 is distinct from the use of the word "review" in Article 21.[1247] In this regard, we observe that, not only does Article 13.1 use the word "investigation" and make an explicit reference to Article 11, but it also makes no reference to the word "review" or to Article 21. For these reasons, we consider that the requirements for carrying out consultations, prescribed in Article 13.1 of the SCM Agreement, do not apply to the conduct of administrative reviews, as governed by Article 21.2 of the SCM Agreement.

4.533 Article 22 of the SCM Agreement, for its part, prescribes the public notice obligations that an investigating authority must meet in the conduct of investigations and reviews. Article 22 provides, in relevant part:

> *Article 22*
>
> *Public Notice and Explanation of Determinations*
>
> 22.1 When the authorities are satisfied that there is sufficient evidence to justify the initiation of an investigation pursuant to Article 11, the Member or Members the products of which are subject to such investigation and other interested parties known to the investigating authorities to have an interest therein shall be notified and a public notice shall be given.
>
> 22.2 A public notice of the initiation of an investigation shall contain, or otherwise make available through a separate report[*], adequate information on the following:
>
> (i) the name of the exporting country or countries and the product involved;
>
> (ii) the date of initiation of the investigation;
>
> (iii) a description of the subsidy practice or practices to be investigated;

[1246] The Appellate Body has observed that the technique of cross-referencing is frequently used in the SCM Agreement, suggesting that, "when the negotiators of the *SCM Agreement* intended that the disciplines set forth in one provision be applied in another context, they did so expressly." (Appellate Body Report, *US – Carbon Steel*, para. 69 and fn 59 thereto)

[1247] See Appellate Body Report, *US – Carbon Steel*, paras. 72 and 105.

(iv) a summary of the factors on which the allegation of injury is based;

(v) the address to which representations by interested Members and interested parties should be directed; and

(vi) the time-limits allowed to interested Members and interested parties for making their views known.

...

22.7 The provisions of this Article shall apply *mutatis mutandis* to the initiation and completion of reviews pursuant to Article 21 and to decisions under Article 20 to apply duties retroactively.

[*fn original][53] Where authorities provide information and explanations under the provisions of this Article in a separate report, they shall ensure that such report is readily available to the public.

4.534 By virtue of the express textual link in Article 22.7, Article 22 applies to both Article 11 investigations and Article 21 reviews. Indeed, in *US – Carbon Steel*, the Appellate Body explained the relationships between Articles 11 and 22, and between Articles 21 and 22, as follows:

> To us, in the same way that Article 22.1 imposes notification and public notice requirements on investigating authorities that have decided, in accordance with the standards set out in Article 11, to initiate an *investigation*, Article 22.1 (by virtue of Article 22.7) also operates to impose notification and public notice requirements on investigating authorities that have decided, in accordance with Article 21, to initiate a *review*.[1248]

4.535 Article 22.7 indicates that the provisions of Article 22 are to apply *mutatis mutandis* to the initiation and completion of Article 21 reviews. The use of the term "*mutatis mutandis*"[1249] in Article 22.7 suggests to us that certain requirements set out in Articles 22.1 through 22.6 of the SCM Agreement, which are fully applicable to the initiation or completion of an Article 11 original investigation, may not be applicable in the same manner, or to the same extent, to Article 21 reviews.[1250]

[1248] Appellate Body Report, *US – Carbon Steel*, para. 112. (emphasis original)

[1249] *Black's Law Dictionary* defines the term "*mutatis mutandis*" as "all necessary changes having been made; with the necessary changes". (*Black's Law Dictionary*, 7th edn, Bryan A. Garner (ed.) (West Group, 1999), p. 1039)

[1250] In a similar vein, we note that two panels discussed the use of the term "*mutatis mutandis*" in Article 12.3 of the Anti-Dumping Agreement, which contains language almost identical to that of

4.536 Having identified the provisions in the SCM Agreement that govern the conduct of administrative reviews, we turn to assessing the circumstances under which an investigating authority may examine new subsidy allegations in the conduct of an administrative review.

4.537 Article 21.1 provides that "[a] countervailing duty shall remain in force only as long as and to the extent necessary to counteract subsidization which is causing injury." As we mentioned above, the disciplines of Article 21, articulated in Article 21.1, relate to "the *duration* of the countervailing duty ('only as long as ... necessary'), its *magnitude* ('only ... to the extent necessary'), and its *purpose* ('to counteract subsidization which is causing injury')".[1251] In the same vein, the second sentence of Article 21.2 grants interested parties the right to request an investigating authority to examine whether the continued imposition of the duty is necessary to offset *subsidization*, and whether the injury would be likely to *continue* or *recur* if the duty were removed or varied, or both. Hence, we read these two provisions as suggesting that the focus of enquiry in an administrative review is on the countervailing duty and whether there is a continuing need for its imposition.

4.538 We note that Articles 21.1 and 21.2 do not confine the enquiry in an administrative review to the subsidies examined in the original investigation. Rather, as noted, the determination of whether to continue imposing a countervailing duty is dependent on an assessment of: (i) the continuing necessity of the countervailing duty to offset what is broadly termed as *subsidization*; and (ii) whether the injury resulting from such *subsidization* is likely to *continue* or *recur* if the duty were *removed* or *varied*, or both.

4.539 We consider that the use of the word "subsidization" in Article 21, as distinct from the word "subsidy" in Article 11.1, allows for a broader scope of review than the precise subsidy or subsidies that were examined in the original investigation, and that resulted in the imposition of the countervailing duty subject of the review. We further consider that the focus of Article 21.2 on whether the injury resulting from such *subsidization* is likely to *continue* or

Article 22.7 of the SCM Agreement. In *US – Corrosion-Resistant Steel Sunset Review*, the panel stated:

> Paragraph 3 of Article 12 states that the provisions of that Article apply *mutatis mutandis* to reviews under Article 11. Therefore, it is clear that the public notice requirements of Article 12 apply *mutatis mutandis* to sunset reviews. However, the use of the term "*mutatis mutandis*" demonstrates that the drafters foresaw that certain provisions of Article 12 could not be applied, at all, or at the very least not in an identical manner, in the case of sunset reviews. The provisions of Article 12 apply in sunset reviews, with whatever changes the nature of sunset reviews may necessitate.

(Panel Report, *US – Corrosion-Resistant Steel Sunset Review*, para. 7.33)

Similarly, in *US – Oil Country Tubular Goods Sunset Reviews*, the panel stated that "the provisions of Article 12 apply to sunset reviews with necessary changes that the nature of sunset reviews may necessitate." (Panel Report, *US – Oil Country Tubular Goods Sunset Reviews*, para. 7.248)

[1251] Appellate Body Report, *US – Carbon Steel*, para. 70. (emphasis original)

recur if the duty were *removed* or *varied*, or both, suggests that an investigating authority may go beyond the particular subsidies examined in the original investigation in the conduct of an administrative review. As we discussed above, the fact that Article 21 calls, in part, for a prospective analysis implies that the investigating authority may also examine events or circumstances that have followed the imposition of the original countervailing duty. Indeed, Article 21.2 uses the word "recur", which we understand as "occur or appear again, periodically or repeatedly".[1252] Hence, the injury resulting from subsidization, which is being addressed by the countervailing duty, may recur due to a new subsidy that is put in place after the imposition of the original countervailing duty. In this regard, we concur with the panel in *US – Carbon Steel* that, in assessing the likelihood of subsidization in the event of revocation of a countervailing duty, an investigating authority may well consider, *inter alia*, the original level of subsidization, any changes in the original subsidy programmes, and "any new subsidy programmes introduced after the imposition of the original" countervailing duty.[1253]

4.540 Accordingly, we understand Articles 21.1 and 21.2 of the SCM Agreement to permit investigating authorities to examine new subsidy allegations in the conduct of an administrative review. Such examination, while subject, *mutatis mutandis*, to the public notice requirements set out in Article 22 of the SCM Agreement, would not be subject to the obligations set out in Articles 11 and 13 of the SCM Agreement.

4.541 Nevertheless, we consider that Articles 21.1 and 21.2 limit the type of new subsidy allegations that may be examined in an administrative review. As discussed above, Article 21.1 provides that a countervailing duty shall remain in force only as long as and to the extent necessary to counteract *subsidization* which is causing injury, while Article 21.2 grants interested parties the right to request an investigating authority to examine whether the continued imposition of the duty is necessary to offset *subsidization*. These provisions expressly link the *subsidization* to the original countervailing duty imposed. This suggests that the only "new subsidies" that may be examined as part of the "subsidization" in an administrative review are those that have a sufficiently close link to the subsidies that resulted in the imposition of the original countervailing duty. Moreover, Article 21.2 requires the investigating authority to assess whether "*the injury* would be likely to continue or recur if *the duty* were removed or varied, or both."[1254] Hence, only the new subsidies that would inform this enquiry may properly be considered by an investigating authority in the conduct

---

[1252] *Shorter Oxford English Dictionary*, 6th edn, A. Stevenson (ed.) (Oxford University Press, 2007), Vol. 2, p. 2495.

[1253] Panel Report, *US – Carbon Steel*, para. 8.96. Although the panel's remarks in this paragraph were made in connection with a sunset review under Article 21.3, the panel's reasoning, in our view, applies equally to the assessment of the likely consequences of removing a countervailing duty pursuant to an administrative review under the similarly worded Article 21.2.

[1254] Emphasis added.

of an administrative review. The use of the words "continue" and "recur", in particular, indicate that there must be a sufficiently close link or similarity between the injury resulting from the original subsidization and the new subsidies being proposed for examination in the administrative review.

4.542 Furthermore, as the Appellate Body has stated, Part V of the SCM Agreement, which houses all of these provisions at issue, is aimed at striking a balance between the right to impose countervailing duties to offset subsidization that is causing injury and the obligations disciplining the use of countervailing measures that Members must respect.[1255] We consider that allowing for an unfettered examination of all types of new subsidy allegations in administrative reviews would upset this delicate balance that Part V of the SCM Agreement seeks to achieve.

4.543 Therefore, in our view, Article 21 requires an investigating authority to establish that there is a sufficiently close nexus between the subsidies that are the subject of the original investigation and the new subsidy allegations that the investigating authority proposes to examine as part of its administrative review. There are several factors that could potentially be taken into consideration on a case-by-case basis in determining whether subsidy allegations that were not at issue in the original investigation or in previous administrative reviews may properly be examined in administrative reviews.[1256] However, India's appeal does not call upon us to determine which of these factors are applicable or ought to have been taken into account in the case before us.

4.7.3.2 Whether the Panel erred in rejecting India's claims that the examination by the USDOC of new subsidy allegations in administrative reviews is inconsistent with Articles 11.1, 13.1, 21.1, 21.2, 22.1, and 22.2 of the SCM Agreement

4.544 India argues, on appeal, that the Panel erred in interpreting Articles 11 and 21 of the SCM Agreement by failing to construe these two provisions harmoniously. According to India, the Panel's assumption that the applicability

---

[1255] Appellate Body Report, *US – Carbon Steel*, para. 74.

[1256] We note that, in the instant dispute, the Panel took into account the fact that the specific new subsidy allegations involved the same product at issue in the original investigation. (See Panel Report, paras. 7.500 and 7.506) We further note that, in response to questioning at the oral hearing, the United States and the European Union suggested that, in their view, for new subsidy allegations to be considered in an administrative review, they should share the following elements with the original subsidies subject of the countervailing duty: (i) the same Member; (ii) the same responding companies (beneficiaries of the subsidies); and (iii) the same products. In addition, the European Union referred to other potential considerations such as the nature of a subsidy, whether the same or a different granting authority or the same or a different subsidy programme is involved, or whether a subsidy has been replaced by another subsidy. (European Union's third participant's submission, paras. 70 and 71)

of Article 21 *ipso facto* excludes the applicability of Articles 11, 13.1, 22.1, and 22.2 does not correspond to a good faith interpretation of Articles 21 and 11. In India's view, the Panel "undermined the reasonable expectations of negotiating partners"[1257] with regard to Article 11 and allowed Members to "frustrate the object and purpose of" Article 11.[1258] For India, the Panel's interpretation opens up a "gaping hole" in the SCM Agreement whereby Members can circumvent the carefully negotiated safeguards under Articles 11, 13, and 22.[1259] Accordingly, since the Panel rejected India's claims under Articles 11.1, 13.1, 22.1, and 22.2 on the basis that these provisions are not applicable to administrative reviews conducted pursuant to Articles 21.1 and 21.2 of the SCM Agreement, India requests us to reverse the Panel's findings in this regard.

4.545 The United States asserts that the Panel was correct in rejecting India's attempt to import and apply the obligations contained in Article 11, 13, or 22 to administrative review proceedings. The United States contends that, in addition to the structure of the SCM Agreement separating the processes of investigation and review, the text of Articles 11.1, 13.1, 22.1, and 22.2 expressly limits the application of these provisions to the original investigation, just as Articles 21.1 and 21.2 apply in the context of review proceedings. The United States adds that India's challenge of the Panel's findings is based on the erroneous proposition that an investigating authority may not levy countervailing duties pursuant to administrative reviews on subsidy programmes that were not examined in the original investigation.[1260] The United States argues that, as the requirements articulated in Articles 11.1, 13.1, 22.1, and 22.2 are limited in their application to original investigations[1261], it follows that these requirements are not applicable to the USDOC's conduct of its administrative reviews.

4.546 India's claims focus on the following statements made by the Panel regarding the relationship between Articles 11 and 21 of the SCM Agreement:

> [T]he issue before the Panel is whether the USDOC was entitled, under Articles 21.1 and 21.2 of the SCM Agreement, to consider new subsidy allegations – i.e. subsidy programmes not formally examined in the original investigation – in the administrative reviews at issue, or whether, as India argues, new subsidy allegations could only be considered in the context of an investigation initiated under Article 11.1 of the SCM Agreement, and undertaken consistently with Articles 13.1, 22.1, and 22.2 of the SCM Agreement. In other words, we must decide whether the

---

[1257] India's appellant's submission, para. 637 (referring to Panel Report, *Korea – Procurement*, para. 7.93). (emphasis omitted)

[1258] India's appellant's submission, para. 637 (quoting Panel Report, *Korea – Procurement*, para. 7.94, in turn quoting *Yearbook of the International Law Commission, 1966*, Vol. II, p. 211).

[1259] India's appellant's submission, para. 637.

[1260] United States' appellee's submission, para. 577.

[1261] United States' appellee's submission, para. 583.

> scope of USDOC's administrative reviews was necessarily circumscribed and limited to the particular subsidy programmes that had been formally examined in the original investigation. If the USDOC was authorized to examine new subsidy allegations under Articles 21.1 and 21.2, we need not further consider India's claims. Conversely, if we find that the USDOC was not authorized to consider new subsidy allegations in administrative reviews, we would have to go on to examine whether the USDOC acted consistently with Articles 11.1, 13.1, 22.1 and 22.2 in the investigation and reviews at issue. We understand that this is the first time a panel has been faced with this specific question.[1262]

4.547 We also recall the Panel's response to India's request for clarification at the interim review stage. India requested the Panel to clarify whether the Panel had exercised judicial economy with regard to India's claims under Articles 11.1, 13.1, 22.1, and 22.2 of the SCM Agreement. Additionally, India requested the Panel to make a specific finding on whether the USDOC had complied with these provisions, arguing that its claims under these provisions were entirely independent from India's other claims relating to new subsidy allegations.[1263] The Panel "decided not to accommodate India's request"[1264], clarifying that it had not exercised judicial economy with regard to India's claims under Articles 11.1, 13.1, 22.1, and 22.2 of the SCM Agreement. Rather, the Panel explained that, as the USDOC was entitled under Articles 21.1 and 21.2 of the SCM Agreement to examine new subsidy allegations in the administrative reviews at issue, there was no need to examine the provisions at issue that regulate investigations.[1265]

4.548 For the reasons discussed above, we do not agree with India that the requirements set out in Articles 11.1 and 13.1 of the SCM Agreement apply to administrative reviews, carried out pursuant to Articles 21.1 and 21.2 of the SCM Agreement. In particular, we recall that nothing in the text of Articles 11 and 13 expressly imports the requirements of those provisions to the conduct of administrative reviews. Moreover, as the Appellate Body found in *Mexico – Anti-Dumping Measures on Rice*, the conditions set out in Article 21.2 of the SCM Agreement are "exhaustive" and Members are not allowed to condition the right of interested parties to an administrative review upon requirements other than those set out in Article 21.2.[1266]

4.549 Furthermore, we do not share India's view that Article 11 is the sole provision in the SCM Agreement that deals with the examination of the "existence, degree and effect of any alleged subsidy", and therefore that Articles 11.1 and 13.1 provide for the manner in which new subsidies are to be

---

[1262] Panel Report, para. 7.501.
[1263] Panel Report, para. 6.166.
[1264] Panel Report, para. 6.168.
[1265] *Ibid.*
[1266] Appellate Body Report, *Mexico – Anti-Dumping Measures on Rice*, para. 315.

considered in a review under Article 21. As we have discussed above, Articles 21.1 and 21.2 of the SCM Agreement permit an investigating authority to examine, in certain circumstances, new subsidy allegations in the conduct of an administrative review. With that in mind, we recall the Appellate Body's explanation that the scope of enquiry provided for under Article 11 is distinct from that provided for under Article 21 of the SCM Agreement. In an original investigation carried out under Article 11 of the SCM Agreement, the investigating authority must establish that all conditions set out in the SCM Agreement for the imposition of countervailing duties are fulfilled. In an administrative review, however, the investigating authority must address only those issues that have been raised before it by the interested parties or, in the case of an investigation conducted on its own initiative, those issues that warranted the examination.[1267] We are not persuaded that the examination of new subsidies in an administrative review alters these fundamentally different scopes of inquiry under Articles 11 and 21 of the SCM Agreement. Accordingly, we find that the Panel did not err in rejecting India's claims under Articles 11.1 and 13.1 of the SCM Agreement on the premise that the requirements set out in these provisions do not apply to administrative reviews, carried out pursuant to Articles 21.1 and 21.2 of the SCM Agreement.

4.550 However, we have expressed the view that, by virtue of the express textual link in Article 22.7 of the SCM Agreement, the notification and explanation obligations set out in Article 22 apply *mutatis mutandis* to administrative reviews. Accordingly, we find that the Panel's interpretation is erroneous insofar as it suggests that the obligations under Articles 22.1 and 22.2 are not applicable to administrative reviews carried out pursuant to Articles 21.1 and 21.2 of the SCM Agreement. In addition, we observe that the Panel's rejection of India's claim under Articles 22.1 and 22.2 concerning the USDOC's 2004, 2006, and 2007 administrative reviews is premised on the Panel's erroneous interpretation of the relationship between Articles 21 and 22 of the SCM Agreement. As a consequence, we also find that the Panel erred in rejecting India's claims that the USDOC acted inconsistently with Articles 22.1 and 22.2 when examining new subsidy allegations in the 2004, 2006, and 2007 administrative reviews.

4.551 This leads us to India's request that we complete the legal analysis and find that, in initiating its 2004, 2006, and 2007 administrative reviews, and with particular respect to eight new subsidy allegations[1268], the USDOC acted inconsistently with its obligations under Articles 22.1 and 22.2 of the

[1267] Appellate Body Report, *US – Lead and Bismuth II*, para. 63; and Panel Report, *Japan – DRAMs (Korea)*, para. 7.350.

[1268] The eight new subsidy allegations that are the subject of India's claims relate to the following programmes: Target Plus Scheme (TPS); Status Certificate programme; Export Promotion Zones & Export Oriented Unit (EPZ & EOU); Export Promotion Zones (EPZ); Income Tax under 10A & 10B; Market Development Assistance; Market Access Initiative; and Long-term Loans from GOI. (India's appellant's submission, para. 655; response to questioning at the oral hearing)

SCM Agreement. The Appellate Body has stressed that completion of the legal analysis can only be undertaken where there are factual findings by the panel, or undisputed facts on the panel record that provide the Appellate Body with a sufficient basis for its own legal analysis.[1269] The Appellate Body has also declined to complete the legal analysis where that would involve addressing claims that the panel had not examined at all[1270], particularly where, at the appellate review stage, the participants did not sufficiently address the issues needed to complete the legal analysis, including the probative value of the evidence not considered by the panel.[1271]

4.552 Turning to the instant dispute, we take note of India's assertion that, during the 2004, 2006, and 2007 administrative reviews, the USDOC conducted investigations into eight alleged new subsidy programmes without issuing any public notice containing the "description of the subsidy practice or practices to be investigated".[1272] India contends that the USDOC failed to comply with Articles 22.1 and 22.2 of the SCM Agreement. The United States, for its part, contends that, for each of its administrative reviews, the USDOC published a notice of initiation in the *Federal Register*, consistent with Article 22.1.[1273] Furthermore, the GOI and interested parties were "notified" of newly alleged subsidies, because they received those allegations directly by means of the USDOC's new subsidy memoranda.[1274] Where new subsidies were not alleged and therefore the USDOC did not issue a new subsidy memorandum, any new subsidy programmes were notified to the GOI and interested parties through questionnaires issued by the USDOC, and were publicized in the preliminary and final review determinations.[1275]

4.553 Based on the arguments and evidence put forward by India and the United States, it is apparent to us that the parties have divergent views as to what constitutes a sufficient public notice for the purpose of meeting the obligations under Articles 22.1 and 22.2 of the SCM Agreement, and whether the USDOC complied with those obligations. However, the Panel, having determined that the

---

[1269] See Appellate Body Reports, *Korea – Dairy*, para. 108; *Canada – Autos*, para. 145; *EC – Asbestos*, paras. 78-81; *US – Hot Rolled Steel*, paras. 174 and 180; *Canada – Dairy (Article 21.5 – New Zealand and US)*, para. 98; *US – Softwood Lumber IV*, para. 118; *EC – Selected Customs Matters*, paras. 278, 285, and 286; *US/Canada – Continued Suspension*, paras. 620 and 735; *US – Continued Zeroing*, paras. 193-195; and *Australia – Apples*, paras. 385 and 402.

[1270] Appellate Body Reports, *EC – Asbestos*, paras. 79 and 82; *US – Section 211 Appropriations Act*, para. 343; *EC – Poultry*, para. 107; *EC – Export Subsidies on Sugar*, para. 337.

[1271] Appellate Body Report, *Japan – DRAMs (Korea)*, para. 142.

[1272] India's appellant's submission, para. 656. (emphasis omitted)

[1273] United States' appellee's submission, paras. 612 and 613 (referring to Panel Exhibits USA-47; USA-80; USA-81; and USA-82 (see table of Panel Exhibits, at pp. 13-16 of this Report)).

[1274] United States' appellee's submission, paras. 612 and 613 (referring to Panel Exhibits USA-69; USA-78; IND-15B; IND-24; IND-25; IND-26; and IND-27 (see table of Panel Exhibits, at pp. 13-16 of this Report)).

[1275] United States' appellee's submission, para. 614 (referring to India's appellant's submission, para. 655; and Panel Exhibits IND-17; IND-32; and IND-37 (see table of Panel Exhibits, at pp. 13-16 of this Report)).

obligations under Article 22 do not apply to administrative reviews, did not examine this specific issue. Moreover, having reviewed the Panel record, we do not find sufficient arguments and evidence specific to the eight new subsidy allegations to which India's claim relates that would assist us in addressing this issue. For these reasons, we find that we are unable to complete the legal analysis in respect of India's claim as it relates to Articles 22.1 and 22.2 of the SCM Agreement.

4.7.3.3 Whether the Panel acted inconsistently with Articles 11 and 12.7 of the DSU

4.554 India argues that the Panel breached its duties under Articles 11 and 12.7 of the DSU to conduct an objective assessment of the matter before it and to provide a "basic rationale" for its findings.[1276] India alleges that the Panel breached these duties by narrowing the scope of India's claim by focusing on whether Articles 21.1 and 21.2 of the SCM Agreement permit the examination of new subsidy allegations in administrative review proceedings. In so doing, the Panel exercised false judicial economy by failing to address separately the "independent claims" of India under Articles 11.1, 13.1, 22.1, and 22.2 of the SCM Agreement.[1277] Consequently, India requests us to reverse the Panel's finding rejecting India's claims under Articles 11.1, 13.1, 22.1, and 22.2 of the SCM Agreement, and further requests us to complete the analysis with respect to these claims.

4.555 For the United States, the crux of India's complaint is that the Panel has misinterpreted Article 21 of the SCM Agreement as being exclusive of Article 11. The United States considers this to be a claim of legal error, and not a challenge to the Panel's objectivity.[1278] Hence, India's claim under Article 11 of the DSU should be rejected on that basis.[1279] As regards Article 12.7 of the DSU, the United States posits that, although India may not agree with the Panel's basic rationale underpinning its findings under Articles 11, 13, and 22 of the SCM Agreement, the Panel's Report reveals that this rationale was nonetheless provided. Therefore, India's appeal under Article 12.7 also should be rejected.[1280]

4.556 We observe that India relies on the same arguments in support of its discrete claims under Articles 11 and 12.7 of the DSU. Nevertheless, given that these two provisions provide for distinct duties to be undertaken by panels, we first address India's claim under Article 11 of the DSU before turning to its claim under Article 12.7 of the DSU.

1276 India's appellant's submission, para. 627.

1277 India's appellant's submission, paras. 622-626.

1278 United States' appellee's submission, para. 597 (referring to Appellate Body Reports, *China – Rare Earths*, para. 5.173; and *EC – Fasteners (China)*, para. 442).

1279 United States' appellee's submission, para. 597.

1280 United States' appellee's submission, para. 602.

4.557 We recall that a claim that a panel has failed to conduct an "objective assessment of the matter before it" required by Article 11 of the DSU is "a very serious allegation"[1281], and the Appellate Body has deemed it unacceptable for an appellant to simply recast factual arguments that it made before the panel in the guise of an Article 11 claim.[1282] India principally contends that the Panel acted inconsistently with Article 11 of the DSU by creating an "artificial dependency in India's claims" – i.e. India's claims under Articles 21.1 and 21.2, on the one hand, and India's claims under Articles 11.1, 13.1, 22.1, and 22.2, on the other hand.[1283] As a result, the Panel did not respond to the claims raised by India under Articles 11.1, 13.1, 22.1, and 22.2 because it assumed that the requirements in these provisions do not apply to administrative reviews conducted pursuant to Article 21 of the SCM Agreement.

4.558 We have considered above India's claim that the Panel failed to interpret correctly the relationship between Articles 11 and 21 of the SCM Agreement by finding them to be mutually exclusive. In conducting this analysis, the Panel made clear its view that the obligations under Articles 11.1, 13.1, 22.1, and 22.2 would be applicable only if the USDOC was authorized to examine new subsidy allegations under Articles 21.1 and 21.2 of the SCM Agreement. The Panel further found that the USDOC's examination of the new subsidy allegations at issue in its administrative reviews is proper, and that the requirements in Articles 11.1, 13.1, 22.1, and 22.2 therefore do not apply. Accordingly, as we see it, the Panel did not ignore India's claims; rather, it rejected them on the basis of its interpretation of Article 21 of the SCM Agreement. Consequently, we do not consider that India has demonstrated an independent claim under Article 11 of the DSU that the Panel failed to assess the matter before it objectively.

4.559 India further contends that the Panel breached its duty under Article 12.7 of the DSU because it did not provide a "basic rationale" for its finding that Articles 11 and 21 of the SCM Agreement are "mutually exclusive".[1284] We recall that the fact that the rationale set out by a panel is not one that an appellant agrees with is not sufficient to conclude that the panel failed to set out the basic rationale for its findings and recommendations as required by Article 12.7 of the DSU.[1285] Nor does Article 12.7 require panels to expound at length on the reasons for their findings and recommendations.[1286]

4.560 India's argument under Article 12.7 of the DSU appears to reiterate India's disagreement with the Panel's interpretation that Articles 11 and 21 of the

1281 Appellate Body Reports, *China – Rare Earths*, para. 5.227 (quoting Appellate Body Report, *EC – Poultry*, para. 133).

1282 Appellate Body Reports, *China – Rare Earths*, para. 5.178 (referring to Appellate Body Report, *EC – Fasteners (China)*, para. 442, in turn referring to Appellate Body Reports, *US – Steel Safeguards*, para. 498; and *Chile – Price Band System (Article 21.5 – Argentina)*, para. 238).

1283 India's appellant's submission, para. 624.

1284 India's appellant's submission, para. 626.

1285 Appellate Body Report, *Korea – Alcoholic Beverages*, para. 168.

1286 Appellate Body Report, *Mexico – Corn Syrup (Article 21.5 – US)*, para. 109.

SCM Agreement are mutually exclusive. That interpretation formed the basis of the Panel's finding rejecting India's claims under Articles 11.1, 13.1, 22.1, and 22.2 of the SCM Agreement. Although India may not agree with the Panel's finding rejecting India's interpretative position, the Panel nevertheless provided an explanation. On that basis, we do not consider that India has demonstrated that the Panel failed to set out the basic rationale for its findings and recommendations.

4.561 In sum, we *reject* India's claims that the Panel acted inconsistently with Articles 11 and 12.7 of the DSU.

4.7.4 Conclusion

4.562 For all of the above reasons, we conclude as follows in respect of the Panel's finding set out in paragraphs 7.508 and 8.3.j of its Report. While we *uphold* the finding of the Panel rejecting India's claims that the examination by the USDOC of new subsidy allegations in administrative reviews relating to the imports at issue is inconsistent with Articles 11.1, 13.1, 21.1, and 21.2 of the SCM Agreement, we *reverse* the finding of the Panel rejecting India's claims that the examination by the USDOC of new subsidy allegations in administrative reviews relating to the imports at issue is inconsistent with Articles 22.1 and 22.2 of the SCM Agreement. However, we *find* that we are unable to complete the legal analysis in respect of India's claim as it relates to Articles 22.1 and 22.2 of the SCM Agreement.

4.8 Cumulative Assessment of Imports in Countervailing Duty Investigations

4.8.1 Claims under Article 15 of the SCM Agreement

4.563 The United States requests us to reverse the Panel's findings and conclusions in section 7.6.1 of the Panel Report that the measure at issue, Section 1677(7)(G) of the US Statute, is inconsistent with Article 15.3[1287] and with Articles 15.1, 15.2, 15.4, and 15.5[1288] of the SCM Agreement "as such" and "as applied" in the original investigation at issue. The United States argues that, in reaching these findings, the Panel erred in its interpretation of these provisions and also alleges that the Panel acted inconsistently with Article 11 of the DSU in finding that Section 1677(7)(G) of the US Statute is inconsistent "as such" with Article 15 of the SCM Agreement.

4.8.1.1 The Panel's findings

4.564 Before the Panel India argued that Section 1677(7)(G) of the US Statute requires the US International Trade Commission (USITC) to assess cumulatively

1287 Panel Report, para. 7.356.
1288 Panel Report, para. 7.369.

the effects of subsidized imports with the effects of non-subsidized imports subject to anti-dumping investigations, and is therefore inconsistent with Article 15.3 and with Articles 15.1, 15.2, 15.4, and 15.5 of the SCM Agreement. The United States contended that these provisions of Article 15 are silent with regard to whether an investigating authority may cumulate the effects of subsidized imports with the effects of non-subsidized imports subject to anti-dumping investigations, and that they therefore do not prohibit such cumulative assessment.

4.565 The Panel began by setting out its interpretation of Article 15.3 and of Articles 15.1, 15.2, 15.4, and 15.5 of the SCM Agreement. The Panel considered that the issue before it was whether the SCM Agreement permits the cumulative assessment of the effects of imports that are subject to a countervailing duty investigation with the effects of imports that are *not* subject to a countervailing duty investigation, but that are subject to a parallel anti-dumping investigation. The Panel referred to this particular kind of cumulative assessment of the effects of subsidized and dumped imports from different sources as "cross-cumulation".[1289] The Panel also noted that other forms of cumulative assessment involving subsidized and dumped imports are possible. The Panel clarified that, in the light of the scope of the claims raised by India in this dispute, its findings would be limited to "'cross-cumulation' of the effects of subsidized imports with the effects of non-subsidized, dumped imports".[1290]

4.566 With regard to the interpretation of Article 15.3 of the SCM Agreement, the Panel noted that the fact that imports from more than one country are "simultaneously subject to countervailing duty investigations" is a necessary pre-condition for a cumulative assessment to be undertaken consistently with that provision. Accordingly, the Panel found that, under Article 15.3, the effects of imports that are not subject to a countervailing duty investigation cannot be assessed cumulatively with those of imports that are subject to a countervailing duty investigation. The Panel rejected the United States' argument that Article 15.3 does not address, and therefore does not regulate, cross-cumulation of the effects of subsidized imports with the effects of non-subsidized, dumped imports. For the Panel, the words "simultaneously subject to countervailing duty investigations" indeed regulate cross-cumulation in that they require that the assessment under Article 15.3 of the effects of the imports be limited to imports that are subject to countervailing duty investigations.

4.567 The Panel further considered that the context of other paragraphs of Article 15 of the SCM Agreement, as well as Article VI:6(a) of the GATT 1994, support its view that only the effects of imports subject to simultaneous countervailing duty investigations may be assessed cumulatively for purposes of an injury analysis in a countervailing duty investigation. In particular, the Panel relied on the fact that Articles 15.1, 15.2, 15.4, and 15.5 refer consistently to

---

1289 Panel Report, para. 7.339.

1290 Panel Report, fn 570 to para. 7.339.

"subsidized imports", and thus expressly limit the imports to be considered under Article 15. Regarding Article VI:6(a) of the GATT 1994, the Panel noted that the provision concerns both anti-dumping and countervailing duties, and that the phrase "effects of the dumping or subsidization, as the case may be", refers to injury caused either by the effect of the subsidy (one "case") or by the effect of dumping (the other "case"), and not to the effects of the subsidy *and* of dumping, cumulatively.[1291]

4.568 Furthermore, the Panel found that, contrary to the United States' argument, the Appellate Body's findings in *EC – Tube or Pipe Fittings* and *US – Oil Country Tubular Goods Sunset Reviews* do not support the proposition that the object and purpose of the SCM Agreement suggests that the "cross-cumulation" at issue is consistent with the obligations of the SCM Agreement. The Panel explained that these reports addressed the rationale for cumulation of the effects of dumped imports from several sources, but did not address the issue of cross-cumulation of the effects of dumped and subsidized imports.[1292]

4.569 Turning next to the interpretation of Articles 15.1, 15.2, 15.4, and 15.5 of the SCM Agreement, the Panel considered the main question to be whether the use of the term "subsidized imports" in these provisions limits the scope of the investigating authority's injury assessment to subsidized imports only. The Panel noted that this question was closely related to the question addressed in its analysis of Article 15.3, in which it had already considered the provisions of Articles 15.1, 15.2, 15.4, and 15.5 of the SCM Agreement as relevant context. In keeping with its earlier finding, the Panel found that the use of the term "subsidized imports" in these provisions limits the scope of the investigating authority's injury assessment to subsidized imports only.

4.570 With respect to the measure at issue, the Panel stated that "Section 1677(7)(G) requires, in certain situations, the USITC to cumulate the effects of subsidized imports with the effects of dumped, non-subsidized imports."[1293] The Panel did not provide further details as to which specific situations it was referring to in this statement. The Panel noted, however, that it was "undisputed that, in the [countervailing duty] investigation at issue, the USITC cumulated the effects of subsidized imports from India with the effects of non-subsidized, dumped imports from China, Kazakhstan, the Netherlands, Romania, Taiwan, and Ukraine, which were only subject to parallel [anti-dumping] investigations".[1294]

[1291] Panel Report, paras. 7.347 and 7.348.
[1292] Panel Report, paras. 7.353 and 7.354.
[1293] Panel Report, paras. 7.340 and 7.358. See also para. 7.322.
[1294] Panel Report, fn 596 to para. 7.356 and fn 611 to para. 7.369.

4.8.1.2 Article 15 of the SCM Agreement

4.571 On appeal, the United States contends that the Panel erred in its interpretation of Article 15.3 of the SCM Agreement in finding that "cross-cumulation" of the effects of subsidized imports with the effects of non-subsidized, dumped imports is inconsistent with this provision. The United States maintains that the fact that Article 15.3 does not specifically authorize an investigating authority to cumulate the effects of subsidized imports with those of dumped imports does not, in itself, indicate that such cross-cumulation is prohibited by the SCM Agreement. Rather, Article 15.3 is silent on the issue of whether cumulation of dumped and subsidized imports is permissible. The United States further contends that the context provided by Article 3.3 of the Anti-Dumping Agreement and by Article VI:6(a) of the GATT 1994 supports an interpretation of Article 15.3 permitting cross-cumulation of the effects of subsidized imports with the effects of dumped imports.

4.572 Moreover, the United States alleges that the Panel erred in finding that the consistent reference to "subsidized imports" in Articles 15.1, 15.2, 15.4, and 15.5 of the SCM Agreement limits the scope of the injury assessment to the effects of subsidized imports only. According to the United States, this finding of the Panel was based, in large part, on the Panel's "flawed reasoning" with respect to Article 15.3.[1295] For the United States, however, none of the provisions in Article 15 expressly prohibits the practice of cross-cumulation, or otherwise addresses a situation in which both anti-dumping and countervailing duty investigations are occurring simultaneously.

4.573 The United States further alleges that the Panel acted inconsistently with Article 11 of the DSU in finding that Section 1677(7)(G) of the US Statute requires, in certain situations, the USITC to cumulate the effects of subsidized imports with the effects of dumped, non-subsidized imports.[1296] The United States contends that the Panel's analysis of Section 1677(7)(G) consists merely of the assertion that it requires cross-cumulation, and alleges that the Panel provided no explanation describing how it came to its conclusion regarding the meaning of that section of the US Statute.

4.574 India requests us to uphold the Panel's finding that Section 1677(7)(G) is inconsistent "as such" and "as applied" with Article 15.3 and with Articles 15.1, 15.2, 15.4, and 15.5 of the SCM Agreement. India submits that the Panel's analysis is supported by the text and context of the provisions, as well as by the object and purpose of the SCM Agreement.

4.575 India contends that, in the light of the reference to imports "simultaneously subject to countervailing duty investigations", Article 15.3 cannot be construed as being silent on the issue of cumulating subsidized

---

[1295] United States' other appellant's submission, paras. 117 and 118.

[1296] United States' other appellant's submission, para. 122 (referring to Panel Report, paras. 7.322, 7.339, 7.340, and 7.358).

imports with non-subsidized imports; rather, it must be understood as prohibiting such cross-cumulation. Even assuming, *arguendo*, that Article 15.3 was silent on the issue of cross-cumulation, such silence must be interpreted as prohibiting cross-cumulation. Otherwise, cumulation of subsidized imports from different sources would be subject to several conditions, while cumulation of subsidized imports with non-subsidized imports from different sources would be entirely at the discretion of the investigating authority.

4.576 With regard to Section 1677(7)(G), India submits that it stipulates that the effects of all imports from countries covered by anti-dumping or countervailing duty investigations initiated on the same day must be assessed cumulatively. India maintains that the Panel reached its conclusion on the meaning of US law on the basis of the evidence submitted by India, which the United States had not challenged. India further argues that the United States cannot be permitted to raise indirectly on appeal a factual issue in the form of a claim under Article 11 of the DSU.

4.577 The United States' appeal calls for us to consider certain issues relating to the interpretation of specific elements of Articles 15.3 and of Articles 15.1, 15.2, 15.4, and 15.5 of the SCM Agreement. We turn first to Article 15.3, which sets out disciplines for conducting an injury and causation analysis. The provision stipulates:

> Where imports of a product from more than one country are simultaneously subject to countervailing duty investigations, the investigating authorities may cumulatively assess the effects of such imports only if they determine that *(a)* the amount of subsidization established in relation to the imports from each country is more than *de minimis* as defined in paragraph 9 of Article 11 and the volume of imports from each country is not negligible and *(b)* a cumulative assessment of the effects of the imports is appropriate in light of the conditions of competition between the imported products and the conditions of competition between the imported products and the like domestic product.

4.578 The central element of Article 15.3 is the provision that "investigating authorities may cumulatively assess" the effects of "such imports". The term "such imports" refers to the first clause of Article 15.3, which describes a situation "[w]here imports of a product from more than one country are simultaneously subject to countervailing duty investigations". The last clause of Article 15.3 stipulates the conditions that must be fulfilled in order for such cumulative assessment to be permitted. In particular, investigating authorities may engage in such cumulative assessment only if: "*(a)* the amount of subsidization established in relation to the imports from each country is more than *de minimis* and the volume of imports from each country is not negligible"; *and* "*(b)* a cumulative assessment of the effects of the imports is appropriate in the light of the conditions of competition between the imported products and the like domestic product."

4.579 Article 15.3 refers to imports "simultaneously subject to countervailing duty investigations".[1297] The provision that investigating authorities may, if the conditions set out in the last clause of Article 15.3 are fulfilled, cumulatively assess the effects of "such" imports thus requires that the imports be "subject to countervailing duty investigations". Conversely, the effects of imports other than such subsidized imports must not be incorporated in a cumulative assessment pursuant to Article 15.3. The text is clear in stipulating that being subject to countervailing duty investigations is a prerequisite for the cumulative assessment of the effects of imports under Article 15.3.

4.580 Our interpretation of Article 15.3 is supported by the context provided by other paragraphs of Article 15, under which the Panel made additional specific findings. Article 15 of the SCM Agreement is entitled "Determination of Injury". It contains several paragraphs setting out various obligations of Members with regard to the determination of injury in the context of a countervailing duty investigation.[1298] Article 15.1 stipulates that "[a] determination of injury for purposes of Article VI of GATT 1994 shall be based on positive evidence and involve an objective examination". As such, Article 15.1 is an overarching provision setting forth Members' fundamental substantive obligations in the context of a determination of injury and informing the more detailed obligations in the subsequent paragraphs of Article 15 concerning the determination of injury by an investigating authority.[1299] In *China – GOES*, the Appellate Body held that the provisions of Article 15 contemplate a logical progression of inquiry leading to an investigating authority's ultimate injury and causation determination. The Appellate Body further explained that this inquiry entails a consideration of the volume of subject imports and their price effects, and requires an examination of the impact of such imports on the domestic industry as revealed by a number of economic factors. These various elements are then linked through a causation analysis between the subject imports and the injury to the domestic industry, taking into account all factors that are being considered and evaluated.[1300]

4.581 Article 15.1 of the SCM Agreement stipulates that a determination of injury shall be based on positive evidence and involve an objective examination of both the volume and effect of the *subsidized imports* on prices in the domestic market for like products, and of the consequent impact of *these imports* on the domestic producers of such products. We note, in particular, the references to

---

[1297] For ease of reference, we refer in this section of the Report to "imports … simultaneously subject to countervailing duty investigations" also as "subsidized imports", and to "imports … simultaneously subject to anti-dumping investigations" also as "dumped imports".

[1298] The word "injury" is defined in footnote 45 of the SCM Agreement as meaning, unless otherwise specified, "material injury to a domestic industry, threat of material injury to a domestic industry or material retardation of the establishment of such an industry".

[1299] See Appellate Body Report, *Thailand – H-Beams*, para. 106, in the context of Article 3.1 of the Anti-Dumping Agreement.

[1300] Appellate Body Report, *China – GOES*, para. 128.

"subsidized imports" in the first part of the provision and to "these imports" in the latter part of the provision. We understand the words "these imports" to refer to the "subsidized imports" in the first part of the provision. By referring to "subsidized imports", rather than to "imports" generally, Article 15.1 requires that the injury analysis in the framework of Article 15, including Article 15.3, be limited to consideration of injury caused by "subsidized imports", rather than covering effects of imports in general.

4.582 We note that Article 3.1 of the Anti-Dumping Agreement contains a similar requirement with regard to the injury determination in an anti-dumping investigation, and the language of this provision is virtually identical to that of Article 15.1 of the SCM Agreement. Thus, we consider that Article 3.1 of the Anti-Dumping Agreement and relevant jurisprudence provide useful guidance for the interpretation of Article 15.1 of the SCM Agreement. With respect to Article 3.1 of the Anti-Dumping Agreement, the Appellate Body has held:

> It is clear from the text of Article 3.1 that investigating authorities must ensure that a "determination of injury" is made on the basis of "positive evidence" and an "objective examination" of the volume and effect of imports that *are dumped* – and to the exclusion of the volume and effect of imports that *are not dumped*.[1301]

In our view, the same rationale applies in the context of Article 15.1 of the SCM Agreement. Thus, investigating authorities must ensure that a determination of injury in countervailing duty investigations is made on the basis of "positive evidence" and an "objective examination" of the volume and effect of imports that *are subsidized*.

4.583 Turning next to Article 15.2 of the SCM Agreement, we note that, in keeping with the general principle set out in Article 15.1, it also refers specifically to the volume of the "subsidized imports" and the effect of "such imports", rather than to imports in general. Thus, Article 15.2 also does not allow an investigating authority to include the effects of imports that are not subsidized in an injury analysis pursuant to Article 15 of the SCM Agreement.

4.584 Similarly, Article 15.4 requires that, when evaluating all relevant economic factors pursuant to this provision, an investigating authority must ensure that it is examining the impact of the *subsidized imports*, to the exclusion of other non-subsidized imports. Moreover, Articles 15.2 and 15.4 are linked through a causation analysis between subject imports and the injury to the domestic industry pursuant to Article 15.5 of the SCM Agreement, which requires the investigating authority to establish that "*the subsidized imports* are, through the *effects of subsidies*, causing injury".[1302] In this regard, the investigating authority shall examine "any known factors other than the

[1301] Appellate Body Report, *EC – Bed Linen (Article 21.5 – India)*, para. 111. (emphasis original)
[1302] Emphasis added.

subsidized imports which at the same time are injuring the domestic industry". The injuries caused by these other factors must not be attributed to the subsidized imports. We agree with the Panel that the term "any known factors other than the subsidized imports" in Article 15.5 includes non-subsidized, dumped imports.[1303] Accordingly, consideration of the effects of non-subsidized, dumped imports in an injury analysis would not comport with the non-attribution requirement of Article 15.5 of the SCM Agreement.

4.585 Moreover, provisions throughout Part V of the SCM Agreement refer consistently to "subsidies" and "subsidized imports". For instance, Article 11.2(iv) stipulates that the initiation of a countervailing duty investigation must be based on, *inter alia*, evidence showing that alleged injury to a domestic industry "is caused by subsidized imports through the effects of the subsidies". As discussed above, Article 15 sets out the specific rules governing an investigating authority's injury determination so as to ascertain whether injury to the domestic industry is caused by the "subsidized imports". Neither Article 11, nor Article 15, contemplates that countervailing duties could be imposed to address injury caused by imports other than the subsidized imports.

4.586 In sum, the reference in Article 15.3 to "products ... simultaneously subject to countervailing duty investigations" indicates that investigating authorities must examine the volume, price effect, and consequent impact of imports that are subsidized, and must exclude from their assessment the volume, price effect, and consequent impact of imports that are *not* subsidized. The overarching requirement under Article 15.1 that an injury determination be based on positive evidence and involve an objective examination of the volume and the effect of subsidized imports and the impact of such imports on domestic producers confirms this interpretation. Furthermore, the references to "subsidized imports" in Articles 15.2, 15.4, and 15.5, as well as various references to "subsidized imports" in other provisions of Part V of the SCM Agreement, further confirm that the imposition of a countervailing duty is consistent with the SCM Agreement only if adopted to counteract injury caused by subsidized imports. Accordingly, we consider that Article 15.3 and Articles 15.1, 15.2, 15.4, and 15.5 of the SCM Agreement require that the injury analysis in the context of a countervailing duty determination be limited to consideration of the effects of subsidized imports.

4.8.1.3 Review of the Panel's analysis

4.587 With these considerations in mind, we turn to the United States' appeal of the Panel's interpretation of Article 15 of the SCM Agreement. We recall that, in the light of the scope of the claims raised by India in this dispute, the Panel's analysis focused on "'cross-cumulation' of the effects of subsidized imports with the effects of non-subsidized, dumped imports". The Panel found that Article

[1303] Panel Report, para. 7.368.

15.3 of the SCM Agreement does not authorize investigating authorities, when making an injury determination in a countervailing duty investigation, to assess cumulatively the effects of imports that are not subject to simultaneous countervailing duty investigations with the effects of imports that are subject to countervailing duty investigations.[1304] In support of its allegations of error, the United States contends that an analysis focusing solely on the injurious effects of either dumped or subsidized imports, when both types of unfairly traded imports are injuring the domestic industry at the same time, would necessarily prevent the investigating authority from "adequately taking into account" the injurious effects of "all unfairly traded imports" from various sources, and would render the authority's injury analysis incomplete.[1305]

4.588 In particular, the United States contends that the Panel erred in rejecting its argument that Article 15.3 is silent on the issue of whether cumulation of the effects of dumped and subsidized imports is permissible. For the United States, the fact that Article 15.3 of the SCM Agreement does not specifically authorize an investigating authority to cumulate the effects of subsidized imports with those of dumped imports does not, in itself, indicate that such cross-cumulation is prohibited by the SCM Agreement.

4.589 At the outset of our analysis, we refer to our interpretation of the framework of the injury analysis as set out in the various paragraphs of Article 15. We have found that Article 15 is not silent on the question of cumulation of the effects of subsidized imports with the effects of non-subsidized imports. As we have explained above, Article 15.3 provides that investigating authorities may, if the conditions set out in the last clause of Article 15.3 are fulfilled, cumulatively assess the effects of imports that are simultaneously subject to countervailing duty investigations. It follows that a cumulative assessment pursuant to Article 15.3 must not encompass the effects of non-subsidized imports. We therefore agree with the Panel's statement that imports being subject to simultaneous countervailing duty investigations "is a necessary pre-condition for a cumulative assessment to be undertaken consistently with Article 15.3".[1306]

4.590 The United States further alleges that the Panel erred in finding that the consistent reference to "subsidized imports" in Articles 15.1, 15.2, 15.4, and 15.5 of the SCM Agreement limits the scope of the injury assessment to the effects of subsidized imports only. According to the United States, this finding of the Panel was based, in large part, on the Panel's "flawed reasoning" with respect to Article 15.3.[1307] For the United States, however, none of the provisions in Article 15 expressly prohibits the practice of cross-cumulation, or otherwise addresses a situation in which both anti-dumping and countervailing duty investigations are occurring simultaneously.

1304 Panel Report, para. 7.344.
1305 United States' other appellant's submission, para. 107.
1306 Panel Report, para. 7.341. (fn omitted)
1307 United States' other appellant's submission, para. 118.

4.591 Based on our interpretation of Articles 15.1, 15.2, 15.4, and 15.5 of the SCM Agreement set out above, we agree with the Panel's finding that the consistent use of the term "subsidized imports" in these provisions limits the scope of the investigating authority's injury assessment to subsidized imports only.[1308] Indeed, we have noted that these provisions of Article 15 contain consistent references to "subsidies" and "subsidized imports", requiring investigating authorities to ensure that their examinations are directed at the effects of subsidized imports and exclude non-subsidized imports. We note, in addition, our finding above that the context provided by various other provisions of the SCM Agreement further confirms this interpretation of the provisions of Article 15 of the SCM Agreement.

4.592 The United States further argues that Article 3.3 of the Anti-Dumping Agreement, as interpreted by the Appellate Body in *EC – Tube or Pipe Fittings*, supports its view that cross-cumulation is permitted under the SCM Agreement. In particular, the United States refers to the Appellate Body's statement that the provision concerning cumulation in Article 3.3 of the Anti-Dumping Agreement reflects a recognition that "a domestic industry confronted with dumped imports originating from several countries may be injured by the cumulated effects of those imports, and that those effects may not be adequately taken into account in a country-specific analysis of the injurious effects of dumped imports."[1309] The United States asserts that the Appellate Body's reasoning concerning the rationale for cumulative assessment in anti-dumping duty investigations applies with equal force to the situation in the present case.[1310] The United States further contends that the Appellate Body report in *US – Oil Country Tubular Goods Sunset Reviews* supports its position, because, in that case, the Appellate Body found cumulation of the effects of imports from several countries in sunset reviews under Article 11.3 of the Anti-Dumping Agreement to be permissible, even though it is not expressly authorized in that Agreement.[1311]

4.593 We recall that, in *EC – Tube or Pipe Fittings*, the Appellate Body addressed the cumulative assessment of dumped imports from various sources. That case did not involve cumulation of the effects of dumped products with those of subsidized, non-dumped imports; rather, it involved cumulation of the effects of dumped imports from several countries. Similarly, the Appellate Body report in *US – Oil Country Tubular Goods Sunset Reviews* addresses cumulation of the effects of dumped imports from several countries. However, the issue before us is a different one, as the present case relates to cumulation of the effects of dumped imports with those of subsidized, *non-dumped* imports. The rationale of the Appellate Body's findings in *EC – Tube or Pipe Fittings* and *US*

[1308] Panel Report, para. 7.360.

[1309] United States' other appellant's submission, para. 106 (quoting Appellate Body Report, *EC – Tube or Pipe Fittings*, para. 116).

[1310] United States' other appellant's submission, para. 107.

[1311] United States' other appellant's submission, para. 104 (referring to Appellate Body Report, *US – Oil Country Tubular Goods Sunset Reviews*, paras. 294-300).

– *Oil Country Tubular Goods Sunset Reviews* provides no basis for including *non-subsidized* imports within a cumulative assessment of the effects of *subsidized* imports from several countries in a countervailing duty investigation pursuant to Article 15 of the SCM Agreement. The text of both Article 3.3 of the Anti-Dumping Agreement and Article 15.3 of the SCM Agreement is clear in that it refers to "dumped imports" and "imports ... subject to countervailing duty investigations", respectively, and thus covers cumulation of dumped imports from several countries (in the case of Article 3.3 of the Anti-Dumping Agreement) and of subsidized imports (in the case of Article 15.3 of the SCM Agreement). Thus, we see no basis in the text of Article 15.3 of the SCM Agreement for cumulatively assessing the effects of subsidized imports with those of non-subsidized imports.

4.594 The United States further argues that "Article 15 must allow an investigating authority to take account of the effects that all unfairly traded imports are having on a domestic industry"[1312], and that the group of "unfairly traded imports" must include both dumped and subsidized products where anti-dumping and countervailing duty investigations are conducted simultaneously. In this regard, we note that the phrase "unfairly traded products" or similar language is not used in Article 15 of the SCM Agreement. Accordingly, we see no basis in the text of Article 15 for the proposition that, for the purposes of an injury determination pursuant to Article 15, an investigating authority may consider a single group of "unfairly traded imports" rather than considering "imports simultaneously subject to countervailing duty investigations" or "subsidized imports", as stipulated in Article 15.3, or in Articles 15.1, 15.2, 15.4, and 15.5, respectively.

4.595 In addition, the United States submits that an analysis focusing solely on the effects of either dumped or subsidized imports alone would prevent the investigating authority from adequately taking into account the injurious effects of all unfairly traded imports, and consequently frustrate the purpose of both the SCM Agreement and the Anti-Dumping Agreement.[1313]

4.596 The Panel addressed this argument by noting that the various provisions of Article 15 refer to "subsidized imports" in setting out the requirements for injury determinations. In particular, the Panel held:

> It is clear to us that the *object* of the analysis to be made under Article 15 is injury caused by "subsidized imports", and not injury caused by "unfairly traded imports". In our view, it would not be reasonable to conclude that Article 15, in specifying criteria for an examination of injury based on the effects of subsidized imports,

---

[1312] United States' other appellant's submission, para. 121.

[1313] United States' other appellant's submission, paras. 112-115; Panel Report, para. 7.352 (referring to United States' first written submission to the Panel, paras. 122 and 126; and opening statement at the second Panel meeting, para. 56).

> would nevertheless allow – or at least not prevent – the inclusion of non-subsidized imports in that analysis without at least an indication in the text to that effect. While imports subject to an anti-dumping investigation may be unfairly traded, they are clearly not subsidized imports, and the United States does not contend otherwise.[1314]

We see no reason to find fault with the Panel's analysis in this respect. The Panel's reasoning based on the text of Article 15, in particular with respect to the use of the term "subsidized imports" in that provision, comports with our interpretation of Article 15 of the SCM Agreement set out above.

4.597 Finally, we note the United States' argument that Article VI:6(a) of the GATT 1994 supports its reading that the cross-cumulation at issue in this dispute is consistent with the provisions of Article 15 of the SCM Agreement. Article VI:6(a) of the GATT 1994 stipulates:

> No Member shall levy any anti-dumping or countervailing duty on the importation of any product of the territory of another Member unless it determines that the effect of the dumping or subsidization, as the case may be, is such as to cause or threaten material injury to an established domestic industry, or is such as to retard materially the establishment of a domestic industry.

4.598 The United States relies in particular on the phrase "as the case may be" in Article VI:6(a). For the United States, this language recognizes that "there may be situations in which it 'may be the case' that the unfair trade practices covered by an authority's injury determination may involve dumping, subsidization, or both unfair trade practices."[1315]

4.599 We examine the phrase "as the case may be" in Article VI:6(a) within the structure of that provision, referring to "the effect of the dumping or subsidization, as the case may be". In particular, we observe that this clause refers to two elements, "dumping" and "subsidization", and connects these two elements with the word "or". To us, the use of "or", as well as the use of the singular "the effect", indicates that the provision refers separately to "dumping" or to "subsidization". Read in this context, the phrase "as the case may be" clarifies that injury may be caused by either the effect of the subsidy (one "case") or the effect of dumping (the other "case").[1316] We therefore agree with the Panel that the phrase "as the case may be" refers to one of two alternatives expressly listed in this provision, and that a third alternative posited by the United States – "dumped and subsidized imports" or "unfairly traded imports" – is not present in Article VI:6(a).[1317] Accordingly, we do not see Article VI:6(a)

[1314] Panel Report, para. 7.343. (emphasis original)
[1315] United States' other appellant's submission, para. 110.
[1316] Panel Report, para. 7.347 (referring to India's second written submission to the Panel, para. 65).
[1317] Panel Report, para. 7.347.

of the GATT 1994 as supporting the proposition that non-subsidized imports may be taken into account in an injury determination pursuant to Article 15 of the SCM Agreement.

4.600 For all the above reasons, we *find* that the Panel did not err in finding that Article 15.3 and Articles 15.1, 15.2, 15.4, and 15.5 of the SCM Agreement do not authorize investigating authorities to assess cumulatively the effects of imports that are not subject to simultaneous countervailing duty investigations with the effects of imports that are subject to countervailing duty investigations.[1318]

4.8.2 Claims under Article 11 of the DSU

4.601 The United States alleges that the Panel acted inconsistently with Article 11 of the DSU in finding that Section 1677(7)(G) of the US Statute "requires, in certain situations, the USITC to cumulate the effects of subsidized imports with the effects of dumped, non-subsidized imports".[1319] The United States maintains that, where a Member challenges another Member's legislation as such, Article 11 of the DSU requires a panel "to examine the meaning and scope of the municipal law at issue"[1320] and "to conduct a detailed examination of [the domestic] legislation in assessing its consistency with WTO law".[1321] According to the United States, however, the Panel failed to address the terms of Section 1677(7)(G) and failed to provide any reasoning as to why it requires, in certain situations, the USITC to assess cumulatively the effects of subsidized imports with the effects of dumped, non-subsidized imports.[1322] The United States therefore requests us to reverse the Panel's findings that Section 1677(7)(G) of the US Statute is "as such" inconsistent with Articles 15.1, 15.2, 15.3, 15.4, and 15.5 of the SCM Agreement.[1323]

4.8.2.1 The Panel's findings regarding Section 1677(7)(G)

4.602 The Panel separately assessed whether Section 1677(7)(G) is "as such" and "as applied" consistent with Article 15.3, and with Articles 15.1, 15.2, 15.4, and 15.5 of the SCM Agreement, respectively. In both assessments the Panel first set out the issue before it. Immediately thereafter, the Panel stated in its analysis under Article 15.3 that, "[i]n [its] view, Section 1677(7)(G) requires, in certain situations, the USITC to cumulate the effects of subsidized imports with

1318 Panel Report, sections 7.6.1.5.1 and 7.6.1.5.2.

1319 Panel Report, paras. 7.340 and 7.358. See also paras. 7.322 and 7.339.

1320 United States' other appellant's submission, para. 123 (quoting Appellate Body Report, *US – Countervailing and Anti-Dumping Measures (China)*, para. 4.98).

1321 United States' other appellant's submission, para. 123 (quoting Appellate Body Report, *US – Hot-Rolled Steel*, para. 200).

1322 United States' other appellant's submission, para. 126.

1323 United States' other appellant's submission, para. 122.

the effects of dumped, non-subsidized imports."[1324] Similarly, at the beginning of its analysis relating to Articles 15.1, 15.2, 15.4, and 15.5, the Panel stated that "[i]t is clear ... that Section 1677(7)(G) requires, in certain situations, the USITC to cumulatively assess the effects of subsidized imports with the effects of dumped, non-subsidized imports."[1325] Moreover, we note that in the subsection entitled "Factual background" at the beginning of the section in the Panel Report relating to Article 15 of the SCM Agreement, the Panel qualified Section 1677(7)(G) as a provision that "requires the USITC to cumulatively assess, for purposes of material injury, the effects of dumped and subsidized imports on the domestic industry".[1326] Beyond these statements, the Panel did not engage with the question of whether, to what extent, or under which circumstances Section 1677(7)(G) requires the USITC to assess cumulatively the effects of subsidized imports with the effects of dumped, non-subsidized imports.

4.8.2.2 Arguments raised on appeal

4.603 The United States maintains that the Panel's statements identified above comprise the whole of the Panel's analysis with regard to the Section 1677(7)(G) of the US Statute. None of these statements are preceded or followed by an explanation describing how the Panel arrived at its conclusions regarding the meaning of the law. For the United States, the Panel's assessment consists of mere assertions only, and the Panel therefore failed to comply with its duty under Article 11 of the DSU.[1327]

4.604 The United States maintains that, while Section 1677(7)(G) explicitly provides for cumulation "with respect to all countries subject to [anti-dumping] petitions filed on the same day, and with respect to all countries subject to [countervailing duty] petitions filed on the same day", it is "on its face ... not definitive"[1328] with regard to cross-cumulation. For the United States, the Panel therefore erred in finding that Section 1677(7)(G)(i) requires, in certain situations, cross-cumulation, and is thus inconsistent with Article 15.3 of the SCM Agreement.

4.605 India responds that, by using the word "shall", the measure at issue mandates that all imports from countries covered by anti-dumping or countervailing duty investigations initiated on the same day must be cumulatively assessed. India emphasizes that the United States did not contest this reading of the measure before the Panel. Furthermore, India maintains that

[1324] Panel Report, para. 7.340.
[1325] Panel Report, para. 7.358.
[1326] Panel Report, para. 7.322.
[1327] United States' other appellant's submission, paras. 127 and 128.
[1328] United States' other appellant's submission, para. 96.

the interpretation of the US law at issue "is a matter of fact"[1329], and that the Panel was therefore entitled to reach its conclusion on the basis of the evidence submitted by India.

4.606 For India, the text of the measure at issue is self-evident and, in the light of the fact that the United States did not contest India's reading of the measure, no additional explanation by the Panel was required. India submits that the production of the text of a measure, alone, may be considered adequate to establish a *prima facie* case[1330] and that evidence beyond the text of the measure needs to be considered only where the text of the measure is unclear.[1331]

4.8.2.3 Review of the Panel's analysis of Section 1677(7)(G)

4.607 Before turning to evaluate the claim before us, we recall the standard articulated by the Appellate Body concerning a panel's duty under Article 11 of the DSU. We have addressed this standard above.[1332] In particular, with regard to assessing a Member's municipal law, the Appellate Body has found that, "[a]s part of their duties under Article 11 of the DSU, panels have the obligation to examine the meaning and scope of the municipal law at issue in order to make an objective assessment of the matter before it."[1333] Moreover, in order to make an "objective assessment of the applicability of specific provisions of the covered agreements to a measure properly before it", a panel must "thoroughly scrutinize the measure before it, both in its design and in its operation, and identify its principal characteristics".[1334] In this vein, the Appellate Body has also held that "a proper determination of which provision of the WTO agreements applies to a given measure must be grounded in a proper understanding of the measure's relevant characteristics."[1335] Furthermore, we recall that, in *US – Countervailing and Anti-Dumping Measures (China)*, the Appellate Body held that, "in ascertaining the meaning of municipal law, a panel should undertake a holistic assessment of all relevant elements, starting with the text of the law and including, but not limited to, relevant practices of administering agencies."[1336]

4.608 The United States alleges that the Panel acted inconsistently with its obligation to conduct an objective assessment of the matter pursuant to Article

[1329] India's appellee's submission, para. 71 (referring to Appellate Body Report, *India – Patents (US)*, para. 66; and Panel Report, *US – Section 301 Trade Act*, para. 7.18).

[1330] India's appellee's submission, para. 73 (referring to Appellate Body Reports, *US – Oil Country Tubular Goods Sunset Reviews*, para. 263; *US – Carbon Steel*, para. 157; *Chile – Price Band System (Article 21.5 –Argentina)*, para. 135; and *Mexico – Anti-Dumping Measures on Rice*, para. 269).

[1331] India's appellee's submission, para. 73 (referring to Appellate Body Report, *US – Carbon Steel*, para. 157).

[1332] See *supra*, section 4.3.1.3.

[1333] Appellate Body Report, *US – Countervailing and Anti-Dumping Measures (China)*, para. 4.98.

[1334] Appellate Body Reports, *China – Auto Parts*, para. 171.

[1335] Appellate Body Report, *US – Large Civil Aircraft (2nd complaint)*, para. 586.

[1336] Appellate Body Report, *US – Countervailing and Anti-Dumping Measures (China)*, para. 4.101.

11 of the DSU. In particular, the United States claims that the Panel failed to address the terms of Section 1677(7)(G) and failed to provide any reasoning as to why it requires, in certain situations, the USITC to assess cumulatively the effects of subsidized imports with the effects of dumped, non-subsidized imports.

4.609 We note that the Panel set out the text of Section 1677(7)(G) in subsection 7.7.2 of its Report, entitled "Factual background". The Panel asserted that Section 1677(7)(G) "requires the USITC to cumulatively assess, for purposes of determining material injury, the effects of dumped and subsidized imports on the domestic industry when certain conditions are met."[1337] The Panel then turned to its interpretation of Article 15.3 and of Articles 15.1, 15.2, 15.4, and 15.5 of the SCM Agreement. At the outset of each analysis, the Panel stated that, in its view, "Section 1677(7)(G) requires, in certain situations, the USITC to [cumulate / cumulatively assess] the effects of subsidized imports with the effects of dumped, non-subsidized imports."[1338] Without addressing further the content of Section 1677(7)(G), the Panel concluded that Section 1677(7)(G) is inconsistent with Article 15.3 and with Articles 15.1, 15.2, 15.4, and 15.5 of the SCM Agreement "as such" and "as applied" in the original investigation at issue.[1339]

4.610 We have set out above the obligations of a panel pursuant to Article 11 of the DSU. In particular, we have recalled the finding of the Appellate Body in *US – Countervailing and Anti-Dumping Measures (China)* that, "in ascertaining the meaning of municipal law, a panel should undertake a holistic assessment of all relevant elements, starting with the text of the law and including, but not limited to, relevant practices of administering agencies."[1340]

4.611 In the present case, the Panel did not make an assessment of the measure at issue. The Panel neither analysed the text of Section 1677(7)(G) nor considered any relevant practice. The Panel asserted that Section 1677(7)(G) requires, in certain situations, the USITC to cumulate the effects of subsidized imports with the effects of dumped, non-subsidized imports. However, the Panel failed to specify what it considered those "certain situations" to be. Nor did the Panel provide reasons based on the text of the measure as to why it required the USITC to cumulate the effects of subsidized imports with the effects of dumped, non-subsidized imports.

4.612 We note that, before the Panel, the parties do not seem to have engaged in much discussion about whether Section 1677(7)(G) requires or permits cross-cumulation of the volume and effects of subsidized and non-subsidized imports. India submitted that, "in cases where only a sub-set of countries subject to [anti-dumping] investigations are subject to simultaneous [countervailing-duty]

[1337] Panel Report, para. 7.322.
[1338] Panel Report, paras. 7.340 and 7.358.
[1339] Panel Report, paras. 7.356 and 7.369.
[1340] Appellate Body Report, *US – Countervailing and Anti-Dumping Measures (China)*, para. 4.101.

investigations, Section 1677(7)(G) *requires* the cumulative assessment of the effects of subsidized imports with the effects of imports not subject to simultaneous [countervailing duty] investigations."[1341] In contrast, the United States maintained that the provisions of Section 1677(7)(G) "*permit* the [USITC] to cumulate subsidized or dumped imports from multiple countries subject to antidumping or countervailing duty investigations if certain criteria are met".[1342] In its subsequent submissions to the Panel, the United States did not revert to the issue of whether Section 1677(7)(G) "requires" or "permits" such a cumulative assessment, nor did it raise any objection to India's characterization of this provision.

4.613 However, the limited nature of the parties' submissions as to the meaning of the measure at issue cannot absolve the Panel from its duties to determine the meaning of municipal law, to engage in an objective assessment of the matter, and to reflect the considerations that led to its conclusion in its report. This is particularly so where the challenge involves a Members' legislation and thus a measure of general and prospective application. Without ascertaining the precise meaning of the measure, a panel cannot find that such measure will necessarily be inconsistent with a Member's obligations under the covered agreements. An "objective assessment" of a measure in the light of such a claim requires a thorough analysis of the measure, which must also be reflected in the panel report.

4.614 Moreover, we consider that it does not comport with the standard of Article 11 of the DSU for the Panel to have found that Section 1677(7)(G) requires "in certain situations" the USITC to cumulate the effects of subsidized imports with the effects of dumped, non-subsidized imports, without specifying these situations. This finding provides the basis for the Panel's conclusions that Section 1677(7)(G) is inconsistent with Article 15.3 and with Articles 15.1, 15.2, 15.4, and 15.5 of the SCM Agreement. Having found that Section 1677(7)(G) is inconsistent with these provisions, the Panel made a recommendation pursuant to Article 19.1 of the DSU, that the United States bring the measure into conformity with its obligations under the SCM Agreement. However, in the light of the vagueness of the Panel's finding regarding the extent to which the measure at issue is inconsistent with the United States' obligations under the SCM Agreement, the scope of the Panel's recommendation pursuant to Article 19.1 of the DSU remains unclear. Consequently, the implementation obligation of the United States is ill-defined. In failing to articulate clearly the scope of its finding of inconsistency, the Panel failed to comply with its duties under Article 11 of the DSU, including to make such findings as will assist the DSB in making the

[1341] Panel Report, para. 7.324 (referring to India's first written submission to the Panel, paras. 109-115 and 497-499; opening statement at the first Panel meeting, paras. 21, 41, and 42; second written submission to the Panel, paras. 52 and 56; and opening statement at the second Panel meeting, para. 18). (emphasis added)

[1342] United States' first written submission to the Panel, para. 86. (emphasis added)

recommendations or in giving the rulings provided for in the covered agreements.

4.615 Accordingly, we *find* that the Panel failed to comply with its duty under Article 11 of the DSU to conduct an objective assessment of the matter before it. We consequently *reverse* the Panel's findings, in paragraphs 7.356, 7.369, 8.2.c, and 8.2.d of the Panel Report, that Section 1677(7)(G) of the US Statute is inconsistent "as such" with Article 15.3, and with Articles 15.1, 15.2, 15.4, and 15.5 of the SCM Agreement.[1343]

4.616 Having reversed these findings of the Panel, we turn to consider whether we are in a position to complete the legal analysis. We note that the Appellate Body has completed the legal analysis with a view to facilitating the prompt settlement and effective resolution of the dispute[1344] when sufficient factual findings by the panel and undisputed facts on the panel record allowed it to do so.[1345] In order to complete the legal analysis in the present case, the focus of our analysis is on the text of the measure at issue.

4.617 We begin by considering the text of Section 1677(7)(G) of the US Statute, which provides, in relevant part:

> (G) Cumulation for determining material injury
>
> (i) In general

For purposes of clauses (i) and (ii) of subparagraph (C), and subject to clause (ii), the Commission shall cumulatively assess the volume and effect of imports of the subject merchandise from all countries with respect to which–

> (I) petitions were filed under section 1671a(b) or 1673a(b) of this title on the same day,
>
> (II) investigations were initiated under section 1671a(a) or 1673a(a) of this title on the same day, or
>
> (III) petitions were filed under section 1671a(b) or 1673a(b) of this title and investigations were initiated under section 1671a(a) or 1673a(a) of this title on the same day,
>
> if such imports compete with each other and with domestic like products in the United States market.

[1343] Panel Report, paras. 7.356 and 7.369.

[1344] See Appellate Body Reports, *Australia – Salmon*, paras. 117-136; *US – Wheat Gluten*, paras. 80-92; and *Canada – Aircraft (Article 21.5 – Brazil)*, paras. 43-52.

[1345] See Appellate Body Reports, *US – Gasoline*, p. 19, DSR 1996:I, p. 18; *Canada – Periodicals*, p. 24, DSR 1997:I, p. 469; *EC – Poultry*, para. 156; *EC – Hormones*, para. 222; *US – Shrimp*, paras. 123 and 124; *Japan – Agricultural Products II*, para. 112; *US – FSC*, para. 133; *Australia – Salmon*, paras. 117 and 118; *US – Lamb*, paras. 150 and 172; *US – Section 211 Appropriations Act*, para. 352; *EC and certain member States – Large Civil Aircraft*, paras. 1174-1178; and *US – Large Civil Aircraft (2nd complaint)*, paras. 1272-1274.

4.618 In order to assess whether Section 1677(7)(G) is inconsistent with Article 15.3, as well as with Articles 15.1, 15.2, 15.4, and 15.5 of the SCM Agreement, we turn to consider whether Section 1677(7)(G) indeed requires the USITC to cumulate the effects of subsidized imports with the effects of dumped, non-subsidized imports.

4.619 We note that Section 1677(7)(G) refers to Section 1671a of the US Statute, which is entitled "Procedures for initiating a countervailing duty investigation". Section 1671a provides for two types of initiation procedures, namely, the procedures for initiation of a countervailing duty investigation by the investigating authority itself pursuant to Section 1671a(a), and the procedures for initiating a countervailing duty investigation upon petition of domestic producers of the like product pursuant to Section 1671a(b).[1346]

4.620 The other provision referred to in Section 1677(7)(G) is Section 1673a of the US Statute, entitled "Procedures for initiating an anti-dumping duty investigation". It provides for two types of initiation procedures, namely, the procedures for initiation of an anti-dumping duty investigation by the investigating authority itself pursuant to Section 1673a(a), and the procedures for initiating an anti-dumping duty investigation upon petition of domestic producers pursuant to Section 1673a(b).[1347]

[1346] Section 1671a(a) and (b) of the US Statute provide in relevant part:

> § 1671a. Procedures for initiating a countervailing duty investigation
>
> (a) Initiation by administering authority
>
> A countervailing duty investigation shall be initiated whenever the administering authority determines, from information available to it, that a formal investigation is warranted into the question of whether the elements necessary for the imposition of a duty under section 1671(a) of this title exist.
>
> (b) Initiation by petition
>
> (1) Petition requirements
>
> A countervailing duty proceeding shall be initiated whenever an interested party described in subparagraph (C), (D), (E), (F), or (G) of section 1677(9) of this title files a petition with the administering authority, on behalf of an industry, which alleges the elements necessary for the imposition of the duty imposed by section 1671(a) of this title, and which is accompanied by information reasonably available to the petitioner supporting those allegations. The petition may be amended at such time, and upon such conditions, as the administering authority and the Commission may permit.

[1347] Section 1673a(a) and (b) of the US Statute provide in relevant part:

> § 1673a. Procedures for initiating an antidumping duty investigation
>
> (a) Initiation by administering authority
>
> (1) In general
>
> An antidumping duty investigation shall be initiated whenever the administering authority determines, from information available to it, that a formal investigation is warranted into the question of whether the elements necessary for the imposition of a duty under section 1673 of this title exist.
>
> ...
>
> (b) Initiation by petition
>
> (1) Petition requirements

4.621 From a joint reading of Section 1677(7)(G) with the provisions of the US Statute referenced therein, it appears that the provision requires an investigating authority to "cumulatively assess the volume and effect of imports of the subject merchandise from all countries" in any of the following three scenarios:

a. petitions to initiate countervailing duty investigations *or* anti-dumping duty investigations are filed on the same day;

b. countervailing duty investigations *or* anti-dumping duty investigations are initiated by the investigating authority on the same day; or

c. petitions to initiate countervailing duty investigations *or* anti-dumping duty investigations are filed on the same day *and* countervailing duty investigations *or* anti-dumping duty investigations are initiated by the investigating authority.

4.622 We note that the word "or" appears in all three scenarios to connect the references to countervailing duty investigations and anti-dumping duty investigations. In addition, in the third scenario, the word "and" is used to connect references to countervailing duty investigations or anti-dumping duty investigations initiated by the investigating authority *and* such investigations initiated upon petition of domestic producers.

4.623 The word "or" may have a different meaning depending on the context in which it is used. It may be used in an exclusive sense, meaning *one or the other, but not both*. Alternatively, it may be used in an inclusive sense, meaning *either one or the other, or both in combination*. Both usages of the word "or" are common and, accordingly, dictionary definitions accommodate both usages.[1348] Moreover, the Appellate Body has previously addressed the different usages of the word "or" in other provisions of the covered agreements and has found that "'or' can be exclusive, and 'or' can also be inclusive".[1349]

4.624 Turning to the specific context in which the word "or" is used in Section 1677(7)(G), we note that, when read in an exclusive sense, the word "or" used in the first scenario – i.e. petitions are filed under Section 1671a(b) (countervailing duties) or 1673a(b) (anti-dumping duties) on the same day – would suggest that the USITC "shall cumulatively assess" the volume and effects of imports *either* within the context of countervailing duty investigations

> An antidumping proceeding shall be initiated whenever an interested party described in subparagraph (C), (D), (E), (F), or (G) of section 1677(9) of this title files a petition with the administering authority, on behalf of an industry, which alleges the elements necessary for the imposition of the duty imposed by section 1673 of this title, and which is accompanied by information reasonably available to the petitioner supporting those allegations. The petition may be amended at such time, and upon such conditions, as the administering authority and the Commission may permit.

[1348] Oxford English Dictionary online, <http://www.oed.com/view/Entry/132129>.

[1349] Appellate Body Report, *US – Line Pipe*, para. 164, with regard to Article 2.1 of the Agreement on Safeguards.

initiated by petition on the same day, *or* within the context of anti-dumping duty investigations initiated by petition on the same day. Similarly, under the second scenario, – i.e. where investigations are initiated under Section 1671a(a) (countervailing duties) or 1673a(a) (anti-dumping duties) on the same day – the word "or" read in the exclusive sense would suggest that the USITC "shall cumulatively assess" the volume and effects of imports *either* within the context of countervailing duty investigations initiated by the authority on the same day, *or* within the context of anti-dumping duty investigations initiated by the authority on the same day. Read in that way, the authority would *not* be required to cumulate the volume and effects of dumped and subsidized imports under the first and second scenario.[1350]

4.625 We now turn to the third scenario, i.e. petitions are filed under Section 1671a(b) or 1673a(b) (countervailing duties or anti-dumping duties) of this title *and* investigations are initiated under section 1671a(a) or 1673a(a) (countervailing duties or anti-dumping duties) of this title on the same day. In this scenario, even if the word "or" is read in its exclusive sense, cumulation of the volume and effects of dumped and subsidized imports would be required if, on the same day, countervailing duty investigations are initiated by petition *and* anti-dumping duty investigations are initiated by the authority, or vice-versa. This is so because Section 1677(7)(G)(iii) expressly refers to a situation where petitions are filed *and* investigations are initiated with respect to anti-dumping duties and countervailing duties on the same day. In that situation, the investigating authority would be required to assess cumulatively the volume and effect of imports of the subject merchandise from all countries with respect to which the conditions of the third scenario are fulfilled. Thus, Section 1677(7)(G)(iii) requires cumulation of the volume and effects of dumped and subsidized imports in the event that the conditions set out in that provision are fulfilled.

4.626 Accordingly, if the word "or" is read in its exclusive sense throughout the provision of Section 1677(7)(G), cumulation of the volume and effects of dumped and subsidized imports would be required only under Section 1677(7)(G)(iii). However, if the word "or" is read in its inclusive sense – i.e. as

---

[1350] We note, however, that India has referred to a statement in the USITC's preliminary determination at issue, which indicates that, in that determination, the agency read the word "or" in Section 1677(7)(G) in the inclusive sense and thus considered itself required to assess cumulatively the volume and price effects of all imports subject to countervailing duty and anti-dumping investigations initiated on the same day:

> For purposes of evaluating the volume and price effects for a determination of material injury by reason of the subject imports, section 771(7)(G)(i) of the Act requires the Commission to assess cumulatively the volume and effect of imports of the subject merchandise from all countries as to which petitions were filed and/or investigations self-initiated by Commerce on the same day, if such imports compete with each other and with domestic like products in the US market.

(USITC Final Determinations (Panel Exhibit IND-9), pp. 9-10 (referring to Section 1677(7)(G))) The Panel referred to this determination in footnote 531 to paragraph 7.323 of its Report.

meaning *either one or the other, or both in combination* – then the word "or" in Section 1677(7)(G) would indicate that the authority shall cumulate the volume and effects of dumped and subsidized imports under Section 1677(7)(G)(i), (ii), and (iii).

4.627 It follows from this analysis that, regardless of whether the word "or" is interpreted in the "inclusive" sense or in the "exclusive" sense, Section 1677(7)(G) requires, to some extent, cumulation of the volume and effects of dumped and subsidized imports. If the word "or" is interpreted in the "exclusive" sense, such cumulation would be required only in the third scenario. In contrast, if the word "or" is read in in the "inclusive sense", it would generally be required under all three scenarios. Even if the word "or" is read in the "exclusive" sense, the use of the word "and" in Section 1677(7)(G)(iii) requires cumulation of the volume and effects of dumped and subsidized imports when the conditions of that clause are met.

4.628 In the light of the above analysis, we consider that it is unclear whether Section 1677(7)(G)(i) and (ii) requires the USITC to cumulate the effects of subsidized imports with the effects of dumped, non-subsidized imports. In the absence of an analysis by the Panel to this effect, and given the paucity of evidence regarding the application of the measure at issue on the Panel record, we are unable to complete the legal analysis with regard to the measure in these respects.

4.629 However, due to the use of the word "and" in Section 1677(7)(G)(iii), it is clear under either reading of the word "or" in this clause that, on its face, this Section requires the USITC to cumulate the effects of subsidized imports with the effects of dumped, non-subsidized imports when petitions to initiate countervailing duty investigations *or* anti-dumping duty investigations are filed on the same day *and* countervailing duty investigations *or* anti-dumping duty investigations are initiated by the investigating authority. Consequently, we *find* that Section 1677(7)(G)(iii) of the US Statute to be inconsistent "as such" with Article 15.3 and with Articles 15.1, 15.2, 15.4, and 15.5 of the SCM Agreement.

5. FINDINGS AND CONCLUSIONS

5.1 For the reasons set out in this Report, the Appellate Body:

a. with respect to the Panel's findings regarding the term "public body" under Article 1.1(a)(1) of the SCM Agreement:

i. *reverses the Panel's finding, in paragraphs 7.89 and 8.3.c.i of the Panel Report, rejecting India's claim that the USDOC's determination that the NMDC is a public body is inconsistent with Article 1.1(a)(1) of the SCM Agreement; and*

ii. *completes the legal analysis and finds that the USDOC's determination that the NMDC is a public body is inconsistent with Article 1.1(a)(1) of the SCM Agreement;*

b. with respect to the Panel's findings regarding financial contribution under Article 1.1(a)(1)(i) and (iii) of the SCM Agreement:

   i. *upholds the Panel's finding, in paragraphs 7.241 and 8.3.d.i of the Panel Report, rejecting India's claim that the USDOC's determination that the GOI provided goods through the grant of mining rights for iron ore and coal is inconsistent with Article 1.1(a)(1)(iii) of the SCM Agreement; and*

   ii. *upholds the Panel's finding, in paragraphs 7.297 and 8.3.e.ii(1) of the Panel Report, rejecting India's claim that the USDOC's determination that the SDF Managing Committee provided direct transfers of funds is inconsistent with Article 1.1(a)(1)(i) of the SCM Agreement;*

c. with respect to the Panel's "as such" findings regarding benefit under Article 14(d) of the SCM Agreement:

   i. *upholds the Panel's finding, in paragraph 7.35 of the Panel Report, rejecting India's claim that the US benchmarking mechanism is inconsistent with Article 14(d) of the SCM Agreement because it fails to require investigating authorities to assess the adequacy of remuneration from the perspective of the government provider before assessing whether a benefit has been conferred on the recipient;*

   ii. *upholds, albeit for different reasons, the Panel's finding, in paragraph 7.46 of the Panel Report, rejecting India's claim that the US benchmarking mechanism is inconsistent "as such" with Article 14(d) of the SCM Agreement because it excludes the use of government prices as benchmarks;*

   iii. *upholds the Panel's finding, in paragraph 7.52 of the Panel Report, rejecting India's claim that the use of "world market prices" as Tier II benchmarks provided for in Section 351.511(a)(2)(ii) of the US Regulations is inconsistent "as such" with Article 14(d) of the SCM Agreement; and*

   iv. *upholds, albeit for different reasons, the Panel's finding, in paragraph 7.63 of the Panel Report, rejecting India's claim that the mandatory use of "as delivered" benchmarks provided for in Section 351.511(a)(2)(iv) of the US Regulations is inconsistent "as such" with Article 14(d) of the SCM Agreement;*

d. with respect to the Panel's "as applied" findings regarding benefit under Article 14 of the SCM Agreement:

i. *declares moot and of no legal effect the Panel's alternative findings, in paragraphs 7.160-7.165 of the Panel Report, on the ex post rationales put forward by the United States to justify the USDOC's failure to consider certain domestic pricing information in assessing whether the NMDC provided iron ore for less than adequate remuneration;*

ii. *reverses the Panel's findings, in paragraphs 7.189 and 7.192 of the Panel Report, rejecting India's claims that the USDOC's exclusion of the NMDC's export prices in determining a Tier II benchmark is inconsistent with Article 14(d) and the chapeau of Article 14 of the SCM Agreement; and completes the legal analysis and finds that the USDOC's exclusion of such prices is inconsistent with Article 14(d) and the chapeau of Article 14 of the SCM Agreement;*

iii. *reverses the Panel's findings, in paragraphs 7.183 and 7.185 of the Panel Report, rejecting India's claim that the USDOC's use of "as delivered" prices from Australia and Brazil in assessing whether the NMDC provided iron ore for less than adequate remuneration is inconsistent with Article 14(d) of the SCM Agreement; and completes the legal analysis and finds that the USDOC's use of such prices is inconsistent with Article 14(d) of the SCM Agreement;*

iv. *upholds the Panel's finding, in paragraph 7.260 of the Panel Report, rejecting India's claim that the USDOC's construction of government prices for iron ore and coal is inconsistent with Articles 1.1(b) and 14(d) of the SCM Agreement; and*

v. *reverses the Panel's finding, in paragraph 7.313 of the Panel Report, rejecting India's claim as it relates to the USDOC's determination that loans provided under the SDF conferred a benefit within the meaning of Articles 1.1(b) and 14(b) of the SCM Agreement, and finds that it is unable to complete the legal analysis;*

e. with respect to the Panel's findings regarding specificity under Article 2.1(c) of the SCM Agreement:

i. *upholds the Panel's finding, in paragraph 7.135 of the Panel Report, that there was no obligation on the USDOC to establish that only a "limited number" within the set of "certain enterprises" actually used the subsidy programme;*

ii. *upholds the Panel's finding, in paragraph 7.126 of the Panel Report, rejecting India's argument that specificity must be established on the basis of discrimination in favour of "certain enterprises" against a broader category of other, similarly situated entities; and*

iii. *upholds the Panel's finding, in paragraph 7.133 of the Panel Report, rejecting India's argument that, if the inherent characteristics of the subsidized good limit the possible use of the subsidy to a certain industry, the subsidy will not be specific unless access to this subsidy is further limited to a subset of this industry;*

f. with respect to the Panel's findings regarding the use of "facts available" under Article 12.7 of the SCM Agreement:

i. *modifies the Panel's interpretation of Article 12.7 of the SCM Agreement, in Section 7.7.5.1 of the Panel Report, and finds that Article 12.7 requires an investigating authority to use facts available that reasonably replace the missing necessary information with a view to arriving at an accurate determination, and that this also includes an evaluation of available evidence;*

ii. *finds that the Panel failed to comply with its duty under Article 11 of the DSU to make an objective assessment of the matter before it, and therefore reverses the Panel's finding, in paragraphs 7.445 and 8.3.h of the Panel Report, that India failed to establish a prima facie case that Section 1677e(b) of the US Statute and Section 351.308(a)-(c) of the US Regulations are inconsistent "as such" with Article 12.7 of the SCM Agreement; and completes the legal analysis and finds that India has not established that Section 1677e(b) of the US Statute and Section 351.308(a)-(c) of the US Regulations are inconsistent "as such" with Article 12.7 of the SCM Agreement; and*

iii. *upholds the Panel's finding, in paragraph 7.450 of the Panel Report, that India failed to establish a prima facie case of inconsistency with Article 12.7 of the SCM Agreement;*

g. with respect to the Panel's findings regarding the USDOC's examination of new subsidy allegations in administrative reviews:

i. *upholds the Panel's finding, in paragraphs 7.508 and 8.3.j of the Panel Report, rejecting India's claims that the USDOC's examination of new subsidy allegations in administrative reviews related to the imports at issue is inconsistent with Articles 11.1, 13.1, 21.1, and 21.2 of the SCM Agreement; and*

ii. *reverses the Panel's finding, in paragraphs 7.508 and 8.3.j of the Panel Report, rejecting India's claims that the USDOC's examination of new subsidy allegations in administrative reviews related to the imports at issue is inconsistent with Articles 22.1 and 22.2 of the SCM Agreement, and finds that it is unable to complete the legal analysis in this regard;*

h. with respect to the Panel's findings regarding "cross-cumulation" under Article 15.3 and Articles 15.1, 15.2, 15.4, and 15.5 of the SCM Agreement:

   i. *finds that the Panel did not err in finding that Article 15.3 and Articles 15.1, 15.2, 15.4, and 15.5 of the SCM Agreement do not authorize investigating authorities to assess cumulatively the effects of imports that are not subject to simultaneous countervailing duty investigations with the effects of imports that are subject to countervailing duty investigations; and*

   ii. *finds that the Panel failed to comply with its duty under Article 11 of the DSU to make an objective assessment of the matter before it, and therefore reverses the Panel's findings, in paragraphs 7.356, 7.369, 8.2.c, and 8.2.d of the Panel Report, that Section 1677(7)(G) of the US Statute is inconsistent "as such" with Article 15.3 and Articles 15.1, 15.2, 15.4, and 15.5 of the SCM Agreement; and completes the legal analysis and finds that Section 1677(7)(G)(iii) is inconsistent "as such" with Article 15.3 and Articles 15.1, 15.2, 15.4, and 15.5 of the SCM Agreement;*

i. except for the findings in paragraphs 5.1.f.ii and 5.1.h.ii above, otherwise *rejects* all of India's claims that the Panel failed to make an objective assessment of the matter before it, and therefore acted inconsistently with Article 11 of the DSU; and

j. with respect to the Panel's findings identified in paragraphs 5.1.c and 5.1.g above, *rejects* India's claims that the Panel failed to provide a basic rationale for its findings, and therefore acted inconsistently with Article 12.7 of the DSU.

5.2 The Appellate Body *recommends* that the DSB request the United States to bring its measures found in this Report, and in the Panel Report as modified by this Report, to be inconsistent with its obligations under the SCM Agreement into conformity with that Agreement.

ANNEX 1

WORLD TRADE ORGANIZATION

WT/DS436/6

15 August 2014

(14-4711)

Page: 1/16

Original: English

UNITED STATES – COUNTERVAILING MEASURES ON CERTAIN HOT-ROLLED CARBON STEEL FLAT PRODUCTS FROM INDIA

Notification of an Appeal by India Under Article 16.4 and Article 17 of the Understanding on Rules and Procedures Governing the Settlement of Disputes (DSU), and Under Rule 20(1) of the Working Procedures for Appellate Review

The following notification, dated 8 August 2014, from the Delegation of India, is being circulated to Members.

---

1. Pursuant to Articles 16.4 and 17 of the *Understanding on Rules and Procedures Governing the Settlement of Disputes* ("DSU") and Rule 20 of the *Working Procedures for Appellate Review* (WT/AB/WP/6) ("Working Procedures"), India hereby notifies the Dispute Settlement Body of its decision to appeal certain issues of law and legal interpretation in the Panel Report in *United States - Countervailing Measures On Certain Hot-Rolled Carbon Steel Flat Products From India* (WT/DS436) ("Panel Report").

2. Pursuant to Rules 20(1) and 21(1) of the Working Procedures, India files this Notice of Appeal *together* with its Appellant's Submission with the Appellate Body Secretariat.

3. Pursuant to Rule 20(2)(d)(iii) of the Working Procedures, this Notice of Appeal provides an *indicative* list of the paragraphs of the Panel Report containing the alleged errors of law and legal interpretation by the Panel in its report, without prejudice to India's ability to rely on other paragraphs of the Panel Report in its appeal.

4. India seeks review by the Appellate Body of the errors of law and legal interpretation by the Panel in its Report and requests findings by the Appellate Body as noted below.

I. THE PANEL HAS COMMITTED LEGAL ERRORS IN SECTIONS 7.2.3 – 7.2.5 OF ITS REPORT AND IN CONNECTED FINDINGS IN SECTION 7.3.3 OF ITS REPORT

5. The Panel erred in its interpretation and application of Article 14(d) of the SCM Agreement and/or failed to make an objective assessment pursuant to Article 11 of the DSU, and/or falsely exercised judicial economy, in so far as the Panel found that 19 CFR § 351.511(a)(2)(i)-(iii) is not "as such" inconsistent with Article 14(d) of the SCM Agreement. In particular, the Panel erred because:

- it incorrectly interpreted Article 14(d) in finding that Article 14(d) does not require an assessment as to 'adequacy' of remuneration actually received by the 'government' provider of goods prior to determining the quantum of benefit[1];
- it incorrectly interpreted Article 14(d) in finding that government transactions can be completely ignored by investigating authorities in assessing the "prevailing market conditions" under Article 14(d) and instead, can be presumptively rejected[2];
- it incorrectly interpreted Article 14(d) in finding that investigating authorities can use out of country benchmarks without first finding that the market is distorted by governmental interference or influence[3];
- it did not make an objective assessment of the matter before it by failing to evaluate India's claim that 19 CFR § 351.511(a)(2)(ii) is inconsistent with Article 14(d) for requiring the use of out-of-country benchmarks without first exhausting all possible source of in-country benchmarks[4];
- it did not make an objective assessment of the matter before it by failing to provide a basic rationale as required under Article 12.7

1 Panel Report, para. 7.35.
2 *Ibid.* paras. 7.39, 7.42, 7.44, 7.46 and 7.189.
3 *Ibid.* paras. 7.47, 7.49-7.50.
4 Panel Report, para. 7.52.

of the DSU, as to the manner in which out of country benchmarks may be resorted to even in situations other than governmental influence in the market[5];

- it did not make an objective assessment of the matter before it, in finding that the method under 19 CFR § 351.511(a)(2)(ii) "must" relate to the prevailing market conditions in the country of provision merely because the parent legislation reproduces Article 14(d)[6], despite finding that the actual words used in 19 CFR § 351.511(a)(2)(ii) do not "necessarily provide[sic] the type of analysis of 'prevailing market conditions'..."[7];
- it incorrectly applied Article 14(d) in finding that 19 CFR § 351.511(a)(2)(ii) must automatically reflect the prevailing market conditions in the country of provision merely because the parent United States' legislation 19 U.S.C. 1677(5)(E)(iv) reproduces Article 14(d)[8];
- it did not make an objective assessment of the matter before it, by failing to evaluate and assess India's claim that 19 CFR § 351.511(a)(2)(i)-(iii) is inconsistent 'as such' with Article 14(d) for mandating an affirmative finding of benefit merely because the government's price in question is less than a benchmark price, without assessing whether the government price or the price difference, if any, is in accordance with 'commercial considerations'[9];
- it did not make an objective assessment of the matter before it, by failing to assess India's claim that 19 CFR § 351.511(a)(2)(i)-(iii) is inconsistent "as such" with Article 14(d) because a government price that is considered 'adequate' under a method consistent with Article 14(d), i.e. 19 CFR § 351.511(a)(2)(iii) [Tier III], would nonetheless be held inadequate under 19 CFR § 351.511(a)(2)(i)-(ii);

6. For these reasons, India requests the Appellate Body to *reverse* the Panel's finding that 19 CFR § 351.511(a)(2)(i)-(iii) is not "as such" inconsistent with Article 14(d) of the SCM Agreement.

7. Further, the Appellate Body must, where necessary, *complete the legal analysis* and find that:

- 19 CFR § 351.511(a)(2)(i) to (iii) is inconsistent with the *first sentence* of Article 14(d) as it fails to assess adequacy of

[5] Panel Report, para. 7.50.
[6] *Ibid.* para. 7.51.
[7] *Ibid.* para. 6.5.
[8] *Ibid.* para. 7.51.
[9] *Ibid.* paras. 6.57, 6.61 and footnote 195.

remuneration to the government provider prior to determining the quantum of benefit;

- 19 CFR § 351.511(a)(2)(i) is inconsistent with the *second sentence* of Article 14(d) for disregarding government prices not set in accordance with competitive bidding in assessing the "prevailing market conditions" in the country of provision;
- 19 CFR § 351.511(a)(2)(ii) is inconsistent with Article 14(d) as it mandates investigating authorities to apply out of country benchmarks to calculate benefit without first determining that the market is distorted by governmental interference or influence;
- 19 CFR § 351.511(a)(2)(ii) is inconsistent with Article 14(d) as it mandates investigating authorities to apply out of country benchmarks without first exhausting all possible sources of in-country benchmarks
- 19 CFR § 351.511(a)(2)(ii) is inconsistent with Article 14(d) as it fails to prescribe any mechanism to adjust world market prices to the prevailing market conditions in the country of provision of goods;
- 19 CFR § 351.511(a)(2)(i) to (ii) is inconsistent with the second sentence of Article 14(d) as it mandates an affirmative finding of benefit merely because the government price is less than a benchmark price, without assessing whether the government price is in accordance with 'commercial considerations' or whether the price difference, if any, is otherwise justified by 'commercial considerations';
- 19 CFR § 351.511(a)(2)(i) to (iii) is inconsistent with Article 14(d) as a government price consistent with 19 CFR § 351.511(a)(2)(iii) will be rejected if a benchmark is available under 19 CFR § 351.511(a)(2)(i) or (ii), as the case may be;

8. Consequently, the Appellate Body must also find that all determinations by the United States in the underlying investigation are inconsistent with Article 14(d) since all the determinations apply 19 CFR § 351.511(a)(2)(i)-(iii).

II. THE PANEL HAS COMMITTED LEGAL ERRORS IN SECTION 7.2.6 OF ITS REPORT

9. The Panel erred in its interpretation and application of Article 14(d) of the SCM Agreement and/or failed to make an objective assessment pursuant to Article 11 of the DSU, and/or falsely exercised judicial economy in so far as the Panel found that 19 CFR § 351.511(a)(2)(iv) is not "as such" inconsistent with Article 14(d) of the SCM Agreement. In particular, the Panel erred because:

- it did not make an objective assessment of the matter before it by narrowing India's actual claim against 19 CFR § 351.511(a)(2)(iv)[10];
- having interpreted Article 14(d) of the SCM Agreement as mandating an assessment of the "general conditions of the relevant market, in the context of which the market operators engage in sale transactions"[11], it failed to apply its own standard to assess whether 19 CFR § 351.511(a)(2)(iv) falls short of this mandate;
- it incorrectly interpreted and applied Article 14(d) of the SCM Agreement in finding that contractual terms of government transactions can *ipso facto* be excluded in assessing the "prevailing market conditions"[12];
- it failed to make an objective assessment of the matter before it by incorrectly assessing India's claim that 19 CFR § 351.511(a)(2)(iv) of the United States' law is "*as such*" inconsistent with Article 14(d) on the basis of existence of import transactions in a *given investigation*[13];
- it incorrectly interpreted and applied Article 14(d) of the SCM Agreement in finding that the mere presence of one or more import transactions into the country of provision justifies the calculation of benefit at delivered prices level in *all* cases[14] without a qualitative assessment of the entire market comprising both imports and domestic transactions.
- it failed to make an objective assessment of the matter before it by not providing a basic rationale as required under Article 12.7 of the DSU, to justify the rejection of India's "as such" claim against 19 CFR § 351.511(a)(2)(iv)[15];

10. For these reasons, India requests the Appellate Body to *reverse* the Panel's finding that 19 CFR § 351.511(a)(2)(iv) is not "as such" inconsistent with Article 14(d) of the SCM Agreement.

11. Further, the Appellate Body must, where necessary, *complete the legal analysis* and find that:

- 19 CFR § 351.511(a)(2)(iv) is inconsistent with Article 14(d) as it mandatorily requires benefit calculation at delivered prices level in *all cases* even where the "prevailing market conditions" is not sales at delivered levels;

---

10 Panel Report, paras. 6.80, 6.84 and 7.60.
11 *Ibid.* para. 7.60.
12 *Ibid.* para. 7.61.
13 *Ibid.* para. 7.62.
14 Panel Report, para. 7.62.
15 *Ibid.*

- 19 CFR § 351.511(a)(2)(iv) is inconsistent with Article 14(d) as it affirmatively find 'benefit' in every case where out of country benchmarks are used simply because of the difference in freight;
- 19 CFR § 351.11(a)(2)(iv) is inconsistent with Article 14(d) because it countervails comparative advantages where out of country benchmarks are used.

12. Consequently, the Appellate Body must also find that all determinations by the United States in the underlying investigation since 2004 are inconsistent with Article 14(d) as all such determinations apply 19 CFR § 351.511(a)(2)(iv).

III. THE PANEL HAS COMMITTED LEGAL ERRORS IN SECTION 7.7.5.1 OF ITS REPORT

13. The Panel erred in its interpretation and application of Article 12.7 of the SCM Agreement and/or failed to make an objective assessment pursuant to Article 11 of the DSU, and/or falsely exercised judicial economy in so far as the Panel found that 19 USC § 1677e(b) and 19 CFR § 351.308 ("AFA provisions") are not "as such" inconsistent with Article 12.7 of the SCM Agreement. In particular, the Panel erred because:

- it incorrectly interpreted Article 12.7 of the SCM Agreement in finding that an investigating authority need not engage in a comparative evaluation of all the available evidence to select the most fitting or most appropriate information[16].
- it erred in its interpretation and application of Article 12.7 of the SCM Agreement in rejecting India's claim[17] that the AFA provisions are "as such" inconsistent with Article 12.7 of the SCM Agreement as they *require* drawing the worst possible inference (including the imposition of the highest possible duty margin) against a non-cooperating party in *all* cases of non-cooperation;
- it did not make an objective assessment of the matter before it in finding that "any adverse inference drawn by the USDOC will in fact be based on the facts available" and that "nothing in the US provisions at issue suggest that the USDOC is not required to take into account all substantiated facts on record or to apply 'facts available' that do not reasonably replace the missing information"[18] because it limited itself to the text of the AFA provisions and consequently, disregarding "other domestic interpretative tools" placed on record by India;

---

[16] *Ibid.* paras. 7.438-439, 7.440-441.

[17] *Ibid.* paras. 7.440-444.

[18] *Ibid.* paras. 7.440-442 & 7.444.

14. For these reasons, India requests the Appellate Body to *reverse* the Panel's finding that the AFA provisions are not "as such" inconsistent with Article 12.7 of the SCM Agreement.

15. Further, the Appellate Body must, where necessary, *complete the legal analysis* and find that:

- Article 12.7 of the SCM Agreement requires investigating authorities to engage in a comparative evaluation of all the available evidence to select the most fitting or most appropriate information;
- Article 12.7 does not permit investigating authorities to draw adverse inferences (including the imposition of highest possible duty margin) in *all cases* of non-cooperation;
- the AFA provisions are "as such" inconsistent with Article 12.7 of the SCM Agreement as it fails to *require* USDOC to engage in a comparative evaluation of all the available evidence to select the most fitting or most appropriate information; and
- the AFA provisions are "as such" inconsistent with Article 12.7 of the SCM Agreement as it *requires* adverse inferences (including in the form of highest possible subsidy margins), to be drawn in *all cases* of non-cooperation.

16. Consequently, the Appellate Body must also find that all determinations by the United States in the underlying investigation applying the AFA provisions are inconsistent with Article 12.7 of the SCM Agreement.

IV. THE PANEL HAS COMMITTED LEGAL ERRORS IN SECTION 7.3.1 OF ITS REPORT

17. The Panel erred in its interpretation and application of Article 1.1(a)(1) of the SCM Agreement and/or failed to make an objective assessment pursuant to Article 11 of the DSU, and/or falsely exercised judicial economy in so far as the Panel upheld the United States' determination that NMDC is a 'public body'. In particular, the Panel erred because:

- it did not make an objective assessment of the matter before it by failing to evaluate the implications of the United States' admission before the Panel in *US – Antidumping and Countervailing Duties (China)* that in the underlying investigation in this dispute, NMDC was held to be public body merely on the basis of GOI shareholding[19];

---

[19] Panel Report, para. 6.90.

- it did not make an objective assessment of the matter before it by failing to consider the totality of the evidence and / or did not treat all evidence in an even-handed manner in finding that the USDOC considered factors beyond GOI shareholding in NMDC while concluding NMDC to be a public body, despite the USDOC expressly stating in its determination that such consideration is not required as a matter of its domestic law[20];
- it did not make an objective assessment of the matter before it by considering the USDOC's determination in the 2007 AR to be relevant in assessing the USDOC's determination in the 2004 and 2006 AR[21];
- it did not make an objective assessment of the matter before it by accepting the United States' *ex post facto* explanation that the reference to NMDC being "governed by" the GOI in the 2004 AR determination, implied that the USDOC considered factors other than GOI shareholding while determining NMDC to be a "public body"[22];
- it did not make an objective assessment of the matter before it and exceeded its authority by *suo moto* providing "additional support" to the USDOC's finding that NMDC is a 'public body' for being under the "administrative control" of the GOI, despite the express acknowledgement of the United States that the USDOC's determination did not refer to the "administrative control" of NMDC[23];
- it exceeded its authority by giving a finding on the implication of 'Miniratna' or 'Navaratna' status of NMDC[24] rather than limiting itself to an assessment as to whether the USDOC ought to have considered 'Miniratna' or 'Navaratna' status of NMDC as being relevant evidence;
- it incorrectly applied Article 1.1(a)(1) of the SCM Agreement in finding that the alleged involvement of GOI in the appointment of NMDC's directors is more 'substantive' and meaningful than GOI's shareholding in NMDC[25];
- it incorrectly applied Article 1.1(a)(1) of the SCM Agreement in finding that *nomination* of directors can be equated with *appointment* of chief executive officers and that there is no

---

20 *Ibid.* paras. 6.96, 7.81 and footnote 244.
21 *Ibid.* para. 7.83.
22 Panel Report, paras. 6.93, 7.82 and footnote 245.
23 *Ibid.* para. 7.82, 7.87 and 6.100.
24 *Ibid.* para. 7.88.
25 *Ibid.* para. 7.85.

distinction between *nomination* of directors by government and *appointment* of directors by the government, in assessing whether the GOI had "meaningful control" over the NMDC[26];

- it incorrectly applied Article 1.1(a)(1) in finding that involvement in NMDC's Board of Directors along with GOI's shareholding was sufficient to fulfill the requirement of "meaningful control"[27] as was referred to by the Appellate Body in *US – Antidumping and Countervailing Duties (China).*
- it incorrectly interpreted Article 1.1(a)(1) of the SCM Agreement in finding that "meaningful control" of NMDC by the GOI would be sufficient to determine that NMDC is a public body[28].

18. For these reasons, India requests the Appellate Body to *reverse* the Panel's finding in affirming USDOC's determination that NMDC is a public body within the meaning of Article 1.1(a)(1) of the SCM Agreement.

19. Further, the Appellate Body must, where necessary, *complete the legal analysis* and find that:

- "meaningful control" of an entity by a government will not be sufficient to conclude such entity as a 'public body' within the meaning of Article 1.1(a)(1) of the SCM Agreement in all cases.
- shareholding by government and appointment of directors by the government, *de hors* other factors, is not sufficient to conclude that an entity is "meaningfully controlled" by the government for the purposes of Article 1.1(a)(1) of the SCM Agreement in all cases; and
- the USDOC determination that NMDC is a public body within the meaning of Article 1.1(a)(1) of the SCM Agreement, is incorrect;

20. Consequently, the Appellate Body must also find that the imposition of CVD based on the NMDC program since 2004 is inconsistent with Article 1.1(a)(1) of the SCM Agreement.

V. THE PANEL HAS COMMITTED LEGAL ERRORS IN SECTION 7.3.2 OF ITS REPORT

21. The Panel erred in its interpretation and application of Articles 1.2 and 2 of the SCM Agreement and/or failed to make an objective assessment pursuant to Article 11 of the DSU, and/or falsely exercised judicial economy in so far as

---

26 *Ibid.*

27 *Ibid.* paras. 7.80-7.89.

28 *Ibid.* paras. 7.81, 7.85-7.86 and 7.89.

the Panel upheld the United States' determination that sale of iron ore by NMDC was *de facto* specific. In particular, the Panel erred because:

- it incorrectly interpreted and applied Article 2.1 of the SCM Agreement in finding that a program can be held to be *de facto* specific even without establishing that the program in question 'discriminates' between the similarly-situated entities[29];
- it incorrectly interpreted and applied the term of "use of a subsidy programme by a limited number of certain enterprises as it appears in Article 2.1(c) of the SCM Agreement[30];
- it did not make an objective assessment of the matter before it by limiting the circumstances in which negotiating history can be relied upon to interpret a treaty[31];
- it did not make an objective assessment of the matter before it by specifically relying upon the findings of the Panel in *US – Softwood Lumber IV*[32], without recording and assessing the "cogent reasons" offered by India for not following said findings for subsidies covered under Article 1.1(a)(1)(iii) of the SCM Agreement;
- it incorrectly interpreted Article 2.1(c) in finding that an alleged subsidy under Article 1.1(a)(iii) can be *de facto* specific merely based on limitations inherent in the nature of the goods allegedly provided or purchased by the government[33].

22. For these reasons, India requests the Appellate Body to *reverse* the Panel's finding that the United States did not act inconsistently with Articles 1.2 and 2.1 in concluding that the sale of iron ore by NMDC was *de facto* specific.

23. Further, the Appellate Body must, where necessary, *complete the legal analysis* and find that:

- a program can be *de facto* specific under Article 2.1(c) of the SCM Agreement only if there is governmental action that 'discriminates' between similarly-situated entities;
- a program can be *de facto* specific under Article 2.1(c) of the SCM Agreement on the basis that it is "use[d] by" a "limited number *of* certain enterprises", only when the subsidy in question is *used* by a smaller set within the larger set of "certain enterprises";
- A program pertaining to provision of goods, cannot be *de facto* specific under Article 2.1(c) of the SCM Agreement if the

29 Panel Report, para. 7.121-7.124.
30 *Ibid.* 7.135.
31 *Ibid.* para. 7.130.
32 *Ibid.* para. 7.131.
33 *Ibid.* para. 7.127-7.133.

determination of *de facto* specificity is solely based on the inherent characteristics of goods in question; and

- the United States acted inconsistently with Articles 1.2, 2.1(c) and 2.4 of the SCM Agreement in finding that the sale of iron ore by NMDC is *de facto* specific.

24. Consequently, the Appellate Body must also find that the imposition of CVD based on the NMDC program since 2004 is inconsistent with Articles 1.2, 2.1 and 2.4 of the SCM Agreement.

VI. THE PANEL HAS COMMITTED LEGAL ERRORS IN SECTION 7.3.3 OF ITS REPORT AND IN CONNECTED FINDINGS IN SECTION 7.4.6.2 OF ITS REPORT

25. The Panel failed to make an objective assessment of the matter before it pursuant to Article 11 of the DSU in so far as the Panel has given findings on the *ex post facto* justifications of the United States for rejecting certain domestic sales information as relevant benchmarks[34], despite expressly recognizing such justifications as *ex post facto*[35]. Accordingly, India requests the Appellate Body to *reverse* the Panel's finding[36] to address the *ex post facto* justifications of the United States and *render moot* the Panel's findings and observations[37] on the United States' *ex post facto* justifications.

26. In the alternative, conditional upon the Appellate Body rejecting the aforesaid requests of India, India submits that the Panel erred in its interpretation and application of Articles 12.1, 12.4, 12.7 and 14 of the SCM Agreement and/or failed to make an objective assessment pursuant to Article 11 of the DSU in so far as the Panel upheld the United States' *ex post facto* justification that the domestic sales information can be rejected as relevant benchmarks. In particular, the Panel erred because:

- it incorrectly interpreted Article 14(d) of the SCM Agreement to find that government prices can *ipso facto* be rejected without first finding that the market is distorted by governmental interference or influence[38];
- it incorrectly interpreted and applied Articles 12.1 and 14(d) of the SCM Agreement in finding that an investigating authority has sufficient discretion to disregard pricing information merely because such information does not pertain to 'actual transactions'[39];

34 Panel Report, paras. 7.159-7.165.
35 *Ibid.* paras. 7.154-7.156.
36 *Ibid.* para. 7.159.
37 *Ibid.* paras. 7.159-165.
38 *Ibid.* para. 7.160.
39 *Ibid.* para. 7.162.

- it incorrectly applied Articles 12.1, 12.7 and 14 of the SCM Agreement in finding that the United States can *completely* reject the price quote of a private party merely because it did not specify the exact iron ore content, even though it indicated the grade of iron ore[40];
- it incorrectly applied Articles 12.1, 12.7 and 14 of the SCM Agreement by finding that the United States could reject information relating to possible in-country benchmarks based on certain alleged defects in the price without ever highlighting and seeking clarifications on such defects during the course of the investigation[41];
- it incorrectly applied Articles 12.1, 12.4 and 14 of the SCM Agreement by finding that the United States could reject the allegedly confidential private party quote supplied by Tata as a relevant benchmark even for Tata[42].

27. The Appellate Body is requested to *reverse* the Panel's findings and observations on the United States' *ex post facto* justifications for rejecting certain domestic sales information as relevant benchmarks and instead, find that:

- an investigating authority cannot disregard domestic pricing information merely because such information does not pertain to 'actual transactions';
- the alleged rejection of in-country benchmarks by the United States merely because those benchmarks related to government transactions, is inconsistent with Article 14(d);
- the alleged rejection of in-country benchmarks by the United States merely because it did not specify the exact iron content, even though it did indicate "low grade" and "high grade" is inconsistent with Articles 12.1, 12.7 and 14 of the SCM Agreement;
- the alleged rejection of in-country benchmarks by the United States, based on certain alleged defects in the price without ever highlighting and seeking clarifications on such defects during the course of the investigation, is inconsistent with Articles 12.1, 12.7 and 14 of the SCM Agreement; and
- the failure by the United States to apply the allegedly confidential private party quote supplied by Tata as a relevant benchmark even for Tata is inconsistent with Articles 12.1, 12.4 and 14 of the SCM Agreement.

---

[40] Panel Report, para. 7.163.

[41] *Ibid.* para. 7.164.

[42] *Ibid.* para. 7.165.

28. Further, the Panel erred in its interpretation and application of Articles 14 of the SCM Agreement and/or failed to make an objective assessment pursuant to Article 11 of the DSU, and/or falsely exercised judicial economy in so far as the Panel upheld the United States' determination that sale of iron ore by NMDC conferred a benefit. In particular, the Panel erred because:

- it failed to consider the totality of the evidence and / or did not treat all evidence in an even-handed manner in finding the Brazilian and Australian prices of iron ore, inclusive all charges for delivery to steel producers in India, as relevant benchmarks on the basis that NMDC allegedly sets its domestic prices in light of what iron purchasers are willing to pay to import[43];
- it incorrectly interpreted and applied Article 14(d) of the SCM Agreement incorrectly in finding that the existence of an import transaction of iron ore from Brazil into India must necessarily mean that the price of iron ore from Brazil, inclusive of all charges for delivery to steel producers in India, will reflect 'prevailing market conditions' for iron ore in India[44], without a qualitative assessment of the entire market comprising both import and domestic transactions for iron ore;
- it incorrectly interpreted and applied Article 14(d) of the SCM Agreement in finding that inclusion of charges associated with international transit in the benchmark price does not nullify and countervail India's comparative advantage[45];
- it incorrectly applied Article 14(d) of the SCM Agreement in finding that export prices of the government provider in question can *ipso facto* be rejected as a relevant benchmark[46];
- it did not make an objective assessment of the matter before it in upholding the USDOC determinations under challenge by referring to record evidence which was never relied upon by the USDOC itself in its determination[47];
- it did not make an objective assessment of the matter before it, by failing to assess whether the USDOC 'adequate[ly]' explained its inconsistent treatment of NMDC's export prices as a relevant benchmark, as required under the chapeau to Article 14 of the SCM Agreement;
- it did not make an objective assessment of the matter before it, by failing to assess whether the USDOC has transparently and

---

[43] *Ibid.* para. 7.182.
[44] Panel Report, para. 7.181-7.183.
[45] *Ibid.* para. 7.185.
[46] *Ibid.* para. 7.189.
[47] *Ibid.* para. 7.182.

adequately explained why NMDC export prices are not 'world market prices' within the meaning of United States' national implementing regulations, viz. 19 CFR § 351.511(a)(2)(ii)[48].

29. For these reasons, India requests the Appellate Body to *reverse* the Panel's finding that the United States did not act inconsistently with Article 14 of the SCM Agreement in concluding that the sale of iron ore by NMDC conferred a benefit.

30. To the extent the Panel's findings in relation to the NMDC program are reiterated in the context of grant of mining rights for iron ore and coal[49], India requests the Appellate Body to *reverse* the same as well.

31. Further, the Appellate Body must, where necessary, *complete the legal analysis* and find that, in relation to the sale of iron ore by NMDC and the grant of mining rights for iron ore by the GOI:

- the United States acted inconsistently with Article 14(d) of the SCM Agreement by presumptively rejecting NMDC export prices as a relevant benchmark to determine the existence and quantity of 'benefit';
- the United States acted inconsistently with Article 14(d) of the SCM Agreement by using prices of iron ore from Brazil, inclusive of all charges for delivery to steel producers in India, as the benchmark price to determine the existence and quantity of 'benefit';
- the United States acted inconsistently with Article 14(d) of the SCM Agreement by using prices of iron ore from Australia, artificially adjusted to include all charges for delivery to steel producers in India, as the benchmark price to determine the existence and quantity of 'benefit'; and
- the United States acted inconsistently with the chapeau to Article 14 of the SCM Agreement by failing to transparently and adequately explain why NMDC export prices are not 'world market prices' within the meaning of United States' national implementing regulations, viz. 19 CFR § 351.511(a)(2)(ii).

32. Consequently, the Appellate Body must also find that:

- the United States acted inconsistently with Article 14(d) of the SCM Agreement by using a benchmark price inclusive of all charges for delivery to steel producers in India, as the benchmark price to determine the existence and quantity of 'benefit' in respect of the Captive Mining of Iron Ore program;

48 *Ibid.* para. 7.189-192.
49 *Ibid.* para. 7.263-265.

- the United States acted inconsistently with Article 14(d) of the SCM Agreement by using a benchmark price inclusive of all charges for delivery to a steel producer in India, as the benchmark price to determine the existence and quantity of 'benefit' in respect of the Captive Mining of Coal program.

33. Consequently, the Appellate Body must also find that the imposition of CVD for the NMDC program since 2004, and the imposition of CVD for the Captive Mining of Iron Ore and Coal programs, is inconsistent with Article 14(d) and the chapeau to Article 14 of the SCM Agreement.

VII. THE PANEL HAS COMMITTED LEGAL ERRORS IN SECTION 7.4.3 OF ITS REPORT

34. The Panel erred in its interpretation and application of Article 1.1(a)(1)(iii) of the SCM Agreement and/or failed to make an objective assessment pursuant to Article 11 of the DSU, and/or falsely exercised judicial economy in so far as the Panel upheld the United States' determination that the grant of mining rights amounts to the 'provision' of the mined minerals. In particular, the Panel erred because:

- it disregarded material evidence necessary to make an objective assessment of the matter before it, by finding as irrelevant, the fact that the royalty paid to the GOI by miners contributes an insignificant 9.03 % of the final cost of the mined mineral[50];
- it incorrectly applied Article 1.1(a)(iii) of the SCM Agreement in finding that "allow[ing] the beneficiary to extract government-owned minerals from the ground, and then us[ing] those minerals for [the beneficiary's] own purpose" means that the "GOI's grant of the right to mine is reasonably proximate to the use or enjoyment of the minerals by the mining entity"[51].

35. For these reasons, India requests the Appellate Body to *reverse* the Panel's finding that the United States did not act inconsistent with Article 1.1(a)(iii) of the SCM Agreement in concluding that the grant of mining rights amounts to 'provision' of the mined mineral.

36. Further, the Appellate Body must, where necessary, *complete the legal analysis* and find that:

- the United States acted inconsistently with Article 1.1(a)(iii) of the SCM Agreement in finding that grant of mining rights to iron ore and coal, amounts to 'provision' of iron ore and coal.

---

50 Panel Report, para. 6.133.
51 *Ibid.* paras. 7.237-7.238.

37. Consequently, the Appellate Body must also find that the imposition of CVD based on the Captive Mining of Iron ore programme and the Captive Mining of coal program is inconsistent with Article 1.1(a)(1)(iii) of the SCM Agreement.

VIII. THE PANEL HAS COMMITTED LEGAL ERRORS IN SECTION 7.4.2 OF ITS REPORT

38. The requests contained in this part are made conditional upon the United States filing an appeal against the Panel decision in Section 7.4.1 of the Panel Report and the Appellate Body reversing the Panel's finding in Section 7.4.1.3 of the Panel Report.

39. The Panel failed to fulfill its duty under Article 11 of the DSU and/or falsely exercised judicial economy in so far as the Panel did not assess[52] India's claim under Article 2.1 of the SCM Agreement against the USDOC's determination that the grant of mining rights for iron ore is *de facto* specific. India requests the Appellate Body to find that the Panel erred in exercising judicial economy in this case.

40. Further, the Appellate Body must *complete the legal analysis* and find that:

- the United States acted inconsistently with Articles 1.2, 2.1 and 2.4 of the SCM Agreement in finding that grant of mining rights to iron ore was *de facto* specific.

41. Consequently, the Appellate Body must also find that the imposition of CVD based on the Captive Mining of Iron ore programme is inconsistent with Articles 1.2, 2.1 and 2.4 of the SCM Agreement.

IX. THE PANEL HAS COMMITTED LEGAL ERRORS IN SECTION 7.4.6 OF ITS REPORT

42. Further, the Panel erred in its interpretation and application of Articles 14 of the SCM Agreement and/or failed to make an objective assessment pursuant to Article 11 of the DSU, and/or falsely exercised judicial economy in so far as the Panel upheld the United States' determination the GOI conferred a benefit in granting mining rights for iron ore and coal. In particular, the Panel erred because:

- it incorrectly interpreted and applied Article 14(d) of the SCM Agreement in finding that a term 'remuneration' need not be the

52 Panel Report, para. 8.4.a.

actual recompense received by the GOI for the grant of mining rights, but can also be notional[53];

- it incorrectly interpreted and applied Article 14(d) of the SCM Agreement in finding that the USDOC was permitted to calculate quantum of benefit on the basis of a fictional constructed price of extracted iron ore (inclusive of the miner's costs and reasonable profits)[54];
- it did not make an objective assessment of the matter before it by determining that India's claim pertaining to "good faith" interpretation is outside the Panel's terms of reference[55].

43. For these reasons, India requests the Appellate Body to *reverse* the Panel's finding that the United States did not act inconsistently with Article 14 of the SCM Agreement in concluding that the GOI conferred a benefit in granting mining rights for iron ore and coal.

44. Further, the Appellate Body must, where necessary, *complete the legal analysis* and find that:

- the 'remuneration', the adequacy of which is to be assessed under Article 14(d) of the SCM Agreement, can only be the actual recompense received by the GOI and cannot be fictional / notional;
- the costs incurred and profits earned by a miner cannot be considered as part of 'remuneration', the adequacy of which is to be assessed under Article 14(d) of the SCM Agreement;
- the United States acted inconsistently with Article 14(d) of the SCM Agreement in finding that the GOI conferred a benefit in granting mining rights for iron ore and coal; and
- the United States acted inconsistently with Article 14(d) of the SCM Agreement by using prices of coal from Australia, inclusive all charges for delivery to the steel producer in India, as the benchmark price to determine the existence and quantity of 'benefit'.

45. Consequently, the Appellate Body must also find that the imposition of CVD based on the Captive Mining of Iron ore programme and the Captive Mining of coal program is inconsistent with Article 14(d) of the SCM Agreement.

---

53 Panel Report, para. 7.260.
54 *Ibid.*
55 *Ibid.* para. 7.261.

X. THE PANEL HAS COMMITTED LEGAL ERRORS IN SECTION 7.5.1 OF ITS REPORT

46. Further, the Panel erred in its interpretation and application of Articles 1.1(a)(1) of the SCM Agreement and/or failed to make an objective assessment pursuant to Article 11 of the DSU, and/or falsely exercised judicial economy in so far as the Panel upheld the United States' determination that the SDF program was a subsidy within the meaning of Article 1.1(a)(1) of the SCM Agreement. In particular, the Panel erred because:

- it did not make an objective assessment of the matter before it, by assuming a meaning for the phrase '*direct*' '*transfer*' of funds as it appears in Article 1.1(a)(1)(i) of the SCM Agreement, without ever interpreting it in accordance with customary rules of interpretation[56];
- it did not make an objective assessment of the matter before it, by assuming a meaning for the term '*transfer* of funds' as it appears in Article 1.1(a)(1)(i) of the SCM Agreement, without ever interpreting the term in accordance with customary rules of interpretation[57];
- it incorrectly interpreted and applied Article 1.1(a)(1)(i) of the SCM Agreement in finding that the USDOC could have reasonably determined the SDF Managing Committee to have '*direct[ly]*' transferred SDF loans merely on the basis that the SDF Managing Committee decides on the issuance, terms and waivers of the SDF loans[58] after finding that the actual transfer is done by an intermediary or intervening private party, i.e. the JPC;
- it incorrectly interpreted and applied Article 1.1(a)(1)(i) of the SCM Agreement in finding that the 'transfer' of funds need not involve the government having title to the funds in question and / or resulting in a charge on the public account[59].

47. For these reasons, India requests the Appellate Body to *reverse* the Panel's finding that the United States did not act inconsistently with Article 1.1(a)(1) of the SCM Agreement in concluding that the SDF loans constituted a subsidy.

48. Further, the Appellate Body must, where necessary, *complete the legal analysis* and find that:

---

[56] Panel Report, paras. 7.292-293.

[57] *Ibid.* paras. 7.295-296

[58] *Ibid.* paras. 7.292-293.

[59] *Ibid.* paras. 7.294-296.

- '*direct* transfer of funds' under Article 1.1(a)(1)(i) of the SCM Agreement excludes *government* transferring funds to the beneficiary through an intermediate private body;
- 'direct *transfer* of funds' under Article 1.1(a)(1)(i) of the SCM Agreement only covers situations where the funds so transferred are owned by the government and / or results in a charge on the public account;
- the United States acted inconsistently with Article 1.1(a)(1) of the SCM Agreement in determining that the SDF program is a "direct transfer of funds" by the SDF Managing Committee.

49. Consequently, the Appellate Body must also find that the imposition of CVD based on the SDF program is inconsistent with Article 1.1(a)(1) of the SCM Agreement.

XI. THE PANEL HAS COMMITTED LEGAL ERRORS IN SECTION 7.5.2 OF ITS REPORT

50. Further, the Panel erred in its interpretation and application of Article 14 of the SCM Agreement and/or failed to make an objective assessment pursuant to Article 11 of the DSU, and/or falsely exercised judicial economy in so far as the Panel failed to appreciate that the benchmark used under Article 14(d) must be 'comparable' to the terms of the loan program itself. In particular, the Panel erred because:

- it did not objectively assess the matter before it in finding that the SDF funds are not producer funds as the funds were sourced from a levy on the consumers and the levy was always destined only towards the SDF funds[60];
- it incorrectly interpreted Article 14(b) and 1.1(b) in finding that the USDOC did not have to account for the entry deposits made to the SDF program by the beneficiaries, while determining that the SDF program conferred a 'benefit'[61].

51. For these reasons, India requests the Appellate Body to *reverse* the Panel's finding that the United States did not act inconsistently with Article 14 of the SCM Agreement in concluding that the SDF loans conferred a benefit.

52. Further, the Appellate Body must, where necessary, *complete the legal analysis* and find that the USDOC violated Articles 14(b) and 1.1(b) in determining that the SDF program conferred a benefit without accounting for the entry deposits made to the SDF program by the beneficiaries.

---

60 Panel Report, para. 7.311 and footnote 526.

61 *Ibid.* paras. 311-312.

XII. THE PANEL HAS COMMITTED LEGAL ERRORS IN SECTION 7.7.5.2.1 OF ITS REPORT

53. Further, the Panel erred in its interpretation and application of Article 12.7 of the SCM Agreement and/or failed to make an objective assessment pursuant to Article 11 of the DSU, and/or falsely exercised judicial economy in so far as the Panel found that the United States did not act inconsistently with Article 12.7 of the SCM Agreement when applying the highest non-*de minimis* subsidy margin in 230 instances in the underlying investigation[62]. In particular, the Panel erred in its interpretation of Article 12.7 of the SCM Agreement and applied the incorrect standard to assess the claim[63]. Further, even when applying its erroneous interpretation of Article 12.7, the Panel incorrectly applied its own standard in rejecting India's claim and imposed an unnecessary burden on India[64].

54. Therefore, India requests the Appellate Body to *reverse* the Panel's finding that the 230 instances in the underlying investigation of applying the *highest* non-*de minimis* subsidy margin pursuant to the AFA provisions is inconsistent with Article 12.7 of the SCM Agreement. Further, the Appellate Body must, where necessary, *complete the legal analysis* and find that the United States acted inconsistently with Article 12.7 of the SCM Agreement by applying the *highest* non-*de minimis* subsidy margin in the 230 instances highlighted by India.

55. Further, India would like to reiterate its earlier request that the Appellate Body also find that the AFA provisions are "as such" inconsistent with Article 12.7 of the SCM Agreement as it requires adverse inferences (including the imposition of highest possible subsidy margins) to be drawn in *all cases* of non-cooperation.

XIII. THE PANEL HAS COMMITTED LEGAL ERRORS IN SECTION 7.7.5.2.9 OF ITS REPORT

56. The Panel failed to make an objective assessment pursuant to Article 11 of the DSU by failing to consider India's submissions in totality, when concluding that India had not made out a *prima facie* case in respect of the 2013 Sunset Review of the USDOC against Essar, ISPAT, SAIL and Tata[65]. Therefore, India requests the Appellate Body to *reverse* the Panel's finding.

57. Further, the Appellate Body must, if necessary, *complete the legal analysis* and find that *all of* the US DOC's determinations in the 2013 Sunset

---

[62] *Ibid.* paras. 7.448-7.449.

[63] *Ibid.*

[64] *Ibid.* Para. 449.

[65] Panel Report, paras. 7.479-7.481.

Review against Essar, ISPAT, SAIL and Tata, are inconsistent with Article 12.7 of the SCM Agreement.

58. In the alternative, the Appellate Body must find that, at a minimum, the USDOC's determinations in the 2013 sunset review are inconsistent with Article 12.7 of the SCM Agreement to the extent they repeat those instances from the previous ARs that have already been found to be inconsistent with Article 12.7 of the SCM Agreement.

XIV. THE PANEL HAS COMMITTED LEGAL ERRORS IN SECTION 7.8.4 OF ITS REPORT

59. The Panel failed to make an objective assessment pursuant to Article 11 and/or falsely exercised judicial economy, in so far as the Panel failed to assess India's claims that the investigation into new subsidies in the course of administrative reviews by the United States in the underlying investigation is inconsistent with Articles 11.1, 13.1, 22.1 and 22.2 of the SCM Agreement[66]. In particular, the Panel erred because:

- it did not objectively assess the matter before it by failing to asses India's claims under Articles 11.1, 13.1, 22.1-22.2 of the SCM Agreement merely because new subsidies were examined under Article 21[67] and by failing to provide a "basic rationale" as required under Article 12.7 of the DSU in this respect;
- it incorrectly interpreted Articles 11 that Article 11 is inapplicable to Article 21 proceedings ignoring the textual meaning that Article 11 would apply anytime where a Member studies the existence, degree or effect of a subsidy, irrespective of how the proceeding is designated under the domestic law;
- it incorrectly interpreted Articles 11 and 21 in assuming that the applicability of Article 21 *ipso facto* excludes applicability of Articles 11, 13.1, 22.1-22.2[68].

60. Therefore, India requests the Appellate Body to *reverse* the aforesaid findings of the Panel.

61. Further, the Appellate Body must, if necessary, *complete the legal analysis* and find that the United States acted inconsistently with Articles 11.1, 13.1, 22.1 and 22.2 of the SCM Agreement by investigating new subsidies in the course of administrative reviews in the underlying investigation.

---

66 *Ibid.* para. 7.501.
67 *Ibid.* paras. 7.501, 7.507, 7.508, 7.168.
68 *Ibid.*

XV. THE PANEL HAS COMMITTED LEGAL ERRORS IN ITS PRELIMINARY RULING

62. Conditional upon the Appellate Body rejecting all the requests made by India in sections IV and V above, the Appellate Body is requested to assess India's appeal in this part. In other words, in the event the Appellate Body finds that the United States did not violate Article 1.1(a)(1) ***or*** Articles 2 and 1.4 of the SCM Agreement, the Appellate Body is requested to assess India's appeal in this part, relating to the Panel's ruling on the United States' preliminary request contained in section 1.3.3 of the Panel Report.

63. The Panel erred in its application of Articles 4.6 and 6.2 of the DSU and/or failed to make an objective assessment pursuant to Article 11 of the DSU, in so far as the Panel found that India's claim under Section XII.C.1 and Section XII.C.2 of India's First Written Submissions are outside the Panel's terms of reference. In particular, the Panel erred because:

- it did not make an objective assessment of the matter before it in accordance with Article 11 and 3.2 of the DSU by failing to record and follow, without offering cogent reasons, the previously adopted findings in *Korea - Dairy* that the respondent bears the initial burden to prove it was actually prejudiced by the allegedly incomplete Panel Request of the complainant;
- it did not make an objective assessment of the matter before it in accordance with Article 11 and 3.2 of the DSU by failing to record and follow, without offering cogent reasons, the previously adopted finding of the Panel in *US – Lamb*, that the questions circulated by India during consultations is one of the relevant "attendant circumstances" in assessing India's Panel Request[69].
- it did not make an objective assessment of the matter before it in accordance with Article 11 and 3.2 of the DSU by failing to examine the legal basis of India's submission that a reference to the term 'initiated' in India's Panel Request must be understood in the light of footnote 37 to the SCM Agreement[70].
- it incorrectly applied Article 6.2 of the DSU in finding that India's Panel Request excludes claims under Article 11 relating to the "alleged initiation of an investigation or the manner in which an investigation was conducted"[71];

64. For these reasons, India requests the Appellate Body to *reverse* the Panel's finding that India's claims under Section XII.C.1 and Section XII.C.2 of India's First Written Submissions are not within the Panel's terms of reference.

---

69 Panel Report, para. 1.37.

70 *Ibid.* footnote 39.

71 *Ibid.* paras. 1.34 and 1.38.

65. Further, the Appellate Body must, where necessary, *complete the legal analysis* to find that:

- in assessing a Member's Panel Request under Article 6.2 of the DSU, questions circulated by the Parties during the course of consultations held under Article 4 of the DSU, is one of the relevant "attendant circumstances" to be considered.
- with respect to an objection raised under Article 6.2 of the DSU, the respondent bears the initial burden to prove it was actually prejudiced by the allegedly incomplete Panel Request of the complainant.
- India's claims in Section XII.C.1 and Section XII.C.2 of India's First Written Submissions are within the Panel's terms of reference; and
- the United States violated Articles 11.1-11.2, 11.9 of the SCM Agreement by initiating investigations into NMDC and TPS programs in the 2004 AR without sufficient evidence as to the existence, amount and nature of said subsidies.

ANNEX 2

WORLD TRADE ORGANIZATION

WT/DS436/7

18 August 2014

(14-4762)

Page: 1/2

Original: English

UNITED STATES – COUNTERVAILING MEASURES ON CERTAIN HOT-ROLLED CARBON STEEL FLAT PRODUCTS FROM INDIA

Notification of an Other Appeal by the United States Under Article 16.4 and Article 17 of the Understanding on Rules and Procedures Governing the Settlement of Disputes (DSU), and Under Rule 23(1) of the Working Procedures for Appellate Review

The following notification, dated 13 August 2014, from the Delegation of the United States, is being circulated to Members.

Pursuant to Article 16 of the *Understanding on Rules and Procedures Governing the Settlement of Disputes* ("DSU") and Rule 23 of the *Working Procedures for Appellate Review*, the United States hereby notifies its decision to appeal to the Appellate Body certain issues of law covered in the Report of the Panel on *United States – Countervailing Measures on Certain Hot-Rolled Carbon Steel Flat Products from India* (WT/DS436/R) and certain legal interpretations developed by the Panel in this dispute.

(1) The United States seeks review by the Appellate Body of the Panel's legal interpretation of the term "public body" under Article 1.1(a)(1) of the *Agreement on Subsidies and Countervailing Measures* ("SCM Agreement") that "[t]he relevant entity must be shown to have been vested with governmental authority, or to have actually exercised such authority through the performance of governmental functions."[1] The United States respectfully requests that the Appellate Body modify this interpretation and clarify that an entity may be a public body within the meaning of Article 1.1(a)(1) if a government controls that entity such that the government can use the entity's resources as its own. In that circumstance, when the entity conveys economic resources, it is the government's own resources that are being conveyed.

(2) The United States seeks review of the Panel's legal conclusions that 19 U.S.C. §1677(7)(G) is inconsistent with Articles 15.3 and 15.1, 15.2, 15.4, and 15.5 of the SCM Agreement, both "as such" and "as applied" in the original investigation at issue in this dispute.[2] These findings are in error, and are based on erroneous findings on issues of law and related legal interpretations, including the Panel's conclusions that "Article 15.3 establishes a necessary pre-condition for cumulative assessment of the effects of the imports in question ... rather than a limitation on the scope of application of Article 15.3"[3]; that the term "subsidized imports" in other provisions of Article 15 constitutes an "express limitation of the imports to be considered" in an injury analysis[4]; and that the context provided by Article VI:6(a) of the *General Agreement on Tariffs and Trade 1994* ("GATT 1994") and Article 3.3 of the *Agreement on Implementation of Article VI of the General Agreement on Tariffs and Trade 1994* ("AD Agreement") does not support the use of cross-cumulation.[5] The United States respectfully requests that the Appellate Body reverse the Panel's findings and conclude that 19 U.S.C. §1677(7)(G) is not inconsistent with Articles 15.3 and 15.1, 15.2, 15.4, and 15.5 of the SCM Agreement "as such" or as applied in the original investigation at issue in this dispute.

---

1 Panel Report, para. 7.80.

2 Panel Report, paras. 7.356, 7.369, 8.2(c), and 8.2(d).

3 Panel Report, paras. 7.343 and 7.341.

4 Panel Report, paras. 7.346 and 7.360.

5 Panel Report, paras. 7.347-7.351.

(3) The United States also seeks review of the Panel's conclusion that 19 U.S.C. §1677(7)(G) "requires, in certain circumstances, the [U.S. International Trade Commission] to cumulate the effects of subsidized imports with the effects of dumped, non-subsidized imports."[6] This finding is based on the Panel's failure to make "an objective assessment of the matter before it, including an objective assessment of the facts of the case" as required by Article 11 of the DSU because the Panel's conclusion is not based on any evaluation of the measure at issue, including its text or other evidence bearing on its meaning. For this reason also, the United States respectfully requests that the Appellate Body reverse the Panel's findings and conclude that 19 U.S.C. §1677(7)(G) is not inconsistent "as such" with Articles 15.3 and 15.1, 15.2, 15.4, and 15.5 of the SCM Agreement.

6 Panel Report, paras. 7.322, 7.339, 7.340, and 7.358.

ANNEX 3

ORGANISATION MONDIALE DU COMMERCE

ORGANIZACIÓN MUNDIAL DEL COMERCIO

WORLD TRADE ORGANIZATION

Appellate Body

United States – Countervailing Measures on Certain Hot-Rolled Carbon Steel Flat Products from India

AB-2014-7

Procedural Ruling

1. On 8 August 2014, India filed a Notice of Appeal in the above proceedings. On 11 August 2014, the Appellate Body Division hearing this appeal received a letter from the United States requesting an extension of the deadline for filing its appellee's submission in these appellate proceedings, due to the size and complexity of India's appeal. The United States noted that India's Notice of Appeal appeared to include at least 67 separate claims of error. The United States requested that the deadline for filing its appellee's submission be extended by one week, to 2 September 2014.

2. On 12 August 2014, we invited India and the third parties to comment in writing on the request by 12 noon, 15 August 2014. We received responses from India and the European Union. The European Union supported the request made by the United States and made its own consequential request that the deadline for filing the third participants' notifications and written submissions also be extended by a week. India referred to the importance of prompt settlement of disputes, but did not object to the United States' request. To the extent that the Division were to accept the United States' request, India asked that it be accorded equal treatment in filing its own appellee's submission. India further supported the European Union's request that the deadline for filing the third participants' notifications and written submissions also be extended.

3. Having considered the United States' request and the comments provided by India and the European Union, the Division has decided, pursuant to Rule 16 of the Working Procedures for Appellate Review, to extend the date for filing the appellees' submissions to Monday, 1 September 2014. Consequently, we have also decided to extend the date for filing the third participants' notifications and written submissions to Wednesday, 3 September 2014. The Appellate Body may provide additional explanation regarding this ruling in its Report.

4. Attached is an updated Working Schedule for Appeal, which includes the revised dates for filing the appellees' submissions and the third participants' notifications and written submissions. Further details regarding the date of the oral hearing and the date of the circulation of the Report will be provided to the participants and the third participants in due course.

United States – Countervailing Measures on Certain Hot-Rolled Carbon Steel Flat Products from India

AB-2014-7

Revised Working Schedule

Process	*Rule*	*Date*
Notice of Appeal	Rule 20	Friday, 8 August 2014
Appellant's Submission	Rule 21(1)	Friday, 8 August 2014
Notice of Other Appeal	Rule 23(1)	Wednesday, 13 August 2014
Other Appellant's Submission	Rule 23(3)	Wednesday, 13 August 2014
Appellees' Submissions	Rules 22 and 23(4)	Monday, 1 September 2014
Third Participants' Submissions	Rule 24(1)	Wednesday, 3 September 2014
Third Participants' Notifications	Rule 24(2)	Wednesday, 3 September 2014

Cumulative List of Published Disputes